Talks with Ramana Maharshi

On Realizing Abiding Peace and Happiness

Talks with
Ramana Maharshi

On Realizing Abiding Peace and Happiness

InnerDirections
PUBLISHING

InnerDirections Publishing

INNER DIRECTIONS FOUNDATION
P.O. Box 130070
Carlsbad, California 92013
Tel: 800 545-9118 • 760 599-4075
www.InnerDirections.org

SECOND EDITION
First edition published 2000
Second revised edition 2001

Book & cover design by Joan Greenblatt
Printed in Canada on recycled paper

ISBN: 1-878019-00-7

Library of Congress Catalog Card Number: 99-75497

Self-Inquiry directly leads to Realization by removing the obstacles which make you think that the Self is not already realized.

CONTENTS

FOREWORD

The Sage of the Century

By Ken Wilber

I am often asked, "If you were stranded on a desert island and had only one book, what would it be?" The book you are now holding in your hands — *Talks with Ramana Maharshi* — is one of the two or three I always mention. And *Talks* tops the list in this regard: it is the living voice of the greatest sage of the twentieth century and, arguably, the greatest spiritual realization of this or any time.

One of the many astonishing things about these *Talks* is how remarkably unwavering is the tone and style, the voice itself — not in the sense that it is fixed and rigid, but rather that it speaks with a full-blown maturity from the first word to the last. It is as if — no, it is certainly the case that — Ramana's realization came to him fully formed — or perhaps we should say, fully formless — and therefore it needed no further growth. He simply speaks from and as the absolute, the Self, the purest Emptiness that is the goal and ground of the entire manifest world, and yet is not other to that world. Ramana, echoing Shankara, used to say:

> The world is Illusory;
> Brahman alone is real;
> Brahman is the world.

This profound realization is what separates Ramana's genuine enlightenment from today's many pretenders to the throne — deep ecology, ecofeminism, Gaia revivals, Goddess worship, ecopsychology, systems theory, web-of-life notions — none of which have grasped the first two lines, and therefore, contrary to their sweet pronouncements, do not really understand the third, either. And it is exactly by all those who are thus in love merely with the manifest world — from capitalists to socialists, from green polluters to green peacers, from egocentrics to ecocentrists — that

Ramana's message needs so desperately to be heard.

What and where is this Self? How do I abide as That? There is no doubt how Ramana would answer those — and virtually all other — questions: Who wants to know? What in you, right now, is aware of this page? Who is the Knower that knows the world but cannot itself be known? Who is the Hearer that hears the birds but cannot itself be heard? Who is the Seer that sees the clouds but cannot itself be seen?

And so arises *Self-Inquiry,* Ramana's special gift to the world. I *have* feelings, but I am not those feelings. Who am I? I *have* thoughts, but I am not those thoughts. Who am I? I *have* desires, but I am not those desires. Who am I?

So you push back into the source of your own awareness — what Ramana often called the "I-I," since it is aware of the normal I or ego. You push back into the Witness, the I-I, and you rest as That. I am not objects, not feelings, not desires, not thoughts.

But then people usually make a rather unfortunate mistake in this Self-Inquiry. They think that if they rest in the Self or Witness, they are going to see something, or feel something, something really amazing, special, spiritual. But you won't see anything. If you see something, then that is just another object — another feeling, another thought, another sensation, another image. But those are all objects; those are what you are *not*.

No, as you rest in the Witness — realizing, I am not objects, I am not feelings, I am not thoughts — all you will notice is a sense of Freedom, a sense of Liberation, a sense of Release — release from the terrible constriction of identifying with these little finite objects, the little body and little mind and little ego, all of which are objects that can be seen, and thus are not the true Seer, the real Self, the pure Witness, which is what you really are.

So you won't see anything in particular. Whatever is arising is fine. Clouds float by in the sky, feelings float by in the body, thoughts float by in the mind — and you can effortlessly witness all of them. They *all* spontaneously arise in your own present, easy, effortless awareness. And this witnessing awareness is not itself anything specific you can see. It is just a vast, background sense of Freedom — or *pure Emptiness* — and in that pure Emptiness, which you are, the entire manifest world arises. You *are* that Freedom, Openness, Emptiness — and not any little finite thing that arises in it.

Resting in that empty, free, easy, effortless witnessing, notice that the clouds are arising in the vast space of your awareness. The clouds are arising within you — so much so, you can taste the clouds, you are one with the clouds, it is as if they are on the side of your skin, they are so close. The sky and your awareness have become one, and all things in the sky are floating effortlessly through your own awareness. You can kiss the sun, swallow the mountain, they are that close. Zen says "Swallow the Pacific Ocean in a single gulp," and that's the easiest thing in the world, when inside and outside are no longer two, when subject and object are non-dual, when the looker and looked at are One Taste. And so:

The world is illusory, which means you are not any object at all — nothing that can be seen is ultimately real. You are *neti, neti*, not this, not that. And under no circumstances should you base your salvation on that which is finite, temporal, passing, illusory, suffering-enhancing and agony-inducing. *Brahman alone is real*, the Self (unqualifiable Brahman-Atman) alone is real — the pure Witness, the timeless Unborn, the formless Seer, the radical I-I, radiant Emptiness — is what is real and all that is real. It is your condition, your nature, your essence, your present and your future, your desire and your destiny, and yet it is always ever-present as pure Presence, the alone that is Alone.

Brahman is the world, Emptiness and Form are not-two. *After* you realize that the manifest world is illusory, and *after* you realize that Brahman alone is real, *then* can you see that the absolute and the relative are not-two or nondual, then can you see that *nirvana* and *samsara* are not-two, then can you realize that the Seer and everything seen are not-two — all of which really means, the sound of those birds singing! The entire world of Form exists nowhere but in your own present Formless Awareness: you can drink the Pacific in a single gulp, because the entire world literally exists in your pure Self, the everpresent great I-I.

Finally, and most importantly, Ramana would remind us that the pure Self — and therefore the great Liberation — *cannot be attained*, anymore than you can attain your feet or acquire your lungs. You are *already* aware of the sky, you *already* hear the sounds around you, you *already* witness this world. One hundred percent of the enlightened mind or pure Self is present right now — not ninety-nine percent, but one hundred percent. As Ramana constantly pointed out, if the Self (or knowledge of the Self) is something that comes into existence — if your realization has a beginning in time — then that is merely another object, another passing, finite, temporal state. There is no reaching the Self — it is reading this page. There is no looking for the Self — it is looking out of your eyes right now. There is no attaining the Self — it is reading these words. You simply, absolutely, cannot attain that which you have never lost. And if you do attain something, Ramana would say, that's very nice, but it's not the Self.

So, if I may suggest, as you read the following words from the world's greatest sage: if you think you don't understand Self or Spirit, then rest in that which doesn't understand, and just that is Spirit. If you think you don't quite "get" the Self or Spirit, then rest in that which doesn't quite get it, and just that is Spirit.

Thus, if you think you understand Spirit, that is Spirit. If you think you don't, that is Spirit. And so we can leave with Ramana's greatest and most secret message: the enlightened mind is not hard to attain but impossible to avoid. In the dear Master's own words:

> There is neither creation nor destruction,
> Neither destiny nor freewill;
> Neither path nor achievement;
> This is the final truth.

PREFACE

When InnerDirections Publishing undertook the joyful task of bringing out a Western edition of *Talks with Sri Ramana Maharshi,* it became clear that this was a profoundly significant project — one that evoked in all who worked on it attitudes of the deepest respect and privilege. It was a task that was achieved through the help of many, beginning with the support and encouragement of Sri V. S. Ramanan, the President of Sri Ramanasramam.

Our goal was to publish an edition in which readability of the text was of primary importance. To begin with, we redesigned the page layout to make the selections easier to follow. The dialogues have now been fully placed in chronological order; the line breaks between the talks generally represent a change in questioner or in the nature of the talk. Next, some of the dated language of British India was carefully modified to reflect phrasing familiar to the contemporary Western reader. Finally, almost all of the text within parenthesis now contains the comments of the original compiler, while words within brackets contain editorial additions specific to this edition.

Those who contributed to the editorial process were deeply touched by the depth and clarity of these dialogues. Dr. Robert Powell's editing is a testimony to his special ability to make words easier to understand, without changing their intrinsic meaning. We also appreciate the invaluable proofreading assistance provided by Linda Hubly, Amelia Kahaney, Phyllis Kahaney, and Joan Loomis. Special thanks to Dr. Mohan Ram and Sri Samudrala Krishnamacharyulu for help with the Sanskrit portions.

Only a few "talks" were removed: those that had duplicate passages throughout the book, and a few that were exceedingly technical in nature. Sanskrit terminology was standardized wherever possible, using familiar transliterations. Words were never changed for the sake of alteration. In fact, the original fragrance and genius of the book is eminently more readable and accessible now.

In the final analysis, this book is a gift to you, the reader. By catching the spirit of these dialogues, you may find your life transformed. Though these words were spoken decades ago, they transmit the essential means to access our original nature, here and now. They are as clear and fresh as the day they were spoken by a remarkable sage who lived at the Southern foothills of the sacred hill, Arunachala.

INTRODUCTION

*"Whatever be the means adopted, you must at last return to the Self,
so why not abide as the Self here and now?"*
— Ramana Maharshi

In the ancient township of Tiruchulli, in a dry, dusty corner of South India, legend speaks of Lord Shiva saving the land from a deluge on three separate occasions. By planting his trident into the earth, Shiva created a hole for the water to flow into. At the place where he planted his trident stands the large temple of *Bhuminatheswara* (Lord of the Earth). Just across the street from this old temple is the house where young Venkataraman was born in December 1879. Though destined to become one of the great sages of modern times, there were no outward signs that would reveal his forthcoming Realization.

After the death of his father, Venkataraman's family moved to the famous temple town of Madurai so that they could be under the watchful eye of a paternal uncle. It was here that the "Awakening" would take place, that waves of spiritual fervor would overtake him while reading the *Periapuranam*, the lives of the sixty-three Tamil saints. From his childhood, there was a continual inner throbbing of "Arunachala, Arunachala," as if the Self — his real Being — was reminding him of his forgotten nature. Once, when a visiting relative recounted his recent pilgrimage to Tiruvannamalai (a temple town where the solitary, sacred hill Arunachala rises above the South Indian plains), young Venkataraman became astonished and overwhelmed that Arunachala was in fact a place on earth — a place one could actually go to.

Shortly after this time, during a hot July day when Venkataraman was just sixteen, he faced his own mortality. One day, when everyone else was away from home, the young boy became completely overcome with the fear of death. Rather than panic or retreat into fear, Venkataraman had the remarkable presence of mind to face the situation, then and there. He dra-

matized the death occurrence to be able to help bring the experience to its
ultimate conclusion, by holding his breath, stiffening his body, and allowing no sound to escape his lips.

To die before death is to face the void; the emptiness in which the content of the mind has no ground on which to endure. It is rare for one to face
the void without recoiling back into form. Venkataraman, like the Buddha,
was determined to stay the course. Upon firm investigation into the nature
of his "I-sense," his former self died, and the infinite Self, the Eternal "I,"
rose to take its place — the true resurrection.

After this experience, Venkataraman stopped going out to play with
friends and preferred solitude. He says of this period:

"I would often sit alone and become absorbed in the Self, the Spirit,
the force or current which constituted me. I would continue in this
despite the jeers of my elder brother who would sarcastically call
me 'Sage' or 'Yogi' and advise me to retire into the jungle like the
ancient *Rishis*."

When his brother reprimanded him in August of that year for behav-
ing like a *sadhu*, while enjoying the amenities of home life, Venkataraman
recognized the truth of his brother's words. He rose to his feet, claiming
that he had to return to school and left for Arunachala. He said of his state
at that time:

"When I left home, I was like a speck swept on by a tremendous
flood; I knew not my body or the world, whether it was day or night."

Providence guided the young sage on his journey home. The vibration
in his heart, of "Arunachala, Arunachala," acted as a guiding light.

Absorbed in the bliss of Being, he sat and slept in various places around
the Hill and in the temple — sometimes moving when groups of young
rascals would pelt him with stones. Just as a light cannot be hidden under
a bushel, the light of Venkataraman's realization became evident, attract-
ing a few earnest seekers. Those were people who wanted to bathe in the
peace of his presence — a peace that gently settled upon one, lifting one
from the persistent cycle of thought.

Ganapathi Muni, a great Sanskrit scholar and yogi, had his doubts
cleared by the young sage who was then living on the slopes of the
Arunachala Hill. Deeply impressed and touched by his great wisdom, the
Muni proclaimed that Venkataraman should subsequently be known as
Bhagavan Sri Ramana Maharshi.

Just as Ramana realized the Self without prior spiritual or philosophical instruction, he attached little importance to theoretical study. His teachings are uniquely suited to modern life and provide for a balanced synthesis of head and heart. Maharshi consistently guided the seeker back to the source of abiding happiness — one's own Self.

The teachings of Ramana Maharshi are among the clearest and most direct of the *advaitic* (nondualistic) teachings originating from India. *Advaita* simply means "not two." Ramana taught that we exist as the Supreme Self at all times. We need only awaken to this reality by seeking the source of the ego, or "I-thought," and abide in the Self that we always are. He referred to this method as Self-Inquiry.

Ramana always encouraged people to lead life in the most natural manner. There was no question of engaging or disengaging in activity — all happens according to destiny. The primary consideration is to be free from the "I-am-the-doer" illusion.

The path of Self-Inquiry liberates one from the never-ending fear and disorder resulting from taking the ego to be real. By becoming free of the ego-illusion, one experiences true freedom and supreme peace. It is a path that takes one from the apparent duality of the individual and the world to the bliss of one's real nature.

Through this awakening to Self-awareness, even by imperfect glimpses, one begins to sense a Reality not limited to the ego's world. And, this current of Awareness, is ultimately revealed as the Self — Pure Consciousness.

Though we often refer to the teaching of Ramana Maharshi as a "path," it is truly pathless. When we abide in our true Being, we turn our back on time — on becoming; and consequently on spending time purifying the very mind and ego structures that only need to be discarded. Maharshi observes:

"You impose limitations on your true nature of Infinite Being, and then weep that you are but a finite creature. Then you take up this or that *sadhana* (spiritual practice) to transcend the nonexistent limitations. But if your *sadhana* itself assumes the existence of the limitations, how can it help you to transcend them?"

Those who surrounded Ramana during his lifetime came from very diverse cultural and social backgrounds. What they had in common was a sincere aspiration to experience true inner peace and freedom. Maharshi never saw anyone as separate from himself and had no disciples in the traditional sense. He regularly said that the Guru was not the physical form, and that guidance would continue after the demise of the Guru's body. Therefore, there was no need to create a lineage, or provide for transmission to carry on successorship.

After years of living in caves upon the Arunachala hill, the Maharshi moved down to its base, near the burial place of his mother. After a short time, a small ashram began to take shape around him, and what is now the current Sri Ramanasramam had its modest beginning. Seekers from all backgrounds and religions came to bask in his presence.

Ramana sat in a modest hall, available day and night to answer questions from sincere seekers. His only possessions were a loincloth and a towel. Maharshi never asked anything of anyone. He never traveled, gave formal talks, or wrote books. He spontaneously answered questions asked of him and was unconcerned regarding the comings and goings of visitors. Yet, he meticulously attended to detail when engaged in the work that he did each day. Whether it was preparing food in the kitchen, stitching a notebook out of leftover paper, or going through ashram proofs, Maharshi always taught mindfulness by example. What's more remarkable is that throughout all the years he lived at the Ashram, he never had a private room or separate accommodation. He slept and lived in the Hall — the same location that visitors occupied days and evenings with him. Only much later toward the last year of his life, when his health was frail, was a small room constructed for his use.

Whoever came to the hermitage to sit in Ramana's presence — whatever their religious or cultural background — all felt he belonged to them. And indeed he did, for "I" is common to all people, and the investigation into its true nature reveals a Unity that is universal — beyond mind-made differences.

Throughout the more than fifty-four years that Maharshi guided seekers from various parts of the world, he never swerved from the essential task of bringing the questioner back to the truth of his or her own Existence. Whatever form the question would take, Ramana would patiently and gently lead the questioner back to the "one who questions."

The legacy of Ramana Maharshi lives in his teachings. The directness and simplicity of the approach appeal to many people, especially in our time. Since wherever we may be our own Self is always available, there are no special requirements for investigating who we truly are.

In 1949, it was detected that Maharshi had malignant sarcoma in his left arm. In spite of intense medical care, on April 14, 1950, his physical end was evident. In the evening, as devotees sat outside the room built specially for his convenience during this final illness, they spontaneously began to sing the refrain to one of his stirring hymns to Arunachala. Arthur Osborne (biographer of Ramana and editor of his written works) writes about that evening:

"On hearing it, Ramana's eyes open and shone, he gave a brief smile of indescribable tenderness. From the outer corner of his eyes, tears of bliss rolled down. One more deep breath, and no more.
At that very moment — 8:47 p.m. — an enormous star trailed slowly across the sky passing to the northeast peak of Arunachala. The meteor was noted as far away as Bombay."

Many of those who had the good fortune to benefit from his physical presence begged him not to leave; Ramana made it very clear that he was not the body, so there was no concern for his leaving. He told those around him:

"They say that I am dying, but I am not going away. Where could I go? I am here."

One of the great collections of dialogues between the Sage and his inquirers is contained in the book you now hold in your hands. Carefully recorded in English, by Munagala S. Venkataramiah, the wisdom in these "talks" will certainly guide us to that profound clarity if we open ourselves completely to it. Only the thirst for true freedom is required. The words of Ramana Maharshi are the mirror of wisdom; whenever we turn to them we see the reflection of our true nature:

"There is no greater mystery than the following: Ourselves being the Reality, we seek to gain reality. We think there is something hiding our Reality, and that it must be destroyed before the Reality is gained. That is ridiculous. A day will dawn when you will yourself laugh at your past efforts. That which will be on the day you laugh is also here and now."

Matthew Greenblatt
September 1, 1999

INTRODUCTION TO THE INDIAN EDITION

These "Talks" cover a period of four years, 1935-1939, and were all recorded by Sri Munagala S. Venkataramiah (Swami Ramanananda Saraswati), a long-standing disciple of Sri Ramana Maharshi. Though Telugu by birth, he speaks English and Tamil fluently and is conversant with Sanskrit. These are necessary qualifications for one who wished to record the conversations of Sri Bhagavan with his various disciples and visitors.

The four years covered here were the days when the Asramam reached the summit of its glory. Maharshi's health was on the whole good and the Hall, where he sat, was open day and night to welcome one and all. Visitors flocked there from every corner of the world; there was hardly a country not represented at one time or another. The war naturally interfered with this influx, though the number of Indian visitors steadily increased as time went by. But it was these conversations, many with Westerners, that were specially interesting: the modern tendency towards materialism and irreligion, on which the West often prides itself, met its match here. Sri Bhagavan glowed like the sun, and even those who did not understand him or agree with his words were fascinated, and could not help but be elevated by his presence.

Though Sri Venkataramiah was fully qualified for the work, to follow Sri Bhagavan was no easy task once he started to talk. He had such a command of his subject that he was never at a loss for a word in whichever language he might happen to be speaking; so few notes could be taken, the listeners being too busy trying not to lose a word of what was being said. Sri Venkataramiah acted as interpreter for the many English-speaking people who flocked to the Asramam, as Sri Bhagavan was reluctant to say more than a few words in that language, though he knew it sufficiently well to read English newspapers and magazines. But to act as interpreter was an even more difficult task than just recording; the flow of words was so steady that no interval was left in which their meaning could be conveyed to the ardent questioner. Often Sri Bhagavan had to be asked to wait while his words were conveyed to the anxious listener. So the difficulties of making this record can easily be imagined; only one who had sat for years at the feet of the Master and had thoroughly absorbed his philosophy and the way he expounded it, was competent for the task. Sri Venkataramiah, the ideal person for this, had luckily been found.

That the language used here is not always elegant is admitted, this was to be expected in the circumstances; doubtless it could have been corrected, but it has been left much as it was, as it was felt that a certain spontaneity it now possesses would otherwise be lost. Though the conversations were in various South Indian languages, most of it was recorded in English, the rest in Tamil and Telugu, which passages have been translated for the purpose of this book. The completed notes were often shown the questioners for verification, but the whole had the seal of approval of Sri Bhagavan himself, as the records were always shown him for his approval or the necessary alteration after they had been entered in the notebook. Thus we may be sure that here we have the exact teaching of the Master, and reading them we once again sit at his feet in the Old Hall, drinking in every word that falls from his lips; enraptured by his smile, the movement of his delicate hands, and his actions; for he was a true artist, often acting the part of the story he was telling so better to drive home his point.

Some may be inclined to criticize this book as monotonous, but, this supposed monotony is deliberate, for some new point is always brought out however similar the talk may seem. Sri Bhagavan always stressed the one essential truth that was necessary for Liberation: that there is only one Self and nothing but the Self. Know that and everything else is known. This cannot be repeated too often.

Doubtless an intellectual grasp of this fact sets one on the path, but, the path once started, mental knowledge must then become actual experience. To know a thing absolutely, not just superficially, one must *be* that thing, otherwise knowledge is incomplete. As I pointed out, we are always nothing but the Self, but associating ourselves with the ignorance of limitation, with an ego, we forget the Seer and identify ourselves with the seen. But what can we do about it? The habit is so long-standing; birth after birth has been imagined, century after century has been fabricated by the mind, which has thus steeped itself more and more in ignorance. It now finds itself disinclined and, even if willing, almost unable to disentangle itself from the thralls of the play-world it has created.

You are the Self, he tells us, nothing but the Self, anything else is just imagination, so BE the Self here and now. There is no need to run off to a forest or shut oneself in a room; carry on with your essential activities but free yourself from association with the doer of them. Self is the witness, you are That.

Example after example is given in these talks, in language to suit all tastes and mentalities. The reading of the book automatically drives one inward to the Source; that is itself a sufficient *sadhana*. Do not delude yourself, you are already That, there is nothing more to be obtained, only false association to be shed, limitation to be recognized as illusory.

His method of doing this is well known: Self-inquiry. Always and at all times seek for the source of the ego, the apparent actor, and on the attainment of that goal, he tells us, the ego will drop away of its own accord, and nothing will be left but the all-blissful Self.

What more is there to say, but to advise one and all to read this book and try and make it a part of themselves? Not one word is to be passed over lightly, or one conversation to be dismissed as superfluous. It is all pure gold. And here again we find the ever-living Sri Ramana Maharshi before us in person, teaching us in his own inimitable words for our benefit and delight.

Sadhu Arunachala
(Major A.W. Chadwick, O.B.E.)
Sri Ramanasramam
January 1, 1955

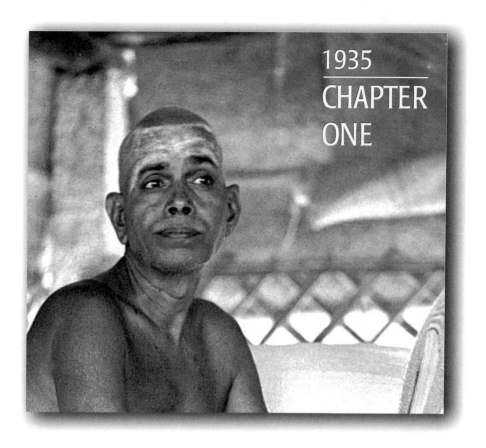

Mr. Evans-Wentz: Is solitude necessary for a *jnani?*

M. Solitude is in the mind of man. One might be in the thick of the world and maintain serenity of mind; such a one is in solitude. Another may stay in a forest, but still be unable to control his mind. He cannot be said to be in solitude. Solitude is a function of the mind. A man attached to desire cannot get solitude wherever he may be; a detached man is always in solitude.

D. So then, one might be engaged in work and be free from desire and stay in solitude. Is that right?

M. Yes. Work performed with attachment is a shackle, whereas work performed with detachment does not affect the doer. He is, even while working, in solitude.

Chapter One − 1935

January 6, 1935

Mrs. M.A. Piggot, an English lady, who had read *A Search in Secret India*, came to see Maharshi. The services of a disciple as interpreter were provided. At the time, there were many visitors in the Hall, including some ladies with their infants. The place resounded with noise. At length silence prevailed. Suddenly, Maharshi, who seemed to be looking at infinite space, was heard to say softly, "Monkey!" A little baby was then discovered in the doorway (unobserved by the mother who was seated on the other side of the door) with a large monkey standing on his hind legs, who with both hands was fondling the child not hurting it in the slightest, both being at peace with each other in Maharshi's presence. When Maharshi's voice was heard, the monkey jumped away adroitly and disappeared. The incident greatly impressed the lady.

January 7, 1935

Mrs. Piggot asked: Is a Master necessary for realization?

Maharshi: The realization is the result of the Master's Grace more than teachings, lectures, meditation, etc. They are only secondary aids, whereas the former is the primary and essential cause.

Devotee: What are the obstacles to realization of the Self?

M. They are habits of mind (*vasanas*).

D. How to overcome these mental habits?

M. By realizing the Self.

D. That is a vicious circle.

M. It is the ego which raises such difficulties, creating obstacles and then suffers from the perplexity of apparent paradoxes. Find out who makes the inquiries and the Self will be found.

D. What are the aids for realization?

M. The teachings of the scriptures and of realized souls.

D. Can such teachings be discussions, lectures, and meditations?

M. Yes, but all these are only secondary aids, whereas what's essential is the Master's Grace.

D. How long will it take for one to get that?

M. Why do you want to know?

D. To give me hope.

M. Even such a desire is an obstacle. The Self is ever there; there is nothing without it. Be the Self and the desires and doubts will disappear. The Self is the witness in the sleep, dream, and waking states of existence. These states belong to the ego. The Self transcends even the ego. Did you not exist in sleep? Did you know then that you were asleep or unaware of the world? It is only in the waking state that you describe the experience of sleep as being unawareness; therefore the consciousness when asleep is the same as that when awake. If you know what this waking consciousness is, you will know the consciousness which witnesses all the three states. Such consciousness may be found by seeking the consciousness as it was in sleep.

D. In that case, I fall asleep.

M. No harm.

D. It is a blank.

M. For whom is the blank? Find out. You cannot deny yourself at any time. The Self is ever there and continues in all states.

D. Should I remain as if in sleep and be watchful at the same time?

M. Yes. Watchfulness is the waking state. Therefore the state will not be one of sleep, but sleepless sleep. If you go the way of your thoughts you will be carried away by them and you will find yourself in an endless maze.

D. So, then, I must go back tracing the source of thoughts.

M. Quite so; in that way the thoughts will disappear and the Self alone will remain. In fact there is no inside or outside for the Self. They are also projections of the ego. The Self is pure and absolute.

D. It is understood intellectually only. Is not intellect a help for realization?

M. Yes, up to a certain stage. Even so, realize that the Self transcends the intellect — the latter must itself vanish to reach the Self.

D. Does my realization help others?

M. Yes, certainly. It is the best help possible. But there are no others to be helped. For a realized being sees only the Self, just like a goldsmith estimating the gold in various jewels. When you identify yourself with the body, then only the forms and shapes are there. But when you transcend your body, the others disappear along with your body-consciousness.

D. Is it so with plants, trees, etc.?

M. Do they exist at all apart from the Self? Find out. You think that you see them. The thought is projected from your Self. Find out wherefrom it arises. Thoughts will cease to arise and the Self alone will remain.

D. I understand theoretically. But they are still there.

M. Yes. It is like a cinema show. There is the light on the screen, and the shadows flitting across impress the audience as the enactment of some piece. Similarly it will be, if in the same play an audience is also shown. The seer and the seen, will then only be the screen. Apply it to yourself. You are the screen, the Self has created the ego, the ego has its accretions of thoughts which are displayed as the world, the trees, plants, etc., about which you are asking. In reality, all these are nothing but the Self. If you see the Self, the same will be found to be all, everywhere, and always. Nothing but the Self exists.

D. Yes, I still understand only theoretically. Yet the answers are simple, beautiful, and convincing.

M. Even the thought, "I do not realize" is a hindrance. In fact, the Self alone is.

JANUARY 8, 1935

An old man came and sat in the Hall. Maharshi was reading Sarma's sanskrit version of Arunachala Akshara Manamalai (*the first of the* Five Hymns to Arunachala). *The man asked softly*: It is said that realization is beyond expression; and expression always fails to describe the realization. How is that?

M. The point has been mentioned in *Arunachala Ashtakam* (Verse 3), where it is admitted that, although the expression of realization is impossible, still its existence is indicated.

(*Soon thereafter there were visible signs of emotion in the man. His breath was deep and hard and he fell on the floor prostrating himself humbly, getting up only after one or two minutes. Remaining calm for a short period, he left the place. Evidently the man had experienced some illumination. He sought confirmation from Maharshi, who responded fittingly. He found confirmation, and humbly and feelingly acknowledged the divine intercession on his behalf.*)

A question was asked about the Upanishadic *passage, "the Supreme Spirit is subtler than the subtlest and larger than the largest."*

M. Even the structure of the atom has been found by the mind. Therefore, the mind is subtler than the atom. That which is behind the mind, namely the individual soul, is subtler than the mind. Further, the Tamil saint

Manikavachakar has said of the specks dancing in a beam of sunlight, that if each represents a universe, the whole sunlight will represent the Supreme Being.

JANUARY 19, 1935

Mr. Douglas Ainslie (Grant Duff), is an aristocratic English gentleman, seventy years old, and nephew of a former Governor of Madras. An author and poet, formerly attached to the British Legation in Athens, Paris, and The Hague, he came to Madras as a guest of Government House. He came to see Maharshi with a letter of introduction from Paul Brunton. The next day he returned and remained a little less than an hour in the Hall. On both days practically no words were exchanged, only gaze meeting gaze. His habits are abstemious; he remains without food of any kind till 1:00 p.m. and then lunches; he is said to have coffee and biscuits in the evening and retires without any further food. He has been a bachelor all along, walks a few miles a day on an empty stomach, speaks little, and is very graceful in his movements. His voice is low and soft and his words appear to come from the heart. He has friends among whom may be counted the late Sir John Woodroffe, Sir Sarvepalli Radhakrishnan, and Prof. Thomas, Sanskrit Professor in Oxford University. He expressed a desire to hear the *Vedas*. On Monday a letter arrived from Riga and the questions therein happened to coincide with those the European visitor asked, relating to the existence of departed souls and how best to serve them.

The reply sent to Riga was read out to him. Tamil songs from Maharshi's *Truth Revealed* and the *Vedas* were repeated in his presence. He considered the recitations magnificent. He came the next afternoon and to the wonder of others, had an experience on the previous night which he repeated to Maharshi. It was that he had seen something like an electric light within himself, in the Heart-center on the right side. He added further that he had seen the sun shining within. Maharshi smiled a little and then had a translation of *Atma-Vidya* (Self-Knowledge) read out to him in which occurs a cryptic saying that realization consists in reaching the *Atman* (Self) which is the expanse of consciousness (*chidvyoman*) as distinguished from the mind, which is the expansion of *chittavyoman*. This explanation appealed to him.

Speaking of him later, Maharshi remarked: Just think of an old man of seventy not choosing to live peacefully in his own house on the income he had earned! How intense has been his earnestness that he left his native land, dared a sea voyage of 6000 miles, and faced the hardships of long railway journeys in a foreign land. Ignorant of the language, undergoing the vicissitudes of a lonely life, he submitted to the inclemency of a hot climate in surroundings that were uncongenial, and to which he was unaccustomed. He could have been happy in his own house. It is his longing for internal peace that has brought him here.

(Quite so! The intensity of his earnestness is revealed by his illuminating experiences here within four days of his arrival, people say.)

With regard to the question concerning departed souls: So long as a man identifies himself with his gross body, the thought materialized as gross manifestations must be real to him. Because his body is imagined to have originated from another physical being, the other exists as truly as his own body. Having existed here once it certainly survives death, because the offspring is still here and feels he has been born of the other. Under these circumstances the other world is true; and the departed souls are benefited by prayers offered for them. On the other hand, considered in a different way, the One Reality is the Self from whom has sprung the ego, which contains within itself the seeds of predispositions acquired in previous births. The Self illumines the ego, the predispositions, and also the gross senses, whereupon the predispositions appear to the senses to have materialized as the universe, and become perceptible to the ego, the reflection of the Self. The ego identifies itself with the body, and so loses sight of the Self, and the result of this inadvertence is dark ignorance and the misery of the present life. The fact of the ego rising from the Self and forgetting it is birth. So, it may be said that the birth of the individual had killed the mother. The present desire to regain one's mother is in reality the desire to regain the Self, which is the same as realizing oneself, or the death of the ego; this is surrender unto the mother, so she may live eternally.

Maharshi then read out from the Tamil version of Yoga Vasishta *the story of Deerga Tapasi who had two sons, Punya and Papa. After the death of the parents, the younger one mourned the loss and the elder brother consoled him as follows:*
"Why do you mourn the loss of our parents? I shall tell you where they are; they are only within ourselves and are ourselves. For the life-current has passed through innumerable incarnations, births and deaths, pleasures and pains, etc., just as the water current in a river flows over rocks, pits, sands, elevations and depressions on its way, but still the current is unaffected. The pleasures and pains, births and deaths, are like undulations on the

surface of seeming water in the mirage of the ego. The only reality is the Self from where the ego appears, and runs through thoughts which manifest themselves as the universe and in which the mothers and fathers, friends and relatives appear and disappear. They are nothing but manifestations of the Self, so that one's parents are not outside the Self. So there is no reason to mourn. Learn it, realize it and be happy."

JANUARY 24, 1935

Mr. W.Y. Evans-Wentz, an English research scholar of Oxford University, brought a letter of introduction from Mr. Paul Brunton and arrived on a visit.

He was tired after his journey and required rest. He is quite accustomed to the Indian way of living, having visited this country several times. He learned the Tibetan language and helped in the translation of the *Tibetan Book of the Dead,* the *Life of Milarepa*, the greatest of Tibetan Yogis, and a third book on the *Tibetan Secret Doctrines.*

In the afternoon Mr. Evans-Wentz began to ask a few questions, relating to yoga. He wanted to know if it was right to kill animals such as tigers, deer, etc., and use their skins for yoga posture (asana).

M. The mind is the tiger or the deer?

D. If everything is illusion, then one can take lives?

M. To whom is illusion? Find that out! In fact, everyone is a "killer of the Self" (*atmahan*) every moment of his life.

D. Which posture (*asana*) is the best?

M. Any *asana*, possibly *sukha asana* (easy posture or the half-lotus position). But that is immaterial for *jnana,* the path of Knowledge.

D. Does posture indicate temperament?

M. Yes.

D. What are the properties and effects of the tiger's skin, wool, or deerskin, etc.?

M. Some have found them out and related them in yoga books. They correspond to conductors and non-conductors of magnetism, etc. But it is all immaterial for the Path of Knowledge (*Jnana Marga*). Posture really means location and steadfastness in the Self. It is internal. The others refer to external positions.

D. Which time is most suitable for meditation?

M. What is time?

D. Tell me what it is!

M. Time is only an idea. There is only the Reality. Whatever you think it is, it looks like that. If you call it time, it is time. If you call it existence, it is existence, and so on. After calling it time, you divide it into years, months, days and nights, hours, minutes, etc. Time is immaterial for the Path of Knowledge. But some of these rules and disciplines are good for beginners.

D. What is *Jnana Marga?*

M. Concentration of the mind is in a way common to both Knowledge and Yoga. Yoga aims at union of the individual with the universal, the Reality. This Reality cannot be new. It must exist even now, and it does exist.

Therefore, the Path of Knowledge tries to find out how *viyoga* (separation) came about. Separation is from the Reality only.

D. What is illusion?

M. To whom is the illusion? Find that out. Then illusion will vanish.

Generally people want to know about illusion and do not examine to whom it occurs. It is foolish. Illusion is outside and unknown. But the seeker is considered to be known and is inside. Find out what is immediate, intimate, instead of trying to find out the distant and unknown.

D. Does Maharshi advise any physical posture for Europeans?

M. It may be advisable. However, it must be clearly understood that meditation is not prohibited in the absence of *asanas,* or prescribed times, or any accessories of the kind.

D. Does Maharshi have any particular method to impart to Europeans in particular?

M. It is according to the mental equipment of the individual. There is indeed no hard and fast rule.

Mr. Evans-Wentz began to ask questions, mostly relating to yoga preliminaries, to all of which Maharshi replied that they are aids to yoga, which is itself an aid to Self-realization, the goal of all.

D. Is work an obstruction to Self-realization?

M. No. For a realized being the Self alone is the Reality, and actions are only phenomenal, not affecting the Self. Even when he acts he has no sense of being an agent. His actions are involuntary and he remains a witness to them without any attachment.

There is no aim for this action. Even one who is still practicing the Path of Wisdom (*jnana*) can practice while engaged in work. It may be difficult in the earlier stages for a beginner, but after some practice it will soon be effective and the work will not be found a hindrance to meditation.

D. What is the practice?
M. Constant search for "I," the source of the ego. Find out "Who am I?" The pure "I" is the reality, the Absolute Existence-Consciousness-Bliss. When That is forgotten, all miseries crop up; when that is held fast, miseries do not affect the person.
D. Is not *brahmacharya* (celibacy) necessary for realization of the Self?
M. *Brahmacharya* is "living in *Brahman*." It has no connection with celibacy as commonly understood. A real *brahmachari*, that is one who lives in *Brahman*, finds bliss in *Brahman*, which is the same as the Self. Why then should you look for other sources of happiness? In fact, the turning away or "non-recognition " or "non-realization" of the Self has been the cause of all misery.
D. Celibacy is a *sine qua non* for yoga?
M. So it is. Celibacy is certainly an aid to realization among so many other aids.
D. Is it then not indispensable? Can a married man realize the Self?
M. Certainly; it is a matter of fitness of mind. Married or unmarried, a man can realize the Self, because that is here and now. If it were not so, but attainable only by some efforts at some other time, and if it were new and something to be acquired, it would not be worthy of pursuit. Because what is not natural cannot be permanent, either. But what I say is that the Self is here and now and alone.
D. God being immanent in all, one should not take life of any kind. Is society right in taking the life of a murderer? Can the State do so? Christian countries are beginning to think it is wrong to do so.
M. What is it that prompted the murderer to commit the crime? The same power awards him the punishment. Society or the State is only a tool in the hands of that power. You speak of one life taken away; but what about innumerable lives lost in wars?
D. Quite so. Loss of lives is wrong anyway. Are wars justified?
M. For a realized man, the one who remains ever in the Self, the loss of one or several or all lives either in this world or in all the three worlds makes no difference. Even if he happens to destroy them all, no sin can touch such a pure soul.

"He who is free from the notion of ego, whose intellect is unattached, though he annihilates all the worlds, he slayeth not, nor is he bound by the results of his actions."
— *Bhagavad Gita* 18.17

D. Do not one's actions affect the person in after-births?

M. Are you born now? Why do you think of other births? The fact is that there is neither birth nor death. Let him who is born think of death and a palliative therefore.

D. How long did it take Maharshi to realize the Self?

M. This question is asked because the name and form are perceived. These are the perceptions consequent on the identification of the ego with the gross body.

If the ego identifies itself with the subtle mind, as in a dream, the perceptions are subtle, also. But in sleep there are no perceptions. Was there not the ego still? Unless it was, there cannot be the memory of having slept. Who was it that slept? You did not say in your sleep that you slept. You say it now in your wakeful state. The ego therefore is the same in wakefulness, dream, and sleep. Find out the underlying Reality behind these states. In that state there is Being alone. There is no you, nor I, nor he; no present, nor past, nor future. It is beyond time and space, beyond expression.

It is ever there.

Just as a plantain tree produces shoots at its roots, before yielding fruits and perishing, and these shoots, being transplanted, do the same again, so also the original primeval Master of antiquity (Dakshinamurti), who cleared the doubts of his *rishi* disciples in silence, has left shoots which are ever multiplying. The Guru is a shoot of that Dakshinamurti. The question does not arise when the Self is realized.

D. Does Maharshi enter *nirvikalpa samadhi?*

M. If the eyes are closed, it is *nirvikalpa;* if open, it is (though differentiated, still in absolute repose) *savikalpa.* The ever-present state is the natural state, *sahaja.*

JANUARY 26, 1935

Mr. Evans-Wentz asked. There are yogis with occult powers. What does Maharshi think of them?

M. The powers are known by hearsay or by exhibition. Thus, they are in the realm of the mind only.

D. Mr. Brunton mentions a yogi in Madras who is said to hold communion with his Master in the Himalayas.

M. It is no more marvelous than telepathy — so commonly known. Telepathy cannot exist without the hearer and remote vision without the seer. What is the difference between hearing from far and from near? It is only the hearer who matters. Without him there cannot be hearing; without the seer there cannot be vision.

D. So you want me to consider the subject and not the object.

M. The subject and object appear only after the mind has arisen. The mind comprises them and also the occult powers.

D. Can the manifestations of light (*jothis*) be seen on Arunachala Hill?

M. Yes.

D. Is there any psychic effect in visiting sacred places like Mt. Kailas, Benares, etc.?

M. Yes.

D. Is there any benefit accruing by dying in Benares?

M. Yes, the meaning will be clear if the real Benares and real dying are understood.

D. You mean that they are in the Self?

M. Yes.

D. There are six centers in the body and there are corresponding centers in the world.

M. Yes. What is in the world is in the body; and what is in the body is in the world also.

D. Is the sacredness of Benares a matter of faith, or is it intrinsically also real?

M. Both.

D. Some people are attracted to one place of pilgrimage and others to another. Is it according to their temperaments?

M. Yes. Just consider how all of you born in different places and living in other lands are gathered here today? What is the Force which has attracted you here? If this is understood, the other Force is also understood.

JANUARY 29, 1935

Mr. Grant Duff asked: Where are memory and forgetfulness located?

M. In the mind (*chitta*).

JANUARY 30, 1935

Mr. Evans-Wentz: Is solitude necessary for a *jnani*?

M. Solitude is in the mind of man. One might be in the thick of the world and maintain serenity of mind; such a one is in solitude. Another may stay in a forest, but still be unable to control his mind. He cannot be said to be in solitude. Solitude is a function of the mind. A man attached to desire cannot get solitude wherever he may be; a detached man is always in solitude.

D. So then, one might be engaged in work and be free from desire and stay in solitude. Is that right?

M. Yes. Work performed with attachment is a shackle, whereas work performed with detachment does not affect the doer. He is, even while working, in solitude.

D. They say there are many saints in Tibet who remain in solitude and are still very helpful to the world. How can that be?

M. It can be so. Realization of the Self is the greatest help that can be rendered to humanity. Therefore, the saints are said to be helpful, though they remain in forests. But it should not be forgotten that solitude is not in forests only. It can be had even in towns, in the thick of worldly occupations.

D. Is it not necessary that the saints should mix with people and be helpful to them?

M. The Self alone is the Reality; the world and the rest of it are not. A realized being does not see the world as different from himself.

D. Thus then, the saint's realization leads to the uplift of humanity without the latter being aware of it. Is that so?

M. Yes. The help is imperceptible but is still there. A saint helps the whole of humanity, unknown to the latter.

D. Would it not be better if he mixed with others?

M. There are no others to mix with. The Self is the one and only Reality.

D. If there were a hundred Self-realized men, would it not be to the greater benefit of the world?

M. When you say "Self" you refer to the unlimited, but when you add "men" to it, you limit the meaning. There is only one Infinite Self.

D. Yes, yes, I see! Sri Krishna has said in the *Gita* that work must be performed without attachment and such work is better than idleness. Is it *Karma Yoga*?

M. What is said is given out to suit the temperaments of the hearers.

D. In Europe, it is not generally understood that a man in solitude can be helpful. They imagine that only men working in the world can be useful. When will this confusion cease? Will the European mind continue wading in the morass or will it realize the truth?

M. Never mind Europe or America. Where are they except in your mind? Realize your Self and then all is realized.

If you dream and see several men, and then wake up and recall your dream, do you try to ascertain if the persons of your dream creation are also awake?

D. What does Maharshi think of the theory of universal illusion (*Maya*)?

M. What is *Maya?* It is only Reality.

D. Is not *Maya* illusion?

M. *Maya* is used to signify the manifestations of the Reality. Thus *Maya* is only Reality.

D. Some say that Sri Shankaracharya was only intellectual and not realized. Is that so?

M. Why worry about Shankaracharya? Realize your own Self. Others can take care of themselves.

D. Jesus Christ cured people of their diseases. Is that only an occult power (*siddhi*)?

M. Was Jesus aware at the time that he was curing men? He could not have been conscious of his powers. There is a story related as follows: Jesus had once cured a man of his blindness. The man turned wicked in the course of time. Meeting him after some years, Jesus observed his wickedness and asked him why he was so. He replied saying that, when he was blind, he could not commit any sin. But after Jesus had cured him of blindness, he grew wicked and Jesus was responsible for his wickedness.

D. Was not Jesus a Perfected Being possessing occult powers?

M. He could not have been aware of his powers.

D. Is it not good to acquire them, such as telepathy, etc.?

M. Telepathy enables one to see and hear from afar. They are all the same, hearing and seeing. Whether one hears from near or far does not make any difference in the hearing. The fundamental factor is the hearer, the subject. Without the hearer or the seer, there can be no hearing or seeing. The latter are functions of the mind. The occult powers (*siddhis*) are therefore only in the mind. They are not natural to the Self. That which is not natural, but acquired, cannot be permanent, and is not worth striving for.

A man is possessed of limited powers and is miserable; he wants to expand his powers so that he may be happy. But consider if it will be so. If with limited perceptions, one is miserable, with extended perceptions the misery must increase proportionately. Occult powers will not bring happiness to anyone, but will make him all the more miserable!

Moreover, what are these powers for? The would-be occultist (*siddha*) desires to display the *siddhis* so that others may appreciate him. He seeks appreciation, and if it is not forthcoming, he will not be happy. There must be others to appreciate him. He may even find another possessor of higher powers. That will cause jealousy and breed unhappiness. The higher occultist may meet a still higher *siddha* and so on, until one will appear who blows up everything in a trice. Such is the highest adept and He is God or the Self.

Which is the real power? Is it to increase prosperity or bring about peace? That which results in peace is the highest perfection.

D. But ordinary people in Europe and America would not appreciate such an attitude and would desire a display of powers and instructions by lectures, etc.

M. Lectures may entertain individuals for a few hours without improving them. Silence, on the other hand, is permanent and benefits the whole of humanity.

D. But silence is not understood.

M. It does not matter. By silence, eloquence is meant. Oral lectures are not so eloquent as silence. Silence is unceasing eloquence. The Primal Master, Dakshinamurti, is the ideal. He taught his *rishi* disciples by silence.

D. But then there were disciples for him. It was all right. Now it is different. They must be sought after and helped.

M. That is a sign of ignorance. The power which created you has created the world. If it can take care of you, it can similarly take care of the world, also.

D. What does Bhagavan think of the "lost soul" mentioned by Jesus Christ?

M. Think what there is to be lost. Is there anything to lose? What matters is only that which is natural. Such must be eternal and cannot be experienced. That which is born must die; that which is acquired must be lost. Were you born? You are ever existent. The Self can never be lost.

D. Buddha advises the eightfold path as being the best so that none might be lost.

M. Yes. This is called *Raja Yoga* by the Hindus.

D. Is yoga advised for a spiritual aspirant?

M. Yoga helps control of mind.

D. But does it not lead to occult powers which are said to be dangerous?

M. But you qualified your question by the words "a spiritual aspirant."

JANUARY 31, 1935

Mr. Ellappa Chettiar, a member of the Legislative Council of Madras Presidency and an influential Hindu, asked: Why is it said that the knowledge born of hearing is not firm, whereas that born of contemplation is firm?

M. On the other hand, it is said that hearsay knowledge (*paroksha*) is not

Chapter One—1935

firm, whereas that born of one's own realization (*aparoksha*) is firm.

It is also said that hearing helps the intellectual understanding of the Truth, that meditation makes the understanding clear, and finally that contemplation brings about realization of the Truth. Furthermore, they say also that all such knowledge is not firm, and that it is firm only when it is as clear and intimate as a gooseberry in the hollow of one's palm.

There are those who affirm that hearing alone will suffice. A competent person who had already, perhaps in previous incarnations, qualified himself, realizes and abides in peace as soon as he hears the Truth told him only once, whereas the person not so qualified must pass through the stages prescribed above, before falling into *samadhi*.

Mrs. Piggott returned from Madras for a further visit. She asked questions relating to diet regulation.
D. What diet is prescribed for a *sadhaka* (one engaged in spiritual practices)?
M. *Sattvic* food in limited quantities.
D. What is *sattvic* food?
M. Bread, fruits, vegetables, milk, etc.
D. Some people take fish in North India. May it be done?
   (*No answer was made by Maharshi.*)
D. We Europeans are accustomed to a particular diet; change of diet affects health and weakens the mind. Is it not necessary to keep up physical health?
M. Quite necessary. The weaker the body, the stronger the mind grows.
D. In the absence of our usual diet, our health suffers and the mind loses strength.
M. What do you mean by strength of mind?
D. The power to eliminate worldly attachment.
M. The quality of food influences the mind. The mind feeds on the food consumed.
D. Really! How can the Europeans adjust themselves to *sattvic* food only?
M. (*Pointing to Mr. Evans-Wentz*) You have been taking our food. Do you feel uncomfortable on that account?
Mr. Evans-Wentz: No. Because I am accustomed to it.
D. What about those not so accustomed?
M. Habit is only adjustment to the environment. It is the mind that matters. The fact is that the mind has been trained to think certain foods tasty and good. The food material is to be had in both vegetarian and non-vegetarian diet equally well. But the mind desires such food as it is accustomed to and considers tasty.

D. Are there restrictions for the realized man in a similar manner?

M. No. He is steady and not influenced by the food he takes.

D. Is it not killing life to prepare a meat diet?

M. *Ahimsa* stands foremost in the code of discipline for the yogis.

D. Even plants have life.

M. So too the slabs you sit on!

D. May we gradually get ourselves accustomed to vegetarian food?

M. Yes. That is the way.

FEBRUARY 2, 1935

Mr. Evans-Wentz continued: May one have more than one spiritual Master?

M. Who is a Master? He is the Self after all. According to the stages of development of the mind, the Self manifests as the Master externally. The famous ancient saint Avadhuta said that he had more than twenty-four Masters. The Master is one from whom one learns anything. The Guru may be sometimes inanimate, as in the case of Avadhuta. God, Guru, and the Self are identical.

A spiritual-minded man thinks that God is all-pervading and takes God for his Guru. Later, God brings him in contact with a personal Guru and the man recognizes him as all in all. Lastly, the same man by the Grace of the Master is made to feel that his Self is the Reality and nothing else. Thus, he finds that the Self is the Master.

D. Does Sri Bhagavan initiate his disciples?

(Maharshi kept silent.)

Thereafter, one of the devotees took it upon himself to answer, saying: Maharshi does not see anyone outside his Self. So there are no disciples for him. His Grace is all-pervading and he communicates his Grace to any deserving individual in silence.

D. How does booklore help in Self-realization?

M. Only so far as to make one spiritually minded.

D. How far does intellect help?

M. Only so far as to make one sink the intellect into the ego, and the ego into the Self.

Mrs. Piggott: Why do you take milk, but not eggs?

M. The domesticated cows yield more milk than necessary for their calves and they find it a pleasure to be relieved of the milk.

D. But the hen cannot contain the eggs?

M. But there are potential lives in them.

D. Thoughts cease suddenly, then "I-I" rises up as suddenly and continues. It is only in the feeling and not in the intellect. Can it be right?

M. It is certainly right. Thoughts must cease and reason disappear for "I-I" to rise up and be felt. Feeling is the prime factor and not reason.

D. Moreover, it is not in the head but in the right side of the chest.

M. It ought to be so. Because the Heart is there.

D. When I see outside, it disappears. What is to be done?

M. It must be held tight.

D. If one is active with such remembrance, will the actions be always right?

M. They ought to be. However, such a person is not concerned with the right or wrong of his actions. His actions are God's and therefore they must be right.

D. Why then the restrictions on food?

M. Your present experience is due to the influence of the atmosphere you are in. Can you have it outside this atmosphere? The experience is spasmodic. Until it becomes permanent, practice is necessary. Restrictions of food are aids for such experience to be repeated. After one gets established in truth, the restrictions drop away naturally. Moreover, food influences the mind and it must be kept pure.

The lady told a disciple later: I feel the vibrations from him more intensely and I am able to reach the "I"- center more readily than before.

On a former occasion B.V. Narasimha Swami, author of Self-Realisation, *asked*: Who am I? How is it to be found?

M. Ask yourself this question. The body (*annamaya kosa*) and its functions are not "I." Going deeper, the mind (*manomaya kosa*) and its functions are not "I."

The next step takes one to the question: "Wherefrom do these thoughts arise?" The thoughts may be spontaneous, superficial, or analytical. They operate in the intellect. Then, who is aware of them? The existence of thoughts, their clear conceptions, and their operations become evident to the individual. The analysis leads to the conclusion that the individuality of the person is operative as the perceiver of the existence of thoughts and of their sequence. This individuality is the ego, or as people say, "I." *Vijnanamaya kosa* (intellect) is only the sheath of "I" and not the "I" itself.

Inquiring further, the questions arise: "Who is this 'I'? Wherefrom does it come?" "I" was not aware in sleep. Simultaneously, with its rise, sleep changes to dream or wakefulness. But I am not concerned with the dream just now. Who am I now, in the wakeful state? If "I" originated from sleep, then the "I" was covered up with ignorance. Such an ignorant "I" cannot be what the scriptures say or the wise ones affirm. "I" am beyond even "sleep"; "I" must be now and here and what I was all along in sleep and dreams also, without the qualities of such states. "I" must therefore be the unqualified substratum underlying these three states (*anandamaya kosa* transcended).

"I" is, in brief, beyond the five sheaths. Next, the residuum after discarding all that which is not-self is the Self, *Sat-Chit-Ananda*.

D. How is that Self to be known or realized?

M. Transcend the present plane of relativity. A separate being (Self) appears to know something apart from itself (non-Self). That is, the subject is aware of the object. The seer is *drik*; the seen is *drisya*.

There must be a unity underlying these two, which arises as "ego." This ego is of the nature of *chit* (intelligence); *achit* (insentient object) is only negation of *chit*. Therefore, the underlying essence is akin to the subject and not the object. Seeking the *drik*, until all *drisya* disappears, the *drik* will become subtler and subtler, until the absolute *drik* alone survives. This process is called *drisya vilaya* (the disappearance of the objective world).

D. Why should the objects (*drisya*) be eliminated? Cannot the Truth be realized even keeping the object as it is?

M. No. Elimination of *drisya* means elimination of the separate identities of subject and object. The object is unreal. All *drisya* (including ego) is the object. Eliminating the unreal, Reality survives. When a rope is mistaken for a snake, it is enough to remove the erroneous perception of the snake for the truth to be revealed. Without such elimination, truth will not dawn.

D. When and how is the disappearance of the objective world (*drisya vilaya*) to be effected?

M. It is complete when the relative subject, namely the mind, is eliminated. The mind is the creator of the subject and the object and the cause of the dualistic idea. Therefore, it is the cause of the wrong notion of limited self and the misery consequent on such an erroneous idea.

D. What is this mind?

M. Mind is one form of the manifestation of life. A block of wood or a subtle machine is not called mind. The vital force manifests as life activity and also as the conscious phenomena known as the mind.

D. What is the relationship between mind and object? Is the mind contacting something different from itself, *viz.*, the world?

M. The world is "sensed" in the waking and the dream states, or is the object of perception and thought, both being mental activities. If there were no such activities as waking and dreaming thought, there would be no "perception" or inference of a "world." In sleep, there is no such activity, and "objects and world" do not exist for us. Hence, "reality of the world" may be created by the ego in its act of emergence from sleep; and that reality may be swallowed up or disappear by the soul resuming its nature in sleep. The emergence and disappearance of the world are like the spider producing a gossamer web and then withdrawing it. The spider here underlies all the three states — waking, dreaming, and sleep; such a spider in the person is called *Atman* (Self), whereas the same with reference to the world (which is considered to issue from the sun) is called *Brahman* (Supreme Spirit). He that is in man is the same as He that is in the sun. (*Sa yaschayam purushe yaschasavaditye sa ekah.*)

While Self or Spirit is unmanifest and inactive, there are no relative dualities; e.g., subject and object — *drik* and *drisya*. If the inquiry into the ultimate cause of manifestation of mind itself is pushed on, mind will be found to be only the manifestation of the Real which is otherwise called *Atman* or *Brahman*. The mind is termed *sukshma sarira* or "thought-body"; and *jiva* is the individual soul. The *jiva* is the essence of the growth of individuality; personality is referred to as *jiva*. Thought or mind is said to be its phase, or one of the ways in which the *jiva* manifests itself — the earlier stage or phase of such manifestation being vegetative life. This mind is always seen as being related to, or acting on, some non-mind or matter, and never by itself. Therefore mind and matter co-exist.

D. How shall we discover the nature of the mind *i.e.*, its ultimate cause, or the noumenon of which it is a manifestation?

M. Arranging thoughts in the order of value, the "I"-thought is the all-important thought. Personality-idea or thought is also the root or the stem of all other thoughts, since each idea or thought arises only as someone's thought and is not known to exist independently of the ego. The ego therefore exhibits thought activity. The second and the third persons do not appear except to the first person. Therefore, they arise only after the first person appears, so all the three persons seem to rise and sink together. Trace, then, the ultimate cause of "I" or personality. The "I" idea arises to an embodied ego and should be related to a body or organism. Has it a location in the body or a special relation to any particular spot, just as speech and libido have their centers in the brain? Similarly, does "I" have any center in the brain, blood, or viscera? Thought-life is seen to center around the brain and the spinal cord which in turn are fed by the blood circulating in them, carrying nutrients and oxygen which are transformed into nerve matter. Thus, the vegetative life — including circulation, respiration, alimentation — or the vital force, is said to be (or reside in) the core or essence of the organism. Thus the mind may be regarded as a manifestation of the vital force which again may be conceived as residing in the Heart.

D. Now for the art of eliminating the mind and developing intuition in its stead, are they two distinct stages with a possibly neutral ground which is neither mind nor intuition? Or does the absence of mental activity necessarily involve Self-realization?

M. To the *abhyasi* (practitioner) there are two distinctive stages. There is a neutral ground of sleep, coma, faint, insanity, etc., in which the mental operations either do not exist or consciousness of Self does not prevail.

D. Taking the first part first, how is the mind to be eliminated or relative consciousness transcended?

M. The mind is by nature restless. Begin liberating it from its restlessness; give it peace, make it free from distractions, train it to look inward, and make all this a habit. This is done by ignoring the external world and removing the obstacles to peace of mind.

D. How is restlessness removed from the mind?

M. External contacts — contacts with objects other than itself — make the mind restless. Loss of interest in non-Self (*vairagya*) is the first step. Then the habits of introspection and concentration will follow. They are characterized by control of external senses, internal faculties (*sama, dama,* etc.), ending in *samadhi* (undistracted mind).

D. How are they practiced?

M. An examination of the ephemeral nature of external phenomena leads to dispassion (*vairagya*). Hence inquiry (*vichara*) is the first and foremost step to be taken. When *vichara* continues automatically, it results in a contempt for wealth, fame, ease, pleasure, etc. The "I"-thought becomes clearer for inspection. The source of "I" is the Heart — the final goal. If, however, the aspirant is not temperamentally suited to *Vichara Marga* (the introspective analytical method), he must develop *bhakti* (devotion) to an ideal — maybe God, Guru, humanity in general, ethical laws, or even the idea of beauty. When one of these takes possession of the individual, other attachments grow weaker; *i.e.,* dispassion develops. Attachment for the ideal simultaneously grows and finally holds the field. Thus *ekagrata* (concentration) grows simultaneously and imperceptibly — with or without visions and direct aids.

In the absence of inquiry and devotion, the natural sedative *pranayama* (breath regulation) may be tried. This is known as *Yoga Marga.* If life is imperiled, the whole interest centers around the one point, the saving of life. If the breath is held, the mind cannot afford to (and does not) jump at its pets — external objects. Thus there is rest for the mind so long as the breath is held. All attention being turned on breath or its regulation, other interests are lost. Again, passions are attended with irregular breathing, whereas calm and happiness are attended with slow and regular breathing. A paroxysm of joy is in fact as painful as one of pain, and both are accompanied by ruffled breaths. Real peace is happiness. Pleasures do not form happiness. The mind improves by practice and becomes finer just as the razor's edge is sharpened by stropping. The mind is then better able to tackle internal or external problems. If an aspirant is unsuited temperamentally for the first two methods, and circumstantially (on account of age) for the third method, he must try the *Karma Marga* (doing good deeds, for example, social service). His nobler instincts will become more evident and he derives impersonal pleasure. His smaller self is less assertive and has a chance of expanding its good side. The person becomes duly equipped for one of these three paths. His intuition may also develop directly by this single method.

D. Can a line of thought or a series of questions induce Self-hypnotism? Should it not be reduced to a single point analyzing the unanalyzable, elementary, vaguely perceived and elusive "I"?

M. Yes. It is really like gazing into vacancy or a dazzling crystal or light.

D. Can the mind be fixed to that point? How?

M. If the mind is distracted, ask the question promptly, "To whom do these distracting thoughts arise?" That takes you back to the "I"-point immediately.

D. How long can the mind stay or be kept in the Heart?

M. The period extends by practice.

D. What happens at the end of the period?

M. The mind returns to the present normal state. Unity in the Heart is replaced by a variety of phenomena perceived. This is called the outgoing mind. The Heart-going mind is called the resting mind.

D. Is all this process merely intellectual or does it predominantly exhibit feeling?

M. The latter.

D. How do all thoughts cease when the mind is in the Heart?

M. By force of will, with strong faith in the truth of the Master's teaching to that effect.

D. What is the good of this process?

M. 1. Conquest of the will — development of concentration.

    2. Conquest of passions — development of dispassion.

    3. Increased practice of virtue — (*samatva*) equality to all.

D. Why should one adopt this self-hypnosis by thinking on the unthinkable point? Why not adopt other methods like gazing into a light, holding one's breath, listening to music, hearing internal sounds, repetition of the sacred syllable (*Pranava*) or other mantras?

M. Light-gazing stupefies the mind and produces catalepsy of the will for the time being, yet secures no permanent benefit. Breath control benumbs the will only. Temporarily listening to sounds produces similar results — unless the mantra is sacred and secures the help of a higher power to purify and elevate the thoughts.

D. What is the relationship between the regulation of thought and that of the breath?

M. Thought and respiration, circulation, etc. (vegetative) activities are both different aspects of the same — the individual life. Both depend upon (or metaphorically, "reside" or "inhere" in) life. Personality and other ideas spring from it like the vital activity. If respiration or other vital activity is forcibly repressed, thought also is repressed. If thought is forcibly slowed down and pinned to a point, the vital activity of respiration is also slowed down, made even, and confined to the lowest level compatible with sustenance of life. In both cases, the distracting variety of thought is temporarily at an end. The interaction is noticeable in other ways also. Take the will to live. That is thought-power. It sustains life when other vitality is almost exhausted and delays death. In the absence of such willpower, death is accelerated. So thought is said to carry life with it in the flesh and from one fleshy body to another.

D. Are there any aids to concentration and casting off distractions?

M. Physically the digestive and other organs are to be kept free from irritation. Therefore, food is regulated in both quantity and quality. Non-irritants are eaten, avoiding chilies, excess of salt, onions, wine, opium, etc. Avoid constipation, drowsiness and excitement, and all foods that induce them. Mentally take interest in one thing and fix the mind on it. Let such interest be all-absorbing to the exclusion of everything else. This is dispassion (*vairagya*) and concentration. God or mantra may be chosen. The mind gains strength to grasp the subtle and merge into it.

D. Distractions result from inherited tendencies. Can they be cast off too?

M. Yes. Many have done so. Believe it! They did so because they believed they could. *Vasanas* (predispositions) can be obliterated. It is done by concentration on that which is free from *vasanas* and yet is their core.

D. How long is the practice to continue?

M. Till success is achieved and until yoga-liberation becomes permanent. Success begets success. If one distraction is conquered, the next is conquered and so on, until all are finally conquered. The process is like reducing an enemy's fort by slaying its manpower — one by one.

D. What is the goal of this process?

M. Realizing the Real.

D. What is the nature of Reality?

M. 1. Existence without beginning or end — eternal.

  2. Existence everywhere, endless, infinite.

  3. Existence underlying all forms, all changes, all forces, all matter, and all spirit.

  The many change and pass away (phenomena), whereas the One ever endures (noumenon).

  4. The one displacing the triads, *i.e.,* the knower, the knowledge and the known. The triads are only appearances in time and space, whereas the Reality lies beyond and behind them. They are like a mirage over the Reality. They are the result of delusion.

D. If "I" is also an illusion, who then casts off the illusion?

M. The "I" casts off the illusion of "I" and yet remains as "I." Such is the paradox of Self-realization. The realized do not see any contradiction in it. Take the case of *bhakti*. I approach *Ishvara* and pray to be absorbed in Him. I then surrender myself in faith and by concentration. What remains afterwards? In place of the original "I," perfect self-surrender leaves a residuum of God in which the "I" is lost. This is the highest form of devotion (*parabhakti*), surrender (*prapatti*), or the height of dispassion (*vairagya*).

  You give up this and that of "my" possessions. If you give up "I" and "mine" instead, all are given up in one stroke. The very seed of possession is lost: thus the evil is nipped in the bud. Dispassion must be very strong to do this. Eagerness must be equal to that of a man kept under water trying to rise to the surface for his life.

D. Can this trouble and difficulty be lessened with the aid of a Master or an *Ishta Devata* (God chosen for worship)? Can they give the power to see our Self as it is — to change us into themselves — to take us into Self-realization?

M. *Ishta Devata* and Guru are aids — very powerful aids on this path. But an aid to be effective requires effort on your part also. Your effort is a *sine qua non*. It is you who should see the sun. Can spectacles and the sun see for you? You yourself have to see your true nature. Not much aid is required for doing it!

D. What is the relation between my free will and the overwhelming might of the Omnipotent?

    1. Is omniscience of God consistent with ego's free will?

    2. Is omnipotence of God consistent with ego's free will?

    3. Are the natural laws consistent with God's free will?

M. Yes. Free will is the present appearing to a limited faculty of sight and will. The same ego sees its past activity as falling into a course of "law" or rules — its own free will being one of the links in that course of law.

Omnipotence and omniscience of God are then seen by the ego to have acted through the appearance of its own free will. So he comes to the conclusion that the ego must go by appearances. Natural laws are manifestations of God's will and they have been laid down.

D. Is study of science, psychology, physiology, philosophy, etc. helpful for:

    1. This art of yoga-liberation?

    2. The intuitive grasp of the unity of the Real?

M. Very little. Some knowledge is needed for yoga and it may be found in books. But practical application is the thing needed. Personal example, personal touch, and personal instructions are the most helpful. As for the other, a person may laboriously convince himself of the truth to be intuited, i.e., its function and nature, but the actual intuition is akin to feeling and requires practice and personal contact. Mere book learning is not of any great use. After realization all intellectual loads are useless burdens and are thrown overboard as jetsam. Jettisoning the ego is necessary and natural.

D. How does dreaming differ from waking?

M. While dreaming, one takes on different bodies; one re-enters this body when dreaming of sense contacts.

D. What is happiness? Is it inhering in the *Atman* or in the object, or in the contact between the subject and the object? But we do not see happiness in our affairs. When does it actually arise?

M. When there is contact of a desirable sort or its memory, and when there is freedom from undesirable contacts or their memory, we say there is happiness. Such happiness is relative and is more appropriately called pleasure.

But people want absolute and permanent happiness. This does not reside in objects, but in the Absolute. It is Peace free from pain and pleasure — a neutral state.

D. In what sense is happiness our real nature?

M. Perfect bliss is *Brahman*. Perfect Peace is of the Self. That alone exists and is conscious. The same conclusion is arrived at when judged metaphysically, and inferred by *Bhakti Marga* (Path of Devotion).

We pray to God for bliss and receive it by Grace. The bestower of bliss must be bliss itself and also Infinite. Therefore, *Ishvara* is the Personal God of infinite power and bliss. *Brahman* is bliss, impersonal, and absolute. The finite egos, deriving their source from *Brahman* and then *Ishvara*, are in their spiritual nature bliss only. Biologically, an organism functions because such functions are attended by happiness. It is pleasure that helps our growth; food, exercise, rest, and gregarious qualities. The psychology (and metaphysics) of pleasure is perhaps this: Our nature is primarily one, whole, and blissful. Take this as a probable hypothesis. Creation is by the entire Godhead breaking into God and Nature (*maya* or *prakriti*). This *maya* is of two parts: (*para*) the supporting essence and (*apara*) the five elements, mind, intellect, and ego (eightfold).

Ego's perfection is suddenly broken at a point and a want is felt, giving rise to a desire to get something or do something. When that want is cured by the fulfillment of that desire, the ego is happy and the original perfection restored. Therefore, happiness may be said to be our natural condition or nature. Pleasure and pain are relative and refer to our finite state, which ever progresses through the satisfaction of our wants. If this relative progress is stopped and the soul merges into *Brahman*, that soul ceases to have relative, temporary pleasure and enjoys perfect peace, bliss. Hence, Self-realization is bliss; it is realizing the Self as the limitless spiritual eye (*jnana dristi*) and not clairvoyance; it is the highest self-surrender. *Samsara* (empirical process) is sorrow.

D. Why then is *samsara* — finite creation and manifestation — so full of sorrow and evil?

M. God's will!

D. Why does God will it so?

M. It is inscrutable. No motive can be attributed to that Power — no desire, no end to achieve can be asserted of that one infinite, all-wise and all-powerful Being. God is untouched by activities, which take place in His presence; compare the sun and the world activities. There is no meaning in attributing responsibility and motive to the One before it becomes many. But God's will for the prescribed course of events is a good solution of the free-will problem. If the mind is restless on account of a sense of the imperfect and unsatisfactory character of what befalls us, or what is committed or omitted by us, then it is wise to drop the sense of responsibility and free will by regarding ourselves as the ordained instruments of the All-wise and All-powerful, to do and suffer as He pleases. He carries all burdens and gives us peace.

On another occasion, the evening was calm and cloudy. It was drizzling occasionally and somewhat cool in consequence. The windows of the Asramam Hall were closed and Maharshi was seated as usual on the sofa. Facing him sat the devotees. Some visitors had come from Cuddalore. A sub-judge, accompanied by two elderly ladies, was among them. The sub-judge began a discussion about the impermanence of all mundane things, by putting the question: Has discrimination between Reality and Unreality (*Sat asat vicharana*) the efficacy in itself to lead us to realization of the one imperishable?

M. As propounded by all and realized by all true seekers, fixity in the Supreme Spirit (*Brahma nishta*) alone can make us know and realize it. It being of us and in us, any amount of discrimination (*vivechana*) can lead us only one step forward, by making us renouncers, by goading us into discarding the seeming (*ubhasa*) as transitory and holding fast to the eternal truth and presence alone.

The conversation turned upon the question as to whether Ishvara Prasad (Divine Grace) is necessary for attaining samrajya (universal dominion) or whether a jiva's honest and strenuous efforts cannot of themselves lead him to That whence there is no return to life and death. Maharshi, with an ineffable smile that lit up his holy face and which was all-pervasive, shining upon the coterie around him, replied in tones of certainty and with the ring of truth: Divine Grace is essential for realization. It leads one to God-realization. But such Grace is vouchsafed only to him who is a true devotee or a yogin, who has striven hard and ceaselessly on the path towards freedom.

D. There are six centers mentioned in the yoga books; but the *jiva* is said to reside in the Heart. Is it not so?

M. Yes. The *jiva* is said to remain in the Heart in deep sleep; and in the brain in the waking state. The Heart need not be taken to be the muscular cavity with four chambers, which propels blood. There are indeed passages in the literature which support this view. There are others who take it to mean a set of ganglia or nerve centers about that region. Whichever view is correct does not matter to us. We are not concerned with anything less than ourself. That we have certainly within us. There could be no doubts or discussions about that.

The Heart is used in the *Vedas* and the scriptures to denote the place whence the notion "I" springs. Does it spring only from that fleshy ball? It springs within us somewhere right in the middle of our being. The "I" has no location. Everything is the Self. There is nothing but that. So the Heart must be said to be the entire body of ourselves and of the entire universe conceived as "I." But to help the practitioner (*abhyasi*) we have to indicate a definite part of the universe, or of the body. So this Heart is pointed out as the seat of the Self. But in truth we are everywhere, we are all that is, and there is nothing else.

D. It is said that Divine Grace is necessary to fully attain undistracted mind (*samadhi*). Is that so?

M. We are God (*Ishvara*). *Ishvara Drishti* (i.e., seeing ourselves as God) is itself Divine Grace. So we need Divine Grace to get God's Grace.

(Maharshi smiles and all devotees laugh together.)

D. There is also Divine Favor (*Ishvara anugraham*) as distinct from Divine Grace (*Ishvara prasadam*). Is that so?

M. The thought of God is Divine Favor! He is by nature Grace (*prasad* or *arul*). It is by God's Grace that you think of God.

D. Is not the Master's Grace the result of God's Grace?

M. Why distinguish between the two? The Master is the same as God and not different from him.

D. When an endeavor is made to lead the right life and to concentrate thought on the Self, there is often a downfall and break. What then is to be done?

M. It will come all right in the end. There is the steady impulse of your determination that sets you on your feet again after every downfall. Gradually the obstacles are all overcome and your current becomes stronger. Everything comes right in the end. Steady determination is what is required.

Mr. N. Natesa Iyer, an orthodox Brahmin, and leader of the Bar in a South Indian town, asked: Are the gods *Ishvara* or *Vishnu* and their sacred regions *Kailasa* or *Vaikuntha* real?

M. As real as you are in this body.

D. Do they possess a *vyavahara satya*, i.e., phenomenal existence, like my body? Or are they fictions like the horn of a hare?

M. They do exist.

D. If so, they must be somewhere. Where are they?

M. Persons who have seen them say they exist somewhere. So we must accept their statement.

D. Where do they exist?

M. In you.

D. Then it is only an idea — that which I can create and control?

M. Everything is like that.

D. But I can create pure fictions e.g., hare's horn or part-truths, e.g. mirage, while there are also facts irrespective of my imagination. Do the gods *Ishvara* or *Vishnu* exist as such?

M. Yes.

D. Is He subject to *pralaya* (cosmic dissolution)?

M. Why? Man becoming aware of the Self transcends cosmic dissolution (*pralaya*) and becomes liberated (*mukta*). Why not God (*Ishvara*) who is infinitely wiser and abler?

D. Do *devas* and *pisachas* (devils) exist similarly?

M. Yes.

D. How are we to conceive of Supreme Consciousness (*Chaitanya Brahman*)?

M. As that which is.

D. Should it be thought of as Self-Effulgent?

M. It transcends light and darkness. An individual (*jiva*) sees both. The Self enlightens i.e., enables such perception; the Self provides the "light" enabling the individual to "see" light and darkness as such.

D. Should it be realized as "I am not the body, nor the agent, nor the enjoyer, etc."?

M. Why these thoughts? Do we now think that we are men, etc.? By not thinking so do we cease to be men?

D. Should one realize it then by the scriptural text such as "There are no differences here?"

M. Why even that?

D. If we think "I am the real," will it do?

M. All thoughts are inconsistent with realization. The correct state is to exclude thoughts of ourselves as well as all other thoughts. Thought is one thing and realization is quite another.

D. Is it not necessary, or at least advantageous, to render the body invisible in one's spiritual progress?

M. Why do you think of that? Are you the body?

D. No. But advanced spirituality must effect a change in the body, must it not?

M. What change do you desire in the body, and why?

D. Is not invisibility evidence of advanced wisdom (*jnana*)?

M. In that case, all those who spoke, who wrote and who passed their lives in the sight of others must be considered ignorant (*ajnanis*)!

D. But did the sages Vasishta and Valmiki possess such powers?

M. It might have been their fate (*prarabdha*) to develop such powers (*siddhis*) side by side with their wisdom (*jnana*). Why should you aim at that which is not essential but apt to prove a hindrance to wisdom? Does the Sage feel oppressed by his body being visible?

D. No.

M. A hypnotist can suddenly render himself invisible. Does that make him into a Sage?

D. No.

M. Visibility and invisibility refer to a seer. Who is that seer? Solve that first. Other matters are unimportant.

D. The *Vedas* contain conflicting accounts of cosmogony. Ether is said to be the first creation in one place; vital energy (*prana*) in another place; something else in yet another; water in still another, and so on. How are these to be reconciled? Do not these impair the credibility of the *Vedas*?

M. Different seers saw different aspects of truths at different times, each emphasizing a particular view. Why do you worry about their conflicting statements? The essential aim of the *Veda* is to teach the nature of the imperishable *Atman* and show us we are That.

D. I am satisfied with that portion.

M. Then treat all the rest as *artha vada* (auxiliary arguments) or expositions for the sake of the ignorant who seek to trace the genesis of things.

D. I am a sinner. I do not perform religious sacrifices (*homas*), etc. Shall I have painful rebirths for that reason? Pray save me!

M. Why do you say you are a sinner? Your trust in God is sufficient to save you from rebirths. Cast all burden onto Him.

In the *Tiruvachakam* it is said: "Though I am worse than a dog, you have graciously undertaken to protect me. This delusion of birth and death is

---

29

maintained by you. Moreover, am I the person to sift and judge? Am I the Lord here? Oh Maheswara! It is for you to roll me through bodies (by births and deaths) or keep me fixed at your own feet." Therefore have faith and that will save you.

D. Sir, I have faith — and yet I encounter difficulties. Weakness and giddiness afflict me after practicing concentration.

M. Breath control (*pranayama*), properly performed, should increase one's strength.

D. I have my professional work and yet I want to be in perpetual *dhyana*. Will they conflict with each other?

M. There will be no conflict. As you practice both and develop your powers you will be able to attend to both. You will begin to look on business as a dream.

> "That which is the night of all beings, for the disciplined man is the
> time of waking; when other beings are waking, then it is night for
> the sage who seeth."
> — *Bhagavad Gita* 11.69

A visitor asked: What to do to get liberation (*moksha*)?

M. Learn what liberation is.

D. Should I do worship (*upasana*) for it?

M. Worship is for mind control (*chitta nirodha*) and concentration.

D. Should I do idol worship? Is there any harm in it?

M. So long as you think you are the body, there is no harm.

D. How to get over the cycle of births and deaths?

M. Learn what it means.

D. Should I not leave my wife and family?

M. How do they harm you? First find out who you are.

D. Should not one give up one's wife, wealth, home?

M. Learn first what *samsara* is. Is all that the cycle (*samsara*)? Have there not been men living among them and getting realization?

D. What are the steps of practical training (*sadhana*) for it?

M. It depends on the qualifications and the nature of the seeker.

D. I am doing idol worship.

M. Go on with it. It leads to concentration of mind. Become one-pointed. All will come out right. People think that freedom (*moksha*) is somewhere yonder and should be sought out. They are wrong. Freedom is only knowing the Self within you. Concentrate and you will get it. Your mind is the cycle of births and deaths (*samsara*).

D. My mind is very unsteady. What should I do?

M. Fix your attention on any single thing and try to hold it there. All will be right.

D. I find concentration difficult.

M. Go on practicing. Your concentration will become as easy as breathing. That will be your crowning achievement.

D. Are not abstinence and pure food helpful?

M. Yes, all that is good.

(Then Maharshi concentrates and silently gazes at vacancy, and thus sets an example to the questioner.)

D. Don't I require yoga?

M. What is it but the means to concentration?

D. To help concentration, is it not good to have some aids?

M. Breath regulation, etc., are such helps.

D. Is it not possible to get a vision of God?

M. Yes. You see this and that. Why not see God? Only you must first know what God is. All are seeing God always, but they do not realize it. You find out what God is. People see, yet see not, because they know not God.

D. Should I not go on with repetition of sacred syllables (*mantra japa*), e.g., Krishna or Rama's name, when worshipping images?

M. Mental *japa* is very good. That helps meditation. Mind gets identified with the repetition and then you get to know what worship (*puja*) really is — losing one's individuality into that which is worshipped.

D. Is the Universal Soul (*Paramatma*) always different from us?

M. That is the common belief, but it is wrong. Think of Him as not different from you, and then you achieve identity of Self with God.

D. Is it not the *Advaita* doctrine to become one with God?

M. Where is becoming? The thinker is all the while the Real. He ultimately realizes the fact. Sometimes we forget our identities, as in sleep and dreams. But God is perpetual consciousness.

D. Is not the Master's guidance necessary, besides idol worship?

M. How did you start it without advice?

D. From sacred books (*puranas*).

M. Yes. Someone tells you of God or Bhagavan himself. In the latter case, God Himself is your Master. What does it matter who the Master is? We really are one with the Master or Bhagavan. The Master is God; one discovers it in the end. There is no difference between human-guru and God-guru.

D. If we have done virtuous action (*punya*) the achievement will not leave us, I hope.

M. You will reap your destiny (*prarabdha*) that way.

D. Will not a wise Master be a great help in pointing out the way?

M. Yes. If you go on working with the light available, you will meet your Master, as he himself will be seeking you.

D. Is there a difference between *prapatti* (self-surrender) and the path of Yoga of the seers?

M. *Jnana Marga* and *Bhakti Marga* (*prapatti*) are one and the same. Self-surrender leads to realization just as inquiry does. Complete self-surrender means that you have no further thought of "I." Then all your predispositions (*samskaras*) are washed away and you are free. You should not continue as a separate entity at the end of either course.

D. Don't we go to Heaven (*svarga*), etc. as the result of our actions?

M. That is as true as the present existence. But if we inquire who we are and discover the Self, what need is there to think of heaven, etc.?

D. Should I not try to escape rebirth?

M. Yes. Find out who is born and who has the trouble of existence now. When you are asleep, do you think of rebirths or even the present existence? So find out whence the present problem arises and there is the solution, also. You will discover that there is no birth, no present trouble or unhappiness, etc. All is That; all is bliss; we are freed from rebirth, in fact. Why fret over the misery of rebirth?

A visitor: The saints Sri Chaitanya and Sri Ramakrishna wept before God and achieved success. Is that not the path to follow?

M. Yes. There was a powerful force (*shakti*) drawing them on through all those experiences. Trust in that immense power to take you to your goal. Tears are often considered a sign of weakness. These great persons were certainly not weak. These manifestations are only passing signs of the great current carrying them on. We must look to the end achieved.

D. Can this physical body be made to disappear into nothingness?

M. Why ask this question? Can you not find out if you are the body?

D. Can we have disappearance from sight (*antardhana*) like the yogis Vasishta or Viswamitra?

M. These are only physical matters. Is that the essential object of our interest? Are you not the Self? Why trouble yourself about other things? Take the essence; reject other learned theories as useless. They who think that physical disappearance matters for our freedom are mistaken. No such thing is needed. You are not the body; what difference does it make whether it disappears in one way or another? There is no great merit in such phenomena. In what does superiority or inferiority consist? Achievement of the Real alone matters. The loss of "I" is the main fact, and not the loss of body. Identity of the Self with the body is the real bondage. Leave off the false notion and perceive the Real intuitively. That alone matters. If you melt a gold ornament before testing it to be gold, what does it matter how it is melted, whole or in parts, or of what shape the ornament was? All that you are interested in is whether it is gold. The dead man sees not his body. It is the survivor that thinks about the manner in which the body is parted from. The realized have no death with or without the body; the realized person is equally aware and sees no difference. To him the one state is not superior to the other. To an outsider also, the fortunes of a liberated person's body need not be of any concern; mind your business. Realize the Self; after realization there will be time to think of what form of death is preferable to you. It is the false identity of the Self with the body that causes the idea of preference, etc. Are you the body? Were you aware of it when you were fast asleep last night? No! What is it that exists now and troubles you? It is "I." Get rid of that and be happy.

A visitor: "The Supreme Spirit (*Brahman*) is Real. The world (*jagat*) is illusion," is the stock phrase of Sri Shankaracharya. Yet others say, "The world is Reality." Which statement is true?
M. Both statements are true. They refer to different stages of development and are spoken from different points of view. The aspirant (*abhyasi*) starts with the definition that that which is real exists always; then he eliminates the world as unreal because it is changing. It cannot be real; "not this, not this!" The seeker ultimately reaches the Self and there finds unity as the prevailing note. Then, that which was originally rejected as being unreal is found to be a part of the unity. Being absorbed in the Reality, the world also is Real. There is only being in Self-realization, and nothing else. Again Reality is used in a different sense and is applied loosely by some thinkers to objects. They say that the reflected (*adhyasika*) Reality admits of degrees which are named:

1. *Vyavaharika satya* (everyday life) — this chair is seen by me and is real.

2. *Pratibhasika satya* (illusory) — illusion of a serpent in a coiled rope. The appearance is real to the man who thinks so. This phenomenon appears at a point of time and under certain circumstances.

3. *Paramartika satya* (ultimate) — Reality is that which remains the same always and without change.

If Reality is used in the wider sense, the world may be said to have everyday life and illusory degrees (*vyavaharika* and *pratibhasika satya*). Some, however, deny even the reality of practical life — *vyavaharika satya* and consider it to be only a projection of the mind. According to them it is only *pratibhasika satya*, i.e., an illusion.

Yogi Ramiah's Account of His Experiences:
Sitting in Maharshi's presence brings peace of mind. I used to sit in *samadhi* for three or four hours. Then I felt my mind took a form and came out from within. By constant practice and meditation, it entered the Heart and was merged into it. I concluded that the Heart is the resting place of mind. The result is peace. When the mind is absorbed in the Heart, the Self is realized. This could be felt even at the stage of concentration (*dharana*).

I asked Maharshi about contemplation. He taught me as follows: When a man dies the funeral pyre is prepared and the body is laid flat on the pyre. The pyre is lit. The skin is burnt, then the flesh, and then the bones until the whole body falls to ashes. What remains thereafter? The mind. The question arises, "How many are there in this body — one or two?" If two, why do people say "I" and not "we"? There is therefore only one. Whence is it born? What is its nature (*svarupa*)? Inquiring thusly, the mind also disappears. Then what remains is seen to be "I." The next question is "Who am I?" The Self alone. This is contemplation. It is how I did it. By this process, attachment to the body (*dehavasana*) is destroyed. The ego vanishes. Self alone shines. One method of getting mind-dissolution (*manolaya*) is association with great ones — the yoga adepts (*yoga arudhas*). They are perfect adepts in *samadhi*. Self-realization has been easy, natural, and perpetual to them. Those moving with them closely and in sympathetic contact gradually absorb the *samadhi* habit from them.

An educated visitor asked Bhagavan about dvaita *and* advaita.
M. Identification with the body is *dvaita*. Non-identification is *advaita*.

An aristocratic and distinguished lady visitor from the North accompanied by her private secretary arrived at noon, waited a few minutes and asked Maharshi soon

34

after he returned to the Hall after lunch: Maharajji, can we see the dead?

M. Yes.

D. Can the yogis show them to us?

M. Yes. They may. But do not ask me to show them to you, for I cannot.

D. Do you see them?

M. Yes, in dreams.

D. Can we realize the goal through yoga?

M. Yes.

D. Have you written on yoga? Are there books on the subject by you?

M. Yes.

After she left, the Master observed: Did we know our relatives before their birth that we should know them after their death?

Someone asked: "What is karma?"

M. That which has already begun to bear fruit is classified as *prarabdha karma* (past action). That which is in store and will bear fruit later is classified as *sanchita karma* (accumulated action). This is multifarious like the grain obtained by villagers as barter for cress (greens). Such bartered grain consists of rice, ragi, barley, etc. Some float on water while others sink. Some of it may be good, bad or indifferent. When the most potent of the multifarious accumulated karma begins to bear fruit in the next birth, it is called the *prarabdha* of that birth.

When one of the present attendants came to Bhagavan for the first time, he asked: What is the way for liberation?

Maharshi replied: The way already taken leads to liberation.

MARCH 28, 1935

Mr. S. Ranganathan, Collector of Vellore and Mr. S.V. Ramamurthi (both with the Indian Civil Service), and Mr. T. Raghaviah, late Diwan of Pudukottah State, visited the Asramam. Mr. Ranganathan asked: Kindly instruct me as to how the mind may be controlled.

M. There are two methods. The one is to see what the mind is; then it subsides. The second is to fix your attention on something; then the mind remains quiet.

(*The questioner repeated the question for further elucidation. The same answer was returned with a little more added. The questioner did not look satisfied.*)

Mr. Raghaviah: Men of the world that we are, we have some kind of grief or another and do not know how to get over it. We pray to God and still are not satisfied. What can we do?

M. Trust God.

D. We surrender; but still there is no help.

M. Yes. If you have surrendered, you must be able to abide by the will of God and not make an issue of what may not please you. Things may turn out differently from what they appear to be. Distress often leads men to faith in God.

D. But we are worldly. There is a wife, there are children, friends and relatives. We cannot ignore their existence and resign ourselves to Divine Will without retaining a little of the personality in us.

M. That means you have not surrendered as professed by you. You must trust only God.

Mr. Ramamurthi: Swamiji, I have read Brunton's book *A Search in Secret India,* and was much impressed by the last chapter, where he says that it is possible to be conscious without thinking. I know that one can think, remaining forgetful of the physical body. Can one think without the mind? Is it possible to gain that consciousness which is beyond thoughts?

M. Yes. There is only one consciousness, which subsists in the waking, dream, and sleep states. In sleep there is no "I." The "I"-thought arises on waking and then the world appears. Where was this "I" in sleep? Was it there or was it not? It must have been there also, but not in the way you feel now. The present is only the "I"-thought, whereas the sleeping "I" is the real "I." It subsists throughout. It is consciousness. If it is known, you will see that it is beyond thoughts.

D. Can we think without the mind?

M. Thoughts may be like any other activity, not disturbing to the Supreme consciousness.

D. Can one read others' minds?

M. Where are others apart from one's own Self?

(The Master as usual told him to find his Self before worrying about others.)

Mr. Raghaviah: How shall we relate the higher experience to the lower experience (meaning spiritual experience to mundane affairs)?

M. There is only one experience. What are the worldly experiences but those built on the false "I"? Ask the most successful man in the world if he knows his Self. He will say "No." What can anyone know without knowing the Self? All worldly knowledge is built upon such a flimsy foundation.

36

Mr. Ramamurthi: How to know the "Real I" as distinct from the "false I"?
M. Is there anyone who is not aware of himself? Each one knows, but yet does not know, the Self. A strange paradox!

The Master later added: If the inquiry is made whether mind exists, it will be found that mind does not exist. That is control of mind. Otherwise, if the mind is taken to exist and one seeks to control it, it amounts to mind controlling the mind, just like a thief turning out to be a policeman to catch the thief, i.e., himself. Mind persists in that way alone, but eludes itself.

APRIL 3, 1935
*Mr. Ekanath Rao, an engineer, asked Sri Bhagavan if solitude is necessary for vi*chara.
M. There is solitude everywhere. The individual is solitary always. His business is to find it within, and not seek it externally.
D. The workaday world is distracting.
M. Do not allow yourself to be distracted. Inquire for whom there is distraction. It will not affect you after a little practice.
D. Even the attempt is impossible.
M. Make it, and it will be found not so difficult.
D. But the answer does not come for the inward search.
M. The inquirer is the answer and there is no other answer. What comes afresh cannot be true. What always is, is true.

APRIL 6, 1935
A visitor asked: The path of realization is difficult. Worldly matters are easy of understanding, whereas this is not.
M. Yes. The mind always seeks external knowledge, leaving aside its own inner Knowledge.
D. A stay of one day with Sri Bhagavan is good; a stay of two days is better, of three days, more so, and so on. If it is a continuous stay here, how shall we get on with our mundane work?
M. Staying here or "elsewhere" must be understood to be the same as "here," and to have the same effect.

APRIL 12, 1935

After hearing the Malayalam version of Upadesa Saram *chanted, Mr. Ramachandra Iyer of Nagercoil asked in a characteristically unsophisticated way about the mind, concentration, and control. The Master said:* The mind is only identity of the Self with the body. It is a false ego that is created; it in turn creates false phenomena and appears to move in them; all these are false. The Self is the only Reality. If the false identity vanishes, the persistence of the Reality becomes apparent. It does not mean that Reality is not here and now. It is always present and eternally the same. It is also in everyone's experience. For everyone knows that he is. "Who is he?" Subjectively, "Who am I?" The false ego is associated with objects; this ego itself is its own object. Objectivity is the falsity. Subject alone is the Reality. Do not confound yourself with the object, namely the body. This gives rise to the false ego, consequently to the world and your movements therein, with the resulting misery. Do not think yourself to be this, that or anything; to be so and so, or to be such and such. Only leave off the falsity. Reality will reveal itself. The scriptures say that the Self is *nityasiddha,* ever present, and yet speak of the removal of *ajnana.* If Self is *nitya* (always) and *siddha* (present), how can there be *ajnana?* For whom is the *ajnana?* These are contradictory. But such statements are only for guiding the earnest seeker. He does not readily understand the only Truth if mentioned in plain words as in *"natwam naham neme janadhipah"* (not Thou, nor I, nor these kings. . .). Sri Krishna declared the Truth, but Arjuna could not grasp it. Later Krishna plainly says that people confound Him with the body, whereas in reality He was not born nor will He die. Still Arjuna required the whole *Gita* for the Truth to be made clear to him.

Look, the Self is only Being, not being this or that. It is simple Being. Be — and there is an end of the ignorance. Inquire for whom is the ignorance. The ego arises when you wake up from sleep. In deep sleep you do not say you are sleeping and that you are going to wake up or that you have been sleeping so long. But still you are there. Only when you are awake you say that you have slept. Your wakefulness comprises sleep also. Realize your pure Being. Let there be no confusion with the body. The body is the result of thoughts. The thoughts will play as usual, but you will not be affected. You were not concerned with the body when asleep; and so you can always remain this way.

Mr. Ekanatha Rao: How can anyone reconcile such activity with wage earning, which is a necessity for worldly people?

M. Actions form no bondage. Bondage arises only with the false notion, "I am the doer." Leave off such thoughts and let the body and senses play their role unimpeded by your interference.

April 20, 1935

A visitor from Kerala expressed his concern for the misery of the world and his opinion that the "Quest for Self" looks selfish in the midst of such suffering. His solution appeared to be selfless work.

M. The sea is not aware of its wave. Similarly the Self is not aware of its ego.

   (*This makes clear what Sri Bhagavan means by quest for the source of ego.*)

A visitor asked Sri Bhagavan: You are Bhagavan. So you would know when I shall get *jnana.* Tell me when I shall be a *jnani.*
Sri Bhagavan replied: If I am Bhagavan there is no one besides the Self — therefore no *jnani* or *ajnani.* If otherwise, I am as good as you are and know as much as yourself. Either way I cannot answer your question.

April 24, 1935

Some men asked the Master questions which ultimately resolved themselves into one — that "I" is not perceptible however much they might struggle. The Master's reply was in the usual strain: Who is it that says that "I" is not perceptible? Is there an ignorant "I," and an elusive "I"? Are there two "I's" in the same person? Ask yourself these questions. It is the mind which says that "I" is not perceptible. Where is that mind from? Know the mind. You will find it a myth. King Janaka said, "I have discovered the thief who had been ruining me so long. I will now deal with him summarily. Then I shall be happy." Similarly it will be with others.
D. How to know the "I"?
M. The "I-I" is always there. There is no knowing it. It is not a new knowledge acquired. What is new and not here and now will be evanescent only. The "I" is always there. There is obstruction to its knowledge and that is called ignorance. Remove the ignorance, and Knowledge shines forth. In fact, this ignorance or even knowledge is not for *Atman.* They are only overgrowths to be cleared off. That is why *Atman* is said to be beyond knowledge and ignorance. It remains as it naturally is — that is all.
D. There is no perceptible progress in spite of our attempts.
M. Progress can be spoken of in things to be obtained afresh. Whereas here it is the removal of ignorance and not acquisition of knowledge. What kind

of progress can be expected in the quest for the Self?

D. How to remove the ignorance?

M. While lying in bed in Tiruvannamalai, you dream in your sleep that you find yourself in another town. The scene is real to you. Your body remains here on your bed in a room. Can a town enter your room, or could you have left this place and gone elsewhere, leaving the body here? Both are impossible. Therefore, your being here and seeing another town are both unreal. They appear real to the mind. The "I" of the dream soon vanishes, then another "I" speaks of the dream. This "I" was not in the dream. Both "I's" are unreal. There is the substratum of the mind which continues all along, giving rise to so many scenes. An "I" rises forth with every thought, and with its disappearance that "I" disappears too. Many "I's" are born and die every moment. The subsisting mind is the real trouble. That is the thief according to King Janaka. Find him out and you will be happy.

(*Sri Bhagavan read out, from the* Prabuddha Bharata, *Kabir's saying that all know that the drop merges into the ocean, but few know that the ocean merges into the drop. This is* para bhakti, *said he.*)

MAY 15, 1935

A wandering monk (sannyasi) *was trying to clear his doubt*: How to realize that all the world is God?

M. If you make your outlook that of wisdom, you will find the world to be God. Without knowing the Supreme Spirit (*Brahman*), how will you find His all-pervasiveness?

Someone inquired about the nature of perception.

M. Whatever state one is in, perceptions partake of that state. The explanation is that in *jagrat* (the waking state) the gross body perceives gross forms and names; in स्वप्न (the dream state) the mental body perceives mental creations in their manifold forms and names; in *sushupti* (deep dreamless sleep), identification with the body being lost, there are no perceptions; similarly in the transcendental state identity, with *Brahman* places man in harmony with everything, and there is nothing apart from his Self.

A question was asked about the nature of happiness.

M. If a man thinks his happiness is due to external causes and possessions, it is reasonable to conclude that his happiness must increase with the increase of possessions and diminish in proportion to their diminution. Therefore, if he is devoid of possessions, his happiness should be *nil*. But what is the actual experience of man? Does it conform to this view?

In deep sleep man is devoid of possessions, including his own body. Instead of being unhappy he is quite happy. Everyone desires to sleep soundly. The conclusion is that happiness is inherent in man and not due to external causes. One must realize his Self in order to access the store of unalloyed happiness.

Maharshi was asked by an educated young man: How can you say the Heart is on the right, when biologists have found it to be on the left?
(The man asked for authority.)
M. Quite so. The physical organ is on the left; that is not denied. But the Heart of which I speak is non-physical and located on the right side. This is my experience; no authority is required by me. Still, you can find confirmation of it in a Malayalam Ayurvedic book and in *Sita Upanishad*; and he produced the quotation from the latter and repeated the text from the former.

Mr. Maurice Frydman, an engineer, remarked on the subject of Grace: A salt doll diving into the sea will not be protected by a waterproof coat.
(It was a very happy simile and was praised as such.)
Maharshi added: The body is the waterproof coat.

*A monk (*sannyasi*) asked how to prevent the mind from being distracted.*
M. You only see objects on forgetting your own Self. If you keep hold of your Self, you will not see the objective world.

*When asked if occult powers (*siddhis*) can be achieved along with omnipotence (*Ishvaratva*) as mentioned in the last verse of* Dakshinamurti Ashtakam, *Maharshi said:* Let omnipotence (*Ishvaratva*) be accomplished first and then the other question may be raised.

Questioner: Can anyone benefit by repeating sacred syllables (mantras) picked up casually?
M. No. He must be competent and initiated in such mantras.
Maharshi illustrated this by the following story:
A King visited his premier in his residence. There he was told the premier was engaged in repetition of sacred syllables (*japa*). The King waited for him and, on meeting him, asked what the *japa* was. The premier

said that it was the holiest of all, *Gayatri*. The King desired to be initiated by the premier, but the latter confessed his inability to initiate him. Therefore, the King learned it from someone else, and meeting the minister later he repeated the *Gayatri* and wanted to know if it was right. The minister said the mantra was correct, but it was not proper for him to say it. When pressed to explain, the minister called to a page close by and ordered him to take hold of the King. The order was however not obeyed. It was repeated several times, but still not obeyed. The King flew into a rage and ordered the same man to hold the minister, and it was done immediately. The minister laughed and said the incident was the explanation required by the King. "How?" asked the King. The minister replied, "The order was the same and the executor also, but the authority was different. When I ordered it, the effect was *nil*, whereas, when you ordered, there was an immediate effect. Similarly with mantras."

Someone inquired: Why is it said in scriptures that the Sage is like a child?
M. A child and a Sage (*jnani*) are similar in a way. Incidents interest a child only so long as they last; he ceases to think of them after they have passed away. So then, it is apparent that they do not leave any impression on the child and he is not mentally affected by them. So it is with a Sage.

A visitor asked how to realize oneself in accordance with Maharshi's instructions, contained in his text Truth Revealed *(verse 8, Supplement). The difficulty lies in controlling the mind.*
M. It is to be done by controlling the breath. If you practice it by yourself without help, then the mind is controlled. Otherwise the mind comes under control spontaneously in the presence of a superior power. Such is the greatness of association with the wise (*satsanga*)

D. Can destiny (karma) ever come to an end?
M. The karmas carry the seeds of their own destruction.

A man asked Maharshi to say something to him. When asked what he wanted to know, he said he knew nothing and wanted to hear something from Maharshi.
M. You know that you know nothing. Find out that knowledge. That is liberation (*mukti*).

A young Brahmin (twenty-five years of age) came on a visit to the Master. At his sight, he became hysterical and shouted *Shivoham, aham Brahma asmi,* "You are God," "You are *Para Brahmam.*" "You are my father," "Father, save me," and so on. His hysterics waxing, he beat his chest violently, alternately with both his hands, shouting *Shivoham, Shivoham.* Then again he shouted hysterically gnashing his teeth, "I will stamp out materialism," as if he was crushing materialism between his teeth. Then he asked. "Either give me power, either give me power —or — or — or — I will . . ." He began as if to throttle himself.

When gently removed by others, he fell prostrate before Sri Bhagavan, saying, "I will take refuge at the feet of my Father. Father! You are Parthasarathi, I am Arjuna. We will stamp out materialism," and so on. He was finally taken away from the presence of Maharshi. He washed himself, took some light refreshment, and quietly seated himself in the Hall for some hours. He abstained from the mid-day meal. In the afternoon, he had another fit when he shouted, "I will chop off the head of Krishna, if he should come here now. He advised me to give up my job, but does not protect my mother. Or let him chop off my head," and so on.

After some hours of quiet, Sri Bhagavan asked Mr. K.L. Sarma to read out a portion of his commentary on *Anubandha* (Appendix to Forty Verses). The gist of it is that people, unable to help themselves, ask for divine powers to be utilized for human welfare. This is similar to the story of a lame man who blustered, saying that he would overpower the enemy if only he were helped onto his legs. The intention is good, but there is no sense of proportion. The young man on hearing it suddenly sprang to his feet, saluting Sri Bhagavan and saying "Father! Father! I was mistaken. Pardon me. Teach me. I shall abide by what you say," and so on. Then, again in the evening he prostrated himself, saying, "I surrender."

A man from Cocanada asked: My mind remains clear for two or three days and then turns dull for the next two or three days; and so it alternates. What is this due to?

M. It is quite natural — the play of brightness (*sattva*), activity (*rajas*) and darkness (*tamas*) alternating. Do not regret the *tamas;* but when *sattva* comes into play, hold on to it fast and make the best of it.

D. What is the Heart?

M. It is the seat (if such could be said of it) of the Self.

D. Is it the physical heart?

M. No. It is the seat wherefrom "I-I" arises.

D. What becomes of the *jiva* after death?

M. The question is not appropriate for a *jiva* now living. A disembodied *jiva* may ask me, if convenient. In the meantime, let the embodied *jiva* solve its present problem and find out who he is. There will be an end of such doubts.

D. What is *dhyana*?

M. The word *dhyana* usually signifies meditation on some object, whereas *nididhyasana* is used for inquiry into the Self. The triads persist until the Self is realized. *Dhyana* and *nididhyasana* are the same so far as the aspirant is concerned, because they involve trinity and are synonymous with *bhakti*.

D. How should *dhyana* be practiced?

M. *Dhyana* serves to concentrate the mind. The predominant idea keeps off all others. *Dhyana* varies according to the individual. It may be on an aspect of God, on a mantra, or on the Self, etc.

JUNE 15, 1935

A young man, Mr. Knowles, came for darshan. *He had read Paul Brunton's two books. He asked:* Buddhists say that "I" is unreal whereas Paul Brunton in *The Secret Path* tells us to get over the "I"-thought and reach the state of "I." Which is true?

M. There are supposed to be two "I's"; the one is lower and unreal, of which all are aware; the other is higher and the real, which is to be realized.

You are not aware of yourself while asleep; you are aware in wakefulness. Waking, you say that you were asleep; you did not know it in the deep-sleep state. So then, the idea of diversity has arisen along with body-consciousness. This body-consciousness arose at some particular moment having an origin and an end. What originates must be something. What is that something? It is the "I"-consciousness. Who am I?, Whence am I? On finding the source, you realize the state of Absolute Consciousness.

D. Who is this "I"? It seems to be only a continuum of sense impressions. The Buddhist idea seems to be so, too.

M. The world is not external. The impressions cannot have an outer origin, because the world can be cognized only by consciousness. The world does not say it exists; it is your impression. Even so, this impression is not consistent and not unbroken. In deep sleep, the world is not cognized; and so it does not exist for a sleeping man. Therefore, the world is the sequence of the ego. Find out the ego. The finding of its source is the final goal.

D. I believe that we should not inflict suffering on other lives. Should we then endure the mosquito bite and submit to it, also?

M. You do not like to suffer yourself. How can you inflict suffering on others? Just keep off mosquitoes since you suffer by their stings.

D. Is it right that we kill other lives, e.g., mosquitoes, bugs?

M. Everyone is a suicide. The eternal, blissful, and natural state has been smothered by this life of ignorance. In this way, the present life is due to the killing of the eternal, pristine Being. Is it not a case of suicide? So then, everyone is a suicide. Why worry about murders and killing?

In the course of a later talk, the visitor said: The world sends impressions and I awake!

M. Can the world exist without someone to perceive it? Which is prior? The Being-consciousness or the rising-consciousness? The Being-consciousness is always there, eternal and pure. The rising-consciousness arises and disappears; it is transient.

D. Doesn't the world exist for others even when I am asleep?

M. Such a world also mocks at you for knowing it without knowing yourself. The world is the result of your mind. Know your mind, then see the world. You will realize that it is not different from the Self.

D. Is not Maharshi aware of himself and his surroundings, as clearly as I am?

M. To whom is the doubt? The doubts are not for the realized; they are only for the ignorant.

June 16, 1935

D. How does a *grihastha* (householder) fare in the scheme of *moksha* (liberation)?

M. Why do you think you are a *grihastha*? If you go out as a *sannyasi*, a similar thought (that you are a *sannyasi*) will haunt you. Whether you continue in the household, or renounce it and go to the forest, your mind haunts you. The ego is the source of thoughts. It creates the body and the world and makes you think you are a *grihastha*. If you renounce the world, it will only substitute the thought *sannyasi* for *grihastha* and the environments of the forest for those of the household. But the mental obstacles always remain. They even increase in new surroundings. There is no help in a change of environment. The obstacle is the mind. It must be overcome whether at home or in the forest. If you can do it in the forest, why not in the home? Therefore, why change the environment? Your efforts can be made even now — whatever environment you may be in.

The environment never abandons you, according to your desire. Look at me. I left home. Look at yourselves. You have come here leaving your home environment. What do you find here? Is this different from what you left? Even if one is immersed in *nirvikalpa samadhi* for years together, when he emerges from it he will find himself in the environment which he is bound to have. That is the reason for Shankaracharya emphasizing *sahaja samadhi* in preference to *nirvikalpa samadhi* in his excellent work *Viveka Chuda-mani.*

One should be in spontaneous *samadhi* — that is, in one's pristine state — in the midst of every environment. Breath control may be internal or external.

Bahih pranayama (external control) is for one not endowed with strength to control the mind. There is no way so sure as that; or a *sadhu's* company. The external practice must be resorted to by a wise man if he does not enjoy a *sadhu's* company. If in a *sadhu's* company the *sadhu,* provides the needed strength, though unseen by others. *Pranayama* need not be exactly as described in *Hatha Yoga.* If engaged in *japa, dhyana, bhakti,* etc., just a little control of breath will suffice to control the mind. The mind is the rider and the breath the horse. *Pranayama* is a check on the horse. By that check, the rider is checked.

Pranayama may be done just a little. To watch the breath is one way of doing it. The mind abstracted from other activities is engaged in watching the breath. That controls the breath, and in its turn the mind is controlled.

If unable to do so, *rechaka* and *puraka* need not be practiced. Breath may be retained a short while in *japa, dhyana,* etc. Then, too, good results will follow.

JUNE 18, 1935

D. Can *advaita* be realized by *japa* of holy names; say Rama, Krishna, etc.?
M. Yes.
D. Is it not a means of an inferior order?
M. Have you been told to make *japa* or to discuss its order in the scheme of things?
(*Silence.*)

Chapter One—1935

June 22, 1935

A youth of twenty asked how to realize the Self. He sat down in silence and waited more than an hour and then was about to leave. While doing so, he again asked:
How to realize Self?

M. Whose Self? Find out.

D. Who am I?

M. Find it yourself.

D. I do not know.

M. Think. Who is it that says "I do not know"? What is not known? In that statement, who is the "I"?

D. Somebody in me.

M. Who is the somebody? In whom?

D. May be some power.

M. Find it.

D. How to realize *Brahman*?

M. Without knowing the Self, why do you seek to know *Brahman*?

D. The *sastras* say *Brahman* pervades all and me, too.

M. Find the "I" in me and then there will be time to think of *Brahman*.

D. Why was I born?

M. Who was born? The answer is the same for all of your questions.

D. Who am I then?

M. (*Smiling.*) Have you come to examine me and ask me? You must say who you are.

D. In deep sleep the soul leaves the body and remains elsewhere. When it re-enters, I awake. Is it so?

M. What is it that leaves the body?

D. The power, perhaps.

M. Find out the power.

D. The body is composed of five elements. What are the elements?

M. Without knowing the Self, how do you aim at knowing the elements?

(*The young man sat awhile and left with permission.*)

The Master remarked later: All right. It will work.

Mr. T.K.S. Iyer, a devotee, was speaking of the chakras. *Sri Bhagavan said*: Atman (the Self) alone is to be realized. Its realization holds all else in its compass. *Shakti*, Ganapati, *siddhis*, etc., are included in it. Those who speak of these have not realized the *Atman*. *Atman* is in the Heart and *is* the Heart itself. The manifestation is in the brain. The passage from the Heart to the brain might be considered to be through *sushumna* or a nerve with any other name.

The *Upanishads* say *pare leena* — meaning that *sushumna* or such *nadis* are all comprised in *para*, i.e., the *atma nadi*. The yogis say that the current rising up to *sahasrara* (brain) ends there. That experience is not complete. For *jnana*, they must come to the Heart. *Hridaya* (Heart) is the alpha and omega.

JULY 4, 1935

Mr. Ranganathan (Indian Civil Service): In *Srimad Bhagavad Gita*, there is a passage, "One's own *dharma* is the best; an alien *dharma* is full of risks." What is the significance of one's own *dharma*?

M. It is usually interpreted to mean the duties of the orders and of the different castes. The physical environment must also be taken into consideration.

D. If *varnasrama dharma* be meant, such *dharma* prevails only in India. On the other hand, the *Gita* should be universally applicable.

M. There is *varnasrama* in some form or other in every land. The significance is that one should hold on to the single *Atman* and not swerve from it. That is its whole gist.

Sva = one's own; i.e., of the Self, of the *Atman*.

Para = the other's; i.e., of the non-self, of the *anatma*.

Atma Dharma is inherence in the Self. There will be no distraction and no fear. Troubles arise only when there is a second to oneself. If the *Atman* is realized to be only unitary, there is no second and therefore no cause for fear. Man, as he is now, confounds the *anatma* (non-Self) *dharma* with *Atma* (the Self) *dharma* and suffers. Let him know the Self and abide in it; then there is an end of fear, and there are no more doubts.

Even if interpreted as *varnasrama dharma*, the significance is only this much. Such *dharma* bears fruit only when done selflessly. That is, one must realize that he is not the doer, but that he is only a tool of some Higher Power. Let that Higher Power do what is inevitable and let me act only according to its dictates. The actions are not mine; therefore, their results cannot be mine, either. If one thinks and acts so, where is the trouble? Be it *varnasrama dharma* or *loukika dharma* (worldly activities), it is immaterial. Finally, it amounts to this:

Sva = *atmanah* (of the Self)

Para = *anatmanah* (of the non-self)

Such doubts are natural. The orthodox interpretation cannot be reconciled with the life of a modern man obliged to work for his livelihood in various capacities.

A man from Pondicherry interposed: Sarva dharman parityajya mamekam saranam vraja *(leaving all duties, surrender to me only).*

Sri Bhagavan: Sarva (all) is only *anatmanah* (of the non-self); the emphasis is only on *ekam* (one). To the man who has a strong hold of the *eka*, where are the *dharmas*? It means "Be sunk in the Self."

D. The *Gita* was taught for action.

M. What does the *Gita* say? Arjuna refused to fight. Krishna said, "So long as you refuse to fight, you have a sense of doership. Who are you to refrain or to act? Give up the notion of doership. Until that sense disappears, you are bound to act. You are being manipulated by a Higher Power. You are admitting it by your own refusal to submit to it. Instead, recognize the Power and submit as a tool. Or (to put it differently), if you refuse you will be forcibly drawn into it. Instead of being an unwilling worker, be a willing one.

"Rather, be fixed in the Self and act according to nature without the thought of doership. Then the results of action will not affect you. That is manliness and heroism."

Thus, "inherence in the Self" is the sum and substance of the *Gita*'s teaching.

Finally, the Master added: If a man is established in the Self, these doubts would not arise. They arise only until he is established there.

D. Then of what use is such reply to the inquirer?

M. The words still have force and will surely operate in due course.

A moulvi (Islamic priest) asked: How does sleep overtake one?

M. If the inquirer knows who is awake in the wakeful condition, he will also know how sleep comes on. The inquiry arises only to the waking man and not to the sleeper. It must be easier to know the waking Self than the sleeping Self.

D. I know how I awoke. But I do not know how sleep comes on. I am aware of my wakeful state. For instance, if anyone takes away my stick I prevent his doing so, whereas I cannot do so in sleep or in dream. The proof of wakefulness is evident. But what is the proof of sleep?

M. Your ignorance is the evidence of sleep; your awareness is that of wakefulness.

D. My wakefulness is known by the opening of my eye. But how does sleep overtake me?

M. In the same way that sleep overtakes you, wakefulness also overtakes you.

D. But I do not perceive how sleep comes on in the same way as I know my wakefulness.

M. Never mind.

D. Please describe what is sleep, without illustrations. Sleep by itself should be known. I want a real picture of sleep.

M. Such a picture is sleep itself.

D. Is it better to reach salvation in being married or in being a hermit?

M. Whatever you think better.

D. Visvamitra had no fall when in the married state, whereas he had a fall in his hermit life. Does it not apply to others, also?

M. Visvamitra was as pure in the hermit life as when married. There was no difference. He was as contaminated when married as when he was a hermit.

D. Was he a *rishi?*

M. When contaminated, he was not a *rishi.*

D. Can he become a *rishi* even afterwards?

M. Yes. By proper *bhakti*, he could become a good *rishi*. Repentance and prayer will set him right.

D. With all your penance for so many years, what have you got?

M. I have got what needs to be got. I see what needs to be seen.

D. Can all see the same?

M. I see only just what all do. It is immanent in all.

D. Is this the way for seeing It?

M. The method may be anything. From whatever directions pilgrims may foregather, they must enter the Kaaba [Muslim shrine at Mecca] only by one route (passage); all gather only to enter the Kaaba.

D. Please tell me two *upadesas* on the way to salvation as known by you.

M. What *upadesa* do I know? Everything is *upadesa*. Worship of God is the only *upadesa*.

JULY 5, 1935

Sri Bhagavan: The silence of solitude is forced. Restrained speech in society amounts to silence. The speaker must come forth before he speaks; if engaged otherwise, speech is restrained. Otherwise the introverted mind is active and not anxious to speak.

Mouna (silence) as a disciplinary measure is meant for limiting mental activities due to speech. If the mind is otherwise controlled, disciplinary *mouna* is unnecessary, for *mouna* then becomes natural.

Vidyaranya has said that twelve years' forced *mouna* brings about absolute *mouna* — that is, makes one unable to speak. It is more like a mute animal than otherwise. That is not *mouna*.

Mouna is constant speech. Inactivity is constant activity.

JULY 6, 1935

Mr. Ekanatha Rao: How is *dhyana* to be practiced — with eyes open or closed?

M. It may be done either way. The point is that the mind must be introverted and kept active in its pursuit. Sometimes it happens that when the eyes are closed, latent thoughts rush forth with great vigor. It may also be difficult to introvert the mind with eyes open, requiring strength of mind to do so. The mind is contaminated when it takes in an object. Otherwise, it is pure. The main factor in *dhyana* is to keep the mind active in its own pursuit without taking in external impressions or thinking of other matters.

Mr. Ekanatha Rao: What is *sphurana* (a kind of indescribable but palpable sensation in the Heart-center)?

M. *Sphurana* is felt on several occasions, such as in fear, excitement, etc. Although it is always and all over [diffused throughout the body], yet it is felt at a particular center and on particular occasions. It is also associated with antecedent causes and confounded with the body. Whereas it is all alone and pure, it is the Self. If the mind is fixed on the *sphurana* and one senses it continuously and automatically, it is realization.

Again, *sphurana* is a foretaste of Realization. It is pure. The subject and object proceed from it. If a person mistakes himself for the subject, objects must necessarily appear as being different from himself. They are periodically withdrawn and projected, creating the world and the subject's enjoyment of the same. If, on the other hand, a man feels himself to be the screen on which the subject and object are projected there can be no confusion, and he can remain watching their appearance and disappearance without any perturbation to the Self.

A high government officer asked: If juniors are promoted over oneself, the mind is perturbed. Will the inquiry "Who am I?" help soothe the mind under such circumstances?

M. Yes. Quite so. The inquiry "Who am I?" turns the mind inward and calms it.

D. I have faith in *murti dhyana* (worship of form). Will it not help me gain *jnana?*

M. Surely it will. *Upasana* helps concentration of mind. Then the mind is free from other thoughts and full of the meditated form. The mind becomes it — and thus quite pure. Then think who is the worshipper. The answer is "I," i.e., the Self. So the Self is gained ultimately.

The present difficulty is that man thinks that he is the doer. But it is a mistake. It is the Higher Power which does everything and man is only a tool. If he accepts that position, he is free from troubles; otherwise he courts them. Take, for instance, the figure in a *gopuram* (temple tower), where it is made to appear to bear the burden of the tower on its shoulders. Its posture and look are a picture of great strain while bearing the very heavy burden of the tower. But consider this. The tower is built on the earth and rests on its foundations. The figure (like Atlas bearing the Earth) is a part of the tower, but is made to look as if it bore the tower. Is it not funny? So is the man who takes on himself the sense of doing.

(*Then, the Malayalam version of* Ulladu Narpadu *was read out by a devotee, for the benefit of the visitor.*)

After hearing it, he asked: What about the reference to duality in practice and unity at the end?

M. Some people think that one must begin practice with a dualistic idea. It refers to them. They say that there is God; the man must worship and meditate; ultimately, the *jiva* merges into God. Others say that the Supreme Being and the *jiva* are always apart and never merge into each other. Howsoever it may be at the end, let us not trouble ourselves about it now. All are agreed that the *jiva* is. Let the man find out the *jiva*, i.e., his Self. Then there will be time to find out if the Self should merge in the Supreme, is a part thereof, or remains different from it. Let us not forestall the conclusion. Keep an open mind, dive within and find out the Self. The truth will itself dawn upon you. Why should you determine beforehand if the finality is unity absolute or qualified, or duality? There is no meaning in it. The ascertainment is now made by logic and by intellect. The intellect derives light from the Self (the Higher Power). How can the reflected and partial light of the intellect envisage the whole and the original Light? The intellect cannot reach the Self, how can it ascertain its nature?

Such is the significance of the reference.

D. One of the stanzas says that the scriptures so scrupulously studied in earlier stages are ultimately of no use. At what stage do they become useless?

M. When their essence is realized. The scriptures are useful to indicate the existence of the Higher Power (the Self) and the way to gain it. Their essence is that much only. When that is assimilated, the rest is useless. But scriptures are voluminous and adapted to the development of the seeker. As one rising up in the scale finds the regions one has passed to be only steps to a higher stage, and so on, the steps ascended becoming *purva paksha* [evidence that establishes a fact] successively until the goal is gained. Then it remains alone, and all the rest becomes useless. That is how the *sastras* become useless. We read so much. Do we remember all that we read? But have we forgotten the essentials? The essential soaks in the mind and the rest is forgotten. So it is with the *sastras*.

The fact is that man considers himself limited and there the trouble arises. This idea is wrong. He can see it for himself. In sleep there was no world, no ego (no limited self), and no trouble. Something wakes up from that happy state and says "I." To that ego, the world appears. Being a speck in the world, he wants more and gets into trouble.

How happy he was before the rising of the ego! Only the rise of the ego is the cause of the present trouble. Let him trace the ego to its source and he will reach that undifferentiated happy state which is sleepless sleep. The Self remains ever the same, here and now. There is nothing more to be gained. Because limitations have wrongly been assumed, there is a need to transcend them. It is like the ten ignorant fools who forded a stream and on reaching the other shore counted themselves to be nine only. They grew anxious and grieved over the loss of the unknown tenth man. A wayfarer, on ascertaining the cause of their grief, counted them all and found them to be ten. But each one of them had counted the others, leaving himself out. The wayfarer gave each in succession a blow telling them to count the blows. They counted ten and were satisfied. The moral is that the tenth man was not got anew. He was all along there, but ignorance caused grief to all of them.

Again, a woman wore a necklace round her neck, but forgot it. She began to search for it and made inquiries. A friend of hers, finding out what she was looking for, pointed out the necklace around the seeker's neck. She felt it with her hands and was happy. Did she get the necklace anew? Here again ignorance caused grief and knowledge happiness.

Similarly, also with the individual and the Self. There is nothing to be gained anew. Ignorance of the Self is the cause of the present misery; knowledge of the Self brings about happiness.

Moreover, if anything is to be got anew it implies its previous absence.

What was once absent might vanish again. So there would be no permanency in salvation. Salvation is permanent because the Self is here and now and eternal.

Thus, man's efforts are directed towards the removal of ignorance. Wisdom seems to dawn, though it is natural and ever present.

The visitor, while taking leave, saluted the Master, and said: It is said that the victim in the tiger's mouth is gone forever.

(*The reference is to a passage in* Who Am I?, *where it is stated that a disciple can never revert to the world after he has once fallen into the field of the Guru's gracious look, as surely as the prey in the tiger's jaws cannot escape.*)

News of someone's death was brought to Sri Bhagavan. He said: Good. The dead are indeed happy. They have got rid of the troublesome overgrowth — the body. The dead man does not grieve. The survivors grieve for the man who is dead. Do men fear sleep? On the contrary, sleep is courted and on waking up every man says that he slept happily. One prepares the bed for sound sleep. Sleep is temporary death; death is longer sleep. Therefore, if a man dies while yet alive he need not grieve over others' death. One's existence is evident with or without the body, as in waking, dream, and sleep. Then why should one desire continuance of the bodily shackles? Let the man find out his undying Self and die and be immortal and happy.

JULY 13, 1935

A visitor: Is the *jagat* (world) perceived even after Self-realization?

M. From whom is this question? Is it from a *jnani* or from an *ajnani?*

D. From an *ajnani.*

M. Realize to whom the question arises. It can be answered if it arises after knowing the doubter. Can the *jagat* or the body say that it is? Or does the seer say that the *jagat* or the body is? The seer must be there to see the objects. Find out the seer first. Why worry yourself now with what will be in the hereafter?

Sri Bhagavan continued: What does it matter if the *jagat* is perceived or not perceived? Have you lost anything by your perception of *jagat* now? Or do you gain anything where there is no such perception in your deep sleep? It is immaterial whether the world is perceived or not.

The *ajnani* sees the *jnani* active and is confounded. The *jagat* is perceived by both; but their outlooks differ. Take the instance of the cinema. There are pictures moving on the screen. Go and hold them. What do you hold? It is only the screen. Let the pictures disappear. What remains? The screen again. So also here. Even when the world appears, see to whom it appears. Hold the substratum of the "I." After the substratum is held, what does it matter if the world appears or disappears?

The *ajnani* takes the world to be real, whereas the *jnani* sees it only as the manifestation of the Self. It is immaterial whether the Self manifests itself or ceases to do so.

JULY 15, 1935

A letter was received containing some learned questions pertaining to memory, sleep, and death. It looked, at first sight, as if they were cogent yet baffling to answer. But when the Master was approached on the subject, he disentangled the skein very nicely, pointing out that all such confusion was due to the non-differentiation of the real "I" from the false "I." The attributes and modes pertain to the latter and not to the former. One's efforts are directed only to remove one's ignorance. Afterwards they cease, and the real Self is found to be always there. No effort is needed to remain as the Self.

JULY 21, 1935

A visitor, Mr. K.S.N. Iyer of the Southern Indian Railway, asked: There is a trifling halting place in my meditation. When I ask myself "Who am I?," my reasoning proceeds as follows: I see my hand. Who sees it? My eye. How to see the eye? In a mirror. Similarly, to see myself, there must be a mirror. "What is to supply the place of the mirror in me?" is my question.

M. Then why do you inquire, "Who am I?" Why do you say you are troubled, and so on? You could as well remain quiet. Why do you rise out of your composure?

D. Inquiring thusly helps me to concentrate. Is concentration the only benefit?

M. What more do you want? Concentration is the thing. What makes you come out of your quiet?

D. Because I am drawn out.

M. Inquiry of "Who am I?" means finding the source of "I." When that is found, that which you seek is accomplished.

(*The gist of Sri Bhagavan's words seem to be that one should make a concerted effort and not give it up baffled, with a defeatist mentality.)*

Dr. Radhakamal Mukerjee, a well-known Professor, a fair man of middle age, with a peaceful look, practicing yoga or meditation, had some occult experiences and desires the mystery to be unraveled by the Master. He wrote a book and had it published by Messrs. Longmans Green & Co., London. He finds Self-realization hard to attain and requires the Master's help. He asked: The *upanishadic* method of meditation has now disappeared. There was a great sage in Bengal who instructed me in it. After long years of discipline and practice, I am having some mystic experiences. I feel sometimes that *Bhuma* (Supreme Consciousness) is infinitude, and that I am finite consciousness. Is that correct?

M. *Bhuma* (Perfection) alone is. It is Infinite. There arises from it this finite consciousness taking on an *upadhi* (limiting adjunct). This is *abhasa* or reflection. Merge this individual consciousness into the Supreme One. That is what should be done.

D. *Bhuma* is an attribute of Supreme Consciousness.

M. *Bhuma* is the Supreme — *yatra naanyat pasyati yatra naanyat srunoti sa bhuma* (where one does not see any other, hears nothing, it is Perfection). It is indefinable and indescribable. It is as it is.

D. There is a vastness experienced. Probably it is just below *Bhuma*, but close to it. Am I right?

M. *Bhuma* alone is. Nothing else. It is the mind that says all this.

D. Transcending the mind, I feel the vastness.

M. Yes — Yes.

The professor turned to the lady seated just a little further away from him and interpreted in Hindi to her.

She: What is the difference between meditation and distraction?

M. No difference. When there are thoughts, it is distraction: when there are no thoughts, it is meditation. However, meditation is only practice (as distinguished from the real state of Peace.)

She: How to practice meditation?

M. Keep off thoughts.

She: How to reconcile work with meditation?

M. Who is the worker? Let him who works ask the question. You are always the Self. You are not the mind. It is the mind which raises these questions. Work proceeds always in the presence of the Self only. Work is no hindrance to realization. It is the mistaken identity of the worker that troubles one. Get rid of the false identity.

Professor: Is the state of non-consciousness close to Infinite consciousness?

M. Consciousness alone remains and nothing more.

D. Sri Bhagavan's silence is itself a powerful force. It brings about a certain peace of mind in us.

M. Silence is never-ending speech. Vocal speech obstructs the speech of silence. In silence, one is in intimate contact with the surroundings. The silence of Dakshinamurti removed the doubts of the four sages. *Mouna vyakhya prakatita tatvam* (Truth expounded by silence). Silence is said to be exposition. Silence is so potent.

For vocal speech, organs of speech are necessary and they precede speech. But the other speech lies even beyond thought. It is, in short, transcendent speech or unspoken words, *para vak*.

D. Is there knowledge in Realization?

M. Absence of knowledge is sleep. There is knowledge in Realization. But this knowledge differs from the ordinary one of the relation of subject and object. It is absolute knowledge. Knowledge has two meanings:

1. *Vachyartha* = *vritti* = Literal meaning.
2. *Lakshyartha* = *Jnana* = *Self* = *Svarupa* = Secondary significance.

D. With *vritti,* one sees knowledge.

M. Quite so; he also confounds *vritti* with knowledge. *Vritti* is a mode of mind. You are not the mind; you are beyond it.

The Lady: There is sometimes an irresistible desire to remain in *Brahma-akara-vritti.*

M. That is good. It must be cultivated until becoming *sahaja* (natural). Then it culminates as *svarupa,* one's own self.

Later, Sri Bhagavan explained: *Vritti* is often mistaken for consciousness. It is only a phenomenon and operates in the region of *abhasa* (reflected consciousness). The Knowledge lies beyond relative knowledge and ignorance, and it is not in the shape of *vritti*. There are no subject and object in it.

Vritti belongs to the *rajasic* (active) mind. The *sattvic* mind (mind in repose) is free from it. The *sattvic* is the witness of the *rajasic*. It is no doubt true consciousness. Still it is called *sattvic* mind because the knowledge of being witness is the function of *abhasa* (reflected consciousness) only. Mind is the *abhasa*. Such knowledge implies mind. But the mind is by itself inoperative. Therefore it is called *sattvic* mind. Such is the *jivanmukta's* state. It is also said that his mind is dead. Is it not a paradox that a *jivanmukta* has a mind and that it is dead? This has to be conceded in argument with ignorant folk.

It is also said that *Brahman* is only the *jivanmukta's* mind. How can one speak of him as *Brahmavid* (knower of *Brahman*)? *Brahman* can never be an object to be known. This is, however, in accordance with common parlance.

Sattvic mind is surmised of the *jivanmukta* and of *Ishvara*. "Otherwise," they argue, "how does the *jivanmukta* live and act?" The *sattvic* mind has to be admitted as a concession to argument.

The *sattvic* mind is in fact the Absolute consciousness. The object to be witnessed and the witness finally merge, and Absolute consciousness alone reigns supreme. It is not a state of *sunya* (blank) or ignorance, but is the *svarupa* (Real Self). Some say that mind arises from consciousness followed by reflection (*abhasa*); others say that the *abhasa* (reflection) arises first followed by the mind. In fact, both are simultaneous.

The Professor asked Sri Bhagavan to extend his Grace to him although he would soon be a thousand miles away. Sri Bhagavan said that time and space are only concepts of mind. But *svarupa* (the Real Self) lies beyond mind, time and space. Distance does not signify anything in the Self.

(*The lady with him was most reluctant to leave the Master and return home.*)
The Master said: Think that you are always in my presence. That will make you feel right.

(*They left after dusk.*)

There were reports of the aforementioned Professor's University lectures in *The Hindu* [newspaper]. The lecturer had emphasized the necessity for birth control and discussed the various possibilities of making man feel his responsibilities so that birth control might be automatic.

The Master, on hearing it, casually remarked: Let them find out the method of dying. (*Here death refers to that of the ego.*)

SEPTEMBER 25, 1935

Mr. K.S.N. Iyer, a railway officer, asked about japa.
M. The utterance and then remembrance and later meditation are the successive stages, finally ending in involuntary and eternal *japa*. The *japakarta* (doer of *japa*) of that kind is the Self. Of all the *japas*, "Who am I?" is the best.

SEPTEMBER 27, 1935

Mr. Ekanatha Rao, the engineer, asked: What about the despondency of not obtaining any encouragement from the Master — much less his Grace?

M. It is ignorance only. The quest must be made as to who is despondent and so on. It is the phantom of the ego arising after sleep which falls prey to such thoughts. In deep sleep, the person was not afflicted. Who is afflicted now while awake? The sleep state is about the normal one. Let him search and find out.

D. But there is no incentive for want of encouragement.

M. Doesn't one find some kind of peace while in meditation? That is a sign of progress. That peace will become deeper and more prolonged with continued practice. It will also lead to the goal. *Bhagavad Gita* — (chap. 14), the final verses — speak of *gunatita* (one who has transcended the *gunas*). That is the final stage.

The earlier stages are *asuddha sattva* (impure being), *misra sattva* (mixed being), and *suddha sattva* (Pure Being).

Of these, the impure being is when one is overpowered by *rajas* and *tamas;* the mixed being is that state in which the being — *sattva* — asserts itself spasmodically; the *suddha sattva* overpowers *rajas* and *tamas.* After these successive stages, there comes the state transcending the *gunas.*

Mr. Maurice Frydman, the engineer, writes in one of his letters: Maharshi is with me not only when I think of Him but also when I am not thinking of Him. Otherwise, how do I live?

Mr. Grant Duff, formerly in a foreign embassy, writes: ". . . pay my respects to Maharshi. He appears to me in my thoughts not only as an *answer* to my question but also as *Presence.*"

SEPTEMBER 29, 1935

Mr. K.S.N. Iyer said he was not convinced that spiritual life could be reconciled with worldly activities. The Master in answer cited some verses from Yoga Vasishta.

> (*The original is said to be millions of verses, of which only 32,000 stanzas are now found in the Sanskrit text. It was condensed to 6000 and called* Laghu Vasishta. *The latter has been rendered in Tamil in 2050 stanzas*).

D. Without the mind concentrating on it, the work cannot be performed satisfactorily. How is the mind to be spiritually disposed and the work be kept going, as well?

M. The mind is only a projection from the Self, appearing in the waking state. In deep sleep, you do not say whose son you are, and so on. As soon as you wake up, you say you are so and so and recognize the world. The world is only *lokah. Lokah* = *lokyate iti lokah* (what is perceived is the world). Which is the eye that sees it? That is the ego which rises and sinks periodically. But you exist always. Therefore, That which lies beyond the ego is consciousness — the Self.

In deep sleep, the mind is merged and not destroyed. That which merges reappears. It may happen in meditation also. But the mind which is destroyed cannot reappear. The yogi's aim must be to destroy it and not to sink in *laya* (dissolution). In the peace of *dhyana, laya* ensues but it is not enough. It must be supplemented by other practices for destroying the mind. Some people have gone into *samadhi* with a trifling thought and after a long time awakened in the trail of the same thought. Such *yogis* have not destroyed the mind. Its destruction is the non-recognition of it being apart from the Self. Even now, the mind *is not*. Recognize it. How can you do it if not in everyday activities? They go on automatically. Know that the mind promoting them is not real but a phantom proceeding from the Self. That is how the mind is destroyed.

The Master, while referring to the Bible for the passage "Be still and know that I am God" (Psalm 46), found in the Ecclesiastes:
   "There is one alone and there is no second," and "The wise man's heart is at the right hand and a fool's heart is at the left."

A man from Masulla asked the Master: How to realize the Self?
M. Everyone has experience of the Self every moment of his life.
D. But the Self is not realized as one would like.
M. Yes. The present experience is *viparita* — different from real. What *is not* is confounded with *what is*.
D. How to find the *Atman*?
M. There is no investigation into the *Atman*. The investigation can only be into the non-self; elimination of the non-self is alone possible. The Self, being always self-evident, will shine forth of itself.

   The Self is called by different names — *Atman*, God, *Kundalini*, mantra, etc. Hold any one of them and the Self becomes manifest. God is no other than the Self. *Kundalini* is now showing forth as the mind. When the mind is traced to its source, it is *Kundalini. Mantra japa* leads to elimination of other thoughts and to concentration on the mantra. The mantra finally merges into the Self and shines forth as the Self.
D. How long is a Guru necessary for Self-realization?

M. Guru is necessary so long as there is the *laghu*. (Pun on Guru = heavy; *laghu* = light). *Laghu* is due to the self-imposed but wrong limitation of the self. God, on being worshipped, bestows steadiness in devotion which leads to surrender. Upon the devotee's surrender, God shows His mercy by manifesting as the Guru. The Guru, otherwise God, guides the devotee, saying that God is in you and He is the Self. This leads to introversion of the mind and finally to realization.

Effort is necessary up to the state of realization. Even then, the Self should spontaneously become evident. Otherwise, happiness will not be complete. Up to that state of spontaneity, there must be effort in some form or another.

D. Our workaday life is not compatible with such efforts.

M. Why do you think that *you* are active? Take the gross example of your arrival here. You left home in a cart, took the train, alighted at the railway station here, got into a cart there and found yourself in this Asramam. When asked, you say that you traveled here all the way from your town. Is it true? Is it not a fact that you remained as you were and there were movements of conveyances all along the way? Just as those movements are confounded with your own, so also are the other activities. They are not your own. They are God's activities.

D. Such idea will lead to blankness of mind and the work will not progress well.

M. Go up to that blankness and tell me afterwards.

D. They say that a visit to Sages helps Self-realization?

M. Yes. So it does.

D. Will not my present visit to you bring it about?

M. (*After a short pause*) What is to be brought about? To whom? Consider, investigate. To whom is this doubt? If the source is traced, the doubt will disappear.

An engineer asked: Animals seem to conform to their own natural laws in spite of their environment and changes, whereas man flouts the social law and is not bound by any definite system. He seems to be degenerating, whereas animals are steady. Is it not so?

M. The *Upanishads* and other scriptures say that human beings are only animals unless they are realized beings. Possibly they are worse, also.

OCTOBER 3, 1935

A very devoted and simple disciple had lost his only son, a child of three years. The next day, he arrived at the Asramam with his family. The Master spoke with reference to them: Training of mind helps one to bear sorrows and bereavements with courage. But the loss of one's offspring is said to be the worst of all griefs. Grief exists only so long as one considers oneself to be of a definite form. If the form is transcended, one will know that the one Self is eternal. There is no death nor birth. That which is born is only the body. The body is the creation of the ego. But the ego is not ordinarily perceived without the body. It is always identified with the body. It is the thought which matters. Let the sensible man consider if he knew his body in deep sleep. Why does he feel it in the waking state? But, although the body was not felt in sleep, did not the Self exist then? How was he in deep sleep? How is he when awake? What is the difference? Ego rises up and that is waking. Simultaneously, thoughts arise. Let him find out to whom are the thoughts. Wherefrom do they arise? They must spring up from the conscious Self. Apprehending it even vaguely facilitates the extinction of the ego. Thereafter, the realization of the one Infinite Existence becomes possible. In that state, there are no individuals other than the Eternal Existence. Hence there is no thought of death or wailing.

If a man considers he is born, he cannot avoid the fear of death. Let him find out if he has been born or if the Self has any birth. He will discover that the Self always exists, that the body which is born resolves itself into thought and that the emergence of thought is the root of all mischief. Find wherefrom thoughts emerge. Then you will abide in the ever-present, inmost Self and be free from the idea of birth or the fear of death.

(*A disciple asked how to do it.*)

M. The thoughts are only *vasanas* (predispositions), accumulated in innumerable previous births. Their annihilation is the aim. The state free from *vasanas* is the primal state — an eternal state of purity.

D. It is not clear yet.

M. Everyone is aware of the eternal Self. He sees so many dying, but still believes himself eternal. Because it is the Truth. Unwillingly, the natural Truth asserts itself. The man is deluded by intermingling the conscious Self with the insentient body. This delusion must end.

D. How will it end?

M. That which is born must end. The delusion is only concomitant with the ego. It rises up and sinks. But the Reality never rises nor sinks. It remains Eternal. The Master who has realized says so; the disciple hears, thinks over his words, and realizes the Self.

There are two ways of putting it: the ever-present Self needs no efforts to be realized; Realization is already there. Illusion alone is to be removed. Some say the word from the mouth of the Master removes it instantaneously. Others say that meditation, etc., is necessary for realization. Both are right; only the standpoints differ.

D. Is *dhyana* necessary?

M. The *Upanishads* say that even the Earth is in eternal *dhyana*.

D. How does karma help? Will it not add to the already heavy load to be removed?

M. Karma done unselfishly purifies the mind and helps to fix it in meditation.

D. What if one meditates incessantly without karma?

M. Try and see. The *vasanas* will not let you. *Dhyana* comes only step by step with the gradual weakening of the *vasanas* by the Grace of the Master.

OCTOBER 15, 1935

Dr. Bernhard Bey, an American chemist who had been interested in Vedanta *for the last twenty years, now in India, came on a visit to the Master. He asked*: How is *abhyasa* to be made? I am trying to find the Light.

(*He himself explained abhyasa as concentration — one-pointedness of mind.*)
The Master asked: What was his *abhyasa* till now?

(*The visitor said he concentrated on the nasal base, but his mind wandered.*)

M. Is there a mind?

Another devotee gently put in: The mind is only a collection of thoughts.

M. To whom are the thoughts? If you try to locate the mind, the mind vanishes and the Self alone remains. Being alone, there can be no one-pointedness or otherwise.

D. It is so difficult to understand this. If something concrete is said, it can be readily grasped. *Japa, dhyana,* etc., are more concrete.

M. "Who am I?" is the best *japa*.

What could be more concrete than the Self? It is within each one's experience every moment. Why should he try to catch anything outside, leaving out the Self? Let each one try to find out the known Self instead of searching for the unknown something beyond.

D. Where shall I meditate on the *Atman*? I mean, in which part of the body?

M. The Self should manifest itself. That is all that is wanted.

A devotee gently added: On the right of the chest, there is the Heart, the seat of the *Atman*.

Another devotee: The illumination is in that center when the Self is realized.

M. Quite so.

D. How to turn the mind away from the world?

M. Is there the world? I mean, apart from the Self? Does the world say that it exists? It is you who say there is a world. Find the Self who says it.

OCTOBER 16, 1935

A question was raised about the differences in the various samadhis.

M. When the senses are merged in darkness, it is deep sleep; when merged in light, it is *samadhi*. Just as a passenger when asleep in a carriage is unaware of the motion, the halting or the unharnessing of the horses, so also a *jnani* in *sahaja samadhi* is unaware of the happenings, waking, dream and deep sleep. Here, sleep corresponds to the unharnessing of the horses. And *samadhi* corresponds to the halting of the horses, because the senses are ready to act just as the horses are ready to move after halting.

In *samadhi*, the head does not bend down because the senses are there though inactive; whereas the head bends down in sleep because the senses are merged in darkness. In *kevala samadhi,* the activities (vital and mental), waking, dream, and sleep, are only merged, ready to emerge after regaining the state other than *samadhi*. In *sahaja samadhi* the activities, vital and mental, and the three states are destroyed, never to reappear. However, others notice the *jnani* active e.g., eating, talking, moving etc. He is not himself aware of these activities, whereas others are aware of his activities. They pertain to his body and not to his Real Self, *svarupa*. For himself, he is like the sleeping passenger — or like a child interrupted from sound sleep and fed, being unaware of it. The child says the next day that he did not take milk at all and that he went to sleep without it. Even when reminded, he cannot be convinced. So, also, in *sahaja samadhi*.

Sushumna pare leena. Here *sushumna* refers to *Tapo Marga*, whereas the *para nadi* refers to *Jnana Marga*.

The Master, relating some stories of the *bhaktas* told how Sri Krishna served Eknath for twelve years, how Panduranga relieved Sakku Bai from her home prison and enabled her to visit Pandharpur. Then he recollected the appearance of a mysterious Moulvi on his way from Madurai to Tiruvannamalai in 1896, how he appeared, spoke, and disappeared suddenly.

Mr. Grant Duff asked the Master if a mongoose had had anything to do with him.
The Master said: Yes. It was the occasion of *Ardra* and *Jayanti*; I was living up
the hill in Skandasramam. Streams of visitors were climbing up the hill
from the town. A mongoose, larger than the ordinary size, of golden hue
(not gray as a mongoose is), with no black spot on its tail as usual with the
wild mongoose, passed these crowds fearlessly. People took it to be a tame
one belonging to someone in the crowd. The animal went straight to
Palaniswami, who was having a bath in the spring by the Virupaksha Cave.
He stroked the creature and patted it. It followed him into the cave, in-
spected every nook and corner and left the place and joined the crowd to
pass up to Skandasramam. I noticed it. Everyone was struck by its attractive appearance and its fearless movements. It came up to me, got on my
lap and rested there some time. Then it raised itself up, looked about and
moved down; it went round the whole place and I followed it lest it should
be harmed by the unwary visitors or by the peacocks. Two peacocks of the
place looked at it inquisitively, whereupon the mongoose moved
nonchalantly from place to place and finally disappeared into the rocks on
the southeast of the Asramam.

The same gentleman asked the Master about the material relation between memory
and will and their relation to the mind.
M. They are functions of the mind. The mind is the outcome of the ego and
the ego is from the Self.

NOVEMBER 6, 1935

The Master gave the true significance of the Christian faith thusly:
 Christ is the ego.
 The Cross is the body.
 When the ego is crucified, and it perishes, what survives is the Absolute
Being (God), ("I and my Father are one") and this glorious survival is called
Resurrection.

Major A.W. Chadwick, an ardent English devotee, asked: Why did Jesus call out
"My God! My God!" while being crucified?
M. It might have been an intercession on behalf of the two thieves crucified with Him. A *jnani* has attained liberation even while alive, here and
now. It is immaterial as to how, where and when he leaves his body. Some
jnanis may appear to suffer, others may be in *samadhi*, while others may

disappear from sight before death. But that makes no difference to their *jnana*. Such suffering is apparent only to the onlooker and not to the *jnani*, for he has already transcended the mistaken identity of the Self with the body.

The same gentleman asked: What is the significance of Christ in the illumination of St. Paul?
M. Illumination is absolute, not associated with forms. After St. Paul became Self-conscious, he identified the illumination with Christ-consciousness.
D. But Paul was not a lover of Christ then?
M. Love or hatred is immaterial. The thought of Christ was there. It is similar to Ravana's case. Christ-consciousness and Self-realization are all the same.

M. *Karpura arati* is symbolic of the burning away of the mind by the light of illumination, *vibhuti* (sacred ashes) is *Shiva* (Absolute Being), and *kumkuma* (vermilion powder) is *Shakti* (consciousness).
   Vibhuti is of two kinds: *Para vibhuti* and *apara vibhuti*. The sacred ashes are of the latter class. The *para* is what remains after all the dross has been burnt away by the Fire of Realization. It is Absolute Being.

Again, the Trinity was explained:
   God the Father represents *Ishvara*
   God the Holy Spirit represents *Atman*
   God the Son represents Guru
   Ishvaro gururatmeti murti bheda vibhagine vyomavad vyapta dehaya dakshinamurtaye namah, meaning that God appears to his devotee in the form of a Guru (son of God), and points out to him the immanence of the Holy Spirit. That is to say that God is Spirit, that this Spirit is immanent everywhere and that the Self must be realized, which is the same as realizing God.

A Bengali visitor asked: How is the mind controlled?
M. What do you call "the mind"?
D. When I sit down to think of God, thoughts wander to other objects. I want to control those thoughts.
M. In the *Bhagavad Gita*, it is said that it is the nature of the mind to wander. One must bring one's thoughts to bear on God. By long practice, the mind

is controlled and made steady.

The wavering of the mind is a weakness arising from dissipation of its energy in the shape of thoughts. When one makes the mind stick to one thought the energy is conserved, and the mind becomes stronger.

D. What is the meaning of the strength of the mind?

M. Its ability to concentrate on one thought without being distracted.

D. How is that achieved?

M. By practice. A devotee concentrates on God; a seeker, follower of the *Jnana Marga*, seeks the Self. The practice is equally difficult for both.

D. Even if the mind is brought to bear on the search for the Self, after a long struggle the mind begins to elude him and the man is not aware of the mischief until after some time.

M. So it would be. In the earlier stages, the mind reverts to the search after long intervals; with continued practice, it reverts after shorter intervals until finally it does not wander at all. It is then that the dormant *shakti* manifests. The *sattvic* mind is free from thoughts, whereas the *rajasic* mind is full of them. The *sattvic* mind resolves itself into the Life-current.

D. Can one keep the mind away from entering into the phase of thoughts before experiencing the current?

M. Yes; the current is pre-existent.

NOVEMBER 7, 1935

A visitor said: Some say that one should practice meditation on gross objects only; it may be disastrous if one constantly seeks to kill the mind.

M. For whom is it disastrous? Can there be anything but disaster apart from the Self?

Unbroken "I-I" is the infinite ocean; the ego, "I"-thought, remains only a bubble on it and is called *jiva*, i.e., individual soul. The bubble, too, is water; when it bursts, it only mixes in the ocean. When it remains a bubble, it is still a part of the ocean. Ignorant of this simple truth, innumerable methods under different denominations, such as *yoga, bhakti, karma* . . . each again with many modifications, are being taught with great skill and in intricate detail only to entice seekers and confuse their minds. So, also, are the religions and sects and dogmas. What are they all for? Only for knowing the Self. They are aids and practices required for knowing the Self.

Objects perceived by the senses are spoken of as immediate knowledge (*pratyaksha*). Can anything be as direct as the Self — always experienced without the aid of the senses? Sense perceptions can only be indirect knowledge, and not direct knowledge. Only one's own awareness is direct knowledge, as is the common experience of one and all. No aids are needed to know one's own Self, i.e., to be aware.

The one Infinite Unbroken Whole (plenum) becomes aware of itself as "I." This is its original name. All other names, e.g., "Om," are later growths. Liberation is only to remain aware of the Self. The *mahavakya* "I am Brahman" is its authority. Though the "I" is always experienced, yet one's attention has to be drawn to it. Then only Knowledge dawns. Thus the need for the instruction of the *Upanishads* and of wise sages.

NOVEMBER 9, 1935

All are aware of their own Self only. Wonder of wonders! They take what *is not* as what *is,* or they see the phenomena apart from the Self. Only so long as there is the knower is there knowledge of all kinds (direct, inferential, intellectual, etc.). Should the knower vanish, they all vanish together with him; their validity is of the same degree as his.

A man prayed to the Master to pardon his sins. He was told it would be enough if he took care to see that his mind did not trouble him.

NOVEMBER 13, 1935

A question was raised by Maj. A.W. Chadwick, as follows: Mr. Edward Carpenter, a certain mystic, has written in a book that he had Self-realization on some occasions and that its effects lasted for some time, only to be gradually lost. On the other hand, *Sri Ramana Gita* says "*Granthi* (knot of ignorance or bondage), snapped once, is snapped forever." In the case of this mystic, the bondage seems to have persisted even after Self-realization. How can that be?

The Master cited Kaivalya *as follows*: The disciple, after realizing the all-shining, unitary, unbroken state of Being-Knowledge-Bliss, surrendered himself to the Master and humbly prayed to know how he could repay the Master's Grace. The Master said: "My reward consists in your permanent unbroken bliss. Do not slip away from it."

D. Having once experienced the Supreme Bliss, how can one stray from it?

M. Oh, it happens! The predisposition adhering to him from time immemorial will draw him out and so ignorance overtakes him.

D. What are the obstacles to remaining steady in unbroken bliss? And how can they be overcome?

M. The obstacles are:

1. Ignorance, which is forgetfulness of one's pure being.
2. Doubt, which consists in wondering if the experience was of the Real or of the unreal.
3. Error, which consists in the "I-am-the-body" idea, and thinking that the world is real. These are overcome by hearing the truth, reflection, and concentration.

The Master continued: Experience is said to be temporary or permanent. The first experience is temporary and by concentration it can become permanent. In the former, bondage is not completely destroyed; it remains subtle and reasserts itself in due course. But in the latter it is destroyed root and branch, never to appear again. The expression *yogabhrashta* (those who have fallen down from yoga) in *Srimad Bhagavad Gita* refers to the former class of men.

D. Is then hearing the Truth meant only for a limited few?

M. It is of two kinds. The ordinary one is to hear it enunciated and explained by a Master. However, the right one is to raise the question for oneself and seek and find the answer in oneself as the unbroken "I-I."

To be reflecting on this experience is the second stage. To remain one-pointed in it is the third stage.

D. Can the temporary experience be called *samadhi?*

M. No. It forms part of the third stage.

D. It looks then as if even hearing the Truth is limited to a very few.

M. Seekers fall into two classes; *kritopasaka* and *akritopasaka*. The former having already overcome their predisposition by steady devotion, and their mind thus made pure, they have had some kind of experience but do not comprehend it; as soon as instructed by a competent Master, permanent experience results.

The other class of seekers need great effort to achieve this end. How will hearing of the Truth, reflection, and concentration help them?

They comprise *upasana* (the nearest approach to Truth) and will end in Self-realization.

The fourth stage is the final one of liberation.

Maj. A.W. Chadwick: Of what nature is the realization of Westerners who relate they have had flashes of cosmic consciousness?

M. It came as a flash and disappeared as such. That which has a beginning must also end. Only when the ever-present consciousness is realized will it be permanent. Consciousness is indeed always with us. Everyone knows "I Am"! No one can deny his own being. The man in deep slumber is not aware; while awake he seems to be aware. But he is the same person. There is no change in the one who slept and the one who is now awake. In deep sleep, he was not aware of his body; there was no body-consciousness. In the wakeful state, he is aware of his body; there is body-consciousness. Therefore, the difference lies in the emergence of body-consciousness and not in any change in the Real Consciousness. The body and body-consciousness arise together and sink together. All this amounts to saying that there are no limitations in deep sleep, whereas there are limitations in the waking state. These limitations are the bondage; the feeling "The body is I" is the error. This false sense of "I" must go. The real "I" is always there. It is *here and now*. It never appears anew and disappears again. That which *is* must also persist forever. That which appears anew will also be lost. Compare deep sleep and waking. The body appears in one state but not in the other. Therefore, the body will be lost. The consciousness was pre-existent and will survive the body. In fact, there is no one who does not say "I Am." The wrong knowledge of "I am the body" is the cause of all the mischief. This wrong knowledge must go. That is realization. Realization is not acquisition of anything new, nor it is a new faculty; it is only removal of all camouflage.

Maj. Chadwick: I try to shake off the body.

M. A man shakes off his clothes and remains alone and free. The Self is unlimited and is not confined to the body. How can the body be shaken off? Where will he leave it? Wherever it is, it is still his.

Maj. Chadwick: (Laughter.)

M. The ultimate Truth is so simple. It is nothing more than being in the pristine state. This is all that need be said.

Still, it is a wonder that to teach this simple Truth there should come into being so many religions, creeds, methods and disputes among them and so on! Oh, the pity! Oh, the pity!

Maj. Chadwick: But people will not be content with simplicity; they want complexity.

M. Quite so. Because they want something elaborate and attractive and puzzling, so many religions have come into existence and each of them is so complex, and each creed in each religion has its own adherents and antagonists.

For example, an ordinary Christian will not be satisfied unless he is told that God is somewhere in the far-off Heavens not to be reached by us un-aided. Christ alone knew Him and Christ alone can guide us. Therefore: Worship Christ and be saved. If told the simple truth — "The Kingdom of Heaven is within you" — he is not satisfied and will read complex and far-fetched meanings into such statements. Mature minds alone can grasp the simple Truth in all its nakedness.

(*Maj. Chadwick later expressed a certain involuntary fear while meditating. He felt the spirit separated from the gross body, and the sensation created fear.*)

M. To whom is the fright? It is all due to the habit of identifying the body with the Self. Repeated experience of separation will make one familiar and the fright will cease.

NOVEMBER 19, 1935

Mr. Ramachandar, a gentleman from Ambala, asked where the Heart is and what Realization is.

M. The Heart is not physical; it is spiritual. *Hridayam* = *hrit+ayam* = This is the center. It is that from which thoughts arise, on which they subsist and where they are resolved. The thoughts are the content of the mind and they shape the universe. The Heart is the center of all. *Yatova imani bhutani jayante* (that from which these beings come into existence) etc., is said to be *Brahman* in the *Upanishads*. That is the Heart. *Brahman* is the Heart.

D. How to realize the Heart?

M. There is no one who even for a trice fails to experience the Self. For no one admits that he ever stands apart from the Self. He is the Self. The Self is the Heart.

D. It is not clear.

M. In deep sleep you exist; awake, you remain. The same Self is in both states. The difference is only in the awareness and the non-awareness of the world. The world rises with the mind and sets with the mind. That which rises and sets is not the Self. The Self is different, giving rise to the mind, sustaining it, and resolving it. So the Self is the underlying principle.

When asked who you are, you place your hand on the right side of the breast and say, "I am." There you involuntarily point out the Self. The Self is thus known. But the individual is miserable because he confounds the mind and the body with the Self. This confusion is due to wrong knowl-edge. Elimination of wrong knowledge is alone needed. Such elimination results in Realization.

D. How to control the mind?

M. What is mind? Whose is the mind?

D. Mind always wanders. I cannot control it.

M. It is the nature of the mind to wander. You are not the mind. The mind springs up and sinks down. It is impermanent, transitory, whereas you are eternal. There is nothing but the Self. To inhere in the Self is the thing. Never mind the mind. If its source is sought it will vanish, leaving the Self unaffected.

D. So one need not seek to control the mind?

M. There is no mind to control if you realize the Self. The mind vanishing, the Self shines forth. In the realized man the mind may be active or inactive; the Self alone remains for him. For the mind, the body and the world are not separate from the Self. They rise from and sink into the Self. They do not remain apart from the Self. Can they be different from the Self? Only be aware of the Self. Why worry about these shadows? How do they affect the Self?

Bhagavan further explained: The Self is the Heart. The Heart is self-luminous. Light arises from the Heart and reaches the brain, which is the seat of the mind. The world is seen with the mind, that is, by the reflected light of the Self. It is perceived with the aid of the mind. When the mind is illumined it is aware of the world. When it is not itself so illumined, it is not aware of the world. If the mind is turned in towards the source of light, objective knowledge ceases and Self alone shines forth as the Heart.

The moon shines by the reflected light of the sun. When the sun has set, the moon is useful for revealing objects. When the sun has risen, no one needs the moon, although the pale disc of the moon is visible in the sky.

So it is with the mind and the Heart. The mind is useful because of its reflected light. It is used for seeing objects. When it is turned inward, the source of illumination shines forth by itself, and the mind remains dim and useless like the moon in daytime.

A sannyasi asked: It is said that the Self is beyond the mind and yet the realization is with the mind. *Mano na manute, Manasa na matam,* and *Manasaivedamaptavyam* (The mind cannot think it. It cannot be thought of by the mind, and the mind alone can realize it). How are these contradictions to be reconciled?

M. *Atman* is realized with *mruta manas* (dead mind) i.e., mind devoid of thoughts and turned inward. Then the mind sees its own source and becomes That. It is not as the subject perceiving an object.

When the room is dark, a lamp is necessary to illumine and eyes to cognize objects. But when the sun is risen there is no need of a lamp, and the objects are seen. To see the sun, no lamp is necessary; it is enough that you turn your eyes towards the self-luminous sun.

Similarly with the mind. To see the objects, the reflected light of the mind is necessary. To see the Heart, it is enough that the mind is turned towards it. Then the mind loses itself and the Heart shines forth.

A gentleman from Ambala asked: What is the rationalistic explanation of Draupadi's sari becoming endless?

M. Spiritual matters cannot be fitted into rationalism. Spirituality is transcendental. The miracle was after Draupadi had surrendered herself. The secret lies in *surrender*.

D. How to reach the Heart?

M. Where are you *now* that you want to reach the Heart? Are you standing apart from the Self?

D. I am in my body.

M. In a particular spot, or all over?

D. All over. I am extending all over the body.

M. Wherefrom do you extend?

D. I do not know.

M. Yes. You are always in the Heart. You are never away from it in order that you should reach it. Consider how you are in deep sleep and in the waking state. These states are also not yours. They are of the ego. The consciousness remains the same and undifferentiated throughout.

D. I understand but I cannot feel it so.

M. Whose is the ignorance? Find it out.

D. All this is so difficult.

M. The idea of difficulty is itself wrong. It will not help you to gain what you want. Again I ask: "Who finds it difficult?"

D. I see that I am coming around to "I."

M. Because you are always that and never away from it. There is nothing so simple as being the Self. It requires no effort, no aid. One has to leave off the wrong identity and be in his eternal, natural, inherent state.

The questioner returned with a request the next day, saying: It is said that one should receive instruction from a Guru. Mere reading of books is not helpful. I have read many books; but there is no practical help derived from such learning. Please tell me what I should do, how I should do it, at what times, in which places, and so on.

(The Master remained silent. His silence seemed to say, "Here and now, be at peace and tranquil. That is all." But the questioner could not interpret it that way; he wanted something concrete.)

The next day Sri Bhagavan said: These people want some *japa, dhyana,* or yoga or something similar. Without their saying what they have been doing so far, what more can be said to them? Again, why *japa,* it's *phalasruti,* etc.? Who is it that makes the *japa?* Who gets the fruits thereof? Can they not look to the Self? Or again, even if instructed by others to do *japa* or *dhyana,* they do it for some time, but are always looking for some results, e.g., visions, dreams, or thaumaturgic powers. If they do not find them, they say they are not progressing or the *tapas* is not effective. Visions, etc., are no signs of progress. Mere performance of *tapas* is its progress also. Steadiness is what is required. Moreover, they must entrust themselves to their mantra or their God and wait for Grace. They don't do so. *Japa* uttered even once has its own good effect, whether the individual is aware or not.

NOVEMBER 28, 1935

Mr. Kishorilal, an officer of the Railway Board, Government of India, hails from Delhi. He looks simple, gentle, and dignified in behavior. He has a gastric ulcer and has arranged for his board and lodging in the town.

Five years ago, he took up the study of devotional literature. He is a *bhakta* of Sri Krishna. He could feel Krishna in all that he saw. Krishna often appeared to him and made him happy. His work was going on without any effort on his part. Everything seemed to be done for him by Krishna himself.

Later he came in contact with a Mahatma who advised him to study *Vedanta* and take to *nirakara upasana,* i.e., devotion to formless Being. He has since read about seven hundred books of philosophy and *Vedanta,* including the *Upanishads, Ashtavakra, Avadhuta,* and *Srimad Bhagavad Gita.* He has also studied Sri Bhagavan's works in English and is much impressed by them.

Once when he was in the jaws of death, no other thought haunted him but that he had not yet visited Sri Bhagavan in his life. So he has come here on a short visit. He prays only for Sri Bhagavan's touch and his Grace.

The Master said to him: Atmaivaham gudakesa, i.e., I am *Atman; Atman* is the Guru; and *Atman* is Grace, also. No one remains without the *Atman.* He is always in contact. No external touch is necessary.

D. I understand. I do not mean external touch.

M. Nothing is more intimate than the *Atman*.

D. Again Sri Krishna appeared to me three months back and said, "Why do you ask me for *nirakara upasana*? It is only *sarva bhutesu cha atmanam sarva bhutani cha atmani.* (The Self in all and all in the Self.)

M. That contains the whole truth. Even this is *oupacharika* (indirect). There is in fact nothing but the *Atman*. The world is only a projection of the mind. The mind originates from the *Atman*. So *Atman* alone is the One Being.

D. Yet it is difficult to realize.

M. There is nothing to realize. It is *nitya suddha buddha mukta* (the Eternal, pure, aware and liberated) state. It is natural and eternal. There is nothing new to gain. On the other hand, a man must lose his ignorance. That is all.

This ignorance must be traced to its origin. To whom is this ignorance? Of what is one ignorant? There are the subject and the object. Such duality is characteristic of the mind. The mind is from the *Atman*.

D. Yes. Ignorance itself cannot exist.

He finally surrendered, saying: Just as a doctor learns what is wrong with the patient and treats him accordingly, so may Sri Bhagavan do with me.

(*He also said that he had lost all inclination to study books and learn from them.*)

M. *Yena asrutam srutam bhavati* (*Chandogya Upanishad*). (By knowing which, all the unknown becomes known.)

Madhavaswami, Bhagavan's attendant: Are there nine methods of teaching the *Mahavakya* "*Tattvamasi*" in the *Chandogya Upanishad*?

M. No. Not so. The method is only one. Uddalaka started teaching "*Sat eva Somya* . . ." (There is only Being . . .) illustrating it with Svetaketu's fast.

1. *Sat*, the Being in the individual, is made obvious by the fast.

2. This (*sat*) Being is similar in all, as honey gathered from different flowers.

3. There is no difference in the *sat* of individuals as illustrated by the state of deep sleep. The question arises — if so, why does not each know it in sleep?

4. Because the individuality is lost, there is only *sat* left. Illustration: rivers lost in the ocean. If lost, is there *sat*?

5. As when a tree is pruned it grows again. That is a sure sign of its life. But is it there even in that dormant condition?

6. Take the instance of salt and water. The presence of the salt in water is subtle. Though invisible to the eye, it is recognized by other senses. How is one to know it? What is the other means?

7. By inquiry; as the example of the man left in the Gandhara forest who regained his home.

8. In evolution and involution, in manifestation and resolution, *sat* alone exists. *Tejah parasyam, devatayam* (the light merges in the Supreme).

9. An insincere man is hurt by the touch of the fire test. His insincerity is brought out by fire. Sincerity is self-evident. A true man or a Self-realized man remains happy, without being affected by the false appearances (namely the world, birth, death, etc.), whereas the false or ignorant man is miserable.

NOVEMBER 29, 1935

Swami Yogananda [author of Autobiography of a Yogi*], with four others, arrived at 8:45 a.m. He looks big, but gentle and well groomed. He has dark flowing hair, hanging over his shoulders. The group had lunch in the Asramam. Mr. C.R. Wright (his secretary) asked*: How shall I realize God?

M. God is an unknown entity. Moreover, He is external. Whereas, the Self is always with you and it *is* you. Why do you leave out what is intimate and go in for what is external?

D. What is the Self again?

M. The Self is known to everyone, but not clearly. You always exist. The Being is the Self. "I Am" is the name of God. Of all the definitions of God, none is indeed so well put as the Biblical statement *"I Am that I Am"* in Exodus (chap. 3). There are other statements, such as *Brahmaivaham, Aham Brahmasmi,* and *Soham.* But none is so direct as the name *Jehovah = I Am.* The Absolute Being is *what is* — it is the Self. It is God. Knowing the Self, God is known. In fact, God is none other than the Self.

D. Why are there good and evil?

M. They are relative terms. There must be a subject to know the good and evil. That subject is the ego. Trace the source of the ego. It ends in the Self.

The source of the ego is God. This definition of God is probably more concrete and more easily understood by you.

D. So it is. How to get bliss?

M. Bliss is not something to be got. On the other hand, you always are bliss. This desire is born of the sense of incompleteness. To whom is this sense of incompleteness? Inquire. In deep sleep, you were blissful. Now you are not so. What is interposed between that bliss and this non-bliss? It is the ego. Seek its source and find you are bliss.

There is nothing new to get. You have, on the other hand, to get rid of your ignorance, which makes you think that you are other than bliss. For whom is this ignorance? It is to the ego. Trace the source of the ego. Then the ego is lost and bliss remains. It is eternal. You are That, here and now. . . That is the master key for solving all doubts. The doubts arise in the mind. The mind is born of the ego. The ego rises from the Self. Search the source of the ego, and the Self is revealed. That alone remains. The universe is only expanded Self. It is not different from the Self.

D. What is the best way of living?

M. It differs according to one's being a *jnani* or *ajnani*. A *jnani* does not find anything different or separate from the Self. All are in the Self. It is wrong to imagine that there is the world, that there is a body in it and that you dwell in the body. If the Truth is known, the universe and what is beyond it will be found to be only in the Self. The outlook differs according to the sight of the person. The sight is from the eye. The eye must be located somewhere. If you are seeing with the gross eyes, you find others gross. If with subtle eyes (i.e., the mind), others appear subtle. If the eye becomes the Self, the Self being infinite, the eye is infinite. There is nothing else to see different from the Self.

(*He thanked Maharshi. He was told that the best way of thanking is to remain always as the Self.*)

Later the Yogi asked: How is the spiritual uplift of the people to be effected? What are the instructions to be given them?

M. They differ according to the temperaments of the individuals and the spiritual ripeness of their minds. There cannot be any instruction *en masse*.

D. Why does God permit suffering in the world? Should He not with His omnipotence do away with it at one stroke and ordain the universal realization of God?

M. Suffering is the way for Realization of God.

D. Should He not ordain differently?

M. It is the way.

D. Are yoga, religion, etc., antidotes to suffering?

M. They help you overcome suffering.

D. Why should there be suffering?

M. Who suffers? What is suffering?

(*No answer. Finally, the Yogi rose up, prayed for Sri Bhagavan's blessings for his own work and expressed great regret for his hasty return. He looked very sincere and devoted and even emotional.*)

In continuation of a previous dialogue (Chandogya Upanishad): Uddalaka explained that all proceeds from *sat* (as illustrated by deep sleep).

The body takes food. Food requires water. Water requires heat to digest the food. (*Tejo mulamanvichcha.*) It is *sat parasyam devatayam* (merged in the Being). If we are *sat sampannah* (merged in the Being), how is it that we do not realize it?

M. Just as the honey gathered from different flowers forms the bulk in a honeycomb, and each drop does not indicate wherefrom it has been collected, so also *sat sampannah* in deep sleep, death, etc., people do not recognize their individualities. They slip into that state unawares. But when they wake up, they regain their original individual characteristics.

D. Honey, though collected from different flowers, becomes the bulk and does not possess individual characteristics. But the individual parts do not also exist in the drops and they do not return to their sources. Whereas the individuals after going into deep sleep wake up as individuals, as formerly. How is that?

M. Just as the rivers discharged into the ocean lose their individualities, still the waters evaporate and return as rain on the hills and through rivers to the ocean, so also the individuals going to sleep lose their individualities and yet return as individuals according to their previous *vasanas* unawares. Thus, even in death, *sat* is not lost.

D. How can that be?

M. See how a tree, whose branches are cut, grows again. So long as the life source is not affected, it will grow. Similarly the *samskaras* sink into the Heart in death: they do not perish. They will at the right time sprout forth from the Heart. That is how the *jivas* are reborn.

D. How does the wide universe sprout forth from such subtle *samskaras* remaining sunk in the Heart?

M. Just as a big banyan tree sprouts from a tiny seed, so the wide universe with names and forms sprouts forth from the Heart.

D. If the origin is *sat*, why is it not felt?

M. The salt in lump form is visible; it is invisible in liquid. Still, its existence is known by taste. Similarly *sat*, though not recognized by the intellect, can still be realized in a different way, i.e., transcendentally.

D. How?

M. Just as a man blindfolded and left by robbers in a jungle inquires about his way home and returns there, so also the ignorant one (blinded by ignorance) inquires of those not so blinded and seeks his own source and returns to it.

"*Vang manasi sampadyate, manah prane, pranastejasi, tejah parasyam devatayam iti.*"

Speech arises from the mind, the mind arises from the *prana* (life-breath), the *prana* arises from the light of consciousness, the light of consciousness arises from the Supreme.

— *Gurupadesa*

D. If so, a *jnani* or an *ajnani* dies in the same manner. Why is an *ajnani* reborn, whereas a *jnani* is not?

M. One enters into *sat* consciously and merges, whereas the other enters unaware and is thrown out unaware, also.

DECEMBER 13, 1935

Two gentlemen from Ambala had been here for a few weeks. Just before taking leave of Sri Bhagavan one of them asked how he should remove the spiritual drowsiness of his friends or of other people in general.

M. Have you removed your own "spiritual drowsiness"? The force which is set up to remove your own "drowsiness" will also operate in other centers. There is the willpower with which you can act on others. But it is on a lower plane and not desirable. Take care of yourself first.

D. How to remove my own "drowsiness"?

M. Whose "drowsiness" is it? Inquire. Turn within. Turn all your inquiries towards search for Self. The force set up within you will operate on others, also.

DECEMBER 14, 1935

An American lady asked Bhagavan what his experiences of samadhi were. When suggested that she should relate her experiences and ask if they were right, she replied that Sri Bhagavan's experiences ought to be correct and should be known, whereas her own were unimportant. She thus wanted to know if Sri Bhagavan felt his body hot or cold in samadhi, if he spent the first three and a half years of his stay at Tiruvannamalai in prayers, and so on.

M. *Samadhi* transcends mind and speech and cannot be described. For example, the state of deep slumber cannot be described; *samadhi* can still less be explained.

D. But I know that I am unconscious in deep sleep.

M. Consciousness and unconsciousness are only modes of the mind. *Samadhi* transcends the mind.

D. Still you can say what it is like.

M. You will know only when you are in *samadhi*.

DECEMBER 17, 1935

Mr. P. Brunton, while reading Upadesa Manjari, *came across the statement that the ego, the world, and God are all unreal. He desired to use a different word for God or at least a qualifying adjective, e.g., the Creative Force or personal God.*

Sri Bhagavan explained that God means *Samashti*, i.e., all that is *plus* the Being — in the same way that "I" means the individual *plus* the Be-ing, and the "world" means the variety plus Being. The Being is in all cases real. The *all*, the *variety* and the *individual* is in each case unreal. So also in the union of the real and the unreal, the mixing up or the false identification is wrong. It amounts to saying *sad-asad-vilakshana*, i.e., transcending the real and the unreal — *sat* and *asat*. Reality is that which transcends all concepts, including that of God. Inasmuch as the name of God is used, it cannot be true. The Hebrew word *Jehovah* (I Am) expresses God correctly. Absolute Being is beyond expression. The word cannot be replaced nor need it be replaced.

The Englishman casually said that in prehistoric ages there was spirituality but not high intellect, whereas intellect has now developed. Sri Bhagavan pointed out that "intellect" raises the question "whose intellect?" The answer is, "the Self." So intellect is a tool of the Self. The Self uses intellect for measuring variety. Intellect is not the Self nor apart from the Self. The Self alone is eternal. Intellect is only a phenomenon. People speak of the development of variety as being the development of intellect. Intellect was always there. *Dhata yatha parvam akalpayat* (The Creator created just as before). Consider your own state, day by day. There is no intellect in dreamless deep sleep. But it is there now. There is no intellect in a child. It develops with age. How could there be manifestation of intellect without its seed

in the sleep state and in the child? Why go to history to teach this fundamental fact? The level of truth of history is only the level of truth of the
individual.

A Telugu gentleman asked about Karma Yoga. Sri Bhagavan said: The person
should act as an actor on the stage. In all actions there is the *sat* as the
underlying principle. "Remember it and act."
He asked about the purity of mind (chitta suddhi). *Sri Bhagavan said:*
   Chitta suddhi is to engage in one thought only to the exclusion of all
others. It is also called one-pointedness of the mind. The practice of meditation purifies the mind.

DECEMBER 23, 1935

Baron Von Veltheim-Ostran, an East German Baron, asked: There should be
harmony between knowledge of the Self and knowledge of the world. They
must develop side by side. Is it right? Does Maharshi agree?
M. Yes.
D. Beyond the intellect and before wisdom dawns there will be pictures of
the world passing before one's consciousness. Is it so?
   Sri Bhagavan pointed out the parallel passage in *Dakshinamurti Stotram*,
to signify that the pictures are like reflections in a mirror; again from the
Upanishad — as in the mirror, so in the world of *manes*, as in the water, so in
the world of Gandharvas; as shadow and sunlight in Brahma Loka.
D. There is spiritual awakening since 1930 all the world over. Does Ma-
harshi agree?
M. The development is according to *your* sight.
   The Baron again asked if Maharshi would induce a spiritual trance and
give him a message which is unspoken but still understandable.
   (*No answer was given.*)

DECEMBER 25, 1935

Mr. M. Frydman: Even without any initial desires there are some strange
experiences for us. Where do they arise from?
M. The desire may not be there now. Enough if it was there before. Though
forgotten by you now, it is bearing fruit in due course. That is how the *jnani*
is said to have *prarabdha* left for him. Of course, it is only according to others' point of view.

D. *Jiva* is said to be bound by karma. Is it so?

M. Let karma enjoy its fruits. As long as you are the doer, so long you are the enjoyer.

D. How to get released from karma?

M. See whose karma it is. You will find you are not the doer. Then you will be free. This requires Grace of God for which you should pray to Him, worship Him, and meditate on Him.

The karma which takes place without effort, i.e., involuntary action, is not binding.

Even a *jnani* is acting as seen by his bodily movements. There can be no karma without effort or without intentions (*sankalpas*). Therefore there are *sankalpas* for all. They are of two kinds: binding — *bandha-hetu*, and *mukti-hetu* — non-binding. The former must be given up and the latter must be cultivated. There is no fruit without previous karma; no karma without previous *sankalpa*. Even *mukti* must be the result of effort so long as the sense of doership persists.

A visitor from Ceylon (Sri Lanka): What is the first step for Realization of Self? Please help me towards it. There is no use in reading books.

Another: This one man's request is that of us all.

M. Quite so. If the Self were to be found in books, it would have been already realized. What wonder can be greater than that we seek the Self in books? Can it be found there?

Of course, books have given readers the sense to ask this question and to seek the Self.

D. Books are utterly useless. They should all be burnt. The spoken word alone is useful. Grace alone is useful.

(*Others spoke according to their own light, until finally they returned to the original question, but Sri Bhagavan remained silent.*)

Mr. Rangachari, a Telugu Pundit in Voorhees' College at Vellore, asked about *nishkama karma* (motionless actions). There was no reply. After a time, Sri Bhagavan went up the hill and a few followed him, including the pundit. There was a thorny stick lying on the way, which Sri Bhagavan picked up; he sat down and began leisurely working at it. The thorns were cut off, the knots were made smooth, and the whole stick was polished with a rough leaf. The entire operation took about six hours. Everyone was wondering at the fine appearance of the stick made of a spiky material.

A shepherd boy appeared on the way as the group became to leave. He had lost his stick and was at a loss. Sri Bhagavan immediately gave the new one in his hand to the boy and passed on.

(*The Pundit said that this was the matter-of-fact answer to his question.*)

At the same time there were four dogs living in the Asramam. Sri Bhagavan said that those dogs would not accept any food not partaken by himself. The pundit put the matter to the test. He spread some food before them; they would not touch it. Then Sri Bhagavan, after a time, put a small morsel of it into his mouth; immediately they fell to and devoured the food.

Later, a man brought two peacocks with their eyes screened. When let loose in Maharshi's presence, they flew away to a distance. They were brought back, but still they flew away. Sri Bhagavan then said, "It is no use trying to keep them here. They are not ripe in their minds like these dogs." However much they tried to keep the peacocks, they would not remain there even a minute.

Talk between the Master and two Moslems, on a previous occasion.
D. Has God a form?
M. Who says so?
D. Well, if God has no form, is it proper to worship idols?
M. Leave God alone because He is unknown. What about you? Have you a form?
D. Yes. I am this and so and so.
M. So then, you are a man with limbs, about three and a half cubits high, with beard, etc. Is that so?
D. Certainly.
M. Then do you find yourself so in deep sleep?
D. After waking, I perceive that I was asleep. Therefore, by inference I remained thus in deep sleep, also.
M. If you are the body, why do they bury the corpse after death? The body must refuse to be buried.
D. No, I am the subtle *jiva* within the gross body.
M. So you see that you are really formless; but you are at present identifying yourself with the body. So long as you are formful, why should you not worship the formless God as being formful?

(*The questioner was perplexed.*)

D. What is reality?

M. Reality must be always real. It is not entangled with forms and names, but is That which underlies these. It underlies limitations, being itself limitless. It is not bound. It underlies unrealities, itself being real. Reality is that which is. It is as it is. It transcends speech and lies beyond such expressions as existence, non-existence, etc.

CHAPTER TWO — 1936

JANUARY 1, 1936

A crowd had gathered here during Christmas.

D. How to attain Unity Consciousness?

M. Being Unity Consciousness how to attain it? Your question is its own answer.

D. What is *Atman* (Self), *anatman* (non-self) and *paramatman* (Supreme Self)?

M. *Atman* is the individual self (*jivatman*); it is ever-present (*nityasiddha*). Each one wants to know the Self. What kind of help does one require to know oneself? People want to see the Self as something new. But it is eternal and remains the same all along. They desire to see it as a blazing light, etc. How can it be so? It is not light, nor darkness (*na tejo, na tamah*). It is only as it is and cannot be defined. The best definition is "I Am that I Am." The *Srutis* speak of the Self as being the size of one's thumb, the tip of the hair, an electric spark, vast, subtler than the subtlest, etc. They have no foundation in fact. It is only Being, but different from the real and the unreal; it is Knowledge, but different from knowledge and ignorance. How can it be defined at all? It is simply *Being*.

Sri Bhagavan said that from the whole Thayumanavar literature, he preferred one stanza:

"Ego disappearing, the 'I-I' spontaneously manifests in full glory."

Then, he cited *Skandar Anubhuti*:

"Not real, nor unreal; not darkness nor light, it is."

One man said that a *siddha* of Kumbakonam claimed to overcome the defects in Sri Shankara's system which deals only with transcendentalism and not the workaday life. One must be able to exercise superhuman powers in ordinary life; that is to say, one must be a *siddha* in order to be perfect.

Sri Bhagavan pointed out a stanza in Thayumanavar which condemns all *siddhis*. Further, he said that Thayumanavar mentions *mouna* (silence) in numerous places, but defines it in only one verse. *Mouna* is said to be that state which spontaneously manifests after annihilation of the ego. That state is beyond light and darkness, but still it is called *light* since no other proper word could be found for it.

JANUARY 3, 1936

Dr. Mohammed Hafiz Syed, a Muslim Professor of Persian and Urdu in the University of Allahabad, asked: What is the purpose of this external manifestation?

M. This manifestation had induced your question.

D. True. I am covered by *maya*. How to be free from it?

M. Who is covered by *maya*? Who wants to be free?

D. Master, being asked "Who?," I know that it is ignorant me, composed of the senses, mind and body. I tried this inquiry "Who?" after reading Paul Brunton's book. Three or four times I was feeling elated, and the elation lasted some time and faded away. How to be established in "I"? Please give me the clue and help me.

M. That which appears anew must also disappear in due course.

D. Please tell me the method of reaching the eternal Truth.

M. You are *That*. Can you ever remain apart from the Self? To be yourself requires no effort since you are always That.

Another impatient questioner postulated and elaborated long premises and finished asking why some children die premature deaths. He required the answer not to satisfy the grown-ups who look on, but the babies who are the victims.

M. Let the victims ask. Why do you ask and desire the answer from the standpoint of a child?

The Muslim Professor asked: When I am here my mind is *sattvic*; as soon as I turn my back on this, my mind hankers after so many objects.

M. Are the objects different from you? There can be no objects without subject.

D. And how shall I know it?

M. Being That, what do you want to know? Are there two selves for the one to know the other?

D. Again, I repeat, Sir, how to know the truth of all this and experience it?

M. There is no gaining of anything new. All that is required is to rid the Self of ignorance. This ignorance consists in the identification of the Self with the non-Self.

D. Yes. I still do not understand. I must have your help. Everyone here is depending on you for your Grace. You yourself must have sought originally the help of a Guru or of God. Extend that Grace to others now and save me.

Before I came here, I desired to see you very much. But somehow I could not find an opportunity to do so. In Bangalore, I made up my mind to return to my place. I met Mr. Frydman and others who sent me here. You have dragged me here. My case is like Paul Brunton's in Bombay, when he was dragged here having canceled his passage home.

I hesitated at first on arrival. I wondered if I would be permitted to approach you and converse with you. My doubts were soon put to rest. I find that all are equal here. You have established equality among all. I dined with you and others. If I should say so to my people in Uttar Pradesh, they would not believe it. The Brahmins would not drink water nor chew *pan* with me. But here you have taken me and others like me into your fold. Though Gandhi is striving hard, he cannot bring about such a state of affairs in the country. I am very happy in your presence.

I regard you as God. I consider Sri Krishna to be the true God because He has said, "Whomsoever one may worship, the worshipper worships me only and I save him." Whereas all others have said, "Salvation is through me (meaning himself) only," Krishna alone is so broad-minded and has spoken like God. You observe the same kind of equality.

JANUARY 4, 1936

Dr. Syed again asked: Should anyone wanting spiritual progress take to action or renunciation (*pravritti-marga* or *nivritti-marga*)?
M. Do you go out of the Self? What is meant by giving up?

An American engineer asked about satsanga *(association with sages).*
M. *Sat* is within us.
D. In the book *Who am I?*, you have said the Heart is the seat of the mind. Is it so?
M. The mind is *Atman*.
D. Is it *Atman* itself or its projection?
M. The same.
D. The Westerners look on the mind as the highest principle, whereas Easterners think the very opposite — why?
M. Where psychology ends, philosophy begins. This is experience; the mind is born, we see it; even without the mind we exist. Everyone's experience

proves it.

D. In deep sleep I do not seem to exist.

M. You say so when awake. It is the mind which speaks now. You exist in deep sleep beyond mind.

D. Western philosophy admits the Higher Self as influencing the mind.

The American engineer asked: Does distance have any effect upon Grace?

M. Time and space are within us. You are always in your Self. How could time and space affect it?

D. In radio, those who are nearer hear sooner. You are Hindu; we are American. Does it make any difference?

M. No.

D. Even thoughts are read by others.

M. That shows that all are one.

JANUARY 5, 1936

There were some French and American visitors to the Asramam. They asked Sri Bhagavan several questions. Among them, one was: What is the message of the East to the West?

M. All attain the same goal.

To another question Sri Bhagavan said: How do you say "I am"? Do you take a light to find yourself? Or did you come to know it by reading books? How? *The questioner said:* By experience.

M. Yes, "experience" is the word. Knowledge implies subject and object. But experience is nonending, eternal.

JANUARY 6, 1936

An elderly gentleman, formerly a co-worker with B.V. Narasimha Swami and author of some Visishtadvaita *work, visited for the first time. He asked about rebirths, if it is possible for the* linga sarira *(subtle body) to get dissolved and be reborn two years after death.*

M. Yes. Surely. Not only can one be reborn, one may be twenty or forty or even seventy years old in the new body though only two years after death. Sri Bhagavan cited Lila's story from *Yoga Vasishta*.

"*Sreyo hi jnanam abhyasat jnanat dhyanam, dhyanat karmaphala tyagah.*"

Knowledge without practice is superior to practice without knowledge. Practice with knowledge is superior to knowledge without practice. *Karmaphala tyagah nishkama karma* as of a *jnani* — action without desire — is superior to knowledge with practice.

Here *jnana* stands for knowledge without practice; *abhyasa* stands for practice without knowledge; *dhyana* stands for practice with knowledge.
D. What is the difference between *yoga* and surrender?
M. Surrender is *Bhakti Yoga*. To reach the source of the "I"-thought is the destruction of the ego, the attainment of the goal, *prapatti* (surrender), *jnana*, etc.

Lakshman Brahmachari from the Sri Ramakrishna Mission asked:
Inquiry of "Who am I?" or of the "I"-thought being itself a thought, how can it be destroyed in the process?
M. When Sita was asked who was her husband among the *rishis* (Rama himself being present there as a *rishi*) in the forest, by the wives of the *rishis*, she denied each one as he was pointed out. Her silence was eloquent.

Similarly, the *Vedas* also are eloquent in *"neti-neti"* (not this-not this) and then remain silent. Their silence is the Real State. This is the meaning of exposition by silence. When the source of the "I"-thought is reached, it vanishes and what remains is the Self.
D. *Patanjali Yoga Sutras* speak of identification.
M. Identification with the Supreme is only another name for destruction of ego.

Mr. Subba Rao asked: What is *mukhya prana* (the chief *prana*)?
M. It is that from which the ego and the *prana* rise. It is sometimes called *kundalini*. Consciousness is not born at any time; it remains eternal. But ego is born; so also the other thoughts. Associated with the Absolute Consciousness they shine forth; not otherwise.
D. What is *moksha* (liberation)?
M. *Moksha* is to know that you were not born. "Be still and know that I am God." To be still is not to think. *Know*, and not *think*, is the key.
D. There are said to be six organs of different colors in the chest of which the Heart is two fingerbreadths to the right of the middle. But the Heart is also formless. Should we then imagine it to have a shape and meditate on it?

M. No. Only the quest "Who am I?" is necessary. What remains all through deep sleep and waking is the same. But in waking there is unhappiness and the effort to remove it. Asked who wakes up from sleep, you say "I." Now you are told to hold fast to this "I." If that is done, the eternal Being will reveal Itself. Investigation of "I" is the point and not meditation on the Heart-center. There is nothing like "within" or "without." Both mean either the same thing or nothing.

Of course there is also the practice of meditation on the Heart-center. It is a mere practice and not investigation. Only the one who meditates on the Heart can remain aware when the mind ceases to be active and remains still; whereas those who meditate on other centers cannot be so aware but infer that the mind was still only after it has become active again.

An educated man asked: Is there an Absolute Being? What is its relation to the relative existence?

M. Are they different from each other? All questions arise only in the mind. The mind arises with waking and subsides in deep sleep. So long as there is a mind, there will be such questions and doubts.

D. There must be stage after stage of progress for gaining the Absolute. Are there grades of Reality?

M. There are no grades of Reality. There are grades of experience for the *jiva* and not of Reality. If anything can be gained anew, it could also be lost, whereas the Absolute is eternal — here and now.

D. If so, why do I remain ignorant of it (*avarana*)?

M. For whom is this ignorance (veiling)? Does the Absolute tell you that it is veiled? It is the *jiva* who says that something veils the Absolute. Find out for whom this ignorance exists.

D. Why is there imperfection in Perfection? That is, how did the Absolute become relative?

M. For whom is this relativity? For whom is this imperfection? The Absolute is not imperfect and cannot ask. The insentient cannot ask the question. Between the two, something has risen up which raises these questions and feels this doubt. Who is it? Is it the one who has now arisen? Or is it the one who is eternal?

Being perfect, why do you feel yourself imperfect? Such is the teaching of all the religions. Whatever may be the experiences, the experiencer is one and the same.

"I" is *purna* — perfection. There is no diversity in sleep. That indicates perfection.

D. Being perfect, why do I not feel it?

M. Nor is imperfection felt in deep sleep. The "I" in sleep being perfect, why does the waking "I" feel imperfect? Because the one who feels imperfect is a spurious offshoot, a differentiation from the Infinite — a segregation from God.

D. I am the same in all the three states. Did this ego submerge me or did I entangle myself with it?

M. Did anything come up without you?

D. I am always the same.

M. Because you see it, this appears to have come up. Did you feel this difficulty in deep sleep? What is new now?

D. The senses and the mind.

M. Who says this? Is it the sleeper? If so, he should have raised the question in deep sleep, also. The sleeper has been lost hold of; some spurious offshoot has differentiated himself and speaks now.

Can anything new appear without that which is eternal and perfect? This kind of dispute is endless; do not engage in it. Turn inward and put a stop to all this. There can be no finality in disputations.

D. Show me that Grace which puts an end to all this trouble. I have not come here to argue. I want only to learn.

M. Learn first what you are. This requires no *sastras*, no scholarship. This is simple experience. The state of *being* is now and here all along. You have lost hold of yourself and are asking others for guidance. The purpose of philosophy is to turn you inward. "If you know your Self, no evil can come to you. Since you asked me, I have taught you."

The ego comes up only holding you (the Self). Hold yourself and the ego will vanish. Until then, the sage will be saying, "There is." The ignorant will be asking, "Where?"

D. The whole problem can be summed up by "Know Thyself."

M. Yes. Quite so.

JANUARY 14, 1936

A question was raised about the Heart.

Sri Bhagavan said that one should seek the Self and realize it. The Heart will play its part automatically. The seat of realization is the Heart. It cannot be said to be either internal or external.

D. Did Bhagavan feel the Heart as the point of Realization in his first or early experience?

M. I began to use the word after seeing literature on the subject. I correlated it with my own experience.

JANUARY 15, 1936

Three European ladies from the Theosophical Conference visited and asked: Is the whole scheme, the Plan, really good? Or is it in the nature of an error, a mistake of which we have to make the best?

M. The Plan is indeed good. The error is on our part. When we correct it in ourselves, the whole scheme becomes all right.

D. Have you any formula to teach us how to bring it about through a remembrance of what we do during sleep?

M. No formula is needed. Everyone has the experience that he slept happily and knew nothing then. Nothing else was experienced.

D. The answer does not satisfy me. We wander in the astral plane in our sleep but we do not remember it.

M. The astral plane relates to dreams, not to deep sleep.

D. What do you consider to be the cause of world suffering? And how can we help to change it, as individuals or collectively?

M. Realize the Real Self. It is all that is necessary.

D. Can we hasten our illumination by doing greater service in the world? And how?

M. As we are not able to help ourselves, so we have to completely surrender ourselves to the Supreme. Then He will take care of us, as well as the world.

D. What do you consider the goal?

M. Self-realization.

D. Is there any way to meet the appointed Guru for each?

M. Intense meditation brings it about.

Dr. G.H. Mees, a young Dutchman, was here for a few days. He asked Sri Bhagavan: I have an impression that in deep sleep, I experience something akin to *samadhi*. Is that so?

M. It is the waking "I" that asks the questions — not the "I" in sleep. If you attain the state of wakeful sleep, which is the same as *samadhi*, while still awake, doubts will not arise.

Samadhi is one's natural state. It is the undercurrent of all three states. This — that is, "I" — is not in those states, but these states are in It. If we get *samadhi* in our waking state, it will persist in the deep sleep state. The distinction between consciousness and unconsciousness belongs to the realm of mind, which is transcended by the state of the Real Self.

D. Is the Buddhist view correct, that there is no continuous entity corresponding to the ideas of the individual soul? Is this consistent with the Hindu notion of a reincarnating ego? Is the soul a continuous entity which reincarnates again and again, or is it a mere mass of mental tendencies — *samskaras?*

M. The Real Self is continuous and unaffected. The reincarnating ego belongs to the lower plane namely, thought. It is transcended by Self-realization.

Reincarnations are due to a spurious offshoot; therefore, they are denied by Buddhists. The present state is due to a mixing up of the *chit* (sentient) with *jada* (insentient).

Lakshman Brahmachari, of the Ramakrishna Mission, asked: Can one imagine oneself as witness of the thoughts?

M. It is not the natural state. It is only an idea (*bhavana*) — an aid to stilling the mind. The Self is ever the witness, whether imagined so or not. There is no need to imagine it except for that purpose. It is best to remain as one's Self.

The Financial Secretary of Mysore asked: Is Paul Brunton's *The Secret Path* useful for Indians as well?

M. Yes — for all.

D. The body, the senses, etc. are not "I." This is common amongst us. But how to practice it?

M. By the threefold method mentioned in the book.

D. Is breath control necessary for inquiry?

M. Not quite.

D. "There is a blankness intervening," the book states.

M. Yes. Do not stop there. See for whom the blankness appears.

D. For devotees there is no blankness, it is said.

M. Even there, there is the latent state, *laya;* the mind wakes up after some time.

D. What is the experience of *samadhi?*

M. It is as it is. For onlookers, it may seem to be a swoon. Even to the practicer, it may appear so in the early experiences. After a few repeated experiences, it will be all right.

D. Do they soothe *nadis* or do they excite them by such experiences?
M. They are excited at first. By continued experience it becomes common and one is no longer excited.
D. Proceeding on safe lines there should be no unpleasantness. Excitement is uncongenial to smooth being and working.
M. A wandering mind is on the wrong track; only a devotional mind is on the right track.

JANUARY 19, 1936

Mr. Ellappa Chettiar, a Member of the Legislative Council from Salem, asked: Is it enough to introvert the mind or should we meditate on "I am *Brahman*"?
M. To introvert the mind is the important thing. Buddhists consider the flow of "I"- thought to be Liberation, whereas we say that such flow proceeds from its underlying substratum — the only Reality.

Why should one be meditating "I am *Brahman*"? Only the annihilation of "I" is Liberation. But it can be gained only by keeping the "I-I" always in view. Hence, the need for investigation of the "I"-thought. If the "I" is not let go, no blank can result to the seeker [the seeker cannot be grounded in reality]. Otherwise, meditation will end in sleep.

There has been only one "I" all along, but what arises from time to time is the false "I"-thought; whereas the intuitive "I" always remains Self-shining, i.e., even before it becomes manifest.

The birth of the gross body does not amount to one's own birth; on the other hand, the birth of the ego is one's own birth.

For liberation, nothing new remains to be gained. It is the original state and this continues unchanged.

D. What is reality?
M. Reality must be always real. It is not entangled with forms and names, but is That which underlies these. It underlies limitations, being itself limitless. It is not bound. It underlies unrealities, itself being real. Reality is that which is. It is as it is. It transcends speech and lies beyond such expressions as existence, non-existence, etc.

The same gentleman, after quoting a verse from Kaivalya, *asked*: Can *jnana* be lost after being once attained?
M. *Jnana*, once revealed, takes time to steady itself. The Self is certainly within the direct experience of everyone, but not as one *imagines* it to be. It

is only as it is. This experience is *samadhi*. Just as fire remains without scorching against incantations or other means, so also the Self remains veiled by *vasanas* and reveals itself only in their absence. Owing to the fluctuation of the *vasanas*, *jnana* takes time to steady itself. Unsteady *jnana* is not enough to check rebirths. *Jnana* cannot remain unshaken side by side with *vasanas*. True, that in the proximity of a great Master, the *vasanas* will cease to be active; the mind becomes still and *samadhi* results, similar to fire not scorching because of other devices. Thus, the disciple gains true knowledge and right experience in the presence of the Master. To remain stabilized in it, further efforts are necessary. He will know it to be his real Being and thus be liberated even while alive. *Samadhi* with closed eyes is certainly good, but one must go further until it is realized that actionlessness and action are not hostile to each other. Fear of loss of *samadhi* while one is active is the sign of ignorance. *Samadhi* must be everyone's natural life.

There is a state beyond both effort and effortlessness. Until it is realized, effort is necessary. After tasting such Bliss even once, one will repeatedly try to regain it. Having once experienced the Bliss of Peace, no one would like to be out of it or engage himself otherwise. It is as difficult for a *jnani* to engage in thoughts as it is for an *ajnani* to be free from them.

The ordinary man says that he does not know himself; he thinks many thoughts and cannot remain without thinking.

No activity of any kind affects a *jnani*; his mind remains ever in eternal Peace.

JANUARY 20, 1936

Mr. Prakasa Rao from Bezwada: Does not illusion become inoperative even before identity with *Brahman* is a fact (*Brahmakaravritti*)? Or does it persist even afterwards?

M. Illusion will not persist after annihilation of the *vasanas*. In the interval between knowledge of the identity and annihilation of the *vasanas*, there will be illusion.

D. How can the world influence a man even after identity with *Brahman*?

M. First do it and see. You can then raise this question, if necessary.

D. Can we know it in the same way as we know our identity?

M. Are you different from the mind? How do you expect it to be known?

D. Can the full scope of the *Chitta* (*Chittavilasa*) be known?

M. Oh! Is this the identity of *Brahman*?

Ignorance vanishing, the residue reveals itself. It is experience, not in the category of knowledge.

JANUARY 23, 1936

Mr. Paul Brunton asked Sri Bhagavan if the Hill here is hollow.

M. The *puranas* say so. When it is said that the Heart is a cavity, penetration into it proves it to be an expanse of light. Similarly, the Hill is one of light. The caves, etc., are covered up by the light.

D. Are there caves inside?

M. In visions I have seen caves, cities with streets, etc., and a whole world in it.

D. Are there *Siddhas*, too, in it?

M. All the *Siddhas* are reputed to be there.

D. Are there only *Siddhas* or others, also?

M. Just like this world.

D. *Siddhas* are said to be in the Himalayas.

M. Kailas is in the Himalayas; it is the abode of Shiva. Whereas this Hill is Shiva Himself. All the paraphernalia of His abode must also be where He Himself is.

D. Does Bhagavan believe that the Hill is hollow, etc.?

M. Everything depends on the individual's viewpoint. You have seen hermitages, etc., on this Hill in a vision. You have described such in your book.

D. Yes. It was on the surface of the Hill. The vision was within me.

M. That is exactly so. Everything is within one's Self. To see the world, there must be a spectator. There could be no world without the Self. The Self is all-comprising. In fact, Self is all. There is nothing besides the Self.

D. What is the mystery of this Hill?

M. Just as you have said in *Secret Egypt*, "The mystery of the pyramid is the mystery of the Self," so also the mystery of this Hill is the mystery of the Self.

Maj. Chadwick: I do not know if the Self is different from the ego.

M. How were you in your deep sleep?

D. I do not know.

M. Who does not know? Is it not the waking Self? Do you deny your existence in your deep sleep?

D. I was and I am; but I do not know who existed in deep sleep.

M. Exactly. The man awake says that he did not know anything in the state of sleep. Now he sees the objects and knows that he is there; whereas in deep sleep there were no objects, no spectator, etc. The same one who is now speaking existed in deep sleep, also. What is the difference between these two states? There are objects and the play of senses now which were not there in sleep. A new entity, the ego, has risen up in the meantime; it plays through the senses, sees the objects, confounds itself with the body, and says that the Self is the ego. In reality, what was in deep sleep continues to exist even now. The Self is changeless; it is the ego that has intervened. That which rises and sets is the ego; that which remains changeless is the Self.

Mr. Prakasa Rao: What is the root cause of *maya*?
M. What is *maya*?
D. *Maya* is wrong knowledge, illusion.
M. For whom is the illusion? There must be one to be deluded. Illusion is ignorance. The ignorant Self sees the objects according to you. When the objects are not themselves present, how can *maya* exist? *Maya* is *ya ma* (*maya* is what is not). What remains is the true Self. If you say that you see the objects, or if you say that you do not know the Real Unity, then are there two selves: one the knower and the other the knowable object? No one will admit of two selves in himself. The awakened man says that he himself was in deep slumber but not aware. He does not say that the sleeper was different from the present one. There is only one Self. That Self is always aware. It is changeless. There is nothing but the Self.
D. What is the astral body?
M. Do you not have a body in your dream? Is it not different from the recumbent body on the bed?
D. Do we survive after death? Does the astral body outlive physical death?
M. Just as in dreams you wake up after several novel experiences, so also after physical death another body is found and so on.
D. They say that the astral body lives for forty years after death.
M. In the present body, you say the dream body is astral. Did you say so in the dream body? What is astral now would appear real then; the present body itself is astral according to that viewpoint. What is the difference between one astral body and another? There is no difference between the two.

Mr. P. Brunton: There are degrees of reality.
M. To say the dream body is unreal now, and to say that this body was unreal in the dream, does not denote degrees of reality. In deep sleep, there

is no experience of the body at all. There is always only one and that is the Self.

Mr. P. Brunton: Why do religions speak of Gods, heaven, hell, etc.?

M. Only to make people realize that they are on a par with this world and that the Self alone is real. The religions are according to the viewpoint of the seeker. Take the *Bhagavad Gita*, for instance: When Arjuna said that he would not fight against his own relatives, his elders, etc., in order to kill them and gain the kingdom, Sri Krishna said, "Not that these, you or I, were not before, are not now, nor will not be hereafter. Nothing was born, nothing was dead, nor will it not be so hereafter" and so on. Later, as he developed the theme and declared that He had given the same instruction to the Sun, through him to Ikshvaku, etc., Arjuna raised the doubt, "How could it be? You were born a few years ago. They lived ages ago." Then, Sri Krishna, understanding Arjuna's standpoint, said: "Yes. There have been so many incarnations of myself and yourself; I know them all but you do not know."

Such statements appear contradictory, yet are correct according to the viewpoint of the questioner. Christ also declared that He was even before Abraham.

D. What is the purpose of such descriptions in religions?

M. Only to establish the Reality of the Self.

D. Bhagavan always speaks from the highest standpoint.

M. *(With a smile)* People would not understand the simple and bare truth — the truth of their everyday, ever-present and eternal experience. That Truth is that of the Self. Is there anyone not aware of the Self? They would not even like to hear it (the Self), whereas they are eager to know what lies beyond — heaven, hell, reincarnation. Because they love mystery and not the bare truth, religions pamper them — only to bring them around to the Self. Wandering hither and thither, you must return to the Self only. Then, why not abide in the Self right here and now?

The other worlds require the Self as a spectator or speculator. Their reality is only of the same degrees as that of the spectator or thinker. They cannot exist without the spectator, etc. Therefore, they are not different from the Self. Even the ignorant man sees only the Self when he sees objects. But he is confused and identifies the Self with the object, i.e., the body and the senses, and plays in the world. Subject and object — all merge in the Self. There is no seer nor objects seen. The seer and the seen are the Self. There are not many selves, either. All are only one Self.

JANUARY 26, 1936

In reply to Miss Leena Sarabhai, a cultured Indian lady of high standing, Sri Bhaga-
van said: The state of equanimity is the state of bliss. The declaration in the
Vedas "I am This or That," is only an aid to gain equanimity of mind.

D. So, it is wrong to begin with a goal, is it?

M. If there is a goal to be reached, it cannot be permanent. The goal must
already be there. We seek to reach the goal with the ego, but the goal exists
before the ego. What is in the goal is prior even to our birth, i.e., the birth of
the ego. Because we exist, the ego appears to exist, too.

If we look on the Self as the ego then we become the ego, if as the mind
we become the mind, if as the body we become the body. It is the thought
which builds up sheaths in so many ways. The shadow on the water is
found to be shaking. Can anyone stop this shaking? If it should cease to
shake, you would not notice the water but only the light. Similarly, take no
notice of the ego and its activities but see only the light behind it. The ego is
the I-thought. The true "I" is the Self.

D. It is one step to realization.

M. Realization is already there. The state free from thoughts is the only real
state. There is no such action as Realization. Is there anyone who is not
realizing the Self? Does anyone deny his own existence? Speaking of realization, it implies two selves — the one to realize, the other to be realized.
What is not already realized is sought to be realized. Once we admit our
existence, how is it that we do not know our Self?

D. Because of the thoughts — the mind.

M. Quite so. It is the mind that stands between and veils our happiness.
How do we know that we exist? If you say because of the world around us,
then how do you know that you existed in deep sleep?

D. How to get rid of the mind?

M. Is it the mind that wants to kill itself? The mind cannot kill itself. So
your business is to find the real nature of the mind. Then you will know
that there is no mind. When the Self is sought, the mind is nowhere. Abiding in the Self, one need not worry about the mind.

D. How to get rid of fear?

M. What is fear? It is only a thought. If there is anything besides the Self,
there is reason to fear. Who sees the second (anything external)? First the
ego arises and sees objects as external. If the ego does not rise, the Self
alone exists and there is no second (nothing external). For anything external to oneself implies the seer within. Seeking it there will induce no doubt,
no fear — not only fear; all other thoughts centered round the ego will

disappear along with it.

D. This method seems to be quicker than the usual one of cultivating qualities allegedly necessary for salvation (*sadhana chatushtaya*)?

M. Yes. All bad qualities center round the ego. When the ego is gone, Realization results by itself. There are neither good nor bad qualities in the Self. The Self is free from all qualities. Qualities pertain to the mind only. The Self is beyond quality. If there is unity, there will also be duality. The numeral one gives rise to other numbers. The truth is neither one nor two. It is as it is.

D. The difficulty is to be in the thought-free state.

M. Leave the thought-free state to itself. Do not think of it as pertaining to you. Just as when you walk, you involuntarily take steps, so too in your actions; but the thought-free state is not affected by your actions.

D. What is it that is discriminative in action?

M. Discrimination will be automatic, intuitive.

D. So intuition alone matters; intuition develops, also.

M. Those who have discovered great Truths have done so in the still depths of the Self.

The ego is like one's shadow thrown on the ground. If one attempts to bury it, it will be foolish. The Self is only one. If limited, it is the ego. If unlimited, it is Infinite and is the Reality.

The bubbles are different from one another and numerous, but the ocean is only one. Similarly, the egos are many, whereas the Self is one and only one.

When told that you are not the ego, realize the Reality. Why do you still identify yourself with the ego? It is like saying "Don't think of the monkey while taking medicine" — it is impossible. Similarly it happens with common folk. When the Reality is mentioned, why do you continue to meditahte *Sivoham* (I am Shiva) or *Aham Brahmasmi* (I am *Brahman*)? The significance must be traced and understood. It is not enough to repeat the bare words or think of them.

Reality is simply loss of the ego. Destroy the ego by seeking its identity. Because the ego is no entity, it will automatically vanish and Reality will shine forth by itself. This is the direct method, whereas all other methods are done retaining the ego. In those paths there arise so many doubts and the eternal question remains to be tackled. But in this method, the final question is the only one and it is raised from the very beginning. No *sadhanas* are necessary for engaging in this quest.

There is no greater mystery than the following: Ourselves being the

Reality, we seek to gain reality. We think there is something hiding our Reality, and that it must be destroyed before the Reality is gained. That is ridiculous. A day will dawn when you will yourself laugh at your past efforts. That which will be on the day you laugh is also here and now.

D. So it is a great game of pretending?

M. Yes.

In *Yoga Vasishta* it is said, "What is Real is hidden from us, but what is false is revealed as true." We are actually always experiencing the Reality only; still, we do not know it. Is it not a wonder of wonders?

The quest "Who am I?" is the axe with which to cut off the ego.

JANUARY 27, 1936

A Gujerati gentleman said he was concentrating on sound (nada) *and wished to know if the method was right.*

M. Meditation on *nada* is one of several approved methods. The adherents claim a very special virtue for it. According to them, it is the easiest and most direct method. Just as a child is lulled to sleep by lullabies, so *nada* soothes one to the state of samadhi. Similarly, just as a king sends his state musicians to welcome his son on his return from a long journey, so also *nada* takes the devotee into the Lord's Abode in a pleasing manner. *Nada* helps concentration. After it is felt, the practice should not be made an end in itself. *Nada* is not the objective; the subject should be firmly held, otherwise a blank will result. Although the subject is there even in the blank state, he would not be aware of the cessation of *nada* of different kinds. In order to be aware even in that blank state, one must remember his own self. *Nada upasana* (meditation on sound) is good, but even better if associated with investigation (*vichara*). In that case, the *nada* is made up of *chinmaya* and also *tanmaya* (Knowledge and Self). *Nada* helps concentration.

JANUARY 28, 1936

In reply to a sadhu *who asked if* bhakti *consisted in forgetting the body, etc., Sri Bhagavan said*: What do you care about the body? Practice *bhakti* and don't worry about what happens to the body.

Mrs. and Mr. Kelly, an elderly couple from America, and others in their company desired to know what they should do to gain concentration in view of the discomforts of sitting, mosquito stings, etc.

M. The discomforts will not bother you if your concentration is right. Do not mind the discomforts. Keep your mind steady in meditation. If you haven't the strength and endurance to bear mosquito stings, how do you hope to gain realization of the Self? Realization must be amidst all the turmoil of life. If you make yourself comfortable and go to bed you will fall asleep. Face the troubles but keep yourself steady in meditation.

JANUARY 31, 1936

The American gentleman is a little hard of hearing. Accustomed to being self-reliant from his youth, he naturally feels worried due to his hearing becoming defective.
M. You were not self-reliant; you were ego-reliant. It is good that ego-reliance is banished and you become truly Self-reliant.

There is no cause for worry. Subjugation of the senses is a necessary preliminary for Self-realization. One sense is subdued for you by God Himself. So much the better.

The questioner said he appreciated the humor, but that his self-respect still suffered.
M. The Self is only one. Do you feel hurt if you blame yourself or scorn yourself for your errors? If you hold the Self there is no second person to scorn you. When you see the world, you have lost hold of the Self. On the contrary, hold the Self and the world will not appear.

FEBRUARY 1, 1936

Mrs. Kelly desired to know how she could best learn to meditate. Sri Bhagavan asked if she had made japa (telling beads as Roman Catholics do).
D. No.
M. Have you thought of God, His qualities, etc.?
D. I have read, talked, etc. about such themes.
M. Well, if the same is revolved in the mind without open expression through the senses it is meditation.
D. I mean meditation as signified in *The Secret Path* and *Who am I?*
M. Long for it intensely so that the mind melts in devotion. After the camphor burns away, no residue is left. The mind is the camphor; when it has resolved itself into the Self without leaving even the slightest trace, it is Realization of the Self.

FEBRUARY 4, 1936

Some Peshawaris, among them a Judicial Commissioner and a young man well-read and earnest, with a strong belief in the existence of Paramatman *(Supreme Self) as different from the* Jivatman *(individual self), raised some questions. Sri Bhagavan clinched his various doubts by this one statement:* Remove the *upadhis* (adjuncts), *jiva* and *parama*, from the *Atman* and tell me if you still find any difference. If later these doubts still persist, ask yourself, "Who is the doubter? Who is the thinker?" Find him. These doubts will vanish.

FEBRUARY 5, 1936

The next day a question was asked about pranayama.

M. *Pranayama* according to *jnana* is:

Na aham — "I am not this" — is out-breathing

Koham — "Who am I?" — is in-breathing

Soham — "I am He" — is retention of breath

This is *vichara*. This *vichara* brings about the desired result.

For one not so advanced as to engage in it, some meditation brings about suspension of breath and the mind ceases to be restless. Control of mind spontaneously affects control of breath; rather, *kevala kumbhaka* (spontaneous retention of breath, without attention to inhalation or exhalation) results.

For one unable to do this also, regulation of breath is prescribed for making the mind quiescent. Quiescence lasts only so long as the breath is controlled, so it is transient. The goal is clearly not *pranayama*. It extends to *pratyahara, dharana, dhyana,* and *samadhi*. Those stages deal with the control of mind. Such control becomes easier for one who previously had practiced *pranayama*. *Pranayama* leads him to the higher stages involving control of mind. Therefore, control of mind is the aim of yoga, also.

A more advanced man will naturally go directly to control of mind without wasting his time in practicing control of breath. A simple development of *pranayama* alone may confer *siddhis*, which so many hanker for.

When asked if there are any food restrictions, Sri Bhagavan said:
"Mita hita bhuk" — agreeable food in moderate quantity.

When asked about the efficacy of bhakti, *Sri Bhagavan answered:* So long as there is *vibhakti*, there must be *bhakti*. So long as there is *viyoga*, there must be *yoga*. So long as there is duality, there must be God and devotee. Similarly also in *vichara*: so long as there is *vichara*, there is duality. But in merging into the Source there is unity only. So it is with *bhakti*, too. Realizing the God of devotion, there will be unity only. God, too, is thought of in and by the Self. So God is identical with the Self. If one is told to have *bhakti* for God and he does so straightaway, it is all right. But there is another kind of man who turns around and says: "There are two, I and God. Before knowing the far-off God, let me know the more immediate and intimate 'I'." For him, the *Vichara Marga* has to be taught. There is in fact no difference between *bhakti* and *vichara*.

The same man again asked about the nature of samadhi *and the means to it.*
M. When the one who asks about the nature of *samadhi* and the method of getting into it vanishes, *samadhi* will result.

Major A.W. Chadwick: It is said that one look of a Mahatma is enough; that idols, pilgrimages, etc. are not so effective. I have been here for three months, but I do not know how I have benefited by the look of Maharshi.
M. The look has a purifying effect. Purification cannot be visualized. Just as a piece of coal takes long to be ignited, a piece of charcoal takes a short time, and a mass of gunpowder is instantaneously ignited, so it is with grades of men coming in contact with Mahatmas.

Mr. S.S. Cohen: I get into meditation and reach a point which may be called "peace" and a contemplative mood. What should be the next step?
M. Peace is Self-realization. Peace need not be disturbed. One should aim at peace only.
D. But I do not have the satisfaction.
M. Because your peace is temporary. If made permanent, it is called Realization.

FEBRUARY 9, 1936
D. Is solitude helpful for practice?
M. What do you mean by solitude?
D. To keep away from others.
M. Why should that be done? It is actuated only by fear. Even in solitude there is fear of intrusion by others and of the solitude being spoiled. Moreover, how are thoughts to be erased in solitude? Should it not be done in the present environment?
D. But the mind is distracted now.

M. Why do you let the mind? Solitude amounts to making the mind still, which can be done in a crowd, too. Mere physical solitude cannot efface one's thoughts. Practice does it. The same practice can be made here, too.

D. In the quest of "I," the seeker, at a certain stage, is directed to keep the mind in a negative attitude for Grace to enter. How can a negative yield a positive result?

M. The Self is always there — not to be newly got.

D. I mean to ask, what has been done in the negative attitude to deserve Grace?

M. Are you asking this question without Grace? Grace is in the beginning, middle, and end. Grace is the Self. Because of false identification of the Self with the body, the Guru is considered to be with body. But from the Guru's point of view, the Guru is only the Self. The Self is one only. He states that the Self alone is. Is not then the Self your Guru? Where else would Grace come from? It is from the Self alone. Manifestation of the Self is a manifestation of Grace and *vice versa*. All these doubts arise because of the wrong outlook and consequent expectation of things external to oneself. Nothing is external to the Self.

D. All our questions are from our standpoint and Sri Bhagavan's replies are from his standpoint. The questions are not only answered, but are also undermined.

FEBRUARY 11, 1936

Mr. Frydman: Janaka was a *jnani* and still he ruled his dominions. Does not action require activity of the mind? What is the rationale of the working of a *jnani's* mind?

M. You say, "Janaka was a *jnani* and yet active, etc." Does Janaka ask the question? The question is in your mind only. The *jnani* is not aware of anything besides the Self. He has no doubts of any kind.

D. Probably it is like a dream. Just as we speak of our dreams, so they think of their actions.

M. Even the dream, etc. is in your mind. This explanation, too, is in your mind only.

D. Yes. I see. All is *Ramana-Maya* — made up of the Self.

M. If so, there will be no duality and no talk.

D. A man, on realizing the Self, can help the world more effectively. Isn't that right?

M. If the world be apart from the Self.

FEBRUARY 12, 1936

Mr. Cohen wished to know if trance is a sine qua non *for Self-realization.*
M. You are always in the Self — now, in trance, in deep sleep, in Realization. If you lose hold of the Self and identify yourself with the body or the mind, these states appear to overtake you, and it also looks like a blank in trance, etc.; whereas you are the Self and ever-present.

FEBRUARY 13, 1936

An elderly man from Ananthapur, after hearing the Vedas *recited in the Hall, stood up and asked*: It is said that the non-Brahmins should not hear the recital of the *Vedas*.
M. Mind your business. Take care of what you came here for. Why do you waste your time in these matters? "I heard the recital," you say. "Who is that "I"? Without knowing the "I" you are using the word. If its significance is known, there will be no doubt. Find the "I" first and you may afterwards speak of other matters.

Continuing, Sri Bhagavan said: The *smritis* (scriptures) say something. They are not appropriate now. I will reform the world, rewrite the *smritis*. Saying so, people are cutting capers in the world from time immemorial. Such reformers have come and gone; but the ancient *smritis* still stand. Why waste time over such matters? Let each one mind his own business. All will be well.

FEBRUARY 23, 1936

A middle-aged woman from Maharashtra, who had studied *Jnaneswari*, *Bhagavata*, and *Vichara Sagara*, and was practicing concentration between the eyebrows, had felt shivering and fear, and did not progress. She required guidance.

Maharshi told her not to forget the seer. The sight is fixed between the eyebrows, but the seer is not kept in view. If the seer is always remembered, it will be all right.

FEBRUARY 24, 1936

Dr. Henry Hand, an American of about seventy, asked: What is ego?

M. Ego being internal and not external to you, it must be clear to yourself.

D. What is its definition?

M. The definition also must proceed from the ego. The ego is to define itself.

D. What is soul?

M. Find the ego, then the soul will also be found.

D. Are they then the same?

M. Soul can be without the ego; but the ego cannot be without the soul. They are like bubble and the ocean.

D. That clarifies the matter. What is *Atman?*

M. *Atman* and soul are the same.

Another American asked about thought-forms.

M. Trace the source of thoughts; then they will disappear.

D. Thoughts materialize.

M. If there are thoughts, they will materialize. If they disappear, there is nothing to materialize. Moreover, if you are physical, the world is physical and so on. Find out if you are physical.

D. How shall I be useful to God's world?

M. Find out if "I" is different from the divine part of the world. Not being able to help yourself, yet you are seeking the divine part of it to help you help the world. The divinity is directing and controlling you. Where do you go in deep sleep? Where do you come out from?

D. I have been influenced by deeds and thoughts.

M. Thoughts and deeds are the same.

D. Is there any way of sensing superphysical phenomena, e.g., guardian angels?

M. The state of the object is according to the state of the seer.

D. A group of seers see the same.

M. Because there is only one seer behind all, and there is diversity of phenomena. Do you perceive diversity in deep sleep?

D. We see Abraham Lincoln who died long ago.

M. Is there the object without the seer? The experiences may be real; the objects are only according to the seer.

D. An assistant of mine was killed in the war. A photo was taken of another group nine years after his death. His picture appears in the photo. How can that be?

M. Possibly thoughts have materialized . . . go to the root of it.

D. How?

M. If the way is external, directions are possible, but it lies within. Seek within. The Self is always realized. Something not already realized might be sought afresh. But the Self is within your experience.

D. Yes. I realize myself.

M. *Myself.* Are there two — *my* and *self?*

D. I do not mean that.

M. Who is it that has or has not realized?

D. There is only one Self.

M. The question can arise only if there are two. Abandon the wrong identification of the Self with the non-self.

D. I mean the higher stage of consciousness.

M. There are no stages.

D. Why doesn't a man get illumination instantly?

M. The man is illumination itself. He is illumining others.

D. Is your teaching different from that of others?

M. The path is one and the realization is only one.

D. But people speak of so many methods.

M. Depending on their own state of mind.

D. What is yoga?

M. Yoga (union) is for one in *viyoga* (separation). But there is only one. If you realize the Self, there will be no difference.

D. Is there efficacy in bathing in the Ganges?

M. The Ganges is within you. This Ganges does not make you feel cold or shiver. Bathe in it.

D. Should we read *Gita* once in a while?

M. Always.

D. May we read the Bible?

M. The Bible and the *Gita* are the same.

D. The Bible teaches that Man is born in sin.

M. The Man is sin. There was no man-sense in deep sleep. The body-thought brings out the idea of sin. The birth of thought is itself sin.

To another question the Master said: Everyone sees only the Self. The divine forms are only like bubbles in the ocean of Reality, or like pictures moving on a screen.

D. The Bible says that the human soul may be lost.

M. The "I"-thought is the ego and that is lost. The real "I" is "I Am that I Am."

D. There is conflict in the teachings of Aurobindo and of the Mother.

M. First surrender the self and then harmonize the conflicts.

D. What is renunciation?

M. Giving up the ego.

D. Is it not giving up possessions?

M. The possessor, too.

D. The world will change if people will give up their possessions for the benefit of others.

M. First give yourself up and then think of the rest.

In answer to another question, Sri Bhagavan said: The methods appear easy according to the nature of the individual. It depends on what he has practiced before.

D. Can we not get realization instantaneously?

M. Realization is nothing new. It is eternal. There is no question of instantaneous or gradual realization.

D. Is there reincarnation?

M. Reincarnation can be real if you are incarnate now. Even now you are not born.

To another question.

M. The ego is the root of all diseases. Give it up. There will be no disease.

D. If all renounce, will there be a practical world? Who will plough? Who will harvest?

M. Realize first and then see. The help through Realization transcends all the help through words, thoughts and deeds, etc. If you understand your own reality, then that of the *rishis* and Masters will be clear to you. There is only one Master and that is the Self.

D. Why do Masters insist on silence and receptivity?

M. What is silence? It is eternal eloquence.

D. What is a receptive attitude of mind?

M. Not to be distracted in mind.

D. Is there any use in bringing America and India closer by bringing the intelligentsia of the two countries together, say, by exchange of professors, etc.?

M. Such events will take place automatically. There is a Power guiding the destinies of nations. These questions arise only when you have lost touch with Reality. Is America apart from you, or India apart? Get hold of it and see.

D. Sri Ramakrishna prepared Vivekananda. What is the power behind it all?

M. The power is only one in all.

D. What is the nature of that force?

M. Just like iron filings drawn towards a magnet, the force is inside and not outside. Ramakrishna was in Vivekananda. If you think Vivekananda to be a body, Ramakrishna also is a body. But they are not bodies. Vivekananda could not go into *samadhi* had not Ramakrishna been within him.

D. Why should one suffer when stung by a scorpion?

M. What is the cause of the appearance of the body and of the world?

D. It is part of the cosmic mind.

M. Let the cosmic mind worry about such happenings. If the individual wants to know, let him discover his Self.

D. About yogic mysteries of drinking nitric acid, swallowing poisons, walking on fire, etc.: are these due to a state of vibration?

M. Let the physical body question it. You are not physical. Why worry about what you are not. If the Self had any form, it might be affected by objects. But the Self has no form; therefore, it is immune from contact with things.

D. What is the significance of the sea of Love?

M. Spirit, Holy Ghost, Realization, Love, etc. are all synonymous.

D. A very, very illuminating conversation.

Mr. N. Subba Rao: What is *visishtadvaita?*

M. The same as this.

D. They do not admit *maya?*

M. *Sarvam* is *Brahman,* we say. They repeat *Brahman* remains qualified (*visishta*) in all.

D. They say that the world is a reality.

M. We say so, too. Shankaracharya has only said, "Find out the reality behind the world." What is called illusion by one is called changefulness by another. The end is the same in both.

Dr. Hand: Maharshi! Do not think we are bad boys.

M. Do not tell me so. But you need not think you are bad boys.

   (All laughed and dispersed at 5:00 p.m.)

Sri Bhagavan a minute later: If they remain a day longer, they will become silent.

Mr. Subba Rao: Do not men go into *samadhi?*

M. Is there no *samadhi* now?

D. Is it eternal?

M. If not, how can it be real?
D. Then?
M. There is no *then*, no *now*.
D. It appears so.
M. To whom?
D. To the mind.
M. What is mind? Who am I?
  (Silence.)

A man asked if it is possible to ward off old age and disease by the intake of divine force.
M. You can ward off the body itself.
D. How to take in the divine force?
M. It is already there. No need to take it in. It can be done only if it is external to you. But it is only you. There is no taking in or giving out.
D. Is there any necessity to obey physical laws, i.e., dieting?
M. These are in imagination only.

A man was worried because he could not succeed in concentrating the mind.
M. Is it not only One even now? It always remains One only. Diversity lies in your imagination only. Unitary Being need not be acquired.

It was mentioned to Sri Bhagavan that a Self-realized being needs no food, etc.
M. You understand according to your state only.

D. How to control the mind?
M. Catch hold of the mind.
D. How?
M. What is mind? Find it out. It is only an aggregate of thoughts.
D. How to root out the sexual impulse?
M. By rooting out the false idea of the body being Self. There is no sex in the Self.
D. How to realize it?
M. Because you think you are the body, you see another also as a body. Difference in sex arises. But you are not the body. Be the real Self. Then there is no sex.

D. Can a yogi know his past lives?
M. Do you know the present life so well that you wish to know the past?

Find out the present life, then the rest will follow. Even with our present limited knowledge, we suffer so much. Why do you wish to burden yourself with more knowledge and suffer more?

D. Can fasting help realization?

M. But it is temporary. Mental fast is the real aid. Fasting is not an end in itself. There must be spiritual development side by side. Absolute fasting makes the mind weak, too. You cannot derive sufficient strength for the spiritual quest. Therefore, take moderate food and go on practicing.

D. They say that after breaking a month's fast, ten days afterwards the mind becomes pure and steady and remains so forever.

M. Yes, if the spiritual quest has been kept up right through the fast, also.

To another question Master said: The best is heart-to-heart speech and heart-to-heart hearing. That is the best *upadesa.*

D. Is not guidance from Guru necessary?

M. Are you apart from Guru?

D. Is proximity helpful?

M. Do you mean physical proximity? What is the good of it? The mind alone matters. The mind must be contacted.

FEBRUARY 28, 1936

A visitor: What is the difference between meditation (*dhyana*) and investigation (*vichara*)?

M. Both amount to the same. Those unfit for investigation must practice meditation. In this practice, the aspirant, forgetting himself meditates, "I am *Brahman*" or "I am Shiva." Thus, he continues to hold to *Brahman* or Shiva; this will ultimately end on the residual Being as *Brahman* or Shiva which he will realize to be Pure Being, i.e., the Self.

He who engages in investigation starts holding on to himself, asking "Who am I?," and the Self becomes clear to him.

D. Will the knowledge gained by direct experience be lost afterwards?

M. *Kaivalya Navanita* says it may be lost. Experience gained without rooting out the *vasanas* cannot remain steady. Efforts must therefore be made to eradicate all the *vasanas*. Otherwise, rebirth takes place. Some say direct experience results from hearing from one's Master; others say it is from reflection; yet others say from one-pointedness and also from *samadhi*. Though appearing different on the surface, ultimately they mean the same.

Knowledge can remain unshaken only after all the *vasanas* are rooted out.

FEBRUARY 29, 1936

D. How can the grip of the ego be slackened?

M. By not adding new *vasanas* to it.

D. Any amount of *japa* has not slackened the grip!

M. How so! It will duly slacken and vanish.

MARCH 2, 1936

Dr. Hand, the American gentleman, asked: Are there two methods for finding the source of the ego?

M. There are no two sources and no two methods. There is only one source and one method.

D. What is the difference between meditation and inquiry into the Self?

M. Meditation is possible only if the ego is kept up. The method is indirect. There is the ego and the object meditated upon, whereas the Self is only one. Seeking the ego — i.e., its source — ego disappears; what is left over is the Self. This method is the direct one.

D. Then what am I to do?

M. Hold on to the Self.

D. How?

M. Even now you are the Self. But you are confounding this consciousness (or ego) with the absolute consciousness. This false identification is due to ignorance. Ignorance disappears along with ego. Killing the ego is the only thing to accomplish. Realization is already there. No attempt is needed to attain realization. For it is nothing external, nothing new. It is always and everywhere — here and now.

MARCH 3, 1936

Mr. N. Subba Rao stated: The *Visishtudvaitins* say that *Atma Sakshatkara* (Self-realization) is preliminary to *Paramatma Sakshatkara* (God-Realization). The difficulty seems to be considerable.

M. What is *Atma Sakshatkara*? Are there two *Atmas* that one realizes the other? There are not two selves. First get *Atma Sakshatkara* and then judge what follows.

D. The *Bhagavad Gita* says there is God whose body is made up of all the souls.

M. All are agreed on the annihilation of the ego. Let us get to business on the agreed point. *Nanajivatva* (different individualities) are mentioned by

114

some *Advaitins*, also. All that is immaterial to one's spiritual uplift. First realize the Self and then see what lies ahead.

MARCH 7, 1936

Dr. Hand intends to leave the Asramam tomorrow, visit the Himalayas (Hardwar), return here, then proceed to Bombay, and embark for Egypt, Palestine, Europe, and finally to his native land, America.

He wants to go to the peak of the hill and would like Sri Bhagavan to accompany him. Sri Bhagavan might go up as high as is convenient for him and then wait for him to finish the climb — and meet him at an appointed spot on the hill. Sri Bhagavan smiled and asked him if he had heard of the experience of Dr. Beasly.

Dr. Hand: He is my friend. He has told me everything — wonderful! I am older than you, Maharshi. But do not give me up as a back number. I can climb up the hill as a boy would. When did you go to the peak last?

M. About eleven years ago. What did Dr. Beasly say?

D. It is in strict confidence. I shall tell you everything if you are left alone with me.

(Maharshi simply smiled.)

D. Maharshi! Are you conscious of a brotherhood of invisible *rishis?*

M. If invisible, how to see them?

D. In consciousness.

M. There is nothing external in consciousness.

D. Is there not the individuality? I fear to lose my individual being. Is there not in consciousness the consciousness of being human?

M. Why fear to lose individuality? What is your state in dreamless sleep? Are you conscious of your individuality then?

D. It is possible.

M. But what is *your* experience? If individuality is there, would it be deep sleep?

D. That depends on the interpretation. What does Maharshi say?

M. Maharshi cannot speak for *your experience*. He does not force anything down anyone's throat.

D. I know. That is why I like him and his teachings so much.

M. Do you not carefully prepare your bed, and are you not anxious to lose your individuality in deep sleep? Why fear it?

D. What is the *nirvana* of Buddha?

M. Loss of individuality.

D. I dread that loss. Can there not be human consciousness in *nirvana?*
M. Are there two selves in that case? Consider your actual experience of sleep and tell me.
D. I should think it possible to retain individual consciousness in *nirvana.* I fear the loss of individuality.

> (*Later, the questioner went up and round the hill and wandered about fifteen miles between 12:00 noon and 8:00 p.m. He returned tired and gave a very lucid speech on agriculture, social conditions, caste system, spiritual quality of the Indians, etc.*)

MARCH 10, 1936

D. What is *mahat?*
M. The projected light from Absolute Consciousness. Just as a seed swells up before sprouting and then sprouts and grows, so also the Absolute Consciousness projects light, manifests as the ego and grows up as the body and the universe.

> *Chit* — "Absolute"
> *Mahat* — "projected consciousness (swollen seed)"
> *Ahamkara* — "ego"
> *Manas* — "mind"
> *Aham + Idam* — "body + world"

Maj. Chadwick: Is it the same as cosmic consciousness?
M. Yes, it is so before the birth of the ego and the universe. It comprises them all. Just as all the pictures thrown on the screen are visible by the light projected from a spot, so also the body and the other objects are all visible in that reflected consciousness. It is, therefore, also cosmic consciousness.

Again, (in the microcosm) the body and all other objects are contained in the brain. The light is projected on the brain. The impressions in the brain become manifest as the body and the world. Because the ego identifies itself with limitations, the body is considered separate and the world separate.

Lying down on your bed in a closed room with eyes shut you dream of London, the crowds there, and you among them. A certain body is identified as yourself in the dream. London and the rest could not have entered into the room and into your brain; however, such wide space and duration of time were all perceptible to you. They must have been projected from the brain. Although the world appears as so big and the brain so small, is it

116

not a matter of wonder that such a big creation is contained within such small compass as one's brain? Though the screen is limited, still all the pictures of the cinema pass on it and are visible there. You do not wonder how such a lengthy procession of events could be manifest on such a small screen. Similarly with the objects and the brain.

D. Then cosmic consciousness is not the same as realization?

M. Cosmic consciousness is behind the ego. It may be called *Ishvara*, and the ego is *jiva. Ishvara* may also be said to be the Absolute. There is no difference there.

> *Para* = Absolute
> *Ishvara* = Cosmic Consciousness (*Mahat*)
> *Jiva Jagat* = Individual Consciousness and the world

The consciousness which pervades even *Ishvara* is the Absolute one.

D. What is the flame mentioned in *Vichara Sangraham*? It is said to be *Atma Jyoti* and one is directed to find the reality behind it.

M. The *Vedas* mention the flame, *Tasyas sikhaya madhye paramatma vyavasthitah*. That flame is to be identified with the ego-consciousness.

MARCH 11, 1936

Mr. Frydman had asked Swami Ramdas something, to which he replied that there would be no more births for himself. The engineer had pointed out there should be no anxiety regarding rebirth. There will be the same Rama, the same Ramdas, the same search for Rama, and the same bliss of realization. What objection could be there for the repetition of this Rama-Lila? Ramdas had admitted that there could be no objection, that it would be an enjoyment and a game. The engineer further said that Ramdas added that he (Ramdas) had found Rama merged in him and was happy in that union. They are the same, still there was Ramdas, there was Rama, there was the union, there was the Bliss. That is eternal. Saying so, he asked what Sri Bhagavan would comment about it.

M. It is all as true as the present events.

Later, Mr. Frydman said that sleep was a state of oblivion and the wakeful state was the mind's activity. The mind was in a potential state in sleep.

M. Were you not in sleep?

D. Yes, I was. But in a state of oblivion. There must be a witness of oblivion and of the mind which says that "I" am continuous in both states.

M. Who is this witness? You speak of "witness." There must be an object, and a subject who witnesses. These are creations of the mind. The idea of witness is in the mind. If there was the witness of oblivion did he say, "I witness oblivion?" You, with your *mind*, said just now that there must be a witness. Who was the witness? You must reply "I." Who is that "I" again? You are identifying yourself with the ego and say "I." Is this ego "I," the witness? It is the mind that speaks. It cannot be witness of itself. With self-imposed limitations you think that there is a witness of mind and of oblivion. You also say, "I am the witness." That one who witnesses the oblivion must say, "I witness oblivion." The present mind cannot arrogate that position to itself.

The whole position becomes untenable. Consciousness is unlimited. On becoming limited it simply arrogates to itself the position. There is really nothing to witness. It is simple Being.

D. *Yad gatva na nivartante tad dhama paramam mama.* Which is that *dhama?* Is it not the Absolute state beyond cosmic consciousness?
M. Yes.
D. *"Na Nivartante"* would mean not covered by ignorance again.
M. Yes.
D. Does it follow then that those who reach Cosmic Consciousness have not escaped from the clutches of ignorance?
M. That is what is meant by saying that all *lokas,* even the *Brahma loka,* do not release one from rebirth. The *Bhagavad Gita* says: "Reaching Me, there is no rebirth . . . All others are in bondage." Moreover, so long as you think that there is *gati* (movement) — as implied in the word *gatva* (having gone to) — there is *punaravritti* (return), also. Again, *gati* implies your *Purvagamanam* (birth). What is birth? It is birth of the ego.

Once born you reach something; if you reach it, you return, also. Therefore, leave off all this verbiage! *Be as you are.* See who you are and remain as the Self, free from birth, going, coming, and returning.
D. True. However often this truth is heard, still it eludes us and we forget it.
M. Quite so. Reminders are often necessary.

In the course of the day, an interesting photo was missing. Sri Bhagavan appeared concerned about it. Mr. Frydman asked how Sri Bhagavan viewed all these matters. Sri Bhagavan said: Suppose you dream that you are taking me to Poland. You wake up and tell me. "I dreamt so and so. Did you dream that or know it? Or how do you view it?"

D. But you are not aware of the happenings in front of you?

M. These are all workings of the mind, and the questions, also.

Sri Bhagavan related an episode in Sri Rama's search for Sita:
Parvati asked Shiva why Rama, the Perfect Being, was grieving at the loss of Sita. Shiva said that Rama was still Perfect. If the Perfection need be tested and made clear, Parvati might appear as Sita before Rama and see what happened. So she did. Rama ignored her appearance and was still crying out, "Ha! Sita! Ha! Sita!" and moved on like a blind man, without taking any notice of Parvati.

   (*See June 30, 1936.*)

MARCH 13, 1936

A gentleman from Bombay said: I asked the Mother in Sri Aurobindo Ashram the following question: "I keep my mind blank without thoughts arising so that God might show Himself in His true Being. But I do not perceive anything."

   The reply was to this effect: "The attitude is right. The Power will come down from above. It is a direct experience."

   (*So he asked what further he should do.*)

M. *Be what you are.* There is nothing to come down or become manifest. All that is needed is to lose the ego. That *which is* is always there. The blank is seen by you. You are there to see the blank. What are you waiting for? The thought "I have not seen," the expectation to see, and the desire of getting something are all the working of the ego. You have fallen into the snares of the ego. The ego says all that and not *you*. *Be yourself* and nothing more!

M. To imagine *Muladhara* at the bottom, the Heart at the center, or the head at the top or over all these, is completely wrong. In one word, *to think is not your real nature.*

M. In the sacred literature, the following are seen:
   "Said without uttering."
   "Showed remaining still as ever," etc.
   Which is this unspoken word? It is only Silence, *Pranava*, or the *Mahavakya*. These are also called "the Word".
   [The four *Mahavakyas* are: 1. "That art Thou," 2. "I am *Brahman*," 3. "This Self is *Brahman*," and 4. *Prajnana* (Absolute Knowledge) is *Brahman*."]

M. We read a newspaper and all the articles therein, but do not care to know anything about the paper itself. We take the chaff but not the substance. The substratum on which all this is printed is the paper and, if we know the substratum, all else will be known (like a wall and its paintings).
D. You said the only One which exists is the Real. What is that only One?
M. The One only is the *Sat*, the existence that appears as the world, the things that we see, and ourselves.
D. What is *Atman*? Is there a finality for the *Atman*?
M. First learn what is *Atman*. If we know this then we can query as to whether it has a finality or not. Which do you call *Atman*?
D. *Jiva* is *Atman*.
M. Learn what *jiva* is. What is the difference between *jiva* and *Atman*? Is *jiva* itself *Atman* or is there any separate thing as *Atman*? There is an end for what you observe; all things created face destruction. That which is not created has no end. That which exists cannot be observed; it is unobservable. We must find out what it is that appears; the destruction of that which appears is the end. *That which exists, exists forever; that which newly appears is later lost.*
D. What happens after birth in human form; what happens to the *jiva*?
M. Let us know first what we are. We do not understand what we are, and until we know that, there is no room for such a question.

"*Asochyam anvosochas tvam, projnavadamscha bhashase.*"
Your grieve over those who should not be grieved for, and yet speak words about wisdom; wise men do not sorrow over the dead or the living.
— *Bhagavad Gita* 2.11

What is it that had birth? Whom do you call a man? If, instead of seeking an explanation for birth, death, and after-death matters, the question is raised as to "who and how you are now," these questions will not arise. You are the same while asleep (deep sleep), in dream, and in the waking state. Is the "I"-thought *jivu*, or the body *jiva*? Is this thought or nature? Or is the experience that we live, etc., our nature?

"*Yada te mohakalilam, buddhir vyatitarishati*
tada gantasi nirvedam, shrotavyasya shrutasya cha."
When your mind shall cross the mire of delusion, then you will become indifferent as to what has been heard or what is yet to be heard.
— *Bhagavad Gita* 2.52

D. Why is *Atma-vichara* necessary?

M. If you do not do *Atma-vichara*, then *loka vichara* creeps in. That which is not is sought for, but not that which is obvious. When once you have found what you seek, *vichara* (inquiry) also ceases and you rest in it. As long as one is confusing the body with the *Atman*, *Atman* is said to be lost and one is said to seek for it, but the *Atman* itself is never lost. It always exists. A body is said to be *Atman*, an *indriya* is said to be *Atman*, then there is the *Jivatman* and *Paramatman* and what not. There are a thousand and one things called *Atman*. The search for *Atman* is to know that which is really *Atman*.

D. I maintain that the physical body of a man sunk in *samadhi* as a result of unbroken contemplation of the Self becomes motionless for that reason. It may be active or inactive. The mind fixed in such contemplation will not be affected by the body or the senses being restless. A disturbance of the mind is not always the forerunner of physical activity. Another man asserts that physical unrest certainly prevents *nirvikalpa samadhi* or unbroken contemplation. What is your opinion? You are the standing proof of my statement.

M. Both of you are right; you refer to *sahaja nirvikalpa* and the other refers to *kevala nirvikalpa*. In the one case, the mind lies immersed in the Light of the Self (whereas the same lies in the darkness of ignorance in deep sleep). The subject discriminates one from the other — *samadhi*, stirring up from *samadhi*, and activity thereafter, unrest of the body, of the sight, of the vital force and of the mind, the cognizance of objects and activity, are all obstructions for him.

In *sahaja*, however, the mind has resolved itself into the Self and has been lost. Differences and obstructions mentioned above do not therefore exist here. The activities of such a being are like the feeding of a sleep-walker, perceptible to the onlooker (but not to the subject). The driver sleeping on his moving cart is not aware of the motion of the cart, because his mind is sunk in darkness. Similarly, the *sahaja jnani* remains unaware of his bodily activities because his mind is dead — having been resolved in the ecstasy of *Chid Ananda* (the Self).

The two words, contemplation and *samadhi*, have been used loosely in the question.

Contemplation is a forced mental process, whereas *samadhi* lies beyond effort.

Sleep	Kevala	Sahaja
1. Mind alive	1. Mind alive	1. Mind dead
2. Sunk in oblivion	2. Sunk in light	2. Resolved into the Self
	3. Like a bucket with the rope left lying in the water in a well	3. Like a river discharged into the ocean and its identity lost
	4. To be drawn out by the other end of the rope	4. A river cannot be redirected from the ocean

The essence of mind is only *awareness* or consciousness. When the ego, however, dominates it, it functions as the reasoning, thinking or sensing faculty. The cosmic mind, not being limited by the ego, has nothing separate from itself and is therefore *only aware*. This is what the Bible means by "I Am that I Am."

The ego-ridden mind has its strength sapped and is too weak to resist the torturing thoughts. The egoless mind is happy in deep, dreamless sleep. Clearly, therefore, bliss and misery are only modes of mind; but the weak mode is not easily interchangeable with the strong mode. Activity is weakness and consequently miserable; passivity is strength and therefore blissful. The dormant strength is not apparent and therefore not utilized.

The cosmic mind, manifesting in some rare being, is able to effect the linkage in others of the individual (weak) mind with the universal (strong) mind of the inner recess. Such a rare being is called the Guru or "God in manifestation."

MAY 19, 1936

Mr. M. Oliver Lacombe, a middle-aged Frenchman who was on a visit to India (delegated by the Institute of Indian Civilization of the University of Paris) came here from Indo-China. Among others, he wanted to meet Maharshi; he came and stayed here about three hours. He had read, in the Sanskrit original, the Bhagavad Gita, *the* Upanishads, *and the* Sutras *with commentaries by Sri Shankara and Ramanuja. He asked*: Is Maharshi's teaching the same as Shankara's?

M. Maharshi's teaching is only an expression of his own experience and realization. Others find that it tallies with Sri Shankara's.

D. Quite so. Can it be put in other ways to express the same realization?

M. A realized person will use his own language.

Sri Bhagavan added: Silence is the best language.

D. What does Maharshi say about *Hatha Yoga* or *Tantric* practices?

M. Maharshi does not criticize any of the existing methods. All are good for purification of the mind, because the purified mind alone is capable of grasping his method and sticking to its practice.

D. Which is the best of the different yogas, *Karma, Jnana, Bhakti,* or *Hatha?*

M. See stanza 10 of *Upadesa Saram.* To remain in the Self amounts to all these in their highest sense.

In dreamless sleep, there is no world, no ego, and no unhappiness, but the Self remains. In the waking state there are all these; yet, there is the Self. One has only to remove the transitory happenings in order to realize the ever-present beatitude of the Self. Your nature is Bliss. Find that on which all the rest is superimposed and you then remain as the pure Self.

D. Yes. It amounts to the removal of alien limitations for discovering the ever-present Self. That is what Shankara says. There is no attainment or loss.

M. Quite so. (*Aside*) He understands.

D. How is work to be done ordinarily for an aspirant?

M. Without self-identification with the actor. For instance, did you intend visiting this place while in Paris?

D. No!

M. You see how you are acting without your intention to do so? The *Gita* says that a man cannot remain without acting. The purpose of one's birth will be fulfilled whether you will it or not. Let the purpose fulfill itself.

D. Why are there so many methods mentioned? For instance, Sri Ramakrishna says that *bhakti* is the best means for salvation.

M. It is according to the standpoint of the aspirant. You have studied the *Gita.* Sri Krishna said:

"There was never a time when I, and you, and these kings were not; nor will they not be in future. That which is unreal never exists. But that which is real never disappears. All that ever was even now is and will ever be."

"I taught this Truth to Aditya; he taught it to Manu, etc. Arjuna asked: "How can it be? You were born some years back and only recently. How could you have taught Aditya?"

Sri Krishna answered: "Yes. We have had several births in the past. I know mine; whereas, you do not know yours. I tell you what happened in those past births."

Look! Krishna, who began saying there was not I, nor you, nor these kings, says now that he had several births before. Krishna does not contradict Himself, though it looks like it. He conforms to the outlook of Arjuna and speaks to him from his level.

There is a parallel passage in the Bible where Jesus says, "Before Abraham was, I am." The teachings of the Sages are suited to the time, place, people, and other surroundings.

(The visitor said he was leaving with regret.)
Maharshi smilingly interrupted: There is no leaving or returning.
The Frenchman at once said: He has transcended time and space.
(He returned to Pondicherry.)

MAY 30, 1936

There is a pet squirrel in the Hall which usually retires into its cage before nightfall. Just as Maharshi was telling it to retire for the night, a visitor, who had announced that he had attained the transcendent consciousness, suggested that water might be offered to it, since it was likely to be thirsty on this hot evening. His presumption to understand animals evoked no response. He repeated it. After a few minutes silence, Maharshi said: You are probably thirsty after your long meditation in the hot sun on the hotter rocks and you would like to drink a jug of water.
D. Quite so. I have taken water.
M. The squirrel is not so thirsty. Because you were practicing austerities in the heat of the sun, you should feel thirsty. Why prescribe it for the squirrel?
Maharshi added: I noticed him standing on the hot rocks facing the sun with eyes closed. I stood there for a while, but did not want to disturb him and came away. These people do as they please.
D. What I did, I did not intend beforehand. It was spontaneous.
M. Oh! I see! Whatever we others do, we do with intention! You seem to have transcended all!
D. This is not the first time I did so. You yourself inspire me and make me do all these things. Yet you ask me why I did it. How is that?
M. I see. You are doing actions being controlled by me. Then the fruits should be considered similarly to be mine and not yours.
D. So they are undoubtedly. I act not of my free will but inspired by you. I have no will of my own.

M. Enough of this rubbish! So did Duryodhana of old (in the *Mahabharata*) say:

"*Janami dharmam nacha me pravrittih,*
janamyadharmam nacha me nivrittih.
Kenapi devana hridi sthitena,
yatha niyuktosmitatha karomi."

I know what *dharma* (righteousness) is but cannot follow the right path, I know what *adharma* (unrighteousness) is but cannot be free of it.

Lord, it is you who make me act this way,

If You enter my heart I can cheerfully stay on the right path.

What is the difference between you two?

D. I see no difference. But I have no will and act without it.

M. You have risen high above the common run. We others are acting with personal will.

D. How, Sir? You have said in one of your works that action can be automatic.

M. Enough! Enough! You and another visitor behave as transcendental beings! You are both fully learned. You need not learn more. I would not have said all this had you not been coming here frequently. Do as you please. But these eccentricities of the beginner's stage will become known in their true light after some time.

D. But I have been in this state for such a long time.

M. Enough!

Mr. S.S. Cohen, a resident disciple, was speaking of the yoga method. Maharshi remarked: Patanjali's first sutra is applicable to all systems of yoga. The aim is the cessation of mental activities. The methods differ. So long as effort is made towards that goal, it is called yoga. The effort is the yoga.

Cessation can be brought about in so many ways:

1. By examining the mind itself. When the mind is examined, its activities cease automatically. This is the method of *jnana*. The pure mind is the Self.
2. Looking for the source of the mind is another method. The source may be said to be God or Self or consciousness.
3. Concentrating upon one thought makes all other thoughts disappear. Finally, that thought also disappears.
4. *Hatha Yoga.*

All methods are one and the same inasmuch as they tend towards the same goal.

It is necessary to be aware while controlling thoughts; otherwise, sleep will result. That awareness, the chief factor, is indicated by the fact of Patanjali emphasizing *pratyahara* (withdrawal of the senses), *dharana* (concentration), *dhyana* (contemplation), and *samadhi* (absorption) even after *pranayama* (breath control). *Pranayama* makes the mind steady and suppresses thoughts. Then why develop it further? Because awareness is the one necessary factor. Such states can be imitated by taking morphine, chloroform, etc., but they do not lead to *Moksha* because they lack awareness.

JUNE 3, 1936

Maharshi, in the course of conversation, explained: Whoever desires liberation? Everyone wants only happiness — happiness, too, as found in the enjoyment of the senses. This question was asked of a Guru, and the latter answered: "Quite so. That happiness which is the result of enjoyment by the senses is the same as that of liberation. That desire of such liberation is one of the four qualifications for attainment. This is common to all. So all are eligible for this knowledge — Self-knowledge."

In fact, there may not be any individual in the world who possesses all the qualities in perfection necessary for an aspirant as mentioned in *Yoga Sutras*, etc. Still, pursuit of Self-knowledge should not be abandoned.

Everyone is the Self by his own experience. Still, he is not aware; he identifies the Self with the body and feels miserable. This is the greatest of all mysteries. One *is* the Self. Why not abide as the Self and be done with miseries?

In the beginning one has to be told that he is not the body, because he thinks that he is the body only. Whereas he is the body and all else. The body is only a part. Let him know it, finally. He must first discern consciousness from insentience and be the consciousness only. Later, let him realize that insentience is not apart from consciousness.

This is discrimination (*viveka*). The initial discrimination must persist to the end; its fruit is liberation.

Maharshi observed: Free will and destiny are ever-existent. Destiny is the result of past action; it concerns the body. Let the body act as may suit it. How are you concerned? Why do you pay attention to it? Free will and Destiny last so long as the body lasts. But wisdom (*jnana*) transcends both.

The Self is beyond knowledge and ignorance. Should anything happen, it happens as the result of one's past actions, divine will, and other factors.

Mr. Subba Rao, a visitor from Amalapuram, asked: How to control the mind?
M. Get hold of the mind.
D. How?
M. Mind is intangible. In fact, it does not exist. The surest way of control is to seek it. Then its activities cease.

JUNE 6, 1936

Mr. Jharka, a gentleman from the University of Benares, holding the M.A. and M.Sc. degrees, said he was stricken with grief due to bereavement of his wife and children. He sought peace of mind and asked how to get it.
M. It is in the mind that birth and death, pleasure and pain — in short the world and ego — exist. If the mind is destroyed, all these are destroyed, too. Note that it should be *annihilated*, not just made latent. For the mind is dormant in sleep. It does not know anything. Still, on waking up, you are as you were before. There is no end of grief. But if the mind is destroyed, the grief will have no background and will disappear along with the mind.
D. How to destroy the mind?
M. Seek the mind. On being sought, it will disappear.
D. I do not understand.
M. The mind is only a bundle of thoughts. The thoughts arise because there is the thinker. The thinker is the ego. The ego, if sought, will vanish automatically. The ego and the mind are the same. The ego is the root-thought from which all other thoughts arise.
D. How to seek the mind?
M. Dive within. You are now aware that the mind rises up from within. So sink within and seek.
D. I do not yet understand how it is done.
M. You are practicing breath control. Mechanical breath control will not lead one to the goal. It is only an aid. While doing it mechanically, take care to be alert in mind and remember the "I"-thought and seek its source. Then you will find that where the breath sinks, "I"-thought arises. They sink and rise together. The "I"-thought also will sink along with the breath. Simultaneously, another luminous and infinite "I-I" will become manifest, which will be continuous and unbroken. That is the goal. It goes by different names — God, Self, *Kundalini Shakti, Consciousness, Yoga, Bhakti, Jnana,* etc.

D. It's not clear yet.

M. When the attempt is made, it will of itself take you to the goal.

JUNE 9, 1936

A visitor asked about the three methods mentioned in Ramana Gita *(chap. 2).*
Maharshi pointed out that breath retention is an aid to control of mind, i.e., suppression or annihilation of thoughts. One person may practice breath control, inhalation, exhalation and retention, or retention only. Still another type of practicing meditator, on controlling the mind, controls the breath, and its retention automatically results. Watching the inhalation and exhalation is also breath-control. These methods are only apparently threefold. They are really one, because they lead to the same goal. They are, however, adopted according to the stage of the aspirant and his antecedent predisposition or tendencies. Really, there are only two methods: inquiry and devotion. One leads to the other.

D. Seeking the "I," there is nothing to be seen.

M. Because you are accustomed to identify yourself with the body and sight with the eyes, you say you do not see anything. What is there to be seen? Who is to see? How to see? There is only one consciousness which, manifesting as "I"-thought, identifies itself with the body, projects itself through the eyes and sees the objects around. The individual is limited in the waking state and expects to see something different. The evidence of his senses will be the seal of authority. But he will not admit that the seer, the seen, and the sight are all manifestations of the same consciousness — namely, "I-I." Contemplation helps one overcome the illusion that the Self must be visual. In truth, nothing visual exists. How do you feel the "I" now? Do you hold a mirror in front of you to know your own being? The awareness is the "I." Realize it and that is the truth.

D. On inquiry into the origin of thoughts, there is a perception of "I." But it does not satisfy me.

M. Quite right. The perception of "I" is associated with a form, maybe the body. There should be nothing associated with the pure Self. The Self is the unassociated, pure Reality, in whose light the body, the ego, etc. shine. On stilling all thoughts, the pure consciousness remains. Just as on waking from sleep and before becoming aware of the world, there is the pure "I-I." Hold to it without sleeping or allowing thoughts to possess you. If *that* is held firmly, it does not matter, even though the world is seen; the seer remains unaffected by the phenomena.

Chapter Two—1936

Gul and Shirin Byramjee, two Parsi ladies from Ahmedabad, arrived this day. They spoke at night to Maharshi: Bhagavan! We have been spiritually inclined from childhood. We have read several books on philosophy, and are attracted by *Vedanta*. So we read the *Upanishads, Yoga Vasishta, Bhagavad Gita*, etc. We try to meditate, but there is no progress in our meditation. We do not understand how to realize ourselves. Can you kindly help us towards realization?

M. How do you meditate?

D. I begin to ask myself "Who am I?," eliminate body as not "I," the breath as not "I," the mind as not "I," yet I am not able to proceed any further.

M. Well, that is so far as the intellect goes. Your process is only intellectual. Indeed, all the scriptures mention the process only to guide the seeker to know the Truth. The Truth cannot be directly pointed out; hence, this intellectual process.

You see, the one who eliminates all the *not I* cannot eliminate the "I." To say "I am not this" or "I am that," there must be the "I." This "I" is only the ego or the "I"-thought. After the rising up of this "I"-thought, all other thoughts arise. The "I"-thought is therefore the root-thought. If the root is pulled out, all others are uprooted at the same time. Therefore, seek the root "I," question yourself "Who am I?"; find out its source. Then all these [thoughts] will vanish and the pure Self will remain.

D. How to do it?

M. The "I" is always there — in deep sleep, in dream and in wakefulness. The one in sleep is the same as that one who now speaks. There is always the feeling of "I." Otherwise, do you deny your existence? You do not. You say "I am." Find out "who is."

D. Even so, I do not understand. "I," you say, is the wrong "I" now. How to eliminate this wrong "I"?

M. You need not eliminate the wrong "I." How can "I" eliminate itself? All you need to do is find out its origin and abide there. Your efforts can extend only thus far. Then the Beyond will take care of itself. You are helpless there; no effort can reach it.

D. If "I" am always — here and now, why do I not feel so?

M. That is it. Who says it is not felt? Does the real "I" say it or the false "I"? Examine it. You will find it is the wrong "I." The wrong "I" is the obstruction. It has to be removed in order that the true "I" may not be hidden. The feeling that "I have not realized" is the obstruction to realization. In fact, it is already realized; there is nothing more to be realized. Otherwise, the realization would be new; it has not existed so far, it must take place hereafter. But what is born will also die. If realization is not eternal, it is not worth having. Therefore, what we seek is not that which must happen afresh. It is only that which is eternal but not now known, due to obstructions; it is that which we seek. All we need do is to remove the obstruction. That which is eternal is not known, because of ignorance. Ignorance is the obstruction. Get over this ignorance and all will be well.

The ignorance is identical with the "I"-thought. Find its source and it will vanish.

The "I"-thought is like a spirit which, although not palpable, rises up simultaneously with the body, flourishes and disappears with it. The body-consciousness is the wrong "I." Give up this body-consciousness by seeking the source of "I." The body does not say, "I am." It is you who say, "I am the body!" Find out who this "I" is. Seeking its source, it will vanish.

D. Then, will there be bliss?

M. Bliss is concurrent with Being-Consciousness. All the arguments relating to the eternal Being of that Bliss apply to Bliss, also. Your nature is Bliss. Ignorance is now hiding that Bliss. Remove the ignorance for Bliss to be freed.

D. Should we not find out the ultimate reality of the world, individual, and God?

M. These are all conceptions of the "I." They arise only after the advent of the "I"-thought. Did you think of them in your deep sleep? You existed in deep sleep, likewise as you are now speaking. If they are real, should they not be so in your sleep, also? They are only dependent upon the "I"-thought. Again, does the world tell you "I am the world"? Does the body say, "I am the body"? *You* say, "This is the world," "this is the body," and so on. So these are only your conceptions. Find out who you are and there will be an end to all your doubts.

D. What becomes of the body after realization? Does it exist or not? We see realized beings acting like others.

M. This question need not arise now. Let it be asked after realization, if need be. As for the realized beings, let them take care of themselves. Why do you worry about them?

Actually, after realization the body and all else will not appear different from the Self.

D. If always Being-Consciousness-Bliss, why does God place us in difficulties? Why did He create us?

M. Does God come and tell you that He has placed you in difficulties? It is you who say so. It is again the wrong "I." If that disappears, there will be no one to say that God created this or that.

That which *is* does not even say, "I am." For, does any doubt arise that "I am not?" Only in such a case should one be reminding oneself "I am a man." One does not. On the other hand, if a doubt arises whether one is a cow or a buffalo, he has to remind himself that he is not a cow, etc., but "I am a man." This would never happen. Similarly with one's own existence and realization.

JUNE 10, 1936

Some ladies asked if there is rebirth of man as a lower animal.

M. Yes. It is possible, as illustrated by Jada Bharata— the scriptural anecdote of a royal sage, having been reborn as a deer.

D. Is an individual capable of spiritual progress in an animal body?

M. Not impossible, though exceedingly rare.

D. What is Guru's Grace? How does it work?

M. Guru is the Self.

D. How does it lead to realization?

M. *Ishvaro gururatmeti* . . . (God is the same as Guru and Self . . .). A person begins with dissatisfaction. Not content with the world, he seeks satisfaction of desires by prayers to God. His mind is purified; he longs more to know God than to satisfy his desires of the flesh. Then God's Grace begins to manifest. God takes the form of a Guru and appears to the devotee, teaches him the Truth, and purifies the mind by his teachings and contact. The mind gains strength and is able to turn inward. With meditation it is purified yet further, and eventually remains still without the least ripple. That stillness is the Self. The Guru is both exterior and interior. From the exterior he gives a push to the mind to turn inward; from the interior he pulls the mind towards the Self and helps the mind to achieve quietness. That is Grace.

Hence, there is no difference between God, Guru, and Self.

The ladies later asked several questions relating to their present inability to realize the already realized, eternal Self. The sign of Realization would be Bliss, which was absent.

M. There is only one consciousness. But we speak of several kinds of consciousness — body-consciousness, Self-consciousness. They are only relative states of the same Absolute consciousness. Without consciousness, time and space do not exist. They appear in consciousness. It is like a screen on which these are cast as pictures and move as in a cinema show. The Absolute consciousness is our real nature.

D. From where do these objects arise?

M. Just from where you arise. Know the subject first and then ask questions about the object.

D. It is only one aspect of the question.

M. The subject comprehends the object also. That one aspect is all comprehensive. See yourself first and then see the objects. What is not in you cannot appear outside.

D. I am not satisfied.

M. Satisfaction can be only when you reach the Source. Otherwise restlessness remains.

D. Is the Supreme Being with or without attributes?

M. Know first if *you* are with or without attributes.

D. What is *samadhi?*

M. One's own true nature.

D. Why then is effort necessary to attain it?

M. Whose is the effort?

D. Maharshi knows that I am ignorant.

M. Do *you* know that you are ignorant? Knowledge of ignorance is no ignorance.

All scriptures are only for the purpose of investigating if there are two consciousnesses. Everyone's experience proves the existence of only one consciousness. Can that one divide itself into two? Is any division felt in the Self? Awaking from sleep, one finds oneself the same in the wakeful as well as the sleep state. That is the experience of everyone. The difference lies in seeking, in the outlook. Because you imagine that you are the seer as separate from the experience, this difference arises. Experience shows that your being is the same all through.

D. From where did ignorance come?

M. There is no such thing as ignorance. It never arises. Everyone is Knowledge itself. Only Knowledge does not shine easily. The dispelling of ignorance is Wisdom which always exists — e.g., the necklace remaining around the neck though supposed to have been lost; or each of the ten fools failing to count himself and counting only the others. To whom is knowledge or ignorance?

D. Can we not proceed from external to internal?

M. Is there any difference like that? Do you feel the difference — external and internal — in your sleep? This difference is only with reference to the body and arises with body-consciousness ("I"-thought). The so-called waking state is itself an illusion.

Turn your vision inward and then the whole world will be full of Supreme Spirit. The world is said to be illusion. Illusion is really Truth. Even science traces the origin of the universe to one primordial matter — subtle, exceedingly subtle.

God is the same to both those who say the world is real and their opponents. Their outlook is different. You need not entangle yourself in such disputations. The goal is one and the same for all. Look to it.

JUNE 14, 1936

Mr. Cohen wanted an explanation of the term "blazing light" used by Paul Brunton in the last chapter of A Search in Secret India.

M. Since the experience is through the mind only, it appears first as a blaze of light. The mental predispositions are not yet destroyed. The mind is, however, functioning in its infinite capacity in this experience.

As for *nirvikalpa samadhi*, i.e., *samadhi* of non-differentiation (undifferentiated, supreme, beatific repose), it consists of pure consciousness, which is capable of illumining knowledge or ignorance; it is also beyond light or darkness. That it is not darkness is certain; can it, however, be said to be not light? At present, objects are perceived only in light. Is it wrong to say that realization of one's Self requires a light? Here *light* would mean the consciousness which reveals itself as the Self only.

The yogis are said to see visions of colors and lights preliminary to Self-realization by the practice of yoga.

Once, Goddess Parvati practiced austerities for realizing the Supreme. She saw some kinds of lights. She rejected them since they emanated from the Self, leaving the Self as it was ever before. She determined that they were not Supreme. Continuing her austerities, she experienced a limitless light and determined that this also was only a phenomenon and not the Supreme Reality. Still, she continued her austerities until gaining transcendental peace. Parvati realized that it was Supreme, and that the Self was the sole Reality.

The *Taittiriya Upanishad* says, "Seek *Brahman* through penance." Later on, "Penance is *Brahman*." Another *Upanishad* says, "Itself is penance which is again made up of wisdom alone." "There, the sun shines not, nor the moon, nor the stars, nor fire; all these shine forth by Its light."

The Parsi ladies asked for an illustration to explain why the Self, though ever present and most intimate, is not being realized. Maharshi cited the stories of:
1. *Svakanthabharanam katha* — that of the necklace, on the neck itself, not being detected.
2. *Dasama* — of the ten fools who counted only nine, each of them omitting to count himself.
3. The lion's cub, brought up in a herd of goats.
4. Karna not knowing his real parentage.
5. The king's son brought up in a low-class family.

They further asked for Maharshi's opinion of Sri Aurobindo's Yoga, and his claim to have probed beyond the experiences of the Vedic rishis and the Mother's opinion of the fitness of her disciples to begin with the realization of the Upanishadic rishis.
M. Aurobindo advises complete surrender. Let us do that first and await results, and discuss further, if need be, afterwards and not now. There is no use discussing transcendental experiences by those whose limitations are not removed. Learn what surrender is. It is to merge in the source of the ego. The ego is surrendered to the Self. Everything is dear to us because of love of the Self. The Self is that to which we surrender our ego and let the Supreme Power, i.e., the Self, do what it pleases. The ego is already of the Self. We have no rights over the ego, even as it is. However, supposing we had, we must surrender them.
D. What about bringing down divine consciousness from above?
M. As if the same is not already in the Heart? "O, Arjuna, I am in the expanse of the Heart," says Sri Krishna. "He who is in the sun, is also in this man," says a mantra in the *Upanishads*. "The Kingdom of Heaven is within," says the Bible. All are thus agreed that God is within. What is to be brought down? From where? Who is to bring what, and why?
    Realization is only the removal of obstacles to the recognition of the eternal, immanent Reality. Reality *is*. It need not be taken from place to place.
D. What about Aurobindo's claim to start from Self-realization and develop further?
M. Let us first realize and then see.
    The fact is: There is Reality. It is not affected by any discussions. Let us abide as Reality and not engage in futile discussions as to its nature, etc.

JUNE 15, 1936

A sad-looking Punjabi gentleman announced himself to Maharshi as having been directed to him by Sri Shankaracharya of Kamakotipeetam, from Jalesvar near Puri, Jagannath. He is a world tourist. He has practiced Hatha Yoga *and some contemplation along the lines of "I am* Brahman.*" After a few moments a blank prevails, his brain gets heated, and he becomes afraid of death. He wants guidance from Maharshi.*

M. Who sees the blank?

D. I know that I see it.

M. The consciousness overlooking the blank is the Self.

D. That does not satisfy me. I cannot realize it.

M. The fear of death is only after the "I"-thought arises. Whose death do you fear? For whom is the fear? There is the identification of the Self with the body. So long as there is this, there will be fear.

D. But I am not aware of my body.

M. Who says that he is not aware?

D. I do not understand.

(*He was then asked to say what exactly was his method of meditation.*)

D. "*Aham Brahmasmi*" (I am *Brahman*).

M. "I am *Brahman*" is only a thought. Who says it? *Brahman* itself does not say so. What need is there for it to say it? Nor can the real "I" say so. For "I" always abides as *Brahman*. To be saying it is only a thought. Whose thought is it? All thoughts are from the unreal "I," i.e., the "I"-thought. Remain without thinking. So long as there is thought there will be fear.

D. As I go on thinking of it there is forgetfulness, the brain becomes heated, and I am afraid.

M. Yes, the mind is concentrated in the brain and hence you get a hot sensation there. It is because of the "I"-thought. So long as there is thought there will be forgetfulness. There is the thought "I am *Brahman*"; forgetfulness supervenes; then the "I"-thought arises and simultaneously the fear of death. Forgetfulness and thought are for the "I"-thought only. Hold it; it will disappear as a phantom. What remains is the real "I." That is the Self. "I am *Brahman*" is an aid to concentration. It keeps other thoughts away. That one thought alone persists. See whose is that thought. It will be found to be from "I." Wherefrom is the "I"-thought? Probe into it, then the "I"-thought will vanish. The Supreme Self will shine forth of itself and no further effort is needed.

When the one real "I" remains alone, it will not be saying, "I am *Brahman*." Does a man go on repeating "I am a man"? Unless he is challenged, why should he declare himself a man? Does anyone mistake himself for a brute, that he should say, "No. I am not a brute, I am a man"? Similarly, *Brahman* or "I" being alone, there is no one there to challenge it and so there is no need for repeating "I am *Brahman*."

JUNE 17, 1936

Mr. Varma, Financial Secretary of the Posts and Telegraphs Department, Delhi, has read Paul Brunton's A Search in Secret India *and* The Secret Path. *He lost his wife with whom he had led a happy life for eleven or twelve years. In his grief he seeks solace. He cannot find it in reading books and wants to tear them up. He does not intend to ask questions. He simply wants to sit here and derive what solace he can in the presence of Maharshi. Maharshi, as if in a train of thought, spoke now and then to the following effect:* It is said, "The wife is one-half of the body." So her death is very painful. This pain is however due to one's outlook being physical; it disappears if the outlook is that of the Self. The *Brahadaranyaka Upanishad* says, "The wife is dear because of the love of the Self." If the wife and others are identified with the Self, how then will pain arise? Nevertheless, such disasters shake the mind of even philosophers.

We are happy in deep sleep. We remain then as the pure Self. We are the same even now. In such sleep there was neither the wife nor others nor even "I." Now they become apparent and give rise to pleasure or pain. Why should not the Self, which was blissful in deep sleep, continue its blissful nature even now? The sole obstruction to such continuity is the wrong identification of the Self with the body.

The *Bhagavad Gita* says: "The unreal has no being; the real never ceases to be; the truth about both has been perceived by the seers of the essence of things." "The real is ever real, the unreal is ever unreal." Again: "He is not born, nor does He die; nor, having been, ceases He any more to be; unborn, perpetual, eternal, ancient, He is not killed when the body is slain." Accordingly, there is neither birth nor death. Waking is birth and sleep is death.

Was the wife with you when you went out to the office, or in your deep sleep? She was away from you. You were satisfied because of your thought that she was somewhere. Whereas now you think that she is not. The difference lies in the different thoughts; that is the cause of pain. The pain is because of the thought of the wife's non-being. All this is the mischief of the mind. The fellow (the mind) creates pain for himself even when there is pleasure. Both pleasure and pain are mental creations.

Again, why mourn the dead? They are free from bondage. Mourning is the chain forged by the mind to bind itself to the dead.

"What if anyone is dead? What if anyone is ruined? Be dead yourself — be ruined yourself." In that sense, there is no pain after one's death. What is meant by this sort of death? Annihilation of the ego, though the body is alive. If the ego persists, a man is afraid of death. The man mourns another's death. He need not do so if he predeceases him (by waking up from the ego-dream, which amounts to killing the ego-sense). The experience of deep sleep clearly teaches that happiness consists in being without the body. The wise also confirm it, speaking of liberation after the body is given up. Thus, the sage is awaiting the casting off of the body. Just as a laborer carrying a load on his head for the sake of wages bears the burden with no pleasure, carries it to the destination, and finally unburdens himself with relief and joy, so also the sage bears this body, awaiting the right and destined time to discard it. If now you are relieved of one-half of the burden, i.e., the wife, should you not be thankful and be happy for it?

Nevertheless you cannot be so because of your outlook.

Even men who ought to know better and who have known the teaching about liberation after death, etc., glorify liberation along with the body and talk about some mysterious power of keeping the body eternally alive!

There will be no pain if this outlook is given up and the person exists as the Self only. Mourning is not the index of true love. It reflects love of the object, of its shape only, but that is not love. True love is shown by the certainty that the object of love is in the Self and that it can never become non-existent.

(*Maharshi cited the story of Ahalya and Indra from* Yoga Vasishta *in this connection.*)

Still it is true, pain on such occasions can only be assuaged by association with the wise.

JUNE 18, 1936

Maharshi on Self-Illumination: The "I" concept is the ego. "I"-illumination is the realization of the real Self. It is ever shining forth as "I-I" in the intellectual sheath. It is pure Knowledge; relative knowledge is only a concept. The bliss of the blissful sheath is also but a concept. Unless there is the experience, however subtle, one cannot say, "I slept happily." From his intellect, he speaks of his blissful sheath. The bliss of sleep is but a concept to the person. However, the concept of experience is exceedingly subtle in sleep. Experience is not possible without simultaneous knowledge of it (i.e.

relative knowledge).

The inherent nature of the Self is Bliss. Some kind of knowledge has to be admitted, even in the realization of Supreme Bliss. It may be said to be subtler than the subtlest.

The word *vijnana* (clear knowledge) is used to both denote realization of the Self and knowing the objects. The Self is wisdom. It functions in two ways. When associated with the ego, the knowledge is objective (*vijnana*). When divested of the ego and the Universal Self is realized, it is also called *vijnana*. The word raises a mental concept. Therefore, we say that the Self-realized sage knows by his mind, but his mind is pure. Again, we say that the vibrating mind is impure and the placid mind is pure. The pure mind is itself *Brahman*; therefore it follows that *Brahman* is not other than the mind of the sage.

The *Mundaka Upanishad* says: "The knower of *Brahman* becomes the Self of *Brahman*." Is it not ludicrous? To know Him and become Him? They are mere words. The sage is *Brahman* — that is all. Mental functioning is necessary to communicate his experience. He is said to be contemplating the unbroken expanse. Brahma, Suka, and others are also said never to swerve from such contemplation.

Such "contemplation" is again a mere word. How is that to be contemplated unless it is divided (into the contemplator and the contemplated)? When undivided, how is contemplation possible? What function can Infinity have? Do we say that a river after its discharge into the ocean has become an ocean-like river? Why should we then speak of contemplation which has become unbroken, as being that of unbroken Infinity? The statement must be understood in the spirit in which it is made. It signifies the merging into the Infinite.

Self-Illumination or Self-realization is similar to it. The Self is ever shining. What does this "I"-illumination mean then? The expression is an implied admission of mind function.

The gods and the sages experience the Infinite continuously and eternally, without their vision being obscured at any moment. Their minds are surmised by the spectators to function, but in fact they do not. Such surmising is due to the sense of individuality in those who draw inferences. There is no mental function in the absence of individuality. Individuality and mind functions are coexistent. The one cannot remain without the other.

The light of the Self can be experienced only in the intellectual sheath. Therefore, *vijnana* of whatever kind (of object or of the Self) depends on the Self being Pure Knowledge.

Mr. Cohen had been cogitating on the nature of the Heart, and whether the "spiritual heart" beats; if so, how? And if it does not beat, then how is it to be felt?

M. This heart is different from the physical heart; beating is the function of the latter. The former is the seat of spiritual experience. That is all that can be said of it.

Just as a dynamo supplies motive power to whole systems of lights, fans, etc, so the original Primal Force supplies energy to the beating of the heart, respiration, etc.

D. How is the "I-I" consciousness felt?

M. As an unbroken awareness of "I." It is simply consciousness.

D. Can we know it when it dawns?

M. Yes, as consciousness. You are that even now. There will be no mistaking it when it is pure.

D. Why do we have such a place as the "Heart" for meditation?

M. Because you seek consciousness. Where can you find it? Can you reach it externally? You have to find it internally. Therefore, you are directed inward. Again the "Heart" is only the seat of consciousness or the consciousness itself.

D. On what should we meditate?

M. Who is the meditator? Ask that question first. *Remain as the meditator.* There is no need to meditate.

Mr. B.C. Das, a lecturer in physics of Allahabad University, asked: Does not intellect rise and fall with the man?

M. Whose is the intellect? It is man's. Intellect is only an instrument.

D. Yes. Does it survive man's death?

M. Why think of death? See what happens in your sleep. What is your experience there?

D. But sleep is transient whereas death is not.

M. Sleep is intermediate between two waking states, so also death is between two successive births. Both are transient.

D. I mean when the spirit is disembodied, does it carry the intellect with it?

M. Spirit is not disembodied. The bodies differ. It may not be a gross body. It will then be a subtle body, as in sleep, dream, or daydream. Intellect does not alter; the bodies may differ according to circumstances.

D. The spirit-body is the astral body then?

M. The intellect is the astral body now.

D. How can it be?

M. Why not? You seem to think that the intellect cannot be limited like a body. It is only an aggregate of certain factors. What else is the astral body?
D. But intellect is a sheath?
M. Yes. Without intellect, no sheath is cognized. Who says that there are five sheaths? Is it not the intellect that declares thus?

Deep sleep is only the state of nonduality. Can the difference between the individual and Universal souls persist there? Sleep implies forgetfulness of all differences. This alone constitutes happiness. See how carefully people prepare their beds to gain that happiness. Soft cushions, pillows, and all the rest are meant to induce sound sleep, that is to say an end to wakefulness. And yet the soft bed, etc., are of no use in the state of deep sleep itself. The implication is that all efforts are meant only to end ignorance. They have no use after realization.

It is enough that one surrenders oneself. Surrender is to give oneself up to the original cause of one's being. Do not delude yourself by imagining such a source to be some God outside you. One's source is within oneself. Give yourself up to it. That means that you should seek the source and merge in it. Because you imagine yourself to be out of it, you raise the question "Where is the source?" Some contend that the sugar cannot taste its own sweetness and that a taster must taste and enjoy it. Similarly, an individual cannot be the Supreme and enjoy the Bliss of that state; therefore, the individuality must be maintained on the one hand and Godhead on the other so that enjoyment may result! Is God insentient like sugar? How can one surrender oneself and yet retain one's individuality for supreme enjoyment? Furthermore, they say that the soul, reaching the divine region and remaining there, serves the Supreme Being. Can the sound of the word "service" deceive the Lord? Does He not know? Is He waiting for these people's service? Would not He — the Pure Consciousness — ask in turn: "Who are you apart from Me that presume to serve Me?"
They assume that the individual soul becomes pure by being divested of the ego and fit for being the body of the Lord. Thus, the Lord is the Spirit and the purified souls constitute His body and limbs! Can there be a soul for the souls? How many souls are there? The answer must be, "There are many individual souls and One Supreme Soul." What is soul in that case? It cannot be the body, etc. What remains after all these are eliminated must be said to be the soul. Thus, even after realizing the soul as that which cannot be discarded, the Supreme Soul must be known to exist. In that

case, how was the soul realized to be the ultimate reality after discarding all that was alien to it? Should this be right, the soul which was described as that inalienable reality is not the true soul. All such confusion is due to the word "soul" (*atma*). The same word *atma* is used to signify the body, the senses, the mind, the vital principle, the individual soul, and the Supreme Being. This wide application of the word has given rise to the idea that the individual soul (*jivatma*) goes to constitute the body of the Supreme (*Paramatma*).

"I, O Arjuna! am the Self, seated in the heart of all beings; . . . "
— *Bhagavad Gita* 10.20

The stanza shows that the Lord is the *Atma* (Self) of all beings. Does it say, "the Self of the selves"? If, on the other hand, you merge in the Self, there will be no individuality left. You will become the Source itself. In that case what is surrender? Who is to surrender what and to whom? This constitutes devotion, wisdom, and investigation.

Among the Vaishnavites too, Saint Nammalvar says, "I was in a maze, sticking to 'I' and 'mine'; I wandered without knowing my Self. On realizing my Self, I understand that I myself am You and that 'mine' (i.e., my possessions) is only You."

Thus, you see, devotion is nothing more than knowing oneself. The school of Qualified Monism also admits it. Still, adhering to their traditional doctrine, they persist in affirming that the individuals are part of the Supreme — his limbs, as it were. Their traditional doctrine says also that the individual soul should be made pure and then surrendered to the Supreme; then the ego is lost and one goes to the regions of Vishnu after one's death; then, finally, there is the enjoyment of the Supreme (or the Infinite)!

To say that one is apart from the Primal Source is itself a pretension; to add that one divested of the ego becomes pure and yet retains individuality only to enjoy or serve the Supreme, is a deceitful stratagem. What duplicity is this — first to appropriate what is really His, and then pretend to experience or serve Him! Is not all this already known to Him?

JUNE 19, 1936

Mr. B.C. Das, the physics lecturer, asked about free will and destiny.
M. Whose will is it? "It is mine," you may say. You are beyond will and fate. Abide as that and you transcend them both. That is the meaning of conquering destiny by will. Fate can be conquered; it is the result of past ac-

tions. By association with the wise, the bad tendencies are conquered. One's experiences are then viewed in proper perspective.

I exist now. I am the enjoyer. I enjoy fruits of action. I was in the past and shall be in the future. Who is this "I"? Finding this "I" to be pure Consciousness beyond action and enjoyment, freedom and happiness are gained. There is then no effort, for the Self is perfect and there remains nothing more to gain.

So long as there is individuality, one is the enjoyer and doer. But if it is lost, the divine Will prevails and guides the course of events. The individual is perceptible to others who cannot perceive divine force. Restrictions and discipline are for other individuals and not for the liberated.

Freewill is implied in the scriptural injunctions to be good. It implies overcoming fate by wisdom; the fire of wisdom consumes all actions. Wisdom is acquired by association with the wise, or rather, its mental atmosphere.

Man owes his movements to another Power, whereas he thinks that he does everything himself — just like a lame man bluffing that, were he helped to stand up, he would fight and chase away the enemy. Action is impelled by desire; desire arises only after the rise of the ego; and this ego owes its origin to a Higher Power on which its existence depends. It cannot remain apart. Why then prattle, "I do, I act, or I function"?

A Self-realized being cannot help but benefit the world. His very existence is the highest good.

Mr. B.C. Das next asked: Yoga means union. I wonder union of what with what?

M. Exactly. Yoga implies prior division and it means later union of one with another. Who is to be united with whom? You are the seeker, seeking union with something. That something is apart from you. Your Self is intimate to you. You are aware of the Self. Seek it and be it. That will expand as the Infinite. Then there will be no question of yoga, etc. Whose is the separation (*viyoga*)? Find it.

D. Are the stones, etc., destined to be always so?

M. Who sees stones? They are perceived by your senses, which in turn are actuated by your mind. So they are in your mind. Whose mind is it? The questioner must find it himself. If the Self is found, this question will not arise.

The Self is more intimate than the objects. Find the subject, and the

objects will take care of themselves. The objects are seen by different persons according to their outlook and these theories are evolved. But who is
the seer, the cognizer of these theories? It is you. Find your Self. Then there
is an end to these vagaries of the mind.

D. What is the mind?

M. A bundle of thoughts.

D. Wherefrom has it its origin?

M. Consciousness of the Self.

D. Then thoughts are not real.

M. They are not; the only reality is the Self.

Maharshi observed: *Pradakshina* (the Hindu rite of going around an object of
worship) is "All is within me." The true significance of the act of going around
Arunachala is said to be as effective as to circuit the world. That means the
whole world is condensed into this Hill. The circuit around the temple of
Arunachala is equally good; and self-circuit (turning round and round) is
as good as the last. So all are contained in the Self.

> "I remain fixed, whereas innumerable universes becoming con-
> cepts within my mind, rotate within me. This meditation is the
> highest *pradakshina.*"
> — *Ribhu Gita*

*Mr. B.C. Das finally asked why the mind cannot be turned inward in spite of re-
peated attempts.*

M. It is done by practice and dispassion and that succeeds only gradually.
The mind, having been so long a cow accustomed to graze stealthily on
others' estates, is not easily confined to her stall. However much her keeper
tempts her with luscious grass and fine fodder, she refuses the first time;
then she takes a bit, but her innate tendency to stray asserts itself and she
slips away. On being repeatedly tempted by the owner, she accustoms herself to the stall; finally, even if let loose she would not stray. Similarly with
the mind. If once it finds its inner happiness, it will not wander anymore.

Mr. Eknatha Rao, a frequent visitor, asked: Are there not modulations in contemplation according to circumstances?

M. Yes, there are. At times, there is illumination and then contemplation is
easy; at other times, contemplation is impossible even with repeated attempts. This is due to the working of the three *gunas* (qualities in nature).

D. Is it influenced by one's activities and circumstances?

M. Those cannot influence it. It is the sense of doership — *kartrutva buddhi* — that forms the impediment.

J<small>UNE</small> 22, 1936

Maharshi was reading G.U. Pope's translation of Tiruvachakam *and came across the stanzas describing the intense feeling of bhakti as thrilling the whole frame, melting the flesh and bones, etc. He remarked:* Manikavachakar is one of those whose body finally resolved itself in a blazing light, without leaving a corpse behind.

Another devotee asked how that could be. Maharshi said:

The gross body is only the concrete form of the subtle stuff — the mind. When the mind melts away and blazes forth as light, the body is consumed in that process. Nandanar is another whose body disappeared in blazing light.

Maj. Chadwick pointed out that Elijah disappeared in the same way. He desired to know if the disappearance of Christ's body from the tomb was like that.

M. No. Christ's body was left as a corpse which was at first entombed, whereas the others did not leave corpses behind.

In the course of conversation, Maharshi said that the subtle body is composed of light and sound and the gross body is a concrete form of the same. Mr. B.C. Das asked if the same light and sound were cognizable by senses.

M. No. They are supersensual. It is like this:

	Ishvara (Universal)	*Jiva* (Individual)
Gross	Universe	Body
Subtle	Sound and Light — *Nada, Bindu*	Mind and *Prana*
Primal	*Atma* (Self)	*Atma* (Self)
	Param (transcendental)	*Param* (transcendental)

They are ultimately the same.

The subtle body of the Creator is the mystic sound *Pranava*, which is sound and light. The universe resolves into sound and light and then into transcendence — *Param*.

Maharshi gave the meaning of Arunachala:

Aruna = Red, bright like fire.

144

The fire is not an ordinary fire, which is only hot. This is *Jnanagni* (Fire of Wisdom), which is neither hot nor cool.

Achala = A hill.

So it means Hill of Wisdom.

JUNE 29, 1936

Mr. A. Bose, an engineer from Bombay, asked: Does Bhagavan feel for us and show Grace?

M. You are neck-deep in water and yet cry for water. It is as good as saying that one neck-deep in water feels thirsty, or a fish in water feels thirsty, or that water feels thirsty.

D. How may one destroy the mind?

M. Is there a mind in the first place? What you call mind is an illusion. It starts from the "I"-thought. Without the gross or subtle senses, you cannot be aware of the body or the mind. Still, it is possible for you to be without these senses. In such a state, you are either asleep or aware of the Self only. Awareness of Self is ever there. Remain what you truly are and this question will not arise.

D. Is the body consciousness an impediment to realization?

M. We are always beyond the body or the mind. If however, you feel the body as the Self, then it is, of course, an impediment.

D. Is the body or the mind of any use to the Self?

M. Yes, inasmuch as it helps Self-realization.

JUNE 30, 1936

Maharshi has been looking into the Shiva Purana *this day. He says:* Shiva has the transcendental and immanent aspects as represented by His invisible, transcendental being and the *linga* aspect, respectively. The *linga* manifested as Arunachala originally stands even to this day. This manifestation was when the moon was in the constellation of Orion (*Ardra*) in December. However, it was first worshipped on *Shivarathri* (night of *Shiva*) day, which is held sacred even now.

In the sphere of speech, *Pranava* (the mystic sound *Aum*) represents the transcendental (*nirguna*), and the *Panchakshari* (the five-syllable mantra) represents the immanent aspect (*saguna*).

Sri Bhagavan narrated the story of Parvati testing Rama. The story is as follows:

145

Rama and Lakshmana were wandering in the forest in search of Sita. Rama was grief-stricken. Just then, Shiva and Parvati happened to pass close by. Shiva saluted Rama and passed on. Parvati was surprised and asked Shiva to explain why He, the Lord of the Universe, being worshipped by all, should stop to salute Rama, an ordinary human who having missed his consort was grief-stricken and moving in anguish in the wilderness and looking helpless. Shiva then said: "Rama is simply acting as a human being would under the circumstances. He is nevertheless the incarnation of Vishnu, and deserves to be saluted. You may test him if you choose."

Parvati considered the matter, took the shape of Sita, and appeared in front of Rama, as he was crying out the name of Sita in great anguish. He looked at Parvati appearing as Sita, smiled and asked, "Why, Parvati, are you here? Where is Shambu (Shiva)? Why have you taken the shape of Sita?" Parvati felt abashed and explained how she went there to test him and sought an explanation for Shiva saluting him.

Rama replied: "We are all only aspects of Shiva, worshipping Him at sight and remembering Him out of sight."

Ramakrishna Swami, a long-resident disciple, asked Maharshi the meaning of "Twaiyarunachala Sarvam," *a stanza in the* Five Hymns to Arunachala.
Maharshi explained it in detail, saying that the universe is like a painting on a screen — the screen being the red hill, Arunachala. That which rises and sinks is made up of what it rises from. The finality of the universe is the God Arunachala meditating on Him or on the seer, the Self; there is a mental vibration "I" to which all are reduced. Tracing the source of "I," the primal "I-I" alone remains, and it is inexpressible. The seat of Realization is within and the seeker cannot find it as an object outside him. That seat is bliss and is the core of all beings; hence it is called the Heart. The only useful purpose of the present birth is to turn within and realize it. There is nothing else to do.
D. How is annihilation of predispositions to be accomplished?
M. You are in that condition in realization.
D. Does it mean that, holding on to the Self, the tendencies should be scorched as they begin to emerge?
M. They will themselves be scorched if only you remain as you truly are.

Mr. B.C. Das, the physics lecturer, asked: Contemplation is possible only with control of mind and control can be accomplished only by contemplation. Is this not a vicious circle?

M. Yes, they are interdependent. They must proceed side by side. Practice and dispassion bring about the result gradually. Dispassion is practiced to check the mind from being projected outward; practice is to keep it turned inward. There is a struggle between control and contemplation; it is going on constantly within. Contemplation will in due course be successful.

D. How to begin? Your Grace is needed for it.

M. Grace is always there. "Dispassion cannot be acquired, nor realization of the Truth, nor inherence in the Self, in the absence of Guru's Grace," the Master quoted.

Practice is necessary. It is like training a roguish bull confined to his stall by tempting him with luscious grass and preventing him from straying.

Then the Master read out a stanza from *Tiruvachakam*, which is an address to the mind, saying: "O humming bee (namely, mind)! Why do you take the pains of collecting tiny specks of honey from innumerable flowers? There is One from whom you can have the whole storehouse of honey by simply thinking or seeing or speaking of Him. Go within and hum to Him (*hrimkara*)."

D. Should one have a form in one's mind, supplemented with reading or chanting God's name in one's meditation?

M. What is mental conception except as meditation?

D. Should the form be supplemented by repetition of mantras or dwelling on divine attributes?

M. When *japa* is the predominating tendency, vocal *japa* becomes eventually mental, which is the same as meditation.

Mr. Bose: A form means duality. Is that good?

M. One who questions like that had better adopt the path of inquiry. Form is not for him.

D. In my meditation, a blank interposes; I see no figure.

M. Of course not.

D. What about the blank?

M. Who sees the blank? You must be there. There is consciousness witnessing the blank.

D. Does it mean I must go deeper and deeper?

M. Yes. There is no moment when you are not.

JULY 2, 1936

Dr. Popatlal Lohara, a visitor, has studied several books including Upadesa Saram *and visited several saints,* sadhus *and* yogis, *probably fifteen-hundred as he puts their number. A* sadhu *in Trimbak told him he still has debts to pay, which if done, will enable him to have realization. His only debt, as he conceived it, was the marriage of his son. It has since been performed and he now feels himself free from karmic indebtedness. He therefore seeks Sri Bhagavan's guidance for freedom from "mental unhappiness" which persists in spite of his not being indebted.*

M. Which text of *Upadesa Saram* did you read?

D. The Sanskrit text.

M. It contains the answer to your question.

D. My mind cannot be made steady by any amount of effort. I have been trying it since 1918.

The Master quoted from Upadesa Saram: "Merging the mind into the Heart certainly comprises meritorious duty (karma), devotion (*bhakti*), yoga and supreme wisdom (*jnana*)." That is the whole truth in a nutshell.

D. That does not satisfy my search for happiness. I am unable to keep my mind steady.

The Master quoted again from the same book: "Continuous search for what the mind is results in its disappearance. That is the straight path."

D. How to search for the mind then?

M. The mind is only a bundle of thoughts. The thoughts have their root in the "I"-thought. He quoted: "Whoever investigates the origin of the "I"-thought, for him the ego perishes. This is the true investigation. The true "I" is then found shining by itself."

D. This "I"-thought rises from me. But I do not know the Self.

M. All these are only mental concepts. You are now identifying yourself with a wrong "I," which is the "I"-thought. This "I"-thought rises and sinks, whereas the true significance of "I" is beyond both. There cannot be a break in your being. You, who slept, are also now awake. There was no unhappiness in your deep sleep. Whereas it exists now. What is it that has happened now for this difference to be experienced? There was no "I"-thought in your sleep, whereas it is present now. The true "I" is not manifest and the false "I" is parading itself. This false "I" is the obstacle to your right knowledge. Find out wherefrom this false "I" arises. Then it will disappear. You will be only what you are — i.e., absolute Being.

D. How to do it? I have not succeeded so far.

M. Search for the source of the "I"-thought. That is all one has to do. The universe exists on account of the "I"-thought. If that ends, there is an end of misery, also. The false "I" will end only when its source is sought.

Dr. Lohara asked for the meaning of one stanza in Upadesa Saram.
M. The one then in sleep is also now awake. There was happiness in sleep, but misery in wakefulness. There was no "I"-thought in sleep; but there is now, while awake. The state of happiness and of no "I"-thought in sleep exists without effort. The aim should be to bring about that state even now. That requires effort.

Sleep	Wakefulness	Bring about sleep even in the wak-
Effortless	. . .	ing state and that is realization. The effort is directed to extinguishing the "I"-thought and not for ushering in the true "I." For the latter is eternal and requires no effort on your part.
Happiness	No happiness	
No "I"-thought	"I"-thought	

Dr. Lohara: Why does the mind not sink into the Heart even while meditating?
M. A floating body does not readily sink unless some means are adopted for making it do so. Breath control makes the mind quiescent. The mind must be alert and meditation pursued unremittingly even when it is at peace. Then it sinks into the Heart. Or the floating body might be loaded with weights and made to sink. So also association with the wise will make the mind sink into the Heart.

Such association is both mental and physical. The extremely visible being (of the Guru) pushes the mind inward. He is also in the Heart of the seeker and so he draws the latter's inward-bent mind into the Heart.

This question is asked only when the person begins to meditate and finds it difficult. Let him practice breath control just a little and the mind will be purified. It does not now sink into the Heart because the latent tendencies stand as obstacles. They are removed by breath control or association with the wise. In fact, the mind is always in the Heart. But it is restive and moves about on account of latent tendencies. When the tendencies are made ineffective, it will be restful and at peace.

By breath control, the mind will be only temporarily quiescent, because the tendencies are still there. If the mind is transformed into the Self, it will no longer give trouble. That is done by meditation.

A disciple asked how he could recognize his own natural primal condition.

M. Absolute freedom from thoughts is the state conducive to such recognition.

When Sri Bhagavan and Rangaswami, an attendant, were on the rocks, Bhagavan noticed someone in the Asramam rocking in a rocking chair, and remarked to the attendant: Shiva made over all His own possessions to Vishnu and wandered away in the forests and wilderness and cemeteries and lived on begged food. In His view, non-possession is higher on the scale of happiness than possession of things.

D. What is that higher happiness?

M. To be free from anxieties. Possessions create anxieties such as their safeguarding, their utilization, etc. Non-possession does not bring any anxieties in its train. Therefore, Shiva relinquished everything in favor of Vishnu, and He himself went away happy.

Divestment of possessions is the highest happiness.

JULY 3, 1936

A visitor from Tirukoilur asked if study of the sacred books will reveal the Truth.

M. That will not suffice.

D. Why not?

M. *Samadhi* alone can reveal it. Thoughts cast a veil over Reality and so it cannot be clear in states other than *samadhi*.

D. Is there thought in *samadhi*?

M. There will only be the feeling *I Am* and no other thoughts.

D. Is not *I Am* a thought?

M. The egoless "I am" is no thought; it is realization. The significance of "I" is God. The experience of *I Am* is to *Be Still*.

JULY 4, 1936

The Master observed· Being of the nature of Bliss, why does one continue to crave for happiness? To be rid of that craving is itself salvation. The Scriptures say, "You are That." The imparting of that knowledge is their purpose. The realization must be by your finding out who you are and abiding as That, i.e., your Self. To be repeating "I am that" or "not this" is a waste of time. For the worthy disciple, the work lies within himself and not without.

As Bhagavan was descending the Hill, one of the workers just outside the Asramam stopped work and was about to prostrate before the Master. Then the Master said: To engage in your duty is the true prostration.

The Master's Attendant asked: How?

M. To perform one's duty carefully is the greatest service to God.

(*Then, smiling, he entered the Hall.*)

At lunch, a visitor from Nellore asked the Master for a tiny bit of food (prasad) *from his dish.*

M. Eat without thinking of the ego. Then, what you eat becomes Bhagavan's *prasad*.

After lunch, the Master continued humorously: If I had given you one morsel from my plate, each one would ask for a morsel, too. What will be left for me if I distribute the whole plate to others? So you see that it is not devotion. There is no significance in eating a morsel from my plate. Be a true devotee.

JULY 8, 1936

At 8:00 a.m., the pet squirrel was watching for an opportunity to run out. The Master remarked: All wish to rush out. There is no limit to going out. Happiness lies within and not without.

JULY 20, 1936

A visitor asked if one can realize the Truth by learning the scriptures and study of books?

M. No. So long as predispositions remain latent in the mind, realization cannot be achieved. *Sastra* learning is itself a *vasana*. Realization is only in *samadhi*.

A visitor: What is *mouna* (silence)?

M. *Mouna* is not closing the mouth. It is eternal speech.

D. I do not understand.

M. That state which transcends speech and thought is *mouna*.

D. How to achieve it?

M. Hold some concept firmly and trace it back. By such concentration, silence results. When practice becomes natural, it will end in silence. Meditation without mental activity is silence. Subjugation of the mind is meditation. Deep meditation is eternal speech.

D. How will worldly transactions go on if one observes silence?

M. When women walk with water pots on their heads and chat with their companions they remain very careful, their thoughts concentrated on the loads on their heads. Similarly, when a sage engages in activities, these do not disturb him because his mind abides in *Brahman*.

The Master said on another occasion: Only the sage is a true devotee.

D. What is the result of *Rama Japa* (repetition of God Rama's name)?

M. *Ra* is Reality, *Ma* is the mind; their union is the fruit of *Rama japa*. Utterance of words is not enough. The elimination of thoughts is wisdom. It is the Absolute Existence.

A Muslim visitor asked about asana *(physical posture).*

M. Abidance in God is the only true posture.

Mr. T.K.S. Iyer, a disciple, was excited because someone in the town had spoken disparagingly of the Master. He did not retort and came away excited. So he asked Master what penalty should be paid for his failure to defend him.

M. Patience, more patience; tolerance, more tolerance!

On the death of King George V, two devotees were discussing the matter in the Hall. They were very upset. The Master said to them:

Whoever dies or is lost, what is that to you? Die yourself and lose yourself, becoming one with love.

A man brought with him a silver idol of Subrahmanya and copper idols of Valli and Devayanai. He said to Sri Bhagavan: I have been worshipping them for the last ten years but have been rewarded only with calamities. What shall I do with them? When I asked others, they attributed my worries to some defect in the make-up of the idols — for instance, the difference in the metals of their make. Is it so?

M. Did they say it was wrong to worship?

In answer to a question, Maharshi said: There is a state when words cease and silence prevails.

D. How to communicate thought to each other?

M. That is only when there is the notion of two.

D. How to get peace?

M. That is the natural state. The mind obstructs the innate peace. Our investigation is only in the mind. Investigate the mind; then it will disappear.

There is no entity by the name "mind." Because of the emergence of thoughts, we surmise something from which they start; that we term "mind." When we probe to see what it is, there is nothing of the sort. After it has vanished, Peace will be found to remain eternal.

D. What is *buddhi* (intellect)?

M. The thinking or discriminating faculty. These are mere names. Be it the ego, the mind or the intellect, it is all the same. Whose mind? Whose intellect? The ego's. Is the ego real? No. We misapprehend the ego and call it intellect or mind.

D. Emerson says, "Soul answers soul by itself — not by description or words."

M. Quite so. However much you learn, there will be no bounds to knowledge. You ignore the doubter but try to solve the doubts. On the other hand, hold on to the doubter and the doubts will disappear.

D. The question resolves itself to knowing the Self.

M. Quite so.

D. How to know the Self?

M. See what the Self is. What you consider to be the Self is really either the mind or the intellect or the "I"-thought. The other thoughts arise only after the "I"-thought. So hold on to it. The others will vanish, leaving the Self as the residuum.

D. The difficulty lies in reaching it.

M. There is no reaching it at all because it is eternal, here and now. If the Self were to be gained anew, it would not be permanent.

D. How to obtain equanimity or peace or equilibrium of mind? What is the best way?

M. I have already answered it. Investigate the mind. It is eliminated and you remain.

"*Dristim jnanamayim kritva, pasyet Brahmamayam jagat.*"
By making your standpoint that of wisdom, the world will be seen only as God.

So the question is one of outlook. You pervade all. See yourself and all are understood. But you have now lost hold of your Self and go about doubting other things.

D. How to know the Self?

M. Are there two "I"'s? How do you know your own existence? Do you see yourself with these eyes? Question yourself. How does this question arise? Do I remain to ask it or not? Can I find my Self as in a mirror?

Because your outlook has been outward bent, it has lost sight of the Self and your vision is external. The Self is not found in external objects. Turn your look within and plunge down; you will be the Self.

D. The unknowable can be attained only by the Grace of the unknowable.

M. He helps the attainment. That is the Grace.

D. How to check the mind?

M. Will a thief betray himself? Will the mind find itself? The mind cannot seek the mind. You have ignored what is real and are holding on to the mind which is unreal, and trying to find what it is. Was there mind in your sleep? It was not. It is here now. It is therefore impermanent. Can the mind be found by you? The mind is not you. You think you are the mind and therefore ask me how it is checked. If it is there, it can be checked, but it is not. Understand this truth by search. Search for unreality is fruitless. Therefore, seek the reality, i.e., the Self. That is the way to rule over the mind. There is only one thing Real!

D. What is the one Real thing?

M. That is what *is*; the others are only appearances. Diversity is not its nature. We are reading the printed characters on paper, but ignore the paper which is the background. Similarly, you are taken up by the manifestations of the mind and let go the background. Whose fault is it?

D. Is there a limit to the Self?

M. What is the Self?

D. The individual soul is the Self.

M. What is the individual soul? Is there any difference between the two, or are they identical?

Any new appearances are bound to disappear. Anything created will certainly be destroyed. The eternal is not born nor does it die. We are now confounding appearances with reality. Appearance carries its end in itself. What is it that appears newly? If you cannot find it, surrender unreservedly to the substratum of appearances; then, the reality remains as residue.

D. What happens to man after death?

M. Engage yourself in the living present. The future will take care of itself. Do not worry about the future. The state before creation and the process of creation are dealt with in the scriptures in order that you may know the present. Because you say you are born, therefore they say, yes, and add that God created you.

But do you see God or anything else in your sleep? If God is real, why does He not shine forth in your sleep, also? *You are always* — now the same as you were in sleep. You are not different from that one in sleep. But why should there be a difference in the feelings or experiences of the two states?

Did you ask, while asleep, the question regarding your birth? Or, where do I go after death? Why think of all these now in the wakeful state? Let what is born think of its birth and the remedy, its cause and ultimate results.

What is birth? Is it of the "I"-thought or of the body? Is "I" separate from the body or identical to it? How did this "I"-thought arise? Is the "I"-thought your nature or is anything else of your nature?

D. Who is to ask these questions?

M. Exactly — that is it. There is no end to it all.

D. Are we then to keep quiet?

M. Doubts cease when the confusion (*moha*) is surpassed.

D. Your statements amount to cessation of *vichara* — investigation.

M. If *Atma-vichara* (self-investigation) ceases, *loka vichara* (world-investigation) takes its place.

(*Laughter in the Hall.*)

Engage in self-investigation, then the non-self will disappear. The Self will be left over. This is self-investigation of the Self. The one word "Self" is equivalent to the mind, body, man, individual, the Supreme and all else.

Mr. M. Frydman: One imagines things and enjoys them by strength of imagination. Such creations are possible to *Brahma*, the Creator. Can the same statement apply to His creature, man?

M. This is also your thought.

D. Krishnamurti says that man should find out the "I." Then "I" dissolves away, being only a bundle of circumstances. There is nothing behind the "I." His teaching seems to be very much like Buddha's.

M. Yes — yes, beyond expression.

AUGUST 23, 1936

D. The world is materialistic. What is the remedy for it?

M. Materialistic or spiritual, it is all according to your outlook. Make your outlook right. The creator knows how to take care of His creation.

D. What is the best thing to do for ensuring the future?

M. Take care of the present; the future will take care of itself.

D. The future is the result of the present. So, what should I do to make it good? Or should I keep still?

M. Whose is the doubt? Who is it that wants a course of action? Find the doubter. If you hold the doubter, the doubts will disappear. Having lost hold of the Self, the thoughts afflict you; the world is seen, doubts arise, also anxiety for the future.

Hold fast to the Self, then these [doubt and anxiety] will disappear.

D. How to do it?

M. This question is relevant to matters of non-self, but not to the Self. Do you doubt the existence of your own Self?

D. No. But still, I want to know how the Self could be realized. Is there any method leading to it?

M. Make effort. Just as water is obtained by boring a well, so also you realize the Self by investigation.

D. Yes. But some find water readily and others only with difficulty.

M. But you already see the moisture on the surface. You are hazily aware of the Self. Pursue it. When the effort ceases, the Self shines forth.

D. How to train the mind to look within?

M. By practice. The mind is the intelligent phase leading to its own destruction, for Self to manifest.

D. How to destroy the mind?

M. Water cannot be made *dry*. Seek the Self; then only the mind will be destroyed.

AUGUST 29, 1936

D. How to avoid misery?

M. Has misery a shape? Misery is only unwanted thought. The mind is not strong enough to resist it.

D. How to gain such strength of mind?

M. By worship of God.

D. Meditation of the God of Immanence is hard to understand.

M. Leave God alone. Hold your Self.

D. How to do *japa* (repetition of mantras)?

M. It is of two kinds — gross and subtle. The latter is meditation on it, strengthening the mind.

D. But the mind does not get steady for meditation.

M. It is due to lack of strength.

D. *Sandhya* is usually done mechanically. Similarly other religious duties. Is it useful? Is it not better to do *japa,* etc., knowing their meanings?
M. Um! Um!

A Gujarati gentleman asked Sri Bhagavan: They say that choice is offered us to enjoy merits or demerits after our death. Their succession will be according to our choice. Is it so?
M. Why raise these questions relating to events after death? Why ask, "Was I born? Am I reaping fruits of my past karma," and so on? They will not be raised some time from now when you fall asleep. Why? Are you now different from the one in sleep? You are not. Why do these questions arise now and not in sleep? Find out.

A middle-aged, frail-looking man came with a walking stick in his hand, placed it before Bhagavan, bowed low, and sat near Maharshi. He got up and with great humility offered the stick to Bhagavan, saying it was sandalwood.

Sri Bhagavan told him to keep it for himself, since nothing of Bhagavan's can be safeguarded. Being common property but coveted by some, it may be taken away by any visitor with or without Bhagavan's permission. Then the donor may be displeased.

But the man humbly insisted. Sri Bhagavan could not resist his supplications, and said, "Keep it yourself as *prasad* from Bhagavan." The man then requested that the stick might first be taken and then given to him by Sri Bhagavan with blessings. Sri Bhagavan received it, smelled it, said it was fine, nodded, and handed it back to the man, saying, "Keep it. It will make you always remember me."

A Maharani Sahiba spoke in a gentle and low voice, but quite audibly: Maharajji, I have the good fortune to see you. My eyes have had the pleasure of seeing you, my ears the pleasure of hearing your voice.
I am blessed with everything that a human being could have.
(*Her Highness's voice choked. With great strength of mind she rallied and pro ceeded slowly.*)
I have all that I want, a human being would want . . . But . . . But . . . I . . . I . . . do not have peace of mind . . . Something prevents it. Probably my destiny . . .

There was silence for a few minutes. Then Maharshi in his usual sweet manner spoke: All right. What need be said has been said. Well. What is destiny? There is no destiny. Surrender, and all will be well. Throw all responsibility onto God. Do not bear the burden yourself. What can destiny do to you then?

D. Surrender is impossible.

M. Yes. Complete surrender is impossible in the beginning. Partial surrender is certainly possible for all. In the course of time, that will lead to complete surrender. Well, if surrender is impossible, what can be done? There is no peace of mind. You are helpless to bring it about. It can be done only by surrender.

D. Partial surrender — well — can it undo destiny?

M. Oh, yes! It can.

D. Is not destiny due to past karma?

M. If one is surrendered to God, God will see to it.

D. This being God's dispensation, how does God undo it?

M. All are in Him only.

D. How is God to be seen?

M. Within. If the mind is turned inward, God manifests as inner consciousness.

D. God is in all — in all the objects we see around us. They say we should see God in all of them.

M. God is in all and in the seer. Where else can God be seen? He cannot be found outside. He should be felt within. To see the objects, mind is necessary. To conceive God in them is a mental operation. But that is not real. The consciousness within, purged of the mind, is felt as God.

D. There are, say, beautiful colors. It is a pleasure to watch them. We can see God in them.

M. They are all mental conceptions.

D. There are more than colors. I mentioned colors only as an example.

M. They are similarly mental.

D. There is the body, also — the senses and the mind. The soul makes use of all these for knowing things.

M. The objects or feelings or thoughts are all mental conceptions. The mind rises after rise of the "I"-thought or ego. Wherefrom does the ego rise? From the abstract consciousness or Pure Intelligence.

D. Is it the soul?

M. Soul, mind, or ego are mere words. There are no entities of the kind. Consciousness is the only truth.

D. Then that consciousness cannot give any pleasure.

M. Its very nature is Bliss. Bliss alone is. There is no enjoyer to enjoy pleasure. Enjoyer and joy — both merge in it.

D. There is pleasure and pain in ordinary life. Should we not remain with only pleasure?

M. Pleasure consists in turning and keeping the mind within; pain in sending it outward. There is only pleasure. Absence of pleasure is called pain. One's nature is pleasure — Bliss (*Ananda*).

D. Is it the soul?

M. Soul and God are only mental conceptions.

D. Is God only a mental conception?

M. Yes. Do you think of God in sleep?

D. But sleep is a state of dullness.

M. If God is real, He must remain always. You remain in sleep and in wakefulness — just the same. If God is as true as your Self, God must be in sleep as well as the Self. This thought of God arises only in the wakeful state. Who thinks now?

D. "I" think.

M. Who is this "I"? Who says it? Is it the body?

D. The body speaks.

M. The body does not speak. If so, did it speak in sleep? Who is this "I"?

D. I within the body.

M. Are you within the body or without?

D. I am certainly within the body.

M. Do you know it to be so in your sleep?

D. I remain in my body in sleep, also.

M. Are you aware of being within the body in sleep?

D. Sleep is a state of dullness.

M. The fact is, you are neither within nor without. Sleep is the natural state of being.

D. Then sleep must be a better state than this.

M. There is no superior or inferior state. In sleep, in dream, and in the wakeful state you are just the same. Sleep is a state of happiness; there is no misery. The sense of want, of pain, etc., arises only in the wakeful state. What is the change that has taken place? You are the same in both, but there is difference in happiness. Why? Because the mind has risen now. This mind rises after the "I"-thought. The "I"-thought arises from consciousness. If one abides in it, one is always happy.

D. The sleep state is the state when the mind is quiet. I consider it a worse state.

M. If that were so, why do all desire sleep?

D. It is the body when tired that goes to sleep.

M. Does the body sleep?

D. Yes. It is the condition in which the wear and tear of the body is repaired.

M. Let it be so. But does the body itself sleep or wake up? You yourself said shortly before that the mind is quiet in sleep. The three states are of the mind.

D. Are they not states of the soul functioning through the senses, etc.?

M. They are not of the soul or of the body. The soul remains always uncontaminated. It is the substratum running through all these three states. Wakefulness passes off, I am; the dream state passes off, I am; the sleep state passes off, I am. They repeat themselves, and yet "I Am" remains. They are like pictures moving on the screen in a cinema show. They do not affect the screen. Similarly, I remain unaffected although these states pass off. If it is of the body, are you aware of the body in sleep?

D. No.

M. Without knowing the body to be there, how can the body be said to be in sleep?

D. Because it is still found after waking up.

M. The sense of body is a thought; the thought is of the mind, the mind rises after the "I"-thought, the "I"-thought is the root-thought. If that is held, the other thoughts will disappear. There will then be no body, no mind, not even the ego.

D. What will remain then?

M. The Self in its purity.

D. How can the mind be made to vanish?

M. No attempt is made to destroy it. To think or wish it is itself a thought. If the thinker is sought, the thoughts will disappear.

D. Will they disappear of themselves? It looks very difficult.

M. They will disappear because they are unreal. The idea of difficulty is itself an obstacle to realization. It must be overcome. To remain as the Self is not difficult.

D. It looks easy to think of God in the external world, whereas it seems difficult to remain without thoughts.

M. That is absurd; to look at other things is easy and to look within is difficult! It must be the very opposite.

D. But I do not understand. It is difficult.

M. The very thought of difficulty is the chief obstacle. A little practice will make you think differently.

D. What is the practice?

M. To find out the source of "I."

D. That was the state before one's birth.

M. Why should one think of birth and death? Are you really born? The rising of the mind is called "birth." After mind, the body-thought arises and the body is seen; then the thought of birth, the state before birth, death, the state after death — all these are only of the mind. Whose is the birth?

D. Am I not now born?

M. So long as the body is considered, birth is real. But the body is not "I." The Self is not born nor does it die. There is nothing new. The sages see everything as being in and of the Self; there is no diversity in it. Therefore, there is neither birth nor death.

D. If sleep is such a good state, why does not one like to be in it always?

M. One is always only in sleep. The present waking state is no more than a dream. Dream can take place only in sleep. Sleep is underlying these three states. Manifestation of these three states is again a dream, which is in turn another sleep. In this way, these states of dream and sleep are endless.

Similar to these states, birth and death also are dreams in a sleep. Realistically speaking, there is no birth and death.

SEPTEMBER 8, 1936

Misses Gulbai and Shirinbai Byramjee, two Parsi ladies, were asking questions around one central point. All their questions really amounted to one: I understand that the Self is beyond the ego. My knowledge is theoretical, not practical. How shall I gain *practical* realization of the Self?

M. Realization is nothing to be got afresh. It is already there. All that is necessary is to be rid of the thought, "I have not realized."

D. Then one need not attempt it.

M. No. Stillness of mind or peace is realization. There is no moment when the Self is not.

So long as there is doubt or the feeling of non-realization, an attempt must be made to rid oneself of these thoughts.

The thoughts are due to identification of the Self with the non-self. When the non-self disappears, the Self alone remains. To make room anywhere, it is enough that things are removed. Room is not brought in afresh. Nay, what's more — room is there even when crowded.

Absence of thoughts does not mean a blank. There must be one to know the blank. Knowledge and ignorance are of the mind; they are born of duality. But the Self is beyond knowledge and ignorance. It is light itself. There is no need to see the Self with another Self; there are no two selves. What is not Self is non-self. The non-self cannot see the Self. The Self possesses no sight or hearing. It lies beyond these — *all alone,* as pure consciousness.

A woman, with her necklace round her neck, imagines it has been lost and goes about searching for it, until she is reminded of it by a friend; she has created her own sense of loss, her own anxiety of search and then her own pleasure of recovery. Similarly, the Self is there all along, whether you search for it or not. Again, just as the woman feels as if the lost necklace has been regained, so also the removal of ignorance and the cessation of false identification reveal the Self which is always present — here and now. This is called realization. It is not new, but amounts to elimination of ignorance and nothing more.

Blankness is the evil result of searching the mind. The mind must be cut off, root and branch. See who the thinker is, who the seeker is. Abide as the thinker, the seeker. All thoughts will then disappear.

D. The ego will remain — the thinker.

M. That ego is pure ego purged of thoughts. It is the same as the Self. So long as false identification persists doubts will persist, questions will arise, and there will be no end to them. Doubts will cease only when an end is put to the non-self. That will result in realization of the Self. There will remain no other there to doubt or ask. All these doubts should be resolved within oneself. No amount of words will satisfy. Hold the thinker. Only when the thinker is not held do objects appear outside or doubts arise in the mind.

Language is only a medium for communicating one's thoughts to another. It is called in only after thoughts arise; other thoughts arise after the "I"-thought rises; the "I"-thought is the root of all conversation. When one remains without thinking, another person is understood by means of the universal language of silence.

Silence is ever-speaking; it is a perennial flow of language; it is interrupted by speaking. These words obstruct that mute language. There is electricity flowing in a wire. With resistance to its passage, it glows as a lamp or revolves as a fan. In the wire, it remains as electric energy. Similarly also, silence is the eternal flow of language, obstructed by words.

What one fails to know by conversation extending to several years can be known in a moment in Silence, or in front of Silence — e.g.,

Dakshinamurti, and his four disciples.

That is the highest and most effective language.

There arose a doubt about "I-I" consciousness being the same as *nirvikalpa samadhi* or anything anterior to it.

Sri Bhagavan said that the tiny hole in the Heart remains always closed, but it is opened by *vichara* with the result that "I-I" consciousness shines forth. It is the same as *samadhi*.

D. What is the difference between fainting and sleep?

M. Sleep is sudden and overpowers the person forcibly. A faint is slower, and there is a tingle of resistance kept up. Realization is possible in a faint and impossible in sleep.

D. What is the state just before death?

M. When a person gasps for breath, it indicates that the person is unconscious of the body; another body has been held and the person swings to and fro. While gasping, there is a more violent gasp at intervals and that indicates the oscillation between the two bodies due to the present attachment not having been completely snapped. I noticed it in the case of my mother and of Palaniswami.

D. Does the new body involved in that state represent the next reincarnation of the person?

M. Yes. While gasping, the person is in something like a dream, not aware of the present environment.

Compiler's note: It must be remembered that Sri Bhagavan had been with his mother from 8:00 a.m. to 8:00 p.m. until she passed away. He was all along holding her head with one hand, the other hand placed on her bosom. What does it signify? He said later, that there was a struggle between him and his mother, until her spirit reached the Heart.

Evidently the soul passes through a series of subtle experiences, and Sri Bhagavan's touch generates a current which turns the soul back from its wandering into the Heart.

The *samskaras*, however, persist and a struggle is kept up between the spiritual force set up by his touch and the innate *samskaras*, until the latter are entirely destroyed and the soul is led into the Heart to rest in eternal Peace, which is the same as Liberation.

Its entry into the Heart is signified by a peculiar sensation perceptible to the Mahatma — similar to the tinkling of a bell.

When Maharshi attended on Palaniswami on his deathbed, he took away his hand after the above signal. But Palaniswami's eyes opened immediately, signifying that the spirit had escaped through them, thereby indicating a higher rebirth, but not Liberation. Having once noticed it with Palaniswami, Maharshi continued touching his mother for a few minutes longer — even after the signal of the soul passing into the Heart — and thus ensured her Liberation. This was confirmed by the look of perfect peace and composure on her features.

SEPTEMBER 15, 1936

Sri Bhagavan said: The *jnani* says, "I am the body"; the *ajnani* says, "I am the body"; what is the difference? "I am" is the truth. The body is the limitation. The *ajnani* limits the "I" to the body. "I" remains independent of the body in sleep. The same "I" is now in the wakeful state. Though imagined to be within the body, "I" is without the body. The wrong notion is not "I am the body." "I" says so. The body is insentient and cannot say so. The mistake lies in thinking that "I" is what "I" is not. "I" is not insentient. "I" cannot be the inert body. The body's movements are confounded with "I," and misery is the result. Whether the body works or not, "I" remains free and happy. The *ajnani*'s "I" is the body only. That is the whole error. The *jnani*'s "I" includes the body and everything else. Clearly, some intermediate entity arises and gives rise to the confusion.

Mr. Vaidyanatha Iyer, a lawyer, asked: If the *jnani* says, "I am the body," what happens to him in death?

M. He does not identify himself with the body even now.

D. But you said just before that the *jnani* says, "I am the body."

M. Yes. His "I" includes the body. For there cannot be anything apart from "I" for him. If the body falls away, there is no loss for the "I." "I" remains the same. If the body feels dead, let it raise the question. Being inert, it cannot. "I" never dies and does not ask the question. Who then dies? Who asks questions?

D. For whom are all the *sastras* then? They cannot be for the real "I." They must be for the unreal "I." The real one does not require them. It is strange that the unreal should have so many *sastras* for him.

M. Yes. Quite so. Death is only a thought and nothing more. He who thinks raises troubles. Let the thinker tell us what happens to him in death. The real "I" is silent. One should not think "I am this — I am not that." To say "this or that" is wrong. They are also limitations. Only "I am" is the truth.

Silence is "I." If one thinks "I am this," another thinks "I am this" and so on; there is a clash of thoughts and so many religions are the result. The truth remains as it is, not affected by any statements, conflicting or otherwise.

D. What is death? Is it not the falling away of the body?

M. Do you not desire it in sleep? What goes wrong then?

D. But I know I shall wake up.

M. Yes — thought again. There is the preceding thought, "I shall wake up." Thoughts rule the life. Freedom from thoughts is one's true nature — Bliss.

SEPTEMBER 22, 1936

Conversing with R. Seshagiri Rao, a visitor, Maharshi remarked that a Self-realized sage (Atma jnani) *alone can be a good* karma yogi:

After the sense of doership has gone, let us see what happens. Sri Shankara advised inaction. But did he not write commentaries and take part in disputation? Do not trouble yourself about doing action or otherwise. Know Thyself. Then let us see whose action it is. Let action complete itself. So long as there is the doer, he must reap the fruits of his action. If he does not think himself to be the doer, there is no action for him. He is an ascetic who has renounced worldly life (*sannyasin*).

D. How did the ego arise?

M. It is not necessary to know it. Know the present. Not knowing that, why do you worry about other times?

Maharshi said in reply to a question: Is the world within you or without you? Does it exist apart from you? Does the world come and tell you "I exist"?

The Brahmin questioner resumed: How do we know that action is ours or not?

M. If the fruits of actions do not affect the person, he is free from action.

D. Is intellectual knowledge enough?

M. Unless intellectually known, how to practice it? Learn it intellectually first, then do not stop there. Practice it.

Maharshi then remarked: When you adhere to one philosophical system (*siddhanta*), you are obliged to condemn the others. That is the case with the heads of monasteries (*matadhipatis*).

All people cannot be expected to do the same kind of action. Each one acts according to his temperament and past lives. Wisdom, Devotion, Action (*jnana, bhakti, karma*) are all interlocked. Meditation on forms is according to one's own mind. It is meant for ridding oneself of other forms and confining oneself to one form. It leads to the goal. It is impossible to fix the mind in the Heart to start with, so these aids are necessary initially. Krishna says there is no birth (*janma*) to you, me, etc., and later says he was born before Aditya, etc. Arjuna disputes it. Therefore, it is certain that each one thinks of God according to his own degree of advancement.

You say you are the body in the wakeful state; not the body in sleep. Bodies being several-fold for an individual, should not there be infinite capacities for God? Whichever method one follows, that method is encouraged by the Sages, for it will lead to the goal.

D. Are there heaven (*swarga*) and hell (*naraka*)?
M. There must be *someone* to go there. They are like dreams. We see time and space exist in a dream, also. Which is true, dream or wakefulness?
D. So we must rid ourselves of lust (*kama*), anger (*krodha*), etc.?
M. Give up thoughts. You need not give up anything else. *You* must be there to see anything. It is the Self. Self is ever conscious.
D. Are pilgrimages, etc., good?
M. Yes.
D. What effort is necessary for reaching the Self?
M. "I" should be destroyed. Self is not to be reached. Is there any moment when Self is not? It is not new. Be as you are. What is new cannot be permanent. What is real must always exist.
D. What is sacrifice through wisdom (*jnana yajna*)?
M. Other disciplines exist for it. Practice is for gaining wisdom (*jnana*).
D. Are *jivanmuktas* (living liberated souls) of different kinds?
M. What does it matter if they differ externally? There is no difference in their wisdom (*jnana*).
D. While loyal to one Master, can one respect others?
M. Guru is only one. He is not physical. So long as there is weakness, the support of strength is needed.
D. J. Krishnamurti says, "No Guru is necessary."
M. How did he know? One can say so after realizing but not before.
D. You have gained this state by great effort. What shall we poor souls do?
M. We are in our Self. We are not in the world.
D. Heaven and hell — what are they?
M. You carry heaven and hell with you. Your lust, anger, etc. produce these regions. They are like dreams.
D. The *Gita* says that if a man fixes his attention between the eyebrows and

holds his breath, he reaches the Supreme state. How is that done?

M. You are always in the Self and there is no "reaching" it. The eyebrow is only a place where attention is to be fixed (seat of meditation — *upasanasthana*).

D. You have spoken of the Heart as the seat of meditation?

M. Yes, it is also that.

D. What is the Heart?

M. It is the center of the Self. The Self is the center of centers. The Heart represents the psychic center, not the physical center.

D. The term *jnana* is realized wisdom. The same term is used for the method, also. Why?

M. *Jnana* includes the method since it ultimately results in realization.

D. Is a man to engage in teaching his knowledge, however imperfect?

M. If his *prarabdha* be that way, yes.

In the seventh chapter of the *Gita*, Arjuna asks if karma is a method (*sadhana*). Krishna answers that it is so if done without sense of doership.

So also are karmas approved by scriptures that deny karma. The karma disapproved of by them is that which is done with a sense of doership. Do not leave karma. You cannot do so. Give up the sense of doership. Karma will go on automatically. Or karma will drop away from you. If karma be your lot according to *prarabdha,* it will surely be done whether you will it or not; if karma not be your lot, it will not be done even if you intently engage in it. Janaka, Suka, etc., did also work without *ahamkara* (ego-sense). Karma may be done for fame, or may be done unselfishly and for the public good. Yet even then they want applause. So it is really selfish.

D. What is that one thing, knowing which all doubts are solved?

M. Know the doubter. If the doubter be held, doubts will not arise. *Here the doubter is transcendental.* Again, when the doubter ceases to exist, there will be no doubts arising. From where could they arise? All are *jnanis, jivanmuktas.* Only they are not aware of the fact. Doubts must be uprooted. This means that the doubter must be uprooted. *Here the doubter is the mind.*

D. What is the method?

M. "Who am I?" is the investigation.

D. May we perform *japa?*

M. Why should you think, "I am this"? Investigate and the thoughts will cease. What *is,* namely the Self, will be revealed as the inescapable residue.

D. Is *Hatha Yoga* necessary?

M. It is one of the aids — not that it is always necessary. It depends upon the person. *Vichara* surpasses *pranayama.* In *Yoga Vasishta,* Chudala advises investigation (*vichara*) to Sikhidvaja for killing the ego.

Reality can be reached by holding on to *prana* or intellect. *Hatha Yoga* is the former; *vichara* is the latter.

D. Is there any individuality for the *jnani* after Realization?

M. How can he retain individuality?

Even ordinarily the elders advise *achamana* and *pranayama* before undertaking any work — be it worldly or otherworldly. That means, concentration of mind accomplishes the work.

D. I meditate on *neti-neti* (not this-not this).

M. No — that is not meditation. Find the source. You must reach the source without fail. The false "I" will disappear and the real "I" will be realized. The former cannot exist apart from the latter.

SEPTEMBER 24, 1936

M. Ignorance *(ajnana)* is of two kinds:

1. Forgetfulness of the Self.
2. Obstruction to the knowledge of the Self.

Aids are meant for eradicating thoughts; these thoughts are the re-manifestations of predispositions remaining in seed-form; they give rise to diversity from which all troubles arise. These aids are, hearing the truth from the Master (*sravana*), etc.

The effects of *sravana* may be immediate and the disciple realizes the truth all at once. This can happen only for the well-advanced disciple.

Otherwise, the disciple feels that he is unable to realize the truth, even after repeatedly hearing it. What is it due to? Impurities in his mind: ignorance, doubt, and wrong identity are the obstacles to be removed.

1. To remove ignorance completely, he has to hear the truth repeatedly, until his knowledge of the subject-matter becomes perfect;
2. To remove doubts, he must reflect on what he has heard; ultimately his knowledge will be free from doubts of any kind;
3. To remove the wrong identification of the Self with the non-self (such as the body, the senses, the mind, or the intellect), his mind must become one-pointed.

All these things accomplished, the obstacles are at an end and *samadhi* results; that is, Peace reigns.

Some say that one should never cease to engage in hearing, reflection and one-pointedness. These are not fulfilled by reading books, but only by continued practice to keep the mind withdrawn.

The aspirant may be *kritopasaka* or *akritopasaka*. The former is fit to realize the Self, even with the slightest stimulus: only some little doubt stands in his way; it is easily removed if he hears the truth once from the Master. Immediately he gains the *samadhi* state. It is presumed that he had already completed *sravana*, reflection, etc. in previous births; they are no longer necessary for him.

For the latter all these aids are necessary; for him doubts crop up even after repeated hearing; therefore he must not give up aids until he gains the *samadhi* state.

Sravana removes the illusion of the Self being one with the body, etc. Reflection makes it clear that Knowledge is Self. One-pointedness reveals the Self as being Infinite and Blissful.

Mr. Duncan Greenlees wrote as follows: One at times has had vivid flashes of a consciousness whose center is outside the normal self and which seems to be inclusive. Without concerning the mind with philosophical concepts, how would Bhagavan advise us to work towards getting, retaining and extending those flashes? Does *abhyasa* (practice) in such experiences involve retirement?

Sri Bhagavan answered: Outside . . . for whom is inside or outside? They can exist only so long as there are subject and object. Again, for whom are these two? They both will resolve into the subject. See who is in the subject. The investigation will lead you to pure consciousness, which is beyond the subject.

Normal self is the mind. This mind is with limitations, but pure consciousness is beyond limitations and reached by investigation.

Getting — Self is always there. One seeks to destroy the obstacles to the revelation of the Self.

Retaining — Having once gained the Self, it will be understood to be "Here and Now." It is never lost.

Extending — There is no extending the Self, for it is always without conraction or expansion.

Retirement — Abiding in the Self is solitude, since there is nothing alien to the Self. Retirement must be from one place to another. There is neither the one nor the other apart from the Self. All being the Self, retirement is impossible and inconsistent.

Abhyasa is investigation into the Self.

A devotee asked Maharshi about some disagreeable statements made by a certain man well-known to Maharshi.

M: I permit him to do so. I have permitted him already. Let him do so even more. Let others follow suit. Only let them leave me alone. If because of these reports no one comes to me, I shall consider it a great service done to me. Moreover, if he cares to publish books containing scandals of me, and if he makes money by their sale, it is really good. Such books will sell even more quickly and in larger numbers than others. He is doing me a very good turn.

(Saying so, he laughed.)

There was a reference to the same subject [September 27, 1936] when Maharshi was alone. The villifier seems to be getting into hot water on account of his inconsiderate action. When it was mentioned, Maharshi seemed concerned for the man's safety and said with obvious sympathy: Even if allowed to have his own way of earning money, the man gets into trouble. If he availed himself of our indulgence and acted sensibly, he could have got on well. But what can we do?

An aristocratic lady looking very intelligent and pensive, asked: We had heard of you, Maharajji, as the kindest and noblest soul. We had long desired to have your *darshan*. I came here once before, on the 14th of last month, but could not remain in your holy presence so long as I wished. Being a woman and also young, I could not stand the people around, and so broke away hurriedly after asking one or two simple questions. There are no holy men like you in our part of the country. I am happy as I have everything I want. But I do not have that peace of mind which brings happiness. I now come here seeking your blessing so that I may gain it.

M. *Bhakti* fulfills your desire.

D. I want to know how I can gain that peace of mind. Kindly advise me.

M. Yes — devotion and surrender.

D. Am I worthy of being a devotee?

M. Everyone can be a devotee. Spiritual fare is common to all and never denied to anyone — be the person old or young, male or female.

D. That is exactly what I am anxious to know. I am young and a *grihini* (housewife). There are duties of *grihastha dharma* (the household). Is devotion consistent with such a position?

M. Certainly. What are you? You are not the body. You are Pure Consciousness. *Grihastha dharma* and the world are only phenomena appearing on that Pure Consciousness. It remains unaffected. What prevents you from being your own Self?

D. Yes. I am already aware of the line of teaching of Maharshi. It is the quest for the Self. But my doubt persists whether such quest is compatible with *grihastha* life.

M. The Self is always there. It is you. There is nothing but you. Nothing can be apart from you. The question of compatibility or otherwise does not arise.

D. I shall be more definite. Though a stranger, I am obliged to confess the cause of my anxiety. I am blessed with children. A boy — a good *brahmachari* — passed away in February. I was grief-stricken. I was disgusted with this life. I want to devote myself to spiritual life. But my duties as a *grihini* do not permit me to lead a retired life. Hence my doubt.

M. Retirement means abidance in the Self. Nothing more. It is not leaving one set of surroundings and getting entangled in another set, even leaving the concrete world and becoming involved in a mental world.

The birth of the son, his death, etc., are seen in the Self only.

Recall the state of sleep. Were you aware of anything happening? If the son or the world be real, should they not be present with you in sleep? You cannot deny your existence in sleep. Nor can you deny you were happy then. You are the same person now speaking and raising doubts. You are not happy, according to you. But you were happy in sleep. What has transpired in the meantime that happiness of sleep has broken down? It is the rise of the ego. That is the new arrival in the *jagrat* state. There was no ego in sleep. The birth of the ego is called the birth of the person. There is no other kind of birth. Whatever is born is bound to die. Kill the ego; there is no fear of recurring death for what is already dead. The Self remains even after death of the ego. That is Bliss — that is Immortality.

D. How is that to be done?

M. See for whom these doubts exist. Who is the doubter? Who is the thinker? That is the ego. Hold it. The other thoughts will die away. The ego is left pure; see wherefrom the ego arises. That is pure consciousness.

D. It seems difficult. May we proceed by *Bhakti Marga*?

M. It is according to individual temperament and equipment. *Bhakti* is the same as *vichara*.

D. I mean meditation, etc.

M. Yes. Meditation is on a form. That will drive away other thoughts. The one thought of God will dominate others. That is concentration. The object of meditation is thus the same as that of *vichara*.

D. Do we not see God in concrete form?

M. Yes. God is seen in the mind. The concrete form may be seen. Still it is only in the devotee's mind. The form and appearance of God-manifestation are determined by the mind of the devotee. But it is not the finality. There is still the sense of duality.

It is like a dream-vision. After God is perceived, *vichara* begins. That ends in Realization of the Self. *Vichara* is the ultimate route.

Of course, only a few find *vichara* practicable. Others find *bhakti* easier.

D. Did not Mr. Brunton find you in London? Was it only a dream?

M. Yes. He had the vision. He saw me in his mind.

D. Did he not see this concrete form?

M. Yes, still in his mind.

D. How shall I reach the Self?

M. There is no reaching the Self. If the Self were to be reached, it would mean that the Self is not here and now, but that it should be got anew. What is got afresh, will again be lost. So it will be impermanent. What is not permanent is not worth striving for. So I say, the Self is not reached. You are the Self. You are already That. The fact is that you are ignorant of your blissful state. Ignorance supervenes and draws a veil over the pure Bliss. Attempts are directed only to remove this ignorance. This ignorance consists in wrong knowledge. The wrong knowledge consists in false identification of the Self with the body, the mind, etc. This false identity must go, and what remains only is the Self.

D. How is that to happen?

M. By inquiry into the Self.

D. It is difficult. Can I realize the Self, Maharaj? Kindly tell me. It looks so difficult.

M. You are already the Self. Therefore, realization is common to everyone. Realization knows no difference in the aspirants. This very doubt, "Can I realize?" or the feeling, "I have not realized" are the obstacles. Be free from these, also.

D. But there should be the experience. Unless I have the experience, how can I be free from these afflicting thoughts?

M. These are also in the mind. They are there because you have identified yourself with the body. If this false identity drops away, ignorance vanishes and Truth is revealed.

D. Yet, I find it difficult. There are disciples of Bhagavan who have had his

Grace and realized themselves without any considerable difficulty. I too, wish to have that Grace. Being a woman and living at a great distance, I cannot avail myself of Maharshi's holy company as much as I would wish. Possibly I may not be able to return. I request Bhagavan's Grace. When I am back at my place, I want to remember Bhagavan. May Bhagavan be pleased to grant my prayer!

M. Where are you going? You are not going anywhere. Even supposing you are the body, has your body come from Lucknow to Tiruvannamalai? You had simply sat in the car and one conveyance or another had moved; and finally you say that you have arrived here. The fact is that you are not the body. The Self does not move. The world moves in it. You are only what you are. There is no change in you. So then, even after what looks like departure from here, you are here and there and everywhere. These scenes shift.

As for Grace, it is within you. Were it external, it would be useless. Grace is the Self. You are never out of its operation. Grace is always there.

D. I mean that when I remember your form, my mind should be strengthened and that response should come from your side, too. I should not be left to my individual efforts, which are after all only weak.

M. Grace is the Self. I have already said, "If you remember Bhagavan, you are prompted to do so by the Self." Is not Grace already there? Is there a moment when Grace is not operating in you? Your remembrance is the forerunner of Grace. That is the response, that is the stimulus, that is the Self, and that is Grace. There is no cause for anxiety.

D. Can I engage in spiritual practice, even remaining in *samsara?*

M. Yes, certainly. One ought to do so.

D. Is not *samsara* a hindrance? Do not all the holy books advocate renunciation?

M. *Samsara* is only in your mind. The world does not speak out, saying, "I am the world." Otherwise, it must be ever there — not excluding your sleep. Since it is not in sleep, it is impermanent. Being impermanent, it has no stamina. Having no stamina, it is easily subdued by the Self. The Self alone is permanent. Renunciation is non-identification of the Self with the non-self. On the disappearance of ignorance, the non-self ceases to exist. That is true renunciation.

D. Why did you then leave your home in your youth?

M. That is my *prarabdha* (fate). One's course of conduct in this life is determined by one's *prarabdha.* My *prarabdha* is this way. Your *prarabdha* is that way.

D. Should I not also renounce?

M. If that had been your *prarabdha,* the question would not have arisen.

D. I should therefore remain in the world and engage in spiritual practice. Well, can I get realization in this life?

M. This has already been answered. You are always the Self. Earnest efforts never fail. Success is bound to result.

D. Will Maharshi be pleased to extend Grace to me, also?

(Maharshi smiled and said "Um! Um!" With blessings and salutation, the interview came to a close and the party departed immediately.)

SEPTEMBER 30, 1936

D. Sri Ramakrishna touched Vivekananda and the latter realized Bliss. Is it possible?

M. Sri Ramakrishna did not touch all for that purpose. He did not create *Atma.* He did not create Realization. Vivekananda was ripe. He was anxious to realize. He must have completed the preliminary course in past births. Such is possible for ripe persons only.

D. Can the same miracle be worked for all?

M. If they are fit. Fitness is the point. A strong man controls a weaker man; a strong mind controls a weaker mind. That was what happened in this case. The effect was only temporary. Why did Vivekananda not stay quiet? Why did he wander about after such a miracle? Because the effect was only temporary.

D. How is the mind to dive into the Heart?

M. The mind now sees itself diversified as the universe. If the diversity is not manifest it remains in its own essence; that is the Heart. Entering the Heart means remaining without distractions.

The Heart is the only Reality. The mind is only a transient phase. To remain as one's Self is to enter the Heart.

Because a man identifies himself with the body, he sees the world separate from him. This wrong identification arises because he has lost his moorings and swerved from his original state. He is now advised to give up all these false ideas, trace back his source, and remain as the Self. In that state, there are no differences. No questions will arise.

All the *sastras* are meant only to make man retrace his steps to the original source. He need not gain anything new. He must only give up his false ideas and useless accretions. Instead of doing it, he tries to catch hold of something strange and mysterious because he believes his happiness lies elsewhere. That is the mistake.

If one remains as the Self, there is bliss. Probably he thinks that being quiet does not bring about the state of bliss. That is due to his ignorance. The only practice is to find out "to whom these questions arise."

D. How to control lust, anger, etc.?

M. Whose are these passions? Find out. If you remain as the Self, nothing will be found apart from the Self. Then there will be no need to control, etc.

D. If a person whom we love dies, grief results. Shall we avoid such grief by either loving all alike or by not loving at all?

M. If one dies, it results in grief for the other who lives. The way to get rid of grief *is not to live*. Kill the one who grieves. Who will remain then to suffer? The ego must die. That is the only way.

The two alternatives amount to the same state. When all have become the one Self, who is there to be loved or hated?

D. What is the Sun *marga*? What is the Moon *marga*? Which of them is easier?

M. *Ravi marga* (Sun *marga*) is *jnana*. Moon *marga* is yoga. They think that after purifying the 72,000 *nadis* in the body, *sushumna* is entered, the mind passes up to the *sahasrara*, and there is nectar trickling.

These are all mental concepts. The person is already overwhelmed by world concepts. Other concepts are now added in the shape of this yoga. The object of all these is to rid man of concepts and to make him inhere as the pure Self — i.e., Absolute consciousness, bereft of thoughts! Why not go straight to it? Why add new encumbrances to the already existing ones?

OCTOBER 1, 1936

Mr. F.G. Pearce, Principal, Scindia School (Gwalior), said Bhagavan has stated in the following verse:

"The illiterates are certainly better off than the literates whose egos are not destroyed by the quest of the self."
— Sad-Vidya Anubandham (Supplement, sloka 36)

This being so, could Bhagavan advise a schoolmaster (who feels this to be true) how to carry on education in such a way that the desire for literacy and intellectual knowledge may not obscure the more important search for the Self? Are the two incompatible? If they are not, then from what age, and by what means, can young people best be stimulated towards the search for the Real Truth within?

M. Pride of learning and desire for appreciation are condemned, and not learning itself. Learning leading to search for Truth and humility is good.

The above questioner spent two very precious days near Bhagavan Maharshi (whom he had not seen since — seventeen years ago — he visited Him for a few minutes on the hillside). His duties now compel him to take his body far away again to the north, and it may be years before he can return.

He humbly requests Bhagavan to make a strong link with him, and to continue to help him with his Grace, in the quest of the Self.

(*Maharshi had a gentle smile for this.*)

Mr. Duncan Greenlees quoted a few verses from Srimad Bhagavatam *to the following effect:*

- "See the Self in yourself like the pure ether in all beings, in and out."
- "Unashamed, fall prostrate before even an outcast, a cow or an ass."
- "So long as "I" am not perceived in all, worship all with body and mind."
- "With right knowledge, see all as *Brahma*. This once clear, all doubts are at an end and you will remain withdrawn in the Self."

He then raised the following questions: Is this a true path to realization of the One Self? Is it not easier for some to practice seeing Bhagavan in whatever meets the mind than to seek the super-mental through the mental inquiry "Who am I?"

M. Yes. When you see God in all, do you think of God or do you not? You should certainly keep God in your mind for seeing God all around you. Keeping God in your mind becomes *dhyana* — the stage before realization. Realization is in the Self only. *Dhyana* must precede it. Whether you make *dhyana* of God or of Self, it is immaterial; the goal is the same.

But you cannot escape the Self. You want to see God in all, but not in yourself? If all are God, are you not included in that all? Yourself being God, is it a wonder that all are God? There must be a seer and thinker even for the practice. Who is he?

D. Through poetry, music, *japa, bhajan,* beautiful landscapes, reading the lives of spiritual heroes, etc., one sometimes experiences a true sense of all-unity. Is that feeling of deep, blissful quiet (wherein the personal self has no place) the "entering into the Heart" of which Bhagavan speaks? Will practice of that lead to a deeper *samadhi,* and so ultimately to a full vision of the Real?

M. Again, there is happiness at pleasant sights, etc. It is the happiness inherent in the Self. That happiness is not alien and afar. You are diving into the Pure Self on occasions, which you consider pleasurable. That diving reveals the Self-existent Bliss. But the association of ideas is responsible for foisting this bliss onto other things or happenings. In fact, it is within you. On these occasions you are plunging into the Self, though unconsciously. If you do so consciously, you call it Realization. I want you to dive consciously into the Self, i.e., into the Heart.

D. If the Self is always realized, we should only keep still. Is that so?
M. If you can keep still without engaging in any other pursuits, it is very good. If that cannot be done, where is the use of being quiet so far as realization is concerned? So long as one is obliged to be active, let him not give up the attempt to realize the Self.

A young man from Dindigul spoke to Sri Bhagavan, saying that he had learned in his stay of a few days that all that he need do is to inquire, "Who am I?" He wanted to know if any discipline was to be observed, and started with the question, "Where should I do the inquiry?" meaning if he should do it in Guru sannidhi (the presence of the Master).
M. The inquiry should be from where the "I" is.
D. People labor for gaining the *summum bonum* of life. I think that they are not on the right track. Sri Bhagavan has made considerable *tapas* and achieved the goal. Sri Bhagavan also desires that all should reach the goal and is willing to help them to that end. His vicarious *tapas* must enable others to reach the goal rather easily. They need not undergo all the hardships that Sri Bhagavan has undergone. Their way has been made easy for them by Sri Bhagavan. Am I not right?
Maharshi smiled and said: If that were so everyone would easily reach the goal, but each one must work for himself.

A young man from Mysore gave a written slip to Sri Bhagavan and waited for an answer. He had asked Sri Bhagavan to say where other Mahatmas could be found whom he might approach for guidance. He confessed he had left his home without informing his elders so that he might seek God through Mahatmas. True, he knew nothing of God or of the search for Him. Therefore, he desired to see Mahatmas. Sri Bhagavan simply returned the note, saying: I must answer any and every question. Unless I do so, I am not great.
The boy tore away the slip and wrote another, which said: You are kind to squir-

rels and hares. You fondle them when they struggle to run away from you.
Yet you are indifferent to human beings. For instance, I have left my home
and am waiting for a fortnight. I have had no food some days. I am strug-
gling. Still, you do not care for me.

M. Look here. I am not endowed with clairvoyance. God has not bestowed
that gift on me. What shall I do? How can I answer your questions? People
call me Maharshi and treat me like this. But I do not see myself as a Maharshi. On the other hand, everyone is a Maharshi to me. It is good that
you in this early age are attempting to seek God. Concentrate on Him. Do
your work without desiring the fruits thereof. That is all you should do.

An extract from *A Hermit in the Himalayas* was found in the *Sunday Times*. It
related to recapitulation of past incarnations. In it, Paul Brunton mentioned
the Buddhist methods of gaining that faculty. Sri Bhagavan said, "There is
a class of people who want to know all about their future or their past.
They ignore the present. The load from the past forms the present misery.
The attempt to recall the past is a waste of time."

There was a reference to reincarnation. Reincarnation of Shanti Devi tallies
with the human standards of time. The latest case reported of a boy of
seven is different, however. He recalls his past births. Inquiries go to show
that the previous body was given up ten months ago.

The question arises how the matter stood for six years and two months
previous to the death of the former body. Did the soul occupy two bodies
at the same time?

Sri Bhagavan pointed out that the seven years is according to the boy;
ten months is according to the observer. The difference is due to these two
different *upadhis*. The boy's experience, extending to seven years, has been
calculated by the observer to cover only ten months of his own time.

(*Sri Bhagavan again referred to Lila's story in* Yoga Vasishta.)

Dr. Syed, a Muslim Professor, is here now. A skeptic friend of his confronted
him with the question: "What miracle does your Maharshi work?"

Dr. Syed replied, "Refreshing Peace within is the highest miracle. Maharshi possesses it."

"What is that to us?" the other man asked. He (Dr. Syed) replied, "The
same Peace is bestowed on all visitors to be shared by them. Mr. Paul Brunton
had mentioned it in his book. Everyone feels it every day in Maharshi's
presence."

The whole conversation was mentioned to Sri Bhagavan with the following addition: Parasurama has said that he felt some refreshing peace within when he met Samvritta on the way. So he made him out to be a great saint. Is not such peace the sole criterion of a Mahatma's presence? Is there anything else?

Sri Bhagavan said: A Madhva saint, Tatvaroyar, had composed a *bharani* on his Master, Swarupanand. Pundits objected to the composition, saying that it was reserved for those who have killed more than a thousand elephants in battle, whereas Swarupanand was an idle man sitting somewhere unknown to people and did not deserve that praise. Tatvaroyar asked them all to assemble before his Master so that they might see for themselves if he could slay one thousand elephants at a time. They did so. As soon as they appeared, they were struck dumb and remained in beatific peace for a few days without the least movement. When they regained their senses, they saluted both, the Master and the disciple, saying that they were more than satisfied. Swarupanand surpassed the warriors in that he could subdue their egos, which is a much more formidable task than slaying a thousand elephants.

(*Maharshi said that the moral was clear. Peace is the sole criterion of a Mahatma's presence.*)

OCTOBER 20, 1936

Dr. Syed: Sri Bhagavan says that the Heart is the Self. Psychology has it that malice, envy, jealousy, and all passions have their seat in the heart. How are these two statements to be reconciled?

M. The whole cosmos is contained in one pinhole in the Heart. These passions are part of the cosmos. They are *avidya* (ignorance).

D. How did *avidya* arise?

M. *Avidya* is like *maya* [that which is not is *maya* (illusion)]. Similarly, that which is not is ignorance. Therefore, the question does not arise. Nevertheless, the question is asked. Then ask, "Whose is the *avidya?*" *Avidya* is ignorance. It implies subject and object. Become the subject and there will be no object.

D. What is *avidya?*

M. Ignorance of Self. Who is ignorant of the Self? The self must be ignorant of Self. Are there two selves?

D. Does Bhagavan see the world as part and parcel of Himself? How does he see the world?

M. The Self alone *is* and nothing else. However, it is differentiated owing to ignorance. Differentiation is threefold: 1. of the same kind, 2. of a different kind, and 3. as parts in itself. The world is not another self similar to the Self. It is not different from the Self; nor is it part of the Self.

D. Is not the world reflected on the Self?

M. For reflection, there must be an object and an image. But the Self does not admit of these differences.

D. Doesn't Bhagavan see the world?

M. Whom do you mean by Bhagavan?

D. A *jiva* advanced more than I.

M. If you understand your *jiva*, the other *jiva* is also understood.

D. I do not wish to discuss. I want to learn. Please instruct me.

M. Because you desire to learn, discussion is unavoidable. Leave all this aside. Consider your sleep. Are you aware of bondage or do you seek means for release? Are you aware of the body itself? The sense of bondage is associated with the body. Otherwise there is no bondage, no material to bind with, and no one to be bound. These appear, however, in your wakeful state. Consider to whom they appear.

D. To the mind.

M. Watch the mind. You must stand aloof from it. You are not the mind. And the Self will remain, always.

D. Does Sri Bhagavan believe in evolution?

M. Evolution must be from one state to another. When no differences are admitted, how can evolution arise?

D. Why does Sri Krishna say, "After several rebirths, the seeker gains knowledge and thus knows Me." There must be evolution from stage to stage.

M. How does *Bhagavad Gita* begin? "Neither I was not, nor you, nor these chiefs, etc." "Neither is it born, nor does it die, etc." So there is no birth, no death, no present as you look at it. Reality was, is, and will be. It is changeless. Later, Arjuna asked Sri Krishna how he could have lived before *Aditya*. Then Krishna, seeing Arjuna was confounding Him with the gross body, spoke to him accordingly. The instruction is for the one who sees diversity. In reality, there is neither bondage nor *mukti* for himself or for others, from the *jnani's* standpoint.

D. Are all in liberation?

M. Where is *all*? There is no liberation, either. It could be only if there were bondage. There was really no bondage, and so it follows, there is no liberation.

D. But to evolve through births, there must be practice, years of *abhyasa*.

M. *Abhyasa* is only to prevent any disturbance to the inherent peace. There is no question of years. Prevent this thought at this moment. You are in your natural state whether you make *abhyasa* or not.

Another man asked: Why do not all realize the Self in that case?
M. It is the same question in another guise. Why do you raise this question? Inasmuch as you raise this question of *abhyasa*, it shows you require *abhyasa*. Make it.

But to remain without questions or doubts is the natural state.

God created man; and man created God. They both are the originators of forms and names only. In fact, neither God nor man was created.

OCTOBER 21, 1936

The aristocratic lady again came after a few days, went straight to Bhagavan, saluted him and said: I came last time with my husband and children. I was thinking of their food and time was pressing. So I could not stay here as long as I would have wished. But later I was worried over the hurried nature of the visit. I have returned now to sit quietly and imbibe Sri Bhagavan's Grace. May he give me strength of mind!
(The Hall was already clear of people. She sat on a crude carpet in front of Sri Bhagavan.)

Sri Bhagavan said smilingly: Yes. Silence is perpetual speaking. Ordinary speech hinders that heart-to-heart talk.
(She agreed and sat quietly. Sri Bhagavan was sitting reclining on the sofa. His eyes were fixed in her direction with a gracious smile on his lips. Both remained silent and motionless for about an hour.)

Prasad was distributed. The lady said: Now I want to return. The river between Bangalore and this place is in floods. On my way here, a bus was overturned in the floods. My car came later, and I saw the sad accident. Still, I was not afraid to ford the river. My car came out safely. I would like to return during daytime.

This time I shall not say "it is the last time I shall come," as I did on former occasions. I do not know, but it may be so. Yet Maharshi should give me strength of mind.

I long for *bhakti*. I want more of this longing. Even realization does not matter to me. Let me be strong in my longing.

M. If the longing is there, Realization will be forced on you even if you do not want it. *Subhechcha* is the doorway to realization.

D. Let it be so. But I am content with longing. Even when I am away from this place, I must not relax in my devotion. May Sri Bhagavan give me the necessary strength. Such longing could only be through his Grace. I am personally too weak.

Again, when I was here on a previous occasion I asked several questions. But I could not follow Sri Bhagavan's answers. I thought I would not ask any more questions, but only sit quietly in his presence imbibing Grace, which might be extended to me. So I do not pursue Maharshi with more questions this time. Only let me have his Grace.

M. Your repeated visits to this place indicate the extension of Grace.

She was surprised and said: I was going to ask Maharshi if he called me. For all of a sudden my husband told me this morning: "There are two days free. If you want you may visit Maharshi and return."

I was very agreeably surprised and pleased. I took it to be a call from Maharshi.

(*She also expressed a desire to reside near Maharshi and asked for his blessings.*)
Maharshi said: A Higher Power is leading you. Be led by the same.

D. But I am not aware of it. Please make me aware of it.

M. The Higher Power knows what to do and how to do it. Trust it.

The Muslim Professor asked: It is said one should give up desire. But there are the needs of the body that are irrepressible. What is to be done?

M. An aspirant must be equipped with three requisites:

1. *Ichcha*, 2. *Bhakti*, and 3. *Sraddha*. *Ichcha* means satisfaction of bodily wants without attachment to the body (such as hunger and thirst and evacuation). Unless that is done, meditation cannot progress. *Bhakti* and *Sraddha* are already known.

D. There are two kinds of desires — the baser and the nobler. Is it our duty to transmute the baser one into the nobler?

M. Yes.

D. Well, Bhagavan, you said there are three requisites of which *ichcha* is the satisfaction of natural wants without attachment to the body, etc. I take food three or four times a day, and attend to bodily wants so much so that I am oppressed by the body. Is there a state when I shall be disembodied so that I might be free from the scourge of bodily wants?

M. It is the attachments (*raga, dwesha*) which are injurious. The action is not bad in itself. There is no harm in eating three or four times. But only do not say, "I want this kind of food and not that kind" and so on.

Moreover, you take those meals in twelve hours of the wakeful state whereas you are not eating in the hours of sleep. Does sleep lead you to *mukti*? It is wrong to suppose that simple inactivity leads one to *mukti*.

D. There is said to be *sadeha mukta* (liberated in body) and *videha mukta* (liberated without body).

M. There is no liberation, and where are *muktas*?

D. Do not Hindu *sastras* speak of *mukti*?

M. *Mukti* is synonymous with the Self. *Jivan mukti* (liberation while alive) and *videha mukti* (liberation after the body falls) are all for the ignorant. The *jnani* is not conscious of *mukti* or *bandha* (bondage). Bondage, liberation, and orders of *mukti* are all said for an *ajnani* in order that ignorance might be shaken off. There is only *mukti* and nothing else.

D. It is all right from Bhagavan's standpoint. But what about us?

M. The difference "He" and "I" are the obstacles to *jnana*.

D. But it cannot be denied that Bhagavan is of a high order whereas we are limited. Will Bhagavan make me one with Him?

M. Were you aware of limitations in your sleep?

D. I cannot bring down the state of my sleep in the present state and speak of it.

M. You need not. These three states alternate before the unchanging Self. You can remember your state of sleep. That is your real state. There were no limitations then. After the rise of the "I"-thought, the limitations arose.

D. How to attain the Self?

M. Self is not to be attained because you already *are* the Self.

D. Yes. There is an unchanging Self and a changing one in me. There are two selves.

M. The changefulness is mere thought. All thoughts arise after the arising of the "I"-thought. See to whom the thoughts arise. Then you transcend them and they subside. This is to say, tracing the source of the "I"-thought, you realize the perfect "I-I." "I" is the name of the Self.

D. Shall I meditate on "I am *Brahman*" (*Aham Brahmasmi*)?

M. The text is not meant for thinking, "I am *Brahman*." *Aham* ("I") is known to everyone. *Brahman* abides as *Aham* in everyone. Find out the "I." The "I" is already *Brahman*. You need not think so. Simply find out the "I."

D. Is not discarding of the sheaths mentioned in the *sastras*?

M. After rise of the "I"-thought, there is the false identification of the "I" with the body, the senses, the mind, etc. "I" is wrongly associated with them and the true "I" is lost sight of. In order to shift the pure "I" from the contaminated "I," this discarding is mentioned. But it does not mean exactly discarding of the non-self, but it means the finding of the real Self.

The real Self is the Infinite "I-I," *i.e.*, "I" is perfection. It is eternal. It has no origin and no end. The other "I" is born and also dies. It is impermanent. See to whom are the changing thoughts. They will be found to arise after the "I"-thought. Hold the "I"-thought. They subside. Trace back the source of the "I"-thought. The Self alone will remain.

D. It is difficult to follow. I understand the theory. But what is the practice?

M. The other methods are meant for those who cannot take to the investigation of the Self. Even to repeat *Aham Brahmasmi* or think of it, a doer is necessary. Who is it? It is "I." *Be* that "I." It is the direct method. The other methods also will ultimately lead everyone to this method of investigation of the Self.

D. I am aware of the "I." Yet my troubles are not over.

M. This "I"-thought is not pure. It is contaminated by association with the body and senses. See to whom the trouble is. It is to the "I"-thought. Hold it. Then the other thoughts vanish.

D. Yes. How to do it? That is the whole trouble.

M. Think "I" "I" "I" and hold to that one thought to the exclusion of all others.

OCTOBER 23, 1936

While speaking of the animal companions in the Hall, Sri Bhagavan quoted a Tamil stanza by Avvai.

When the old lady was going along, on one occasion she heard someone praising Kambar. She replied with a stanza:

> "Each is great in its own way. What is Kambar's greatness compared with a bird building its nest so fine, the worms giving lac, the honey-bee building the comb, the ants building cities, and the spider its web?"

Bhagavan then began to describe their activities: While living on the Hill, he had seen a hut built of stones and mud and roofed with thatch. There was constant trouble with white ants. The roof was pulled down and the walls demolished to get rid of the mud, which harbored the ants. Sri Bhagavan saw that the hollows protected by stones were made into towns. These were skirted by walls plastered black and there were roads to neighboring cities, which were similarly skirted with black plastered walls. The roads were indicated by these walls. The interior of the town contained holes in which ants used to live. The whole wall was thus tenanted by white ants which ravaged the roofing materials above.

Sri Bhagavan had also watched a spider making its web and described it. It is seen in one place, then in another, again in a third place. The fiber is fixed at all these points. The spider moves along it, descends, ascends, and goes round and round and the web is finished. It is geometrical. The net is spread out in the morning and rolled up in the evening.

Similarly, the wasps build their nests of lac (crude), and so on.

So then, each animal has got some remarkable instinct. Kambar's learning is not to be wondered at because it is God's will, as it is in the other cases.

Dr. Syed: What is salvation? What did Christ mean by it?
M. Salvation for whom? And from what?
D. Salvation for the individual and from the sorrows of the world.
M. Whose are the sorrows?
D. Of the mind.
M. Are you the mind?
D. I shall now explain how this question arose. I was meditating. I began to reflect on the Grace shown by Christ to some devotees who got salvation. I consider that Sri Bhagavan is similar. Is not salvation the result of similar Grace? That is what I mean by my questions.
M. Yes. Right.
D. The booklet *Who am I?* speaks of *svarupa drishti* (seeing the essence). Then there must be a seer and the seen. How can this be reconciled with the Ultimate Unity?
M. Why do you ask for salvation, release from sorrow, etc.? He who asks for them sees them also. The fact is this. *Drishti* (sight) is consciousness. It forms the subject and object. Can there be *drishti* apart from the Self? The Self is all — *drishti*, etc.
D. How to discern the ego from the perfect "I-I"?
M. That which rises and falls is the transient "I." That which has neither origin nor end is the permanent "I-I" consciousness.
D. Will continuous thought on the Self make the mind more and more refined so that it will not think of anything but the highest?
M. There is the peaceful mind which is the Supreme. When the same becomes restless, it is afflicted by thoughts. Mind is only the dynamic power (*shakti*) of the Self.
D. Are the sheaths (*kosas*) material and different from the Self?

M. There is no difference between matter and spirit. Modern science admits that all matter is energy. Energy is power or force (*shakti*). Therefore, all are resolved in *Shiva* and *Shakti* i.e., the Self and the Mind.

The *kosas* are mere appearances. There is no reality in them as such.

D. How many hours a day should one devote to meditation?

M. Your very nature is meditation.

D. It will be so when ripe, but not now.

M. You become conscious of it later. That does not mean that your nature is now different from meditation.

D. What about practice?

M. Meditation must always be practiced.

D. A Persian mystic says: "There is nothing but God." The Koran says: "God is immanent in all."

M. There is no "all," apart from God, for Him to pervade. He alone is.

D. Is it morally right for a man to renounce his household duties upon realizing that his highest duty is *Atma-chintana* (continuous thought on the Self)?

M. This desire to renounce things is the obstacle. The Self is simple renunciation. The Self has renounced all.

D. It is true from Bhagavan's standpoint. But for us . . . My work demands the best part of my time and energy; often, I am too tired to devote myself to *Atma-chintana*.

M. The feeling "I work" is the hindrance. Inquire, "Who works?" Remember, "Who am I?" The work will not bind you. It will go on automatically. Make no effort either to work or to renounce work. Your effort is the bondage. What is bound to happen will happen.

If you are destined to cease working, work cannot be had even if you hunt for it. If you are destined to work, you cannot leave it; you will be forced to engage in it. So leave it to the Higher Power. You cannot renounce or hold as you choose.

D. How is all-immanent God said to reside in *dahara-kasa* (Ether of the Heart)?

M. Do we not reside in one place? Do you not say that you are in your body? Similarly, God is said to reside in *Hritpundarika* (the heart-lotus). The heart-lotus is not a place. Some name is mentioned as the place of God because we think we are in the body. This kind of instruction is meant for those who can appreciate only relative knowledge.

Being immanent everywhere, there is no particular place God exists.

Because we think we are in the body, we believe that we are born. However, we do not think of the body, of God, or of the method of realization in our deep slumber. Yet in our waking state, we hold on to the body and think we are in it.

The Supreme Being is that from which the body is born, in which it lives, and into which it resolves. However, we think that we reside within the body. Hence, such instruction is given. The instruction means: "Look within."

Mr. G.V. Subbaramiah, a lecturer in English in Nellore, asked:
Brahman is the one by whom all this is pervaded (*yena sarvamidam thatham*). But then, how does Sri Krishna specify the *vibutis* (divine manifestations) in chapter 10 of the *Bhagavad Gita*?
M. The specifications are in reply to a definite question by Arjuna who wanted to know the Lord's *vibhutis* for convenience of worship (*upasana soukaryam*). The fact is that God is all. There is nothing apart from Him.
D. The individual is said to give up decayed bodies (*jirnani sairani*) and take up new ones (*navani*). Would the statement apply to infant deaths, also?
M. You do not know, in the first place, what is *jirnani* and what is *navani*. Secondly, *jirna* and *nava* are relative terms. What is old to a king may be new to a beggar. The truth is that the individuality signifies the state of embodiment till the time of liberation!

Dr. Syed: How is Grace to be obtained?
M. Similar to obtaining the Self.
D. Practically, how is it to be for us?
M. By self-surrender.
D. Grace was said to be the Self. Should I then surrender to my own Self?
M. Yes. To the one from whom Grace is sought. God, Guru, and Self are only different forms of the same.
D. Please explain, so that I may understand.
M. So long as you think you are the individual, you believe in God. On worshipping God, He appears to you as Guru. On serving Guru, He manifests as the Self. This is the rationale.

D. There are widespread disasters in the world, *e.g.*, famine and pestilence. What is the cause of this state of affairs?
M. To whom does all this appear?

D. That won't do. I see misery abound.

M. You were not aware of the world and its sufferings in your sleep; you are conscious of them in your wakeful state. Continue in that state in which you were not afflicted by these. That is to say: when you are not aware of the world, its sufferings do not affect you. When you remain as the Self, as in sleep, the world and its sufferings will not affect you. Therefore, look within. See the Self! There will be an end of the world and its miseries.

D. But that is selfishness.

M. The world is not external. Because you identify yourself wrongly with the body, you see the world outside, and its pain becomes apparent to you. But they are not real. Seek the reality and get rid of this unreal feeling.

D. There are great men, public workers, who cannot solve the problem of the misery of the world.

M. They are ego-centered; hence their inability. If they remained in the Self, they would be different.

D. Why do Mahatmas (enlightened persons) not help?

M. How do you know that they do not help? Public speeches, physical activity, and material help are all outweighed by the silence of Mahatmas. They accomplish more than others.

D. What is to be done by us for ameliorating the condition of the world?

M. If *you* remain free from pain, there will be no pain anywhere. The trouble now is due to your seeing the world externally and also thinking that there is pain there. But both the world and the pain are within you. If you look within there will be no pain.

D. God is perfect. Why did He create the world imperfect? The work shares the nature of the author. But here it appears not so.

M. Who is it that raises the question?

D. I — the individual.

M Are you apart from God that you ask this question?

So long as you consider yourself the body, you see the world as external. The imperfections appear to you. God is perfection. His work also is perfection. But you see it as imperfection because of your wrong identification.

D. Why did the Self manifest as this miserable world?

M. In order that you might seek it. Your eyes cannot see themselves. Place a mirror before them and they see themselves. Similarly with the creation. "See yourself first and then see the whole world as the Self."

D. So it amounts to this — that I should always look within.

M. Yes.

D. Should I not see the world at all?

M. You are not instructed to shut your eyes from the world. You are only to "see yourself first and then see the whole world as the Self." If you consider yourself as the body, the world appears to be external. If you are the Self, the world appears as *Brahman*.

Dr. Syed asked: I have been reading the *Five Hymns to Arunachala*. I find that the hymns are addressed to Arunachala by you. You are an *Advaitin*. How then do you address God as a separate Being?

M. The devotee, God, and the Hymns are all the Self.

D. But you are addressing God. You are specifying this Arunachala Hill as God.

M. You can identify the Self with the body. Should not the devotee identify the Self with Arunachala?

D. If Arunachala is the Self, why should it be specially picked out among so many other hills? God is everywhere. Why do you specify Him as Arunachala?

M. What has attracted you from Allahabad to this place? What has attracted all these people around?

D. Sri Bhagavan.

M. How was I attracted here? By Arunachala. The Power cannot be denied. Again, Arunachala is within and not without. The Self is Arunachala.

D. Several terms are used in the holy books — *Atman, Paramatman, Para,* etc. What is the gradation in them?

M. They mean the same to the user of the words. But they are understood differently by persons according to their development.

D. But why do they use so many words to mean the same thing?

M. It is according to circumstances. They all mean the Self. *Para* means "not relative" or "beyond the relative," that is to say, the Absolute.

D. Should I meditate on the right chest in order to meditate on the Heart?

M. The Heart is not physical. Meditation should not be on the right or the left. Meditation should be on the Self. Everyone knows "I am." Who is the "I"? It will be neither within nor without, neither on the right nor the left. "I am" — that is all.

The Heart is the center from which everything springs. Because you see the world, the body and so on, it is said there is a center for these, which is called the Heart. When you are in the Heart, the Heart is known to be neither the center nor the circumference. There is nothing else. Whose center could it be?

D. May I take it that the Self and the non-self are like a substance and its shadow?

M. Substance and shadow are for the one who sees only the shadow and mistakes it for the substance. But there is neither substance nor shadow for the one who is aware only of the Reality.

D. Buddha, when asked if there is the ego, was silent; when asked if there is no ego, he was silent; asked if there is God, he was silent; asked if there is no God, he was silent. Silence was his answer for all these. *Mahayana* and *Hinayana* schools have both misinterpreted his silence and stated that he was an atheist.

If he were an atheist, why should he have spoken of *nirvana*, of births and deaths, of *karma*, reincarnations, and *dharma*? His interpreters are wrong. Is it not so?

M. You are right.

OCTOBER 27, 1936

The Muslim Professor asked how Vaishnavism *can be reconciled with* Advaitism.

M. The *Vaishnavites* call themselves *Visishtadvaitins*. This is also *Advaita*. Just as the individual body comprises the soul, the ego, and the gross body, so also God comprises *Paramatma*, the world, and the individuals.

D. Does not *bhakti* imply duality?

M. *Swa swarupanusandhanam bhaktirityabhidheeyate* (Reflection on one's own Self is called *bhakti*). *Bhakti* and Self-inquiry are one and the same. The Self of the *advaitins* is the God of the *bhaktas*.

D. Is there a spiritual hierarchy of all the original propounders of religions watching the spiritual welfare of humans?

M. Let them be or let them not be. It is only a surmise at the best. *Atma* is *pratyaksha* (self-evident). Know it and be done with speculation. One may admit such a hierarchy; another may not. But no one can gainsay the *Atma*.

D. What does Sri Bhagavan think of *Pravritti* and *Nivritti margas*?

M. Yes. Both are mentioned. What of it?

D. Which is the better of the two?

M. If you see the Self — pure and simple — it is *nivritti*; if you see the Self with the world, it is *pravritti*. In other words, inward-turned mind (*antarmukhi manas*) is *nivritti*; outward-going mind (*bahirmukhi manas*) is *pravritti*. Anyway, there is nothing apart from the Self. Both are the same.

Similarly, with the spiritual hierarchy; they cannot exist apart from the Self. They are only in the Self and remain as the Self. Realization of the Self is the one Goal of all.

In the course of conversation, someone referred to the fact that when Mr. Brunton and a lady were walking home in the night, they saw a bright glow on half the hill moving slowly and gently from North to South. Sri Bhagavan said: This hill is said to be wisdom in visible shape.

D. How is it visible to the physical eye?

M. Sambandar sang:

"The One who fascinated my heart or the captivator of my heart, I sing of Him in my mind."

The Heart is captivated; consequently, the mind must have sunk into the Heart, and yet there is the remembrance which enables the saint to sing of God later.

Then the experience of a young disciple was mentioned. The young man, educated and in good circumstances, in good health and sober mind, was once facing Sri Bhagavan's picture in his home and meditating on the figure. The figure suddenly appeared animated, which threw the young man into a spasm of fear. He called out for his mother, who came and asked him what the matter was. He was surrounded by his relatives who were perplexed by his appearance. He was aware of their presence, but was still overpowered by a mysterious force which he tried to resist. For a short time, he became unconscious. Fear seized him as he regained consciousness. The people became anxious and tried to bring him round with medicines.

When he later came to Tiruvannamalai, he had some foreboding of similar experience. The proximity of Sri Bhagavan prevented any untoward happening. But whenever he wandered away from the Hall, he found the force almost irresistible and himself in the grip of fear.

Sri Bhagavan said: Is it so? No one told me this before.

A devotee asked, if it was not shaktipata *(descent of divine power)?*

M. Yes, it is. A mad man clings to *samskaras*, whereas a *jnani* does not. That is the only difference between the two. *Jnana* is madness of a kind.

D. But *shaktipata* is said to occur in *karmasamya, i.e.,* when merit and demerit are equal.

M. Yes. *Malaparipaka, karmasamya,* and *shaktipata* mean the same. A man is running the course of his *samskaras;* when taught he is the Self, the teaching affects his mind and imagination runs riot. He feels helpless before the onrushing power. His experiences are only according to his imagination of the state.

"I am the Self," whatever he may conceive it to be. *Shaktipata* alone confers the true and right experience.

When the man is ripe for receiving the instruction and his mind is about to sink into the Heart, the instruction imparted works in a flash and he realizes the Self. Otherwise, there is always the struggle.

Mano-nasa, jnana, and *chittaikagrata* (annihilation of the mind, knowledge and one-pointedness) mean the same.

A lady from Uttar Pradesh arrived with her brother, a woman companion, and a burly bodyguard.

When she came into the Hall she saluted Maharshi with great respect and feeling, and sat down on a wool blanket in front of him. Sri Bhagavan was then reading Trilinga in Telugu on the reincarnation of a boy.

The boy is now thirteen years old and reading in the Government High School in a village near Lucknow. When he was three years old he used to dig here and there; when asked, he would say that he was trying to recover something which he had hidden in the earth. When he was four years old, a marriage function was celebrated in his home. When leaving, the guests humorously remarked that they would return for this boy's marriage. But he turned round and said: "I am already married. I have two wives." When asked to point them out, he requested to be taken to a certain village, and there he pointed to two women as his wives. It was learned that a period of ten months had elapsed between the death of their husband and the birth of this boy.

When this was mentioned to the lady, she asked if it was possible to know the after-death state of an individual. Sri Bhagavan said: Some are born immediately after, others after some lapse of time, a few are not reborn on this earth but eventually get salvation in some higher region, and a very few get absolved here and now.

She: I do not mean that. Is it possible to know the condition of an individual after his death?

M. It is possible. But why try to know it? All facts are only as true as the seeker.

She: The birth of a person, his being and death are real to us.

M. Because you have wrongly identified your own self with the body, you think of the other one also in terms of a body. Neither you nor the other, is the body.

She: But from my own level of understanding, I consider myself and my son to be real.

M. The birth of the "I"-thought is one's own birth; its death is the person's death. After the "I"-thought has arisen, the wrong identity with the body arises. Thinking yourself the body, you give false values to others and identify them with bodies. Just as your body has been born, grows and will perish, so also you think the other was born, grew up and died. Did you think of your son before his birth? The thought came after his birth and persists even after his death. Inasmuch as you are thinking of him, he is your son. Where has he gone? He has gone to the source from which he sprang. He is one with you. So long as you are, he is there, too. If you cease to identify yourself with the body, but see the real Self, this confusion will vanish. You are eternal. The others also will similarly be found to be eternal. Until this truth is realized, there will always be this grief due to false values arising from wrong knowledge and wrong identity.

She: Let me have true knowledge by Sri Bhagavan's Grace.

M. Get rid of the "I"-thought. So long as "I" is alive, there is grief. When "I" ceases to exist, there is no grief. Consider the state of sleep!

She: Yes. But when I take to the "I"-thought, other thoughts arise and disturb me.

M. See whose thoughts they are. They will vanish. They have their root in the single "I"-thought. Hold to it and they will disappear.

Again the Master pointed to the story of *Punya* and *Papa* in *Yoga Vasishta,* where *Punya* consoles *Papa* on the death of their parents and turns him to realizing the Self. Further, creation is to be considered in its two aspects, *Ishvara srishti* (God's creation) and *jiva srishti* (individual's creation). Of these two, the universe is the former; and its relation to the individual is the latter. It is the latter which gives rise to pain and pleasure, irrespective of the former.

A story was mentioned from Panchadasi:

There were two young men in a village in South India. They went on a pilgrimage to North India. One of them died. The survivor, who was earning something, decided to return only after some months. In the meantime, he came across a wandering pilgrim whom he asked to convey the information regarding himself and his dead companion to the village in

South India. The wandering pilgrim did so, but by mistake changed the names. The result was that the dead man's parents rejoiced in his safety and the living one's parents were in grief.

Thus, you see, pain or pleasure has no reference to facts but to mental conceptions. *Jiva Srishti* is responsible for it. Kill the *jiva* and there is no pain or pleasure, but the mental bliss persists forever. Killing the *jiva* is to abide in the Self.

She: I hear all this. It is beyond my grasp. I pray Sri Bhagavan to help me understand it all.

I had been to a waterfall in Mysore. The cascade was a fascinating sight. The waters streamed out in the shapes of fingers trying to grasp the rocks but were rushed on by the current to the depths below. I imagined this to be the state of individuals clinging to their present surroundings. But I cannot help clinging.

I cannot imagine that we are no better than seasonal flowers, fruits and leaves on trees. I love flowers, but still this idea has no hold on me.

(After a few minutes, she pointed out that she had intended to ask Maharshi about death and matters relating to it, but did not however do so. She left after seeing Lakshmi, the cow.)

November 9, 1936

Mr. Cohen: What is will? I mean — where does it fit in, in the five *kosas*?

M. The "I"-thought arises first and then all other thoughts. They comprise the mind. The mind is the object and the "I" is the subject. Can there be will without the "I"? It is comprised in the "I." The "I"-thought is the *vijnanamaya kosa* (intellectual sheath). Will is included in it.

Annamaya kosa is the gross body sheath. The senses with the *prana* and the *karmendriyas* form the *pranamayakosa* (sense-sheath). The senses with the mind form the *manomaya kosa* (mind-sheath). They are the *jnanendryas*. The mind is formed of thoughts only. *Idam* (this) is the object and *aham* ("I") is the subject; the two together form the *vijnanamayakosa* (intellect-sheath).

November 10, 1936

Miss W. Umadevi, a Polish lady and convert to Hinduism, had traveled in Kashmir and brought pictures from that country at which we were looking. Sri Bhagavan humorously remarked: We have seen those places without the trouble of travel.

D. I wish to go to Kailas.

M. One can see these places only if destined. Not otherwise. After seeing all, there will still remain more — if not in this hemisphere, then maybe in the other. Knowledge implies ignorance of what lies beyond what is known. Knowledge is ever limited.

After some time, Sri Bhagavan continued: Appar was old and decrepit and yet began to travel to Kailas. Another old man appeared on the way and tried to dissuade him from the attempt, saying that it was so difficult to reach there. Appar was, however, insistent and said he would risk his life in the attempt. The stranger asked him to dip himself in a tank close by. Appar did so and found Kailas then and there. Where did all this happen? In Tiruvayyar, nine miles from Tanjore. Where is Kailas, then? Is it within the mind or outside it? If Tiruvayyar be truly Kailas, it must appear to others as well. But Appar alone found it so.

Similarly, it is said of other places of pilgrimage in the South that they are the abodes of Shiva, and devotees confirmed that. This was true from their standpoint. Everything is within. There is nothing without.

D. How long does it take a man to be reborn after death? Is it immediately after death, or some time after?
M. You do not know what you were before birth, yet you want to know what you will be after death. Do you know what you are now?

Birth and rebirth pertain to the body. You are identifying the Self with the body. It is a wrong identification. You believe that the body was born and will die, and confound the phenomena relating to the one with the other. Know your real being and these questions will not arise.

Birth and rebirth are mentioned only to make you investigate the question and find out that there are neither births nor rebirths. They relate to the body and not to the Self. Know the Self and do not be perturbed by doubts.

D. Can you help me to get rid of *Maya*?
M. What is *Maya*?
D. Attachment to the world.
M. Did the world exist in your deep sleep? Was there attachment to it?
D. There was not.
M. Were you there or not?
D. Maybe.
M. Then do you deny having existed in sleep?

D. I do not.

M. You are therefore now "the same one as there was in sleep."

D. Yes.

Sleep	Wakefulness
No world	World
No attachment	Attachment
The Self	The Self

What is it then, that raises the question of *Maya* just now?

D. The mind was not in sleep. The world and the attachment to it are of the mind.

M. That is it. The world and the attachment to it are of the mind, not of the Self.

D. I was ignorant in sleep.

M. Who says that he was ignorant? Is he not ignorant now? Is he a *jnani*? Ignorance is now mentioned by the contaminated Self here.

D. Was the Self pure then in sleep?

M. It did not raise any doubts. It did not feel imperfect or impure.

D. Such Self is common to all, even in a dead body.

M. But the man in sleep or in a dead body does not raise questions. Consider who raises questions. It is you. Were you not in sleep? Why was there no imperfection? The pure Self is simple Being. It does not associate itself with objects and become conscious as in the wakeful state. What you now call consciousness in the present state is associated consciousness requiring brain, mind, body, etc., to depend upon. But in sleep, consciousness persisted without these.

D. But I do not know the consciousness in sleep.

M. Who is not aware of it? You admit "I am." You admit "I was" in sleep. The state of Being is your self.

D. Do you mean to say that sleep is Self-realization?

M. It is the Self. Why do you talk of Realization? Is there a moment when the Self is not realized? If there be such a moment, the other moment might be said to be one of Realization. There is no moment when the Self is not nor when the Self is not realized. Why pick out sleep for it? Even now you are Self-realized.

D. But I do not understand.

M. Because you are identifying the Self with the body. Give up the wrong identity and the Self is revealed.

D. But this does not answer my question to help me to get rid of *Maya*, i.e., attachment.

M. This attachment is not found in sleep. It is perceived and felt now. It is not your real nature. On whom are these accretions? If the Real Nature is known, these exist not. If you realize the Self, the possessions are not perceived. That is getting rid of *Maya*. *Maya* is not objective, that it could be gotten rid of in any other way.

NOVEMBER 15, 1936

A certain man, who claims to have been Sri Maharshi's former disciple, has filed a suit in the court praying for a declaration that he is the legitimate Sarvadhikari (manager) of the Asramam.

Sri Maharshi was examined by the Commission. There was a crowd but the proceedings went on smoothly in the room on the Northeast.

The following are a few tidbits from the examination. Sri Bhagavan's answers were quite spontaneous and smooth:

Q. To which *asramam* does Sri Bhagavan belong?

M. *Atiasramam* (beyond the four stages).

Q. What is that?

M. It is beyond the four commonly known *asramas*.

Q. Is it *sastraic*?

M. Yes. It is mentioned in the *sastras*.

Q. Are there others of the same type besides yourself?

M. There may be.

Q. Have there been any?

M. Suka, Rishabha, Jada Bharata, and others.

Q. You left home at an early age because you had no attachment for home and property. But here, there is property in the Asramam. How is that?

M. I do not seek it. Property is thrust on me. I neither love nor hate it.

Q. Are they given to you?

M. They are given to the Swami, whoever he may be. But the body is considered the Swami in the world. That body is this. It reduces itself to myself.

Q. In that case, the attachment to property is now renewed. Is that correct?

M. I do not hate it — that is all I said.

Q. In practical life, it amounts to what I say.

M. Just as we live and move in practical matters.

Q. Do you give *upadesa* (initiation)? Have you ever done it?

M. Visitors ask questions. I answer them as well as I know. It is for them to treat my words as they please.

Q. Is it *upadesa?*

M. How shall I say how others take it?

Q. Have you disciples?

M. I do not give *upadesa* in the ceremonial manner; for instance, keeping a *kumbha,* making *puja* to it, and whispering to the person.

The person may call himself my disciple or devotee. I do not consider anyone to be my disciple. I have never sought *upadesa* from anyone, nor do I give ceremonial *upadesa.* If people call themselves my disciples, I neither approve nor disapprove. In my view all are alike. They consider themselves fit for being called disciples. What can I say to them? I do not call myself a disciple or a Guru.

Q. How did you approve the building of Skandasramam on the Hill, which was temple land, without previously obtaining permission from the authorities?

M. Guided by the same Power which made me come here and reside on the Hill.

Q. When you threw away your cash, etc., within an hour after arrival in this place, you did so because you did not desire possessions. You never touch money. There were no possessions for several years after your arrival here. How is it that donations are now being accepted by the Asramam?

M. This practice grew up at a later stage because a few associates began to use my name to collect funds. I did not approve of their action nor check them. So it is going on. One man leaves, another steps in, but the process goes on. I do not desire that contributions should be accepted. But people do not heed that advice. I do not desire to give ineffective advice I do not, therefore, check them. Since money comes in, property grows spontaneously.

Q. Why do you not sign your name?

M. The author of *Self-Realisation* has furnished his answer to this question. Moreover, by what name am I to be known? I myself do not know. People have given me several names from time to time since my arrival here. If I should sign by one name, all would not understand it. So I used to say to people seeking autographs that, even if they should show my signature, people in general would not believe it to be true.

Q. You do not touch money nor other offerings, I trust.

M. People sometimes place fruits in my hands. I touch them.

Q. If you receive one kind of offering, why should you not receive money, also?

M. I cannot eat money. What shall I do with it? Why should I take that with which I do not know what to do?

Q. Why do visitors stop at the Asramam?

M. They must know why.

Q. You have no objection to anyone coming and staying here, I suppose.

M. No.

Q. You have similarly no objection to any length of their stay.

M. No. If I do not find it agreeable, I will go away. That is all.

A lawyer devotee asked Sri Bhagavan if the previous day's examination by the Commission caused much strain.

M. I did not use my mind and so there was no strain. Let them examine me for a thousand days. I don't mind.

November 16, 1936

D. Does the *tantric sadhana* bring about Self-realization?

M. Yes.

D. Which worship in *Tantra* is the best?

M. It depends on one's temperament.

D. What part does *Kundalini* play in bringing about Self-realization?

M. *Kundalini* rises from any *lakshya* that you have. *Kundalini* is the *prana-shakti* (life-current).

D. Different deities are said to reside in different *chakras*. Does one see them in the course of *sadhana?*

M. They can be seen if so desired.

D. Does the path to Self-realization go through *samadhi?*

M. They are synonymous.

D. It is said that the Guru can make his disciple realize the Self by transmitting some of his own power to him? Is it true?

M. Yes. The Guru does not bring about Self-realization. He simply removes the obstacles to it. The Self is always realized.

D. Is there absolute necessity of a Guru for Self-realization?

M. So long as you seek Self-realization, the Guru is necessary. Guru is the Self. Take Guru to be the Real Self and your self as the individual self. The disappearance of this sense of duality is the removal of ignorance. So long as duality persists in you, the Guru is necessary. Because you identify your-self with the body you think the Guru, too, to be somebody. You are not the body, nor is the Guru. You are the Self and so is the Guru. This knowledge is gained by what you call Self-realization.

D. How can one know whether a particular individual is competent to be a Guru?

M. By the peace of mind found in his presence and by the sense of respect you feel for him.

D. If the Guru happens to turn out incompetent, what will be the fate of the disciple who has implicit faith in him?

M. Each one according to his merits.

D. What are your opinions about social reform?

M. Self-reform automatically brings about social reform. Confine yourself to self-reform. Social reform will take care of itself.

D. What is your opinion about Gandhiji's *Harijan* movement?

M. Ask him.

D. Is it necessary to take a bath if we touch dead bodies?

M. The body is a corpse. So long as one is in contact with it, one must bathe in the waters of the Self.

D. If the *advaita* is final, why did Madhvacharya teach *dvaita*?

M. Is your Self *dvaita* or *advaita*? All systems agree on self-surrender. Attain it first, then there will be time to judge whose view is right or otherwise.

D. Why do you not preach to the people to set them on the right path?

M. You have already decided by yourself that I do not preach. Do you know who I am and what preaching is?

D. Is the shaving of widows among Brahmins not cruel?

M. This may be asked of *Dharma Sastris* or reformers. Reform yourself first and let us then see about the rest.

November 17, 1936

D. How can one become *jitasangadoshah* (free from the stain of association)?

M. By *satsanga* (association with the wise).

"*Satsangatve nissangatvam, nissangatve nirmohatvam, nirmohatve nischalatatvam, nischalatatve jivanmuktih.*"

By association with sages comes non-attachment, from non-attachment comes freedom from desire; from desirelessness comes mental stillness, from mental stillness comes freedom from the ego.

Satsanga means *sanga* (association) with *Sat*. *Sat* is only the Self. Since the Self is not now understood to be *Sat*, the company of the sage who has thus understood it is sought. That is *Satsanga*. Introversion results. Then *Sat* is revealed. For whom is association? For whom is *dosha*?

D. To the Self.

M. No. The Self is pure and unaffected. The impurities affect only the ego.

D. Can the soul remain without the body?

M. It will be so a short time hence — in deep slumber. The Self is bodiless. Even now it is.

D. Can a *sannyasi* remain in the midst of *samsara*?

M. So long as one thinks that he is a *sannyasi*, he is not one. So long as one does not think of *samsara*, he is not a *samsari*; on the other hand, he is a *sannyasi*.

NOVEMBER 18, 1936

D. It is said in *Srimad Bhagavad Gita*: "Realize the Self with pure intellect and also by service to Guru and by inquiry." How are they to be reconciled?

M. *Ishvaro Gururatmeti* — Ishvara, Guru, and Self are identical. So long as the sense of duality persists in you, you seek a Guru considering that he stands apart. He, however, teaches you the truth and you gain the insight.

D. Kindly explain:

"*Ahameko name kaschit nahamanyasya kasyachit naham pasyami yasyaham tam na pasyami yo mama.*"

I am alone; none is mine; of none else am I, I see none to whom I belong, none who is mine.

M. This sloka occurs in different scriptures, holy books, *e.g., Bhagavata, Mahabharata,* etc. It also forms the motto of chapter 11 in *Self-Realisation*. *Aham* — "I," is only one. Egos are different. They are in the One Self. The Self is not affected by the egos. "I" is one only. "I" is the Truth. All that follows is meant to refute the sense of duality.

D. If the Self is itself aware, why am I not aware of the same, even now?

M. There is no duality. Your present knowledge is due to the ego and only relative. Relative knowledge requires a subject and an object, whereas the awareness of the Self is absolute and requires no object.

Remembrance also is similarly relative, requiring an object to be remembered and a subject to remember. When there is no duality, who is to remember whom?

D. What happens to the created ego when the body dies?

M. Ego is "I"-thought. In its subtle form it remains a thought, whereas in its gross aspect it embraces the mind, the senses and the body. They disappear in deep slumber, along with the ego. Still the Self is there; similarly, it will be in death.

Ego is not an entity independent of the Self in order that it must be created or destroyed by itself. It functions as an instrument of the Self and periodically ceases to function. That is to say, it appears and disappears; this might be considered to be birth and death.

Relative knowledge pertains to the mind and not to the Self. It is therefore illusory and not permanent. Take a scientist, for instance. He formulates a theory that the Earth is round and goes on to prove it on an incontrovertible basis. When he falls asleep the whole idea vanishes; his mind is left a blank. What does it matter whether the world remains round or flat when he is asleep? So you see the futility of all such relative knowledge.

One should go beyond such relative knowledge and abide in the Self. Real knowledge is such experience and not apprehension by the mind.

D. Why does not Sri Bhagavan go about and preach the Truth to the people at large?

M. How do you know I am not doing just that? Does preaching consist in mounting a platform and haranguing the people around? Preaching is simple communication of knowledge. It may be done in Silence, too.

What do you think of a man listening to a harangue for an hour and going away without being sufficiently impressed by it so as to change his life? Compare him with another who sits in a holy presence and leaves after some time with his outlook on life totally changed. Which is better: To preach loudly without effect or to sit silently sending forth intuitive forces to play on others?

Again, how does speech arise? There is abstract knowledge (unmanifest). From it arises the ego, which gives rise to thoughts and words successively. So then:

Abstract Knowledge
↓
Ego
↓
Thoughts
↓
Words

Words are, therefore, the great grandson of the original source. If words can produce such an effect, how much more powerful would preaching through silence be! Judge for yourself.

D. Why can we not remain in *sushupti* as long as we like and also be voluntarily in it just as we are in the waking state?

M. *Sushupti* continues in this state, also. We are ever in *sushupti*. That should be consciously gone into and realized in this very state. There is no real going into or coming out of it. Becoming aware of that is *samadhi*. An ignorant man cannot remain long in *sushupti* because he is forced by nature to emerge out of it. His ego is not dead and it will rise up again. But the wise man attempts to crush it in its source. It rises up again and again for him, too, impelled by nature, i.e., *prarabdha*. Both in the *jnani* and *ajnani*, ego sprouts forth, but with this difference: when the *ajnani's* ego rises up it is quite ignorant of its source; he is not aware of his *sushupti* in the dream and *jagrat* states. When the ego of a *jnani* rises up, he enjoys transcendental experience, always keeping his *lakshya* (aim) on its source. This ego is not dangerous; it is like the skeleton of a burnt rope; in this form it is ineffective. By constantly keeping our aim on our source, our ego is dissolved in its source like a doll of salt in the ocean.

D. Sri Ramakrishna says that *nirvikalpa samadhi* cannot last longer than twenty-one days. If persisted in, the person dies. Is that so?

M. When the *prarabdha* is exhausted, the ego is completely dissolved without leaving any trace. This is final liberation. Unless *prarabdha* is completely exhausted, the ego will be rising up in its pure form even in *jivanmuktas*. I still doubt the statement of the maximum duration of twenty-one days. It is said that people cannot live if they fast thirty or forty days. But there are those who have fasted longer, say a hundred days. It means that there is still *prarabdha* for them.

D. How is realization made possible?

M. There is the absolute Self from which a spark proceeds as from fire. The spark is called the ego. In the case of an ignorant man, it identifies itself with an object simultaneously with its rise. It cannot remain independent of such association with objects. This association is *ajnana* or ignorance, whose destruction is the objective of our efforts. If its objectifying tendency is killed, it remains pure and also merges into the source. The wrong identification with the body is *dehatmabuddhi* ("I-am-the-body" idea). This must go before good results can follow.

D. How to eradicate *dehatmabuddhi*?

M. We exist in *sushupti* without being associated with the body and mind. But in the other two states, we are associated with them. If one with the body, how can we exist without the body in *sushupti*? We can separate ourselves from that which is external to us and not from that which is one with us. Hence, the ego is not one with the body. This must be realized in the waking state. *Avasthatraya* (the three states of waking, dream, and deep sleep) should be studied only for gaining this outlook.

The ego in its purity is experienced in intervals between two states or two thoughts. Ego is like that caterpillar which leaves its hold only after catching another. Its true nature can be found when it is out of contact with objects or thoughts. Realize this interval with the conviction gained by the study of *avasthatraya* (the three states of consciousness).

D. How do we go to sleep and how do we wake up?

M. Just at nightfall, the hen clucks and the chicks go and hide themselves under her wings. The hen then goes to roost in the nest with the chicks in her protection. At dawn, the chicks come out and so does the hen. The mother hen stands for the ego, which collects all the thoughts and goes to sleep. At sunrise, the rays emerge forth and are collected again at sunset. Similarly, when the ego displays itself, it does so with all its paraphernalia. When it sinks, everything disappears with it.

D. What does *sushupti* look like?

M. On a cloudy dark night, no individual identification of objects is possible and there is only dense darkness, although the seer has his eyes wide open; similarly, in *sushupti* the seer is aware of simple nescience.

Sri Bhagavan is said to have remarked to an inquisitive person: What is the meaning of this talk of truth and falsehood in the world, which is itself false?

November 27, 1936

A Punjabi gentleman, a doctor by profession, came here with his wife to visit Sri Bhagavan. He was in the Hall when Sri Bhagavan came in after lunch, then asked: How should I meditate? I do not have peace of mind.

M. Peace is our real nature. It need not be attained. Our thoughts must be obliterated.

D. I have been trying to obliterate them, but have not succeeded.

M. The *Gita* method is the only one for it. Whenever mind strays, bring it back to bear on meditation.

D. I cannot bring my mind to meditate.

Another devotee: An elephant when free puts its trunk here and there and feels restless. If a length of chain is given to it, the trunk holds it and is no longer restless. Similarly, mind without an aim is restless; with an aim, it remains at peace.

D. No, no, that is all theory. I have read many books. But no use. It is practically impossible to make the mind concentrate.

M. Concentration is impossible so long as there are predispositions. They obstruct *bhakti*, also.

The interpreter advised the questioner to study Who am I? *The doctor was ready with his protestations:* I have read it, also. I still cannot make my mind concentrate.

M. By practice and dispassion — *abhyasa vairagyabhyam.*

D. *Vairagya* is necessary . . .

M. *Abhyasa* and *vairagya* are necessary. *Vairagya* is the absence of diffused thoughts; *abhyasa* is concentration on one thought only. The one is the positive and the other the negative aspect of meditation.

D. I am not able to do so by myself. I am in search of a *force* to help me.

M. Yes, that is what is called Grace. Individually, we are incapable because the mind is weak. Grace is necessary. *Sadhu seva* is meant only for it. There is however, nothing new to get. Just as a weak man comes under the control of a stronger one, the weak mind of a man comes under control easily in the presence of the strong-minded *sadhus*. That which is — is only Grace; there is nothing else.

D. I request your blessings for the good of myself.

M. Yes — Yes.

(*He left with his wife.*)

November 30, 1936

While discussing karma, *Sri Bhagavan said*: Karma has its fruits (*phala*). They are like cause and effect. The interrelation of a cause and its effect is due to a *Shakti* whom we call God. God is *phala data* (dispenser of fruit).

A visitor had been speaking of the Self having forgotten its true nature. Sri Bhagavan, after some time, said: People speak of memory and oblivion of the Fullness of the Self. Oblivion and memory are only thought-forms. They will alternate so long as there are thoughts. But Reality lies beyond these. Memory or oblivion must be dependent on something. That something must be foreign, too; otherwise there cannot be oblivion. It is called "I" by everyone. When one looks for it, it is not found because it is not real. Hence, "I" is synonymous with illusion or ignorance (*maya, avidya,* or *ajnana*). To know that there never was ignorance is the goal of all spiritual teachings. Ignorance must be of one who is aware. Awareness is *jnana. Jnana* is eternal and natural. *Ajnana* is unnatural and unreal.

D. Having heard this truth, why does not one remain content?
M. Because the *samskaras* have not been destroyed. Unless they cease to exist, there will always be doubt and confusion (*sandeha, viparita*). All efforts are directed to destroying doubt and confusion. To do so, their roots must be cut. Their roots are the *samskaras.* These are rendered ineffective by practice as prescribed by the Guru. The Guru leaves it to the seeker to do this much so that he himself might find out that there is no ignorance. This truth mentioned is in the stage of the hearing of the Truth (*sravana*). That is not *drdha* (firm). For making it unshaken, one has to practice reflection (*manana*) and one-pointedness (*nididhyasana*). These two processes scorch the seeds of *vasanas* so that they are rendered ineffective.

Some extraordinary persons get *drdha jnana* (unshaken knowledge) even on hearing the Truth only once (*sakrchhravana matrena*). This is because they are *krthopasakah* (advanced seekers), whereas the *akrthopasakah* (raw seekers) take longer to gain *drdha jnana* (unshaken knowledge).

People ask: "How did ignorance (*avidya*) arise at all?" We have to say to them: "Ignorance never arose. It has no real being. That which is, is only *vidya* (Knowledge)."
D. Why then do I not realize it?
M. Because of the *samskaras.* However, find out who does not realize and what he does not realize. Then it will be clear that there is no *avidya* (ignorance).

Mr. Sagarmull, a Marwari gentleman and cotton merchant from Bombay, seems learned in Srimad Bhagavad Gita. *He asked:* Srimad Bhagavad Gita *says: Mattah parataram nanyat kinchit and later on sutre manigana iva* — "there is nothing different from Me," and later on, "like beads strung on a thread." If there is nothing but Sri Krishna, how can the world be said to be like "beads on a string"?
M. It means that the *sutra* (string) and the *mani* (jewel beads) are not apart from me. There is no *maniganah* (row of beads) apart from the string (*sutra*) and no string apart from me. The *sloka* emphasizes unity and not multiplic-

ity, which is only on the surface.

D. Unity can only be after merging into Bhagavan. True — but until then there must be diversity. That is *samsara*.

M. Where are we now? Are we apart from Bhagavan? The *samsara* and we are all in Bhagavan.

D. But that is the experience of the *jnanis*. Differentiation persists until *jnana* dawns. So there is *samsara* for me.

M. *Samskara* (predisposition) is *samsara* (cycle of births and deaths).

D. Right. "All this is Vasudeva" — this truth has been forgotten by us. So we cannot identify ourselves with God.

M. Where is forgetfulness?

D. Like *svapna*.

M. Whose *svapna*?

D. *Jiva's*.

M. Who is *Jiva*?

D. It is *Paramatma's*.

M. Let *Paramatma* ask then.

D. I shall make my doubt clear by means of an illustration.

M. Whoever wants the doubt to be illustrated and made clear? Direct experience — *pratyaksha* — does not require examples for elucidation.

D. There is *pratyaksha* and also forgetfulness.

M. What is forgotten and by whom?

D. Listen. One dreams; the dream world disappears on waking.

M. Wake up similarly from the present dream.

D. *Prakrti* (nature) is too powerful.

M. See the *Purusha* (Lord), also. What can *prakrti* do then?

D. There is a *granthi* (knot) between them.

M. Whose is that knot? Is it of the Lord or of Nature? Or of both?

D. Due to *Brahman*.

M. Then *Brahman* must ask or must be asked. To whom is *svapna*? Or the knot? You are always saying, "I ask." Who is that "I"?

D. I do not perceive.

M. "I" is eternal. It would vanish if it were anything particular. It is Perfection. So it is not found as an object.

D. But I am imperfect.

M. Why bring in imperfection? Why are you not perfect? Did you feel imperfection in your sleep? Why do you not remain so even now? Bring sleep into the waking state (*jagrat sushupti*) and you will be all right. *Ya nisa sarva bhootanam . . . pasyato muneh . . .* (That which is night for the ignorant is day for the wise.)

D. Yes, if he is a *muni* (sage).

M. Who is a *muni*? Is he not a man?

D. Do you not feel a slap if given to you? Is there no differentiation? Is it *jnana*?

M. A man under chloroform or under the influence of drink does not feel it. Is he a *jnani*? Is *jnana* inconsistent with that feeling?

D. There is the seer, the seen, and sight. They are not characteristic of *jnana*.

M. In sleep, in trance, in absent-mindedness, there is no differentiation. Do you call it *jnana*? What has happened in these states? Is that which was then, absent now? That which *is* exists forever. The difference is due to the mind. The mind is sometimes present, at other times absent. There is no change in the Reality. Reality is always Bliss — *Ananda*.

D. Bliss is the outcome of practice. What is that practice?

M. *Sadhana* is the inquiry to find out to whom all these doubts arise.

D. It is for the ego (*ahhamkara*).

M. Wherefrom does *ahamkara* arise?

D. Guidance is necessary to show me the way.

M. Go within and find the route. You cannot find it externally; nor should you seek it there.

D. I am unable to find the ego by search. I stop there.

M. How can you get it? It is not apart from you. Leave alone not finding it. Where are you now? Do you mean to say, "I am not"?

D. What or how am I?

M. Do not trouble yourself about it. Let it be as it is. Why do you care? Did you care for the whole or part (*samashti, vyashti*) in your sleep? The same person is present now, too. You are the same in sleep and in waking.

D. Sleep and waking are different states having different effects . . .

M. How does it matter to you? The Self is the same, all through.

D. The mind is not steady in meditation.

M. Whenever it wanders, turn it inward again and again.

D. When *duhka* (misery) overpowers me, inquiry is impossible.

M. Because the mind is too weak. Make it strong.

D. By what means?

M. *Satsanga, Ishvara Aradhana, Pranayama* (association with the wise, worship of God, breath control).

D. What happens then?

M. Misery is removed; that is our aim. You do not *acquire* happiness: your very nature is happiness. Bliss is not newly earned. All that is done is to remove unhappiness. These methods suffice.

D. Association with the wise may strengthen the mind. There must also be practice. What practice should be done?

M. Yes. Practice is necessary, too. Practice means removal of predispositions. Practice is not for fresh gain; it is to kill the predispositions.

D. *Abhyasa* (practice) should give me that power.

M. Practice is power. If thoughts are reduced to a single thought, the mind is said to have grown strong. When practice remains unshaken, it becomes *sahaja* (natural).

D. What is such practice?

M. Inquiring into the Self. That is all. *Atmanyeva vasam nayet* . . . Fix the mind on the Self.

D. What is the aim to be kept in view? Practice requires an aim.

M. *Atman* is the aim. What else can there be? All other aims are for those incapable of *atmalakshya* (having the Self for the aim). They lead you ultimately to *Atma-vichara* (inquiry into the Self). One-pointedness is the fruit of all kinds of practice. One person may get it quickly; another, after a long time. Everything depends on one's practice.

D. Peace is extolled more than anything else. How to gain it?

M. It is your very nature. Forgetfulness never overtakes the Self. The Self is now confounded with non-self and that makes you speak of forgetfulness of the Self, peace, etc. Oblivion will never rear up its head if this confusion is put an end to.

D. How is that done?

M. Inquiry into the Self. One-pointedness means cessation of mental activities. Forgetfulness must be for the self — well, of what? — of the Self? Are there then two selves? Practice removes the *samskaras*.

D. But *samskaras* are infinite and eternal — from beginningless time.

M. This itself is a *samskara*. Give up that idea and all *samskaras* will disappear at once. That is *visranti* (repose), *shanti* (peace). Peace is ever present. But you hold it down and rise over it and thus disturb it. Then you say, "I want peace."

D. Will peace be gradual?

M. Yes. Make the mind still, gradually (*Sanaissanaih uparamet*) says the *Bhagavad Gita*.

After some time, the visitor asked if one Mr. G. had been here on or about the 20th of this month. He himself had heard about Maharshi from him. Mr. G. was full of joy after his visit here.

M. How can I know the names of all these visitors? He might have been. All are full of joy. There is no name, no form ... Name is however needed for *vyavahara* (empirical life).

DECEMBER 5, 1936

D. You spoke of *atiasrama* (beyond the *asramas* — beyond the orders of life) the other day. Is there any authority for it? Is it mentioned anywhere?
M. Yes, in the *Upanishads*, the *Suta Samhita (Skanda Purana)*, *Bhagavata*, *Bharata*, and other works.
D. Are there any restrictions or disciplines for achieving that state?
M. There are characteristics of it mentioned.
D. There are Gurus for each *asrama*. Is there a Guru for *atiasrama*?
M. Yes.
D. But you do not admit a Guru.
M. There is a Guru for everyone. I admit a Guru for me, also.
D. Who is your Guru?
M. The Self.
D. For whom?
M. For myself. The Guru may be internal or external. He may reveal Himself internally or communicate externally.
D. Can the *atiasramis* own property?
M. There is no restriction for them. They may do as they please. *Suka* is said to have married and begotten children, also.
D. The *atiasrami* is like a householder in that case.
M. I have already said that he is above the four recognized *asramas*.
D. If they can marry, own property, etc., they are only *grihastha*.
M. That may be your view.
D. Can they own property and convey the same to others?
M. They may or may not. All depends on their *prarabdha*.
D. Is there any karma for them?
M. Their conduct is not regulated according to any rules or codes.
D. When visitors want to stay here, say two or three days, do they need your permission?
M. Permission from the management is permission from me. The visitors come here for me; the management is for me. Wherever there is mutual agreement, I do not interfere. When visitors come here and I admit them, will others dare go against my wishes? My consent is implied in the actions that take place with mutual understanding.

Sri Bhagavan was shown a stanza in his own handwriting in praise of Himself as Subrahmanya. He said that the handwriting was his own whereas the ideas were Perumalswami's.

D. But do you not agree with the statement made in it?

M. In the same way as an idol is praised as *Subrahmanya.*

DECEMBER 13, 1936

Mr. K K.V. Iyer: There is no way found to go inward by means of meditation.

M. Where else are we now? Our very being is that.

D. Being so, we are ignorant of it.

M. Ignorant of what, and whose is the ignorance? If ignorant of the Self, are there two selves?

D. There are not two selves. The feeling of limitation cannot be denied. Due to limitations . . .

M. Limitation is only in the mind. Did you feel it in deep sleep? You exist in sleep. You do not deny your existence then. The same Self is now and here, in the wakeful state. You are now saying that there are limitations. What has happened is that there are these differences between the two states. The differences are solely due to the mind. There was no mind in sleep, whereas it is now active. The Self exists in the absence of the mind, also.

D. Although it is understood, it is not realized.

M. It will be by and by, with meditation.

D. Meditation is with mind; how can it kill the mind in order to reveal the Self?

M. Meditation is sticking to one thought. That single thought keeps away other thoughts; distraction of mind is a sign of its weakness. By constant meditation it gains strength, i.e., to say, fugitive thought gives way to the enduring background free from thoughts. This expanse devoid of thought is the Self. Mind in purity is the Self.

Sri Bhagavan continued in reply to the former questioner: Everyone says, "I am the body." It is the experience of the sage as also of the ignorant. The ignorant man believes that the Self is confined to the body only, whereas the wise man knows that the body cannot remain apart from the Self. The Self is infinite for him and includes the body.

Mr. Bose said that he felt peace in Maharshi's presence, which lasted for some time but asked why it is not enduring?

M. That Peace is your real nature. Contrary ideas are only superimpositions. This is true *bhakti*, true yoga, and true *jnana*. You may say that this peace is acquired by practice. The wrong notions are given up by practice. That is all. Your true nature always persists. These flashes are only signs of the ensuing revelation of the Self.

In reply to the first questioner, Bhagavan said: The Heart is the Self. It is neither within nor without. The mind is its *shakti*. After emergence of the mind, the universe appears and the body is seen to be contained in it. All these are contained in the Self and cannot exist apart from It.

DECEMBER 14, 1936

Mr. Parkhi: How is meditation to be practiced?

M. Meditation is, truly speaking, *Atmanishtha* (to be fixed as the Self). But when thoughts cross the mind and effort is made to eliminate them, that effort is usually termed "meditation." *Atmanishtha* is your real nature. Remain as you are — that is the aim.

D. But thoughts come up. Is our effort meant to eliminate thoughts only?

M. Yes. Meditation being on a single thought, all other thoughts are kept away. Meditation is only negative in effect inasmuch as thoughts are kept away.

D. It is said *Atma samstham manah krtva* (fixing the mind in the Self). But the Self is unthinkable.

M. Why do you wish to meditate at all? Since you wish to do so, you are told *Atma samstham manah krtva* (fixing the mind in the Self); why do you not remain as you are without meditating? What is that *manah* (mind)? When all thoughts are eliminated, it becomes *Atma samstha* (fixed in the Self).

D. If a form is given, I can meditate on it and other thoughts are eliminated. But the Self is formless.

M. Meditation on forms or concrete objects is said to be *dhyana*, whereas the inquiry into the Self is *vichara* (inquiry) or *nididhyasana*.

Explaining *adhyaropapavadabhyam* (superimposition and its elimination), Sri Bhagavan pointed out that the former turns you inward toward the Self; and then, according to the latter, you know that the world is not apart from the Self.

Mr. Natverlal Parekh, a Gujerati gentleman who had attended the International Religious Conference as a delegate from Baroda, is here on a visit. He is a young man, well-groomed, alert, and quite conscious of his well-earned merit. He presented a note containing some questions to Sri Bhagavan.

D. Pray help me realize *Atma-Paramatma-Satchitananda.*

M. *Atma-Paramatma-Satchitananda* mean one and the same thing — the Self. The Self is eternally realized. Otherwise, there will be no pleasure in it. If it is not eternal, it must have a beginning; what begins will also end, so it is only transient. There is no use seeking for a temporary state of affairs. The fact is that it is the state of effortless, ever-alert Peace. Effortlessness while remaining aware is the state of Bliss, and that is Realization.

D. I do not want intellectual answers. I want them to be practical.

M. Yes. Direct knowledge does not require intellectual discourses. Since the Self is directly experienced by everyone, they are not at all necessary. Everyone says, "I am." Is there anything further to realize?

D. It is not clear to me.

M. You exist. You say, "I am." That means existence.

D. But I am not sure of it, i.e., my existence.

M. Oh! Who then is speaking now?

D. I, surely. But whether I exist or not, I am not sure. Moreover, admitting my existence leads me nowhere.

M. There must be one even to deny the existence. If you do not exist, there is no questioner, and no question could have arisen.

D. Let us take it that I exist.

M. How do you know you exist?

D. Because I think, I feel, I see, etc.

M. So you mean that your existence is inferred from these. Furthermore, there is no feeling, thinking, etc., in sleep and yet there is being.

D. But no. I cannot say that I existed in deep sleep.

M. Do you then deny your existence in sleep?

D. I may be or may not exist in sleep. God only knows.

M. When you wake up from sleep, you remember what you did before falling asleep.

D. I can say I was before and after sleep, but I cannot say if I was in sleep.

M. Do you now say you were asleep?

D. Yes.

M. How do you know unless you remember the state of sleep?

D. It does not follow that I existed in sleep. Admission of such existence leads nowhere.

M. Do you mean a man dies every time that sleep overtakes him and that he resuscitates while waking?

D. Maybe. God alone knows.

M. Let God come and find the solution for these riddles, then. If one were to die in sleep, one would be afraid of sleep, just as one fears death. But in truth, one courts sleep. Why should that be unless there is pleasure in it?

D. There is no positive pleasure in sleep. Sleep is courted only to be rid of fatigue.

M. Well, that is right, "to be free from fatigue." There is one who is free from fatigue.

D. Yes.

M. So you exist in sleep and you now exist, too. You were happy in sleep without feeling, thinking, etc. The same one [you] continues now, why are you not happy?

D. How can it be said there is happiness?

M. Everyone says *Sukhamahamasvapsam* (I slept happily or was blissfully asleep).

D. I do not think they are right. There is no *sukha* (bliss), only absence of sorrow.

M. Your very being is bliss. Therefore, everyone says, "I was blissfully asleep." That means one remains in the primal uncontaminated state in sleep. As for sorrow, there is none. Where is it in order that you might speak of its absence in sleep? The present wrong identification of the Self with the body gives rise to all these misapprehensions.

D. What I want is realization. I currently do not feel my inherent happy nature.

M. This is because the Self is now identified with the non-self. The non-self too is not apart from the Self. However, there is the wrong notion that the body is apart and the Self is confounded with the body. This wrong identification must end for happiness to manifest.

D. I am unable to help myself.

(*The engineer suggested surrender to the Master.*)

D. Agreed.

M. Your nature is happiness. You say that is not apparent. See what obstructs you from your true being. It is pointed out to you that the obstruction is the wrong identity. So eliminate the error. The patient must take the medicine prescribed by the doctor in order that he may be cured.

D. But the patient is too weak to help himself and so places himself uncon-

ditionally in the hands of the doctor.
M. The doctor must be given a free hand and the patient must only remain quiet without saying anything. Similarly, keep quiet. That is effortlessness.
D. That is the most effective medicine, too.

The other questions he wrote down were:
D. Convince me of the existence of God.
M. Realization of the Self amounts to such conviction.
D. How is *prarabdha* (past karma) related to *purushakara* (one's own effort here)?
M. *Prarabdha* is karma (action). There must be a *karta* (doer) for it. See who the *karta* is. *Purushakara* is effort. See who exerts it. There is identity established. The one who seeks to know their relation is himself the link.
D. What is karma and rebirth?
M. See the *karta* (doer) and then the karma (action) becomes obvious. If you are born now, rebirth may follow. See if you are born now.
D. Help me to have *jyotidarshana* (vision of light).
M. *Darshana* (sight) implies *drashta* (seer). Find him and *darshana* (sight) is included in him.

Poovan, a shepherd, says that he knows Sri Bhagavan from thirty years ago, the days of the Virupaksha cave. He would, at times, supply milk to visitors in those days.

Some six years ago he had lost a sheep, for which he was searching for three days. The sheep was pregnant and he had lost all hopes of recovering her, because he thought she had been set upon by wild animals. One day, he was passing by the Asramam when Sri Bhagavan saw him and inquired how he was. The man replied he was looking out for a lost sheep. Sri Bhagavan kept quiet, as is usual with him. Then he told the shepherd to help in lifting some stones, which he did with great pleasure. After the work was finished, Sri Bhagavan told him: "Go this way," pointing to the footpath towards the town. "You will find the stray sheep on the way." So he did and found the lost sheep with two little lambs.

The shepherd now says, "What a Bhagavan is this! Look at the force of his words! He is great! He never forgets even a poor man like me. He remembers my son Manikkam, also with kindness. Such are the great ones! I am happy when I can do any little job for him, such as looking after the cows when they are in heat."

DECEMBER 18, 1936

Mr. Cohen asked: Meditation is with mind in the *jagrat* (waking) state. There is mind in the dream state, also. Why is there no meditation during dreaming? Is it even possible?

M. Ask it in the dream.

After a short silence, Sri Bhagavan continued: You are told to meditate now and find out who you are. Instead of doing that, you ask "Why is there no meditation in dream or in sleep?" If you find out for whom there is *jagrat* (waking), it will be clear that dream and sleep are also for the same one. You are the witness of *jagrat* (waking), *svapna* (dream) and *sushupti* (sleep) — rather, they pass before you. Because you are out of meditation now, these questions arise. Stick to meditation and see if these questions arise.

DECEMBER 23, 1936

A certain visitor formulated a question, saying that meditation is more direct than investigation, because the former holds onto the truth, whereas the latter sifts the truth from untruth.

M. For the beginner, meditation on a form is easier and more agreeable. Practice of it leads to *Atma-vichara*, which consists in sifting Reality from unreality.

What is the use of holding onto truth when you are filled with antagonistic factors?

Atma-vichara directly leads to realization by removing the obstacles which make you think that the Self is not already realized.

DECEMBER 25, 1936

A brahmachari youth who graduated in science has been waiting here for Grace for the last four or five months in order that some job might drop on him like a ripe apple from the tree. He has made no other efforts to secure a job. Yesterday his brother came here to take him away to his parents. But the youth declined to go. An appeal was made to Sri Bhagavan who said: I do not tell anyone to come nor ask him to go. Everyone pleases himself here. He says he finds peace in the Hall and he also wants a job. Evidently, the job must be found in the Hall itself so that his peace may not be disturbed. Peace is not in the Hall. It is in the repose of the Self. It can be gained anywhere.

Some days later, the youth threw away his sacred thread and appeared before Sri Bhagavan with his limbs shaking, which the young man later described as his Bliss (ananda). Sri Bhagavan told him not to make a habit of sitting in front of him in the Hall and ordered him out. Furthermore, he continued: Even a fledgling is protected by the parent birds only until such time as it grows its wings. It is not protected forever. Similarly with devotees. I have shown the way. You must now be able to follow it up and find peace wherever you are.

The young man thinks that Sri Bhagavan gave him upadesa in the following words: "The self (*i.e.* ego) must be subdued by oneself."

The man, however, has refused the offer of a job in one of the local schools and thinks that he has been given a mighty job by the Hill or by Sri Bhagavan. "What that job is the world will know later," he says. He had anticipated all this day's occurrences some months ago and had foretold them to his mother and his friends. He is happy with the events.

Sri Bhagavan, however, compared him to another man who is in no way of the right type. The boy thinks he is Bhagavan in embryo. Later, he went mad and died.

A gentleman enthusiastically recounted several of his experiences on following Sri Bhagavan's instructions and incidentally mentioned that he and Sri Bhagavan were born on the same day of the week and bore the same name . . . Sri Bhagavan completed it, adding: The same Self is in both.

A young man from Trichi, questioned Sri Bhagavan on the mention in Upadesa Manjari *of atyanta vairagyam (total dispassion) as the qualification of a ripe disciple and asked:* What is *vairagya?* Detachment from worldly pursuits and desire for salvation. Is it not so?
M. Who has not got it?

Each one seeks happiness but is misled into regarding pain-associated pleasures as happiness. Such happiness is transient. His mistaken activity gives him short-lived pleasure. Pain and pleasure alternate in the world. To discriminate between pain-producing and pleasure-producing matters and confine oneself to the happiness-producing pursuit only is *vairagya*. What is it that will not be followed by pain? He seeks it and engages in it. Otherwise, man has one foot in the world and another in the spiritual pursuit (without progressing satisfactorily in either field).

A question was again raised regarding the function of the Guru.

M. Because man is not able to help himself, finding himself too weak, he seeks more strength in the shape of a Guru.

Mr. K.R.V. Iyer sought more light on *nada* (sound).

M. He who meditates on it feels it. There are ten kinds of *nadas*. After the final thundering *nada*, the man gets *laya*. That is his natural and eternal state. *Nada, jyoti,* or inquiry thus takes one to the same point. (The former are indirect and the last is direct).

D. The mind becomes peaceful for a short while but re-emerges. What is to be done?

M. The peace often gained must be remembered at other times. That peace is your natural and permanent state. By continuous practice, it will become natural. It is called the "current." That is your true nature.

Nada, visions, etc., imply the existence of *triputi* (the triads of cognizer, cognition, and the cognized). The current resulting from investigation into the Self is *suddha triputi* or pure *triad* — that is to say, undifferentiated triad.

DECEMBER 26, 1936

A Swiss lady described a vision she had of Sri Bhagavan. While sitting with her eyes wide open, she saw Sri Bhagavan's face becoming cherub-like and draped in glorious flowers. She was drawn in love towards that child-like face.

M. The vision is in your mind. Your love is the cause. Paul Brunton saw me as a giant figure; you saw me like a child. Both are visions.

The lady said: Paul Brunton asked me if I had any spiritual experience here, and I denied it. Now this happens.

M. Do not be deceived by visions.

D. If one is miles away in Europe and invokes your aid . . . ,

M. Where is Europe? It is within you.

D. I have come here; I would like Maharshi to go there.

(Saying it, she laughed gently. Silence for some minutes.)

M. You see the physical body and so you find limitations. Time and space operate on this plane. So long as you think of the gross body, there will be differences found as different bodies. On the other hand, knowledge of the real Maharshi will set all doubts at rest.

Are you in India now? Or is India within you? Even now, this notion that you are in India must go. India is within you. In order to verify it, look to your sleep. Did you feel that you were in Europe or in India while asleep? You were nevertheless existing then the same as now.

Space is in you. The physical body is in space, but not you.

Paul Brunton had his eyes closed when he saw the vision, whereas you had your eyes open, you say.

D. Yes. But I never had a vision, whereas he is a psychic.

After a few minutes she asked if it is an advantage or a disadvantage to see visions like this.

M. An advantage.

Sri Bhagavan continued: Probably you had been thinking of a child and that appeared in the vision . . .

D. Yes, only of Shiva — His child-like face . . .

M. That's it.

D. But Shiva is the Destroyer . . . (meaning, not a child).

M. Yes — of sorrows.

After a few minutes, Bhagavan continued: You will shortly go to sleep. On waking up in the morning, you will say, "I slept well and happily." What happened in sleep is your real nature. That continues now, too; otherwise it will not be your real nature. Get the state of sleep even now; it is Shiva.

Have we got a form? Find out before you think of Shiva's form. Did you not exist in sleep? Were you aware of any form then? Were you with form in your sleep? You existed all the same. The "I" which was in sleep is also now present. You were not the body according to your sleep experience. You are the same now — that is, without the body. Being without the body, you were happy in sleep. You are the same now. That which is enduring must alone be your real nature. There was no body but only experience of happiness in sleep. That endures now, too. The Self is bodiless. If you are thus without body, how can Shiva be with body? If you are with body, Shiva also is with body. If you are not, He also is not.

D. Why is He then Shiva?

M. Shiva means embodiment of happiness — of auspiciousness.

(*She was very pleased. After a time, she left.*)

The visitors were talking among themselves and one of them said:

We, though familiar with our traditional teachings, are unable to follow these teachings (*meaning Sri Bhagavan's*). How can the foreigners unfamiliar with our ways follow Sri Bhagavan's teachings so easily?

Sri Bhagavan remarked finally: Visions are better than no visions. People become interested in that way. They do not take to foreign ideas; but once they do, they hold on. So much for their merits.

Sri Bhagavan later referred to Sivaprakasam Pillai's vision: Visions are not external. They appear only internally. If external, they must assert themselves without there being a seer. In that case, what is the warranty for their existence? The seer only.

D. Something concrete is required to meditate upon. How shall we meditate upon "I"?
M. We have become totally rooted in forms and so we require a concrete form for meditating upon. Only that which we contemplate will remain in the end. When you contemplate, the other thoughts disappear. So long as you need to contemplate, there are other thoughts. Where are you? You contemplate because you exist, for the contemplator must contemplate. The contemplation can only be where he is. Contemplation wards off all other thoughts. You should merge yourself in the source. At times we merge in the source unconsciously, as in sleep, death, swoon, etc. What is contemplation? It is merging into the source *consciously*. Then the fear of death, of swoon, etc. will disappear, because you are able to merge into the source *consciously*.

Why fear death? Death cannot mean non-being. Why do you love sleep, but not death? Do you not think now? Are you not existing now? Did you not exist in your sleep? Even a child says that he slept well and happily. He admits his existence in sleep, unconsciously though. So, consciousness is our true nature. We cannot remain unconscious. We, however, say we were unconscious in our sleep because we refer to qualified consciousness. The world, the body, etc., are so imbedded in us that this relative consciousness is taken to be the Self. Does anyone say in his sleep that he is unconscious? He says so now. This is the state of relative consciousness. Therefore, he speaks of relative consciousness and not of abstract consciousness. The consciousness is beyond relative consciousness or unconsciousness.

Again reverting to Tiruvachakam, *Sri Bhagavan said:* All the four foremost saints have expressed their experiences in the very first stanza. 1. Undifferentiated worship, 2. Never-failing remembrance, 3. Unrisen thought, 4. The ego is not, the Self is.

All mean the same.
D. But this truth is not realized.

M. It will be realized in due course. Till then there is devotion (*bhakti*): "Even for a trice you do not leave my mind." Does He leave you any moment? It is you who allow your mind to wander away. He remains ever steady. When your mind is fixed, you say: "He does not leave my mind even for a trice." How ridiculous!

DECEMBER 27, 1936

Mr. Shamanna from Mysore asked Sri Bhagavan: Kindly explain *Aham Sphurana* (the light of "I-I").

M. "I" is not known in sleep. On waking "I" is perceived associated with the body, the world, and non-self in general. Such associated "I" is *Aham vritti*. When *Aham* represents the Self only, it is *Aham Sphurana*. This is natural to the *jnani* and is itself called *jnana* by *jnanis,* or *bhakti* by *bhaktas.* Though ever present, including in sleep, it is not perceived. It cannot be known in sleep all at once. It must be first realized in the waking state, for it is our true nature underlying all the three states. Efforts must be made only in the *jagrat* (waking) state and the Self realized here and now. It will afterwards be understood and realized to be continuous Self, uninterrupted by *jagrat, svapna,* and *sushupti.* Thus it is *akhandakara vritti* (unbroken experience). *Vritti* is used for lack of a better expression. It should not be understood to be literally a *vritti.* In that case, *vritti* will resemble an "ocean-like river," which is absurd. *Vritti* is of short duration; it is qualified, directed consciousness; or absolute consciousness broken up by cognition of thoughts, senses, etc. *Vritti* is the function of the mind, whereas the continuous consciousness transcends the mind. This is the natural, primal state of the *jnani* or the liberated being. That is unbroken experience. It asserts itself when relative consciousness subsides. *Aham vritti* ("I"-thought) is broken, *Aham sphurana* (the light of "I-I") is unbroken, continuous. After thoughts subside, the light shines forth.

DECEMBER 31, 1936

A question was asked regarding untouchability.

M. The Non-self is untouchable. The social untouchability is manmade, whereas the other untouchability is natural and divine.

A question was asked regarding the avatars *of Vishnu.*

M. Let us know our own *avatara;* the knowledge of the other *avatars* will follow.

221

Again there was a question about Ishvara.

M. Existence of *Ishvara* follows from our conception of *Ishvara*. Let us first know whose concept He is. The concept will be only according to the one who conceives. Find out who you are and the other problem will solve itself.

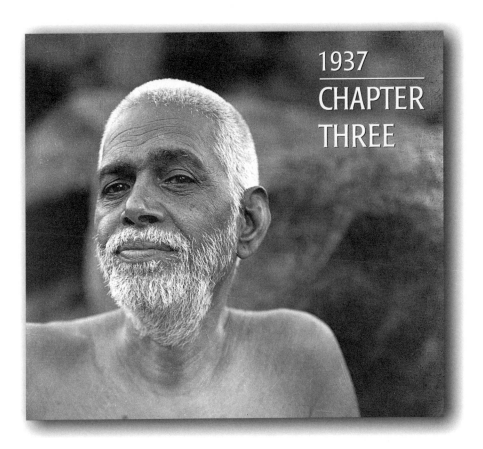

D. When I try to meditate, I am unable to do so because my mind wanders. What am I to do?

M. Your question furnishes the answer. With regard to the first part of the question, you say you concentrate but do not succeed. "You" means "the Self." On what do you concentrate? Where do you fail? Are there two selves, for the one to concentrate on the other? Which is the self now complaining of failure? There cannot be two selves. There is only one Self, and that need not concentrate.

"But then, why is there no happiness?" — you ask. What is it that prevents you from remaining as the Spirit which you are in sleep? You yourself admit it is the wandering mind. Find out the mind. If its "wandering" stops, it will be found to be the Self — your "I"-consciousness which is Spirit eternal. It is beyond knowledge and ignorance.

Chapter Three — 1937

D. What is the difference between *Aham Brahmasmi* (I am *Brahman*) and *Brahmaivaham* (only *Brahman* I am).

M. The former is *Pratyaksha vritti* (direct experience), whereas the latter is *Paroksha jnana* (indirect knowledge). The first begins with the realization of *Aham* ("I"), whereas the latter starts with the hearsay *Brahman* which cannot be apart from the Self, if the same has been realized.

Mr. Greenlees: After leaving this Asramam in October I was aware of Bhagavan's peace enfolding me for about ten days. All the time while busy with work there was an undercurrent of that peace of unity; it was almost like the dual consciousness of being half-asleep during a dull lecture. Then it faded out entirely, and the old stupidities returned.

Work leaves no time for meditation. Is the constant reminder "I Am," trying to feel it while actually at work, enough?

M. It will become constant when the mind gets strengthened. Repeated practice strengthens the mind, and such a mind is capable of holding onto the current. In that case, being engaged in work or not, the current remains unaffected and uninterrupted.

D. No separate meditation is necessary?

M. Meditation is your true nature now. You call it meditation, because there are other thoughts distracting you. When these thoughts are dispelled, you remain alone, i.e., in the state of meditation free from thoughts; and that is your real nature which you are now attempting to gain by keeping out other thoughts. Such repression of other thoughts is now called "meditation." When the practice becomes firm, the real nature shows itself as true meditation.

Other thoughts arise more forcibly when you attempt meditation.

There was an immediate chorus of questions by a few others. Sri Maharshi continued: Yes, all kinds of thoughts arise in meditation. It is but right. What lies hidden in you is brought out. Unless they rise up, how can they be destroyed? They therefore rise up spontaneously in order to be extinguished in due course, thus strengthening the mind.

A visitor: All are said to be *Brahman.*
M. Yes, they are. But so long as you think they are apart, they must be avoided. If on the other hand they are found to be Self, there is no need to say "all." For all that exists is only *Brahman.* There is nothing besides *Brahman.*
D. The *Ribhu Gita* speaks of so many objects as unreal, adding at the end that they are all *Brahman* and thus real.
M. Yes. When you see them as so many they are *asat,* i.e., unreal. But when you see them as *Brahman* they are real, deriving their reality from their substratum, *Brahman.*
D. Why then does *Upadesa Saram* speak of the body, etc., as *jada* i.e. insentient?
M. Inasmuch as you say that they are body, etc., apart from the Self. But when the Self is found, this body, etc. are also found to be in it. Afterwards, no one will ask the question and no one will say they are insentient.
D. *Viveka* is said to be discrimination between the Self and the non-self. What is the non-self?
M. There is no non-self, in fact. The non-self also exists in the Self. It is the Self which speaks of the non-self because it has forgotten itself. Having lost hold of itself, it conceives something as non-self, which is after all nothing but itself.
(*At this point, the discussion between the protagonists of various theories heated up.*)

JANUARY 2, 1937
M. The "I" which rises will again subside. That is the individual "I" or the "I"-concept. That which does not rise will not subside. It *is* and will be forever. That is the universal "I," the perfect "I," or realization of the Self.

At 5:30 p.m., the Swiss lady complained to Sri Bhagavan that she gets a headache upon prolonged meditation.
M. If the meditator and meditation are understood to be the same, there will be no headache or similar complaints.
D. But they are different. How can we consider them to be identical?

M. That is due to your outlook. There is only one and there are no differences. On meditation, the relative consciousness will vanish. That is not annihilation, for Absolute Consciousness arises. The Bible itself says, "The Kingdom of Heaven is within you." If you consider yourself to be the body, there is some difficulty in understanding this statement. On the other hand, if you know who you really are, the Kingdom of Heaven and all are included in your true Self. They are concepts arising after the ego has arisen. *Drishtim jnanamayeem krtva pasyet Brahmamayam jagat* (Turn your look within and make it absolute). With that absolute awareness realized, look without and you will realize the universe as not being apart from the realized Absolute.

Because your outlook is directed externally, you speak of a *without*. In that state you are advised to look *within*. This *within* is relative to the *without* you are seeking. In fact, the Self is neither without nor within.

Speaking of Heaven one thinks of it as above or below, within or without, since one is accustomed to relative knowledge. One seeks only objective knowledge and hence these ideas.

Realistically speaking there is neither up nor down, neither in nor out. If they were real they should be present in dreamless sleep, also. For what is real must be continuous and permanent. Did you feel "in" or "out" in your sleep? Of course not.

D. I do not remember.

M. If there was anything there, then that could be remembered. But you admit your existence then. The same Self is now speaking. The Self who was undifferentiated in sleep is differentiated in the present state, and sees the diversity. The Real Existence is the only One devoid of objective knowledge. That is Absolute consciousness. That is the state of happiness, as admitted by all of us. That state must be brought about even in this waking state. It is called *jagrat sushupti*. That is *mukti*.

D. The ego is the one which reincarnates.

M. Yes, but what is reincarnation? The ego remains the same. New bodies appear and hold it. The ego does not change. It does not leave one body, seek and find another. Just see what happens even to your gross body. Suppose you go to London. How do you do it? You take a conveyance, go to the docks, board the steamer and reach London in a few days. What has happened? The conveyances had moved, but not your body. Still you say that you traveled from one part of the globe to the other. The movements of the conveyances have been superimposed on your body. Similarly with your ego. The reincarnations are superimpositions. For example, what happens in a dream? Do you go to the dream world or does it occur in you? Surely the latter is the case. Just the same with reincarnations. The ego remains changeless all along.

Again, there is no time and space in your sleep. They are concepts which arise after the "I"-thought has arisen. Before the rise of the "I"-thought the concepts are absent. Therefore you are beyond time and space. The "I"-thought is only limited "I." The real "I" is unlimited, universal, beyond time and space. They are absent in sleep. Just on rising up from sleep, and before seeing the objective world, there is a state of awareness which is your pure Self. That must be known.

D. But I do not realize it.

M. It is not an object to be realized. You are That. Who is there to realize, and what?

Mr. V.K. Cholkar, of Poona: It is said "Know thyself" or see who the "I" in you is. What is the way to do it? Is it by simply repeating the mantra mechanically all along or have you to do it, remembering every moment why you are repeating the mantra?

M. You are always repeating the mantra automatically. If you are not aware of the *ajapa* (unspoken chant) which is eternally going on, you should take to *japa*. *Japa* is made with an effort. The effort is meant to ward off other thoughts. Then the *japa* becomes mental and internal. Finally, its *ajapa* and eternal nature will be realized, for it will be found to be going on even without your effort. The effortless state is the state of realization.

Mr. Cholkar again requested instructions from a practical point of view, i.e., suitable to himself.

M. It is not external and therefore need not be sought elsewhere. It is internal and also eternal. It is always realized. But you say you are not aware. It requires constant attention to itself. No other effort is necessary. Your effort is only meant not to allow yourself to be distracted by other thoughts.

(The person was satisfied.)

Mr. Greenlees: Bhagavan said yesterday that while a person is engaged in the search for "God within," one's outer work would go on automatically. In the life of Sri Chaitanya it is explained that while he sought Krishna (the Self) during his lectures to students, he forgot where his body was and went on talking of Krishna. This raises doubt whether work can safely be left to itself. Should one keep part attention on the physical work?

M. The Self is all. Now I ask you: Are you apart from the Self? Can the work go on apart from the Self? Or is the body apart from the Self? None of them could be apart from the Self. The Self is universal. So all the actions will go on whether you engage in them voluntarily or not. Attending to the Self includes attending to the work.

D. The work may suffer if I do not attend to it.

M. Because you identify yourself with the body, you consider that the work is done by you. But the body and its activities, including the work, are not apart from the Self. What does it matter whether you attend to the work or not? Suppose you walk from one place to another. You do not attend to every single step that you take. After a time, however, you find yourself at your destination. You notice how the work, i.e., walking, has gone on without your attention to it. Similarly it is with other kinds of work.

D. Then it is like sleepwalking.

M. Quite so. While a child is fast asleep, his mother feeds him. The child eats the food quite as well, as when awake. But the next morning, he says: "Mother! I did not take food last night." The mother and others know, however, that he did. But he says he did not. He was not aware and yet the action had gone on. Somnambulism is indeed a good analogy for this kind of work.

Take another example: A passenger in a cart has fallen asleep. The bulls move or stand still or are unyoked on the journey. He does not know these occurrences, but finds himself in a different place after waking. He has been blissfully ignorant of the events on the way, but his journey has been completed.

Similarly, with the Self of the person. He is asleep in the body. His waking state is the movement of the bulls, his *samadhi* is their standing still (because *samadhi* = *jagrat sushupti*) i e., to say, he is aware of but not attached to actions. So the bulls are in harness but do not move. His sleep is the unyoking of the bulls, for there is complete suspension of activities corresponding to the release of the bulls from the yoke.

Still another example: Scenes are projected on the screen in a cinema show. But the moving pictures do not affect or alter the screen. The seer pays attention to the pictures and ignores the screen. They cannot remain apart from the screen. Still, its existence is ignored. So also the Self is the screen on which the pictures, namely activities, are going on. Man is aware of the latter, ignoring the former. All the same, he is not apart from the Self. Whether aware or unaware, actions continue.

D. There is an operator in the cinema.

M. The cinema show is made out of insentient materials. The screen, the pictures, lamp, etc., are insentient and require an operator, a sentient agent. In the case of the Self, it is Consciousness itself and therefore self-contained. There cannot be an operator apart.

(*The devotee protested that he did not confuse the body with the operator, as the above answer would imply.*)

M. The functions of the body were kept in mind involving the need for the operator. Because there is the body — a *jada* object — an operator, a sentient agent, is necessary.

Because people think they are *jivas,* Sri Krishna has said that God resides in the Heart as the operator of the *jivas.* In fact, there are no *jivas* and no operator. The Self comprises all. It is the screen, the pictures, the seer, the actor, the operator, the light, and all else. Your confounding it with the body and imagining yourself as the actor amounts to the seer being represented as an actor in a cinema picture. Imagine the actor in the picture asking if he could enact a scene without the screen. Such is the case of the man who thinks of his acting apart from the Self.

D. It is like asking the spectator to act in the cinema picture. Somnambulism seems to be desirable.

M. There is the belief that the crow rolls only one iris into either eye to see any object. It has only one iris, but two eye sockets. Its sight is manipulated according to its desire.

Or, the elephant has one trunk with which it breathes and does things such as drinking water, etc.

Again, serpents are said to use the same apparatus for either seeing or hearing.

Similarly, the actions and states are according to one's point of view. Sleep waking or waking sleep, or dreaming sleep or dreaming wakefulness are about the same.

D. We have to deal with a physical body in a physical waking world. If we sleep while work is done or work when sleep overtakes us, the work will go wrong.

M. Sleep is not ignorance; it is your pure state. Wakefulness is not knowledge; it is ignorance. There is full awareness in sleep; there is total ignorance in waking. Your real nature covers both, and extends beyond. The Self is beyond knowledge and ignorance.

Sleep, dream, and waking are only modes passing before the Self. They proceed whether you are aware or not. That is the state of the *jnani* in whom pass the states of waking, *samadhi,* deep sleep and dream, like the bulls moving, standing or being unyoked when the passenger is asleep, as mentioned before. These questions are from the point of view of the *ajnani;* otherwise they do not arise.

D. Of course they cannot arise for the Self. Who would be there to ask? But unfortunately, I have not yet realized the Self.

M. That is just the obstacle in your way. You must get rid of the idea that you are an *ajnani* yet to realize the Self. You *are* the Self. Was there ever a time when you were apart from the It?

D. So it is an experiment in somnambulism . . . or daydreaming.

(*Bhagavan laughed.*)

JANUARY 3, 1937

In yesterday's answers, Sri Bhagavan said that the Self is pure Consciousness in deep slumber, and he also indicated the Self of the transition from sleep to the waking state as the ideal for realization. He was requested to explain. Sri Bhagavan graciously answered: The Self is pure Consciousness in sleep; it evolves as *aham* ("I") without the *idam* ("this") in the transition stage; and manifests as *aham* ("I") and *idam* ("this") in the waking state. The individual's experience is by means of *aham* ("I") only. So he must aim at realization in the way indicated (i.e., by means of the transitional "I"). Otherwise, the sleep-experience does not matter to him. If the transitional "I" is realized, the substratum is found and that leads to the goal.

Sleep is said to be *ajnana* (ignorance). That is only in relation to the wrong *jnana* (knowledge) prevalent in the wakeful state. The waking state is really *ajnana* (ignorance) and the sleep state is *prajnana* (full knowledge). *Prajnana* is *Brahman*, says the *sruti. Brahman* is eternal. The sleep-experiencer is called *prajna*. He is *Prajnanam* in all the three states. Its particular significance in the sleep state is that He is full of knowledge (*prajnanaghana*). What is *ghana?* There are *jnana* and *vijnana.* Both together operate in all perceptions. *Vijnana* in the *jagrat* is *viparita jnana* (wrong knowledge) i.e., *ajnana* (ignorance). It always coexists with the individual. When this becomes *vispashta jnana* (clear knowledge), It is *Brahman.* When wrong knowledge is totally absent, as in sleep, He remains pure *prajnana* only. That is *Prajnanaghana. Aitareya Upanishad* says *prajnana, vijnana, ajnana, samjnana* are all names of *Brahman.* Being made up of knowledge alone, how is He to be experienced? Experience is always with *vijnana.* Therefore, the pure "I" of the transitional stage must be held for the experience of the *Prajnanaghana.* The "I" of the waking state is impure and is not useful for such experience. Hence the use of the transitional "I," or the pure "I." How is this pure "I" to be realized? *Viveka Chudamani* says, "*Vijnana kose vilasatyajasram vijnana kosa*" (He is always shining forth in the intellectual sheath). *Tripura Rahasya* and other works point out that the interval between two consecutive *sankalpas* (ideas or thoughts) represents the pure *aham* ("I"). Therefore, holding on to the pure "I" one should have the *Prajnanaghana* for aim, and there is the *vritti* present in the attempt. All these have their proper and respective places and at the same time lead to realization.

Again, the pure Self has been described in *Viveka Chudamani* to be beyond *asat*, i.e., different from *asat*. Here *asat* is the contaminated waking "I." *Asadvilakshana* means *sat*, i.e., the Self of sleep. He is also described as different from *sat* and *asat*. Both mean the same. He is also *asesha sakshi* (all-seeing witness).

If pure, how is He to be experienced by means of the impure "I"? A man says, "I slept happily." Happiness was his experience. If not, how could he speak of what he had not experienced? How did he experience happiness in sleep, if the Self was pure? Who is it that speaks of that experience now? The speaker is the *vijnanatma* (ignorant self) and he speaks of *prajnanatma* (pure self). His present statement of the experience of happiness in sleep makes one infer his existence in sleep. How then did he remain? Surely not as in the waking state. He was there very subtly. Exceedingly subtle *vijnanatma* experiences the happy *prajnanatma* by means of the *maya* mode. It is like the rays of the moon seen below the branches, twigs and leaves of a tree.

The subtle *vijnanatma* seems apparently a stranger to the obvious *vijnanatma* of the present moment. Why should we infer his existence in sleep? Should we not deny the experience of happiness and be done with this inference? No. The fact of the experience of happiness cannot be denied, for everyone courts sleep and prepares a nice bed for the enjoyment of sound sleep.

This brings us to the conclusion that the cognizer, cognition, and the cognized are present in all three states, though there are differences in their subtleties. In the transitional state, the *aham* ("I") is *suddha* (pure), because *idam* ("this") is suppressed. *Aham* ("I") predominates.

Why isn't that pure "I" realized now or even remembered? Because of want of acquaintance (*parichaya*) with it. It can be recognized only if it is consciously attained. Therefore, make the effort and gain consciously.

One of the attendants asked about Sri Bhagavan's statement, "Reality and myth are both the same." How is that?

M. The *tantrics* and others of the kind condemn Sri Shankara's philosophy as *maya vada* without understanding him aright. What does he say? He says: 1. *Brahman* is real, 2. the universe is a myth, 3. *Brahman* is the universe.

He does not stop at the second statement but continues to supplement it with the third. What does it signify? The Universe is conceived to be apart from *Brahman* and that perception is wrong. The antagonists point to his illustration of *rajju sarpa* (rope-snake). This is unconditioned superimposition. After the truth of the rope is known, the illusion of snake is removed once and for all.

But they should also take into consideration the conditioned superimposition, e.g., *marumarichika* or *mrigatrishna* (water of mirage).

The mirage does not disappear even after knowing it to be a mirage. The vision is there but the man does not run to it for water. Sri Shankara must be understood in the light of both illustrations. The world is a myth. Even after knowing it, it continues to appear. It must be known to be *Brahman* and not apart.

If the world appears, yet to whom does it appear, he asks. What is your reply? You must say the Self. If not, will the world appear in the absence of the cognizing Self? Therefore, the Self is the reality. That is his conclusion. The phenomena are real as the Self, but are myths apart from the Self.

Now, what do the *tantrics*, etc., say? They say that the phenomena are real because they are part of the Reality in which they appear.

Are not these two statements the same? That is what I meant by reality and falsehood being one and the same.

The antagonists continue: With the conditioned as well as the unconditioned illusions considered, the phenomenon of water in a mirage is purely illusory because that water cannot be used for any purpose. On the other hand, the phenomenon of the world is different, for it is purposeful. How, then, does the latter stand on a par with the former?

A phenomenon cannot be a reality simply because it serves a purpose or purposes. Take a dream, for example. The dream creations are purposeful; they serve the dream-purpose. The dream-water quenches dream-thirst. The dream-creation is, however, contradicted in the waking state. The waking creation is contradicted in the other two states. What is not continuous cannot be real. If real, the thing must ever be real — not real for a short time and unreal at other times.

So it is with magical creations. They appear real and are yet illusory.

Similarly, the universe cannot be real of itself — that is to say, apart from the underlying Reality.

There is fire on the screen in a cinema show. Does it burn the screen? There is a cascade of water. Does it wet the screen? There are tools. Do they damage the screen?

That is why it is said *achchedyoyam, adahyoyam, akledhyoyam* etc. Fire, water, etc. are phenomena on the screen of *Brahman* (*i.e.*, the Self) and they do not affect It.

January 6, 1937

Mr. Parkhi: Many visitors here tell me they get visions or thought-currents from you. I am here for the last month and a half and still have not had the slightest experience of any kind. Is it because I am unworthy of your Grace? If so, I feel it disgraceful that I being *Vasishtakulotpanna* (of the lineage of Vasishta) should not have your Grace, while far-off foreigners have it. Will you kindly suggest some *prayaschitta* (method of expiation) for removing this disgrace?

M. Visions and thought-currents are had according to the state of mind. It depends on the individuals and not upon the Universal Presence. Moreover, they are immaterial. What matters is Peace of Mind.

D. Peace of mind is the result of trance. How is that trance to be had?

M. Trance is only absence of thoughts. That state prevails in sleep. Do you have enduring peace of mind on that account?

D. It is said in the journal maintained in the Asramam that trance is necessary.

M. Trance is not something to be acquired anew. Your natural state is that of trance.

D. But I do not feel it.

M. The fact of your contrary belief is the impediment.

D. Since I have not realized the Self, I do not understand my permanent state of trance.

M. This is only a repetition. That is the obstruction. This arises because you think that the non-self is you. That is the mistake. Do not take the non-self to be the Self. Then the Self will be evident to you.

D. I understand it theoretically but not in practice.

M. There are not two selves — for the self to speak of the non-realization of the Self.

D. It is still theoretical to me. How shall I get the trance?

M. Trance is only temporary in its effects. There is happiness so long as it lasts. After rising from it, the old *vasanas* return. Unless the *vasanas* are destroyed in *sahaja samadhi* (effortless *samadhi*), there is no benefit from trance.

D. But mustn't trance precede *sahaja samadhi*?

M. Trance is the natural state. Although there are activities and phenomena, yet they do not affect the trance. If they are realized to be not apart from the Self, the Self is realized. Where is the use of trance, unless it brings about enduring peace of mind? Know that even now you are in trance whatever happens. That is all.

D. But how shall I do it?

A scholar remarked: Yato vacho nivartante aprapya manasa saha (where words fail to reach, along with the mind).

The questioner retorted: It is also said *manasaiva aptavyam* (to be realized with the mind only).

M. Yes. The Pure Mind; i.e., the mind free from thoughts is the Self. The pure mind is beyond the impure mind.

D. Seen with the subtlest of subtle intellect by subtle seers.

M. What was said of mind applies to this, also.

D. If trance is already my inherent state, why then is it said that trance must be acquired before Realization?

M. It means that one should be aware of his eternal state of trance. Inattentiveness to it is ignorance. *Pramado vai mrtyuh* (inattention is death itself).

D. How can I be attentive without getting trance beforehand?

M. Very well. If you are so anxious for trance, any narcotic will do; a drug habit will be the result, and not liberation. There are *vasanas* in the latent state even in trance. The *vasanas* must be destroyed.

Another devotee: Can there be Self-realization before the *vasanas* are entirely destroyed?

M. There are two kinds of *vasanas:* 1. *bandha hetuh,* causing bondage for the ignorant, and 2. *bhoga hetuh,* giving enjoyment for the wise. The latter do not obstruct realization.

D. Are Self-realized persons — for example, Vamadeva and Jada Bharata — reborn?

M. The Realized ones cannot be reborn. Rebirth is due to *vasanas,* which are binding. But these are destroyed in the state of Self-realization.

D. Are we to take it that they had gone to the stage of *kevala nirvikalpa* but not to *sahaja nirvikalpa*?

M. Yes.

D. If *vasanas* for enjoyment only do not obstruct the state of realization and if one can look upon the events of the world without his state of bliss being distributed, it means that attachment alone is bondage. Am I right?

M. Yes, quite. Attachment is bondage. Attachment disappears with the elimination of the ego.

D. Realization is said to be helped by Guru's Grace.

M. Guru is none other than the Self.

D. Krishna had Sandipini for his Guru and Rama had Vasishta.

M. Guru is said to be external for the seeker. The inward turning of the mind is brought about by the Guru. Since the seeker is outward-bent, he is advised to learn from a Guru whom he will in due course find to be the Self.

D. May I have Guru's Grace?

M. Grace is always there.

D. But I do not feel it.

M. Surrender will make one understand Grace.

D. I have surrendered heart and soul. I am the best judge of my heart. Still I do not feel Grace.

M. If you had surrendered, the questions would not have arisen.

D. I have surrendered. Still questions arise.

M. Grace is constant. Your judgment is the variable. Where else should the fault lie?

D. I must be enabled to surrender myself.

M. Thayumanavar has said: "Glory to Thee for enabling me to discuss so much and follow Thy words so far!"

JANUARY 7, 1937

A Hindi gentleman asked how the fear of death could be overcome.

M. Find out if you were ever born before thinking of death. Only he who is born can die. You are as good as dead even in sleep. What fear is there of death?

D. How are we in sleep?

M. Ask the question during sleep. You recall the experience of sleep only when you are awake. You recall that state by saying, "I slept happily."

D. What is the instrument by which we experience that state?

M. We call it *Mayakarana* as opposed to the *antahkarana* to which we are accustomed in our other states. The same instruments are called differently in the different states, even as the *anandatman* of sleep is termed the *vijnanatman* of the wakeful state.

D. Please furnish me with an illustration for the *Mayakarana* experiencing the *ananda*.

M. How can you say, "I slept happily"? The experience is there to prove your happiness. There could not be any remembrance in the wakeful state in the absence of the experience in the sleep state.

D. Agreed. But please give me an illustration.

M. How can it be described? If you dive into water to recover an article, you speak of its recovery only after rising out of the water. You don't say anything while submerged.

D. I do not have fear in sleep, whereas I have it now.

M. Because *dwiteeyadvai bhavait* — fear is always of a second one. Of what are you afraid?

D. By reason of the perception of the body, the senses, the world, *Ishvara*, doership, enjoyment etc.

M. Why do you see them if they cause fear?

D. Because they are inescapable.

M. But it is the "you" who sees them. For whom is the fear? Is it for them?

D. No, it is for me.

M. Because you see them, you fear them. Do not see them and there will be no fear.

D. What then should I do in the waking state?

M. Be the Self; there will be no second thing to cause fear.

D. Yes. Now I understand. If I see my Self, then the sight is warded off the non-self and there is happiness. Yet there is fear of death.

M. Only the one who is born is to die. See if you were born at all in order that death should threaten you.

Mr. Sridhar, a Hindu from Goa, asked: What is *kousalam* (skill) in *"Yogah karmasu kousalam"* (yoga is skill in action). How is it to be gained?

M. Do your actions without caring for the result. Do not think that you are the doer. Dedicate the work to God. That is the skill and also the way to gain it.

D. *Samatvam yoga uchyate* (Equanimity is yoga). What is that equanimity?

M. It is unity in diversity. The universe is now seen to be diverse. See the common factor (*sama*) in all the objects. When that is done, equality in the pairs of opposites (*dwandwani*) naturally follows. It is the latter which is ordinarily spoken of as equanimity.

D. How is the common factor to be perceived in the diversity?

M. The seer is only one. They [the diverse phenomena] do not appear without the seer. There is no change in the seer, however much the others may change.

> Yogah karmasu kousalam = Skill in work is yoga
> Samatvam yoga uchyate = Equanimity is yoga
> Mamekam saranam vraja = Only surrender to Me
> Ekamevadwiteeyam = One without a second

These represent Karma, Yoga, *Bhakti*, and *Jnana*, and convey the same meaning. They are only the single Truth presented in its different aspects.

Mr. Ekanatha Rao: Is Grace necessary?

M. Yes.

D. How to gain Divine Grace?

M. By surrender.

D. Still I do not feel Grace.

M. Sincerity is wanting. Surrender should not be verbal nor conditional.

(Passages from St. Justinian were read out to illustrate these statements.)

Prayer is not verbal; it is from the Heart. To merge into the Heart is prayer. That is also Grace.

The Alwar says: "I was all along seeking Thee. But on realizing the Self, I find you are the Self. The Self is my all, and so you are my All."

D. Impurities of limitation, ignorance, and desire (*anava, mayika,* and *kamya*) place obstacles in the way of meditation. How to conquer them?

M. By not being swayed by them.

D. Grace is necessary.

M. Yes, Grace is both the beginning and the end. Introversion is due to Grace; Perseverance is Grace; and Realization is Grace. That is the reason for the statement: *Mamekam saranam vraja* (only surrender to Me). If one has entirely surrendered oneself, is there any part left to ask for Grace? He is then swallowed up by Grace.

D. The obstacles are powerful and obstruct meditation.

M. If a Higher Power is recognized and surrendered to, how can any obstacle obstruct you? If you say, "They are powerful," the source of their Power must be held so that they do not obstruct you.

In the course of an informal conversation, Sri Bhagavan pointed out that Self-realization is possible only for the fit. The *vasanas* must be eliminated before *jnana* dawns. One must be like Janaka for *jnana* to dawn, and ready to sacrifice everything for the Truth. Complete renunciation is the index of fitness.

D. Miseries appear in *jagrat* (the waking state). Why should they appear?

M. If you see your Self, they will not appear.

D. If I turn to look who I am, I do not find anything.

M. How did you remain in your sleep? There was no "I"-thought there, and you were happy. On the other hand, in the *jagrat* there are thoughts flowering in the wake of the root-thought "I," and these hide your inherent happiness. Get rid of these thoughts, which are the obstacles to happiness. Your natural state is one of happiness, as evident in your sleep.

D. I do not know anything of my sleep experience.

M. But you know that it was happiness. Otherwise, you would not be saying, "I slept happily." When there is no thought, no "I" and nothing in fact except yourself, you are happy. That is the whole Truth.

This is exactly what is conveyed by the Mahavakya *Tattvamasi* (You are That). Find your Self and then "That" is known.

D. How is that *Brahman*?

M. Why do you want to know of *Brahman* apart from yourself? The scripture says, "You are That." The Self is intimate to you and you cannot be without the Self. Realize It. That is the Realization of *Brahman*, also.

D. But I am unable to do it. I am too weak to realize my Self.

M. In that case, surrender yourself unreservedly and the Higher Power will reveal Itself.

D. What is unconditional surrender?

M. If one surrenders oneself, there will be no one to ask questions or to be thought of. Either the thoughts are eliminated by holding on to the root-thought "I," or one surrenders oneself unconditionally to the Higher Power. These are the only two ways for Realization.

A cultured lady, daughter of a well-known solicitor of Madras, asked: What should one do in order to remain free from thoughts as advised by you? Is it only the inquiry "Who am I?"

M. Only to remain still. Do it and see.

D. It is impossible.

M. Exactly. For the same reason the inquiry "Who am I?" is recommended.

D. Raising the question, no response comes from within.

M. What kind of response would you expect? Are you not there? What more?

D. Thoughts rise up increasingly.

M. Then and there raise the same question, "Who am I?"

D. Should I do so as each thought arises? Is the world our thought only?

M. Leave this question to the world. Let it ask, "How did I come into being?"

D. Do you mean it is not related to me?

M. Nothing is perceived in deep sleep; all these are seen only after waking. Only after thoughts arise does the world comes into being; what can it be but thought?

Another visitor asked: What should we do to make the mind still?

M. First let the mind be gotten hold of and brought here; then we shall consider ways and means of stilling it.

D. I meant to say that it is always changing — even when doing our *japa*.

M. *Japa* is meant only for stilling the mind.

D. What *japa* is good for it?

M. Anything suitable, such as *Gayatri*.

D. Will *Gayatri* do?

M. Can anything excel it? Only those who cannot do it look for others. It contains the whole range of truth in it. Chanting (*japa*) will lead to *dhyana* (meditation) and is a means for realizing the Self.

D. Will half an hour a day do for it?

M. It must be done always, or as long as you can.

While explaining stanza six in Arunachala Ashtaka, *Sri Bhagavan observed the following*:

The final word in the previous stanza asks, "Is there One?" The initial words in the present stanza answer, "Yes, there is the One . . ." It proceeds "Though it is the only One, yet by its wonderful power it gets reflected on the tiny dot "I" (the ego), otherwise known as ignorance or the aggregate of latent tendencies; this reflected light is relative knowledge. This, according to one's *prarabdha* (past karma now fructifying), manifests the inner latent tendencies as the outer gross world and withdraws the gross external world as the subtle internal tendencies; such power is called mind in the subtle plane and brain in the physical plane. This mind or brain acts as the magnifier to that Eternal One Being and shows It forth as the expanded universe. In the waking and dream states, the mind is outward bent and in sleep it is inward bent; with the mind as the medium, the one Supreme Being seems diversified in the waking and dream states and remains withdrawn in the sleep state, or swoon, etc. Therefore, you are only That and cannot be otherwise. Whatever the changes, the same one Being remains as yourself; there is nothing besides yourself."

The previous stanza says: Once exposed to sunlight, a sensitive plate can no longer take on images; similarly, the mind (the sensitive plate), after exposure in Your Light, cannot reflect the world any more. Moreover, the Sun is of You only. Should his rays be so powerful as to prevent images being formed, how much more so should Your Light be? It is thus said that there is nothing apart from the One Being, Yourself.

In the present stanza, the tiny dot equals the ego; the tiny dot made up of darkness is the ego consisting of latent tendencies; the seer or the subject or the ego rising, it expands itself as the seen, the object or the *antahkaranas* (the inner organs). The light must be dim in order to enable the ego to rise up. In broad daylight, a rope does not look like a snake. The rope itself cannot be seen in complete darkness, so there is no chance of mistaking it for a snake. Only in dim light, in dusk, or in light darkened by shadows does the rope "appear" to be a snake. Similarly, it is for the Pure Radiant Being to rise up as the Ego — it is possible only in Its Light diffused through darkness. This darkness is otherwise known as the Original Ignorance (Original Sin). The Light passing through it is called Reflected Light. The Reflected Light on its own merits is commonly known as the Pure Mind or *Ishvara* or God. *Ishvara* is well known to be unified with *Maya*; in other words, the Reflected Light is *Ishvara*.

The other name — Pure Mind — implies impure mind, also. It is the *rajasic* or active mind, or the ego; this too, can be projected from the former *sattvic* mind through another reflection only; thus, the ego is the product of the second darkness (*avidya*). Then comes the *tamasic* or the dull mind in the shape of *antahkaranas* (the inner organs); this appears as the world.

From the standpoint of the gross body, it may be said to shine forth externally as the world by means of the brain.

But the gross body is of the mind only. The mind may be said to consist of four inner organs, or the principle composed of thoughts, or the sixth sense; or combining intellect with the ego, and *chitta* with the mind (i.e. memory-faculty with the thinking faculty), it may be taken to consist of two parts (the ego and the mind). In the latter case, the *vijnanatma* (the intellectual Self) or the ego or the seer forms the subject, and the mental sheath or the seen, the object.

The waking, dream and sleep states have their origin in the Original Darkness (*mula avidya*). With the mind outgoing and deriving experiences from its modes in the waking and dream states, and indrawn in sleep, experiencing with modes of *Maya*, a unique power regulates all activities of the individuals and of the universe. All these are only phenomena passing through the Reflected Light on the substratum of the Self-radiant Being.

Just as a rope-snake cannot be seen in broad daylight, nor rope itself in thick darkness, so also the world appears neither in the *samadhi* state of Self-shining pure Being nor in deep sleep, swoon, etc. Only in Reflected Light (Light mixed with Darkness or knowledge soiled by Ignorance) can the world, *not independent of its Source*, seem to rise up, flourish, and be resolved. Its diversity, too, cannot be exclusive of the Reality, the original Source. Here a play is going on in which the One Single Being becomes manifold, is objectified and then withdrawn. There must be a *Shakti* (Power) to do it, and wonderful, too! She cannot be independent of Her origin. In the Self-shining Pure Being this *Shakti* cannot be seen. Nevertheless, Her actions are only too well known. How sublime!

From Her sublime original activity (i.e., power vibrating), *sattva*-filled reflection results; from it the *rajasic* ego; then *tamasic* thought-forms which are commonly known as knowledge, or the light corresponding to the magnifying lens. Just as the artificial light is projected through a lens onto the screen, so also the Reflected Light passes through thought (the magni-fier) before expanding as the world beyond it; furthermore, thought — it-self the world in seed form — seems to be the wide external world. Such is the extraordinary Power! In this way *Ishvara*, individual, and the world are only of the Reflected Light, having the Self-shining single Being for sub-stratum.

Now, what is this "I"-thought (the ego)? Is it the subject or the object, in the scheme of things?

Inasmuch as it witnesses all other objects in the waking and dream states, or at any rate we think that it does, it must be considered to be the subject. On realizing the Pure Self, however, it will be an object only.

Whose is this "I"-thought (the ego)? This investigation forms the *vichara*.

"I"-thought and "this-thought" are both emanations from the same light. They are related to *rajoguna* and *tamoguna* respectively. In order to have the Reflected Light (pure *sattva*), free from *rajas* and *tamas*, it must shine forth as "I-I," unbroken by "this"-thought. This pure state momentarily inter-venes between sleep and waking. If prolonged, it is cosmic consciousness, or even *Ishvara*. This is the only passage to the Realization of the Self-shin-ing Supreme Being.

Again, there are two kinds of experiences in deep sleep as recollected after waking — that is, "I slept *happily, unaware* of anything." Happiness and ignorance are the experiences. Thus we see the Power modified as *avarana* (darkness) and *vikshepa* (diversity). The mind is the result of *vikshepa*.

JANUARY 10, 1937

Some Reminiscences

1. While in Skandasramam, Sri Bhagavan saw a white toad, small and long, at a distance of about ten feet from him. Sri Bhagavan stared at it and it stared at him. Suddenly, it took a long jump and lodged itself precisely on one of the eyes of Sri Bhagavan, who quickly closed it and so was not injured.

2. There were two peacocks that used to strut with their feathers spread out like a spangled fan. A cobra, too, used to take part in the pastime and raised its hood and moved about in their midst.

3. Sri Bhagavan says that the peacock, as soon as it sights a green lizard, goes straight to it and meekly places its neck down before the lizard which bites it off and kills the peacock.

4. Rangaswami Iyengar was once out on the hill. A leopard was nearby. He threw a stone. It turned towards him. He hurried away for his life. Sri Bhagavan met him on the way and asked what the matter was. Iyengar simply said "leopard" as he was running. Sri Bhagavan went where the beast was and it moved away soon after. All this happened at the time of the plague. Leopards used to roam freely by the side of the temple, sometimes in twos and threes.

5. Sri Bhagavan said, "A frog is often compared to a yogi. It remains quiet for a long time, the only sign of life being the rhythmic movement of the underskin below the neck.

   "Again, frogs can remain for extraordinary long periods with their animation suspended. They are said to swallow their tongues. Swallowing the tongue is also a yogic practice. The animation is suspended. The yogi does not die but the tongue must be drawn out by someone else before life activity is resumed. It is a wonder how the frog brings out the swallowed tongue and resumes activity."

JANUARY 11, 1937

6. While reading "Raghuveeran" — *Ramayana* written in easy Malayalam prose — there was a passage relating how Hanuman reached Lanka mentally before he crossed over physically to that island. Sri Bhaga-

van emphasized the point that the mental approach accomplishes the purpose earlier than physical action.

7. Sri Bhagavan related the following funny anecdote: Ezhuthachan, a great Malayali saint and author, had a few fish concealed on him when he entered the temple. An enemy reported it to the worshippers in the temple. The man was searched and taken to the king. The king asked him "Why did you take the fish into the temple?" He replied: "It is not my fault. I had it concealed in my clothes. The others exposed the fish in the temple. The fault lies in exposure. Excreta within the body are not considered filthy; but when excreted, they are considered filthy. So also with this."

JANUARY 12, 1937

Mr. Rama Sastri from Guntur District composed eight slokas on Sri Bhagavan and read them out with feeling. The Sastri then prayed for guidance: I am a *samsari* unfit for *Jnana Marga.* The affairs of the world are distracting me. Please instruct me what to do.
M. Think of Bhagavan. How would the affairs of the world distract Him? You and they are in Him.
D. May I do *nama smarana?* What *nama* shall I take?
M. You are Rama Sastri. Make that name significant. Be one with Rama.

JANUARY 13, 1937

In answer to a question by a long-time attendant, Sri Bhagavan said: Everybody complains of the restlessness of the mind. Let the mind be found and then they will know. True, when a person sits down to meditate thoughts rush up by the dozen. The mind is only a bundle of thoughts. The attempt to push through the barrage of thoughts is unsuccessful. If one can by any means abide in the Self, it is good. For those who are unable to do so, chanting or meditation (*japa* or *dhyana*) is prescribed. It is like giving a piece of chain to an elephant to hold in its trunk. The trunk of the elephant is usually restless. It puts it out in all directions when taken out in the streets. If given a chain to carry, the restlessness is checked. Similarly with the restless mind. If made to engage in *japa* or *dhyana*, other thoughts are warded off; and the mind concentrates on a single thought. It thus becomes peaceful. It does not mean, however, that peace is gained without a prolonged

243

struggle; the other thoughts must be fought out.

Here is another illustration: Suppose a cow plays a rogue and strays into neighbors' fields to graze. She is not easily weaned from her stealthy habit. Think how she can be kept in the stall. If forcibly tethered in the stall, she simply bides her time to play the rogue. If she is tempted with fine grass in the stall, she takes one mouthful on the first day and again waits for the opportunity to run away. The next day she takes two mouthfuls; so she takes more and more on each succeeding day, until finally she is weaned from her wicked tendencies. When entirely free from bad habits, she might be safely left free and she would not stray into neighbors' pasture land. Even when beaten in the stall, she does not leave the place. Similarly with the mind. It is accustomed to stray outward by the force of the latent *vasanas* manifesting as thoughts. So long as there are *vasanas* contained within, they must come out and exhaust themselves. The thoughts comprise the mind. Searching what the mind is, the thoughts will recoil and the seeker will know they arise from the Self. It is the aggregate of these thoughts that we call "mind." If one realizes that the thoughts arise from the Self and abide in their source, the mind will disappear. After the mind ceases to exist and the bliss of peace has been realized, one will find it as difficult to bring out a thought as he now finds it difficult to keep out all thoughts. Here the mind is the cow playing the rogue; the thoughts are the neighbors' pasture; one's own primal being free from thoughts is the stall.

The bliss of peace is too good to be disturbed. A man fast asleep hates to be awakened and ordered to mind his business. The bliss of sleep is too enthralling to be sacrificed to the work born of thoughts. The thought-free state is one's primordial state and full of bliss. Is it not miserable to leave it for the thought-ridden and unhappy one?

If one wants to abide in the thought-free state, a struggle is inevitable. One must fight one's way through before regaining one's original state. If one succeeds in the fight and reaches the goal, the enemy, namely the thoughts, will all subside in the Self and disappear entirely. The thoughts are the enemy. They amount to the creation of the Universe. In their absence, there is neither world nor God the Creator. The Bliss of the Self is the single Being only.

When Prahlada was in *samadhi,* Vishnu thought within Himself:

"This *asura* (demon) being in *samadhi,* all the *asuras* are in peace. There is no fight, no trial of strength, no search for power, nor the means for gaining power. In the absence of such means for power — *yaga, yajna,* etc., i.e., the gods are not thriving; there is no new creation, nor even is any existence justified. So I will wake him up; then the *asuras* will rise up and their original nature will manifest itself. The gods will challenge them; the *asuras* and others will then seek strength and adopt the means for its acquisition. *Yajnas*, etc., will flourish; the gods will thrive, there will be more and more of creation, more of fight, and I shall have enough to do."

So Vishnu awakened Prahlada, blessing him with eternal life and *jivanmukti*. *Deva-asura* fight was resumed and the old order of things was restored so that the universe continues in its eternal nature.

D. How could God Himself wake up the *asura* element and bring about constant warfare? Is not Pure Goodness the nature of God?

M. Goodness is only relative. Good always implies bad; they ever coexist. The one is the obverse of the other.

The audience in the Hall were very attentively listening. One of them, a sincere devotee of Sri Bhagavan, was so impressed by it that he soon lost himself. He later described his experience as follows: I was long wondering where the "current" starts, within the body or elsewhere. Suddenly, my body grew tenuous until it disappeared. The inquiry "Who am I?" went on very clearly and forcibly. The sound of "I-I-I" alone persisted. There was one vast expanse and nothing else. There was a hazy perception of the occurrences in the Hall. I knew that people stood up to salute at the end of the Vedic chant. I wanted to stand but the thought soon deserted me. I was again lost in the one expanse. The experience continued until I heard the voice of Sri Bhagavan. That made me collect myself. Then I stood up and saluted. The strange feeling continued for more than half an hour. I cannot forget it; it is still haunting me.

Sri Bhagavan listened to his words and was silent for some minutes. A few observations fell from his lips: One may seem to go out of the body, but the body itself is not more than our thought. There can be no body in the absence of thought; no outgoing or incoming in the absence of body. However, owing to habit, the feeling of going out arises.

A particle of hail falling on the surface of the sea melts away and becomes water, wave, froth, etc., in the sea. Similarly, the subtle intellect, rising up as the tiny dot (ego) from the heart and bulging out, finally enters into and becomes one with the Heart.

Though milk remains as wide as the sea, can you drink it with a mouth as wide as the sea? You can suck it only through the tiny capillaries of the paps.

Nammalvar, the Vaishnavite saint, has said: "Only my Self is you." What does it mean? "Before I realized my Self, I was wandering looking out for You; having now realized my Self, I see that you are my Self." How will this fit in with qualified monism? It must be explained thusly: "Pervading my Self, you remain as the *antaryamin* (Immanent Being). Thus, I am a part of your body and you are the owner of the body (*sariri*)."

Having given up one's own body as not being oneself, why should one become another's (God's) body? If one's body is not the Self, other bodies also are non-self. The protagonists of qualified monism think that individuality is necessary to experience the Bliss. Individuality, i.e., "I"-ness, should not be lost. Aha! The Self is not the body, but your Self becomes the body of God! Is it not absurd?

Or if you make *prapatti* (surrender yourself) to God, you have made yourself over to Him and you are His and no longer yours. If He is in need of a body, let Him look out for Himself. You need not say He is the owner of a body.

JANUARY 17, 1937

A European gentleman began in measured tones and spoke clearly and slowly:
Why should individuals remain caught up in the affairs of this world and reap troubles as a result? Should they not be free? If they are in the spiritual world, they will have greater freedom.

M. The world is only spiritual. Since you are identifying yourself with the physical body, you speak of this world as being physical and the other world as spiritual. Whereas, that which is, is only spiritual.

D. Do the disembodied souls, i.e., the spirits, have a deeper insight and enjoy greater freedom?

M. Because you identify yourself with this body, you speak of the disembodied souls as being spirits. From these limitations, you talk of their limitations and seek to know their capacities. Even the disembodied souls have subtle bodies; otherwise, you would not say "disembodied souls." Disembodiment means "divested of this gross body." Inasmuch as you endow them with individuality they are centered in their subtle bodies. Their limitations will be according to their own state. Just as you feel the burden of your limitations, they also feel the burden of their limitations. What I meant by spirit and spiritual world is the Absolute Spirit and not relative. If you realize yourself as Spirit, you will see that this world is only spiritual and not physical.

D. Are their bodies temporary as our bodies are? Do they reincarnate?

M. These questions arise because you think yourself to be the body. This body has birth and death, and when it falls another body arises which is called "reincarnation." But are you that body? If you find you are not this body but the spirit, you will be free from gross or subtle bodies, and then there will be no limitations. Where is the world, physical or spiritual, in the absence of any limitations? How will the question of reincarnation arise?

Again, consider it from another point of view: You create a dream-body for yourself in your dream and act with that dream-body. The same is falsified in the waking state. At present, you think you are this body and not the dream-body. In your dream, this body is falsified by the dream-body. So that, you see, neither of these bodies is real since each of them is true for a time only and false at other times. That which is real must be real forever. But you say "I." This "I"-consciousness is present throughout the three states. There is no change to it. That is alone real. The three states are false; they are only for the mind. It is the latter which obstructs your vision of yourself. Your true nature is that of Infinite Spirit. That was the case in your sleep. You note the limitations in the other two states. What is the difference due to? There was no mind in sleep, but it is present in the dream and the waking states. The feeling of limitation is the work of the mind. What is mind? Find it. If you search for it, it will vanish by itself, for it has no real existence. It is comprised of thoughts and it disappears with the cessation of those thoughts.

D. Do I remain then?

M. What is your experience in sleep? There were no thoughts, no mind, and yet you remained then.

D. When I try to meditate, I am unable to do so because my mind wanders. What am I to do?

M. Your question furnishes the answer. With regard to the first part of the question, you say you concentrate but do not succeed. "You" means "the Self." On what do you concentrate? Where do you fail? Are there two selves, for the one to concentrate on the other? Which is the self now complaining of failure? There cannot be two selves. There is only one Self, and that need not concentrate.

"But then, why is there no happiness?" — you ask. What is it that prevents you from remaining as the Spirit which you are in sleep? You yourself admit it is the wandering mind. Find out the mind. If its "wandering" stops, it will be found to be the Self — your "I"-consciousness which is Spirit eternal. It is beyond knowledge and ignorance.

D. I am hard-worked and find little time to practice concentration. Are there any aids for it? Is control of breath a good aid?

M. *Prana* and mind arise from the same source. The source can be reached by holding the breath or tracing the mind. If you cannot do the latter, the former will no doubt be helpful. The regulation of breath is mastered by watching its movements.

If the mind is watched, thoughts cease. Peace results and it is your true nature. King Janaka said: "I have now found the robber (namely the mind) who has been robbing me of my 'I-ness.' I will instantly kill this thief." The perturbation owing to thoughts appears to rob the Self of its peace. This perturbation is the mind. When that ceases, the mind is said to take flight. The Self remains as the undisturbed substratum.

Another person interposed: The mind must kill itself.

M. Yes, if there be the mind. A search for it discloses its non-existence. How can anything that does not exist be killed?

D. Is not mental *japa* better than oral *japa*?

M. Oral *japa* consists of sounds. The sounds arise from thoughts. For one must think before one expresses the thoughts in words. The thoughts form the mind. Therefore, mental *japa* is better than oral *japa*.

D. Should we not contemplate the *japa* and repeat it orally, also?

M. When the *japa* becomes mental, where is the need for its sounds?

Japa, becoming mental, becomes contemplation. *Dhyana*, contemplation and mental *japa* are the same. When thoughts cease to be promiscuous and one thought persists to the exclusion of all others, it is said to be contemplation. The object of *japa* or *dhyana* is the exclusion of several thoughts and to confine oneself to one single thought. Then that thought too vanishes into its source — absolute Consciousness, i.e., the Self. The mind engages in *japa* and then sinks into its own source.

D. The mind is said to be from the brain.

M. Where is the brain? It is in the body. I say that the body itself is a projection of the mind. You speak of the brain when you think of the body. It is the mind which creates the body, the brain in it, and also ascertains that the brain is its seat.

D. Sri Bhagavan has said in one of the works that the *japa* must be traced to its source. Is it not the mind that is meant?

M. All these are only the workings of the mind. *Japa* helps to fix the mind to a single thought. All other thoughts are subordinated until they disappear. When it becomes mental, it is called *dhyana*. *Dhyana* is your true nature. It is however called *dhyana* because it is made with effort. Effort is necessary so long as thoughts are promiscuous. Because you are with other thoughts, you call the continuity of a single thought "meditation" or *dhyana*. If that *dhyana* becomes effortless it will be found to be your real nature.

In the morning, Sri Bhagavan read out a short passage from St. Estella in the Tamil Ramakrishna Vijayam. Its purport is:

"Your enemies are lust, passion, etc. If you feel injured, turn within and find out the cause of the injury. It is not external to you. The external causes are mere superimpositions. If you cannot injure yourself, will the all-merciful God injure you in any manner?"

(Sri Bhagavan further said that St. Estella was a good saint whose teachings were quite sound.)

Sri Bhagavan, being asthmatic, is hoarse. Oranges were brought as offerings. Pieces were distributed as usual. Sri Bhagavan was clearing his throat and was obliged to spit out the orange from his mouth. He said that he had to spit it out. A gentleman said: Probably, it does not suit Sri Bhagavan's health.

M. Would you say so if *you* had brought the fruits, instead of the other person?

JANUARY 18, 1937

Mrs. Roorna Jennings, an American lady of the International Peace League, asked Sri Bhagavan about the spread of Peace in the world.

Sri Bhagavan replied that if one gains the Peace of the Self it will spread itself without any effort on the part of the individual. When one is not peaceful, how can that one spread peace in the world?

Mrs. Jennings asked if it wasn't true that the East has a scientific approach to Realization of the Self.

M. You are already the Self. No elaborate science is necessary to establish it.

D. I understand the general truth of it. But there must be a practical method for it which I call "science."

M. The cessation of such thoughts is the realization of the Self. One does not see the world or one's own body, being away from the Self. Always being the Self, one sees everything else. God and the world are all in the Heart. See the Seer and everything will be found to be the Self. Change your outlook. Look within. Find the Self. Who is the substratum of the subject and the object? Find it and all problems are solved!

(The lady was then told of the pamphlet, Who am I? *She agreed to read it before asking further questions of Sri Bhagavan.)*

JANUARY 20, 1937

Sri Bhagavan said he felt no sensation in his legs, though they were massaged. "If they serve the purpose of walking, what does it matter if sensation is lost?" he asked. Then, in the course of conversation, he related that a ray of light has been found which, when projected, does not reveal the operator but enables him to witness the scene. So it is with *siddhas.* They are only pure light and can see others but cannot be seen by others. For example Prabhulinga, while touring in the North, came across Goraknath. The latter displayed his yogic powers e.g., when his arm was cut by a sword and the sword was blunted without inflicting injury on him. This is making the body proof against injury (*kayasiddhi*). Prabhulinga offered himself to be cut. When the sword was thrust, it passed right through his body as if it were air and there was no injury on the body. Gorak was astonished and offered himself as the disciple of Prabhulinga.

JANUARY 21, 1937

D. How will the sexual impulse cease to be?

M. When differentiation ceases.

D. How can it be effected?

M. The "opposite" sex, and its relation, are only mental concepts. The *Upanishad* says that all are dear because the Self is beloved of all. One's happiness is within; the love is of the Self only. It is only within; do not think it to be without. Then differentiation ceases to operate.

JANUARY 22, 1937

A merchant, who seems to have studied the Upanishads *and* Srimad Bhagavad Gita, *asked some questions:*

D. How to realize the Self?

M. The Self is always directly perceived. There is no moment when it is not. How then is it to be ascertained? Find out the Self. You are that.

D. But it is said the heart-knots are cut away and all doubts end when the

Supreme is found. The word *drishti* is used.

M. To *be* the Self is the same as *seeing* the Self. There are no two selves for the one to see the other.

(Later, he continued the same question of investigation into the Self.)

D. How to realize the Self?

M. It is already realized. One should know this simple fact. That is all.

D. But I do not know it. How shall I know it?

M. Do you deny your existence?

D. No. How can that be done?

M. Then the truth is admitted.

D. Yet, I do not see. How shall I realize the Self?

M. Find out who says "I."

D. Yes. I say "I."

M. Who is this "I"? Is it the body or someone besides the body?

D. It is not the body, but someone besides.

M. Find out.

D. I am unable to do so. How shall I find it?

M. You are now aware of the body. You were not aware of the body in deep sleep. Still, you remained in sleep. After waking up, you behold the body and say, "I cannot realize the Self." Did you say so in your sleep? Because you were undivided (*akhanda*) then, you did not say so. Now that you are contracted within the limits of the body, you say, "I have not realized." Why do you limit your Self and then feel miserable? Be of your true nature and happy. You did not say "I" in sleep. You say so now. Why? Because you hold to the body. Find out wherefrom this "I" comes. Then the Self is realized.

The body, being insentient, cannot say "I." The Self, being infinite, cannot say "I" either. Who then says "I"?

D. I do not yet understand. How to find the "I"?

M. Find out wherefrom this "I" arises. Then this "I" will disappear and the infinite Self remains. This "I" is only the knot between the sentient and the insentient. The body is not "I," the Self is not "I." Who, then, is the "I"? Wherefrom does it arise?

D. Wherefrom *does* it arise?

M. Find out.

D. I do not know. Please enlighten me.

M. It is not from without. It is from within. Where does it come from? If from elsewhere, you can be led there. Being within, you must find it out yourself.

D. From the head?

M. Does the concept of "head" arise after the "I," or does "I" arise from the head? If "I" is in the head, why do you bend it when sleep overpowers you? "I" is ever constant. So also, must its seat be. If the head bends at one time and is erect at another, how can it be the seat of "I"? Your head is laid flat in sleep. When awake, it is raised up. Can it be the "I"?

D. Which is it, then?

M. "I" comes from within. When asleep, there is no "I." Just before waking, there is the "I"-thought.

D. The heart-knot is said to be between the eyebrows.

M. Some say "between the eyebrows"; others, "at the coccyx," and so on. All these are from the standpoint of the body. The body comes after the "I"-thought.

D. But I cannot divest myself of the body.

M. So you admit that you are not the body.

D. If there is pain in this body, I feel it; but not if another body is injured. I cannot get over this body.

M. This identity is the cause of such feeling. That is the *hridaya granthi* (heart-knot).

D. How is this knot to go?

M. For whom is the knot? Why do you want it to go? Does it ask or do you ask?

D. It cannot ask; I am asking.

M. Who is that "I"? If that is found, the knot will not remain.

D. The knot is concomitant with the body. The body is due to birth. How is rebirth to cease?

M. Who is born? Is the Self born? Or is it the body?

D. It is the body.

M. Then let the body ask how its rebirth may cease.

D. It will not ask. So I am asking.

M. Whose is the body? You were without it in your deep sleep. After the "I"-thought arose, the body arose. The first birth is that of the "I"-thought. The body has its birth subsequent to the "I"-thought. So its birth is secondary. Get rid of the primary cause and the secondary one will disappear by itself.

D. How is that "I"-thought to be checked from rising?

M. By Self-quest.

D. I try to understand, but without success. Can I find the Self by means of *japa*? If so, please tell me how.

M. What *japa*? Why should you make artificial *japa*? You can find out the eternal and natural *japa* always going on within you.

D. Some *upadesa* (instruction) will probably help me.

M. If I say "Repeat Rama, Rama" to one who has not struggled through books like you, he will do it and stick to it. If I say so to one like you who has read much and is investigating matters, you will not do it for long, because you will think, "Why should I do it? Above all, who am I that should be repeating the mantra? Let me find who I am before I proceed further"; and so you will stop *japa* and begin investigation.

D. It is said: "The senses are outgoing (*paranchikhani*); inward turned (is) sight (*avrittachakshuh*)." What is *avrittachakshuh* (inward-turned sight)?

M. It does not mean replacement of the eyeball in the opposite direction. What is *chakshuh*?

D. The eye.

M. Does the eye see or anyone behind it? If the eye could see, does a corpse see? The one who is behind the eye sees through the eye. He is indicated by the word *chakshuh*.

D. *Divya chakshuh* (divine eye) is necessary to see the glory of the God. This physical eye is the ordinary *chakshuh*.

M. Oh! I see. You want to see million-sun splendor and the rest of it!

D. Can we not see the glory as million-sun splendor?

M. Can you see the single sun? Why do you ask for millions of suns?

D. It must be possible to do so by divine sight. "Where the sun shines not, etc. That is My Supreme abode" (*Bhagavad Gita*). Therefore, there is a state where this sun is powerless. That state is that of God.

M. All right. Find Krishna and the problem is solved.

D. Krishna is not alive.

M. Is that what you have learned from the *Gita*? Does He not say that He is eternal? Of what are you thinking? His body?

D. He taught others while alive. Those around Him must have realized. I seek a similar living Guru.

M. Is *Gita* then useless after He withdrew His body? Did He speak of His body as Krishna?

Natwewaham jatu nasam . . . (Never I was not . . .).

D. But I want a living Guru who can state the truth firsthand.

M. The fate of the Guru will be similar to the fate of Krishna.

(*The questioner retired.*)

Later, Sri Bhagavan said: Divine sight means Self-luminosity. The word *divya* shows it. The full word means the Self. Who is to bestow a divine eye? And who is to see? Again, people read in the books, "hearing, reflection and one-pointedness are necessary." They think that they must pass through *savikalpa samadhi* and *nirvikalpa samadhi* before attaining Realization. Hence all these questions. Why should they wander in that maze? What do they gain in the end? It is only cessation of the trouble of seeking. They find that the Self is eternal and self-evident. Why should they not get that repose even this very moment?

A simple man, not learned, is satisfied with *japa* or worship. A *jnani* is of course satisfied. The whole trouble is for the bookworms. Well, well. They will also get on.

Mr. K.R.V. Iyer: How is the mind to be purified?

M. The *sastras* say: "By karma, *bhakti* and so on." My attendant asked the same question once before. He was told, "By karma dedicated to God." It is not enough that one thinks of God while doing the karma, but one must unceasingly think of Him. Then alone will the mind become pure.

(*The attendant applies it to himself and says, "It is not enough that I serve Sri Bhagavan physically. But I must unceasingly remember Him."*)

To another person, who asked the same question, Bhagavan replied: The quest of the Self means the "I-am-the-body" idea must vanish. (*Atma-vichara* = disappearance of *dehatma buddhi*.)

JANUARY 23, 1937

Mrs. Jennings, an American lady, asked the following questions:

D. Is not affirmation of God more effective than the quest, "Who am I?" Affirmation is positive, whereas the other is negation. Moreover, it indicates separateness.

M. So long as you seek to know how to realize, this advice is given to find your Self. Your seeking the method denotes your separateness.

D. Is it not better to say, "I am the Supreme Being" than ask, "Who am I?"

M. Who affirms? There must be one to do it. Find that one.

D. Is not meditation better than investigation?

M. Meditation implies mental imagery, whereas investigation is for the Reality. The former is objective, whereas the latter is subjective.

D. There must be a scientific approach to this subject.

M. To avoid unreality and seek Reality is scientific.

D. I mean there must be a gradual elimination, first of the mind, then of the intellect, and finally of the ego.

M. The Self alone is Real. All others are unreal. The mind and intellect do not remain apart from you.

The Bible says, "Be still and know that I am God." Stillness is the sole requisite for realization of the Self as God.

D. Will the West ever understand this teaching?

M. There is no question of time and space. Understanding depends on ripeness of mind. What does it matter if one lives in the East or the West?

(*Sri Bhagavan referred the lady to a few stanzas in* Truth Revealed *and to* Thayumanavar. *She retired.*)

Later Sri Bhagavan said the whole Vedanta *is contained in two Biblical statements:* "I Am that I Am" *and* "Be still and know that I am God."

Mr. K.S.N. Iyer, a Railway Officer, said to Sri Bhagavan that the compiler of Cosmic Consciousness *considers realization to be possible only within certain age limits in an individual's life.*

M. Does anyone say, "I must come into being before or after a certain age?" He is here and now. Statements like this are misleading because people come to believe that they cannot realize the Self in this incarnation and must take their chances in another. It is all absurd.

With regard to Shiva Visishtadvaita, *(i.e.,* Shaiva Siddhanta*), Sri Bhagavan said: Garudoham bhavana,* "I am Garuda" — conception does not make a *garuda* of a man. All the same, the poisonous effects of snakebite are cured. Similarly with the *Shivoham bhavana* (I-am-Shiva) conception. One is not transformed into Shiva, but the ruinous effects of the ego are put to an end. Or the person retains his individuality but remains pure, i.e., fit for constituting a part of the body of Shiva. This way he can enjoy the Supreme Bliss. That is liberation, say the *Shaiva Siddhantis*. This simply betrays the love of their individuality and is in no way the true experience of liberation.

Mr. Bose began: After return of body-consciousness . . .

M. What is body-consciousness? Tell us that first. Who are you apart from consciousness? Body is found because there is body-consciousness which arises from "I"-consciousness, which in turn arises from consciousness.

Consciousness → "I"-consciousness → body-consciousness → body.

There is always consciousness and nothing but that. What you are now considering to be body-consciousness is due to superimposition. If there is only consciousness and nothing but it, the meaning of the Scripture *Atmanastu kamaya sarvam priyam bhavati* (All are dear because of the love of the Self) becomes clear.

A question arises as to why there should be suicides in that case. Why does one do it? Because he is unhappy and desires to put an end to his unhappiness. He actually does it by ending association with the body which represents all unhappiness. For there must be a killer to kill the body. He is the survivor after suicide. That is the Self.

Mrs. Jennings: Sri Bhagavan says that the state of Realization is freedom from the tyranny of thoughts. Have not the thoughts a place in the scheme of things — maybe on a lower plane?

M. The thoughts arise from the "I"-thought, which in turn arises from the Self. Therefore, the Self manifests as "I" and other thoughts. What does it matter if there are thoughts or no thoughts?

D. Are good thoughts helpful for Realization? Are they not authentic *via media,* a lower rung of the ladder, to Realization?

M. Yes, this way. They keep off bad thoughts. They must themselves disappear before the state of Realization.

D. But are not creative thoughts an aspect of Realization and therefore helpful?

M. Helpful only in the way as stated before. They must all disappear in the Self. Thoughts, good or bad, take you farther and not nearer, because the Self is more intimate than thoughts. You are the Self, whereas the thoughts are alien to the Self.

D. So the Self finally absorbs its own creation, which had helped its Realization. Whereas civilization wrongly worships and so separates and "short-circuits" its own creations, which had helped its advance.

M. Are you not distinct from thoughts? Do you not exist without them? But can the thoughts exist without you?

D. Is civilization generally, slowly but surely, advancing in the right direction towards this Self-realization?

M. Civilization is in the order of things. It will finally resolve itself — as all others — in the Realization of the Self.

D. Is a fine type of primitive man nearer to Realization than a civilized man governed by intellect and thought?

M. A realized man may look a savage, but a savage is not a realized man.

D. Is it right to think that *all* that happens to us is God's ordainment, and therefore only good?

M. Of course it is. Yet all others and God are not apart from the Self. How can thoughts of them arise when you remain as the Self?

D. Is "surrender" accepting all physical annoyances such as ants, mosquitoes, snakes, etc. and, in accepting, willing or ceasing to be really hurt by them?

M. Whatever it is, is it apart from you, the seer or the thinker?

A Parsi lady intervened: If they are not apart, do we not feel the sting of the ants?

M. Whom does the ant sting? It is the body. You are not the body. So long as you identify yourself with the body, you see the ants, plants, etc. If you remain as the Self, there are no others apart from the Self.

D. The body feels the pain of the sting.

M. If the body feels it, let it ask. Let the body take care of itself. How does it matter to you?

The American lady again: Does complete surrender mean that all noise and disturbance in our environment, even during meditation, must be accepted? Or should we seek a cave in a mountain for solitude? Didn't Bhagavan do this?

M. There is no going or returning. The Self is said to be unaffected by the elements, infinite, eternal. It cannot move. There is no place to move for the Self.

D. But, in the process of finding the Self, is this seeking external help spiritually legitimate?

M. The error lies in the identification of the Self with the body. If Bhagavan is the body, you may ask that body. But understand him whom you address as Bhagavan. He is not the body. He is the Self.

The American lady referred to an article in Harijan *where it is said that everything is God and nothing belongs to the individual, and so on.*

M. Everything, the individual, God, and all are only the Self.

> *(She then read some lines from Shelley and asked if Shelley was not a realized soul.)*
>
> "Within a cavern of man's trackless spirit
> Is throned an Image so intensely fair
> That the adventurous thoughts that wander near it
> Worship, and as they kneel, tremble and fear
> The splendour of its presence, and the light
> Penetrates their dreamlike frame

Till they become charged with the strength of flame."

M. Yes. The lines are excellent. He must have realized what he wrote.
(*The lady thanked Sri Bhagavan and retired.*)

At 11:00 p.m., a party from Guntur, in Andhra Pradesh, arrived, consisting of a middle-aged woman with a sad but firm look, her mother, and two men. They requested an audience with Sri Bhagavan. The woman said to Sri Bhagavan: When my son was in the womb, my husband died. The son was born posthumous. He grew up all right for five years. Then he was attacked by infantile paralysis. At the age of nine, he became bedridden. Nevertheless, he was bright and cheerful. For two years, he remained in that condition and now they say he is dead. I know he is only sleeping and will awake soon. When they told me he had collapsed, I was shocked. I saw in a vision a *sadhu* who appeared to pass his hands over the child's body and the child awoke refreshed. I believe that *sadhu* is yourself. Please come and touch the boy so that he may get up.
Sri Bhagavan asked what the doctor said.
She replied: They say he is dead. But what do they know? I have brought the boy all the way from Guntur to this place.
Someone asked: How? Is the corpse brought here?
She: They said that the corpse would be taken by paying special rates at one-half rupee per mile. We have paid 150 rupees for it, and brought it as luggage.
M. If your vision is correct the boy will wake up tomorrow.
She: Please touch him. May I bring him into the compound?
(*The others protested and persuaded them to leave. They left and the next morning the corpse was reported to have been cremated.*)

When asked, Sri Bhagavan said: It is said of some saints that they revived the dead. They, too, did not revive all the dead. If that could be done, there would be no world, no death, no cemetery, etc.
One man asked: The mother's faith was very remarkable. How could she have had such a hopeful vision and still be disappointed? Can it be a superimposition attendant on her child's love?
M. She and her child not being real, how can the vision alone be a superimposition?
D. Then how is it to be explained?
(*No answer.*)

D. Even as the hand is cut off, one must remain unaware of it because the *Bhagavad Gita* declares that the Self is different from the body.

M. Does *jnana* consist in being unaware of the pain of injury?

D. Should he not remain unaware of pain?

M. Major operations are performed under anesthetics, keeping the patient free from pain. Does the patient gain *jnana*, too, at the same time? Insensibility to pain cannot be *jnana*.

D. Should not a *jnani* (a sage) be insensible to pain?

M. Physical pain only follows body-consciousness; it cannot exist in the absence of body-consciousness. Mind, being unaware of the body, cannot be aware of its pains or pleasures. Read the story of Indra and Ahalya in *Yoga Vasishta*; there, death itself is said to be an act of mind.

Pains are dependent on the ego; they cannot be without the "I," but "I" can remain without them.

D. *Vichara Sagara* relates four obstacles to Self-realization.

M. Why only four? Some say there are nine. Sleep is one of them. What is sleep? It is only the obverse of waking. It cannot be independent of waking. Sleep is unalloyed Self. Do not think you are awake; sleep cannot be, nor the three states. Only forgetting the Self you say you dreamed. Can anything exist in the absence of the Self? Why do you leave it out and hold the non-self?

As the mind tends to go out, turn it inward then and there. It goes out owing to the habit of looking for happiness outside oneself; but the knowledge that the external objects are not the cause of happiness will keep it in check. This is *vairagya* or dispassion. Only after perfect *vairagya*, the mind becomes steady.

The mind is only a mixture of knowledge and ignorance or of sleep and waking. It functions in five ways:

1. *Kshipta* (active)
2. *Moodha* (dull)
3. *Vikshipta* (distracted)
4. *Kashaya* (latent)
5. *Ekagrya* (one-pointed)

Of these, *kashaya* is only the latency of tendencies and not the tendencies themselves such as attachment, repulsion, etc.

Yourself being *ananda* (bliss), why should you enjoy it saying, "Ah! How blissful!" This is *rasasvada*.

During the marriage ceremonies, a virgin feels happy as a bride without experiencing the embrace of man: this is *rasasvada*.

D. *Jivanmukti* (liberated while alive) itself being *ananda* . . .

Sri Bhagavan interrupted: Do not look for *sastras*. What is *jivanmukti*? What is *ananda*? Liberation itself is in doubt. What are all these words? Can they be independent of the Self?

D. We have no experience of all this.

M. What is not, is always lost; what is, is ever present, here and now. This is the eternal order of things. Example: A necklace around the neck.

Sri Bhagavan continued after an interval: Destroy the power of mind by seeking it. When the mind is examined, its activities cease automatically.

Looking for the source of mind is another method. The source may be said to be God or Self or Consciousness.

Concentrating on one thought, all other thoughts disappear; finally, that thought also disappears. It is necessary to be *aware* while controlling thoughts, otherwise it will lead to sleep.

D. How to seek the mind?

M. Breath control may do as an aid, but can never lead to the goal itself. While doing it mechanically, take care to be alert in mind and remember the "I"-thought and seek its source. Then you will find that where the breath sinks, the "I"-thought arises. They sink and rise together. The "I"-thought also will sink along with the breath. Simultaneously, another luminous and infinite "I—I" will manifest and it will be continuous and unbroken. That is the goal. It goes by different names — God, Self, *Kundalini-Shakti*, consciousness etc., etc.

When the attempt is made, it will of itself take you to the goal.

M. Free will and Destiny last as long as the body lasts. But wisdom transcends both, for the Self is beyond knowledge and ignorance.

M. The mind is a bundle of thoughts. The thoughts arise because there is the thinker. The thinker is the ego. The ego, if sought, will automatically vanish. The ego and the mind are the same. The ego is the root-thought from which all other thoughts arise.

D. There are times when persons and things take on a vague, almost transparent, form as in a dream. One ceases to observe them as from outside, but is passively conscious of their existence, while not actively conscious of any kind of selfhood. There is a deep quietness in the mind. Is it, at such times, ready to dive into the Self? Or is this condition unhealthy, the result of self-hypnotism? Should it be encouraged as a means of getting temporary peace?

M. There is consciousness along with quietness in the mind; this is exactly the state to be aimed at. The fact that the question has been framed on this point, without realizing that it is the Self, shows that the state is not steady but casual.

The word "diving" is appropriate to the state of outgoing tendencies when the mind is to be diverted and turned within, so as to dive below the surface of externalities. But when deep quietness prevails without obstructing the consciousness, where is the need to dive? If the state is not realized as the Self, the effort to do so may be called "diving." The state may in that way be said to be suitable for realization or "diving." Thus the last two questions in the paragraph are unnecessary.

D. The mind continues to feel partial towards children, possibly because of the form sometimes used to personify the ideal. How can this preference be outgrown?

M. Hold the Self. Why think of children and reactions towards them?

D. This third visit to Tiruvannamalai seems to have intensified the sense of egoism in me and made meditation less easy. Is this an unimportant passing phase or a sign that I should avoid such places henceforth?

M. It is imaginary. This place or another is within you. Such imaginations must end so that the places have nothing to do with the activities of the mind. Even your surroundings are not of your own accord; they are there as a matter of course. You must rise above them and not get involved.

Sri Shankara's Path to Liberation Through Discrimination
The current issue of The Vision *contains Sri Ramana Maharshi's preface to Shankaracharya's* Viveka Chudamani *(Crown Gem of Discrimination), translated by Mr. S. Krishna.*

Every being in the world yearns to be always happy, free from the taint of sorrow, and desires to get rid of bodily ailments which are not of his true nature. Further, every one cherishes the greatest love for himself; and this love is not possible in the absence of happiness. In deep sleep, though devoid of everything, one has the experience of being happy. Yet, due to the ignorance of the real nature of one's own being, which is happiness itself, people flounder in the vast ocean of material existence. They forsake the right path that leads to happiness, and act under the

mistaken belief that the way to be happy consists of obtaining the pleasures of this and the other world.

A Safe Guide

But alas, that happiness which does not have the taint of sorrow is not
realized. It is precisely for the purpose of pointing out the straight path
to happiness that Shiva took on the guise of Sri Shankaracharya, and
wrote the commentaries on the three scriptural authorities (*Prasthana
Traya*) of the *Vedanta*, which extol the excellence of this bliss, and dem-
onstrated it by his own example in life. These commentaries, however,
are of little use to those ardent seekers who are intent upon realizing
the bliss of absolution, but are lacking in scholarship for studying them.

It is for such as these that Sri Shankara revealed the essence of the
commentaries in this short treatise, "The Crown Gem of Discrimination", explaining in detail the points that have to be grasped by those
who seek absolution, and thereby directing them to the true and straight
path.

Learning Won't Do

Sri Shankara observes that it is hard indeed to attain human birth, and
one should (having attained it) strive for the realization of the bliss of
liberation, which is truly the nature of one's being. By *jnana* or Knowledge alone is bliss realized, and *jnana* is achieved only through *vichara*,
or steady enquiry. In order to know this method of enquiry, says Sri
Shankara, one should seek the favor of a Guru. He then proceeds to
describe the qualities of the Guru and his *sishya*, and how the latter
should approach and serve his Master. He further emphasizes that in
order to realize the bliss of liberation, one's own individual effort is an
essential factor. Mere book learning never yields this bliss, which can
be realized only through enquiry or *vichara*, and which consists of *sravana*
or devoted attention to the precepts of the Guru, *manana* or deep contemplation, and *nididhyasana* or the cultivation of steady poise in the
Self.

The Three Paths

The three bodies — physical, subtle, and causal — are non-self and are
unreal. The Self, or "I," is quite different from them. It is due to ignorance that the sense of the Self or the "I"-notion is foisted on that which
is not Self, and this indeed is bondage. Since bondage arises from igno-

rance, liberation results from Knowledge. To know this from the Guru is *sravana*.

To reject the three bodies consisting of the five sheaths (physical, vital, mental, gnostic, and delectant) as not "I," and to extract through subtle enquiry of "Who am I?" that which is different from all the three bodies, existent as one and universal in the heart as *Aham* or "I," denoted by the word *Tvam* (in the Scriptural dictum "*Tat-tvam-asi*" — That thou art), this process of subtle enquiry is *manana* or deep contemplation.

The Beatitude

The world of name and form is but an adjunct of *Sat* or *Brahman*, and not being different from it is rejected as such and is affirmed as nothing else but *Brahman*. The instruction by the Guru to the disciple of the *Mahavakya, Tat-tvam-asi*, which declares the identity of the Self and the Supreme, is *upadesa*. The disciple is then enjoined to remain in the beatitude of *Aham-Brahman* — "I," the Absolute. Nevertheless, the old tendencies of the mind sprout up thick and strong and form an obstruction (to that state of beatitude). These tendencies are threefold and egoism, which is their root, flourishes in the externalized and differentiating consciousness caused by the forces of *vikshepa* or dissipation (due to *rajas*), and *avarana* or envelopment (due to *tamas*).

Churning the Mind

To install the mind firmly in the heart until these forces are destroyed, and to awaken with unswerving, ceaseless vigilance the true and cognate tendency which is characteristic of the *Atman* — expressed by the dicta, *Aham Brahmasmi* (I am *Brahman*), and *Brahmaivaham* (*Brahman* alone am I) — is termed *nididhyasana* or *atmanusandhana*, i.e., constancy in the Self. This is otherwise called *Bhakti, Yoga*, and *Dhyana*.

Atmanusandhana has been likened to churning the curd to draw forth butter, the mind being compared to the churning rod, the heart to the curd, and the practice of constancy in the Self to the process of churning. Just as by churning the curd butter is extracted and by friction fire is kindled, by unswerving vigilant constancy in the Self — ceaseless, like the unbroken filamentary flow of oil — is generated the natural or changeless trance or *nirvikalpa samadhi*, which readily and spontaneously yields that direct, immediate, unobstructed, and universal perception of *Brahman*, which is at once Knowledge and Experience and which transcends time and space.

Limitless Bliss

This is Self-Realization; cut asunder is the *hridaya granthi* or the Knot of the Heart. The false delusions of ignorance, the vicious and age-long tendencies of the mind, which constitute this knot, are destroyed. All doubts are dispelled and the bondage of karma is severed.

Thus has Sri Shankara, in this "Crown Gem of Discrimination," described *samadhi* or trance transcendent, which is the limitless bliss of liberation, beyond doubt and duality, and has at the same time, indicated the means for its attainment. To realize this state of freedom from duality is the *summum bonum* of life: and he alone that has won it is a *jivanmukta* (the liberated one while yet alive), and not he who merely has a theoretical understanding of what constitutes *purushartha* or the desired end and aim of human endeavor.

Final Freedom

Thus, the *jivanmukta* is declared to be free from the bonds of three-fold karmas (*sanchita, agami,* and *prarabdha*). The disciple who has reached this stage then relates his personal experience. The liberated one is free indeed to act as he pleases, and when he leaves the mortal frame attains absolution, and returns not to this "birth which is death."

Sri Shankara thus describes Realization that connotes liberation as two-fold, i.e., *jivanmukti* and *videha mukti*, referred to above. Moreover, in this short treatise, written in the form of a dialogue between a Guru and his disciple, he has considered many relevant topics.

FEBRUARY 6, 1937

While speaking to Mr. G. Shanmugham, a very sincere lawyer devotee, Bhagavan observed: The *sastras* say that one must serve a Guru for twelve years for getting Self-realization. What does Guru do? Does he hand it over to the disciple? Is not the Self always realized? What does the common belief mean then? The man is always the Self and yet he does not know it. He confounds it with the non-self, viz. the body etc. Such confusion is due to ignorance. If ignorance is wiped out, the confusion will cease to exist and the true knowledge will unfold. By remaining in contact with realized sages, man gradually loses his ignorance until its removal is complete. The eternal Self is thus revealed.

This is the meaning conveyed by the story of Ashtavakra and Janaka. The anecdotes differ in different books. We are not concerned with names and embellishments. The *tattva*, i.e., the moral, must not be lost sight of. The disciple surrenders himself to the Master. That means there is no vestige of individuality retained by the disciple. If the surrender is complete, all sense of individuality is lost and there is thus no cause for misery. The eternal being is only happiness. That is revealed.

Without understanding it correctly, people think the Guru teaches the disciple something like *"Tat-tvam-asi"* and that the disciple realizes "I am *Brahman*." In their ignorance, they conceive of *Brahman* as something more huge and powerful than anything else. With a limited "I," the man is so stuck up and wild. What will be the case if the same "I" grows up enormous? He will be enormously ignorant and foolish! This false "I" must perish. Its annihilation is the fruit of Guru *seva*. Realization is eternal, and it is not newly brought about by the Guru. He helps in the removal of ignorance — that is all.

FEBRUARY 7, 1937

Dr. Subramania Iyer, Retired Health Officer of Salem, read out a passage which contained the instructions that one should know that the world is transitory, that worldly enjoyments are useless, that one should therefore turn away in disgust from them, restrain the senses, and meditate on the Self to realize it.

Sri Bhagavan observed: How does one know the world to be transitory? Unless something permanent is held, the transitory nature of the world cannot be understood. Because the man is already the Self, and the Self is the Eternal Reality, his attention is drawn to it; and he is instructed to rivet his attention on the Eternal Reality, the Self.

M. Thought rises up as the subject and object. "I" alone being held, all else disappears. It is enough, but only to the competent few.

Others argue, "Quite so. The world existing during my sleep existed before my birth and will exist after my death. Do not others see it? How can the world cease to be if my ego does not appear?" The genesis of the world and the different schools of thought are meant to satisfy such people.

D. Nevertheless, being only products of intellect, they cannot turn the mind inward.

M. Just for this reason, the scriptures speak of an "inturned look," "one-pointed look," and so on.

The Self, being always the Self, why should only a *dhira* be illumined? Does it mean a man of courage? No, *dhih* = intellect; *rah* = watch, protection. So *dhira* is the one who always keeps the mind inward bent without letting it loose.

FEBRUARY 8, 1937

D. What is *turiya*?

M. There are three states only: waking, dream and sleep. *Turiya* is not a fourth one; it is what underlies these three. But people do not readily understand it. Therefore, it is said that this is the fourth state and the only Reality. In fact, it is not apart from anything, for it forms the substratum of all happenings; it is the only Truth, your very Being. The three states appear as fleeting phenomena on it and then sink into it alone. Therefore, they are unreal.

The pictures in a cinema show are only shadows passing over the screen. They make their appearance, move forward and backward, change from one to another, and are therefore unreal, whereas the screen all along remains unchanged. Similarly with paintings: the images are unreal and the canvas is real. So, also with us: the world phenomena, within or without, are only passing phenomena not independent of our Self. Only the habit of looking on them as being real and located outside ourselves is responsible for hiding our true being and showing forth the others. The ever-present only Reality, the Self, being found, all other unreal things will disappear, leaving behind the knowledge that they are no other than the Self.

Turiya is only another name for the Self. Aware of the waking, dream and sleep states, we remain unaware of our own Self. Nevertheless, the Self is here and now, and it is the only Reality. There is nothing else. So long as identification with the body lasts, the world seems to lie outside us. Only realize the Self and the things of the world *are not*.

An American lady, a theosophist, asked: What are the means by which the approach to my Master may be made nearer?

M. How far away are you now from him?

D. I am away from him, but I want to get closer.

M. If you first know your Self, you may then find out how far away the other is. Who are you now? Are you the personality?

D. Yes, I am the personality.

M. Is the personality independent of the Self?

D. Sometimes.

M. At what times?

D. I mean I have some flashes of the reality and at other times I do not.

M. Who is aware of those flashes?

D. I, I mean my personality.

M. Is this personality aware as being apart from the Self?

D. Which Self?

M. Which do you consider the personality to be?

D. The lower self.

M. Then I mean to ask whether the lower self is aware independently of the Higher Self?

D. Yes, at times.

M. Who feels that she is away from the Master, just now?

D. The Higher Self.

M. Does the Higher Self have a body that says the Master is away from it? Does it speak through your mouth? Are you apart from that?

D. Can you kindly advise me how I can train myself to be aware of what I do even without the body, as in sleep?

M. Awareness is your nature. In deep sleep or in waking, it is the same. How can it be gained afresh?

D. But I do not remember what I did in my sleep.

M. Who says, "I do not remember?"

D. I say it now.

M. You were the same then; why do you not say so in your sleep?

D. I do not remember what I said in my sleep.

M. You say, "I know, I remember," in the wakeful state. This same personality says, "I did not know — I did not remember in sleep." Why doesn't this question arise in sleep?

D. I do not know what happens in sleep. That is the reason I ask now.

M. The question affects the sleeping phase and must be raised there. It does not affect the waking phase and there is no apparent reason for it.

The fact is you have no limitations in sleep, and no question arises. Whereas now you put on limitations, identify yourself with the body and questions of this kind arise.

D. I understand, but do not realize it (i.e., unity in variety).

M. Because you are in diversity, you say you understand unity — that you have flashes, remember things, etc.; you consider this diversity to be real. On the other hand, Unity is the reality, and the diversity is false. It must go before unity reveals itself — its reality. It is always real. It does not send flashes of its being in this false diversity. On the contrary, this diversity obstructs the truth.

Then some others pursued the conversation.
M. Removal of ignorance is the aim of practice, and not acquisition of Realization. Realization is ever present, here and now. Were it to be acquired anew, Realization would be understood as being absent at one time and present at another. In that case, it is not permanent, and therefore not worth the attempt. But Realization is permanent and eternal and is here and now.
D. Grace is necessary for the removal of ignorance.
M. Certainly. But Grace is all along there. Grace is the Self. It is not something to be acquired. All that is necessary is to know its existence. For example, the sun is brightness only. It does not see darkness. Whereas others speak of darkness fleeing on the sun's approach. Similarly, ignorance also is a phantom and not real. Because of its unreality, its unreal nature being found, it is said to be removed.

Again, the sun is there and also bright. You are surrounded by sunlight. Still, if you would know the sun, you must turn your eyes in its direction. So also Grace is found by practice alone, although it is here and now.
D. By the desire to surrender constantly, increasing Grace is experienced, I hope.
M. Surrender once for all and be done with the desire. So long as the sense of doership is retained, there is the desire; that is also personality. If this goes, the Self is found to shine forth pure.

The sense of doership is the bondage, and not the actions themselves.

"Be still and know that I am God." Here stillness is total surrender without a vestige of individuality. Stillness will prevail and there will be no agitation of mind. Agitation of mind is the cause of desire, the sense of doership and personality. If that is stopped, there is quiet. There, "Knowing" means "Being." It is not the relative knowledge involving the triad knowledge, subject and object.
D. Is the thought "I am God" or "I am the Supreme Being" helpful?
M. "I Am that I Am." *I Am* is God — not thinking, "I am God." Realize *I Am* and do not think *I am*. "Know I am God" it is said, and not "Think I am God."

Later Sri Bhagavan continued: It is said, "I Am that I Am." That means a person must abide as the "I." He is always the "I" alone. He is nothing else. Yet he asks, "Who am I?" A victim of illusion would ask, "Who am I?" and not a man fully aware of himself. The wrong identity of the Self with the non-self makes you ask, "Who am I?"

Later still: There are different routes to Tiruvannamalai, but Tiruvannamalai is the same by whichever route it is gained. Similarly, the approach to the subject varies according to the personality. Yet the Self is the same. But, still being in Tiruvannamalai, if one asks for the route, it is ridiculous. So also, being the Self, if one asks how to realize the Self, it looks absurd. You *are* the Self. Remain as such. That is all. The questions arise because of the present wrong identification of the Self with the body. That is ignorance. This must go. On its removal, the Self alone *is.*

D. Does not education make a sage more useful to the world than illiteracy?
M. Even a learned man must bow before the illiterate sage.

Illiteracy is ignorance: education is learned ignorance. Both of them are ignorant of their true aim; whereas a sage is not ignorant because there is no aim for him.

D. Why should there be sleep in the world?
M. Owing to sin only.
D. Can it be destroyed?
M. Yes.
D. It ends only after making itself felt, they say.
M. Why then devotion to God?
D. How can sleep be destroyed?
M. Be not aware of its activities and effects.
D. How can it be done?
M. Only by inquiry of the Self.

FEBRUARY 12, 1937

A Scene in the Hall: It is 8:20 p.m., Sri Bhagavan has returned from supper and stretched himself out on the sofa. The light is dim; there are three men sitting on the floor. One is busy copying something from a journal, another is wrapped in meditation, and the third is looking around, having nothing to do. The Hall is silent but for occasional clearing of the throat by Sri Bhagavan.

Madhavaswami, the attendant devotee, slips in noiselessly with a sheaf of betel leaves in hand. He moves to the table. Sri Bhagavan, who is reclining on the sofa, sees him and calls out, yet kindly: "Sh, Sh, what are you doing?"

The attendant softly murmurs, "Nothing," and leaves the betel there and fumbles.

M. I do not want it. (The attendant softly settles down on the floor). Kasturi pill — one after another, every day. The bottle will be empty — and more is ordered. I don't want it.

A devotee skillfully blames the olla podrida *of the day-meal for the indifferent health of Sri Bhagavan.*
M. No — no — It was well made. It was good.

After a few minutes, the attendant slips out and returns with a bottle in hand, goes near Sri Bhagavan and stretches out a pill saying, "Cumin seed pill." Sri Bhagavan softly murmur, "It contains lime juice: lime juice is not good for this."

A devotee, Rangaswami Iyengar, has in the meantime become wide-awake from his meditation and looks on. The attendant is still holding out his hand with the pill. Sri Bhagavan continues, "Who is to munch it?"

Rangaswami Iyengar, "It need not be munched. It may be kept in the mouth and sucked." The attendant hastily agrees, "Yes — yes — it is only to be sucked."

M. Give it to him (pointing to Rangaswami Iyengar). Let him munch it or suck it. I do not want it.

(*The attendant returns disappointed, squats on the floor, and again rises up.*)
M. Eh! — Eh! What do you do? I do not want.

The attendant moves up to the medicine chest, murmuring: Kasturi pill — it will be effective.
Sri Bhagavan: I shall soon be right even without it. Do not take it out. Eh! — Eh! — keep it there — I won't take it — do what you like.

(*The attendant again settles down and all remain silent before retiring to bed.*)

FEBRUARY 13, 1937
At about 7:30 a.m., Sri Bhagavan was climbing up the hill after breakfast. Padananda went and prostrated, stood up and said: All right, I have had darshan . . . I shall return.

Sri Bhagavan smilingly: Whose *darshan?* Why don't you say that you gave *darshan* to me?

At about 9:00 a.m., a devotee from Poona (Mr. Parkhi) saluted Sri Bhagavan and read out his ashtaka *(verse) praying to Sri Bhagavan for Grace. The piece finished with a prayer for quick liberation (*jhatiti mukti*) and the devotee emphasized it.*
M. *Mukti,* i.e., liberation, is not to be gained hereafter. It is there forever, here and now.
D. I agree, but I do not experience it.
M. The experience is here and now. One cannot deny one's own self.
D. That means existence and not happiness.
M. Existence = Happiness = Being. The word *mukti* (liberation) is so provoking. Why should one seek it? He believes that there is bondage and therefore seeks liberation. But the fact is that there is no bondage but only liberation. Why call it by a name and seek it?
D. True — but we are ignorant.
M. Only remove ignorance. That is all there is to be done.

FEBRUARY 14, 1937
The aristocratic gentleman from Lucknow has written to Mr. Paul Brunton that his wife has since lost that peace of mind which she had gained by her visits to Sri Bhagavan, so he desires that Sri Bhagavan may be pleased to restore the same peace.
M. It is due to weakness of mind that peace once gained is later lost.

Mudaliar Swami, son of the lady who brings bhiksha every day to Sri Bhagavan, related the following interesting incident:
While Sri Bhagavan was staying in Virupaksha Cave, he and Mudaliar Swami were walking together behind the Skandasramam site. There was a huge rock about fifteen feet high. It was a cleft; a girl (a shepherdess) was standing there crying. Sri Bhagavan asked the reason for her sorrow. She said, "A sheep of mine has slipped into this cleft, so I am crying." Sri Bhagavan descended into the cleft, took the sheep on his shoulders, climbed up to the surface, and delivered the sheep to her. Mudaliar Swami says that it was a very remarkable feat for any human being.

Mr. Subbaramiah, a college professor from Nellore, asked about mukti.
M. All questions relating to *mukti* are inadmissible, because *mukti* means release from bondage, which implies the present existence of bondage. There

is no bondage and therefore no *mukti*, either.

D. The *sastras* speak of it and its grades.

M. The *sastras* are not meant for the wise because they do not need them; the ignorant do not want them. Only the *mumukshus* look up to the *sastras*. That means that the *sastras* are neither for wisdom nor for ignorance.

D. Vasishta is said to be a *jivanmukta*, whereas Janaka was a *videhamukta*.

M. Why speak of Vasishta or Janaka? What about oneself?

There were many new visitors this day. Two of them were speaking of Ganapati Muni in Sri Bhagavan's presence.

Sri Bhagavan added a few words to their talk: Some say that *jnana* and *upasana* are the two wings with which to fly to *mukti*. What is *jnana*? What is *upasana*? *Jnana* is ever-present. That is the ultimate goal, also. When an effort is made the effort is called *upasana*; when it is effortless, it is *jnana*, which is the same as *mukti*.

After some discussion among themselves, a visitor said: Some Superior Power must help us to shake off the externalities.

Sri Bhagavan said: Who sees the externalities? Do *they* say that they exist? If so, let the world say that it exists.

If the world is a projection from the interior, it must be recognized that it is projected simultaneously with the "I"-thought. Either way, the "I" is the fundamental basis knowing which all else is known.

Another mentioned that Ganapati Muni used to say that he could even go to Indra-loka and say what Indra was doing, but he could not go within and find the "I."
Sri Bhagavan added that Ganapati Muni used to say that it was easy to move forward, but impossible to move backward.

Then Sri Bhagavan remarked: However far one goes, there he is. Where is moving backward? The same truth is contained in the mantra in *Isa-Upanishad*.

In reply to a query how Ganapati Muni became an asu kavi (inspired poet), Sri Bhagavan said: It is said that while he was making *tapasya*, Shiva appeared and gave him milk or honey to drink, after which he became *asu kavi*.

FEBRUARY 20, 1937

A European civilian, Mr. Dodwell, Deputy Secretary of Finance in the Madras

*Government, arrived with his wife before 1:00 p.m. and stayed in the Hall till about
3:30 p.m. The lady asked:* The spiritual leaders in the West say that the spiritual center is in India. Is there any contact among the spiritual leaders in India? Or is contact possible between the leaders of the East and the West?
M. What do you mean by spiritual center?
D. The spiritual center is the seat of spiritual leaders.
M. What do you understand by "spiritual leaders?"
D. In the West there is a crisis. Scientific knowledge is far advanced. Such knowledge is used for generating destructive forces. There is a movement for making them constructive. When thus diverted, it will be for the good of the world. The leaders of this movement are the redeemers.
M. By "spiritual leaders," we understand this to mean those who are "spiritual" as opposed to those who are "physical." Spirit is unlimited and formless. Such too, is the spiritual center. There is only one such center. Whether in the West or in the East, the center cannot differ; nor has it any locality. Being unlimited, it includes the leaders, the men, the world, the forces of destruction and of construction. There is no differentiation. You speak of contact because you are thinking of the embodied beings as spiritual leaders. The spiritual men are not bodies; they are not aware of their bodies. They are only spirit, limitless and formless. There is always unity among them and all others; nay, they comprise all.
   The Spirit is the Self. If the Self is realized, these questions cannot arise at all.

Mrs. Jinarajadasa from Adyar: Self-realization sounds so easy, yet is so difficult in practice.
M. What can be easier? The Self is more intimate than anything else. If that cannot be realized, is it easy to realize what is apart and farther away?
D. Self-realization is so illusory. How can it be made permanent?
M. The Self can never be illusory. It is the only Reality. That which appears will also disappear and is therefore impermanent. The Self never appears and disappears and is therefore permanent.
D. Yes — true. You know that in the Theosophical Society they meditate to seek the Masters to guide them.
M. The Master is within. Meditation is meant for the removal of ignorance, of the wrong idea that he is without. If he were a stranger whose advent you await, he is bound to disappear also. Where is the use of a transient being like that?
   However, as long as you think that you are an individual or that you are

the body, so long is the Master necessary, and he will appear with a body. When this wrong identification ceases, the Master will be found to be the Self.

There is a stanza in *Kaivalya*:

"My Lord! You had remained as my Self within, protecting me in all my past incarnations. Now, by your Grace, you have manifested yourself as my Master and revealed yourself as the Self."

Just see what happens in sleep. There is no ego, no India, no seekers, no Master, etc.; and yet you are, and happy, too.

The ego, India, seekers, etc., appear now; but they are neither apart from nor independent of you.

There was a large group of visitors on account of the election holidays, and some of these also joined in the discussion. One of them asked about reincarnation.

M. Reincarnation can only be so long as there is ignorance. There is no incarnation either now, nor was there before, nor will be hereafter. This is the truth.

D. What is the ego-self?

M. The ego-self appears and disappears and is transitory, whereas the real Self is permanent. Though you are actually the true Self, yet you wrongly identify the real Self with the ego-self.

D. How does the mistake come about?

M. See if it has come about.

D. One has to sublimate the ego-self into the true Self.

M. The ego-self does not exist at all.

D. Why then does it give us trouble?

M. To whom is the trouble? The trouble also is imagined. Trouble and pleasure are only for the ego.

D. Why is the world so wrapped up in ignorance?

M. Take care of yourself only. Let the world take care of itself. See your Self. If you are the body, there is the gross world, also. If you are Spirit, all is Spirit alone.

D. It will hold good for the individual, but what of the rest?

M. Do it first and then see if the question arises afterwards.

D. Is there *avidya*?

M. For whom is it?

D. For the ego-self.

M. Yes, for the ego. Remove the ego; *avidya* is gone. Look for it; the ego vanishes. The real Self alone remains. The ego professing *avidya* is not to be seen. There is no *avidya* in reality. All *sastras* are meant to disprove the existence of *avidya*.

D. How did the ego arise?

M. Ego is not. Otherwise, do you admit of two selves? How can there be *avidya* in the absence of the ego? If you begin to inquire, the *avidya*, which is already non-existent, will be found not to be or you will say it has fled away.

Ignorance pertains to the ego. Why do you think of the ego and also suffer? What is ignorance again? It is that which is non-existent. However, the worldly life requires the hypothesis of *avidya*. *Avidya* is only our ignorance and nothing more. It is ignorance or forgetfulness of the Self. Can there be darkness before the Sun? Similarly, can there be ignorance before the Self-evident and Self-luminous Self? If you know the Self, there will be no darkness, no ignorance, and no misery.

It is the mind that feels the trouble, misery, etc. Darkness never comes nor goes. See the Sun and there is no darkness. Similarly, see the Self and *avidya* will be found not to exist.

D. Sri Ramakrishna and others practiced concentration.

M. Concentration and all other practices are meant for recognizing the absence, i.e., non-existence, of ignorance. No one can deny his own being. Being is knowledge, i.e., awareness. That awareness implies absence of ignorance. Therefore, everyone naturally admits non-existence of ignorance. And yet, why should he suffer? Because he thinks he is this or that. That is wrong. "I am" alone is; and not "I am so and so," or "I am such and such." When existence is absolute, it is right; when it is particularized, it is wrong. That is the whole truth.

See how each one admits that he is. Does he look into a mirror to know his being? His awareness makes him admit his existence or being. But he confuses it with the body, etc. Why should he do so? Is he aware of his body in his sleep? No, yet he himself does not cease to be in sleep. He exists there though without the body. How does he know that he exists in sleep? Does he require a mirror to reveal his own being now? Only be aware, and your being is clear in your awareness.

D. How is one to know the Self?

M. "Knowing the Self" means "Being the Self." Can you say that you do not know the Self? Though you cannot see your own eyes and though not provided with a mirror to look in, do you deny the existence of your eyes? Similarly, you are aware of the Self even though the Self is not objectified. Or, do you deny your Self because it is not objectified? When you say, "I cannot know the Self," it means absence in terms of relative knowledge, because you have been so accustomed to relative knowledge that you identify yourself with it. Such wrong identity has forged the difficulty of not knowing the obvious Self because it cannot be objectified; so you ask, "How is one to know the Self?" Your difficulty is centered in "How?" Who is to know the Self? Can the body know it?

Let the body answer. Who says that the body is perceived now?

In order to meet this kind of ignorance, the *sastras* formulate the theory of God's *lila* or *krida* (play). God is said to emanate as the mind, the senses, and the body and to play. Who are you to say that this play is a trouble to you? Who are you to question the doings of God?

Your duty is *to be*, and not *to be this or that*. "I Am that I Am" sums up the whole truth. The method is summed up in "Be Still." What does "stillness" mean? It means, "destroy yourself." Because any form or shape is the cause of trouble. Give up the notion that "I am so and so." Our *sastras* say: *ahamiti sphurati* (it shines as "I").

D. What is *sphurana* (shining)?

M. (*Aham-aham*) "I-I" is the Self; (*Aham idam*) "I am this" or "I am that" is the ego. Shining is there always. The ego is transitory. When the "I" is kept up as "I" alone it is the Self; when it flies at a tangent and says "this," it is the ego.

D. Is God apart from the Self?

M. The Self is God. "I Am" is God. "I am the Self, O Gudakesa!" (*Ahamatma Gudakesa*). [*Bhagavad Gita*.]

This question arises because you are holding the ego-self. This will not arise if you hold the True Self. For the Real Self will not and cannot ask anything. If God be apart from the Self, He must be a Self-less God, which is absurd.

D. What is *namaskara* (prostration)?

M. Prostration means "subsidence of the ego." What is "subsidence?" To merge into the source of its origin. God cannot be deceived by outward genuflections, bowings, and prostrations. He sees if the individuality is there or not.

Mr. Shamanna: Is there a sixth sense to feel "I Am?"

M. Do you have it in your sleep? There is only one being functioning through the five senses. Or do you mean that each sense is independent of the Self and there are five selves admitting of a sixth to control them? There is a power working through these five senses. How can you deny the existence of such Power? Do you deny your existence? Do you not remain even in sleep where the body is not perceived? The same "I" continues to be now; so we admit our existence, whether there is the body or not. The senses work periodically. Their work begins and ends. There must be a substratum on which their activities depend. Where do they appear and merge? There must be a single substratum. Were you to say that the single unit is not perceived, it is an admission of it being single — for you say that there is no second one to know it.

All these discussions are only to get rid of ignorance. When that is done, everything will be clear. It is a matter of competence, or ripeness.

D. Cannot Grace hasten such competence in a seeker?

M. Leave it to Him. Surrender unreservedly. One of two things must be done. Either surrender because you admit your inability and also require a Higher Power to help you; or investigate into the cause of misery, go into the source and merge into the Self. Either way, you will be free from misery. God never forsakes one who has surrendered (*Mamekam saranam vraja*).

D. What is the drift of the mind after surrender?

M. Is the surrendered mind raising the question? (*Laughter.*)

The Nellore Professor asked about vishvarupa darshana.

M. V*ishvatma darshana* is *vishvarupa darshana,* i.e., the universal Self or the cosmic Self is the cosmos. Sri Krishna started the discourse in chapter 2 (*Bhagavad Gita*), saying, "I have no form." In chapter 11, He says, "See my form as the Universe." Is it consistent? Again he says, "I transcend the three worlds," but Arjuna sees the three worlds in Him. Sri Krishna says, "I cannot be seen by men, Gods, etc."; yet Arjuna sees himself and the Gods in Him. No one could see, and yet Arjuna was endowed with divine sight to see Him. Does it not look like a maze of contradictions?

The answer is that the understanding is wrong. *Sthula dristi* (bodily understanding) on the physical plane is absurd. *Jnana dristi* (subtle understanding) is necessary. That is why Arjuna was given *divya chakshuh* (divine sight). Can such sight be gross? Will such interpretation lead you to a right understanding?

Sri Krishna says *Kalosmi,* "I am Time." Does Time have a shape?

If the universe be His form should it not be one and unchanging? Why does He say to Arjuna, "See in me whatever you desire to see?" That means that His form is according to the desires of the seer. They speak of "divine sight" and yet paint the scene, each according to his own view. There is the seer also in the seen. What is all this? Even a hypnotist can make you see strange scenes. You call this a trick, whereas the other you call divine. Why this difference? Anything seen cannot be real. That is the truth.

As Sri Bhagavan was continuing in the same strain, a visitor asked how to overcome the identity of the Self with the body.

M. What about sleep?

D. There is ignorance prevailing.

M. How do you know your ignorance in sleep? Did you exist in sleep, or not?

D. I do not know.

M. Do you deny your existence in sleep?

D. I must admit it by my reasoning.

M. How do you infer your existence?

D. By reasoning and experience.

M. Is reasoning necessary for experience? (*Laughter.*)

D. Is meditation analytical or synthetical?

M. Analysis or synthesis is in the region of intellect. The Self transcends the intellect.

Before leaving at 3:30 p.m., Mrs. Dodwell raised a second question, asking what is meant by neti-neti.

M. There is now wrong identification of the Self with the body, senses, etc. You proceed to discard these, and this is *neti*. This can be done only by holding to the one which cannot be discarded. That is *iti* alone.

FEBRUARY 21, 1937

A Marathi lady, a casual visitor then taking leave, was almost on the point of bursting into tears. She asked: I know that *mukti* is impossible in one life. Still, may I not have peace of mind in this life?

The Master looked at her very kindly and said smiling softly: Life and all else are in *Brahman* alone. *Brahman* is here and now. Investigate.

D. I have been practicing meditation for a number of years. Yet my mind is not steady and cannot be brought to bear on meditation.

Again looking steadily at her, the Master said: Do it now and all will be right.

A young girl of nine or ten, whose mother is a Research Scholar in Sanskrit at the University of Madras, accompanied by Mr. Maurice Frydman, met Sri Bhagavan in Palakothu at about noon. Sri Bhagavan, as was usual with him, kindly smiled at her. She asked Sri Bhagavan: Why is there misery on earth?

M. Due to Karma.

D. Who makes karma bear fruits?

M. God.

D. God makes us do karma and gives bad fruits for bad karma. Is it fair?

(*Sri Bhagavan almost laughed and was very pleased with her. Later he was coaxing her to read something on returning to the Hall. Since then he is watching her.*)

FEBRUARY 22, 1937

A Marathi gentleman and wife, past middle age, were on a visit here. They are quiet and simple people. Both of them tearfully took leave and the gentleman even sobbed out a prayer for Sri Bhagavan's Grace. Sri Bhagavan gazed at them, with his lips parted showing a row of white teeth. His eyes also had a tear in them.

Sri Bhagavan was in the cattle-shed. People were working and he watched their work for a short time. Then someone came and said that a large number of visitors were waiting in the Hall. Sri Bhagavan in his calm way said: "Yes — yes, you do your work. Let me go for mine. People are waiting for me. Let me go." Then he left the place.

FEBRUARY 23, 1937

There was a group of three middle-aged Andhras on a visit to Sri Bhagavan. One of them kneeled and asked: I am performing *Hatha Yoga,* namely *basti, dhauti, neti,* etc. I find a blood vessel hardened in the ankle. Is it a result of yoga?

M. The blood vessel would have hardened under any circumstances. It does not trouble you as much now as it would otherwise. *Hatha Yoga* is a cleansing process. It also helps peace of mind, after leading you to *pranayama.*

D. May I do *pranayama?* Is it useful?

M. *Pranayama* is an aid for the control of mind. Only you should not stop with *pranayama.* You must proceed further to *pratyahara, dharana, dhyana,* and *samadhi.* Full results are reaped finally.

Another member of the group asked: How are lust, anger, acquisitiveness, confusion, pride, and jealousy overcome?

M. By *dhyana.*

D. What is *dhyana*?

M. *Dhyana* is holding on to a single thought and putting off all other thoughts.

D. What is to be meditated upon?

M. Anything that you prefer.

D. Shiva, Vishnu, and Gayatri are said to be equally efficacious. Which should I meditate upon?

M. Anyone you like best. They are all equal in their effect. But you should stick to one.

D. How to meditate?

M. Concentrate on that one whom you like best. If a single thought prevails, all other thoughts are put off and finally eradicated. So long as diversity prevails, there are bad thoughts. When the object of love prevails, only good thoughts hold the field. Therefore, hold on to one thought only. *Dhyana* is the chief practice.

A little later, Sri Bhagavan continued: Dhyana means fight. As soon as you begin meditation, other thoughts will crowd together, gather force, and try to sink the single thought to which you try to hold. The good thought must gradually gain strength by repeated practice. After it has grown strong, the other thoughts will be put to flight. This is the battle royal always taking place in meditation.

One wants to rid oneself of misery. It requires peace of mind, which means absence of perturbation owing to all kinds of thoughts. Peace of mind is brought about by *dhyana* alone.

D. What is the need then for *pranayama*?

M. *Pranayama* is meant for one who cannot directly control the thoughts. It serves like a brake to a car. But one should not stop with it, as I said before, but must proceed to *pratyahara, dharana,* and *dhyana*. After the fruition of *dhyana*, the mind will come under control even in the absence of *pranayama*. The *asanas* (postures) help *pranayama*, which helps *dhyana* in its turn, and peace of mind results. Herein lies the purpose of *Hatha Yoga*.

Later Sri Bhagavan continued: When *dhyana* is well established, it cannot be given up. It will go on automatically whether engaged in work, play or enjoyment. It will persist in sleep, too. *Dhyana* must become so deep-rooted that it will be natural to one.

D. What rite or action is necessary for the development of *dhyana*?

M. *Dhyana* is itself the action, the rite and the effort. It is the most intense and potent of all. No other effort is necessary.

D. Is not *japa* necessary?

M. Is *dhyana* not *vak* (speech)? Why is japa necessary for it? If *dhyana* is gained, there is no need for anything else.

D. Is not a vow of silence helpful?

M. A vow is only a vow. It may help *dhyana* to some extent. But what is the good of keeping the mouth closed and letting the mind run riot? If the mind is engaged in *dhyana,* where is the need for speech?

Nothing is as good as *dhyana.* Should one take to action with a vow of silence, where is the good of the vow?

D. What is *Jnana Marga* (path of Knowledge)?

M. I have been saying it for so long. What is *jnana? Jnana* means realization of the Truth. It is done by *dhyana. Dhyana* helps you hold on to Truth to the exclusion of all thoughts.

D. Why are there so many Gods mentioned?

M. The body is only one. Still, how many functions are performed by it? The source of all the functions is only one. It is in the same way with the Gods.

D. Why does a man suffer misery?

M. Misery is due to multifarious thoughts. If the thoughts are unified and centered on a single item there is no misery, but happiness results. Then, even the thought, "I do something" is absent; nor will there be an eye on the fruit of action.

D. Hair standing on end, sobbing voice, joyful tears, etc., are mentioned in *Atma Vidya Vilasa* and other works. Are these found in *samadhi,* or before, or after?

M. All these are the symptoms of exceedingly subtle modes of mind (*vrittis*). Without duality they cannot remain. *Samadhi* is Perfect Peace where these cannot find a place. After emerging from *samadhi* the remembrance of the state gives rise to these symptoms. In *Bhakti Marga* (path of devotion), these are the precursors to *samadhi.*

D. Are they not so in the path of *jnana?*

M. Maybe. There is no definiteness about it. It depends on the nature of the individual. Individuality entirely lost, these cannot find a place. But even the slightest trace of it being present, these symptoms become manifest.

Manikavachakar and other saints have spoken of these symptoms. They say tears rush forth involuntarily and irrepressibly. I had the same experience when staying in Virupaksha cave.

D. The sleep state is said to be the experience of bliss yet, on recollection, the hairs do not stand on end. Why should they do so, if the *samadhi* state is recollected?

M. *Samadhi* means sleep in the waking state (*jagrat sushupti*). Bliss is overpowering and the experience is very clear, whereas it is different in sleep.

D. Can we put it that in sleep there is no unhappiness, nor happiness, i.e., the experience is neither negative nor positive.

M. But the recollection is positive — "I slept happily," says the man. So there must be the experience of happiness in sleep.

D. Is Bliss the absence of unhappiness, or is it something positive?

M. It is positive. Loss of unhappiness and the rise of happiness are simultaneous.

D. Can it be that the recollection of happiness in sleep is not clear and so there is no ecstasy, etc.?

M. The Bliss of *samadhi* is a perfectly clear experience and its recollection also is similar. But the experience of sleep is otherwise.

FEBRUARY 28, 1937

His Highness The Maharajah of Mysore had a private interview with Sri Bhagavan in the newly built bathroom from 9:15 to 9:30 a.m. He saluted Sri Bhagavan placing his head on Sri Bhagavan's feet and said: I have read Sri Bhagavan's life and long had a desire to meet him, but my circumstances are such that intentions of this kind cannot easily be carried into effect. Nor can I stay here as other disciples can, considering my obligations. While I remain here for about fifteen minutes, I shall now pray only for Thy Grace.

(*On departure H.H. again saluted Sri Bhagavan as before and left after presenting two fine shawls and some money to the office.*)

MARCH 13, 1937

H.H. The Maharajah of Travancore had an interview from 4:30 p.m. to 5:15 p.m.

Their Highnesses the Maharajah and the Maharani of Travancore, who arrived at Tiruvannamalai by the 8 a.m. train, visited the Asramam at 4:15 p.m. The public was barred from the Hall where Bhagavan sat. Even devotees who were visiting the Hall daily were excluded, by a sad mistake, from the interview. The Royal party was introduced to Sri Bhagavan by a retired District Magistrate. Two aides-de-camp, the Private Secretary to H.H. the

Maharajah, some officials of the Travancore State, and an Advocate of Mylapore, were present. The discussion started by the District Magistrate went on about *manas*, concentration, Realization, purpose of creation, etc. Her Highness put forth some questions expressing her doubts and they were all dealt with by Sri Bhagavan. H.H. the Maharajah also took part in the discussion. The whole conversation was in Tamil and Malayalam.

During the visit of the Royal Family of Travancore, Her Highness appeared very cultured, vivacious, and conversant with Malayalam, Tamil, and English. Most of the questions were put by Her Highness. One of these was: What is the purpose of creation?

M. It is to give rise to this question; investigate the answer, and finally abide in the Supreme or rather the primal source of all, including the Self. The investigation will resolve itself into one of quest for the Self and cease only after the non-self is sifted away and the Self realized in all its purity and glory.

D. How is the investigation to start?

M. The Self is plain to all and the starting equally plain.

D. What is the starting point for one in my stage of development?

M. Each one has some method of *upasana* or *japa*. If that is pursued in all sincerity with due perseverance, it will automatically lead to the investigation of the Self.

    (*The writer of these notes was not present and the above was gathered from one of the attendants of Sri Maharshi.*)

MARCH 21, 1937

A middle-aged Canarese visitor asked about akarma *(actionless act).*

M. Whatever one does after the ego has vanished is *akarma*.

A learned Telugu visitor, who had composed a song in praise of Sri Bhagavan, read it out, placed it at his feet, and saluted. After some time, he asked for upadesa.

M. The *upadesa* is contained in *Upadesa Saram* (The Essence of Instruction).

D. But oral and personal instruction is more valuable.

M. If there is anything new and hitherto unknown, *upadesa* will be appropriate. Here it happens to be stilling the mind and remaining free from thoughts.

D. It looks impossible.

M. But it is precisely the pristine and eternal state of all.

D. It is not perceived in our everyday active life.

M. Everyday life is not divorced from the Eternal State. So long as the daily life is imagined to be different from the spiritual life, these difficulties arise. If the spiritual life is correctly understood, the active life will be found to be no different from it.

Can the mind be found by the mind when looking for it as an object? The source of the mental functions must be sought and gained. That is the Reality.

One does not know the Self owing to the interference of thoughts. The Self is realized when thoughts subside.

D. "Only one in a million pursues *sadhanas* to completion." (*Bhagavad Gita* 7. 3).

M. "Whenever the turbulent mind wavers, then and there pull it and bring it under control" (*Bhagavad Gita* 6.26). "Seeing the mind with the mind" (*manasa mana alokya*), so proclaim the *Upanishads*.

D. Is the mind an *upadhi* (limiting adjunct)?

M. Yes.

D. Is the seen (*drisya*) world real (*satya*)?

M. It is true to the same degree as the seer (*drashta*). Subject, object and perception form the triad (*triputi*). There is a reality beyond these three. These appear and disappear, whereas the truth is eternal.

D. These *triputi sambhava* are only temporal.

M. Yes, if one recognizes the Self even in temporal matters, these will be found to be non-existent, rather inseparate from the Self; and they will be going on at the same time.

MARCH 22, 1937

A middle-aged Andhra visitor: Man is said to be divine. Why then does he have regrets?

M. Divinity refers to the essential nature. The regrets are of *Prakriti*.

D. How is one to overcome regrets?

M. By realizing the Divinity in him.

D. How?

M. By practice.

D. What kind of practice?

M. Meditation.

D. Mind is not steady while meditating.

M. It will be all right by practice.

D. How is the mind to be steadied?
M. By strengthening it.
D. How to strengthen it?
M. It grows strong by *satsanga* (company of the wise).
D. Shall we add prayers, etc.?
M. Yes.
D. What of the one who has no regrets?
M. He is an accomplished Yogi. There is no question about him.
D. People cite disasters, earthquakes, famines, etc., to disprove God. How shall we meet their contention?
M. Wherefrom have they come — those who argue?
D. They say, "Nature."
M. Some call it "Nature" — others "God."
D. Are we to keep anything for a rainy day or live a precarious life for spiritual attainments?
M. God looks after everything.

MARCH 27, 1937

In the course of conversation with a visitor from Andhra Pradesh, Sri Bhagavan quoted:

"Asamsayam mahabaho mano durnigraham chalam
Abhvasena tu Kaunteya vairagyena cha grhyate."
Without doubt, O mighty-armed Hero,
the mind is restless, hard to curb.
Yet by constant effort, Partha
matched with detachment — curbed it *is*.
— *Bhagavad Gita 6.35*

To explain vairagya, *Sri Bhagavan again quoted:*
"Sankalpaprabhavan kamams tyaktva sarvan aseshatah
Manasaivendriyagramam viniyamya samantatah."
Having abandoned without exception
all longing born of thought for self,
Having drawn in by mind alone
his team of senses from all sides.
— *Bhagavad Gita 6.24*

As for practice (abhyasa):

"Sanaissanairuparamet buddhya dhritigrhitaya
Atmasamstham manah krtva na kinchidapi chintayet."
By slow approaches let him come to rest,
   with patient, rock-poised Will;
His mind at home in Selfhood pure,
   let him create no *thought* at all.
— *Bhagavad Gita* 6.25

Again for jnana:
   "Yato yato nischarati manas chanchalam asthiram
   Tatastato niyamyaitad atmanyeva vasam nayet."
Though over and over the fickle mind,
   all restlessness, a-wandering goes,
Still over and over let him regain control,
   and bring it back to the Self alone.
— *Bhagavad Gita* 6.26

APRIL 2, 1937

A gentleman from Kerala, asked Sri Bhagavan for an explanation of Atma-Vidya *("Self-Knowledge"). Sri Bhagavan explained this short piece of five stanzas as follows:* Chidambaram is the famous place of pilgrimage associated with Nandanar who sang that *Atma-Vidya* is most difficult of attainment. Muruganar (a longstanding devotee of Sri Bhagavan) began however by stating that *Atma-Vidya* is the *easiest* of attainments. *Ayye atisulabham* is the burden of the song. In explanation of this extraordinary statement, he argued that *Atma* being the Self is eternally obvious, even to the least of men. The original statement and the subsequent reasoning are incompatible, because there need be no *attainment* if the Self is the substratum of all selves and so obvious, too. Naturally, he could not pursue the theme further and laid the first four lines composed by him before Sri Bhagavan for completion.

Sri Bhagavan admitted the truth of the disciple's statement and pointed out why the Self, though obvious, is hidden. It is the wrong identity of the Self with the body, etc.

D. How did the wrong identity arise?

M. Due to thoughts. If these thoughts are put to an end, the real Self should shine forth of itself.

D. How are these thoughts to be ended?

M. Find out their basis. All of them are strung on the single "I"-thought. Quell it; then all others are quashed. Moreover, there is no use knowing all except the Self. If the Self is known, all others become known. Hence, Self-realization is the primary and sole duty of man.

D. How to quell the "I"-thought?

M. If its source is sought, it does not arise and thus is quelled.

D. Where and how to find it?

M. It is in fact the consciousness which enables individuals to function in different ways. Pure Consciousness is the Self. All that is required to realize the Self is to "Be Still."

D. What can be easier than that?

M. So *Atma-Vidya* is the easiest of attainments.

A European gentleman asked: How do you answer the question, "Who are you?"

M. Ask yourself the question, "Who am I?"

D. Please tell me how you have found it. I shall not be able to find it myself. The "I" is the result of biological forces. It results in silence. I want to know how the Master finds it.

M. Is it found only by logic? The scientific analysis is due to intellect.

D. According to J.C. Bose, nature does not make any difference between a worm and a man.

M. What is Nature?

D. It is that which exists.

M. How do you know the existence?

D. By my senses.

M. "My" implies your existence. But you are speaking of another's existence. You must exist to speak of "my senses." There cannot be "my" without "I."

D. I am a poor creature. I come to ask you, Great Master that you are, what this existence is. There is no special significance in the word *existence*. He exists, I exist, and others exist. What of that?

M. The existence of anyone posited shows your own existence. "Existence is your nature."

D. There is nothing strange in anything existing.

M. How do you know its existence — rather than your own existence?

D. What is new in the existence of anything? I take up your book and read there that the one question one should ask oneself is "Who am I?" I want to know "Who are you?" I have my own answer. If another says the same, and so do millions of others, there is the probability of the Self. I want a positive answer to the question, and no playing with words.

M. In this way, you are in the region of probabilities at best.

D. Yes. There are no certainties. Even God cannot be proved to be an absolute certainty.

M. Leave God alone for the time being. What of yourself?

D. I want confirmation of the Self.

M. You seek the confirmation from others. Each one though addressed as "you," styles himself "I." The confirmation is only from "I." There is no "you" at all. All are comprised in "I." The other can be known only when the Self is posited. The others do not exist without the subject.

D. Again, this is nothing new. When I was with Sir C. V. Raman, he told me that the theory of smell could be explained from his theory of light. Smell need no longer be explained in terms of chemistry. Now, *there* is something new; it is progress. That is what I mean when I say there is nothing new in all the statements I hear now.

M. "I" is never new. It is eternally the same.

D. Do you mean to say that there is no progress?

M. Progress is perceived by the outgoing mind. Everything is still when the mind is introverted and the Self is sought.

D. The Sciences — what becomes of them?

M. They all end in the Self. The Self is their finality.

(*It was 5:00 p.m.; Sri Bhagavan left the Hall and the gentleman left for the station.*)

Mr. Bose, the Bengali engineer, asked the meaning of the last stanza of Atma-Vidya ("*Self-Knowledge*").

Sri Bhagavan explained on the following lines: There is the world perceived; the perception is only apparent. It requires location for existence and light. Such *existence* and *light* are simultaneous with the rise of mind. So the physical existence and illumination are part of mental existence and illumination. The latter is not absolute, for the mind rises and sinks. The mind has its substratum in the Self, which is self-evident; i.e., its existence and self-luminosity are obvious. That is absolute being, continuous in the sleep, waking, and dream states.

The world consists of variety, which is the function of the mind. The mind shines by reflected light — i.e. light reflected from the Self. Just as the pictures in a cinema show are seen only in diffused, i.e. artificial light, but not in a strong glare or in thick darkness, so also the world pictures are perceptible only in diffused, i.e. reflected light of the Self through the darkness of *avidya* (ignorance). The world cannot be seen either in pure ignorance as in sleep, or in pure light as in Self-realization. *Avidya* is the cause of variety.

The engineer said that he understood only intellectually.
M. Because intellect holds you at present, i.e. you are in the grip of intellect in the waking state when you discuss these matters.
  (Later, it was added that Grace is needed for Realization.)
The engineer asked how Grace is to be obtained.
M. Grace is the Self. It is not manifest because of ignorance prevailing. With *sraddha*, it will become manifest.
  Sraddha (faith), Grace, Light, Spirit are all synonymous with the Self.

APRIL 5, 1937

A Telugu gentleman, subdued in appearance, but learned in philosophy, asked Sri Bhagavan about monolaya. *Sri Bhagavan said that everything is contained in* Upadesa Saram, *a copy of which the man was holding in his hand.*
D. What is mind?
M. See what it is.
D. It is *sankalpa vikalpatmaka* (made up of thoughts and their changes).
M. Whose *sankalpa* (thought)?
D. *Sankalpa* is the nature of the mind.
M. Of what is the *sankalpa*?
D. Of the externalities.
M. Quite so. Is that your nature?
D. It is of the mind.
M. What is your nature?
D. *Suddha Chaitanya* (Pure Conscious Light).
M. Then why do you worry about *sankalpa* and the rest?
D. The mind is admitted to be changing and unsteady (*chanchala* and *asthira*).
M. It is also said in the same place that the mind is to be introverted and made to merge into the Self; that the practice must be long because of slowness and must be continued until it is totally merged in the Self.
D. I want *prasad*, i.e., Grace, for it.
M. It is always with you. All that is required of you is not to confound yourself with the extrovert mind but to abide as the Self. That is *prasad*.
  (The gentleman saluted and retired.)

Lokesananda, a sannyasi, *asked Sri Bhagavan:* Is there *prarabdha* for a *jivanmukta?*
M. Who is the questioner? From whom does the question proceed? Is it a *jivanmukta* who is asking?
D. No, I am not a *mukta* as yet.
M. Then why not let the *jivanmukta* ask the question for himself?
D. The doubts are for *me.*
M. Quite so. The *ajnani* has doubt, but not a *jnani.*

The conversation turned to *vasanas.* Sri Bhagavan said that good tendencies and bad ones (*suvasana* and *kuvasana*) are concomitant — the one cannot exist without the other. Maybe one class predominates. Good tendencies (*suvasana*) are cultivated and they must also be finally destroyed by *jnana.*

A young prodigy was mentioned. Sri Bhagavan remarked that latent impressions of previous births (*purva janma samskara*) were strong in him.
D. How does it manifest as the ability to cite well-known saints? Is it *vasana* in the form of a seed only?
M. Yes. Predisposition (*samskara*) is acquired knowledge and kept in stock. It manifests under favorable circumstances. One with strong *samskara* understands the thing when presented to him much quicker than another with no *samskara* or weak *samskara.*
D. Does it hold good with inventors, also?
M. "There is nothing new under the sun." What we call inventions or discoveries are merely rediscoveries by competent men with strong *samskara* in the directions under consideration.
D. Is it so with Newton, Einstein, etc.?
M. Certainly. But the *samskaras*, however strong, will not manifest unless in a still mind. It is within the experience of everyone that his attempts to rake up his memory fail, whereas something flashes in the mind when he is calm. Mental quiet is necessary even for remembrance of forgotten things. The so-called genius is one who worked hard in his past births and acquired knowledge and kept it in store as *samskaras.* He now concentrates his mind until it merges in the subject. In that stillness, the submerged ideas rise up. That requires favorable conditions, too.

APRIL 6, 1937

Mr. Venkata Rao, an Andhra gentleman, in the course of conversation with Sri Bhagavan, was told:

Until you gain *jnana* you cannot understand the state of a *jnani*. There is no use asking about the work of Ishvara and the rest. Some ask why Shiva went naked in Daruka forest and spoiled the chastity of the *rishi's* wives. The *puranas*, which record this incident, have also said that Shiva had previously saved the *Devas* and the universe by consuming the poison *halahala* at the time of churning the ocean of milk. He, who could save the world from the deadly poison and lead the sages to emancipation, had also wandered nude amongst their women. Their actions are incomprehensible to ordinary intellects. One must be a *jnani* to understand a *jnani* or *Ishvara*.

D. What is the relation between *bhakti* and *jnana*?

M. The eternal, unbroken, natural state is *jnana*. Does it not imply love of Self? Is it not *bhakti*?

D. Idol worship does not seem good. They worship the formless God in Islam.

M. What is their conception of God?

D. As Immanence, etc.

M. Is not God even then endowed with attributes? Form is only one kind of attribute. One cannot worship God without some notions. Any *bhavana* (idea) presupposes a God with attributes (*saguna*). Moreover, what is the use of discussing the form or formlessness of God? Find out if you have a form. You can then understand God.

D. I admit I have no form.

M. All right. You have no form in sleep, but in the waking state you identify yourself with a form. See which is your real state. That is understood to be without form on investigation. If you know your Self to be formless by your *jnana*, should you not concede the same amount of *jnana* to God and understand Him to be formless?

D. But there is the world for God.

M. How does the world appear? How are we? Knowing this, you know God. You will know if He is Shiva, or Vishnu or any other or all put together.

D. Is *Vaikuntha* in *Paramapada*, i.e., in the transcendent Self?

M. Where is *Paramapada* or *Vaikuntha* unless in you?

D. *Vaikuntha*, etc. appear involuntarily.

M. Does this world appear voluntarily?

(*The questioner returned no answer.*)

M. The self-evident "I," ignoring the Self, goes about seeking to know the non-Self. How absurd!

D. This is *Sankhya Yoga*. Being the culmination of all kinds of other yogas, how can it be understood to start with? Is not *bhakti* antecedent to it?

M. Has not Sri Krishna started the *Gita* with *Sankhya*?

D. Yes. I understand it now.

In Sri Ramakrishna's "Life" it is said that an idol, Ramlal, was animate. Is it true?

M. Can you account for the animation of this body? Is the movement of the idol more mysterious than the movement of this body?

D. Metal does not move itself.

M. Is not the body a corpse? You will probably consider it a mystery if the corpse moves. Is that so?

Three persons came on a short visit. The eldest of them asked: There is one process of creation mentioned in the *Upanishads* and another in *Puranas.* Which of them is true?

M. They are many, and meant to indicate that the creation has a cause and a creator should be posited so that one might seek the cause. The emphasis is on the purpose of the theory and not on the process of creation. Moreover, the creation is perceived by someone. There are no objects without the subject; that is the objects do not come and tell you that they are, rather it is you who say that the objects exist. The objects are therefore what the seer makes of them. They have no existence independent of the subject. Find out what *you* are and then you understand what the world is. That is the object of the theory.

D. The soul is only a small particle whereas creation is so huge. How can we surmise it?

M. The particle speaks of the huge creation; where is the contradiction?

Later Sri Bhagavan continued:

There are so many theories, scriptural and scientific. Have they reached any finality? They cannot. *Brahman* is said to be subtler than the subtlest, wider than the widest. *Anu* is an atom, infinitesimal. It ends in subtle perception. The subtlety is of the *sukshma* body, i.e., the mind. Beyond the mind there is the Self. The greatest of things are also conceptions, the conceptions are of the mind; beyond the mind there is the Self. So the Self is subtler than the subtlest.

There may be any number of creation theories. All of them extend outwardly. There will be no limit to them because time and space are unlimited. They are, however, only in the mind. See the mind; time and space are transcended and the Self is realized.

Creation is explained scientifically or logically to one's own satisfaction. But is there any finality about it? Such explanations are called *krama srishti* (gradual creation). On the other hand, *drishti srishti* (simultaneous or sudden creation) is *yugapad srishti*. Without the seer, there are no objects seen. Find the seer and the creation is comprised in him. Why look outward and go on explaining the phenomena, which are endless?

With regard to presents to Sri Bhagavan, he observed: Why do they bring presents? Do I want them? Even if I refuse, they thrust presents on me. What for? If I accept them, I must yield to their wishes. It is like giving a bait to catch the fish. Is the angler anxious to feed the fish? No, he is anxious to feed on the fish.

Swami Lokesananda asked: What is the relation between Brahman *and* Ishvara?
M. *Brahman* is called *Ishvara* in relation to the world.
D. Is it possible to speak to *Ishvara* as Sri Ramakrishna did?
M. When we can speak to each other, why should we not speak to *Ishvara* in the same way?
D. Then why does it not happen with us?
M. It requires purity and strength of mind and practice in meditation.
D. Does God become evident if the above conditions exist?
M. Such manifestation is as real as your own reality. In other words, when you identify yourself with the body as in *jagrat*, you see gross objects; when in the subtle body or in a mental plane as in *svapna*, you see objects equally subtle; in the absence of identification as in *sushupti*, you see nothing. The objects seen bear a relation to the state of the seer. The same applies to visions of God.

By long practice, the figure of God, as meditated upon, appears in dreams and may later appear in *jagrat* also.
D. Is that the state of God-realization?
M. Listen to what happened once, years ago.

There was a saint by name of Namdev. He could see, talk, and play with Vithoba as we do with one another. He used to spend most of his time in the temple playing with Vithoba.

On one occasion, the saints had gathered together, among whom was Jnandev of well-established fame and eminence. Jnandev asked Gora Kumbhar (a potter-saint) to use his proficiency in testing the soundness of baked pots and find out which of the assembled saints was properly baked clay. So Gora Kumbhar took his stick and gently struck each one's head [jokingly] as if to test. When he came to Namdev, the latter protested in a huff; all laughed and hooted. Namdev was enraged and sought Vithoba in the temple. Vithoba said that the saints knew best; this unexpected reply upset Namdev all the more.

He said: You are God. I converse and play with you. Can there be anything more to be gained by man?

Vithoba persisted: The saints know.

Namdev: Tell me if there is anything more real than you.

Vithoba: We have been so familiar with each other that my advice will not have the desired effect on you. Seek the beggar-saint in the forest and know the truth.

Accordingly, Namdev sought out the particular saint mentioned by Vithoba. Namdev was not impressed with the holiness of the man for he was nude, dirty and was lying on the floor with his feet resting on a *linga*. Namdev wondered how this could be a saint. The saint, on the other hand, smiled at Namdev and asked, "Did Vithoba send you here?" This was a great surprise to Namdev, who was now more inclined to believe the man to be great. So Namdev asked him: "You are said to be a saint; why do you desecrate the *linga*?" The saint replied: "Indeed I am too old and weak to do the right thing. Please lift my feet and place them where there is no *linga*." Namdev accordingly lifted the saint's feet and placed them elsewhere. But there was again a *linga* below them. Wherever the feet were placed, then and there appeared a *linga* underneath. Namdev finally placed the feet on himself and he turned into a *linga*. Then Namdev understood that God was immanent and learned the truth and departed. He went home and did not go to the temple for several days. Vithoba now sought him out in his home and asked why Namdev would not go to the temple to see God. Namdev said: "Is there a place where He is not?"

The moral of the story is clear. Visions of God have their place below the plane of Self-realization.

D. When I read Sri Bhagavan's works, I find that investigation is said to be the one method for Realization.
M. Yes, that is *vichara*.
D. How is that to be done?
M. The questioner must admit the existence of his self. "I Am" is the Realization. To pursue the clue until Realization is *vichara*. *Vichara* and Realization are the same.
D. It is elusive. What shall I meditate upon?

M. Meditation requires an object to meditate upon, whereas there is only the subject without the object in *vichara*. Meditation differs from *vichara* in this respect.

D. Is not *dhyana* one of the efficient processes for Realization?

M. *Dhyana* is concentration on an object. It fulfills the purpose of keeping away diverse thoughts and fixing the mind on a single thought, which itself must also disappear before Realization. But Realization is nothing new to be acquired. It is already there, but obstructed by a screen of thoughts. All our attempts are directed towards this screen and then Realization is revealed.

If a true seeker is advised to meditate, many may go away satisfied with the advice. But someone among them may turn around and ask, "Who am I to meditate on an object?" Such a one must be told to find the Self. That is the finality. That is *vichara*.

D. Will *vichara* alone suffice in the absence of meditation?

M. *Vichara* is the process and the goal, also. "I Am" is the goal and the final Reality. To hold to it with effort is *vichara*. When spontaneous and natural, it is Realization.

The same sannyasi *visitor, Swami Lokesananda, asked about* samadhi. *Maharshi's replied:*

1. Holding on to Reality is *samadhi.*
2. Holding on to Reality with effort is *savikalpa samadhi.*
3. Merging in Reality and remaining unaware of the world is *nirvikalpa samadhi.*
4. Merging in Ignorance and remaining unaware of the world is sleep. (Head bends but not in *samadhi*).
5. Remaining in the primal, pure natural state without effort is *sahaja nirvikalpa samadhi.*

D. It is said that one remaining in *nirvikalpa samadhi* for 21 days must necessarily give up the physical body.

M. *Samadhi* means passing beyond *dehatma buddhi* (I-am-the-body idea), and non-identification of the body with the Self is a foregone conclusion.

There are said to be persons who have been immersed in *nirvikalpa samadhi* for a thousand years or more.

Later, Sri Bhagavan continued: The intricate maze of philosophy of different schools is said to clarify matters and reveal the Truth. But in fact they create confusion where no confusion need exist. To understand anything, there must be the Self. The Self is obvious. Why not remain as the Self? What need to explain the non-self?

I was indeed fortunate that I never took to it [philosophy]. Had I taken to it, I would probably be nowhere — always in confusion. My *purva vasanas* (former tendencies) directly took me to the inquiry, "Who am I?" It was indeed fortunate.

APRIL 11, 1937

D. There is a short account of the spiritual experiences of St. Theresa, in the March issue of *Prabuddha Bharata*. She was devoted to a figure of the Madonna, which became animated to her sight, and she was in bliss. Is it the same as *Shaktipata*?

M. The animated figure indicates depth of meditation (*dhyana bala*). *Shaktipata* prepares the mind for introversion. There is a process of concentration of mind on one's own shadow, which in due course becomes animated, and answers questions put to it. That is due to strength of mind or depth of meditation. Whatever is external is also transitory. Such phenomena may produce joy for the time being, but abiding peace, i.e., *shanti,* does not result. This is obtained only by the removal of *avidya* (ignorance).

D. How is the mind to be stilled?

M. Looking at the mind with the mind, or fixing the mind in the Self, brings the mind under control of the Self.

D. Is there any yoga, i.e., a process to this end?

M. *Vichara* (investigation) alone will do it.

D. How is *poorna Brahman* to be attained? What is the method best suited to a *grihastha* (householder)?

M. You have already said *poorna*, i.e., perfection. Are you apart from *poorna*? If apart from it, will it be *poorna*? If not apart, how does the question arise? The knowledge that *Brahman* is *poorna* and that you are not apart from it is the finality. See it and you will find that you are not a *grihastha* or any limited being.

D. What are the *tattvas*?

M. Knowledge of *poorna Brahman* will elucidate the other matters automatically.

APRIL 12, 1937

A Dutch lady, Mrs. Gongrijp, an ardent Theosophist, who had worked long in Java and is now living in Adyar, Madras, came here for a short visit. She asked: Theosophy speaks of *tanha,* meaning thirst for rebirth. What is its cause?

M. Thirst for rebirth is the desire to be reborn so as to end successive births. The spirit is at present moribund; it must be revived so that rebirth may take place after the present apparent death. Forgetfulness of your real nature is the present death; remembrance of it is the rebirth. It puts an end to successive births. Yours is eternal life.

D. I take *tanha* to mean "clinging to life" — the desire for eternal life.

M. No doubt it is so. How does the desire arise? Because the present state is unbearable. Why? Because it is not your true nature. Had it been your real nature no desire would disturb you. How does the present state differ from your real nature? You are Spirit in truth. However, that spirit wrongly identifies itself with the gross body. The body has been projected by the mind; the mind itself has originated from the spirit. If the wrong identification ceases, there will be peace and permanent, indescribable bliss.

D. Life is of the body and rebirth is to incarnate in another body.

M. Mere change of body produces no effect. The ego associated with this body is transferred to another body. How can that satisfy anyone?

Moreover, what is life? Life is existence, which is your Self. That is life Eternal. Otherwise, can you imagine a time when you are not?

That life is now conditioned by the body and you wrongly identify your being with that of the body. You are life unconditioned. These bodies attach themselves to you as mental projections and you are now afflicted by the "I am-the-body" idea. If this idea ceases, you are purely your Self.

Where or how were you before being born? Were you in sleep? How were you in that state? You existed then, too, without the body. Therefore, the ego arises, and then the mind which projects the body. "I-am-the-body" idea is the result. Because the body exists, you say that it was born and it will die, and transfer the idea to the Self, saying that you are born and you will die. In fact, you remain without the body in sleep; but now you remain with the body. The Self can remain without the body, but the body cannot exist apart from the Self.

"I-am-the-body" thought is ignorance; that the body is not apart from the Self is knowledge. That is the difference between knowledge and ignorance.

The body is a mental projection; the mind is the ego, and the ego rises from the Self. So the body-thought is distracting and strays away from the

Self. For whom is the body or the birth? It is not for the Self, the Spirit. It is for the non-self which imagines itself separate. So long as there is the sense of separation, there will be afflicting thoughts. If the original source is regained and the sense of separation put to an end, there is peace.

Consider what happens when a stone is thrown up. It leaves its source and is projected upward, tries to come down and stays in motion until it regains its source, where it is at rest. So, also, the waters of the ocean evaporate and form clouds which are moved by winds. These condense into water, fall as rain and the waters roll down the hill in streams and rivers, until they reach their original source, the ocean, where they are at peace. Thus, you see, wherever there is a sense of separateness from the source there is agitation and movement until the sense of separateness is lost. So it is with yourself. Now that you identify yourself with the body, you think that you are separate from the Spirit — the true Self. You must regain your source before the false identity ceases and you are happy.

Gold is not [in itself] an ornament, but an ornament is comprised of nothing but gold. Whatever shape the ornament may assume and however different the ornaments are, there is only one reality, namely gold. So also with the bodies and the Self. The single reality is the Self. To identify oneself with the body and yet to seek happiness is like attempting to cross a river on the back of an alligator. The bodily identity is due to extroversion and the wandering of the mind. To continue in that state will only keep one in an endless tangle and there will be no peace. Seek your source, merge in the Self, and remain all alone.

Rebirth means discontent with the present state, and desire to be born where there will be no discontent. Births, being of the body, cannot affect the Self. The Self remains even after the body perishes. The discontent is due to wrong identification of the Eternal Self with the perishable body. The body is a necessary adjunct of the ego. If the ego is killed, the eternal Self is revealed in all its glory.

The body is the Cross. Jesus, the son of man, is the ego or "I-am-the-body" idea. When he is crucified, he is resurrected as the Glorious Self — Jesus, the Son of God! "*Give up this life if thou wouldst live.*"

D. Fear is consequent on the possibility of non-existence; it pertains to the body. One is not aware of the body in sleep. One is not afraid of but courts sleep, whereas one dreads death. Why this difference between the two outlooks?

M. Desire of sleep or fear of death is when the mind is active and not in the respective states themselves. The mind knows that the body entity persists and reappears after sleep. Therefore, sleep is not attended with fear but the pleasure of non-bodily existence is sought. Whereas the mind is not sure of reappearance after the so-called death and dreads it.

APRIL 14, 1937

The body is in the mind, which has the brain for its seat, which again functions by light borrowed from another source, as admitted by the yogis themselves in their fontanel theory. The *jnani* further argues: if the light is borrowed, it must come from its native source. Go to the source directly and do not depend on borrowed resources. Just as an iron ball comes into being separate from the fiery mass of iron, and later cools down giving up the fire, it must again be made fiery to unite with the original mass. So, the cause of separation must also form the factor of reunion.

If there is an image reflected there must be a source and also accessories like the sun and a pot of water for reflection. To do away with the reflection, either the surface is covered up corresponding to reaching the fontanel according to the yogis, or the water is drained away, which is called *tapas* (*Tapo Brahmeti — tapas* is *Brahman*). That is to say, the thoughts or the brain activities are made to cease. This is *Jnana Marga*.

All these are, however, based on the assumption that the *jiva* is separate from the Self or *Brahman*. But are we in fact separate? "No," says the *jnani*. The ego is simply wrong identity of the Self with the non-self, as in the case of a colorless crystal and its colored background. If the background is removed the crystal shines in its original purity. So it is with the Self and the *antahkaranas* (organs of cognition).

Still, the illustration is not quite appropriate. For the ego has its source from the Self and is not separate like the background from the crystal. Having its source from the Self, the ego must only be retraced for it to merge in its source.

The center of the ego and its core are called the Heart, the same as the Self.

A gentleman asked if the yogis also reach the anahata *and thus realize the Heart-center as is done by the* jnanis *but in a different way.*
M. *Anahata* is not the same as the Heart-center. If so, why should they wander further on to *Sahasrara*? Moreover, the question arises because of the sense of separateness persisting in us. We are never away from the Heart-

center. Before reaching *anahata* or after passing it, one is only in the center. Whether one understands it or not, one is not away from the center. Practice of yoga or *vichara* is done, always remaining in the center only.

D. What is to be our *sadhana*?

M. *Sadhana* for the *sadhaka* is the *sahaja* of the *siddha*. *Sahaja* is the original state, so that *sadhana* amounts to removal of the obstacles to realization of this abiding truth.

D. Is concentration of mind one of the *sadhanas*?

M. Concentration is not thinking one thing. It is, on the other hand, putting off all other thoughts that obstruct the vision of our true nature. All our efforts are only directed to lifting the veil of ignorance. At present, it appears difficult to quell the thoughts. On the other hand, in the regenerate state it will be found more difficult to call in thoughts. For are there things to think of? There is only the Self. Thought can function only if there are objects. But there are no objects. How can thoughts arise at all?

The habit makes us believe that it is difficult to cease thinking. If the error is found out, one would not be foolish enough to exert oneself unnecessarily by way of thinking.

D. Is not Grace more effective than *abhyasa* (practice)?

M. Guru simply helps you in the eradication of ignorance. Does he hand over Realization to you?

D. We are ignorant.

M. Inasmuch as you say you are ignorant, you are wise. Is he a madman who says that he is mad?

Guru's Grace is like a hand extended to help you out of water, or it makes your way easier for the removal of ignorance.

D. Is it not like a medicine to cure the disease of *avidya*?

M. What is medicine for? It is only to restore the patient to his original state of health. What is this talk of Guru, Grace, God, etc.? Does the Guru hold you by the hand and whisper something in your ear? You imagine him to be like yourself. Because you are with a body, you think that he is also a body in order to do something tangible to you. His work lies within. How is Guru gained? God, who is immanent, in his Grace takes pity on the loving devotee and manifests Himself as a being according to the devotee's standard. The devotee thinks that he is a man and expects a relationship as between bodies. But the Guru, who is God or Self incarnate, works from within, helps man to see the error of his ways, guides him in the right path until he realizes the Self within.

After such realization, the disciple feels, "I was so worried before. I am after all the Self, the same as before but not affected by anything; where is he who was miserable? He is nowhere to be seen."

What should we do now? Only act upon the words of the Master, work within. The Guru is both within and without. So he creates conditions to drive you inward and prepares the interior to drag you to the center. Thus he gives a push from without and exerts a pull from within so that you may be fixed at the center.

In sleep, you are centered within. Simultaneously, with waking your mind rushes out, thinking this, that and all else. This must be checked. It is possible only for the agent who can work both within and without. Can he be identified with a body? We think that the world can be conquered by our efforts. When frustrated externally and driven internally, we feel "Oh! Oh. There is a power higher than man." The existence of the higher power must be admitted and recognized. The ego is a very powerful elephant and cannot be brought under control by anyone less than a lion, who is no other than the Guru in this instance; whose very look makes the elephant tremble and die. We will know in due course that our glory lies where we cease to exist. In order to gain that state, one should surrender oneself saying, "Lord. Thou art my Refuge!" The Master then sees, "This man is in a fit state to receive guidance," and so guides him.

D. What is self-surrender?

M. It is the same as self-control; control is effected by removal of *samskaras* which imply the functioning of the ego. The ego submits only when it recognizes the Higher Power. Such recognition is surrender or submission, or self-control. Otherwise, the ego remains stuck up like the image carved on a tower, making a pretence by its strained look and posture that it is supporting the tower on its shoulders. The ego cannot exist without the Power, but thinks it acts of its own accord.

D. How can the rebellious mind be brought under control?

M. Either seek its source so that it may disappear or surrender that it may be struck down.

D. But the mind slips away from our control.

M. So be it. Do not think about it. When you recollect yourself, bring it back and turn it inward. That is enough.

No one succeeds without effort. Mind control is not one's birthright. The successful few owe their success to their perseverance.

A passenger in a train keeps his load on the head by his own folly. Let him put it down; he will find the load reaches the destination just the same. Similarly, let us not pose as doers, but resign ourselves to the guiding Power.

D. Swami Vivekananda says that a spiritual Guru can transfer spirituality substantially to the disciple.

M. Is there a substance to be transferred? Transfer means eradication of the sense of being the disciple. The Master does it. Not that the man was something at one time and metamorphosed later into another.

D. Is not Grace the gift of the Guru?

M. God, Grace, and Guru are all synonymous and also eternal and immanent. Is not the Self already within? Is it for the Guru to bestow it by his look? If a Guru thinks so, he does not deserve the name.

The books say that there are so many kinds of *diksha* (initiation). They also say that the Guru makes some rites with fire, water, *japa*, mantras, etc. and call such fantastic performances *dikshas*, as if the disciple (*sishya*) becomes ripe only after such processes are gone through by the Guru.

If the individual is sought, he is nowhere to be found. Such is the Guru. Such is Dakshinamurti. What did he do? He was silent; the disciples appeared before him. He maintained silence; the doubts of the disciples were dispelled, which means that they lost their individual identities. That is *jnana* and not all the verbiage usually associated with it.

Silence is the most potent form of work. However vast and emphatic the *sastras* (scriptures) may be, they fail in their effect. The Guru is quiet and peace prevails in all. His silence is vaster and more emphatic than all the *sastras* put together. These questions arise because of the feeling that having been here so long, heard so much, tried so hard, one has not gained anything. The work proceeding within is not apparent. In fact, the Guru is always within you.

Thayumanavar says: "Oh Lord! Coming with me all along the births, never abandoning me and finally rescuing me!" Such is the experience of Realization.

Srimad Bhagavad Gita says the same in a different way, "We two are not only now but have ever been so."

D. Does not the Guru take a concrete form?

M. What is meant by *concrete*? Because you identify your being with your body, you raise this question. Find out if you are the body.

The *Gita* says: *param bhavam ajanantah* (9.11) — that those who cannot understand the transcendental nature (of Sri Krishna) are fools, deluded by ignorance.

The Master appears to dispel that ignorance. As Thayumanavar puts it, he appears as a man to dispel the ignorance of a man, just as a deer is used as a decoy to capture the wild deer. He has to appear with a body in order to eradicate our ignorant "I-am-the-body" idea.

APRIL 15, 1937

Mr. Bose, the Bengali Engineer, has since read Gaudapada Karikas *and Sir S. Radhakrishnan's* Indian Philosophy, *and so asked the following questions:* Is there any genuine difference between the dream experience and the waking state?

M. Because you find the dream creations transitory in relation to the waking state, there is said to be a difference, but this difference is only apparent and not real.

D. Is the waking state independent of existing objects?

M. Were it so, the objects must exist without a seer; that is to say, the object must tell you that it exists. Does it do so? For example, does a cow moving in front of you say that she is moving? Or do you say of your own accord, "There is a cow moving?" The objects exist because of the seer cognizing them.

D. Gaudapada in *Mandukya Karikas* says that there is no difference between the two states from the standpoint of Reality-Absolute.

M. Of course not.

D. I believe Bhagavan also says so. Prof. Radhakrishnan in his *Indian Philosophy* says that in his *Brahma Sutra* Commentary, Sri Shankara makes a distinction between the two states. Is it a fact? If so, what is it? How can there be any distinction from the viewpoint of reality? So long as the mind exists in any form, there will be distinction. But from the standpoint of *Atman*, nondual *Brahman*, can there be any distinction?

M. The dream is for the one who says he is awake. In fact, wakefulness and dream are equally unreal from the standpoint of the Absolute.

D. In pure *Advaita* can evolution, creation or manifestation have any place? What about the theory of *vivarta*, according to which *Brahman* appears as the world without forgetting its essential nature, like the rope appearing as a snake?

M. There are different methods of approach to prove the unreality of the universe. The example of the dream is one among them. *Jagrat, svapna*, and *sushupti* are all treated elaborately in the scriptures in order that the Reality underlying them might be revealed. It is not meant to accentuate differences among the three states. The purpose must be kept clearly in view.

Now they say that the world is unreal. Of what degree of unreality is it? Is it like that of a son of a barren mother or a flower in the sky, mere words without any reference to facts? But the world is a fact and not a mere word.

The answer is that it is a superimposition on the one Reality, like the appearance of a snake on a coiled rope seen in dim light.

But here, too, the wrong identity ceases as soon as a friend points out that it is a rope. Whereas in the matter of the world, it persists even after it is known to be unreal. How is that? Again, the appearance of water in a mirage persists even after knowledge of the mirage is recognized. So it is with the world. Though knowing it to be unreal, it continues to manifest.

But the water of the mirage is not sought to satisfy one's thirst. As soon as one knows that it is a mirage, one gives it up as useless and does not run after it for procuring water.

D. Not so with the appearance of the world. Even after it is repeatedly declared to be false, one cannot avoid satisfying one's wants from the world. How can the world be false?

M. It is like a man satisfying his dream-wants by dream-creations. There are objects, there are wants, and there is satisfaction. The dream-creation is as purposeful as the *jagrat* world and yet it is not considered real.

Thus we see that each of these illustrations serves a distinct purpose in establishing the stages of unreality. The realized sage finally declares that in the regenerate state the *jagrat* world also is found to be as unreal as the dream world is found to be in the *jagrat* state.

Each illustration is to be understood in its proper context and should not be studied as an isolated statement. It is a link in a chain. The purpose of all these is to direct the seeker's mind towards the one Reality underlying them all.

D. Is there that difference in the philosophy of Shankara and Gaudapada which the learned Professor wants us to believe?

M. The difference is only in our imagination.

D. Sir S. Radhakrishnan writes:

> The general idea pervading Gaudapada's work that bondage and liberation, the individual soul and the world are all unreal, makes a caustic critic observe that the theory which has nothing better to say than that an unreal soul is trying to escape from an unreal Supreme Good, may itself be an unreality. It is one thing to say that the unchangeable reality expressing itself in the changing universe without forfeiting its nature is a mystery, and another to dismiss the whole changing universe as a mere mirage. If we have to play the game of life we cannot do so with the conviction that the play is a show and all the prizes in it are mere blanks. No philosophy can consistently hold such a theory and be at rest with itself. The greatest condemnation of such a theory is that

we are obliged to occupy ourselves with objects the existence and value of which we are continually denying in theory. It only shows that there is something else which includes and transcends the world but it does not imply the world is a dream.

M. As was already said, the purpose of the whole philosophy is to indicate the underlying Reality — whether of the *jagrat*, *svapna* and *sushupti* states, or the individual souls, the world and God.

Three outlooks are possible:

1. The *Vyavaharika*: The man sees the world in all its variety, surmises the creator, and believes in himself as the subject. All these are thus reduced to the three fundamentals, *jagat*, *jiva*, and *Ishvara*. He learns the existence of the creator and tries to reach Him in order to gain immortality. If one is thus released from bondage, there are all other individuals existing as before who should work out their own salvation. He more or less admits the One Reality underlying all these phenomena. The phenomena are due to the play of *maya*. Maya is the *shakti* of *Ishvara* or the activity of Reality. Thus, the existence of different souls, objects, etc., does not clash with the *advaitic* point of view.

2. The *Pratibhasika*: The *jagat*, *jiva*, and *Ishvara* are all cognized by the seer only. They do not have any existence independent of him. So there is only one *jiva*, be it the individual or God. All else is simply a myth.

3. The *Paramarthika*: i.e., *ajatavada* (no-creation doctrine) which admits of no second. There is no reality or absence of it, no seeking or gaining, no bondage or liberation and so on.

The question arises: why then do all the *sastras* speak of the Lord as the creator? How can the creature that you are create the creator and argue that the *jagat*, *jiva*, and *Ishvara* are mental conceptions only?

The answer is as follows: You know in this *jagrat* (waking) state your father is dead, and that several years have elapsed since his death. However, you see him in your dream and recognize him to be your father, of whom you were born and who has left patrimony to you. Here the creator is in the creature. Again, you dream that you are serving a king and that you are a part in the administrative wheel of the kingdom. As soon as you wake up, all of them have disappeared leaving you, the single individual, behind. Where were they all? Only in yourself. The same analogy holds good in the other case, also.

D. In the *Vyavaharika*, above mentioned, how does *maya* come in?

M. *Maya* is only *Ishvara-Shakti* or the activity of Reality.

D. Why does it become active?

M. How can this question arise? You are yourself within its fold. Are you standing apart from that universal activity in order to ask this question? The same Power is raising this doubt in order that all doubts may finally cease.

D. The dream world is not purposeful as the *jagrat* world, because we do not feel that wants are satisfied.

M. You are not right. There are thirst and hunger in the dream, also. You might have had your fill and kept over the remaining food for the next day. Nevertheless, you feel hungry in the dream. This food does not help you. Your dream-hunger can be satisfied only by eating dream-food. Dream-wants are satisfied by dream-creations only.

D. We recollect our dreams in our *jagrat*, but not *vice versa*.

M. Not right again. In the dream, you identify yourself with the one now speaking.

D. But we do not know that we are dreaming as apart from waking as we do now.

M. The dream is the combination of *jagrat* and *sushupti*. It is due to the *samskaras* of the *jagrat* state. Hence, we remember dreams at present. *Samskaras* are not formed contrariwise; therefore, we are not aware of the dream and *jagrat* simultaneously. Still, everyone will recollect strange perplexities in a dream. One wonders whether he dreams or is awake. He argues and determines that he is only awake. When really awake, he finds it was all only a dream.

In the course of another conversation, Sri Bhagavan said. Visions add zest to meditation and nothing more.

April 16, 1937

Mr. Krishnamurti, an Andhra gentleman, asked: When making *tapas* (austerities), on what object must we fix our sight? Our mind is fixed on what we utter.

M. What is *tapas* for?

D. For Self-realization.

M. Quite so. *Tapas* depends on the competency of the person. One requires a form to contemplate. But it is not enough. For can anyone ever keep looking at an image? So the image must be implemented by *japa*. *Japa* helps fixing the mind on the image, in addition to the eyesight. The result of these efforts is concentration of mind, which ends in the goal. He becomes what he thinks. Some are satisfied with the name of the image. Every form must have a name. That name denotes all the qualities of God. Constant *japa* puts off all other thoughts and fixes the mind. That is *tapas*. One-pointedness is the *tapas* wanted.

The question as to what *tapas* is was asked in order to know what purpose to serve. It will take the form required for the purpose.

D. Are not physical austerities also *tapas*?

M. Maybe one form of it. They are due to *vairagya* (dispassion).

D. I have seen a man with his arm lifted all his life.

M. That is *vairagya*.

D. Why should one afflict his body for this purpose?

M. You think it is affliction whereas it is a vow, and for the other man it is an achievement and a pleasure.

Dhyana may be external or internal or both. *Japa* is more important than external form. It must be done until it becomes natural. It starts with effort and is continued until it proceeds of itself. When natural it is called Realization.

Japa may be done even while engaged in other activity. That which *is*, is the One Reality. It may be represented by a form, a *japa*, *mantra*, *vichara*, or any kind of attempt. All of them finally resolve themselves into that One Single Reality. *Bhakti*, *vichara*, *japa* are only different forms of our efforts to keep out unreality. The unreality is an obsession at present. Reality is our true nature. We are wrongly persisting in unreality — that is, thoughts and worldly activities. Cessation of these will reveal the Truth. Our attempts are directed towards keeping them out. It is done by thinking of the Reality only. Although it is our true nature, it looks as if we are thinking of the Reality. What we do really amounts to the removal of obstacles for the revelation of our true Being. Meditation or *vichara* is thus a reversion to our true nature.

D. Are our attempts sure to succeed?

M. Realization is our nature. It is nothing new to be gained. What is new cannot be eternal. Therefore, there is no need for doubting if one would lose or gain the Self.

While speaking of the brain and the Heart, Sri Bhagavan recalled an incident from the old days: Kavyakantha Ganapati Muni once argued that the brain was the most important center and Sri Bhagavan maintained that the Heart was even more so. There were others watching the discourse. A few days later Sri Bhagavan received a letter containing a short poem in English on that discourse from a young boy, N. S. Arunachala, who had not yet matriculated.

That poem is remarkable for its poetic imagination. Sri Bhagavan, Kavyakantha, and the assemblage of other persons are represented as the Heart, the brain, and the body respectively, and again as the sun, the moon, and the earth. The light from the sun is reflected by the moon, and the earth is illumined. Similarly, the brain acts by consciousness derived from the Heart and the body is thus protected. This teaching of Sri Bhagavan is found in *Ramana Gita*, also. The Heart is the most important center from which vitality and light radiate to the brain, thus enabling it to function. The *vasanas* are enclosed in the Heart in their subtlest form, later flowing to the brain which reflects them highly magnified, corresponding to a cinema show at every stage. That is how the world is said to be nothing more than a cinema show.

Sri Bhagavan further added: Were the *vasanas* in the brain instead of the Heart, they would be extinguished if the head is cut off so that reincarnations would come to an end. But it is not so. The Self obviously safeguards the *vasanas* in its closest proximity, i.e., within itself in the Heart, just as a miser keeps his most valued possessions (treasure) with himself and never out of reach. Hence the place where the *vasanas* are is the Self, i.e., the Heart, and not the brain (which is only the theater for the play of the vasanas from the greenroom of the Heart).

APRIL 17, 1937

There was some reference to the excerpt from the Modern Psychological Review *wondering if any instruments could be of use in detecting the Heart-center and if proper subjects were available for recording the experience of the adepts on the spiritual path, and so on. While others were speaking, Sri Bhagavan said:* In the incident mentioned in the book *Self-Realisation*, where I became unconscious and symptoms of death supervened, I was aware all along. I could feel the action of the physical heart stopped and equally the action of the Heart-center unimpaired. This state lasted about a quarter of an hour.

We asked if it was true that some disciples have had the privilege of feeling Sri Bhagavan's Heart-center to be on the right by placing their hands on Sri Bhagavan's chest. Sri Bhagavan said, "Yes."

(*Mr. Viswanatha Iyer, Narayana Reddi, and others have said they felt Sri Bhagavan's Heart-center to be on the right by placing their hands on his chest.*)

A devotee rightly observed that if hands could feel and locate the Heart-center, delicate scientific instruments would certainly be able to do so.

D. The Heart is said to be on the right, on the left or in the center. With such differences of opinion, how are we to meditate on *Hridaya*?

M. You *are* and it is a fact. *Dhyana* is by you, of you, and in you. It must go on wherever you are. It cannot be outside you. So you are the center of *dhyana* and that is the Heart.

A location is, however, given to it with reference to the body. You know that you *are*. Where are you? You are in the body and not out of it. Yet not the whole body. Though you pervade the whole body, still you admit of a center from which all your thoughts start and wherein they subside. Even when the limbs are amputated, you are there but with defective senses. So a center must be admitted. That is called the Heart. The Heart is not merely the center, but the Self. Heart is only another name for the Self.

Doubts arise only when you identify it with something tangible and physical. The scriptures describe it as the source of 101 *nadis*, etc. In *Yoga Vasishta*, Chudala says that *kundalini* is composed of 101 *nadis*, thus identifying one with the other.

Heart is no conception, no object for meditation. But it is the seat of meditation; the Self remains all alone. You see the body in the Heart, the world in it. There is nothing separate from it. So all kinds of effort are located there only.

APRIL 18, 1937

A casual visitor asked: What is *nishta*? How is the look to be directed between the eyebrows?

M. How do we see these things? There is a light by which they are seen. Your question amounts to asking how that light is seen.

D. What is the significance of the spot between the eyebrows?

M. That is mentioned as if to say: "Do not see with your eyes."

D. What is regulation of breath for?

M. Only to control the mind.

After a few minutes, Sri Bhagavan continued: The mind functions both as light and as objects. If divested of things, the light alone remains.

D. But we must know that there is such light.

M. Sight or cognition is impossible without such light. How do you cognize anything in sleep? Our cognition pertains to the present state because there is light. Light is the essential requisite for sight. It is plain in our daily life. Among the lights, sunlight is the most important. Hence they speak of the glory of millions of suns.

D. There is light if we press the eyelids with our fingers.

Another questioner: What is the use of seeing such a light?

M. It is done lest we forget the goal. The practice helps one not to divert the attention to other pursuits.

The object is seen or the light is recognized because there is the subject to do so. How does it affect the subject whether the objects are seen or not? If the light, i.e., the cognizer or the consciousness, is seen, there will be no object to be seen. Pure light, *i.e.,* Consciousness alone remains.

D. Why then is the regulation of breath necessary?

M. Control of breath or its regulation is only for controlling the mind so that it does not wander.

D. Is it for control of mind only?

M. It is not enough that light is seen; it is also necessary to have the mind engaged in a single activity, *e.g.,* the elephant trunk and the chain.

D. How long will it take for one to gain *Chintamani* (The celestial gem granting all the wishes of its owner)?

M. The example of *Chintamani* is found in *Yoga Vasishta. Chintamani* signifies the Real nature of the Self. The story is as follows:

A man was making *tapasya* for gaining *Chintamani.* A gem mysteriously fell into his hands. He thought that it could not be *Chintamani* because his efforts had been too short and too little to gain the gem. He discarded it and continued the *tapas.* Later, a *sadhu* placed before him a brilliant pebble with facets cut. The man was taken in by its appearance but found it could not fulfill his desires as he originally supposed. Similarly, the Self being inherent, should not be sought elsewhere.

Queen Chudala illustrated King Sikhidhvaja's error by this story: The King had *vairagya* even while ruling his kingdom and could have realized the Self if only he had pushed his *vairagya* to the point of killing the ego. He did not do so, but came to the forest, had a timetable of *tapas* and yet did not improve even after eighteen years of *tapas*. He had made himself a victim of his own creation. Chudala advised him to give up the ego and realize the Self, which he did, and was liberated.

It is clear from Chudala's story that *vairagya* accompanied by ego is of no value, whereas all possessions in the absence of ego do not matter.

APRIL 19, 1937

A respectable and orthodox gentleman asked about Sri Chakra.

M. It has a deep significance. There are forty-three corners with sacred syllables in them. Its worship is a method for concentration of mind. The mind is wont to move externally; it must be checked and turned within. Its habit is to dwell on names and forms, for all external objects possess names and forms. Such names and forms are made of symbolic mental conceptions in order to divert the mind from external objects and make it dwell within itself. The idols, mantras, *yantras*, are all meant to give food to the mind in its introvert state, so that it may later become capable of being concentrated, after which the superb state is reached automatically.

APRIL 20, 1937

Mr. Cohen, a resident disciple, has been thinking for some days about a book called *Nirvana* written by a prominent Theosophist, in which the author claims to reach *nirvana* every night after going to sleep. He claims to see his own Master and other Masters of the Theosophical Society as bright lights within the ocean of light, which is *nirvana*. He asked Sri Bhagavan how that could be possible, considering the *Advaitic* teaching that the *nirvanic* experience is the same as that of the pure consciousness of Being.

M. *Nirvana* is Perfection. In the Perfect State there is neither subject nor object — nothing to see, nothing to feel, nothing to know. Seeing and knowing are the functions of the mind. In *nirvana*, there is nothing but the blissful pure consciousness "I Am."

D. How then can a prominent T. S. leader, who claims clairvoyance of a high order, praise the author for his supposed correct and vivid description of *nirvana*, and why is the T. S. so obsessed by the idea of "Service?"

M. Well, Theosophy and kindred movements are good inasmuch as they make a man unselfish and prepare him for the highest truth. Service, like prayers, *japas*, and even business done in God's name, leads to the highest goal — Self-realization.

311

D. But after how long? And why should a man who is ready for the Absolute knowledge stick to the knowledge of the relative?

M. Everything happens in its own time. The one who is ready for the Absolute knowledge will be made somehow to hear of it and follow up on it. He will realize that *Atma-vidya* (Self-knowledge) is the highest of all virtues and also the end of the journey.

Then, asked about the difference between external and internal nirvikalpa samadhis, *the Master said:* External *samadhi* is holding on to the Reality while witnessing the world, without reacting to it from within. There is the stillness of a waveless ocean. Internal *samadhi* involves loss of body-consciousness.

D. Is loss of body-consciousness a requisite to the attainment of *sahaja samadhi*?

M. What is body-consciousness? Analyze it. There must be a body and consciousness limited to it which together make up body-consciousness. These must lie in another Consciousness, which is absolute and unaffected. Hold it. That is *samadhi*. It exists when there is no body-consciousness because it transcends the latter; it also exists when there is the body-consciousness. So it is always there. What does it matter whether body-consciousness is lost or retained? When lost, it is internal *samadhi*: when retained, it is external *samadhi*. That is all.

A person must remain in any of the six *samadhis* so that *sahaja samadhi* may be easy for him.

D. The mind does not sink into that state even for a second.

M. A strong conviction is necessary that I am the Self, transcending the mind and the phenomena.

D. Nevertheless, the mind proves to be a restraint against attempts to sink it.

M. What does it matter if the mind is active? It is so only on the substratum of the Self. Hold the Self, even during mental activities.

D. I cannot go within sufficiently deep.

M. It is wrong to say so. Where are you now if not in the Self? Where should you go? All that is necessary is the stern belief that you are the Self. Say rather that the other activities throw a veil on you.

D. Yes, it is so.

M. That means that the conviction is weak.

D. I understand that the "I" is only artificial (*krtrima*); my attempts at realizing the real "I" are unavailing because the artificial "I" is brought into action for realizing the other.

M. *Viveka Chudamani* makes it clear that the artificial "I" of the *vijnana kosa* is a projection and through it one must look to the significance (*vachya*) of "I," the true principle.

D. Saint Theresa and others saw the image of Madonna animated. It was external. Others see the images of their devotion in their mental sight. This is internal. Is there any difference in degree in these two cases?

M. Both indicate that the person has strongly developed meditation. Both are good and progressive. There is no difference in degree.

The one has a conception of divinity and draws mental images and feels them. The other has the conception of divinity in the image and feels it in the image. The feeling is within in both instances.

APRIL 21, 1937

With reference to the location of the Heart-center on the right side of the human body, Sri Bhagavan said: I had been saying all along that the Heart-center was on the right, notwithstanding the refutation by some learned men that physiology taught them otherwise. I speak from experience. I knew it even in my home during my trances. Again, during the incident related in the book *Self-Realisation*, I had a very clear vision and experience. All of a sudden a light came from one side erasing the world vision in its course until it spread all round until the vision of the world was completely cut out. I felt the muscular organ on the left had stopped working; I could understand that the body was like a corpse, that the circulation of blood had stopped, and the body became blue and motionless. Vasudeva Sastri embraced the body, wept over my death, but I could not speak. All the time, I was feeling the Heart-center on the right working as well as ever. This state continued fifteen or twenty minutes. Then, suddenly, something shot out from the right to the left resembling a rocket bursting in air. The blood circulation was resumed and normal condition restored. I then asked Vasudeva Sastri to move along with me and we reached our residence.

The *Upanishads* say that 101 *nadis* terminate in the Heart and 72,000 originate from them and traverse the body. The Heart is thus the center of the body. It can be a center because we have been accustomed to think that we remain in the body. In fact the body and all else are in that center only.

A middle-aged man prostrated himself before Sri Bhagavan, who asked him about his well-being. After a few minutes, Sri Bhagavan recalled an incident saying that this was the only person whom Sri Bhagavan had slapped; it happened about thirty years ago.

Sri Bhagavan was living in Mulaippal Tirtha. There was a Jada Swami living in the neighborhood (*Mamarathu Guhai*). This boy, who was about eight years of age, used to play pranks on everyone, including Sri Bhagavan. One day, he went to Maharshi and said that Jada Swami wanted a bucket. Without waiting for permission, he took away the bucket. Palani Swami, the attendant, was not there. So Sri Bhagavan followed the boy to Jada Swami's place. Before Bhagavan reached the place, the boy had told the other that Brahmanaswami had sent him a bucket. Jada Swami was wondering why! In a few minutes, Maharshi reached the place and learned what had happened. So he raised his hand to give the boy a slap but the mind would not yield to slapping. But he argued within himself and determined that the urchin should be slapped and so he did.

There is a Tamil stanza by Avvai. It is an address of the prana *to the stomach, its meaning being*:
> "O stomach! How difficult it is to get on with you! You cannot starve when no food is available, nor can you take more and keep it in reserve when food is plenty! You will take only what you want and when you want; thus you are troublesome to me, allowing me no rest."

Sri Bhagavan altered it thusly; stomach addresses the prana:
> "O *Prana*! How troublesome you are to me! You never allow me to rest but continue loading me with food off and on. It is so difficult to get on with you."

(Saying it Sri Bhagavan laughed. Sri Bhagavan often says that he is made to eat more than is good for him.)

MAY 21, 1937

Sri Bhagavan, while speaking of the marriage ceremony among the Brahmins, said that the *Kasiyatra* (pilgrimage to the holy city of Varanasi) represents the bridegroom to be a *vairagi-purusha* (person of non-attachment). It is therefore right that he should be given a *kanya* (virgin) for leading a householder's life. It follows that a *vairagi* can alone be a good householder.

314

Once, on a cold day, Sri Bhagavan was sitting in a cave on the hill with his hands folded on his breast as a protection against the cold. Some Andhra visitor had come; he broke a coconut and poured the cold juice on Sri Bhagavan's head as *abhisheka* (offering to a sacred image); Sri Bhagavan was surprised.

A visitor asked: While making *nama-japa* and after continuing it for an hour or more I fall into a sleep-like state. On waking, I recollect that my *japa* has been interrupted. So I proceed again.

M. "Like sleep." That is right. It is the natural state. Because you are now associated with the ego you consider the natural state to be something which interrupts your work. You must repeat the experience until you realize that it is your natural state. You will then find that *japa*, etc., is extraneous. Still, it will be going on automatically. Your present doubt is due to the false identity.

Japa means clinging to one thought to the exclusion of all other thoughts. That is the purpose of *japa*; it leads to *dhyana*, which ends in Self-realization.

Mr. G. V. Subbaramiah, a devotee, has written some short poems, which are interesting. Some of them refer to a child. Sri Bhagavan said God becomes a child, and *vice versa*. That means that the *samskaras* are yet latent in the child and thus its innocence is complete. When they are eradicated even a grown up man becomes a child once again, and thus remains God.

The author said: The child creates the "home" atmosphere.

Sri Bhagavan: Yes. The children are always in the "home." We too are there but are dreaming and imagining that we are outside the home.

Sri Bhagavan added: I have rendered the word "youth" (*yuva*) in *Dakshinamurti Stotra* as "child" (*bala*). This seems more appropriate.

To be reborn is to become a child over again. One must be reborn before gaining *jnana, i.e.,* recovering the natural state.

Asked if Sri Bhagavan had read Kamba Ramayana, *Sri Bhagavan said:* No. I have not read anything. All my learning is limited to what I learned before my fourteenth year. Since then, I have had no inclination to read or learn. People wonder how I speak of *Bhagavad Gita*, etc. It is due to hearsay. I have not read the *Gita* nor waded through commentaries for its meaning. When I hear a *sloka* (verse), I think its meaning is clear and I say it. That is all and nothing more. Similarly with my other quotations. They come out naturally. I realize that the Truth is beyond speech and intellect. Why then should I project the mind to read, understand and repeat stanzas, etc.? Their purpose is to know the Truth. The purpose having been gained, there is no further use engaging in studies.

Someone remarked: If Sri Bhagavan had been inclined to study, there would not be a saint today.
M. Probably all my studies were finished in past births and I was satiated. There is therefore no *samskara* operating now in that direction.

The week before the *Mahapuja* (June 3, 1937) brought many visitors including some relatives of Sri Bhagavan. Among them is an elderly lady — the widow of Subba Iyer in whose house Sri Bhagavan was living when he left home in August, 1896. Old memories revived when Sri Bhagavan saw her.

He remembered how on a festive occasion he was asked to help her in making some *modakas* (delicacies), but he hesitated and finally refused, because he was obliged to change his clothes and he could put on only *koupina* (loincloth), which made him feel shy. He was reprimanded by his uncle and this lady.

The uncle's wife said with humility and gentleness: Quite. No wonder that one destined for this high state could not do such humble work in those days.

Then Sri Bhagavan remarked: If I refused to wear *koupina* once, I am now made to pay the penalty by wearing it always.

(*The lady recalled how Sri Ramana was suffering from headache for several days at a time.*)

Sri Bhagavan said: Yes, yes! It was the month before I left Madurai. It was not headache, but an inexpressible anguish which I suppressed at the time; these were, however, the outward symptoms which I said were due to headache. I remember how anxious you grew on account of my "headache." You used to rub some ointment on my forehead every day. My anguish continued until I left Madurai and reached this place.

JUNE 4, 1937

A lawyer from Cuddalore quoted as follows: "Neither the sun shines there, nor the moon, nor the stars nor lightning. How can fire shine there? All these luminaries shine in His Light only. With His Light, all these shine forth!" He asked, what does "with His Light" mean? Does all else shine on account of Him, or in His Light?

Sri Bhagavan said: There is only He. He and His Light are the same. There is no individual to perceive other things, because the perceiver and the perceived are only He. The sun, the moon, etc., shine forth. How? Do they come and tell you they shine forth or does another apart from them say so?

D. Of course I say that they shine forth.

M. Therefore, they shine on account of you. Again, consciousness is necessary to know that they shine forth. That consciousness is your Self or you. So then you or your consciousness is the same as He and His Light, by which all else shines forth.

D. Is that Light like sunlight?

M. No. The sunlight is *jada* (insentient). You are aware of it. It makes objects perceptible and chases away darkness, whereas consciousness is that Light which makes not only light but also darkness perceptible. Darkness cannot exist before sunlight, but it can remain in the Light of Consciousness. Similarly, this consciousness is pure Knowledge in which both knowledge and ignorance shine.

D. If God is all, why does the individual suffer for his actions? Are not the actions prompted by Him, for which the individual is made to suffer?

M. He who thinks he is the doer is also the sufferer.

D. But the actions are prompted by God and the individual is only His tool.

M. This logic is applied only when one suffers, but not when one rejoices. If the conviction prevails always, there will be no suffering, either.

D. When will the suffering cease?

M. Not until individuality is lost. If both the good and bad actions are His, why should you think that the enjoyment and suffering are yours alone? He who does good or bad also enjoys pleasure or suffers pain. Leave it there and do not superimpose suffering on yourself.

A resident devotee, Kunju Swami, related an observation of Sri Maharshi after the robbery in the Asramam in 1923.

Some disciples were asking why the robbers should be allowed to molest even sadhus and why the sadhus would not protect themselves and their dependents from the robbers.

Sri Bhagavan observed: There were *rishis* like Vishvamitra who could duplicate the universe if they wished. They lived during the lifetime of Ravana who caused agony even to Sita and Rama, among others. Could not Vishvamitra have destroyed Ravana by his occult powers? Though capable, he kept still. Why? The occurrences are known to the sages, but pass away without leaving an impression on their minds. Even a deluge will appear a trifle to them; they do not care for anything.

Dr. Venkata Rao, a visitor from Guntur, asked: A Guru asks his disciple to do things contrary to ethical principles. The disciple, having accepted the person as the Master, desires to please the Master but his moral sense obstructs him. What should he do under the circumstances?

(*No reply.*)

I shall make myself clear. The Guru asked his disciple to commit a theft and the disciple did not do it. The Master then said, "I wanted to test you to see if you had completely surrendered yourself or retained your individuality. It is now clear what it is." Is the Guru right in ordering the disciple that way?

(*Still no reply.*)

Another person observed: There are persons on whom I refuse to sit in judgment. Still I cannot help wondering whether they deserve the appellation of Gurus. They appear bogus men. If they were really worthy, they would not order their disciples in that way.

M. But the person says, "It is only for a test."

The questioner continued: Should it be carried out?

M. Your original statement contains the answer to your question.

Both the questioners jointly asked: The action is disagreeable. Can it be done?

M. The question might be referred to the person himself, i.e., the Guru. He is responsible for the situation.

A young man asked: I try to cultivate willpower, but do not succeed. How should I set about it?

(*No answer.*)

D. I came here three years ago and Sri Bhagavan said that willpower is necessary for strength of mind. Since then I have been wanting to cultivate it, but without success.

(*No answer.*)

D. During these years, I have had four or five reverses. They upset me considerably. There is always the fear of failure haunting my attempts. This results in lack of faith in myself, which certainly foredooms my efforts to failure. Nothing, in fact, succeeds like success; and also nothing foils one's attempts like failure. Hence my question.

(*No answer.*)

D. Is not willpower necessary for success? It should ensure success and also rule out failure.

(*No answer.*)

D. I try to gain willpower. After these years, I find myself only where I began. There is no progress.

(*No answer.*)

D. What are the means for gaining willpower?

M. Your idea of willpower is success insured. Willpower should be understood to be the strength of mind which makes it capable of meeting success or failure with equanimity. It is not synonymous with certain success. Why should one's attempts always be attended by success? Success breeds arrogance and man's spiritual progress is thus arrested. Failure, on the other hand, is beneficial, inasmuch as it opens his eyes to his limitations and prepares him to surrender himself. Self-surrender is synonymous with eternal happiness. Therefore, one should try to gain equipoise of mind under all circumstances. That is willpower. Again, success and failure are the results of *prarabdha* (past actions, currently bearing fruit) and not of willpower. A man may be doing only good and noble actions and yet prove a failure. Another may do otherwise and yet be uniformly successful. This does not mean that willpower is present in the one and not in the other.

D. Is it not said in the book *Truth Revealed* (*Ulladu Narpadu*) that the world is a product of the mind?

M. Yes.

D. Does it not follow that the mind grown strong brings the world under control?

M. The mind in its external activities gives rise to the world. Such activities fritter away the strength of the mind. Its strength lies in being confined to itself with the external activities arrested.

D. There is an idiot who cannot count up to ten. His mind certainly does not operate as does that of a thinker. Is the former a better man than the latter?

M. Who says he is an idiot? Your mind in its wandering says so.

D. Is willpower gained by divesting oneself of thoughts?

M. Rather by confining oneself to a single thought. Ultimately, this will also disappear, leaving Pure Consciousness behind. Concentration helps one to it.

D. So then, it is gained by directing the mind and concentrating it. The personality has nothing to do with it.

M. Personality is the root-cause of external activities. It must sink for gaining the highest good.

In the course of conversation with a learned man who asked about Purusha *and* Prakriti, *Sri Bhagavan said:* Purusha *and* Prakriti *are only the bifurcation of the one Supreme. They are surmised because the student has the sense of duality deeply rooted. The same* Gita *also says that* Purushottama *lies beyond* Purusha *and* Prakriti.

D. What are *para nadi, Sushumna nadi* and, the Heart?

M. But *Sushumna* resolves into the *para* (*Sushumnatu pareleena*). Heart is usually understood to be the muscular organ lying on the left of the chest. The *Modern Psychological Review* speaks of the physical organ on the left and the Heart center on the right. The Bible says that a fool's heart is on the left and a wise man's on the right. *Yoga Vasishta* says that there are two hearts; the one is *samvit* (consciousness); and the other the blood vessel.

D. What is *Anahata*?

M. *Anahata* is the *chakra* lying behind the heart. It is not *samvit. Lalita Sahasranama* states, "*Anahata chakrasthayai namo namah*" (Salutations to the core situated in *Anahata*) and the next mantra *Hrit* (in the Heart). Thus it is clear that *Anahata* is not the same as *Hrit*.

M. Willpower or any other power is gained by practice (*abhyasa*).

D. Is success not dependent on Guru's Grace?

M. Yes, it is. Is not your practice itself due to such Grace? The fruits are the result of the practice and follow it automatically. There is a stanza in *Kaivalya*, which says: "O Guru! You have been always with me watching me through several reincarnations, and ordaining my course until I was liberated." The Self manifests externally as Guru when the occasion arises; otherwise, He is always within, doing the needful.

June 12, 1937

Mr. Das, of Allahabad University: Has the food which one usually takes anything to do with increase or decrease of one's spirituality? That is, does it influence spirituality for good or bad?

M. Yes. *Sattvic* (pure) food in moderate quantity is helpful for spiritual development.

D. For a *grihi*, i.e., a man of the world (householder), what conduct in life will help him *most* spiritually?

M. *Dhyana* or *bhakti*, which mean the same thing.
D. What is meant by taking the name of God? How to reconcile the following two ideas?
   1. The Bible says: "Do not take the name of God in vain."
   2. The Hindu *sastras* enjoin taking the name of God all the time.
M. One should not use the name of God artificially and superficially without feeling. To use the name of God, one must call upon Him and surrender to Him unreservedly. After such surrender the name of God is constantly with the man.
D. What are the fundamental tests for discovering men of great spirituality, since some are reported to behave like insane people?
M. The *jnani's* mind is known only to the *jnani*. One must be a *jnani* oneself in order to understand another *jnani*. However, the peace of mind, which permeates the saint's atmosphere, is the only means by which the seeker understands the greatness of the saint.

His words or actions or appearance are no indications of his greatness, for they are normally beyond the comprehension of ordinary people.
D. Has man any freewill or is everything in his life predestined and preordained?
M. Freewill holds the field in association with individuality. As long as individuality lasts, so long there is freewill. All the *sastras* are based on this fact, and they advise directing the freewill in the right channel.

Find out to whom freewill or destiny matters. Abide in it. Then these two are transcended. That is the only purpose of discussing these questions. To whom do these questions arise? Find out and be at peace.
D. Are intellect and emotion, like the physical body, growths with the birth of man; and do they dissolve or survive after death?
M. Before considering what happens after death, just consider what happens in your sleep. Sleep is only the interval between two waking states. Do they survive that interval?
D. Yes, they do.
M. The same holds good for death, also. They represent body-consciousness and nothing more. If you are the body, they always hold on to you. If you are not the body, they do not affect you. The one who was in sleep is now in the waking state, just speaking. You were not the body in sleep. Are you the body now? Find it out. Then the whole problem is solved.

Similarly, that which is born must die. Whose is the birth? Were you born? If you say you were, of whose birth are you speaking? It is the body which was born and it is that which will die. How do birth and death affect the eternal Self?

Think and inquire to whom the questions arise. Then you will know.

D. It is said that the Universe consists of light and sound. Are these two constituents like the light and sound in the physical world? Can they be seen and heard with the physical organs— eye and ear? Or are they to be experienced only subjectively?

M. Light and sound correspond to *bindu* and *nada* in *Tantric* terminology, and to the mind and life-current in the *Vedantic*. They are gross, subtle, and transcendental. The organs can perceive the gross aspect; the other aspects are not so perceptible. The subtle can be inferred and the transcendental is only transcendental.

D. Hinduism accepts reincarnation of the *jiva*. What happens to it during the interval between death of one body and birth of the next one?

M. Solve this question by referring to the state of sleep. What happens to you in sleep?

D. I do not know.

M. Yet you exist. Therefore, existence beyond knowledge and ignorance is indicated. Although ignorance was prevailing, according to your present idea, yet you did not say so in sleep. You continued to exist all the same. Mere ignorance does not rule out the fact of your existence.

D. In the practice of meditation, are there any signs of the nature of subjective experience or otherwise, which will indicate the aspirant's progress towards Self-realization?

M. The degree of freedom from unwanted thoughts and the degree of concentration on a single thought are the measure to gauge one's progress.

D. Is it necessary to take to *sannyasa* for Self-realization?

M. *Sannyasa* is to renounce one's individuality. This is not the same as tonsure and ochre robes. A man may be a *grihi*; yet, if he does not think he is a *grihi*, he is a *sannyasi*. On the contrary, a man may wear ochre robes and wander about; yet if he thinks he is a *sannyasi*, he is not. To think of *sannyasa* defeats its own purpose.

Sri Bhagavan remarked: People see the world. The perception implies the existence of a seer and the seen. The objects are alien to the seer. The seer is intimate, being the Self. People do not, however, turn their attention to finding out the obvious seer but run about analyzing the seen. The more the mind expands, the farther it goes and renders Self-realization more difficult and complicated. One must directly see the seer and realize the Self.

D. So then, it amounts to synthesizing phenomena and finding the one underlying Reality.

M. Why do you still consider the phenomena? See who is the seer. Synthesis means engaging the mind in other pursuits. That is not the way to Realization.

D. I want to eliminate the non-self so that the Self may be realized. How shall I do it? What are the characteristics of the non-self?

M. There is one who says that the non-self must be eliminated. Who is he?

D. I mean this man. When I travel from Calcutta to Madras, I must know Madras so that I may not get off at an intermediate station out of ignorance. There are the signboards and the timetable to guide me in my travel. But what is the guide in my search for the Self?

M. It is all right for the journey. You know how far away you are from Madras. Can you tell me how far away you are from the Self in order that you should seek it?

D. I do not know.

M. Are you ever divorced from the Self? Is it possible to be divorced? Are not all these alien to you — and the Self the most intimate? Where should you go to gain the Self?

D. I am now away from the Self. I must retrace my steps in order to regain it.

M. How far away? Who says he is apart? Can there be two selves?

D. It is said that individuals are modifications of the Self, just as ornaments are of gold.

M. When a man speaks in terms of ornaments, ignoring their substance as gold, he is told that they are gold. But here the man is consciousness and speaks of himself as its modification. Do you remain apart from Self that you speak of yourself as Its modification?

D. Cannot gold be imagined to say that it has become an ornament?

M. Being insentient, it does not say so. But the individual is sentient and cannot function apart from consciousness. The Self is Pure Consciousness. Yet man identifies himself with the body, which is itself insentient and does not say "I am the body" of its own accord. Someone else says so. The unlimited Self does not. Who else is he that says so? A spurious "I" arises between the Pure Consciousness and the insentient body and imagines itself limited to the body. Seek this and it will vanish as a phantom. That phantom is the ego, or the mind, or the individuality.

All the *sastras* are based on the rise of this phantom, whose elimination is their purpose. The present state is mere illusion. Disillusionment [waking up from illusion] is the goal and nothing more.

D. The mind is said to be a bundle of thoughts.

M. Because it functions on account of a single root — the "I"-thought. □□ has no real existence as a separate entity.

"*Manasantu kim margane krte naiva manasam marga arjavat.*"

When the mind unceasingly investigates its own nature, it transpires that there is no such thing as mind. This is the direct path for all.

— *Upadesa Saram* (17)

D. Are not thoughts projections from the mind?

M. In that case, the mind is taken to be synonymous with the "I"-thought or the ego.

DECEMBER 15, 1937

Sri Bhagavan has selected ten stanzas from the famous work of Sri Shankara — Shivananda Lahari — *describing devotion (*bhakti):

1. What is *bhakti*?

   Just as the *ankola* fruit falling from the tree rejoins it or a piece of iron is drawn to a magnet, so also thoughts, after rising up, lose themselves in their original source. This is *bhakti*. The original source of thoughts is the feet of the Lord, *Ishvara*. Love of His Feet forms *bhakti*. (61)

2. Fruit of *bhakti*:

   The thick cloud of *bhakti*, formed in the transcendental sky of the Lord's Feet, pours down a rain of Bliss (*ananda*) and fills the lake of mind to overflowing. Only then the *jiva*, always transmigrating to no useful end, has his real purpose fulfilled. (76)

3. Where to place *bhakti*?

   Devotion to gods, who have themselves their origin and end, can result in fruits similarly with origin and end. In order to be in Bliss everlasting, our devotion must be directed to its source, namely the Feet of the ever-blissful Lord. (83)

4. *Bhakti* is a matter only for experience and not for words:

   How can Logic or other polemics be of real use? Can the *ghatapatas*

324

(favorite examples of the logicians, meaning the pot and the cloth) save you in a crisis? Why then waste yourself thinking of them and in discussion? Stop exercising the vocal organs and giving them pain. Think of the Feet of the Lord and drink the nectar! (6)

5. Immortality is the fruit of Devotion:
   At the sight of him who in his heart has fixed the Lord's Feet, Death is reminded of his bygone disastrous encounter with Markandeya and runs away.
   All other gods worship only Shiva, placing their crowned heads at His feet. Such involuntary worship is only natural to Shiva.
   Goddess Liberation, His consort, always remains part of Him. (65)

6. If only Devotion be there, the conditions of the *jiva* cannot affect him. However different the bodies, the mind alone is lost in the Lord's Feet. Bliss overflows! (10)

7. Devotion always unimpaired:
   Wherever or however it be, only let the mind lose itself in the Supreme. It is Yoga! It is Bliss! Or the Yogi or the Bliss incarnate! (12)

8. *Karma Yoga* also is *Bhakti*:
   To worship God with flowers and other external objects is troublesome. Only lay the single flower, the heart, at the feet of Shiva and remain at Peace. Not to know this simple thing and to wander about! How foolish! What misery! (9)

9. This *Karma Yoga* puts an end to one's *samsara*:
   Whatever the order of life (*asrama*) of the devotee, only once thought of, Shiva relieves the devotee of his load of *samsara* and takes it on Himself. (11)

10. Devotion is *Jnana*:
    The mind losing itself in Shiva's Feet is Devotion. Ignorance lost! Knowledge! Liberation! (91)

DECEMBER 16, 1937

A few ladies came from Bangalore. One among them asked: The world is composed of differences, from our point of view. How shall we be able to get over these differences and comprehend the One Essence of all things?

M. The differences are the result of the sense of doership (*kartritva*). The fruits will be destroyed if the root is destroyed. So relinquish the sense of doership; the differences will vanish and the essential reality will reveal itself.

In order to give up the sense of doership, one must find out who the doer is. Inquire within; the sense of doership will then vanish. *Vichara* (inquiry) is the method.

DECEMBER 22, 1937

A Marathi gentleman asked: I have read much about Self-realization; I do *japa, puja,* etc., but nothing seems to satisfy me. Can Sri Bhagavan kindly guide me?

M. What is it that you seek to gain? Everyone seeks happiness. Happiness is one's lot in everyday sleep. Bring about that state of happiness even in the waking state. That is all.

D. I do not follow. How is it to be done?

M. *Atma-vichara* is the way.

D. It seems too difficult to adopt, being so intangible. What shall I do if I feel unfit for this method of inquiry?

M. Guidance is there. It is for individuals to avail themselves of it.

DECEMBER 25, 1937

A Telugu gentleman stood up and asked: The mind is said to be pure when all its *vasanas* are wiped out. It is also the finality. When there is something to be gained, is it not duality?

M. Let the mind be first made pure. If the same question arises thereafter, the answer may then be sought.

DECEMBER 26, 1937

An Andhra visitor asked: What is sleep?

M. Why, you experience it every day.

D. I want to know exactly what it is, so that it may be distinguished from *samadhi.*

M. How can you know sleep when you are awake? The answer is to go to

sleep and find out.
D. But I cannot know it in this way.
M. This question must be raised in sleep.
D. But I cannot raise the question then.
M. So, that is sleep.

Sri Bhagavan went out for a few minutes. On his return, the same man asked: Self-realized *jnanis* are seen to take food and do actions like others. Do they similarly experience the states of dream and sleep?
M. Why do you seek to know the state of others, maybe *jnanis*? What do you gain by knowing about others? You must seek to know your own real nature.
    Who do you think that you are? Evidently, the body.
D. Yes.
M. Similarly, you take the *jnani* to be the visible body upon which the actions are superimposed by you. That makes you ask these questions. The *jnani* himself does not ask about the dream or sleep state. He has no doubts himself. The doubts are in you. This must convince you of your wrong premises. The *jnani* is not the body. He is the Self of all.
    The sleep, dream, *samadhi*, etc., are all states of the *ajnanis*. The Self is free from all these. Here lies the answer to the earlier question, also.
D. I sought to know the state of *sthita prajnata* (unshaken knowledge).
M. The *sastras* are not for the *jnani*. He has no doubts to be cleared. The riddles are for *ajnanis* only. The *sastras* are for them alone.
D. Sleep is the state of nescience and so it is said of *samadhi*, also.
M. *Jnana* is beyond knowledge and nescience. There can be no question about that state. It is the Self.

Mr. Thomas, Professor of Sanskrit, University of Oxford, presided over the Oriental Conference in Trivandrum. On his way to Calcutta he visited Sri Bhagavan. He is an elderly gentleman with a broad forehead and a quiet manner. He speaks softly and slowly. He evinces great interest in oriental literature, especially Sanskrit. He had heard of the richness of Tamil. He wanted to know which of the English translations of Srimad Bhagavad Gita *was the best. The Hall was crowded and a few people mentioned, each with his own opinion, Thibaut's, Mahadeva Sastri's, Telang's, etc. Sri Bhagavan made mention of F. T. Brooks. Mr. Thomas desires one in metrical form because it is the proper vehicle for the rasa (essence) contained in it. Rasa is also Peace, he said.*
M. Yes. *Brahman* is only *rasa.*

D. *Rasa* is also Bliss.

M. *Rasa, Ananda,* Peace are all names for the same Bliss.

The Professor was shown Mr. Grant Duff's speech in the Philosophical Conference held in Paris. Later the book Dharma *by Dr. G.H. Mees was placed in his hands, on seeing which he asked what Sri Bhagavan thought of castes.*

M. The castes relate to bodies and not to the Self. The Self is Bliss. To realize Bliss, one realizes the Self. No need to worry oneself about caste, etc.

D. The *ahamkar* ("I"-sense) is also called the Self.

M. *Ahamkar* is limited, whereas the Self is beyond it.

D. There is much literature in English relating to Eastern philosophy and religion. There are different exponents. The system of Ramanuja is well presented. Prof. Radhakrishnan expounds the *advaitic* system. He lays more stress on experience than on evidence. Shankara shows a highly developed mind.

A discussion followed on direct perception. The Professor spoke of mental perception as being different from sensory perception.

M. To infer one's existence, no other evidence is necessary. The *indriyas* (senses) and the mind arising from the ego cannot serve as evidence relating to the Self. The Self is their basis. They do not exist independently of the Self. One's own existence is self-evident. Bliss is the Self. All become dear, only owing to the love of Self.

D. Love postulates duality. How can the Self be the object of love?

M. Love is not different from the Self. Love of an object is of an inferior order and cannot endure, whereas the Self *is* Love; in other words, God is Love.

D. It is also the Christian idea.

Professor Thomas asked Sri Bhagavan which of the methods was the best for the attainment of the goal. Is not Patanjali's the best?

M. *Yogas chitta vritti nirodhah* (Yoga is to check the mind from changing), which is acceptable to all. That is also the goal of all. The method is chosen according to one's own fitness. The goal for all is the same. Yet different names are given to the goal only to suit the process preliminary to reaching the goal. *Bhakti, Yoga, Jnana* are all the same. *Svasvarupanusandhanam bhaktirity abhidheeyate* (Self-contemplation is called *bhakti*).

D. Does Sri Bhagavan advocate *advaita*?

M. *Dvaita* and *advaita* are relative terms. They are based on the sense of duality. The Self is as it is. There is neither *dvaita* nor *advaita*. "I Am that I Am." Simple Being is the Self.

D. This is not *mayavada*.

M. The mind is *maya*. Reality lies beyond the mind. So long as the mind functions, there is duality, *maya*, etc. Once it is transcended, Reality shines forth. Although it is said to shine forth, Self-effulgence is the Self.

D. It is *Satchitananda*.

M. *Sat-Chit-Ananda* is said to indicate that the Supreme is not *asat* (different from unreal), not *achit* (different from insentient) and not *anananda* (different from unhappiness). Because we are in the phenomenal world we speak of the Self as *Satchitananda*.

D. *Aham* "I" applies to the individual and also to *Brahman*. It is rather unfortunate.

M. It is *upadhi bheda* (owing to different limiting adjuncts). The bodily limitations pertain to the *aham* ("I") of the *jiva*, whereas the universal limitations pertain to the *aham* ("I") of *Brahman*. Take off the *upadhi* (limiting adjunct); the "I" (*aham*) is pure and single.

D. Does Bhagavan give *diksha* (initiation)?

M. *Mouna* (silence) is the best and most potent *diksha*. That was practiced by Sri Dakshinamurti. Touch, look, etc., are all of a lower order. Silence *(mouna diksha)* changes the hearts of all. There is no Guru and no disciple. The *ajnani* confounds his body with the Self, and so he takes the other's body for the Guru. But does the Guru think his body to be the Self? He has transcended the body. There are no differences for Him. So the *ajnani* cannot appreciate the standpoint of Guru and of *sishya*.

D. Is there then no difference between the one and the other?

M. There are differences from the standpoint of the phenomenal world, but not from that of Reality.

    (*The Professor was thankful. He hoped to appreciate Sri Bhagavan's writings better after having seen and conversed with him.*)

In the course of conversation, Sri Bhagavan said: Upasana and *dhyana* are possible only so long as there is the mind and they must cease with the cessation of the mind. They are mere preliminaries to final eradication of thoughts and the stillness of mind.

D. *Shaiva Siddhanta* postulates three fundamentals as being eternal. Is it opposed to *Vedanta*?

M. The three entities are *jiva*, God, and bondage. Such trinities are common in all religions. They are true so long as the mind is operative; they are mere creations of the mind. One can postulate God only after the mind arises. God is not different from the Self. The Self is objectified as God. So also with Guru.

The Professor returned in the evening and asked something about good actions. He further wondered why Brahman *is said to be* Satchitananda, *but not God. Sri Bhagavan said:*

Sat denotes being beyond *sat* and *asat*,

Chit beyond both *chit* and *achit*,

Ananda beyond both bliss and non-bliss.

What is it, then? Even if not *sat* or *asat*, it must be admitted to be *sat* only. Compare the term *jnana*. It is the state beyond knowledge and ignorance. Yet *jnana* is not ignorance but knowledge. So also with *Satchitananda*.

D. It favors the one aspect.

(*After a word about* Atma-vichara, *he took leave saying he would not trouble Sri Maharshi any further, although he had several doubts yet to be cleared and that he wanted to make* nididhyasana *of what he had heard so far.*)

A judge from Mysore asked: Upasana and *dhyana* were said to be due to mental activities. Cessation of activities was also said to be Realization. Now, how to realize without *upasana* or *dhyana*?

M. They are preliminaries. Such action will lead to the desired inaction.

D. The Heart is said to be experienced on the right. Physiologically, it is on the left.

M. Spiritual experience is spoken of.

D. Is it the psychic heart?

M. Yes.

D. How to know that it is on the right?

M. By experience.

D. Is there any indication to that effect?

M. Point out to yourself and see.

DECEMBER 28, 1937

Being Christmas holidays, there is a great rush of visitors from far and near. A group of them sat down and two among them asked the following questions:

D. Do you know English?

(*Prompted to ask questions, he continued.*)

D. Have you realized your Self?
Sri Bhagavan smiled and said: Go on, continue.
D. Have you experienced *nirvikalpa samadhi*?
  (He was asked to finish his questions.)
D. Can you enter into *nirvikalpa samadhi* at will? Is it not important for sages to influence their surroundings?

Another man asked: Can Sri Bhagavan help us realize the Truth?
M. Help is always there.
D. Then there is no need to ask questions. I do not feel the ever-present help.
M. Surrender and you will find it.
D. I am always at your feet. Will Bhagavan give us some *upadesa* to follow? Otherwise, how can I get the help living six hundred miles away?
M. That *Sadguru* is within.
D. *Sadguru* is necessary to guide me to understand it.
M. The *Sadguru* is within.
D. I want a visible Guru.
M. That visible Guru says that He is within.
D. Can I throw myself at the mercy of the *Sadguru*?
M. Yes. Instructions are necessary only so long as one has not surrendered oneself.
D. Is no particular time necessary for meditation?
M. Meditation depends on strength of mind. It must be unceasing, even while engaged in work. A particular time is meant for novices.
D. Will *Sadguru* place his hand on my head to assure me of his help? I will have the consolation that his promise will be fulfilled.
M. A bond will be the next requisition and a suit will be filed if you imagine no help forthcoming. (*Laughter.*)
D. May I come near, Sir? (*For blessing.*)
M. Such doubts should not arise in you. They contradict your statement of surrender. *Sadguru* is always on your head.
D. Surrender comes after effort.
M. Yes, it becomes complete in due course.
D. Is a teacher necessary for instructions?
M. Yes, if you want to learn anything new. But here you have to unlearn.
D. Yet a teacher is necessary.
M. You have already got what you seek elsewhere. So no teacher is necessary.

D. Is there any use of the man of Realization for the seeker?

M. Yes. He helps you get rid of your delusion that you are not realized.

D. So, tell me how.

M. The paths are meant only to dehypnotize the individual.

D. Dehypnotize me. Tell me what method to follow.

M. Where are you now? Where should you go?

D. I know "I am"; but I do not know what I am.

M. Are there two "I's" then?

D. It is begging the question.

M. Who says this? Is it the one who is, or is it the other who does not know what he is?

D. I am, but do not know what or how.

M. "I" is always there.

D. Does the "I" undergo any transformation, say in death?

M. Who witnesses the transformation?

D. You seem to speak *Jnana Yoga*. This is *Jnana Yoga*.

M. Yes, it is.

D. But surrender is *Bhakti Yoga*.

M. Both are the same.

After some time, the man continued: Then I have to conclude that I am Consciousness and that nothing occurs except by my presence.

M. It is one thing to conclude it by reasoning and another thing to be convinced.

The other man continued: I shall wait three months and see if help is forthcoming. Now, may I have your assurance?

M. Is this what is asked by one who has surrendered?

Four visitors retired. The same man continued to say: Fulfill your promise. (*Laughter.*)

He also said: God has given me enough for bread and butter and I am happy. In addition, I want peace of mind. Hence this request.

DECEMBER 29, 1937

Two ladies and two gentlemen arrived from Sri Lanka. One of them asked: Have you realized God? If so, in what shape?

M. Who remains there to see God? The question might well be if one has known oneself.

D. I have known myself.

M. Is the "I" different from the Self that you say, has known the Self?

D. I know the Self as identical with the body. If the Self is different from the body, let Bhagavan tell me how to see the Self separate from the body. He has realized God. He can teach me.

M. Why should the Self be separated from the body? Let the body remain as it is.

D. The soul when disembodied can see through all bodies.

M. Are there others, then? Or is there even your own body? Consider your sleep — you do not know your body at that time. But still, you are there all the same. Did you then perceive the world through this or other bodies? Nevertheless, you cannot deny your existence in sleep. There must be a subject to see the world and the subject must also be limited. If unlimited, how can there be others beside the unlimited Self?

D. Does God have any limits?

M. Leave God alone. What limits were there for your Self in your sleep?

D. Death must then be the highest state.

M. Yes. We are now living in Death. Those who have limited the unlimited Self have committed suicide by putting on such limitations.

D. Concentrate on the Self, you say. How to do it?

M. If that is solved, everything else is solved.

D. Know thyself, you say. How to know the Self?

M. You now know that you are the body.

D. *Raja Yoga* realizes through the body, senses, etc., and Sri Bhagavan advises realization by thinking. This is *Jnana Yoga*.

M. How can you think without the body?

D. God does not think?

M. Why then did you start asking, "In what shape did you see God?"

D. God must be felt through the senses.

M. Are you not feeling God?

D. Is everybody feeling God always?

M. Yes.

D. Then what is realization?

M. Realization is to get rid of the delusion that you have not realized.

D. I don't catch the point.

(*They left, having taken a snapshot.*)

D. What is *vishvarupa*?

M. It is to see the world as the Self of God. In the *Bhagavad Gita*, God is said to be various things and beings, and also the whole universe. How to realize or see it thusly? Can one see one's Self? Though not seen, can the Self be denied? What is the Truth?
D. Is it then wrong to say that some have seen it?
M. It is true in the same degree as you are. The *Gita* begins saying that no one was born; in the fourth chapter, it says:

> "The numerous incarnations, yours and mine, have taken place;
> I know them but you do not."
> — *Bhagavad Gita* 4.5

Of these two statements, which is the truth? The instruction is according to the listener's understanding. If the second chapter contains the whole Truth, why should so many more chapters follow?

In the Bible, God says "I Am before Abraham." He does not say "I was" but "I Am."

M. People read of Vivekananda having asked Sri Ramakrishna, "Have you seen God?" and imitate him now. They also ask, "Have you realized God?"

I ask what is *realization*.

Realization implies perfection. When you are limited, your perception also is limited. Your knowledge is thus imperfect. Of what value is that imperfect knowledge?

In *Vishvarupa Darshan*, Arjuna is told to see whatever he desired and not what was presented before him. How can that *darshan* be real?

December 30, 1937

A visitor asked: For beginners like me, which is most suited: either worship of qualified God or contemplation of "I am *Brahman?*"
M. The answer is contained in the question. The question itself shows it to be worship of qualified God.
D. "I" is felt in the waking and dream states but not in deep sleep. Why so?
M. If so, does it not exist in deep sleep?
D. Because there are mental modes in these two states, and no such mode in the other.

1938

CHAPTER FOUR

M. What is to be done? Reality is One only. How can It be realized? Realization is thus an illusion. Practice seems to be necessary. Who is to practice? In looking for a doer, the act and the accessories will disappear.

Moreover, if Realization is not present here and now, how can It, newly obtained, be of any use? What is permanent must be eternally present. Can it be newly acquired and be permanent also?

Realize what is present here and now. The sages did so before and still do that only. Hence they say that it looks as if it were newly acquired. Once veiled by ignorance and later revealed, Reality looks as if newly realized. But it is not new.

CHAPTER FOUR — 1938

JANUARY 3, 1938

D. Rama asks: "*Brahman* being pure, How can *maya* arise from Him and veil Him, also?" Vasishta replies: "In the pure mind associated with strong dispassion, this question will not arise." Of course in *advaita* (nondualistic) philosophy, there can be no place for *jiva, Ishvara,* and *maya*. Oneself sinking into the Self, the *vasanas* (latent tendencies) will entirely disappear, leaving no room for such a question.

M. The answers will be according to the capacity of the seeker. It is said in the second chapter of the *Gita* that no one is born or dies; but in the fourth chapter, Sri Krishna says that numerous incarnations of His and of Arjuna had taken place, all known to Him but not to Arjuna. Which of these statements is true? Both are correct, but from different standpoints. Now the question is raised: "How can *jiva* rise up from the Self?" I will answer. Only know your real Being; then you will not raise this question.

Why should a man consider himself separate? How was he before being born or how will he be after death? Why waste time in such discussions? What was your form in deep sleep? Why do you consider yourself an individual?

D. My form remains subtle in deep sleep.

M. As is the effect so is the cause. As is the tree, so is its seed. The whole tree is contained in the seed, which later manifests as the tree. The expanded tree must have a substratum, which we call *maya*. As a matter of fact, there is neither seed nor tree; there is only Being.

D. *Vasanakshaya* (total end of all predispositions) — *Mano nasa* (annihilation of mind) — *Atma-sakshatkara* (Realization of the Self); they seem to be interdependent.

M. The different expressions have only one meaning; they differ according to the individual's progress. Dispassion, Realization — all mean the same thing; also, they say "practice and dispassion." Why practice? Because the modes of mind once subside and then rise up; again subside and rise up, and so on.

D. Beginningless predisposition makes one do wrong. Without *jnana*, this predisposition cannot vanish. But *jnana* appears almost impossible. Expiation alone cannot undo all the karma; for how much expiation will be needed! Look where we will! Everything looks difficult, even impossible. Association with the wise seems to be the only cure of all ills.

M. What is to be done? Reality is One only. How can It be realized? Realization is thus an illusion. Practice seems to be necessary. Who is to practice? In looking for a doer, the act and the accessories will disappear.

Moreover, if Realization is not present here and now, how can it, newly obtained, be of any use? What is permanent must be eternally present. Can it be newly acquired and be permanent also?

Realize what is present here and now. The sages did so before and still do that only. Hence they say that it looks as if it were newly acquired. Once veiled by ignorance and later revealed, Reality looks as if newly realized. But it is not new.

D. *Karma, bhakti, yoga,* and *jnana* and their subdivisions only confuse the mind. To follow the elders' words seems to be the only right thing to do. What should I hold? Please tell me. I cannot sift the *srutis* and *smritis*; they are too vast. So please advise me.

(No answer.)

D. Without logic, without learned terminology, please instruct me in the way to the Bliss of Self. Let it be of Guru's Grace only.

M. Have a clear idea of your requirement. Who seeks to gain what? Then ask the method.

D. Bliss manifests occasionally, but I am unable to describe it. At times there is illumination, but is it the Reality? If so, how to make it permanent? The method must be simple. Please make it clear without logic, learned discussions or mystifying words.

(No answer.)

Another visitor asked: Please tell me which is the most efficacious of all the methods, e.g., prayer to God, Guru *anugraha* (Master's Grace), concentration of mind, etc.

M. The one is the consequence of the other. Each leads to the next stage; they form a continuous whole. God, Guru, and Self are not different; they are one and the same. Therefore, the methods offer no choice.

Mr. Pannalal (Indian Civil Service), a high Government official from Allahabad, with his wife, a highly cultured lady, and Mr. Brijnarayan, a retired judge, were on a visit for a week. The night prior to their departure, they wished to have their doubt cleared, which was: We had a great sage for our Guru. He advised us to "take the name of Hari," saying that it is all in all; no effort is necessary for concentrating the mind. Concentration will come of itself if Harinam is persisted in. So we are doing it. The Guru passed away. We felt like a rudderless ship in mid-ocean. In our anxiety to find a safe guide, we read and heard of you and so desired to come here. Our desire has been fulfilled after two years' longing. On coming here and hearing Sri Bhagavan, we understand that the Master teaches *Atma-vichara* (self-quest). This is the method of Knowledge (*Jnana Marga*), whereas the other Master taught us *Bhakti Marga* (devotion). What shall we do now? Are we to give up the other method and take to this new one? If once we change, shall we not change many more times according to the Masters we meet? What progress can be made by such frequent changes? Pray remove this doubt and bless us.

The Master referred the gentleman to the following article in the September issue of *The Vision*, a journal from Anandashram, Kanhangad:

Literal translation of Namdev's "Philosophy of the Divine Name."
1. The Name densely permeates the sky and the lowest regions and the entire universe. Who can tell to what depths in the nether regions and to what height in the heavens It extends? The ignorant undergo the eighty-four lakhs of species of births, not knowing the essence of things. Namdev says the Name is immortal. Forms are innumerable, but the Name is all that.

2. The Name itself is form; and form itself is Name. There is no distinction between Name and form. God became manifest and assumed Name and form. Hence the Name the *Vedas* have established. Beware, there is no mantra beyond the Name. Those who say otherwise are ignorant. Namdev says the Name is Keshava Himself. This is known only to the loving devotees of the Lord.

3. The all-pervading nature of the Name can only be understood when one recognizes his "I." When one's own name is not recognized, it is impossible to get the all-pervading Name. When one knows oneself, then one finds the Name everywhere. To see the Name as different from the Named creates illusion. Namdev says, "Ask the Saints."

4. None can realize the Name by practice of knowledge, meditation, or austerity. Surrender yourself first at the feet of the Guru and learn to know that "I" myself is that Name. After finding the source of that "I," merge your individuality in that oneness, which is Self-existent and devoid of all duality. That which pervades beyond *dvaita* and *dvaitatita*, that Name has come into the three worlds. The Name is *Parabrahman* itself, where there is no action arising out of duality.

JANUARY 8, 1938

While explaining a stanza of his own, Sri Bhagavan observed:
The sun illumines the universe, whereas the Sun of Arunachala is so dazzling that the universe is obscured and an unbroken brilliance remains. But it is not realized in the present state and can be realized only if the lotus of the heart blossoms. The ordinary lotus blossoms in the light of the visible sun, whereas the subtle Heart blossoms only before the Sun of Suns. May Arunachala make my heart blossom so that His unbroken brilliance may shine all alone!

Further on, Sri Bhagavan continued:
The mirror reflects objects; yet they are not real because they cannot remain apart from the mirror. Similarly, the world is said to be a reflection in the mind as it does not remain in the absence of mind. The question arises: if the universe is a reflection, there must be a real object known as the universe in order that it might be reflected in the mind. This amounts to an admission of the existence of an objective universe. Truly speaking, it is not so.

Therefore, the dream illustration is set forth. The dream world has no objective existence. How, then, is it created? Some mental impressions should be admitted. They are called *vasanas*. How were the *vasanas* in the mind? The answer is: they are subtle. Just as a whole tree is contained potentially in a seed, so the world is in the mind.

Then this question arises: A seed is the product of the tree, which must have existed once in order that it may be reproduced. So the world also must have been there some time. The answer is: No! There must have been several incarnations to gather the impressions, which are remanifested in the present form. I must have existed before as I do now. The direct way to find an answer will be to see if the world is there. Admitting the existence of the world, I must admit a seer who is no other than myself. Let me find myself so that I may know the relation between the world and the seer. When I seek the Self and abide as the Self, there is no world to be seen. What is the Reality then? The seer only, and certainly not the world.

Such being the truth, man continues to argue on the basis of the reality of the world. Whoever asked him to accept a legal brief for the world?

Yoga Vasishta clearly defines Liberation as the abandonment of the false and remaining as Being.

A visitor asked: The illustration of the mirror relates to the sense of sight only. The world is perceived by the other senses, as well. Can the unreality be established in relation to the other senses, also?

M. A figure on the screen in the cinema show appears to watch the whole world. What is the reality behind the subject and the object in the same show? An illusory being watches an illusory world.

D. But I am the witness of the show.

M. Certainly you are. You and the world are as real as the cinema figure and the cinema world.

An advocate visitor: The mind becomes aware of the world through the senses. When the senses are active, one cannot help feeling the existence of the world. How can *Karma Yoga* be of any use for pure awareness?

M. The world is perceived by the mind through the senses. It is of the mind. The seer sees the mind and the senses as within the Self and not apart from it. The agent, remaining unaffected by the actions, gets more purified until he realizes the Self.

JANUARY 9, 1938

Explaining a stanza in Akshara Manamalai, *Sri Bhagavan said that mouna is the highest form of upadesa. It signifies "silence" as master, disciple, and practicer. Three sannyasins, who were visiting Sri Bhagavan, began a discussion:*

D. If one remains quiet, how is action to proceed? Where is the scope for *Karma Yoga*?

M. Let us first understand what karma is, whose karma it is, and who is the doer. Analyzing them and inquiring into their truth, one is perforce obliged to remain as the Self in peace. Nevertheless, the actions will go on.

D. How will the actions go on if I do not act?

M. Who asks this question? Is it the Self or another? Is the Self concerned with action?

D. No, not the Self. It is another, different from the Self.
M. So it is plain that the Self is not concerned with actions, and therefore the question does not arise.
D. I agree.

Another asked: What is the state of the realized man? Is he not acting?
M. The question implies that the realized man is not the questioner. Why should you concern yourself with another? Your duty is to look to yourself and not ask of others.
D. The scriptures hold him up as the ideal.
M. Certainly. He is the ideal. You should realize the Self. Even if his state is now described, your understanding of it will be only according to your capacity. You admit that your capacity is limited. The scriptures say that the realized state admits of no limits. So then, the only way to understand this state is to realize the Self and experience the state. If the question arises afterwards, the answer will be found.

Another visitor asked: Differentiation is made between the sentient and the insentient (*chit* and *jada*) in the opening verse of *Upadesa Saram*.
M. The *Upadesa* is from the standpoint of the hearer. There is no truth in the insentient (*jada*). One whole consciousness (*chit*) prevails all alone.

JANUARY 24, 1938

Mr. Grant Duff was in the Hall. Sri Bhagavan was mentioning some new publications, including Maha Yoga. *He also remarked that Mr. Duff, having read* Sat Darshana Bhashya, *would be surprised at the different view of* Maha Yoga. *Both claim to represent Sri Bhagavan's philosophy; but they differ so much that* Maha Yoga *actually condemns the other.*

Someone cited the curious claim of Sat Darshana Bhashya *that individuality is retained even after loss of the ego. Sri Bhagavan remarked:* What is to be done? The *Upanishads* say, "Brahmavid Brahmaiva bhavati" (Knower of *Brahman* becomes *Brahman*). There is more than one *Brahmavid* at a time. "Are all of them the same? Are they not separate?", so ask some persons. They look to the bodies only. They do not look to the realization. There is no difference in the realization of *Brahmavid*. That is the Truth. But when the question is raised from the standpoint of the body, the reply is bound to be "Yes. They are different." This is the cause of the confusion.

Mr. Duff: The Buddhists deny the world; the Hindu philosophy admits its existence, but says it is unreal. Am I right?

M. The difference of view is according to the difference in the angles of vision.

D. They say that *Shakti* creates the world. Is the knowledge of unreality due to the unveiling of *maya*?

M. All admit *Shakti's* creation. What is the nature of the Creatrix? It can only be in conformity with the nature of the creation. The Creatrix is of the same nature as Her creation.

D. Are there degrees of illusion?

M. Illusion is itself illusory. Illusion must be seen by one beyond it. Can such a seer be subject to illusion? Can he then speak of degrees of illusion?

There are scenes floating on the screen in a cinema show. Fire appears to burn buildings to ashes. Water seems to wreck vessels. But the screen on which the pictures are projected remains unscorched and dry. Why?

Because the pictures are unreal and the screen is real.

Reflections pass through a mirror, but the mirror is not in any way affected by the quality or quantity of the reflections on it. So the world is a phenomenon on the single Reality, which is not affected in any manner. Reality is only one.

The discussion about illusion is due to the difference in angle of vision. Change your angle of vision to one of *jnana* and then find the universe to be only *Brahman*. Being now in the world, you see the world as such. Get beyond it and this will disappear: the Reality alone will shine.

Sri Bhagavan said that a saint, Namah Shivaya, who was formerly living in Arunachala, must have undergone considerable difficulties. For he sang a song saying:

"God proves the devotee by means of severe ordeals. A washerman beats the cloth on a slab, not to tear it, but only to remove the dirt."

JANUARY 25, 1938

A musician came into the Hall and began to sing Tyagaraja Kirtanas *in Telugu. One of them says:*

"Find the source of the sound which is transcendental (*muladhara sabda*) by diving deep like a pearl-diver diving for pearls."

Then, he sang another song:
> "For a man who has controlled his mind, where is the use of
> *tapasya*? Give up the 'I-am-the-body' idea and realize 'I am not;
> Thou art all.'"

This song was translated to Mr. Duff, who was then in the Hall. Mr. Duff asked: Is
it necessary to control one's breath? What becomes of the man who has not
practiced breath-control?
M. Breath-control is only an aid for diving deep. One may as well dive
down by control of mind. On the mind being controlled, the breath becomes controlled automatically. One need not attempt breath-control; mind-
control is enough. Breath-control is recommended for the man who cannot
control his mind straightaway.
>   *Naham* — I am not this — corresponds to *rechaka*
>   *Koham* — Who am I? (search for the I) — corresponds to *puraka*
>   *Soham* — He am I (the Self alone) — corresponds to *kumbhaka*.
So these are the functions of *pranayama*.

Again the three formula are:
>   *Na — Aham* (Not — I).
>   *Ka — Aham* (Who — I).
>   *Sa — Aham* (He — I).
>   Delete the prefixes and hold on to the common factor in all of them.
That is *Aham* — "I," that is the gist of the whole matter.

Later on Sri Bhagavan referred to the songs and said: Tyagaraja says it well. The
mind should be controlled. The question arises "What is mind?" He himself answers in the next couplet, saying that it is the "I-am-the-body" idea.
The next question is how control is effected. He answers again, saying "By
complete surrender. Realize that I am not and that all is He." The song is
fine and compact. He also mentions the other method, namely, control of
breath.

JANUARY 31, 1938
*After Mr. Duff had left, there was a reference to his visit to the Ashram. Sri Bhaga-
van remarked*: Some *Shakti* draws people from all parts of the globe to this
center.
A devotee aptly said: That *Shakti* is not different from Sri Bhagavan.

Sri Bhagavan immediately remarked: What *Shakti* drew me here originally? The same *Shakti* that draws all others, as well.

Sri Bhagavan was, happily, in the mood to relate the following stories:
1. There was a king with a devoted queen. She was a devotee of Sri Rama and yearned that her husband should similarly be a devotee. One night, she found that the king mumbled something in his sleep. She kept her ears close to his lips and heard the word "Rama" repeated continually as in *japa*. She was delighted and next day ordered the minister to hold a feast. The king having partaken of the feast, asked his wife for an explanation. She related the whole occurrence and said that the feast was in gratitude to God for the fulfillment of her long cherished wish. The king was, however, annoyed that his devotion should have been found out. Some say that having thus betrayed God, he considered himself unworthy of God and so committed suicide. It means that one should not openly display one's piety. We may take it that the king told the queen not to make a fuss over his piety and they lived happily together.

2. Thondaradipodi (*Bhaktanghrirenu*) Alwar: One who delights in the dust of the feet of devotees. A devotee (of this name) was keeping a plot of land in which he grew *tulasi*, the sacred basil, made garlands of it, and supplied the same to the God in the temple. He remained a bachelor and was respected for his life and conduct. One day two sisters, who lived by prostitution, walked near the garden and sat under a tree. One of them said, "How disgusting is my life that I soil my body and mind every day. This man's life is most desirable." The other replied, "How do you know his mind? Maybe he is not as good as he appears to be. The bodily functions may be forcibly controlled and the mind may be reveling in riotous thoughts. One cannot control one's *vasanas* as easily as the physical frame."

   The former said, "The actions are only the indices of the mind. His life shows his mind to be pure."

   The other said, "Not necessarily. His mind has not been proved as yet."

   The first challenged her to prove his mind. She accepted. The second desired to be left alone with only a shred of garment in which to clothe herself. The first sister returned home, leaving the other alone with flimsy clothing. As the latter continued to remain under the

344

tree, she appeared penitent and humble. The saint noticed her and approached her after some time. He asked what had happened to her that she appeared in such low spirits. She pleaded penitence for her past life, desired to lead a purer and nobler life and finished with a prayer to him to accept her humble services in the garden or attendance on himself. He advised her to return home and lead a normal life. But she protested. So he detained her for watering the *tulasi* plants. She accepted the function with delight and began to work in the garden.

One rainy night, this woman was found standing under the eaves of the thatched shed in which the saint was. Her clothes were dripping and she was shivering with cold. The Master asked why she was in such a pitiable state. She said that her place was exposed to the rains and so she sought shelter under the eaves and that she would retire as soon as the rain ceased. He asked her to move into the hut and later told her to change her wet clothes. She did not have dry clothes to put on, so he offered her some of his own clothing. She wore them. Later she begged permission to massage his feet. He consented. Eventually, they embraced.

The next day she returned home, had good food, and wore fine clothes. She still continued to work in the garden.

Sometimes, she used to remain in her home, a long time. Then this man began to visit her there, until he finally lived with her. Nevertheless, he did not neglect the garden nor the daily garlands for God.

There occurred a public scandal regarding his change of life. God then resolved to restore him to his old ways and so assumed the shape of the saintly devotee himself. He appeared to the *dasi* (courtesan) and secretly offered her a rich present, an anklet of God.

She was very pleased with it and hid it under her pillow. He then disappeared. All these events were secretly observed by a maidservant in the house.

The ornament was found missing in the temple. The worshipper reported the loss to the proper authorities. They offered a tempting reward for anyone who would furnish a clue leading to the recovery of the lost property. The maidservant provided the clue and claimed the reward. The police recovered the ornament and arrested the *dasi* who said that the devotee gave it to her. He was then roughly handled. A supernatural voice said, "I did it. Leave him alone."

The king and all the others were surprised. They fell prostrate at the man's feet and set him free. He then led a better and nobler life.

3. Kaduveli Sidhar was famed as a very austere hermit. He lived on the dry leaves fallen from trees. The king of the country heard of him, saw him, and offered a reward for the one who would prove this man's worth. A rich *dasi* agreed to do it. She began to live near the recluse and pretended to attend to him. She gently left pieces of *pappadam* along with the dry leaves picked by him. When he had eaten them, she began to leave other kinds of tasty food along with dry leaves. Eventually, he took good tasty dishes supplied by her. They became intimate and a child was born to them. She reported the matter to the king.

The king wanted to know if she could prove their mutual relationship to the general public. She agreed and suggested a plan of action. Accordingly, the king announced a public dance performance by that *dasi* and invited the people to it. They gathered there and she also appeared, but not before she had given a dose of laxative to the child and left it in charge of the saint at home.

The dance was at its height here; the child was crying at home for the mother. The father took the babe in his arms and went to the dancing performance. She was dancing hilariously. He could not approach her with the child. She noticed the man and the babe. She contrived to kick her legs in the dance so as to unloose one of her anklets just as she approached the place where the saint was. She gently lifted her foot and he tied the anklet. The public shouted and laughed. But he remained unaffected. Yet to prove his worth, he sang a Tamil song meaning:

> "For victory, let go my anger! I release my mind when it rushes away. If it is true that I sleep day and night quite aware of my Self, may this stone burst into twain and become the wide expanse!"

Immediately, the stone (idol) burst with a loud noise. The people were astounded.

Sri Bhagavan continued: Thus he proved himself an unswerving *jnani*. One should not be deceived by the external appearance of a *jnani*. Thus *Vedantachudamani* (v. 181) means:

Although a *jivanmukta* associated with body may, owing to his *prarabdha*, appear to lapse into ignorance or wisdom, yet he is only pure like the ether (*akasha*) which is always itself clear whether covered by dense clouds or cleared of clouds by currents of air. He always revels in the Self alone, like a loving wife taking pleasure with her husband alone, though she attends to him with things obtained from others (by way of fortune, as determined by her *prarabdha*). Though he remains silent like one devoid of learning, yet his supineness is due to the implicit duality of the *vaikhari vak* (spoken words) of the *Vedas*; his silence is the highest expression of the realized nonduality which is, after all, the true content of the *Vedas*. Though he instructs his disciples, yet he does not pose as a teacher in the full conviction that the teacher and disciple are mere conventions born of illusion (*maya*), and so he continues to utter words (like *akasvani*). If, on the other hand, he mutters words incoherently like a lunatic, it is because his experience is inexpressible like the words of lovers in embrace. If his words are many and fluent like those of an orator, they represent the recollection of his experience, since he is the unmoving nondual One, without any desire awaiting fulfillment. Although he may appear grief-stricken like any other man in bereavement, yet he evinces just the right love of and pity for the senses which he earlier controlled before he realized that they were mere instruments and manifestations of the Supreme Being. When he seems keenly interested in the wonders of the world, he is only ridiculing the ignorance born of superimposition. If he appears indulging in sexual pleasures, he must be taken to enjoy the ever-inherent Bliss of the Self which, divided Itself into the Individual Self and the Universal Self, delights in their reunion to regain Its original Nature. If he appears wrathful, he means well to the offenders. All his actions should be taken to be only divine manifestations on the plane of humanity. There should not arise even the least doubt as to his being emancipated while yet alive. He lives only for the good of the world.

Sri Bhagavan now warned the hearers against the mistake of disparaging a jnani *for his apparent conduct, and again cited the story of Parikshit:*

He was a stillborn child. The ladies cried and appealed to Sri Krishna to save the child. The sages round about wondered how Krishna was going to save the child from the effects of the arrows (*apandavastra*) of Asvatthama. Krishna said, "If the child be touched by one eternally celibate (*nityabrahmachari*), the child would be brought to life." Even Suka dared not touch the child. Finding no one among the reputed saints bold enough to touch the child, Krishna went and touched him, saying, "If I am eternally celibate (*nityabrahmachari*), may the child be brought to life." The child began to breathe and later grew up to be Parikshit.

Just consider how Krishna, surrounded by 16,000 *gopis* (milkmaids), is a *brahmachari*! Such is the mystery of *jivanmukti*! A *jivanmukta* is one who does not see anything separate from the Self.

If, however, a man consciously attempts to display *siddhis*, he will receive only kicks.

FEBRUARY 3, 1938

Miss Umadevi, a Polish lady convert to Hinduism, asked Sri Bhagavan: I once told Sri Bhagavan how I had a vision of Shiva at about the time of my conversion. A similar experience recurred to me at Courtallam. These visions are momentary, but they are blissful. I want to know how they might be made permanent. Without Shiva, there is no life in what I see around me. I am so happy to think of Him. Please tell me how His vision may be everlasting to me.

M. You speak of a vision of Shiva. Vision is always of an object. That implies the existence of a subject. The value of the vision is the same as that of the seer. (That is to say, the nature of the vision is on the same plane as that of the seer.) Appearance implies disappearance, also. Whatever appears must also disappear. A vision can never be eternal, but Shiva is eternal.

The *pratyaksha* (vision) of Shiva to the eye signifies the existence of the eyes to see; the *buddhi* (intellect) lying behind the sight; the seer behind the *buddhi* and the sight; and, finally, the Consciousness underlying the seer. This vision is not as real as one imagines it to be, because it is not intimate and inherent; it is not first-hand. It is the result of several successive phases. Of these, Consciousness alone does not vary. It is eternal. It is Shiva. It is the Self.

Vision implies a seer. The seer cannot deny the existence of the Self. There is no moment when the Self as Consciousness does not exist, nor can the seer remain apart from Consciousness. This Consciousness is the eternal Being and the only Being. The seer cannot see himself. Does he deny his existence because he cannot see himself with the eyes as *pratyaksha* (in vision)? No! So, *pratyaksha* does not mean seeing, but Being.

"To Be" is to realize — hence "I Am that I Am." I Am, is Shiva. Nothing else can be without Him. Everything has its being in Shiva and because of Shiva.

Therefore, inquire "Who am I?" Sink deep within and abide as the Self.

That is Shiva as Being. Do not expect to have visions of Him repeated. What is the difference between the objects you see and Shiva? He is both the subject and the object. You cannot be without Shiva. Shiva is always realized *here and now*. If you think you have not realized Him, it is wrong. This is the obstacle for realizing Shiva. Give up that thought also, and realization is there.

D. Yes. But how shall I affect it as quickly as possible?

M. This is the obstacle for realization. Can there be the individual without Shiva? Even now, He is you. There is no question of time. If there be a moment of non-realization, the question of realization can arise. But as it is, you cannot be without Him. He is already realized, ever realized and never non-realized.

Surrender to Him and abide by His will whether he appears or vanishes; await His pleasure. If you ask Him to do as *you* please, it is not surrender but command to Him. You cannot have Him obey you and yet think that you have surrendered. He knows what is best and when and how to do it. Leave everything entirely to Him. His is the burden: you have no longer any cares. All your cares are His. Such is surrender. This is *bhakti*.

Or, inquire to whom these questions arise. Dive deep in the Heart and remain as the Self. One of these two ways is open to the aspirant.

Sri Bhagavan added: There is no being who is not conscious and therefore who is not Shiva. Not only is he Shiva, but also all else of which he is aware or not aware. Yet he thinks in sheer ignorance that he sees the universe in diverse forms. But if he sees his Self, he is not aware of his separateness from the universe; in fact, his individuality and the other entities vanish although they persist in all their forms. Shiva is seen as the universe. But the seer does not see the background itself. Think of the man who sees only the cloth and not the cotton of which it is made; or of the man who sees the pictures moving on the screen in a cinema show and not the screen itself as the background; or again the man who sees the letters which he reads but not the paper on which they are written. The objects are thus Consciousness and forms. But the ordinary person sees the objects in the universe but not Shiva in these forms. Shiva is the Being assuming these forms and the Consciousness seeing them. That is to say, Shiva is the background underlying both the subject and the object, and again Shiva in Repose and Shiva in Action, or Shiva and Shakti, or the Lord and the Universe. Whatever it is said to be, it is only Consciousness whether in repose or in action. Who is there that is not conscious? So, who is not realized? How then can questions arise doubting realization or desiring it? If "I" am not *pratyaksha* to me, I can then say that Shiva is not *pratyaksha*.

These questions arise because you have limited the Self to the body; only then the ideas of *within* and *without*, of subject and object, arise. The objective visions have no intrinsic value. Even if they are everlasting, they cannot satisfy the person. Uma has Shiva always with Her. Both together form *Ardhanariswara*. Yet she wanted to know Shiva in His true nature. She made *tapas*. In her *dhyana*, she saw a bright light. She thought: "This cannot be Shiva, for it is within the compass of my vision. I am greater than this light." So she resumed her *tapas*. Thoughts disappeared. Stillness prevailed. She then realized that Being is Shiva in His true nature.

Muruganar cited Appar's stanza:
> "To remove my darkness and give me light, Thy Grace must work through me only."

Sri Bhagavan mentioned Manikavachakar's:
> "We do *bhajana* and the rest. But we have not seen nor heard of those who had seen Thee."

One cannot see God and yet retain individuality. The seer and the seen unite into one Being. There is no cognizer, nor cognition, nor the cognized. All merge into One Supreme Shiva only!

FEBRUARY 4, 1938

Mr. S. S. Suryanarayana Sastri, Reader in Philosophy, Madras University, arrived this night. He had a doubt, which he said had been cleared on reading Sarma's commentary on "Self-Knowledge." The doubt was: How can the world be an imagination or a thought? Thought is a function of the mind. The mind is located in the brain. The brain is within the skull of a human being, who is only an infinitesimal part of the universe. How, then, can the universe be contained in the cells of the brain?

Sri Bhagavan answered by saying: So long as the mind is considered to be an entity of the kind described, the doubt will persist. But what is mind? Let us consider. The world is seen when the person wakes up from sleep. It comes after the "I"-thought. The head rises up. So the mind has become active. What is the world? It is objects spread out in space. Who comprehends it? The mind. Is not the mind, which comprehends space, itself space (*akasha*)? The space is physical ether (*bhutakasha*). The mind is mental ether (*manakasha*), which is contained in transcendental ether (*chidakasha*). The mind is thus the ether principle, *akasha tattva*. Being the principle of knowledge (*jnana tattva*), it is identified with ether (*akasha*) by metaphysics. Considering it to be ether (*akasha*), there will be no difficulty in reconciling the apparent contradiction in the question. Pure mind (*suddha manas*) is ether (*akasha*). The dynamic and dull (*rajas* and *tamas*) aspects operate as gross objects, etc. Thus, the whole universe is only mental.

Again, consider a man who dreams. He goes to sleep in a room with doors closed so that nothing can intrude on him while asleep. He closes his eyes when sleeping so that he does not see any object. Yet, when he dreams, he sees a whole region in which people live and move about with himself among them. Did this panorama get in through the doors? It was simply unfolded to him by his brain. Is it in the sleeper's brain, or in the brain of the dream individual? It is in the sleeper's brain. How does it hold this vast country in its tiny cells? This must explain the oft-repeated statement that the whole universe is a mere thought or a series of thoughts.

A Swami asked: I feel toothache. Is it only a thought?

M. Yes.

D. Why can I not think that there is no toothache and thus cure myself?

M. When engrossed in other thoughts, one does not feel the toothache. When one sleeps toothache is not felt.

D. But toothache remains all the same.

M. Such is the firm conviction of the reality of the world that it is not easily shaken off. The world does not become for that reason any more real than the individual himself.

D. Now there is the Sino-Japanese war. If it is only in imagination, can or will Sri Bhagavan imagine the contrary and put an end to the war?

M. The Bhagavan of the questioner is as much a thought as the Sino-Japanese war.

(*Laughter.*)

FEBRUARY 7, 1938

Mr. Dhar (Indian Civil Service), a high Officer, and his wife, both young, highly cultured and intelligent, are on a visit here, but they fell ill since their arrival. Mrs. Dhar desired to know how meditation could become steady.

M. What is meditation? It consists in expulsion of thoughts. All the present troubles are due to thoughts and are themselves thoughts. Give up thoughts.

That is happiness and also meditation.

D. How are thoughts given up?

M. The thoughts are for the thinker. Remain as the Self of the thinker and there is an end of thoughts.

Mr. Dhar asked Sri Bhagavan why Brahma, who is Perfection, creates and puts us to ordeals for regaining Him.

M. Where is the individual who asks this question? He is in the universe and included in the creation. How does he raise the question when he is bound in the creation? He must go beyond it and see if any question arises then.

FEBRUARY 8, 1938

Three ladies are on a short visit here, Mrs. Hearst from New Zealand, Mrs. Craig and Mrs. Allison from London. One asked: What is the best way to work for world peace?

M. What is world? What is peace, and who is the worker? The world is not in your sleep and forms a projection of your mind in your *jagrat* (waking state). It is therefore an idea and nothing else. Peace is absence of disturbance. The disturbance is due to the arising of thoughts in the individual, who is only the ego rising up from Pure Consciousness.

To bring about peace means to be free from thoughts and abide as Pure Consciousness. If one remains at peace oneself, there is only peace all about.

D. If it is a question of doing something one considers wrong, and thereby saving someone else from a great wrong, should one do it or refrain?

M. What is right and wrong? There is no standard by which to judge something to be right and another to be wrong. Opinions differ according to the nature of the individual and according to the surroundings. They are again ideas and nothing more. Do not worry about them. But get rid of thoughts. If you always remain in the right, then right will prevail in the world.

D. What should one think of when meditating?

M. What is meditation? It is expulsion of thoughts. You are perturbed by thoughts that rush in one after another. Hold on to one thought so that others are expelled. Continuous practice gives the necessary strength of mind to engage in meditation.

Meditation differs according to the degree of advancement of the seeker. If one is fit for it one might directly hold the thinker; and the thinker will automatically sink into his source, namely Pure Consciousness.

352

If one cannot directly hold the thinker, one must meditate on God; and in due course, the same individual will have become sufficiently pure to hold the thinker and sink into absolute Being.

One of the ladies was not satisfied with this answer and asked for further elucidation.
Sri Bhagavan then pointed out that to see wrong in another is one's own wrong. The discrimination between right and wrong is the origin of the sin. One's own sin is reflected outside and the individual in ignorance superimposes it on another. The best course for one is to reach the state in which such discrimination does not arise. Do you see wrong or right in your sleep? Did you not exist in sleep? Be asleep even in the wakeful state, abide as the Self, and remain uncontaminated by what goes on around you.

Moreover, however much you might advise them, your hearers may not rectify themselves. Be in the right yourself and remain silent. Your silence will have more effect than your words or deeds. That is the development of willpower. Then the world becomes the Kingdom of Heaven, which is within you.

D. If one is to withdraw oneself, why is there the world?

M. Where is the world and where does one go withdrawing oneself? Does one fly in an airplane beyond space? Is it withdrawal?

The fact is this: the world is only an idea. What do you say: Are you within the world or is the world within you?

D. I am in the world; I am part of it.

M. That is the mistake. If the world were to exist apart from you, does it come and tell you that it exists? No, you see it exist. You see it when you are awake and not when asleep. If it exists apart from you, it must tell you so and you must be aware of it even in your sleep.

D. I became aware of it in my *jagrat*.

M. Do you become aware of yourself and then of the world? Or do you become aware of the world and then of yourself? Or do you become aware of both simultaneously?

D. I must say simultaneously.

M. Were you or were you not, before becoming aware of yourself? Do you admit your continued existence before and when you become aware of the world?

D. Yes.

M. If always existing yourself, why are you not aware of the world in sleep if it exists apart from the Self?

D. I become aware of myself and of the world, also.

M. So you become aware of yourself. Who becomes aware of whom? Are there two selves?

D. No.

M. So you see that it is wrong to suppose that Awareness has passing phases. The Self is always aware. When the Self identifies itself as the seer, it sees objects. The creation of the subject and the object is the creation of the world. Subjects and objects are creations in Pure Consciousness. You see pictures moving on the screen in a cinema show. When you are intent on the pictures, you are not aware of the screen. But the pictures cannot be seen without the screen behind. The world stands for the pictures and Consciousness stands for the screen. The Consciousness is pure. It is the same as the Self, which is eternal and unchanging. Get rid of the subject and object, and Pure Consciousness alone remains.

D. But why did Pure *Brahman* become *Ishvara* and manifest the universe if He did not mean it?

M. Did *Brahman* or *Ishvara* tell you so? You say that *Brahman* became *Ishvara*, and so on. This, too, you did not say in your sleep. Only in your *jagrat* state you speak of *Brahman, Ishvara,* and universe. The *jagrat* state is a duality of subject and object — owing to the rise of thoughts. So they are your thought-creations.

D. But the world exists in my sleep even though I am not aware.

M. What is the proof of its existence?

D. Others are aware of it.

M. Do they say so to you when you are in sleep, or do you become aware of others who see the world in your sleep?

D. No, but God is always aware.

M. Leave God alone. Speak for yourself. You do not know God. He is only what you think of Him. Is He apart from you? He is that Pure Consciousness in which all ideas are formed. You are that Consciousness.

FEBRUARY 10, 1938

Mrs. Dhar: Sri Bhagavan advises practice of inquiry even when one is engaged in external activities. The finality of such inquiry is the realization of the Self, and consequently the breath must stop. If the breath should stop, how will the work go on? In other words, how will the breath stop when one is working?

M. There is confusion between the means and the end (i.e., *sadhana* and *sadhya*). Who is the inquirer? The aspirant and not the *siddha*. Inquiry signifies that the inquirer considers himself separate from inquiry.

So long as this duality lasts, the inquiry must be continued, i.e., until the individuality disappears and the Self is realized to be only the eternal Being (including both inquiry and inquirer).

The Truth is that the Self is constant and unintermittent Awareness. The object of inquiry is to find the true nature of the Self as Awareness. Let one practice inquiry so long as separateness is perceived.

Once realization arises, there is no further need for inquiry. The question will also not arise. Can awareness ever think of questioning who is aware? Awareness remains pure and simple.

The inquirer is aware of his own individuality. Inquiry does not stand in the way of his individual awareness; nor does external work interfere with such awareness. If work, seemingly external, does not obstruct the individual awareness, will the work, realized to be not separate from the Self, obstruct the uninterrupted Awareness of the Self, which is One without a second, and which is not an individual separate from work?

Mrs. Dhar: I form part of the creation and so remain dependent. I cannot solve the riddle until I become independent. Yet I ask Sri Bhagavan, should He not answer the question for me?

M. Yes. It is Bhagavan that says, "Become independent and solve the riddle yourself. It is for you to do it." Again: where are you now that you ask this question? Are you in the world, or is the world within you? You must admit that the world is not perceived in your sleep although you cannot deny your existence then. The world appears when you wake up. So where is it? Clearly the world is your thought. Thoughts are your projections. The "I" is first created and then the world. The world is created by the "I," which in its turn rises up from the Self. The riddle of the creation of the world is thus solved if you solve the creation of the "I." So I say, find your Self.

Again, does the world come and ask you "Why do 'I' exist? How was 'I' created?" It is you who ask the question. The questioner must establish the relationship between the world and himself. He must admit that the world is his own imagination. Who imagines it? Let him again find the "I" and then the Self.

Moreover, all the scientific and theological explanations do not harmonize. The diversities in such theories clearly show the uselessness of seeking such explanations; they are purely mental or intellectual and nothing more. Still, all of them are true according to the standpoint of the individual. There is no creation in the state of realization. When one sees the Self, the world is not seen. So see the Self and realize that there has been no creation.

Mrs. Dhar has been laid up and is unable to go to the Hall and so feels unhappy. This was mentioned to Sri Bhagavan. He said: Well, thinking like this keeps her always in the Presence. This is better than remaining in the Hall and thinking of something else.

FEBRUARY 11, 1938
The following article, "Contact with Saints," which appeared in The Vision *(published by Anandashram) was read out to Sri Bhagavan.*

A Danger
"Seek the company of saints by all means, but do not remain indefinitely with them. The adage 'familiarity breeds contempt' applies even in their case," writes Swami Ramdas in an article in *The Vision.*

"Spiritual growth is, no doubt, largely dependent on suitable association. Company of saints is, therefore, held to be essential for a seeker after truth. But it must not be understood that the seeker should permanently stick on to them.

"He may, for a brief period, remain in their contact and, thereby drawing inspiration and guidance, get himself thoroughly awakened to the consciousness of the indwelling Reality. It would be well for him to depart from them before the light and inspiration that he has received diminishes or disappears.

May Turn Scoffers
"There are many cases known to the writer and many others of which he has heard and read, in which such continued dwelling in the company of saints has not only cooled down the ardor and aspiration of the seekers but also turned them into scoffers and skeptics. The fall of a *sadhaka* from faith, purity, and aspiration does him incalculable harm.

"A young plant growing beneath the shade of a full-grown giant tree does not develop strength and stature. Its growth will be dwarfed, shriveled, and diseased. Whereas if the same plant were put into the open ground directly exposed to the storms, heat, cold, and other rigors of changing weather, it is bound to grow into a mighty tree drawing sustenance from both above and below.

Stifled Growth

"This analogy of the plant aptly illustrates the stunted life of a seeker who is attached merely to the outward personality of a saint and spends all his days in close association with him. Here the initiative for free expression of his unique spiritual possibilities is stifled. He fails to cultivate the fundamental qualities for his advancement — fearlessness, self-dependence, and endurance. The one great Guide that should control his mind, speech, and body should be the almighty Spirit within him. To surrender to this Spirit and become its very embodiment is his goal. To stand on his own legs, struggle and grow by his own strength and experience, and lastly to hand himself over to God by his own endeavor brings true liberation and peace.

"From what has been said above, it must not be construed that reflection is cast upon the greatness and efficacy of the company of God-realized souls. Such a contact is the most effective means for a rapid spiritual evolution of the soul. In fact, the Grace of saints is an invaluable aid for *sadhana* and without it the condition of the aspirant is like a bird beating in vain its wings against the bars of the cage for freedom. Saints are the saviors and liberators. The Hindu conception of a saint is that he is the very embodiment of God himself. So honor him, derive the rare benefit of his society, serve him with a frank and pure heart, listen intently to his words of advice, and strive to act up to them and achieve the fullest knowledge of the Truth you are in quest of. But seek not to remain attached to his person and lose the spiritual gifts you obtained from him by first contacts."

Maharshi listened and remained silent. He was requested to say if contact with saints could be a danger. He then quoted a Tamil stanza, which says that contact with the Guru should be kept up till videha mukti *(liberation at death). He also stated "Where is the* Satpurusha? *He is within." Then he quoted another stanza meaning:*

"O Master, Who has been within me in all my past incarnations and Who manifested as a human being, only to speak the language understood by me and lead me."

FEBRUARY 12, 1938

Mrs. Rosita Forbes was said to be in India. Sri Bhagavan said: The explorers seek happiness in finding curiosities, discovering new lands and undergoing risks in adventures. They are thrilling. But where is pleasure found? Only within. Pleasure is not to be sought in the external world.

FEBRUARY 13, 1938

Sri Bhagavan said that the nondual idea is advised, but not *advaita* in action. How will one learn *advaita* if one does not find a Master and receive instructions? Is there not duality then? That is the meaning.

FEBRUARY 14, 1938

Quoting Alexander Selkirk's soliloquy, Sri Bhagavan said: The happiness of solitude is not found in retreats. It may be had even in busy centers. Happiness is not to be sought in solitude or in busy centers. It is in the Self.

FEBRUARY 17, 1938

Observing the moon before the rising sun, Sri Bhagavan remarked: See the moon and also the cloud in the sky. There is no difference in their brilliance. The moon looks only like a speck of cloud. The *jnani's* mind is like this moon before sunlight. It is there, but not shining of itself.

FEBRUARY 18, 1938

As Sri Bhagavan was going through the letters, which arrived today, he read out one of them as follows: A Brahmin boy working in a household went to sleep as usual In his sleep, he cried out. When he woke up, he said that he felt his *prana* going out of the body through the mouth and nostrils. So he cried. Soon after, he found himself dead and the soul taken to *Vaikunta* where God Vishnu was surrounded by other gods and devotees with prominent *Vaishnavite* marks on their foreheads. Vishnu said, "This man should be brought here at two o'clock tomorrow. Why has he been brought here now?" The boy then woke up and related his experience. The next day, at two o'clock, he passed away.

Mrs. Dhar had been anxious to ask some questions and get help from Sri Bhagavan. She approached him with great hesitation and gently related her troubles: My attempts at concentration are frustrated by sudden palpitations of the heart and accompanying hard, short and quick breaths. Then my thoughts also rush out and the mind becomes uncontrollable. Under healthy conditions I am more successful, and my breath comes to a standstill with deep concentration. I had long been anxious to get the benefit of Sri Bhagavan's proximity for the successful culmination of my meditation, and so came here after considerable effort. I fell ill here. I could not meditate and so I felt depressed. I made a determined effort to concentrate my mind, even though I was troubled by short and quick breaths. Though I am partly successful, it does not satisfy me. The time for my leaving this place is drawing near. I feel more and more depressed as I contemplate departing. Here I find people obtaining peace by meditation in the Hall, whereas I am not blessed with such peace. This itself has a depressing effect on me.

M. This thought, "I am not able to concentrate," is itself an obstacle. Why should the thought arise?

D. Can one remain without thoughts rising all the twenty-four hours of the day? Should I remain without meditation?

M. What is "hours?" It is a concept. Each question of yours is prompted by a thought.

Your nature is Peace and Happiness. Thoughts are the obstacles to realization. One's meditation or concentration is meant to get rid of obstacles and not to gain the Self. Does anyone remain apart from the Self? No! The true nature of the Self is declared to be Peace. If the same peace is not found, the non-finding is only a thought which is alien to the Self. One practices meditation only to get rid of these alien fancies. So, then, a thought must be quelled as soon as it rises. Whenever a thought arises, do not be carried away by it. You become aware of the body when you forget the Self. But can you forget the Self? Being the Self, how can you forget it? There must be two selves for one to forget the other. It is absurd. So the Self is not depressed; it is not imperfect, it is ever happy. The contrary feeling is a mere thought which has actually no stamina in it. Be rid of thoughts. Why should one attempt meditation? Being the Self, one remains always realized — only be free from thoughts.

You think that your health does not permit your meditation. This depression must be traced to its origin. The origin is the wrong identification of the body with the Self. The disease is not of the Self. It is of the body. But the body does not come and tell you that it is possessed by the disease. It is you who say so. Why? Because you have wrongly identified yourself with the body.

The body itself is a thought. Be as you really are. There is no reason to be depressed.

Mrs. Dhar was called away and she retired. The question was however pursued as follows:

D. Sri Bhagavan's answers do not permit us to put further questions, not because our minds are peaceful but we are unable to argue the point. Our discontent is not at an end. For the physical ailments to go, the mental ailments should go. Both go when thoughts go. Thoughts do not go without effort. Effort is not possible with the present weakness of mind. The mind needs Grace to gain strength. Grace must manifest only after surrender. So all questions, wittingly or unwittingly, amount to asking for Sri Bhagavan's Grace.

M. (*Smiling.*) Yes.

D. Surrender is said to be *bhakti*. But Sri Bhagavan is known to favor inquiry for the Self. There is thus confusion in the hearer.

M. Surrender can take effect only when done with full knowledge. Such knowledge comes after inquiry. It ends in surrender.

D. The knowledge of the Supreme Being is after transcending the individual self. This is *jnana*. Where is the need for surrender?

M. Quite so. There is no difference between *jnana* and surrender. (*Smile.*)

D. How is the questioner satisfied then? The only alternative left is association with the wise or devotion to God (*satsanga* or *Ishvara bhakti*).

M. (*Smiling*) Yes.

FEBRUARY 21, 1938

In the course of the conversation, Sri Bhagavan spoke appreciatingly of the services of Palaniswami and Ayyaswami — his former attendants.

He said that they raised in the garden two crude platforms, which were occupied by himself and Palaniswami; they were most comfortable. They were made of straw and bamboo mats and were even more comfortable than the sofa here. Palaniswami used to pass through the footpath between rows of prickly pear to bring begged food every night from Kizhnathoor. Though Sri Bhagavan protested, Palaniswami persisted in doing so. He was free from greed or attachment of any kind. He had earned some money by service in the Straits Settlements and deposited his small savings with some-

one in the town from whom he used to draw in emergencies. He was offered a comfortable living in his native village, which he refused, and continued to live with Sri Bhagavan until the end.

Ayyaswami had worked under a European in South Africa and was
clean, active, and capable. He could manage even ten ashrams at a time.
He was also free from any attachment or greed. He was loyal to Palaniswami,
even fond of him. He was more capable than the other.

Annamalai first visited Maharshi in Virupaksha cave; he later went to
Kovilur and studied some Tamil scriptures. He returned to Skandasramam.
He died in January 1922, in his twenty-ninth year. In the meantime, he had
composed thirty-six stanzas in Tamil full of significance and fervor.

(*Sri Bhagavan had them read out and briefly explained their meaning.*)

March 5, 1938

A passage from Arunachala Mahatmya *(the Glory of Arunachala) was read out.
It related to Pangunni (a lame sage) who had his legs made whole by the Grace of Sri
Arunachala. Sri Bhagavan then related the story of a man who he had seen while
living in Gurumurtham:*
The man was Kuppu Iyer. His legs were useless and he could not walk. He
was once on his way to Vettavalam, moving on his buttocks. An old man
suddenly appeared before him and said "Get up and walk. Why do you
move on your buttocks?" Kuppa Iyer was excited and beside himself. Involuntarily, he rose up and walked freely. After going a short distance, he
looked behind to see the stranger who made him walk. But he could not
find anyone. He narrated the incident to all those who were surprised to
see him walk. Any old man in the town can bear witness to Kuppa Iyer
regaining the use of his legs.

Again, a girl from the girl's school was waylaid and robbed of her jewels. Suddenly an old man appeared on the scene, rescued the girl, escorted
her to her home, and then disappeared.

Often such mysterious happenings occur in Tiruvannamalai.

March 6, 1938

Sri Bhagavan explained to a retired Judge of the High Court some points in the
Upadesa Saram *as follows:*
1. Meditation should remain unbroken as a current. If unbroken, it is
   called *samadhi or kundalini shakti.*

2. The mind may be latent and merge in the Self; it must necessarily rise up again. After it rises up, one finds oneself only as ever before. For in this state the mental predispositions are present in latent form to remanifest under favorable conditions.

3. The mind activities can be completely destroyed. This differs from the former mind, for here the attachment is lost, never to reappear. Even though the man sees the world after he has been in the *samadhi* state, the world will be taken only at its worth, that is to say it is the phenomenon of the One Reality. The True Being can be realized only in *samadhi*; what was then is also now. Otherwise, it cannot be Reality or Ever-present Being. What was in *samadhi* is here and now, too. Hold it and it is your natural condition of Being. *Samadhi* practice must lead to it. Otherwise, how can *nirvikalpa samadhi* be of any use in which a man remains as a log of wood? He must necessarily rise up from it sometime or other and face the world. But in *sahaja samadhi*, he remains unaffected by the world.

So many pictures pass over the cinema screen: fire burns away everything, water drenches all, but the screen remains unaffected. The scenes are only phenomena, which pass away leaving the screen as it was. Similarly the world phenomena simply pass on before the *jnani*, leaving him unaffected.

You may say that people find pain or pleasure in worldly phenomena. It is owing to superimposition. This must not happen. With this end in view, practice is made.

Practice lies in one of the two courses: devotion or knowledge. Even these are not the goals. *Samadhi* must be gained; it must be continuously practiced until *sahaja samadhi* results. Then there is nothing more to do.

Mr. Vaidyalingam, an employee of the National Bank, said: By meditation, manifestation disappears and *ananda* results. However, it is short-lived. How is it made ever-abiding?

M. By scorching the predispositions.

D. Is not the Self the witness only (*sakshimatra*)?

M. "Witness" is applicable when there is an object to be seen. Then it is duality. The Truth lies beyond both. In the mantra, *sakshi cheta kevalo nirgunascha*, the word *sakshi* must be understood as *sannidhi* (presence), without which there could be nothing. See how the sun is necessary for daily activities. He does not however, form part of the world actions; yet they cannot occur without the sun. He is the witness of the activities. So it is with the Self.

MARCH 7, 1938

Yogi Ramiah: All actions take place owing to *Shakti*. How far does *Shakti* go? Can she effect anything without one's own effort?

M. The answer to the question depends on what the *Purusha* is understood to be. Is he the ego or the Self?

D. *Purusha* is *svarupa*.

M. But he cannot make any *prayatna* (effort).

D. *Jiva* is the one who makes the *prayatna*.

M. So long as egoity lasts, *prayatna* is necessary. When egoity ceases, actions become spontaneous. The ego acts in the presence of the Self. It cannot exist without the Self.

The Self makes the universe what it is by His *Shakti,* yet He does not Himself act. Sri Krishna says in the *Bhagavad Gita,* "I am not the doer and yet actions go on." It is clear from the *Mahabharata* that he effected very wonderful actions. Yet He says that He is not the doer. It is like the sun and the world actions.

D. He is without *abhimana* (attachment) whereas the *jiva* is with *abhimana*.

M. Yes. Being attached, he acts and also reaps the fruits. If the fruits are according to his desire he is happy; otherwise, he is miserable. Happiness and misery are due to his attachment. If actions were to take place without attachment, there would be no expectation of fruit.

D. Can actions take place spontaneously without individual effort? Should we not cook our food in order to eat it later?

M. *Atman* acts through the ego. All actions are due to efforts only. A sleeping child is fed by his mother. The child eats food without being wide-awake and then denies having taken food in sleep. However, the mother knows what happened. Similarly, the *jnani* acts unawares. Others see him act, but he does not know it himself. Owing to fear of Him, the wind blows, etc. That is the order of things. He ordains everything and the universe acts accordingly, yet He does not know. Therefore, He is called the great Doer. Every embodied being (*ahamkari*) is bound by *niyama* (observance). Even Brahma cannot transgress it.

(*This devotee later explained the significance of his question. He hears Sri Bhagavan say that the world goes on and the individual needs are met by Divine Will.*

But he finds that Sri Bhagavan wakes up the Ashramites at about 4:00 a.m. to cut vegetables for the day's curry. He wanted to have the doubt cleared for his own benefit and the question was not meant for general discussion.)

MARCH 10, 1938

As Sri Bhagavan was going out, the following Vedic chant was heard from a hut:
"*Antaraditya manasa jvalantam — Brahmana vindat.*"
The interior sun, the Self, shines though the mind.

Sri Bhagavan drew our attention to it and remarked: In the *Taittiriya Upanishad*, also, He is said to be made of gold, etc. What does it all mean? Although the sun and the other luminaries are said to be self-luminous, yet they do not shine forth of themselves but by the light of the Supreme Being (*na tatra suryo . . . vibhati.*) So long as they are said to be separate from *Brahman*, their "Self-luminosity" is the luminosity of *Brahman*. All these mantras mentioning the sun, etc. speak only of *Brahman*.

Yogi Ramiah asked: A Master is approached by an aspirant for enlightenment. The Master says that *Brahman* has no qualities, nor stain, nor movement, etc. Does he not then speak as an individual? How can the aspirant's ignorance be wiped off unless the Master speaks in this way? Do the words of the Master as an individual amount to Truth?
M. To whom should the Master speak? Whom does he instruct? Does he see anyone different from the Self?
D. But the disciple is asking the Master for elucidation.
M. True, but does the Master see him as different? The ignorance of the disciple consists in not knowing that all are Self-realized. Can anyone exist apart from the Self? The Master simply points out that ignorance lies there and therefore does not stand apart as an individual.

What is Realization? Is it to see God with four hands, bearing conch, wheel, club, etc.? Even if God should appear in that form, how is the disciple's ignorance wiped out? The truth must be eternal realization. The direct perception is ever-present Experience. God Himself is known as directly perceived. It does not mean that He appears before the devotee as said above. Unless the Realization is eternal, it cannot serve any useful purpose. Can the appearance with four hands be eternal realization? It is phenomenal and illusory. There must be a seer. The seer alone is real and eternal.

Let God appear as the light of a million suns: Is it *pratyaksha?*

To see it, the eyes, the mind, etc. are necessary. It is indirect knowledge, whereas the seer is direct experience. The seer alone is *pratyaksha.* All other perceptions are only secondary knowledge. The present superimposition of the body as "I" is so deep-rooted that the vision before the eyes is considered *pratyaksha* (direct perception), but not the seer himself. No one wants realization because there is no one who is not realized. Can anyone say that he is not already realized or that he is apart from the Self? No. Evidently, all are realized. What makes him unhappy is the desire to exercise extraordinary powers. He knows that he cannot do so. Therefore, he wants God to appear before him, confer all His powers on the devotee, and keep Himself in the background. In short, God should abdicate His powers in favor of the man.

D. It is all right for *mahatmas* like Sri Bhagavan to speak out so plainly. Because the Truth does not swerve from you, you consider it easy for all others. Nevertheless, the ordinary folk have a real difficulty.

M. Then does anyone say that he is not the Self?

D. I meant to say that no one else has the courage to put things straight like Maharshi.

M. Where is the courage in stating things as they are?

As a European Countess was leaving for Europe tonight, she requested him to bless her and her family.

M. You do not go anywhere away from the Presence as you imagine. The Presence is everywhere. The body moves from place to place, yet it does not leave the one Presence. So no one can be out of sight of the Supreme Presence. Since you identify one body with Sri Bhagavan and another body with yourself, you find two separate entities and speak of going away from here. Wherever you may be, you cannot leave Me.

To illustrate it: The pictures move on the screen in a cinema show; but does the screen itself move? No. The Presence is the screen: you, I, and others are the pictures. The individuals may move, but not the Self.

D. The *avatars* are said to be more glorious than the self-realized *jnanis.* *Maya* does not affect them from birth; divine powers are manifest, new religions are started, and so on.

Sri Bhagavan quoted the following:

"Jnani tvatmaiva me matam.

Sarvam khalvidam brahma."

When the Self alone is seen within then nothing is seen to be apart from the Self.

How is an avatar different from a jnani; or how can there be an avatar as distinct from the universe?

D. The eye (*chakshu*) is said to be the repository (*ayatana*) of all forms; so the ear (*srotra*) is of all sounds, etc. The one *Chaitanya* operates as all; no miracles are possible without the aid of the senses (*indriyas*). How can there be miracles at all? If they are said to surpass human understanding, so are the creations in dreams. Where then is the miracle?

The distinction between *avataras* and *jnanis* is absurd. "Knower of *Brahman* becomes *Brahman* only" is otherwise contradicted.

M. Quite so.

March 15, 1938

A large group of Punjabis arrived here in a pilgrim special. They came to Ramanasramam at about 8:45 a.m. and sat quietly for a long time. At about 9:20 one of them said: Your reputation has spread in the Punjab. We have traveled a long distance to have your *darshan*. Kindly tell us something by way of instruction.

(There was no oral reply. Sri Bhagavan smiled and gazed on.)

After some time, the visitor asked: Which is the best — the *yoga*, the *bhakti* or the *jnana* path?

(Still Sri Bhagavan smiled and gazed as before. He left the Hall for a few minutes and the visitors began to disperse. A sprinkling of them continued to sit in the Hall. A longstanding disciple told the visitor that Sri Bhagavan had answered him by his Silence, which was even more eloquent than words.)

After Sri Bhagavan returned, the visitor began to speak a little. In the course of his speech, he said: It is all right for those who believe in God. Others ask — Is there a God?

M. Are you there?

D. Quite so. That is the question. I see before my eyes a battalion of soldiers passing. Therefore, I am. The world must have been created by God. How shall I see the Creator?

M. See yourself, who sees these, and the problem is solved.

D. Is it to sit silently or read sacred books or concentrate the mind? *Bhakti*

366

helps concentration. People fall at the feet of the *bhakta*. If it does not happen, he feels disappointed and his *bhakti* fades.

M. The longing for happiness never fades. That is *bhakti*.

D. How shall I get it more quickly? Suppose I concentrate two hours today? If I try to lengthen the period the next day, I fall asleep because I get tired of the job.

M. You do not get tired in sleep. The same person is now present here. Why should you be tired now? Because your mind is restless and wanders — it gets tired, and not you.

D. I am a businessman. How shall I get on with business and have peace of mind, also?

M. This is also a thought. Give up this thought also and remain as your true Self.

D. It is said: "Do your duty without any expectation of results. How shall I acquire that frame of mind?"

M. You need not aspire for or get any new state. Get rid of your present thoughts, that is all.

D. How shall I get the *bhakti* necessary for it?

M. It is *bhakti* to get rid of thoughts, which are only alien to you (the Self).

D. What is thought-force, mesmerism, etc.? There was a doctor in Paris — called Dr. Coué. He was illiterate, yet was able to cure many incurable diseases by will-force. He used to say: "Generate power to cure yourself. The power is within you."

M. It is through the same willpower that the seat of all diseases, the body, has arisen.

D. So it is said thoughts manifest as objects.

M. This thought must be for *mukti* (liberation).

D. God must enable us to get rid of the other thoughts.

M. This is again a thought. Let that which has incarnated raise the question. You are not that because you are free from thoughts.

Another visitor from Rawalpindi asked: The *Atman* is formless. How shall I concentrate on it?

M. Leave alone the *Atman* which you say is formless or intangible. Mind is tangible to you. Hold the mind and it will do.

D. Mind itself is very subtle and is also the same as the *Atman*. How shall we know the nature of the mind? You have said that all supports are useless. What should be our stand then?

M. Where does your mind stand?

D. Where does it stand?
M. Ask the mind itself.
D. I ask you now. Should we concentrate on mind then?
M. Um!
D. But what is the nature of the mind? It is formless. The problem is perplexing.
M. Why are you perplexed?
D. The *sastras* want us to concentrate and I cannot do it.
M. Through what *sastras* have we known our existence?
D. It is a matter of experience. But I want to concentrate.
M. Be free from thoughts. Do not hold on to anything. They do not hold you. Be yourself.
D. I do not yet understand as to where I take my stand and concentrate. Can I meditate on my mind?
M. Whose mind?
D. My own mind?
M. Who are you? The question now resolves itself all right.
  (*All retired for lunch.*)

The visitor returned at 2:30 p.m. and pursued the same question.
D. Maharshi advises the seeker to get rid of thoughts. On what should I concentrate the mind after all the thoughts are expelled? I do not see where I stand then and on what I should concentrate.
M. For whom is the concentration?
D. For the mind.
M. Then concentrate the mind.
D. On what?
M. Answer the question yourself. What is the mind? Why should you concentrate?
D. I do not know what the mind is. I ask Maharshi.
M. Maharshi does not seek to know the mind. The questioner must question the mind itself as to what it is.
D. Maharshi advises that the mind should be divested of thoughts.
M. This is itself a thought.
D. When all thoughts disappear, what then remains?
M. Is the mind different from thoughts?
D. No. The mind is made up of thoughts. My point is this: When all thoughts are got rid of, how shall I concentrate the mind?
M. Is not this also a thought?

D. Yes, but I am advised to concentrate.

M. Why should you concentrate? Why should you not allow your thoughts free play?

D. The *sastras* say that the thoughts, thus playing free, lead us astray — that is, to unreal and changeful things.

M. So then, you want not to be led to unreal and changeful things. Your thoughts are unreal and changeful. You want to hold the Reality. That is exactly what I say. The thoughts are unreal. Get rid of them.

D. I understand now. Yet there is a doubt. "Not a trice can you remain inactive." How shall I be able to rid myself of thoughts?

M. The same *Gita* says: "Although all actions take place, I am not the doer." It is like the sun towards the world activities. The Self always remains actionless, whereas thoughts arise and subside. The Self is Perfection; it is immutable; the mind is limited and changeful. You need only cast off your limitations. Your perfection thus stands revealed.

D. Grace is necessary for that.

M. Grace is ever present. The only thing necessary is that you surrender to It.

D. I surrender and pray that even if I go wrong, I may be forcibly drawn to it.

M. Is this surrender? Surrender to be complete must be unquestioning.

D. Yes, I surrender. You say I must dive into the ocean of the Self like a pearl diver into the sea.

M. Because you are now thinking that you are out of the ocean of Consciousness.

D. I practice *pranayama*. It generates heat in the body. What should I do?

M. The heat will pass away when the mind gains calm.

D. That is true but most difficult.

M. This is again a thought, which is an obstacle.

Someone remarked: It is said that those who live or die within a thirty-mile radius of Arunachala, get *mukti* (Liberation) unasked. It is also admitted that only by *jnana* is liberation obtained. The *purana* also remarks that *Vedanta Vijnana* is difficult to get. So *mukti* is difficult. But life or death round about the Hill bestows *mukti* so easily. How can that be?

M. Shiva says, "By My command." Those who live here need no initiation, *diksha*, etc., but get *mukti*. Such is the command of Shiva.

D. The *purana* also says that those who are born here are Shiva's group of followers, such as ghosts, spirits, disembodied beings, etc.

M. So it is said of other *khetras* (sacred places), as well, e.g., Tiruvarur,

Chidambaram.

D. How does mere life or death here confer *mukti?* It is difficult to understand.

Sri Bhagavan:

"*Darsanad Abhrasadasi jananat Kamalalaye, Kasyantu maranan muktih smaranad Arunachalam.*"

To see Chidambaram, to be born in Tiruvarur, to die in Benares, or merely think of Arunachala, is to be assured of Liberation.

Jananat Kamalalaye means, "by being born in *Kamalalaya.*" What is it? It is the Heart.

Similarly, *Abhrasadasi* — Seat of Consciousness. Again, *Kasi* is the Light of Realization. Remembering Arunachala completes the verse. It must be understood in the same sense.

D. So *bhakti* is necessary.

M. Everything depends on one's outlook. One sees that all born in Tiruvarur or visiting Chidambaram, or dying in Benares, or contemplating Arunachala, are *muktas.*

D. I think of Arunachala, but still am not a *mukta.*

M. Change of outlook is all that is necessary. See what such a change did for Arjuna. He had the vision of the Cosmic Self. Sri Krishna says: "Gods and saints are eager to see my Cosmic Form. I have not fulfilled their desire. Yet I endow divine sight by which you can see that Form." Well, having said so, does He show what He is? No. He asks Arjuna to see in Him all that he desires to see. If that were His real form, it must be changeless and known for what it is worth. Instead, Arjuna is commanded to see whatever he desires. So where is the Cosmic Form? It must be in Arjuna.

Furthermore, Arjuna finds Gods and saints in that form and they are praising the Lord. If the form is withheld from the Gods and saints as stated by Krishna, who are they of Arjuna's vision?

D. They must be in his imagination.

M. They are there because of Arjuna's outlook.

D. Then the outlook must be changed by God's Grace.

M. Yes. That happens to *bhaktas.*

D. A man dreams of a tiger, takes fright and wakes up. The dream tiger appears to the dream ego, who is also frightened. When he wakes up, how is it that that ego disappears, and the man wakes up as the waking ego?

M. That establishes that the ego is the same. Dream, wakefulness, and sleep are passing phases for the same ego.

D. It is so difficult to spot the mind. The same difficulty is shared by all.
M. You can never find the mind through mind. Pass beyond it in order to find it non-existent.
D. Then one must directly go to seek the ego. It is so?
M. That's it.

Mind, ego, intellect are all different names for one single inner organ (*antahkarana*). The mind is only the aggregate of thoughts. Thoughts cannot exist but for the ego. So all thoughts are pervaded by ego (*aham*). Seek wherefrom the "I" rises, and the other thoughts will disappear.
D. What remains cannot be "I," but Pure Consciousness.
M. Quite so. You start seeking happiness. On analysis, you find that misery is caused by thoughts. They are called the mind. While trying to control the mind, you seek the "I" and get fixed in Being-Knowledge-Bliss.

Another devotee: What, then, is the mind?
M. Mind is consciousness, which has assumed limitations. You are originally unlimited and perfect. Later, you take on limitations and become the mind.
D. It is *avarana* (veiling), then. How does this happen?
M. To whom is the *avarana*? It is the same as *avidya* (ignorance), ego, or the mind.
D. *Avarana* means obscuration. Who is obscured? How does it arise?
M. The limitation is itself obscuration. No questions will arise if limitations are transcended.

MARCH 16, 1938

The Heart of the *Upanishads* is construed as *Hridayam,* meaning: This (is) the center. That is, it is where the mind rises and subsides, the seat of Realization. When I say that it is the Self, people imagine it is within the body. When I ask where the Self remains in one's sleep, they seem to think it is within the body, but unaware of the body and its surroundings like a man confined in a dark room. To such people, it is necessary to say that the seat of Realization is somewhere within the body. The name of the center is the Heart; but it is confounded with the physical heart organ.

When a man dreams, he creates himself (i.e., the *ahamkara*, the seer) and his surroundings. All of them are later withdrawn into himself. The one became many, along with the seer. Similarly, the one becomes many in the waking state. The objective world is really subjective. An astronomer discovers a new star at immeasurable distance and announces that its light takes thousands of years to reach the earth. Well, where is the star, in fact? Is it not in the observer? But people wonder how a huge globe, larger than the Sun, at such a distance, can be contained in the brain-cells of a man. The space, the magnitudes, and the paradox are all in the mind only. How do they exist there? Inasmuch as you become aware of them, you must admit a light, which illumines them. These thoughts are absent in sleep but rise up on waking. So this light is transient, having an origin and an end. The consciousness of "I" is permanent and continuous. So this cannot be the aforementioned light. It is different but has no independent existence. Therefore, it must be *abhasa* (reflected light). The light in the brain is thus reflected knowledge (*abhasa samvit*) or reflected being (*abhasa sat*). The true knowledge (*Samvit*) or Being (*Sat*) is in the center called Heart (*Hridaya*). When one wakes up from sleep it is reflected in the head, and so the head is no longer lying prone but rises up. From there, the consciousness spreads all over the body and so the superimposed "I" functions as the wakeful entity.

The pure light in the brain is *suddha manas* (the pure mind) which later becomes contaminated and is *malina manas,* the one ordinarily found.

All these are, however, contained in the Self. The body and its counterparts are in the Self. The Self is not confined in the body, as is commonly supposed.

Sri Maharshi read out the following news item from a paper: A forest guard armed with a rifle was going in the jungle and noticed two bright spots in a thicket. On closer approach to find out what they were, he was face to face with a huge tiger within a few yards of him. He threw down his gun, and assumed a prayerful attitude towards the jungle king. The tiger stood up and slowly moved away without injuring him.

MARCH 21, 1938

Dr. Stanley Jones, a Christian missionary, visited Maharshi. He writes books and also lectures. He has two Ashrams under his control in North India. Another gentleman and two ladies accompanied him. At present, he is writing a book, "On the Indian Road" and wants to meet the spiritually great men in India so that he may collect material for this work. He wishes to know how the Indian sages have proceeded and what they have found as their experience of divinity. So he asked several questions. The following is only a short sketch of his interview:

D. What is your quest? What is the goal? How far have you progressed?

M. The goal is the same for all. But tell me why you should be in search of a goal? Why are you not content with the present condition?

D. Is there then no goal?

M. Not so. What makes you seek a goal? It is a counter-question to be answered by you.

D. I have my own ideas of these subjects. I want to know what Maharshi has to say.

M. Maharshi has no doubts to be cleared.

D. Well, I consider the goal to be realization by the lower mind of the higher mind so that the Kingdom of Heaven might endure here on earth. The lower mind is incomplete and must be made perfect by realization of the higher mind.

M. So then you admit a lower mind which is incomplete and which seeks realization of the higher so that it may become perfect. Is that lower mind apart from the higher mind? Is it independent of the other?

D. The Kingdom of Heaven was brought down on Earth by Jesus Christ. I consider him to be the Kingdom personified. I want everyone to realize the same. He said: "I am hungry with other men's hunger" and so on. Mutual partnership in pleasure and pain is the Kingdom of Heaven. If that Kingdom is universalized, everyone will feel at one with the rest.

M. You speak of the differences between the lower and the higher minds, pleasures and pains. What becomes of these differences in your sleep?

D. But I want to be wide awake.

M. Is this your wide-awakened state? It is not. It is only a dream in your long sleep. All are in sleep, dreaming of the world and things and actions.

D. This is all *Vedantic* stuff for which I have no use. The existing differences are not imaginary; they are real. However, what is that real waking? Can Maharshi tell us what he has found it to be?

M. Real waking lies beyond the three states of waking, dream and sleep.

D. I am really awake and know that I am not asleep.

M. Real waking lies beyond the plane of differences.

D. What is the state of the world, then?

M. Does the world come and tell you "I exist?"

D. No. But the people in the world tell me that the world needs spiritual, social, and moral regeneration.

M. You see the world and the people in it. They are your thoughts. Can the world be apart from you?

D. I enter into it with love.

M. Before entering in this manner, do you stand aloof?

D. I am identified with it and yet remain apart. Now I came here to ask Maharshi and hear him. Why does he ask me questions?

M. Maharshi has replied. His reply amounts to this: Real waking does not involve differences.

D. Can such realization be universalized?

M. Where are differences there? There are no individuals in it.

D. Have you reached the goal?

M. The goal cannot be anything apart from the Self, nor can it be something to be gained afresh. If that were so, such a goal cannot be abiding and permanent. What appears anew will also disappear. The goal must be eternal and within. Find it within yourself.

D. I want to know your experience.

M. Maharshi does not seek enlightenment. The question is of no use to the questioner. Whether I have realized or not, how does it affect the questioner?

D. Not so. Each one's experience has a human value in it and can be shared by others.

M. The problem must be solved by the questioner himself. The question is best directed to oneself.

D. I know the answer to the question.

M. Let us have it.

D. I was shown the Kingdom of Heaven twenty years ago. It was by God's Grace only. I made no effort for it. I was happy. I want to universalize, moralize, and socialize it. At the same time, I want to know Maharshi's experience of the Divine.

Mrs. Jinarajadasa intervened and spoke softly: We all agree that Maharshi has brought the Kingdom of Heaven on Earth. Why do you press him to answer your questions relating to his realization? It is for you to seek and gain it.

> (*The questioner listened to her, argued slightly, and resumed his questions to Maharshi.*)

After one or two light questions, Major Chadwick spoke sternly: "The Kingdom of Heaven is within you," says the Bible.

D. How shall I realize it?

Major Chadwick: Why do you ask Maharshi to realize it for you?

D. I do not.

Major Chadwick: The Kingdom is within you. You should realize it.

D. It is *within* only for those who hear it.

Major Chadwick: The *Bible* says "within you," and adds no qualifications.
(The questioner felt his conversation was already too long and so retired after thanking Maharshi and others.)

Mrs. Jinarajadasa: How shall we be able to remember the truth experienced in dreams?

M. Your present waking state, your dreams, and your desire to remember are all thoughts. They arise only after the mind has arisen. Were you not existing in the absence of the mind?

D. Yes, I was.

M. The fact of your existence is also your realization.

D. I understand it intellectually. The truth is felt in temporary flashes only. It is not abiding.

M. Such thoughts cover up the state of your eternal realization.

D. The rough and tumble of city life is not congenial to realization. Jungle retreats afford the necessary quiet and solitude.

M. One may be free in a city and yet bound in jungle retreats. It is all in the mind.

D. The mind again is *maya*, I suppose.

M. What is *maya*? The knowledge that the mind is divorced from Reality is *maya*. The mind is in Reality only and not apart. This knowledge is the elimination of *maya*.

Further conversation led to the question whether the mind is identical with the brain. Sri Bhagavan said: The mind is only a force operating on the brain. You are now here and awake. The thoughts of the world and the surroundings are in the brain within the body. When you dream, you create another self that sees the world of dream creation and the surroundings just as you do now. The dream visions are in the dream brain, which in turn is in the dream body. That is different from your present body. You remember the dream now. The brains are, however, different. Yet the visions appear in the mind. The mind, therefore, is not identical with the brain. Waking, dream and sleep are for the mind only.

D. The understanding is intellectual.

M. Intellect, whose intellect? The problem revolves around that question.

You admit that you exist even in the absence of intellect — say, in sleep. How do you know that you exist if you have not realized your existence?

Your very existence is realization. You cannot imagine a time when you were not. So there is no instant when realization is not.

MARCH 22, 1938

A certain man from Madurai asked: How to know the Power of God?

M. You say, "I Am." That is it. What else can say, "I Am?"

One's own being is His Power. The trouble arises only when one says, "I am this or that, such and such." Do not do it — Be yourself. That is all.

D. How to experience Bliss?

M. To be free from thinking "I am now out of Bliss."

D. That is to say free from modes of mind.

M. To be with only one mode of mind to the exclusion of others.

D. But Bliss must be experienced.

M. Bliss consists in not forgetting your being. How can you be otherwise than what you really are? It is also to be the seat of Love. Love is Bliss. Here the Seat is not different from Love.

D. How shall I be all-pervading?

M. Give up the thought, "I am not all-pervading now."

D. How to permeate separate objects?

M. Do they exist independently of "I?" Do they say to you "We are?" You see them. You are, and then the objects are also seen. "Without me, these do not exist" — this knowledge is permeation. Owing to the idea "I am the body," the separate objects are seen as if lying outside. Know that they are all within yourself. Is a piece of cloth independent of yarn? Can the objects remain without me?

D. Which is the best of all the religions? What is Sri Bhagavan's method?

M. All religions and methods are one and the same.

D. But different methods are taught for liberation.

M. Why should you be liberated? Why not remain as you are now?

D. I want to get rid of pain. To be rid of it is said to be liberation.

M. That is what all religions teach.

D. But what is the method?

M. To retrace your way back.

D. Whence have I come?

M. That is just what you should know. Did these questions arise in your sleep? Did you not exist then? Are you not the same being now?

D. Yes, I *was* in sleep; so also the mind, but the senses had merged so I

376

could not speak.

M. Are you *jiva?* Are you the mind? Did the mind announce itself to you in sleep?

D. No. But elders say that the *jiva* is different from *Ishvara.*

M. Leave *Ishvara* alone. Speak for yourself.

D. What about myself? Who am I?

M. That is just it. Know it, then all will be known; if not, ask then.

D. On waking, I see the world and I am not changed from sleep.

M. But this is not known in sleep. Now or then, you remain the same. Who has changed now? Is your nature to be changing or remain unchanging?

D. What is the proof?

M. Does one's own being require proof? Only remain aware of your own self and all else will be known.

D. Why then do the dualists and nondualists always quarrel among themselves?

M. If each one minds his own business, there will be no quarrel.

A European lady, Mrs. Gasque, gave a slip of paper on which was written: "We are thankful to Nature and the Infinite Intelligence for your Presence among us. We appreciate that your Wisdom is founded upon pure Truth and the basic principle of Life and Eternity. We are happy that you remind us to 'Be still and Know That.' What do you consider the future of this Earth?"

M. The answer to this question is contained in the other sheet. *Be still and know that I Am God.* "Stillness" here means, "Being free from thoughts."

D. This does not answer the question. The planet has a future — what is it to be?

M. Time and space are functions of thoughts. If thoughts do not arise, there will be no future or Earth.

D. Time and space will remain even if we do not think of them.

M. Do they come and tell you that they are? Do you feel them in your sleep?

D. I was not conscious in my sleep.

M. And yet you were existing in your sleep.

D. I was not in my body. I had gone out somewhere and jumped in here just before waking.

M. Your having been away in sleep and jumping in now are mere ideas. Where were you in sleep? You were simply what you are, but with the only difference that you were free from thoughts in sleep.

D. Wars are going on in the world. If we do not think, do the wars cease?

M. Can you stop wars? He who made the world will take care of it.

D. God made the world and He is not responsible for its present condition. It is we who are responsible for the present state.

M. Can you stop the wars or reform the world?

D. No.

M. Then why do you worry about what is not possible for you? Take care of yourself and the world will take care of itself.

D. We are pacifists. We want to bring about Peace.

M. Peace is always present. Get rid of the disturbances to Peace. This Peace is the Self. The thoughts are the disturbances. When free from them, you are Infinite Intelligence, i.e., the Self. There is Perfection and Peace.

D. The world must have a future.

M. Do you know what it is in the present? The world and all together are the same, now as well as in the future.

D. The world was made by the operation of Intelligence on ether and atoms.

M. All of them are reduced to *Ishvara* and *Shakti*. You are not now apart from them. They and you are one and the same Intelligence.

After a few minutes, one lady asked: Do you ever intend to go to America?

M. America is just where India is (i.e., in the plane of thought).

Another (Spanish) lady: They say that there is a shrine in the Himalayas which upon entering gives some strange vibrations that heal all diseases. Is that possible?

M. They speak of some shrine in Nepal and also in other parts of the Himalayas where people are said to become unconscious upon entering.

Muruganar asked what prajnana *is.*

M. *Prajnana* (Absolute Knowledge) is that from which *vijnana* (relative knowledge) proceeds.

D. In the state of *vijnana*, one becomes aware of the *samvit* (cosmic intelligence). But is that *suddha samvit* aware by itself without the aid of *antahkaranas* (inner organs)?

M. It is so, even logically.

D. Becoming aware of *samvit* in *jagrat* by *vijnana, prajnana* is not found self-shining. If so, it must be found in sleep.

M. The awareness is at present through *antahkaranas*. *Prajnana* is always shining, even in sleep. If one is continuously aware in *jagrat*, the awareness will continue in sleep, also.

Moreover, it is illustrated thus: A king comes into the hall, sits there, and then leaves the place.

He did not go into the kitchen. Can one in the kitchen for that reason say, "The king did not come here?" When awareness is found in *jagrat*, it must also be in sleep.

Dr. Pande of Indore is on a visit here. He asked leave of Bhagavan to ask questions so that his doubts might be cleared. He wanted to be shown a practical way to realize the Self.

M. A man was blindfolded and left in the woods. He then inquired for directions to Gandhara with everyone he encountered until he finally reached it. So, also, all the ways lead to Self-realization. They are aids to the common goal.

D. *Dhyana* will be easy if there is a *pratikam* (symbol). But the inquiry into the Self does not show any *pratikam*.

M. You admit the existence of the Self. Do you point to the *pratikam* (symbol) and say that it is the Self? Maybe you think the body is the Self. But consider your deep sleep. You do exist then. What is the *pratikam* there? So the Self can be realized without *pratikam*.

D. Quite true. I see the force of your words. But yet are not mantras, etc., helpful?

M. They are helpful. What is mantra? You are thinking of the simple sounds of the mantra. Repetition of the same excludes all other thoughts. The single thought of the *mantra japa* remains. That, too, drops away giving place to the Infinite Self, which is the mantra itself.

Mantra, *dhyana, bkakti*, etc., are all aids and finally lead to *Svarupa*, the Self, which is what they are themselves.

In a few minutes, Maharshi continued: Everyone is the Self, indeed infinite. Yet each one mistakes the body for the Self. To know anything, illumination is necessary. Such illuminating agency can only be in the form of light, which is, however, lighting the physical light and darkness; so then, that other Light lies beyond the apparent light and darkness. It is itself neither light nor darkness, but is said to be Light because It illumines both. It is also Infinite and remains as Consciousness. Consciousness is the Self, of which everyone is aware. No one is away from the Self. So each one is Self-realized. Yet what a mystery it is that no one knows this fundamental fact, and desires to realize the Self. This ignorance is due to the mistaking of the body for the Self. Realization now consists of getting rid of this false idea that one is not realized. Realization is not anything newly acquired. It must be already there in order that it may be permanent. Otherwise, Realization is not worth striving for.

After the false notion "I-am-the-body" or "I have not realized" is removed, Supreme Consciousness or the Self alone is left, which is however called Realization in the present state of knowledge. However, the truth is that Realization is eternal and already there — here and now.

Finally, Realization amounts to elimination of ignorance and nothing more or less.

D. My profession requires my staying in my place. I cannot remain in the vicinity of *sadhus*. Can I have realization, even in the absence of *satsanga*, as necessitated by my circumstances?

M. *Sat* is *aham pratyaya saram* — the Self of selves. The *sadhu* is that Self of selves. He is immanent in all. Can anyone remain without the Self? No. So no one is away from *satsanga*.

APRIL 30, 1938

Mr. Sitaramiah, a visitor: What does *samyamana* mean in the *Patanjali Yoga Sutra*?

M. One-pointedness of mind.

D. By such *samyamana* in the Heart, *chitta samvit* is said to result. What does it mean?

M. *Chitta samvit* is *Atma jnana*, i.e. Knowledge of the Self.

D. I think that celibacy and initiation are prerequisites even for a householder to succeed in self-investigation. Am I right? Or can a householder observe celibacy and seek initiation from a Master on certain occasions only?

M. First ascertain who the wife and the husband are. Then these questions will not arise.

D. Engaged in other pursuits, can the mental activities be checked and the query "Who am I?" pursued? Are they not mutually exclusive?

M. These questions arise only in the absence of strength of mind. As mental activities diminish, the strength of mind increases.

D. Does the karma theory mean that the world is the result of action and reaction? If so, action and reaction of what?

M. Until realization there will be karma, i.e., action and reaction; after realization, there will be no karma and no world.

D. While engaged in *Atma-vichara* (the investigation of the Self), I fall asleep. What is the remedy for it?

M. Do *nama-sankirtana* (sing the name of God).

D. It is ruled out in sleep.

M. True. The practice should be continued while awake. Immediately when you wake up from sleep, you should resume it. The sleeper does not care for *Atma-vichara*. So he need not practice anything. The waking self desires it, and so he must do it.

In the course of conversation, Sri Bhagavan continued: The mind is something mysterious. It consists of *sattva, rajas,* and *tamas.* The latter two give rise to *vikshepa.* In the *sattva* aspect, it remains pure and uncontaminated, so there are no thoughts there and it is identical with the Self. The mind is likeh *akasha* (ether). Just as there are the objects in the *akasha,* so there are thoughts in the mind. One cannot hope to measure the universe and study the phenomena. It is impossible, for the objects are mental creations. Measuring them is similar to trying to stamp with one's foot on the head of the shadow cast by oneself. The farther one moves the farther also the shadow goes. So one cannot plant one's foot on the head of the shadow.

(*Here Sri Bhagavan related several incidents connected with shadows including the pranks of monkeys and a mirror.*)

A child sees his own shadow and tries to hold the head of the shadow. As he bends and puts out his arm, the head moves further. The child struggles more and more. The mother, seeing the struggle, pities the young one. So she takes hold of the young hand and keeps it on his own head and tells the child to observe the head of the shadow caught in the hand. Similarly with the ignorant practicer, trying to study the universe. The universe is only an object created by the mind and has its being in the mind. It cannot be measured as an exterior entity. One must reach the Self in order to reach the universe.

People often ask how the mind is controlled. I say to them, "Show me the mind and then you will know what to do." The fact is that the mind is only a bundle of thoughts. How can you extinguish it by the thought of doing so or by a desire? Your thoughts and desires are part and parcel of the mind. The mind is simply fattened by new thoughts rising up. Therefore, it is foolish to attempt to kill the mind by means of the mind. The only way of doing it is to find its source and hold on to it. The mind will then fade away of its own accord. Yoga teaches, *chitta vritti nirodha* (control of the activities of the mind). But I say *Atma-vichara* (Self-investigation) is the only practical way. *Chitta vritti nirodha* is brought about in sleep, swoon, or by starvation. As soon as the cause is withdrawn, there is recrudescence of thoughts. Of what use is it then? In the state of stupor, there is peace and no misery. But misery recurs when the stupor is removed. So *nirodha* (control) is useless and cannot be of lasting benefit.

How then can the benefit be made lasting? It is by finding the cause of misery. Misery is due to objects. If they are not there, there will be no contingent thoughts and so misery is wiped out. "How will objects cease to be?" is the next question. The *srutis* and the sages say that the objects are only mental creations. They have no substantive being. Investigate the matter and ascertain the truth of this statement. The result will be the conclusion that the objective world is in the subjective consciousness. The Self is thus the only Reality that permeates and also envelops the world. Since there is no duality, no thoughts will arise to disturb your peace. This is Realization of the Self. The Self is eternal, and so also its Realization.

In the course of the talk, Sri Bhagavan also made a few other points clearer:
Abhyasa consists of withdrawal within the Self every time you are disturbed by thought. It is not concentration or destruction of the mind, but withdrawal into the Self.

Dhyana, bhakti, japa, etc., are aids to keep out the multiplicity of thoughts. A single thought prevails which also eventually dissolves in the Self.

The questioner quoted that the mind starved of ideas amounted to realization and asked what the experience is in that state. He himself read out a passage from Mr. Brunton stating that it was indescribable. The answer was there. He again speculated that it must be like looking through an unsilvered mirror, as contrasted with the present experience corresponding to looking at a silvered mirror.

Sri Bhagavan said it was a mirror facing another clear mirror, i.e., no reflection.

MAY 2, 1938

Mr. Ganpatram: How shall I find out "Who am I?"
M. Are there two selves for the one self to find the other?
D. The Self must be only one consisting of two aspects of "I" and *sankalpa* (i.e., of thinker and thought).
After a time, he continued: Please tell me how I shall realize the "I." Am I to

make the *japa*, "Who am I?"

M. No *japa* of the kind is meant.

D. Am I to think, "Who am I?"

M. You have known that the "I"-thought springs forth. Hold the "I"-thought and find its *mula* (source).

D. May I know the way?

M. Do as you have now been told and see.

D. I do not understand what I should do.

M. If it is anything objective, the way can be shown objectively. But this is subjective.

D. I do not understand.

M. What! Do you not understand that you are?

D. Please tell me the way.

M. Is it necessary to show the way in the interior of your own home? This is within you.

D. What do you advise me to do?

M. Why should you do anything and what should you do? Only keep quiet. Why not do so? Each one must act according to his own state.

D. Please tell me what is suitable to me. I want to hear it from you.

(*No answer.*)

A young Englishwoman came here dressed in a Muslim sari. She had evidently been in North India and met Dr. G.H. Mees. Sri Bhagavan read out a stanza called "The Black Sun," from the anniversary issue of The Vision, *written by Swami Bharatananda. After a few minutes, Miss J. asked*: One gathers from the stanza that one should keep on meditating until one gets merged in the state of consciousness. Do you think it right?

M. Yes.

D. I go further and ask: Is it right that one should, by conscious will, go into that state from which there is no return?

(*No answer, dinner bell.*)

In the Afternoon:

D. What is the object of Self-realization?

M. Self-realization is the final goal and it is the end in itself.

D. I mean, what is the use of Self-realization?

M. Why should you seek Self-realization? Why do you not rest content with your present state? It is evident that you are discontented with the present state. The discontent is at an end if you realize the Self.

D. What is that Self-realization which removes the discontent? I am in the world and there are wars in it. Can Self-realization put an end to them?

M. Are you in the world? Or is the world in you?

D. I do not understand. The world is certainly around me.

M. You speak of the world and happenings in it. They are mere ideas in you. The ideas are in the mind. The mind is within you. And so the world is within you.

D. I do not follow. Even if I do not think of the world, the world is still there.

M. Do you mean to say that the world is apart from the mind and it can exist in the absence of the mind?

D. Yes.

M. Does the world exist in your deep sleep?

D. It does.

M. Do you see it in your sleep?

D. No, I don't. But others, who are awake, do.

M. Are you so aware in your sleep? Or do you become aware of the others' knowledge now?

D. In my waking state.

M. So you speak of waking knowledge and not of sleep-experience. The existence of the world in your waking and dream states is admitted because they are the products of the mind. The mind is withdrawn in sleep, and the world is in the condition of a seed. It becomes manifest again upon waking. The ego springs forth, identifies itself with the body, and sees the world. So the world is a mental creation.

D. How can it be?

M. Do you not create a world in your dream? The waking state similarly is a long drawn-out dream. There must be a seer behind the waking and dream experiences. Who is that seer? Is it the body?

D. It cannot be.

M. Is it the mind?

D. It must be so.

M. But you remain in the absence of the mind.

D. How?

M. In deep sleep.

D. I do not know if I exist then.

M. If you were not, how do you recollect yesterday's experiences? Is it possible that there was a break in the continuity of the "I" during sleep?

D. It may be.

M. If so, a Johnson may wake up as a Benson. How will the identity of the individual be established?

D. I don't know.

M. If this argument is not clear, follow a different line. You admit, "I slept well," "I feel refreshed after a sound sleep." So sleep was your experience. The experiencer now identifies himself with the "I" in the speaker. So this "I" must have been in sleep, also.

D. Yes.

M. So "I" was in sleep; if the world was there, did it say that it existed?

D. No. But the world tells me its existence now. Even if I deny its existence, I may knock myself against a stone and hurt my foot. The injury proves the existence of the stone and so of the world.

M. Quite so. The stone hurts the foot. Does the foot say that there is the stone?

D. No. — "I" do.

M. Who is this "I?" It cannot be the body or the mind, as we have seen before. This "I" is the one who experiences the waking, dream, and sleep states. The three states are changes, which do not affect the individual. The experiences are like pictures passing on a screen in the cinema. The appearance and disappearance of the pictures do not affect the screen. Similarly, the three states alternate with one another, leaving the Self unaffected. The waking and dream states are creations of the mind. So the Self covers all. To know that the Self remains happy in its perfection is Self-realization. Its use lies in the realization of Perfection and thus of happiness.

D. Can it be complete happiness to remain Self-realized if one does not contribute to the happiness of the world? How can one be so happy when there is a war in Spain, a war in China? Is it not selfishness to remain Self-realized without helping the world?

M. The Self was pointed out to you to cover the universe and also transcend it. The world cannot remain apart from the Self. If the realization of such Self be called selfishness, that selfishness must cover the world, also. It is nothing contemptible.

D. Does not the realized man continue to live just like a non-realized being?

M. Yes, with this difference: that the realized being does not see the world as being apart from the Self. He possesses true knowledge and the internal happiness of being perfect, whereas another person sees the world apart, feels imperfection, and is miserable. But, otherwise, their physical actions are similar.

D. The realized being also knows that there are wars being waged in the world, just like the other man.

M. Yes.

D. How then can he be happy?

M. Is the cinema screen affected by a scene of fire burning or sea rising? So it is with the Self.

The idea that I am the body or the mind is so deeply ingrained that one cannot get over it, even if convinced otherwise. One experiences a dream and knows it to be unreal on waking. Waking experience is unreal in other states. So each state contradicts the others. They are therefore mere changes taking place in the seer, or phenomena appearing in the Self, which is unbroken and remains unaffected by them. Just as the waking, dream and sleep states are phenomena, so also birth, growth and death are phenomena in the Self, which continues to be unbroken and unaffected. Birth and death are only ideas. They pertain to the body or the mind. The Self exists before the birth of this body and will remain after the death of this body. So it is with the series of bodies taken up in succession. The Self is immortal. The phenomena are changeful and appear mortal. The fear of death is of the body. It is not true of the Self. Such fear is due to ignorance. Realization means True Knowledge of the Perfection and Immortality of the Self. Mortality is only an idea and cause of misery. You get rid of it by realizing the Immortal nature of the Self.

May 3, 1938

The same lady continued: If the world is only a dream, how should it be harmonized with the Eternal Reality?

M. The harmony consists in the realization of its inseparateness from the Self.

D. But a dream is fleeting and unreal. It is also contradicted by the waking state.

M. The waking experiences are similar.

D. One lives fifty years and finds a continuity in the waking experience, which is absent in dreams.

M. You go to sleep and dream a dream in which the experiences of fifty years are condensed within the short duration of the dream, say five minutes. There is also a continuity in the dream. Which is real now? Is the period covering fifty years of your waking state real, or the short duration of five minutes of your dream? The standards of time differ in the two states. That is all. There is no other difference between the experiences.

D. The spirit remains unaffected by the passing phenomena and by the successive bodies of repeated births. How does each body get the life to set it acting?

M. The spirit is differentiated from matter and is full of life. The body is animated by it.

D. The realized being is then the spirit and unaware of the world.

M. He sees the world but not as separate from the Self.

D. If the world is full of pain, why should he continue the world-idea?

M. Does the realized being tell you that the world is full of pain? It is the other one who feels the pain and seeks the help of the wise saying that the world is painful. Then the wise one explains from his experience that if one withdraws within the Self, there is an end of pain. The pain is felt so long as the object is different from oneself. But when the Self is found to be an undivided whole, who and what is there to feel? The realized mind is the Holy Spirit and the other mind is the home of the devil. For the realized being this is the Kingdom of Heaven: "The Kingdom of Heaven is within you." That Kingdom is *here* and *now*.

A group of young men asked: It is said that a healthy mind can be only in a healthy body. Should we not attempt to keep the body always strong and healthy?

M. In that way there will be no end of attention to the health of the body.

D. The present experiences are the result of past karma. If we know the mistakes committed previously, we can rectify them.

M. If one mistake is rectified, there yet remains the whole *sanchita* which is going to give you innumerable births. So that is not the procedure. The more you prune a plant, the more vigorously it grows. The more you rectify your karma, the more it accumulates. Find the root of karma and cut it off.

MAY 4, 1938

Another group of visitors was asking for the method of Realization. In the course of a reply, Sri Bhagavan said: Holding the mind and investigating it is advised for a beginner. But what is mind after all? It is a projection of the Self. See for whom it appears and from where it rises. The "I"-thought will be found to be the root-cause. Go deeper; the "I"-thought disappears and there is an infinitely expanded "I"-consciousness. That is otherwise called

Hiranyagarbha. When it puts on limitations it appears as individuals.

The English lady wished to have a private talk with Sri Bhagavan. She began: I am
returning to England. I leave this place this evening. I want to have the
happiness of Self-realization in my home. Of course, it is not easy in the
West. But I shall strive for it. What is the way to do it?
M. If Realization were something outside you, a way could be shown consistent with the safety of the individual, his capacity, etc. Then questions
such as is it realizable and, if so, in what time, would also arise. But here,
Realization is of the Self. You cannot remain without the Self. The Self is
always realized, but you don't recognize the fact. The Realization is now
obscured by the present world-idea. The world is now seen outside you
and the idea associated with it obscures your real nature. All that is needed
is to overcome this ignorance and the Self stands revealed. No special effort is necessary to realize the Self. All efforts are for eliminating the present
obscuration of the Truth.

A lady is wearing a necklace around her neck. She forgets it, imagines
it to be lost, and impulsively looks for it here, there and everywhere. Not
finding it, she asks her friends if they have found it anywhere, until one
kind friend points to her neck and tells her to feel the necklace around the
neck. The seeker does so and feels happy the necklace is found. Again,
when she meets her other friends, they ask her if her lost necklace was
found. She says "yes" to them, as if it were lost and later recovered. Her
happiness on re-discovering it around her neck is the same as if some lost
property had been recovered. In fact, she never lost it nor recovered it. And
yet she was once miserable and now she is happy. So, also, with the realization of the Self. The Self is always realized. The Realization is now obscured.
When the veil is removed, the person feels happy at rediscovering the ever-
realized Self. The ever-present Realization appears to be a new Realization.

Now, what should one do to overcome the present ignorance? Be eager to have the true knowledge. As this eagerness grows, the wrong knowledge diminishes in strength until it finally disappears.
D. The other day, you were saying that there is no awareness in deep sleep.
But I have on rare occasions become aware of sleep even in that state.
M. Now, of these three factors, the awareness, sleep, and knowledge of it,
the first one is changeless. That awareness, which cognized sleep as a state,
now sees the world also in the waking state. The negation of the world is
the state of sleep. The world may appear or disappear — that is to say, one
may be awake or asleep — but the awareness is unaffected. It is one con-

tinuous whole over which the three states of waking, dream, and sleep pass. Be that awareness even now. That is the Self: that is Realization — there is Peace, there is Happiness.

(*The lady thanked Maharshi and retired.*)

MAY 7, 1938

Mr. Kishorelal Mashruwala, President, of Gandhi Seva Sangh, asked: How is *brahmacharya* to be practiced in order that it may be successfully lived up to?

M. It is a matter of willpower. *Sattvic* food, prayers, etc., are useful aids to it.

D. Young men have fallen into bad habits. They desire to get over them and seek our advice.

M. Mental reform is needed.

D. Can we prescribe any special foods, exercise, etc., to them?

M. There are some medicines. Yogic *asanas* and *sattvic* food are also helpful.

D. Some young persons have taken a vow of *brahmacharya*. They repent of the vow after a lapse of ten or twelve years. Under these circumstances, should we encourage young persons to take the vow of *brahmacharya*?

M. This question will not arise in the case of true *brahmacharya*.

D. Some young men take the vow of *brahmacharya* without knowing its full implications. When they find it difficult to carry out, they seek our advice.

M. They need not take a vow, but they may try it without the vow.

D. Is *naishthika brahmacharya* (life-long celibacy) essential as a *sadhana* for Self-realization?

M. Realization itself is *naishthika brahmacharya*. The vow is not *brahmacharya*. Life in *Brahman* is *brahmacharya* and it is not a forcible attempt at it.

D. It is said that *kama* (desire), *krodha* (anger), etc., vanish in the presence of the Sadguru. Is that so?

M. It is correct. *Kama* and *krodha* must vanish before Self-realization.

D. But all the disciples of a guru are not of the same degree of advancement. There are found to be lapses in a few cases. Who is responsible for such lapses?

M. There is no connection between Self-realization and individual predispositions (*samskara*). It is not always possible to live up to the ideal of the Guru.

D. Do not passions affect Realization?

M. The attempt to cleanse oneself will be automatic.

D. Is it not necessary to wash off all impurities before Realization?

M. *Jnana* will wash them clean.

D. Gandhiji is often perplexed finding his intimate disciples going wrong. He wonders how that could happen and thinks it is due to his own defects. Is it so?

Sri Bhagavan smiled and answered after a few minutes: Gandhiji has struggled so long to perfect himself. All others will be right in due course.

D. Is the Hindu view of reincarnation correct?

M. No definite answer is possible to this question. There are pros and cons for the view. Even the present birth is denied *natvevaham jatu nasam*, etc. (*Bhagavad Gita*). We were never born, etc.

D. Is not individuality *anadi* (without beginning)?

M. Investigate and see if there is any individuality at all. Ask this question after solving this problem. Nammalvar says:

> "In ignorance, I took the ego to be myself; however, with right knowledge, the ego is nowhere and only you remain as the Self."

Both monists and dualists are agreed on the necessity of Self-realization. Let us do it first and then discuss the side issues. *Advaita* or *dvaita* cannot be decided upon on theoretical considerations alone. If the Self is realized, the question will not arise at all. Even Suka had no confidence in his *brahmacharya*, whereas Sri Krishna was sure of his. Self-realization is designated by so many different names — *satya, brahmacharya,* etc. What is natural to the state of Self-realization forms the disciplinary course in the other state. The "I-am-the-body" idea will become extinct only on Self-realization. With its extinction, the *vasanas* will become extinct and all virtues will remain forever.

D. *Samskaras* are said to persist even in a *jnani.*

M. Yes. They are *bhoga hetu* (leading to enjoyment only) and not *bandha hetu* (leading to bondage).

D. This fact is often abused by fakes who pretend to be *sadhus* but lead vicious lives. They say it is *prarabdha* (a remnant of past karma). How shall we distinguish the fakes from the genuine *sadhus*?

M. The one who has given up the idea of being the doer cannot repeat, "This is my *prarabdha*." "*Jnanis* lead different lives" is said for the benefit of others. The *jnanis* cannot make use of this in explanation of their lives and conduct.

After a few minutes, Sri Bhagavan remarked about Mr. Kishorelal's weak body.

Mr. Kishorelal: I am asthmatic. I have never been strong. Even as a baby, I was not fed on my mother's milk.

M. Here the mind is strong and the body is weak.

D. I wanted to practice *Raja Yoga*. I could not do so on account of my physical condition. The mind also began to wander with the movement of the body.

M. If the mind is kept immovable, let the body change as much as it likes.

D. Is it not a handicap to the beginner?

M. Attempts must be made in spite of handicaps.

D. Of course. But they will be momentary.

M. The idea of "momentary" is one among so many other ideas. So long as thoughts persist, this idea also will recur. Concentration is our own nature (Being). There is the effort now; but it ceases after Self-realization.

D. It is said to be the interval between flights of mind.

M. This, too, is due to the activity of the mind.

> (*The devotee submitted that whenever he thought he had found something original, he later discovered he had been forestalled. Sri Bhagavan pointed out that everything remains in germinal form, and so there can be nothing new.*)

May 8, 1938

In a suit by the temple against the Government regarding ownership of the Hill, Sri Bhagavan was cited as a witness and was examined by a commission.

Maharshi said: The buildings or ashrams grow around me. I do not wish for them. I do not ask for them nor prevent their formation. I have known that actions are done even though I did not want them to be done. So I conclude that they *must* happen and I therefore do not say "no."

Question: Is the present Sarvadhikari (Manager) to be your successor?

M. Yes. Only management (i.e., succession here means simple supervision).

Question: Is the work now being carried out by him?

M. He simply supervises the work. The work is being done by others, as well.

May 18, 1938

A visitor from Andhra Pradesh: What will help me in fixing my attention always at thy holy feet?

M. The thought "Am I ever away from the feet?"

D. How is this thought to be fixed?

M. By driving away other thoughts which counteract this.

Sri Bhagavan had gone through *Turn Eastwards* — the whole book of Mademoiselle Pascaline Maillert — and spoke for about an hour on that book. He said that the writing is full of feeling and the writer is sincere. The book is written in simple style and finishes off with remembrance of himself. A few errors here and there might be pointed out for correction in subsequent editions. Nandanar Charitra has been repeated twice under the mistaken notion that the incident was on two different occasions. *Prithvi, Ap,* etc., *lingas* are wrongly located. Sri Bhagavan thinks the book is well written. He interprets *Turn Eastwards* as "Turn to the Source of Light." This book is a good supplement to Mr. Brunton's book.

MAY 29, 1938

A Kerala Brahmin, Professor in the Ernakulam College, had an interesting conversation with Sri Bhagavan. Sri Bhagavan advised surrender to God. The visitor gave a glimpse of an Indian Civil Service Officer. The gentleman, while a student, was an atheist or an agnostic. He is very pious now, and the change has surprised everyone who had known him before.

In further conversation, the following noteworthy points were raised by the visitor: One must become satiated with the fulfillment of desires before they are renounced.

Sri Bhagavan smiled and cut in: Fire might as well be put out by pouring spirit over the flames. (*All laugh.*) The more desires are fulfilled, the deeper grow the *samskaras.* They must become weaker before they cease to assert themselves. That weakness is brought about by restraining oneself and not by losing oneself in desires.

D. How can they be rendered weaker?

M. By knowledge. You know you are not the mind. The desires are in the mind. Such knowledge helps one to control them.

D. But they are not controlled in our practical lives.

M. Every time you attempt satisfaction of a desire, the knowledge comes that it is better to desist. Repeated reminders of this kind will in due course weaken the desires. What is your true nature? How can you ever forget it? Waking, dream, and sleep are mere phases of the mind. They are not of the Self. You are the witness of these states. Your true nature is found in sleep.

D. But we are advised against falling asleep during meditation.

M. It is stupor you must guard against. The sleep which alternates with waking is not true sleep. That waking which alternates with sleep is not true waking. Are you now awake? You are not. You are required to wake up to your real state. You should not fall into false sleep nor keep falsely awake. Hence: *Laye sambodhayecchittam vikshiptam samayet punah.*

What does it mean? That you should not fall into any one of these states but remain amidst them in your true, unsullied nature.

D. The states are of our mind only.

M. Whose mind? Hold it and see.

D. The mind cannot be held. It is that which creates all these. It is known only by its effects and not in its true nature.

M. Quite so. You see the colors of the spectrum. Together they form the white light. But seven colors are seen through the prism. Similarly, the one Self resolves itself into so many phases — mind, body, world, etc. That is, the Self is seen as the mind, the body, or the world. In other words, it becomes whatever you perceive it to be.

D. These instructions are difficult to follow in practice. I will hold on to God and surrender.

M. That is the best.

D. How can I do my duties without attachment? There is my wife; there are my children. I must do my duty towards them. Affection is necessary. Am I right?

M. How do you do your work in the College?

D. (*Laughing*) For wages.

M. Not because you are attached, simply as doing your duty.

D. But my pupils expect me to love them.

M. "Detachment in the interior and attachment in appearance," says *Yoga Vasishta.*

JUNE 9, 1938

A Swami belonging to the Ramakrishna Mission had a very interesting conversation with Sri Bhagavan, in the course of which Sri Bhagavan observed: Avidya (ignorance) is the obstacle for knowing your true nature even at the present moment.

D. How is one to get over *Avidya*?

M. *Ya na vidyate sa avidya* (What is not, is *avidya*). So it is itself a myth. If it really be, how can it perish? Its *being* is false and so it disappears.

D. Although I understand it intellectually, I cannot realize the Self.

M. Why should this thought disturb your present state of realization?

D. The Self is One, yet I do not find myself free from trouble.

M. Who says this? Is it the Self which is only one? The question contradicts itself.

D. Grace is necessary for realization.

M. Inasmuch as you, being a man, now understand that there is a higher power guiding you, it is due to Grace. Grace is within you. *Ishvaro gururatmeti* (*Ishvara,* Guru, and the Self are synonymous).

D. I pray for that Grace.

M. Yes, yes.

JUNE 10, 1938

In the course of a different conversation, Sri Bhagavan said:

> *Sattva* is the light,
> *Rajas* is the subject,
> *Tamas* is the object.

Even the *sattva* light is only reflected light. Were it pure, original Light, there would be no modification in it. *The manokasa* (mind-ether) is reflected as *bhutakasha* (element-ether), and objects are seen as being separate from the subject.

Samadhi is present even in *vyavaharadasa* (practical life). Our activities (*vyavahara*) have no existence apart from *samadhi*. The screen is there when the pictures move past on it and also when they are not projected. Similarly, the Self is always there in *vyavahara* (activity) or in *shanti* (peace).

People often say that a *mukta purusha* should go out and preach his message to the people. They argue, how can anyone be a *mukta* while there is misery by his side? True. But who is a *mukta*? Does he see misery beside him? They want to determine that state of a *mukta* without themselves realizing that state. From the standpoint of the *mukta*, their contention amounts to this: a man has a dream in which he finds several persons. On waking, he asks, "Have the dream individuals also wakened?" It is ridiculous.

Again, a good man says, "It does not matter even if I do not get *mukti*. Or let me be the last man to get it so that I shall help all others to be *muktas* before I am one." It is all very good. Imagine a dreamer saying, "May all these wake up before I do." The dreamer is no more absurd than the amiable philosopher.

The Swami from the Ramakrishna Mission had a few more questions: Swamiji, I went up the hill to see the ashrams where you lived in your youth. I have also read your life story. May I know if you did not then feel that there is God to whom you should pray, or that you should practice something in order to reach this state?

M. Read the life and you will understand. *Jnana* and *ajnana* are of the same degree of truth; that is, both are imagined by the ignorant and are not true from the standpoint of the *jnani*.

D. Is a *jnani* capable of or likely to commit sins?

M. An *ajnani* sees someone as a *jnani* and identifies him with the body. Because he does not know the Self and mistakes his body for the Self, he extends the same mistake to the state of the *jnani*. The *jnani* is therefore considered to be the physical frame.

The *ajnani*, though he is not the doer, imagines himself to be the doer and considers the actions of the body his own; he thinks the *jnani* to be similarly acting when the body is active. But the *jnani* himself knows the Truth and is not confounded. The state of a *jnani* cannot be determined by the *ajnani* and therefore the question troubles only the *ajnani*; it never arises for the *jnani*. If he is a doer, he must determine the nature of the actions. The Self cannot be the doer. Find out who is the doer, and the Self is re-vealed.

D. There could be no *advaita* in actions. That is how the questions arose.

M. But the stanza says there should be. This "do" is applicable only to the practicer and not to the accomplished ones.

D. Yes. I quite see it. Moreover, *advaita* cannot be practiced in one's dealings with the Guru. For, consistently with it, he cannot receive instructions.

M. Yes, the Guru is within and not without. A Tamil saint once said:

"O Guru! Always abiding within me, but manifesting now in human form only to guide and protect me!"

What is within as the Self manifests in due course as Guru in human shape.

D. So it amounts to this: To see a *jnani* is not the same as understanding him. You see the *jnani's* body and not his *jnanam*. One must therefore be a *jnani* to know a *jnani*.

M. The *jnani* sees no one as an *ajnani*. All are only *jnanis* in his sight. In the ignorant state, one superimposes his ignorance on a *jnani* and mistakes him for a doer. In the state of *jnana*, the *jnani* sees nothing separate from the Self. The Self is all shining and only pure *jnana*. So there is no *ajnana* in his sight. There is an illustration of this kind of allusion or superimposition.

Two friends went to sleep side by side. One of them dreamt that both had gone on a long journey and had strange experiences. On waking up he recapitulated them and asked his friend if it was not so. The other one simply ridiculed him saying that it was only his dream and could not affect the other.

So it is with the *ajnani* who superimposes his illusive ideas on others.

Regarding ajnana *in early youth and* jnana *at the present time, Sri Bhagavan said:* There is no *jnana* as it is commonly understood. The ordinary ideas of *jnana* and *ajnana* are only relative and false. They are not real and therefore not abiding. The true state is the nondual Self. It is eternal and abides whether one is aware or not. It is like *kanthabharana* or the tenth man.

D. Someone else points it out.

M. That one is not external. You mistake the body for the Guru. But the Guru does not think himself so. He is the formless Self. That is within you; he appears without only to guide you.

D. When all thoughts are banished and the mind is still or enters into a state of nothingness or emptiness, what is the nature of effort needed on the part of the "seeker" to have a *pratyakshabhava* of the "sought" (e.g., seeing a mango as a mango)?

M. Who sees nothingness or emptiness? What is *pratyaksha?* Do you call perception of mango *pratyaksha?* It involves the play of *karma, karta,* and *karya* (action, doer, and deed). So it is relative and not absolute. Because you see a thing now you say there is nothing afterwards (i.e., when you no longer see it). Both are functions of the mind. What lies behind both these assertions is *pratyaksha.* There is *indriya pratyaksha* (directly perceived by the senses), *manasa pratyaksha* (directly perceived by the mind), and *sakshat pratyaksha* (realized as the very Being). The last alone is true. The others are relative and untrue.

D. If no effort is needed, can the perpetuated state of emptiness of mind be called the state of realization?

M. Effort is needed so long as there is mind. The state of emptiness has been the bone of contention in all philosophies.

D. Is there anything like *pratyakshabhava* in the state of realization or is realization merely felt or experienced as the very Being or *Sthiti* of the soul?

M. *Pratyaksha* is the very being and it is not feeling, etc.

D. Until the seeker realizes that he is the sought, the above questions arise for him.

M. True. See if you are the seeker. The Self is often mistaken for the knower. Is there not the Self in deep sleep, i.e., nescience? Therefore, the Self is beyond knower and knowledge. These doubts are in the realm of mind. To speak from this point of view, the advice is to keep the mind clear, and when *rajas* and *tamas* are wiped off, then the *sattva* mind alone exists. So the "I" vanishes in the *sattva* (*unadhal kan*).

Jnana chakshus does not mean it is an organ of perception like the other sense organs. *Jnanameva chakshuh.* Clairvoyance, etc., are not functions of *jnana chakshus.* So long as there is a subject and an object it is only relative knowledge. *Jnana* lies beyond relative knowledge; it is absolute.

The Self is the source of subject and object. Now ignorance prevailing, the subject is taken to be the source. The subject is the knower and forms one of the triads whose components cannot exist independently of one another. So the subject or the knower cannot be the ultimate Reality. Reality lies beyond subject and object. When realized, there will be no room for doubt.

"*Bhidyate hridayagranthih chhidyante sarvasamsayah.*"

Once the knot of the heart is cut there will no longer be any doubts.

The heart knot is snapped; doubts are set at rest. This is called *pratyaksha* and not what you are thinking of. *Avidya nasa* is alone Self-realization. Self-realization is only *oupacharika*. Self-realization is only a euphemism for elimination of ignorance.

July 12, 1938

A young man from Mysore asked: How did I get this body?

M. You speak of "I" and the "body." There is the relationship between the two. You are not therefore the body. The question does not occur to the body because it is inert. There is an occasion when you are not aware of the body — namely, in deep sleep. The question does not arise then. Nevertheless, you are there in sleep. To whom does the question arise now?

D. The ego.

M. Yes. The body and the ego rise up together and sink together. There is an occasion when you are not associated with the ego: in deep sleep. Presently you are associated with the ego. Of these two states, which is your real state? You are present in sleep and the same "You" is present now, too. Why should the doubt arise now and not then? You are right in saying that it is for the ego. You are not the ego. The ego is intermediate between the Self and the body. You are the Self. Find out the origin of the ego and see if the doubt still persists.

Sri Bhagavan added after a few minutes: The answer, according to *sastras*, will be that the body is due to karma. The question will be how did karma arise? We must say "from a previous body" and so on without end. The direct method of attack is not to depend on mere hypotheses but to ask: "Whose karma is it? Or whose body?" Hence, I answered in this manner. This is more purposeful.

AUGUST 14-16, 1938

Rajendra Prasad, Jamnalal Bajaj, and others are on a visit to Sri Maharshi. Sri J. Bajaj asked: How is the mind to be steadily kept right?

M. All living beings are aware of their surroundings, and therefore intellect must be surmised in all of them. At the same time, there is a difference between the intellect of man and that of other animals, since man not only sees the world as it is and acts accordingly, but also seeks fulfillment of desires and is not satisfied with the existing state of affairs. In his attempt to fulfill his desires, he extends his vision far and wide and yet turns away dissatisfied. He now begins to think and reason.

The desire for permanency of happiness and peace suggests permanency in his own nature. Therefore, he seeks to find and regain his own nature, i.e., his Self. That found, all is found.

Such inward seeking is the path to be gained by man's intellect. The intellect itself realizes after continuous practice that it is enabled to function by some Higher Power. By itself, it cannot reach that Power. So it ceases to function after a certain stage. When it thus ceases to function, the Supreme Power is still left there all alone. That is Realization; that is the finality, the goal.

It is thus plain that the purpose of the intellect is to realize its own dependence upon the Higher Power and its inability to reach the same. So it must annihilate itself before the goal is gained.

D. A *sloka* is quoted which means: "I do not desire kingdoms, etc. Only let me serve Thee forever, and there lies my highest pleasure." Is that right?

M. Yes. There is room for *kama* (desire) so long as there is an object apart from the subject (i.e., duality). There can be no desire if there is no object. The state of no-desire is *moksha*. There is no duality in sleep and also no desire. Whereas there is duality in the waking state and so desire also is there. Because of duality, a desire arises for the acquisition of the object. That is the outgoing mind, which is the basis of duality and of desire. If one knows that Bliss is none other than the Self, the mind becomes inward-turned. If the Self is gained, all the desires are fulfilled. That is the *apta kamah atma kamah akamascha* (fulfillment of desire) of the *Brihadaranyaka Upanishad*. That is *moksha*.

Here, Sri Bajaj tried to make himself clear by saying that what he meant by sadbuddhi was not the same as buddhi. It means: That which holds fast to the good, the right, and the chosen path. He wanted to know how such steadfastness could be gained.

M. What is wanted for gaining the highest goal is loss of individuality. The intellect is co-extensive with individuality. Loss of individuality can only be after the disappearance of *buddhi*, good or bad. The question therefore does not arise.

D. But yet one must know the right thing, choose the right path, practice the right *dharma* and hold fast to it. Otherwise, he is lost.

M. True strength accrues by keeping in the right direction without swerving from it.

D. Difficulties are encountered. How is one to get the necessary strength to overcome the obstacles that beset one's path?

M. By means of devotion and company of the sages.

D. Loss of individuality was just before mentioned as a prerequisite to *moksha*. Now devotion and association with the wise are advised as the methods. Is there not individuality implied in them, e.g., in "I am a *bhakta*," "I am a *satsangi*?"

M. The method is pointed out to the seeker. The seeker has certainly not lost his individuality so far; otherwise, the question would not have arisen. The way is shown to effect the loss of individuality of the seeker; it is thus appropriate.

D. Is the desire for *swaraj* (independence) right?

M. Such desire no doubt begins with self-interest. Yet practical work for the goal gradually widens the outlook so that the individual becomes merged in the country. Such merging of the individuality is desirable, and the related karma is *nishkama* (unselfish).

D. If *swaraj* is gained after a long struggle and terrible sacrifices, is not the person justified in being pleased with the result and elated by it?

M. He must in the course of his work have surrendered himself to the Higher

Power whose might must be kept in mind and never lost sight of. How then, can he be elated? He should not even care for the result of his actions. Then alone the karma becomes unselfish.

D. How can unerring rectitude be ensured for the worker?

M. If he has surrendered himself to God or to Guru, the Power to which he had surrendered will take him on the right course. The worker no longer need concern himself about the rectitude (or otherwise) of the course. The doubt will arise only if he fails to obey the Master in all details.

D. Is there not any Power on earth, which can bestow Grace on Its devotees so that they may grow strong to work for the country and gain *swaraj*?

(Sri Maharshi remained silent. This, he later said, signified that such was the case.)

D. Is not the *tapasya* of the ancient *mahatmas* of the land available for the benefit of its present-day inheritors?

M. It is, but the fact must not be overlooked that no one can claim to be the sole beneficiary. The benefits are shared by all alike.

Is it without such saving Grace that the present awakening has come into being?

After a short pause, Sri Bajaj said: Sri Rajendra Prasad is such a noble and selfless worker for the country that he has sacrificed a very lucrative career for this work. The country needs him. And yet he is not in good health, and is always weak and ailing. Why should there be such cruelty to such a noble son of the country?

(Sri Maharshi simply smiled a benign smile.)

AUGUST 17, 1938

An American gentleman, Mr. J. M. Lorey, has been staying in the Ashram for about two months. He asked: I am leaving tonight. It gives me pain to tear myself away from this place. But I must go to America. I ask for a message from the Master. The Master understands me even better than I do myself. So I pray for a message to keep me up when I am away from the Master.

M. The Master is not outside you, as you seem to imagine. He is *within*, is in fact the Self. Recognize this truth. Seek within you and find Him there. Then you will have constant communion with Him. The message is always there; it is never silent. It can never forsake you nor can you ever move away from the Master.

Your mind is outgoing. Because of that tendency, it sees objects as being outside and the Master among them. But the Truth is different. The Master is the Self. Turn the mind within and you will find the objects there. You will also realize that it is the Master who is your very Self and there is nothing but Him.

Because you identify yourself with the body, you have accepted objects as being outside you. But are you the body? You are not. You are the Self. *There* are all the objects and the whole universe. Nothing can escape the Self. How then can you move away from the Master who is your very Self? Suppose your body moves from place to place; does it ever move away from your Self? Similarly, you can never be without the Master.

(*Mr. Lorey was struck by the answer, although he was already familiar with the Master's ways. He was even visibly moved. He prayed that the Grace of the Master might abide with him.*)

M. The Master being the Self, Grace is inseparable from the Self.

(*Mr. Lorey saluted Sri Maharshi with intense fervor, saying that he might be enabled to realize the Truth.*)

M. Is there any moment when you have not realized the Self? Can you ever be apart from the Self? You are always That.

D. You are the great Master shedding joy and bliss on the world. Your love is indeed unlimited that you choose to abide in the world in human shape! But I wish to know if one should necessarily realize one's Self before being of help to the country and a leader of men.

M. Realize the Self first and the rest will follow.

D. America is now the foremost country in industrial matters, mechanical engineering, scientific advances, and other worldly affairs. Will she come up to the same level in the spiritual life, also?

M. Certainly, she is bound to.

D. Thank God that it will be so! I am a partner in an engineering firm. But it is not of vital concern to me. I try to bring spiritual ideals into the work-a-day life of the firm.

M. That is good. If you surrender yourself to the Higher Power, all will be well. That Power sees your affairs through. Only so long as you think that you are the worker, you are obliged to reap the fruits of your actions. If on the other hand, you surrender yourself and recognize your individual self as only a tool of the Higher Power, that Power will take over your affairs along with the fruits of actions. You are no longer affected by them, and the work goes on unhampered. Whether you recognize the Power or not, the scheme of things does not alter. Only there is a change of outlook. Why should you carry your load on your head when you are travelling in a train? It transports you and your load whether the load is on your head or on the floor of the train. You are not lessening the burden of the train by keeping it on your head, but only strain yourself unnecessarily. Similar is the sense of doership in the world by individuals.

D. I have been interesting myself in metaphysics for over twenty years. But I have not gained any novel experience as so many others claim. I have no powers of clairvoyance, clairaudience, etc. I feel myself locked up in this body and nothing more.

M. It is right. Reality is only one and that is the Self. All the rest are mere phenomena in it, of it, and by it. The seer, the objects, and the sight — all are the Self only. Can anyone see or hear, leaving the Self aside? What difference does it make to see or hear anyone in close proximity or over an enormous distance? The organs of sight and hearing are needed in both cases; so also the mind is required. None of them can be dispensed with in either case. There is dependence one way or another. Why then should there be a glamour about clairvoyance or clairaudience?

Moreover, what is acquired will also be lost in due course. No thing can ever be permanent.

The only permanent thing is Reality; and *that* is the Self. You say, "I am." "I am going," "I am speaking," "I am working," etc. Hyphenate "I am" in all of them. Thus I-Am. *That* is the abiding and fundamental Reality. This truth was taught by God to Moses: "I Am that I Am." "Be still and know that I am God." So "I-Am" is God.

You know that you are. You cannot deny your existence at any moment. For you must be there in order to deny it. This (Pure Existence) is understood by stilling your mind. The mind is the outgoing faculty of the individual. If that is turned within, it becomes *still* in the course of time and that "I Am" alone prevails. "I Am" is the whole Truth.

D. I appreciate the whole answer.

M. Who is there to appreciate what?

To a question about the Heart, Sri Bhagavan said: Leave alone the idea of *right* and *left*. They pertain to the body. The Heart is the Self. Realize it and then you will see for yourself.

(*Mr. Lorey thanked Sri Bhagavan and saluted him before retiring.*)

AUGUST 18, 1938

A visitor asked Sri Bhagavan about the "over-mind," the "super-mind," the "psychic," and the "Divine" of Sri Aurobindo's terminology.

M. Realize the Self or the Divine. Then, all these differences will disappear.

Babu Rajendra Prasad said: I have come here with Mahatma Gandhiji's permission, and I must return to him soon. Can Sri Bhagavan give me any message for him?
M. *Adhyatma shakti* is working within him and leading him on. That is enough. What more is necessary?

AUGUST 19, 1938

Explaining the opening stanza of Sad-Vidya, *Sri Bhagavan said: Sat* (Being) is *Chit* (Knowledge Absolute); also, *Chit* is *Sat*; what *is*, is only one. Otherwise, the knowledge of the world and of one's own being will be impossible. It denotes both being and knowledge. However, both of them are one and the same. On the other hand, be it *Sat* only and not *Chit* also, such *Sat* will only be insentient (*jada*). In order to know it, another *Chit* will be needed; such *Chit* being other than *Sat* cannot be. But it *must be*. Now, taking *Chit* to be *Sat*, since *Sat* is *jada*, *Chit* also becomes *jada*, which is absurd. Again to know it, another *Chit* is required, which is also absurd.

Therefore, *Sat* and *Chit* are one and the same.

AUGUST 22, 1938

An Arya Samajist from Bangalore, with a companion, visited Sri Maharshi. He asked: What is the use of yoga practice? Is it for personal use or universal benefit?
M. Yoga means union of two entities. What are they? Inquire. Use or benefit is in relation to some center. What is it? Inquire.
D. Should there be distinction of castes?
M. Who is it that sees such distinction? Find it out.
D. I find that it is observed in this Ashram. Probably without the approval of Sri Bhagavan, others observe it here.
M. Who are you that speak of others, etc? Did you notice others, etc., in your *sushupti* (deep sleep)?
D. I am the individuality here. I may not see others in my sleep, but I see them now.
M. No doubt you do. But the one who sees now and the one who did not see in sleep are "you" only — the same individual. Why should you notice differences now and be troubled? Be as you were in sleep.

D. That cannot be. I see it now, whereas I do not see it in my sleep. That does not alter the existing state of affairs.

M. Do the objects exist in the absence of the subject?

D. Their existence is independent of the subject.

M. Do you say that they exist, or do they come and announce their existence to you?

D. I know that they exist.

M. So it is your knowledge of them only. Their existence is not absolute.

D. Even if I did not know, they would continue to exist.

M. Do you claim their existence in the absence of your knowledge of them? (*Laughter.*)

D. *Brahman* is equal to all. There cannot be any distinction. Caste distinction is against the highest principle.

M. Why do you drag in *Brahman*? He has no grievances. Let him who has grievances pursue the matter.

D. You are a Mahatma. You cannot admit castes. But how do the people here enforce such distinctions?

M. Did I tell you that I am a *jnani* or a *mahatma*? You are saying it yourself. Nor did I make a grievance of this caste affair.

D. *Paramatma* is the same in all.

M. Why do you bring in all these names? They can take care of themselves. They do not require your help.

D. Mahatma Gandhi also admits equality . . .

M. Gandhi is not here.

D. Aurobindo does not approve of castes. Do you approve of them?

M. As for Aurobindo, you ask him. As for my opinion, how does it matter to you? How will it be of use to you? Have you got any opinion on the matter? That alone will affect you, not the opinion of others.

D. I do not approve of the caste system. Mahatma's opinion is valuable as a guidance. I want your blessings in my attempts.

M. Mahatma has told you to seek and find your Self. You will not do it, but ask for his blessings.

D. I am trying to follow the instructions. But caste distinction is painful. It must go.

M. To whom does it cause pain?

D. To members of society . . .

M. It is you who say it. There are countries where there are no such distinctions of caste. Are they free from trouble? There are wars, internecine struggle, etc. Why do you not remedy the evils there?

D. There are troubles here, also.

M. Differences are always there. There are not only human beings, but also animals, plants, etc. The state of affairs cannot be helped.

D. We do not mind the animals, etc., at present.

M. Why not? If they could speak they would claim equality with you and dispute your claims no less vigorously than human beings.

D. But we cannot help it. It is God's work.

M. If that is God's work, then the other part is your work, is that so?

D. It is a manmade distinction.

M. You need not notice these distinctions. There is diversity in the world. A Unity runs through the diversity. The Self is the same in all. There is no difference in spirit. All the differences are external and superficial. You find out the Unity and be happy.

The pain of diversity is overcome by the joy of the perception of Unity. Moreover, a king may disguise himself as a servant. That makes no difference in the person.

D. I do not object to differences. But the claims of superiority are wrong.

M. There are differences in the limbs of one's body. When the hand touches the foot, the hand is not defiled. Each limb performs its function. Why do you object to differences?

D. The people feel the injustice of caste distinction. It must be rooted out.

M. You can individually arrive at the state where such distinctions are not perceived and be happy. How can you hope to reform the world? Even if you try, you cannot succeed. Kavyakantha Ganapati Sastri offered to initiate Harijans with mantras and make Brahmins of them. But the Harijans did not come forward to accept the offer. That shows they are themselves afflicted by an inferiority complex. Remove that complex first before you try to reform others.

Moreover, why do you go to places where such distinctions are observed and cause pain to yourself? Why should you not seek places where they are not observed and be happy there?

Gandhiji also tries to bring about equality. He too is up against the barrier of an inferiority complex afflicting the lower orders. He cannot enforce his views on others. He observes nonviolence. So matters stand as they are.

D. We must work to obliterate caste distinctions.

M. Then do it. If you have succeeded in the world, then see if the distinctions persist in this place.

D. This must be the first place where I want to effect the reform.

M. Why do you exert yourself so much to effect reforms? Go to sleep and see if there are differences. There you obliterate differences without any effort.

(*Laughter.*)

AUGUST 24, 1938

An Indian Civil Service Officer was in the Hall for a few hours. He asked: Can *ahimsa* (nonviolence) put an end to wars in the world?

> (*Sri Bhagavan did not answer and it was time to go out for the evening walk. The next day when someone else repeated this question, Sri Bhagavan said that the question contained its answer. It is obvious that in a state of perfect* ahimsa, *there can be no war.*)

AUGUST 26, 1938

Mr. MacIver had an interview with Sri Bhagavan and spoke about diksha *(initiation).*

Sri Bhagavan asked: What is this *diksha*?

> (*After a pause.*)

M. *Diksha* is of various kinds, by word, by sight, by touch and so forth.

D. Bhagavan's is *mouna diksha,* is it not?

M. Yes, this is the highest form of *diksha.*

D. Is it applicable to the *Vichara Marga* only?

M. All the *margas* are included in the *Vichara Marga.*

D. Yes, but if one wished to take them separately, it would not be applicable. Would it?

M. No.

D. Supposing one feels the need for aids to Realization? These are to be regarded as belonging to accessory *margas*, are they not?

M. Yes.

D. And for these, then, other *dikshas* would be necessary?

M. Yes

D. From this another question arises: So long as I am at Bhagavan's feet, I cannot be regarded as a faithful Christian.

> (*Sri Bhagavan interrupted, saying that this was the very essence of Christianity.*)

D. Yes, but not in the eyes of the present representatives of the Church. Accordingly, I can no longer look to the side of the Church for aid. Have I Bhagavan's leave to look elsewhere?

M. That is left to you.

(After a pause, Sri Bhagavan spoke to the effect that people who come here are brought by some mysterious Power, which will look to their needs. The conversation practically ended there.)

SEPTEMBER 11, 1938

Sri Bhagavan said: All mistake the mind-consciousness for Self-Consciousness. There is no mind in deep sleep but no one denies his being in sleep. Even a child says on waking, "I slept well," and does not deny his existence. The "I" rises up, the mind turns outward through the five senses and perceives objects; this they call direct perception. Asked if "I" is not directly perceived, they get confused, because "I" does not announce itself as an object in front and only the perception with the senses can be recognized by them as knowledge; this habit is so strong with them. A stanza in *Thevaram* says:

> "O sages, eager to get over all misery, worry not about inferences and examples! Our Light is ever shining forth from within! With mind clear, live in God!"

This is direct perception. Will the ordinary people admit it? They want God to appear in front of them as a bright Being mounted on a bull. Such a vision once originated must also end. It is therefore transient. *Thevaram* speaks of the Eternal and Ever-experienced Being. This *Thevaram* takes one directly to the Reality.

SEPTEMBER 16, 1938

Mr. MacIver, a resident devotee, asked Sri Bhagavan if he might go to Switzerland where a Guru was inviting him. Sri Bhagavan said: Some Force brought him here and the same is taking him to Europe. Let him always remember that the world is only a projection of the mind, and the mind is in the Self. Wherever the body may move, the mind must be kept under control. The body moves, but not the Self. The world is within the Self, that is all.

SEPTEMBER 22, 1938

A question arose if the world is real or unreal, since it is claimed to be both by the *advaitins* themselves. Sri Bhagavan said that it is unreal if viewed as apart from the Self and real if viewed as the Self.

There was some reference to two *slokas* in *Yoga Vasishta* where spiritism in *mlechcha desa* is mentioned. Mr. MacIver said that black magic is more prevalent in the West than is ordinarily known to the observer. The writer then remembered how Mr. Paul Brunton had once said that he actually feared a woman for her association with black magic.

Sri Bhagavan asked if the gentleman had read *Devikalottaram.* He then said that *abhichara prayoga* (black magic) is condemned there. He also added that by such practices one only effects one's own ruin. *Avidya* (ignorance) is itself bad and makes one commit suicide. Why should black magic be added to it?

D. What is the *pratikriya* (remedy) open to the victim of black magic?

M. *Bhakti* (devotion to God).

D. Non-resistance seems to be the only remedy for all kinds of evil such as slander.

M. Quite so. If one abuses another or injures him, the remedy does not lie in sharp retort or resistance. Simply keep quiet. This quiet will bring peace to the injured but make the offender restless until he is driven to admit his error to the injured party.

This black magic is said to have been used even against the greatest saints in India since time immemorial. The *tapasvis* of Daruka forest used it against Shiva Himself.

Then the conversation turned on *Brahmaloka.*

Sri Bhagavan said *Brahmaloka* is the same as *Atmaloka.* Again *Brahmaiva lokah = Brahmalokah* (Brahma is Himself the region) and *Brahma* is *Atma.* So *Brahmaloka* is only the Self.

Loka and *aloka* are synonymous. It is the same as *andamillakkan* in *Ulladu Narpadu. Lokyate iti lokah* (That which is seen is *loka*).

Sri Bhagavan said in the course of conversation: Ahamkriti (the ego) is not the same as *aham.* The latter is the Supreme Reality, whereas the former is the ego. This has to be overcome before the Truth is realized. The Supreme Being is unmanifest and the first sign of manifestation is *Aham Sphurana* (light of "I"). The *Brihadaranyaka Upanishad* says *Aham nama abhavat* (He became "I"-named). That is the original name of Reality.

Mr. V. Gupta, a Telugu Pundit, asked about the operation of Grace: Is it the mind of the Guru acting on the mind of the disciple, or something different?
M. The Highest Form of Grace is Silence (*mouna*). It is also the highest *upadesa*.
D. Vivekananda has also said that silence is the loudest form of prayer.
M. It is so, for the seeker's silence. Guru's silence is the loudest *upadesa*. It is also Grace in its highest form. All other *dikshas* (initiations), e.g., *sparsa*, *chakshus*, are derived from *mouna* (silence). They are therefore secondary. *Mouna* is the primary form. If the Guru is silent, the seeker's mind gets purified by itself.
D. Is it proper to pray to God or Guru when afflicted by worldly ills?
M. Undoubtedly.

M. The *mahavakyas* and their interpretation lead to interminable discussions and keep the minds of the seekers engaged externally. To turn the mind inward, one must directly settle down in the "I." Then there is an end of external activities and perfect Peace prevails.

Later, a passage from the Yoga Vasishta *was read out before Sri Bhagavan, indicating initiation by look and also by touch. Sri Bhagavan observed:* Dakshinamurti observed silence when the disciples approached him. That is the highest form of initiation. It includes other forms. There must be a subject-object relationship in the other *dikshas*. First the subject must emanate and then the object. Unless these two are there, how is the one to look at the other or touch him? *Mouna diksha* is the most perfect; it comprises looking, touching, and teaching. It will purify the individual in every way and establish him in Reality.

An Australian gentleman (Mr. Lowman) is here on a visit. He seems to be studying the Hindu system of philosophy. He started saying that he believed in unity, that the jiva *is in illusion, and so on.*
M. What is the unity you believe in? How can the *jiva* find a place in it?
D. The Unity is the Absolute.
M. The *jiva* cannot find a place in Unity.
D. But the *jiva* has not realized the Absolute and imagines itself separate.
M. *Jiva* is separate because it must exist in order to imagine something.
D. But it is unreal.

M. Any unreal thing cannot produce effects. It is like saying that you killed some animal with the horn of a hare. A hare does not grow horns.

D. I see the absurdity. But I speak from the physical plane.

M. You say, "I." Who is that "I"? Once that is found, you can say whose is the illusion.

A little later, Sri Bhagavan asked: You say you are in the physical plane now. In which plane are you in dreamless sleep?

D. I think in the physical plane again.

M. You say, "I think." That means that you are saying it now while you are awake. Anyway, you admit that you exist in deep sleep, don't you?

D. Yes, but I did not function then.

M. So then, you existed in deep sleep. You are the same one who continues to exist? Are you not?

D. Yes.

M. With this difference — that you did not function in your sleep. Rather you are associated with the thinking faculty in your waking state and you are dissociated from it in sleep. Is it not so?

D. Yes.

M. Which is then your real nature? Is it to be associated with thinking or to be dissociated?

D. I see it now. But I was not aware of my being in sleep.

M. You say so now. You do not say so in your sleep. Or do you deny your being (very existence) in sleep?

D. No.

M. It amounts to this: that you exist in both states. The Absolute Existence is the Self. You are also conscious of the Existence. That Existence is also consciousness (*Sat* and *Chit*). That is your real nature.

D. But thinking is necessary even for realization.

M. *That thinking* is aimed at the elimination of all thinking.

D. Owing to my ignorance, I do not realize the Absolute Existence-Consciousness.

M. Who is the "I?" Whose is the ignorance? Answers to these questions will alone suffice to prove that you are already realized. Is there anyone who denies his own existence? Or can anyone say he did not exist in his sleep? Pure Existence is thus admitted. The admission also implies consciousness. Thus all men are realized. There is no ignorant man at all.

D. Yes, I understand. But I have a small question to ask. The state of Realization is one of desirelessness. If a human being is desireless, he ceases to be human.

M. You admit your existence in sleep. You did not function then. You were not aware of any gross body. You did not limit yourself to this body. So you could not find anything separate from your Self.

Now, in your waking state, you continue to be the same Existence with the limitations of the body added. These limitations make you see other objects. Hence arises desire. But the state of desirelessness in sleep made you no less happy than now. You did not feel any want. You did not make yourself miserable by not entertaining desires. But now you entertain desires because you are limited to this human frame. Why do you wish to retain these limitations and continue to entertain desires?

Sri Bhagavan continued: Does the body tell you that it is there? It is certainly something apart from the body that remains aware. What is it?

Do you say that it is the "I," meaning the ego, which arises simultaneously with the waking of the individual from sleep? Be it so. The body is not sentient. The Absolute does not speak. The ego does. One does not aspire for liberation in sleep. The aspiration arises only in the waking state. The functions of the waking state are those of the ego, which is synonymous with the "I." Find out who this "I" is. On doing so and abiding as "I," all these doubts will be cleared.

SEPTEMBER 28, 1938

Some Congressmen handed over the following questions to Maharshi:
1. How long is India destined to suffer bondage?
2. Have not the sons of India made enough sacrifice for her liberation?
3. Will India get freedom during Mahatma Gandhi's lifetime?

The above questions were not answered categorically. Sri Bhagavan simply remarked: Gandhiji has surrendered himself to the Divine and works accordingly with no self-interest. He does not concern himself with the results but accepts them as they turn up. That must be the attitude of national workers.

D. Will the work be crowned with success?

M. This question arises because the questioner has not surrendered himself.

D. Should we not then think of and work for the welfare of the country?

M. First take care of yourself, and the rest will naturally follow.

D. I am not speaking individually, but for the country.

M. First surrender and see. The doubts arise because of the absence of surrender. Acquire strength by surrender and then your surroundings will be found to have improved to the degree of strength acquired by you.

D. Should we not know if our actions will be worthwhile?

M. Follow the example of Gandhiji in the work for the national cause. "Surrender" is the word.

The following slip was also handed over to Sri Bhagavan: Four of us have come from Coorg. We had gone to Delhi to wait as a deputation on the Working Committee of the Indian National Congress and we are now going back. We are sent from the Coorg Congress Committee; kindly give us some message to the Coorg District Congress Committee and the people of Coorg in general.

   (*When this slip was handed over, Sri Bhagavan said that the same answer holds good here, too. The message is contained in the word "Surrender."*)

September 29, 1938

A visitor asked Sri Bhagavan: I want knowledge.

M. Who wants knowledge?

D. I want it.

M. Who is this "I?" Find the "I" and see later what further knowledge is required.

October 2, 1938

A Pilgrim's special train brought several visitors from Bengal. One of them said that he had read Mr. Paul Brunton's book and since then was anxious to see Sri Bhagavan. He also asked: How shall I overcome my passions?

M. Find their root and then it will be easy.

   (*Later.*)

What are the passions, *Kama* (lust), *krodha* (anger), etc? Why do they arise? On account of likes and dislikes towards the objects seen. How do the objects project themselves in your view? Because of your *avidya*, i.e., ignorance. Ignorance of what? Of the Self. Thus, if you find the Self and abide therein, there will be no trouble owing to the passions.

   (*Later.*)

Again, what is the cause of the passions? Desire to be happy or enjoy pleasure. Why does the desire for happiness arise? Because your nature is

412

happiness itself, and it is natural that you come into your own. This happiness is not found anywhere besides the Self. Do not look for it elsewhere. But seek the Self and abide therein.

Still again, that happiness which is natural is simply rediscovered, so it cannot be lost, whereas the happiness arising from other subjects is external and thus liable to be lost. Therefore, it cannot be permanent and so it is not worth seeking.

Moreover, craving for pleasures should not be encouraged. One cannot put out burning fire by pouring fuel over it. Any attempt to satisfy your craving for the time being so that the passion may later be suppressed is simply foolish.

There are, no doubt, other methods for the suppression of passion. They are: 1. Regulated food, 2. Fasting, 3. Yoga practice, 4. Medicines. But their effects are transitory. The passions reappear with greater force as soon as the check is removed. The only way to overcome them is to eradicate them. That is done by finding their source, as stated above.

Another pilgrim asked: I am a man with a family. Is it possible for those in a family to get release, and if so how?
M. Now, what is "family?" Whose family is it? If the answers to these questions are found, the other questions will solve themselves. Tell me: Are you in the family, or is the family in you?
(*The visitor did not answer.*)
Sri Bhagavan's answer continued: Who are you? You include three aspects of life, namely, the waking, the dream, and the sleep states. You were not aware of the family and their ties in your sleep, and so these questions did not arise then. But now you are aware of the family and their ties, and therefore you seek release. But you are aware of the same person throughout.
D. Because I now feel that I am in the family, it is right that I should seek release.
M. You are right. But consider and say: Are you in the family or is the family in you?

Another visitor interposed: What is family?
M. That's it. It must be known.
D. There is my wife and there are also my children. They are dependent on me. That is the family.
M. Do the members of the family bind your mind? Or do you bind yourself

to them? Do they come and say, "We form your family. Be with us?" Or do you consider them as your family and that you are bound to them?

D. I consider them as my family and feel bound to them.

M. Quite so. Because you think that so-and-so is your wife and so-and-so are your children, you also think that you are bound to them.

These thoughts are yours. They owe their very existence to you. You can entertain these thoughts or relinquish them. The former is bondage and the latter is release.

D. It is not quite clear to me.

M. You must exist in order that you may think. You may think these thoughts or other thoughts. The thoughts change, but not you. Let go of the passing thoughts and hold onto the unchanging Self. The thoughts form your bondage. If they are given up, there is release. The bondage is not external. So no external remedy need be sought for release. It is within your competence to think and become bound or cease thinking and thus be free.

D. But it is not easy to remain without thinking.

M. You need not cease thinking. Only think of the root of the thoughts; seek it and find it. The Self shines by itself. When that is found, the thoughts cease of their own accord. That is freedom from bondage.

D. Yes. I understand it now. I have learned it now. Is a Guru necessary?

M. So long as you consider yourself as an individual, a Guru is necessary to show to you that you are not bound by limitations and that your nature is to be free from limitations.

Another visitor asked: Actions are bondage. One cannot remain without some kind of activity. So bondage goes on increasing. What is one to do under the circumstances?

M. One should act in such a manner that the bondage is not strengthened but gets weakened. That is selfless action.

OCTOBER 3, 1938

A visitor asked Sri Bhagavan: People give some names to God and say that the name is sacred and repetitions of the name bestow merit on the individual. Can that be true?

M. Why not? You bear a name to which you answer. But your body was not born with that name written on it, nor did it say to anyone that it bore such and such a name. And yet a name is given to you and you answer to that name, because you have identified yourself with the name. Therefore, the name signifies something and it is not a mere fiction. Similarly, God's name is effective. Repetition of the name is remembrance of what it signifies, hence its merit.

(The man did not look satisfied. Finally, he wanted to retire and prayed for Sri Bhagavan's Grace.)

Sri Bhagavan now asked how mere sounds assuring him of Grace would satisfy him unless he had faith.

(Both laughed and the visitor retired.)

OCTOBER 4, 1938

A group of respectable ladies from Coorg, were in the Hall. One of them asked: I have received a mantra. People frighten me saying that it may have unforeseen results if repeated. It is only *Pranava*. So I seek advice. May I repeat it? I have considerable faith in it.

M. Certainly, it should be repeated with faith.

D. Will it do by itself? Or can you kindly give me any further instructions?

M. The object of *mantra japa* is to realize that the same *japa* is already going on in oneself even without effort. The oral *japa* becomes mental and the mental *japa* finally reveals itself as being eternal. That mantra is the person's real nature. That is also the state of realization.

D. Can the bliss of *samadhi* be gained thus?

M. The *japa* becomes mental and finally reveals itself as the Self. That is *samadhi*.

D. Please show Grace to me and strengthen me in my efforts!

OCTOBER 13, 1938

A middle-aged person from Andhra Pradesh asked: Is thought of God necessary for fixing one's sight (or making the mind one-pointed)?

M. What is the practice?

D. To fix the look.

M. What for?

D. To gain concentration.

M. The practice gives work for the eye right enough; but where is the work for the mind in the process?

D. What should I do for it?

M. Thought of God, certainly.

D. Does the practice make one ill?

M. Maybe. But all will be rightly adjusted of its own accord.

D. I practiced *dhyana* four hours a day and fixation of sight for two hours. I became ill. Others said it was owing to my practice. So I gave up *dhyana*.

M. Matters will adjust themselves.

D. Is it not better that the gaze of the eye becomes fixed naturally?

M. What do you mean?

D. Is practice necessary to fix the gaze or is it better to let it happen of its own accord?

M. What is practice if it is not an attempt to make something natural? It will become natural after long practice.

D. Is *pranayama* necessary?

M. Yes. It is useful.

D. I did not practice it. But should I undertake it?

M. Everything will be all right with sufficient strength of mind.

D. How shall I get strength of mind?

M. By *pranayama*.

D. Is food regulation also necessary?

M. It is certainly useful.

D. Should my contemplation be on the Infinite or the limited being?

M. What do you mean?

D. May I contemplate on Sri Krishna or Sri Rama alternately?

M. *Bhavana* (ideas or impressions) implies *khanda* i.e., division.

OCTOBER 15, 1938

In the course of conversation, Sri Bhagavan said that Tirujnanasambandar had sung in praise of Arunachala. He also mentions the story briefly as follows:

Jnanasambandar was born in an orthodox family about 1,500 years ago. When he was three years old, his father took him to the temple in Shiyali. He left the boy on the bank of the sacred tank and went in to bathe. As he dipped into the water the boy, not finding his father, began to cry out. Immediately, Shiva and Parvati appeared in a *vimana* (aerial car). Shiva told Parvati to feed the boy with her milk. So she drew out milk in a cup and handed it to the boy. He drank it and was happy.

The father came out of the water and saw the boy smiling with streaks of milk round his lips. He asked the boy what happened. The boy did not answer. He was threatened and the boy sang songs. They were hymns in praise of Shiva, who appeared before him. He sang, "The One with earrings . . . the Robber, who robbed me of my mind . . ."

He thus became one of the most famous *bhaktas* and was much sought after. He led a vigorous and active life and went on pilgrimage to several places in South India. He got married in his sixteenth year. The bride and the bridegroom went to have *darshan* (sight) of God in the local temple soon after the marriage ceremonies were over. A large party went with them. When they reached the temple, the place was a blaze of light and the temple was not visible. There was, however, a passage visible in the blaze of light. Jnanasambandar told the people to enter the passage. They did so. He himself went round the light with his young wife, came to the passage, and entered it as the others had done earlier. The Light vanished, leaving no trace of those who entered it. The temple again came into view as usual. Such was the brief but very eventful life of the sage.

In one of his tours, he had come to Arayaninallur or Tirukoilur, eighteen miles from Tiruvannamalai. The place is famous for its Shiva temple. (*It was here that Sri Bhagavan had that vision of Light on his way to Tiruvannamalai in his seventeenth year. Sri Bhagavan did not then know that the place was sanctified by the feet of Tirujnanasambandar some fifteen centuries ago.*) When the ancient sage was staying in Ariyanainallur, an old man who carried a flower-basket came to him. The young sage asked the old man who he was. The latter replied that he was a servant of Sri Arunachala, the God residing as the Hill here.

Sage: How far is it from here?

Old man: I walk every day from there to here collecting flowers for daily worship. So it is only near.

Sage: Then I shall go with you to that place.

Old man: A rare pleasure, indeed, for me!

They went together, with a large crowd following the Sage. After walking some distance the Sage wanted to ask how much further the place was, but the old man had disappeared. A little later, a gang of thieves waylaid the pilgrims who surrendered all that they had with them. They plodded along and reached their destination. The young Sage fell into contemplation. God appeared and said that the thieves were only His followers and that his needs would be met. Accordingly, the group of pilgrims found all their wants. The Sage had sung hymns in praise of Sri Arunachala. In one of the stanzas, he says:

"You are a dense mass of *jnana*, capable of removing the "I-am-the-body" idea from Your devotees! Herds of gazelles, boars, and bears come down Your slopes in the night to search for food on the plains. Herds of

elephants go from the plains to Your slopes where they may rest. So
different herds of animals meet on Your slopes."

Sri Bhagavan continued: So this Hill must have been a dense forest fifteen-
hundred years ago. It has since been denuded of the forest by woodcut-
ters, etc., through these several centuries.

The account of Sri Arunachala given by the mysterious old man to
Jnanasambandar is contained in 300 *slokas* in Upamanyu's *Bhakta Charita*.
One of the *Archakas* (priest) of the temple had it with him and showed it to
Sri Bhagavan on the occasion of the temple suit within the last few months.
Sri Bhagavan copied the *slokas*.

*The following is taken from the diary of Annamalai Swami, a devotee of Sri Bhaga-
van and resident of Sri Ramanasramam*:
1. That man who is active in the world and yet remains desireless, without losing sight of his own essential nature, is alone a true man.
   (*This was in answer to the Swami who wanted to retire into a cave for practicing meditation*).
2. He asked about *sannyas*. Should not a man renounce everything to
   get Liberation?

M. Even better than the man who thinks "I have renounced everything" is
the one who does his duty but does not think "I do this" or "I am the doer."
Even a *sannyasi* who thinks "I am a *sannyasi*" cannot be a true *sannyasi*,
whereas a householder who does not think "I am a householder" is truly a
sannyasi.

D. One person says one thing one way. Another says the same thing in a
different way. How is the truth to be ascertained?
M. Each one sees his own Self only, always, and everywhere. He finds the
world and God according to what he is.

A Nayanar went to Kalahasti for the *darshan* of God. He saw all the
people there as Shiva and Shakti because he himself was so. Again,
Dharmaputra considered that the whole world was composed of people
having some merit or other and that each of them was even better than he
himself for some reason or other. Whereas Duryodhana could not find even
a single good person in the world. Each reflects his own nature.

D. Is there no way of escape from the miseries of the world?

M. There is only one way, and that consists in not losing sight of one's Self under any circumstances. To inquire "Who am I?" is the only remedy for all the ills of the world. It is also perfect bliss.

Soon after the announcement in the newspapers that Gandhiji was going to fast twenty-one days in the Yerwada jail, two young men came to Sri Bhagavan; they were very excited. They said: Mahatma is now fasting for twenty-one days. We want permission from Sri Bhagavan to run up to Yerwada so that we may also fast as long as he does. Please permit us. We are in a haste to go.
   (*Saying so, they made ready to rush out.*)
Sri Bhagavan smiled and said: It is a good sign that you have such feelings. But what can you do now? Get the strength that Gandhiji has already got by his *tapasya*. You will afterwards succeed.

Sri Bhagavan often used to say, Mouna is the utmost eloquence. Peace is the utmost activity. How? Because the person remains in his essential nature and so permeates all the recesses of the Self. Thus he can call up any power into play, whenever or wherever necessary. That is the highest *siddhi*.

Annamalai asked: Namdev, Tukaram, Tulsidas, and others are said to have seen Maha Vishnu. How did they see Him?
M. In what manner? Just in the same manner as you see me now and I see you here. They would also have seen Vishnu in this way only.
   (*Annamalai records that, on hearing it, his hairs stood on end, and an intense joy overpowered him.*)

Once A. (Annamalai) asked, "How can one be worshipful while engaged in daily work?"
   Sri Bhagavan did not reply. Ten minutes passed. A few girls came for *darshan* of Sri Bhagavan. They began to sing and dance. Their song was to the effect: "We will churn the milk without losing thought of Krishna."
   Sri Bhagavan turned to the Swami and said there was the reply to his question. This state is called *bhakti, yoga,* and *karma*.

M. The person soaked in the "I-am-the-body" idea is the greatest sinner and he is a suicide. The experience of "I-am-the-Self" is the highest virtue. Even a moment's *dhyana* to that effect is enough to destroy all the *sanchita* (accumulated) karma. It works like the sun before which darkness is dispelled. If one remains always in *dhyana*, can any sin, however heinous, survive his *dhyana*?

Once Sri Bhagavan said: Desire constitutes *maya*, and desirelessness is God.

A. asked: What exactly is the difference between worldly activity and *dhyana*?
M. There is no difference. It is like naming one and the same thing by two different words in two different languages. The crow has two eyes but only one iris, which is rolled into either eye as it pleases. The trunk of an elephant is used for breathing and for drinking water. The snake sees and hears with the same organ.

When Sri Bhagavan was going up the hill, the Swami asked: Does the closing or opening of the eyes make any difference during *dhyana*?
M. If you strike against a wall with a rubber ball and you stand at a distance, the ball rebounds, and runs back to you. If you stand near the wall, the ball rebounds and runs away from you. Even if the eyes are closed, the mind follows thoughts.

Once A. asked: There is more pleasure in *dhyana* than in sensual enjoyments. Yet the mind runs after the latter and does not seek the former. Why is it so?
M. Pleasure or pain are aspects of the mind only. Our essential nature is happiness. But we have forgotten the Self and imagine that the body or the mind is the Self. It is that wrong identity that gives rise to misery. What is to be done? This *vasana* is very ancient and has continued for innumerable past births. Hence it has grown so strong. That must go before the essential nature, which is happiness, asserts itself.

A certain visitor asked Sri Bhagavan: There is so much misery in the world because wicked men abound. How can one find happiness?
M. All are gurus to us. The wicked say by their evil deeds, "Do not come near me." The good are always good. So then, all persons are like gurus to us.

A. asked: I often desire to live in solitude where I can find all I want with ease, so that I may devote all my time to meditation only. Is such a desire good or bad?
M. Such thoughts will bestow a *janma* (reincarnation) for their fulfillment. What does it matter where and how you are placed? The essential point is

that the mind must always remain in its source. There is nothing external which is not also internal. The mind is all. If the mind is active, even solitude becomes like a marketplace. There is no use closing your eyes. Close the mental eye, and all will be right. The world is not external to you. The good persons will not care to make plans previous to their actions. Why so? For God who has sent us into the world has His own plan, and that will certainly work itself out.

Many visitors came on one occasion and they all saluted Sri Bhagavan with the single prayer: "Make me a *bhakta*, give me *moksha*."
After they left, Sri Bhagavan said, thinking aloud: All of them want *bhakti* and *moksha*. If I say to them, "Give yourself to me," they will not. How then can they get what they want?

On one occasion, a few devotees were discussing the relative merits of some famous bhaktas. They could not agree, and referred the matter to Sri Bhagavan. He remained silent. The discussion became heated. Finally, Sri Bhagavan said: One cannot know about another or confer bondage or release on another. Each one desires to become famous in the world. It is natural for man. But that desire alone does not bring about the end in view. He who is not accepted by God is certainly humiliated. He who has surrendered himself, body and mind, to God becomes famous all over the world.

A. was once badly distracted by sexual thoughts. He fought against them. He fasted three days and prayed to God so that he might be free from such thoughts. Finally, he decided to ask Sri Bhagavan about it.
Sri Bhagavan listened and remained silent for about two minutes. Then he said: Well, the thoughts distracted you and you fought against them. That is good. Why do you continue to think of them now? Whenever such thoughts arise, consider to whom they arise and they will flee away from you.

A. asked: A person does something good but sometimes suffers pain even in these right activities. Another does something wicked but is happy. Why should that be so?
M. Pain or pleasure is the result of past karma and not of the present karma; pain and pleasure alternate with each other. One must suffer or enjoy them patiently without being carried away by them. One must always try to hold on to the Self. When one is active, one should not care for the results and not be swayed by the pain or pleasure met with occasionally. He who

is indifferent to pain or pleasure can alone be happy.

D. What is the significance of Guru's Grace in the attainment of liberation?
M. Liberation is not anywhere outside you. It is only within. If a man is anxious for deliverance, the Guru within pulls him in and the Guru without pushes him into the Self. This is the Grace of the Guru.

A visitor asked Sri Bhagavan (in writing) the following questions: 1. Were the differences in the world simultaneous with creation, or are they of later growth?, 2. Is the Creator impartial? Why is one born lame, another blind, and so on?, 3. Are the eight Dikpalas (gods of the directions), thirty-three crores of gods, and the seven *rishis* (sages) existent even today?
M. Refer these questions to yourself and the answer will be found.

After a pause, Sri Bhagavan continued: If we first know our Self, then all other matters will be plain to us. Let us know our Self and then inquire concerning the Creator and creation. Without first knowing the Self, to seek knowledge of God, etc., is ignorance. A man suffering from jaundice sees everything yellow. If he tells others that all things are yellow, who will accept his statement?

The creation is said to have an origin. How? Like a tree and the seed from which it has grown. How was the seed produced? From a similar tree. Where is the end to the series of questions? Therefore, one must know one's Self before the world is known.

Sri Bhagavan often speaks of namaskar *(prostration) in the following strain*: This *namaskar* was originally meant by the ancient sages to serve as a means of surrender to God. The act still prevails, but not the spirit behind it. The doer of *namaskar* intends to deceive the object of worship by his act. It is mostly insincere and deceitful. It is meant to cover up innumerable sins. Can God be deceived? The man thinks that God accepts his *namaskar* and that he himself is free to continue his old life. They need not come to me. I am not pleased with these *namaskars.* The people should keep their minds clean; instead of that, they bend themselves or lie prostrate before me. I am not deceived by such acts.

Somerset Maugham, a well-known English author, was on a visit to Sri Bhagavan. He also went to see Maj. Chadwick in his room and there he suddenly became unconscious. Maj. Chadwick requested Sri Bhagavan to see him. Sri Bhagavan went into the room, took a seat, and gazed on Mr. Maugham. He regained his senses and saluted Sri Bhagavan. They remained silent and sat facing each other for nearly an hour. The author attempted to ask questions but did not speak. Maj. Chadwick encouraged him to go ahead. Sri Bhagavan said, "All finished. Heart-talk is all talk. All talk must end in silence only."

(*They smiled and Sri Bhagavan left the room.*)

A man asked Sri Bhagavan: How is it that *Atma-vidya* (Self-knowledge) is said to be the easiest?

M. Any other *vidya* requires a knower, knowledge, and an object to be known, whereas this does not require any of them. It is the Self. Can anything be so obvious as that? Hence it is the easiest. All that you need do is to inquire, "Who am I?" A man's true name is *mukti* (liberation).

There are some buildings in the Ashram. There was a building plan which somehow could not be followed in its entirety. Therefore, A. and the Sarvadhikari (manager) did not agree on many details and there used to be trouble between them. A. was once highly disgusted with the state of affairs. He asked Sri Bhagavan what could be done under the circumstances. Sri Bhagavan said: Which of the buildings was according to a plan made by the people here? God has His own plans and all these go on according to that. No one need worry as to what happens.

The Ashramites once asked Sri Bhagavan: How were we all in our previous births? Why do we not know our own past?

M. God in His mercy has withheld this knowledge from people. If they knew they were virtuous, they would grow proud; in the opposite case, they would be depressed. Both are bad. It is enough that one knows the Self.

Just as a river does not continue its flow after its discharge into the ocean, so also a person loses all movements after he merges in the Self.

D. Sri Bhagavan once recounted how Kavyakantha Ganapati Muni asserted to him that a man could live on three rupees a month. What is Sri Bhagavan's opinion in the matter?

M. A man can live happily only if he knows he requires nothing with which to live.

Maj. Chadwick asked Sri Bhagavan one night: The world is said to become manifest after the mind becomes manifest. There is no mind when I sleep. Is the world non-existent to others at that time? Does it not show that the world is the product of a universal mind? How then shall we say that the world is not material, but only dreamlike?

M. The world does not tell you that it is of the individual mind or the universal mind. It is only the individual mind that sees the world. When this mind disappears, the world also disappears.

There was a man who saw in his dream his father who had died thirty years earlier. Furthermore, he dreamt that he had four more brothers and that his father divided his property among them. A quarrel ensued; the brothers assaulted the man and he woke up in a fright. Then he remembered that he was all alone, he had no brothers, and the father was dead long ago. His fright gave place to contentment. So you see — when we see our Self, there is no world; and when we lose sight of the Self, we get ourselves bound in the world.

A visitor asked: We are advised to concentrate on the spot in the forehead between the eyebrows. Is that right?

M. Everyone is aware, "I am." Leaving aside that awareness, one goes about in search of God. What is the use of fixing one's attention between the eyebrows? It is mere folly to say that God is between the eyebrows. The aim of such advice is help the mind to concentrate. It is one of the forcible methods to check the mind and prevent its dissipation. It is forcibly directed into one channel. It is only a help to concentration.

But the best means of realization is the inquiry "Who am I?" The present trouble is to the mind, and must be removed by the mind only.

D. Are there restrictions to be observed in food?

M. *Sattvic* food taken in moderation.

D. There are several *asanas* mentioned. Which of them is the best?

M. *Nididhyasana* (one-pointedness of the mind) is the best.

A visitor asked: Sri Bhagavan! When I heard of you, a strong desire arose in me to see you. Why should it be so?

M. The desire arose in the same way as the body arises to the Self.

D. What is the purpose of life?

M. To seek to know the significance of life is itself the result of good karma in past births. Those who do not seek such knowledge are simply wasting their lives.

A man asked Sri Bhagavan: Sri Bhagavan can know when I shall become a *jnani*. Please tell me when it will be.

M. If I am Bhagavan, then there is no one apart from me to whom *jnana* should arise or to whom I should speak. If I am an ordinary man like others, then I am as ignorant as the rest. Either way, your question cannot be answered.

When Sri Bhagavan was taking his bath, a few *bhaktas* were around him speaking among themselves. They asked him about the use of *ganja* (hashish). Sri Bhagavan had finished his bath by that time.

He said: "Oh *ganja*! The users feel immensely happy when they are under its influence. How shall I describe their happiness! They simply shout *ananda! Ananda!* . . ." Saying so, He walked as if tipsy. The *bhaktas* laughed. He appeared as if he stumbled, placed his hands round A. and cried "*ananda! ananda!*" (bliss! bliss!)

A. records that his very being was transformed from that time. He had remained an inmate for the past eight years. He further says that his mind now remains at peace.

D. What is the *svarupa* (form) and the *arupa* (formless) mind?

M. When you wake up from sleep a light appears, which is the light of the Self, passing through *Mahatattva*. It is called cosmic consciousness. That is *arupa*. The light falls on the ego and is reflected therefrom. Then the body and the world are seen. This mind is *svarupa*. The objects appear in the light of this reflected consciousness. This light is called *jyoti*.

OCTOBER 21, 1938

There is a statement in the book *Vichara Sangraham* that though a person realizes the Self once he cannot, for that simple reason alone, become a *mukta*. He continues to remain a victim of *vasanas* (latencies). Sri Bhagavan was asked whether the realization referred to was the same as the *jnani's*, and if so, why there should be a difference in their effects.

M. The experience is the same. Every person experiences the Self consciously or unconsciously. The *ajnani's* experience is clouded by his latencies, whereas the *jnani's* is not so. The *jnani's* experience of the Self is, therefore, distinct and permanent.

A practicer may by long practice gain a glimpse of Reality. This experience may be vivid for the time being. And yet he will be distracted by the old *vasanas* and so his experience will not avail him. Such a man must continue his *manana* and *nididhyasana* so that all the obstacles may be destroyed. He will then be able to remain permanently in the Real State.

D. What is the difference between a man who makes no attempts and remains an *ajnani,* and another who gains a glimpse and returns to *ajnana?*

M. In the latter case, a stimulus is always present to goad him on to further efforts until the realization is perfect.

D. The *Srutis* say: *Sakrit vibhatoyam brahmaloka* (This knowledge of *Brahman* shines forth once and forever).

M. They refer to permanent realization and not to the glimpse.

D. How is it possible that a man forgets his very experience and falls back into ignorance?

Sri Bhagavan illustrated it with the following story:

There was a king who treated his subjects well. One of his ministers gained his confidence and misused the influence. All the other ministers and officers were adversely affected and they hit upon a plan to get rid of him. They instructed the guards not to let the man enter the palace. The king noted the minister's absence and inquired about him. He was informed that the man was taken ill and therefore could not come to the palace. The king sent his physician to attend to the minister. False reports were conveyed to the king that the minister was sometimes improving and at other times relapsing. The king wanted to see the patient. But the pundits said that such an action was against *dharma.* Later, the minister was reported to have died. The king was very sorry when he heard the news.

The arrogant minister was kept informed of all the happenings by spies of his own. He tried to foil the other ministers. He waited for the king to come out of the palace so that he might report to the king himself. On one occasion he climbed up a tree, hid himself among the branches, and awaited the king. The king came out that night in the palanquin and the man in hiding jumped down in front of the palanquin and shouted his identity. The companion of the king was equally resourceful. He at once took out a handful of sacred ash (*vibhuti*) from his pocket and scattered it in the air so that the king was obliged to close his eyes. The companion shouted victory (*jai*) to the king and ordered the band to play so that the other man's shout was drowned in the noise. He also ordered the palanquin-bearers to move fast and he himself sang incantations to keep off evil spirits. The king was thus left under the impression that the dead man's ghost was playing pranks on him.

The disappointed man became desperate and retired into the forest for *tapasya* (austerities). After a long time, the king happened to pass by while hunting. He came across the former minister seated, in deep contemplation. But he hastened away from the spot for fear that the ghost should molest him.

The moral of the story is that even though the man was seen in flesh and blood, the wrong notion that he was a ghost prevented right values being assessed. So it is with a forced realization of the Self.

OCTOBER 22, 1938

A group of people came on a visit to Sri Bhagavan. One of them asked: How can I keep my mind in order?

M. A refractory bull is lured to the stall by means of grass. Similarly, the mind must be lured by good thoughts.

D. But it does not remain steady.

M. The bull accustomed to stray takes delight in going astray. However, he must be lured with luscious grass to the stall. Even so, he will continue to trespass into the neighbor's fields. He must gradually be made to realize that the same kind of good grass can be had in his own place. After a time, he will remain in the stall without straying. Later, a time will come when, even if driven out of the stall, he will return to it without going into the neighboring fields. So also the mind must be trained to take to right ways. It will gradually grow accustomed to good ways and not return to wrong ways.

D. What are the good ways to be shown to the mind?

M. Thought of God.

OCTOBER 23 - 26, 1938

Pundit Bala Kak Dhar, a jagirdar *(administrator) from Kashmir, had come all the way from Srinagar to have* darshan *of Sri Bhagavan on Deepavali Day. He gave a bundle of papers to Sri Bhagavan containing an account of his life and position. His talks with Sri Bhagavan were all personal. One of his questions was*: Now that I have had the *darshan* of Sri Bhagavan and it is enough for me, may I throw away all the charms, *tantras,* and *pujas* into the river?

M. Daily *puja* as prescribed in the *dharma sastras* is always good. It is for purification of the mind. Even if one feels oneself too advanced to need such *puja,* still it must be performed for the sake of others. Such action will be an example to one's children and other dependents.

A gentleman from Mysore asked: How is the mind to be kept in the right way?
M. By practice. Give it good thoughts. The mind must be trained in good ways.
D. But it is not steady.
M. The *Bhagavad Gita* says: *Sanaissanairuparamet* (The mind must gradually be brought to a standstill); *Atma samstham manah krtva* (making the mind inhere in the Self); *Abhyasa-vairagyabhyam* (by practice and dispassion).
　　Practice is necessary. Progress will be slow.
D. What is the Self referred to in *Atma samstham* (fixing it in the Self)?
M. Do you not know your Self? You certainly exist. Or do you deny your existence? The question may arise "Who is this Self?" only if you do not exist; but you cannot ask anything unless you exist at the same time. Your question shows that you exist. Find out who you are. That is all.
D. I have read many books. But my mind does not turn to the Self.
M. Because the Self is not in the books, but it is in you. Reading books makes one learned. That is the purpose and its fulfillment.
D. How to accomplish *Atma sakshatkara* (Self-realization)?
M. You are the *Atma* (Self) and that is *sakshat* (here and now), also. Where is the place for *kara* (accomplishment) in it? This question shows that you think you are the non-Self. Or you think that there are two selves, the one to realize the other. It is all absurd.
　　That you identify yourself with the gross body lies at the root of it all. Well, this question arises now. Did it arise in your sleep? Did you not exist then? Certainly you did exist in sleep. What is the difference between these two states that the question should arise now but not in sleep? Now you think that you are the body. You see things around you and you want to see the Self in a similar manner. Such is the force of habit. The senses are mere instruments of perception. *You* are the seer. Remain as the seer only. What else is there to see? Such is the state in deep sleep. Therefore, this question does not arise then.
　　Atma sakshatkara (Self-realization) is thus only *anatma nirasana* (giving up the non-Self).
D. Is there only one Self or are there more selves?
M. This is again due to confusion; you identify the body with the Self. You think: "Here I am, here he is, there is another, and so on." You find many bodies and think they are so many selves. But did you ask in your sleep, "I

am sleeping here, how many are yet there who are awake?" Does any question arise, for that matter? Why does it not arise? Because you are only one and there are not many.

D. What is my *tattva* (truth)?

M. You are yourself the *tattva*. Is there a different one to know the *tattva* of another? How can you exist apart from the *tattva*? The very fact of your existence makes you ask this question. Your very existence is the *tattva*. Give up the attires of the *tattva* and remain in your essential nature. All the Scriptures tell you only not to waste your efforts in non-truth — non-*tattva*. Give up the non-*tattva*. Then *tattva* remains, always shining pure and single.

D. I want to know my *tattva* and my duties.

M. Know your *tattva* first and then you may ask what your duties are. You must exist in order to know and do your duty. Realize your existence and then inquire into your duties.

There is a Tamil paper Arya Dharmam. *An article on* Vairagyam *(non-attachment) appeared in it. Sri Bhagavan read it out in answer to a question. The article was briefly as follows: Vairagya = vi + raga = vigataraga (non-attachment).*

Vairagya is possible only for the wise. However, it is often misapplied by the ordinary folk. For instance, a man often says "I have decided not to go to cinema shows." He calls it *vairagya*. Such wrong interpretation of words and old sayings are not uncommon. Again, we often hear, "Dog seen, stone is not seen, stone seen, dog is not seen." It is ordinarily understood to mean that one cannot find a brickbat to throw at a stray dog. But this popular saying has a much deeper significance. It is based on a story: A certain wealthy man's house was closely guarded. It had also a ferocious dog chained to a pillar at the gate. The dog and the chain were, however, very skillful pieces of art. They were sculptured in stone, but appeared life-like. A pedestrian on the road once took fright at the sight of the ferocious animal and hurt himself in an attempt to dodge it. A kindly neighbor took pity on him and showed him that it was not a living dog. When the man passed by it the next time, he admired the sculptor's skill and forgot his old experience. Thus when he found it to be a dog, he could not see the stone of which it was made; and again, when he found it a piece of sculpture, he did not see any dog to hurt him. Hence the proverb. Compare it with "The elephant hides the wood and the wood hides the elephant." Here it is a wooden elephant.

Atma is always *Sat-Chit-Ananda*. Of these, the first two are experienced in all the states, whereas the last one is said to be experienced in sleep only.

The question arises how the true nature of the Self can be lost in the waking and dream states. It is, really speaking, not lost. In sleep, there is no mind and the Self shines as Itself, whereas in the other two states what shines forth is the reflected light of the Self. *Ananda* is felt after the cessation of thoughts in sleep. It is also manifest on other occasions as love, joy, etc., *priya, moda,* and *pramoda.* But they are all *chitta vrittis* (modes of mind).

When a man is walking in the street, his mind is full of fleeting thoughts. Suppose he passes a bazaar where some fine mangoes are for sale. He likes the mangoes and purchases them. He is anxious to taste them. So he hastens home and eats them and feels happy. When the fleeting thoughts give way to pleasure at the sight of mangoes, it is *priya*; when he gets them as his own, the pleasure is *moda*; lastly, when he eats them, the pleasure is *pramoda.* All three kinds of pleasure are due to the disappearance of other thoughts.

November 3 - 6, 1938

Sri Bhagavan explained to Mr. MacIver the first few stanzas of Sad-Vidya, *as follows:*

1. The first stanza is the auspicious beginning. Why should the subject matter of the piece be brought in here? Can knowledge be other than Being? Being is the core — the Heart. How then is the Supreme Being to be contemplated and glorified? Only to remain as the Pure Self represents auspicious beginning. This speaks of attributeless *Brahman* according to the *Jnana Marga* (method of knowledge).

2. The second stanza is in praise of God with attributes. In the previous verse, to be the one Self is mentioned; in the present verse, surrender to the Lord of all is indicated. Furthermore, the second verse indicates: the fit reader, the subject matter, the relationship, and the fruit. The fit reader is the one who is competent for it. Competence consists of non-attachment to the world and the desire to be liberated.

   All know that they must die some time or other but they do not think deeply over the matter. All have a fear of death; such fear is momentary. Why fear death? Because of the "I-am-the-body" idea. All are fully aware of death, of the body, and its cremation. That the body is lost in death is well known. Owing to the "I-am-the-body" notion, death is feared as being the loss of oneself. Birth and death pertain to the body only; but they are superimposed onto the Self, giving rise to the delusion that birth and death relate to the Self.

In an effort to overcome birth and death, man looks up to the Supreme Being to save him. Thus are born faith and devotion to the Lord. How to worship Him? The creature is powerless and the Creator all-powerful. How to approach Him? To entrust oneself to His care is the only thing left for him; total surrender is the only way. Therefore, he surrenders himself to God. Surrender consists of giving up oneself and one's possessions to the Lord of mercy. Then, what is left over for man? Nothing — neither himself nor his possessions. The body liable to be born and to die having been made over to the Lord; man need no longer worry about it. Then birth and death cannot strike terror. The cause of fear was the body. It is no longer his; why should he fear now? Or where is the identity of the individual to be frightened?

Thus the Self is realized and Bliss results. This is then the subject matter: freedom from misery and gain of Happiness. It is the highest good to be gained. Surrender is synonymous with Bliss itself. This is the relationship.

The "fruit," means to reflect on the subject matter and gain Knowledge which is ever-present, here and now. The stanza ends with "the immortal ones."

3. The five senses mean the subtle functions (*tanmatras*), namely: hearing, touch, seeing, taste, and smell. Variations of these constitute the whole universe; they vary according to the three *gunas* as follows:

Tamas (dullness) — the gross elements
Rajas (activity) — the instruments for knowing objects
Sattva (clearness) — the different kinds of knowledge of the senses.
Also by:
Tamas — the gross objects (the world)
Rajas — the vital airs and the *karmendriyas*
Sattva — the senses.
Karmendriyas are organs of holding, walking, speech, evacuation, and reproduction.

Now consider the ringing of a bell. The sound is related to hearing; the bell is the object, the modification of *tamoguna*. The *rajasic tanmatras*, changing as the vibrations of sound, extend around the bell, then get connected through air with the ear to be felt as sound.

The knowledge recognizing it as sound is the *sattva tanmatra*.

To understand the *tanmatras* as the subject particles of matter is incomplete. They are only the subtle forms of sound, touch, sight, taste, and smell, which form the components of the entire universe. Such is the creation of the world.

For want of proper terminology, these ideas cannot be easily expressed in foreign languages.

4. This stanza says that all are agreed on one point. What is it? The state beyond duality and nonduality, beyond subject and object, beyond *jiva* and God — in short, beyond all differences. It is free from ego. "How to reach it?" is the question. By giving up the world, it says. Here "the world" stands for thoughts relating to it. If such thoughts do not arise, the ego does not rise up. There will be neither subject nor object. Such is the state.

Mr. V.G. Sastri showed a cutting to Sri Bhagavan. It contained a prophecy by Sri Rama Tirtha that India would reach the full height of her former glory before the year 1950. Sri Bhagavan said: Why should we think that India is not already in the height of her glory? The glory is in your thought.

NOVEMBER 7, 1938

In reply to Sri K.L. Sarma, Sri Bhagavan spoke about Dakshinamurti Stotra *as follows*:
I originally intended to write a commentary on it. Mr. Ranganatha Iyer took away my Tamil version of the *stotra* and printed it along with *Appalapattu*. He later asked me to enlarge it. I had the introduction ready. He saw it and took it away for printing. I did not proceed with the work. As for the *stotra*:

Brahma, the creator, created four sons from his mind. They were Sanaka, Sanandana, Sanathkumara, and Sanatsujata. They asked their creator why they were brought into existence. Brahma said: "I must create the universe. But I want to go to do *tapas* for realizing the Self. You are brought forth in order that you may create the universe. That will be by multiplying yourselves." They did not like the idea. They wondered why they should take the trouble on themselves. It is natural for one to seek the source. They therefore wanted to regain their source and be happy. So they did not obey the commands of Brahma but left him. They desired guidance for realization of the Self. They were the best-equipped individuals for Self-realization. Guidance should be only from the best of Masters. Who could it be but Shiva — the *yogiraja*. Shiva appeared before them sitting under the sacred banyan tree. Being *yogiraja*, should He practice yoga? He went into *samadhi* as He sat; He was in Perfect Repose. Silence prevailed. They saw Him. The effect was immediate. They fell into *samadhi* and their doubts were at an end.

Silence is the true *upadesa*. It is the perfect *upadesa*. It is suited only for the most advanced seeker. The others are unable to draw full inspiration from it. Therefore, they require words to explain the Truth. But Truth is beyond words; it does not warrant explanation. All that is possible is to indicate It. How is that to be done?

The people are under an illusion. If the spell is removed, they will realize the Truth. They must be told to realize the falsity of the illusion; then they will try to escape its snares. *Vairagya* will result. They will inquire into the Truth, i.e., seek the Self. That will make them abide as the Self. Sri Shankara, being the *avatar* of Shiva, was full of compassion for fallen beings. He wanted all of them to realize their blissful Self. He could not reach them all with his Silence. So he composed the *Dakshinamurti Stotra* in the form of a hymn so that people might read it and understand the Truth.

What is the nature of the illusion? All are in the grip of enjoyment, i.e., *bhokta, bhogyam, bhoga*. This is due to the wrong notion that *bhogya vastu* (the objects) are real. The ego, the world, and the creator are the fundamentals underlying the illusion. If they are known as not apart from the Self, there will be no more illusion.

The first four stanzas deal with the world. It is shown to be the same as the Master whose Self is that of the seeker, also, or the Master to whom the seeker surrenders himself. The second four stanzas deal with the individual whose Self is shown to be the Self of the Master. The ninth stanza deals with *Ishvara*, and the tenth with the *siddhi* or Realization.

Such is the scheme of the *stotra*.

Which is the *darpana* (mirror) here? A mirror, as we know it, is an insentient object that reflects light. What corresponds to a mirror in an individual? The light of the Self-luminous Self is reflected on the *Mahatattva*. The reflected light is the mind-ether or the pure mind. This illumines the *vasanas* (latencies) of the individual and hence the sense of "I" and "this" arises.

A superficial reading of the *slokas* makes one believe that the bondage, liberation, etc., are all related to the Master, i.e., Sri Dakshinamurti. It is absurd. Surrender to Him is meant.

A visitor asked Sri Bhagavan: Nirguna upasana (meditation on the formless) is said to be difficult and risky. He quoted a verse from the *Bhagavad Gita*, *avyaktahi* etc. (the unmanifest, etc.)
M. What is manifest is considered to be unmanifest and doubt is created. Can anything be more immediate and intimate than the Self? Can anything be plainer?
D. *Saguna upasana* (meditation on form) seems easier.
M. Do what is easy for you.

Multiplicity of individuals is a moot point with most persons. A *jiva* (individual soul) is only the light reflected on the ego. The person identifies himself with the ego and argues that there must be more like him. He is not easily convinced of the absurdity of his position. Does a man who sees many individuals in his dream persist in believing them to be real and inquire after them upon waking?

This argument does not convince the disputant.

Again, there is the moon. Let anyone look at her from any place at any time; she is the same moon. Everyone knows it. Now suppose there are several receptacles of water reflecting the moon. The images are all different from one another and from the moon herself. If one of the receptacles falls to pieces, that reflection disappears. Its disappearance does not affect the real moon or the other reflections. It is similar with an individual attaining Liberation. He alone is liberated.

The sectarian of multiplicity makes his argument against nonduality: "If the Self were single, then if one man is liberated, that would mean all souls are liberated. In practice, this is not the case. Therefore *Advaita*, is incorrect."

The weakness in the argument is that the reflected light of the Self is mistaken for the original Light of the Self. The ego, the world, and the individuals are all due to the person's *vasanas*. When they perish, that person's hallucinations disappear — that is to say, one pitcher is broken and the relative reflection is at an end.

The fact is that the Self is never bound. There can, therefore, be no release for it. All the troubles are for the ego only.

A question was asked why it was wrong to say that there is a multiplicity of *jivas*. *Jivas* are certainly many. For a *jiva* is only the ego and forms the reflected light of the Self. Multiplicity of selves may be wrong but not of *jivas*.

M. *Jiva* is called so because he sees the world. A dreamer sees many *jivas* in a dream but all of them are unreal. The dreamer alone exists and he sees all. So it is with the individual and the world. There is the creed of only one Self, which is also called the creed of only one *jiva*. It says that the *jiva* is the only one who sees the whole world and the *jivas* therein.

D. Then *jiva* means the Self here?

M. So it is. But the Self is not a seer. But here he is said to see the world. So he is differentiated as the *jiva*.

D. Of what use is the fear of death that is common to all?

M. True, it is common to all. Such fear serves no useful purpose because being overpowered by the latent tendencies of the mind man dies a natural death. It does not lead him to non-attachment and he cannot investigate the matter.

D. How, then, are you giving the same instruction without distinction to visitors?

M. What do I say? The ego in each one must die. Let him reflect on it. Is there this ego, or is there not? By repeated reflection, one becomes more and more fit.

Mr. Ranganatha Ayyar, a devotee of fourteen years' standing, is here on a visit. He asked: How long is the interval between one's death and reincarnation?

M. It may be long or short. But a *jnani* does not undergo any such changes; he merges into the universal Being, so says the *Brihadaranyaka Upanishad*. Some say that those who after death pass into the path of light are not reborn, whereas those who after death take the path of darkness are reborn after they have enjoyed the fruits of karma in their subtle bodies.

If one's merits and demerits are equal, they are directly reborn here. Merits outweighing demerits, the subtle bodies go to heavens and are then reborn here; demerits outweighing merits, they go to hells and are afterwards reborn here.

A *yogabrashta* is said to fare in the same manner. All these are described in the *sastras*. But in fact, there is neither birth nor death. One remains only as what one really is. This is the only Truth.

D. What are *asanas* (postures or seats)? Are they necessary?
M. Many *asanas* with their effects are mentioned in the *Yoga Sastras*. The seats are the tiger-skin, grass, etc.; the postures are the "lotus posture," the "easy posture," and so on. Why all these — only to know oneself? "I am the body; the body requires a seat; it is the earth," thinking thusly, he seeks seats. But in sleep, did he think of the support or the bed; the bed on the cot and the cot on the earth? Did he not exist in sleep, too? How was he then?

The truth is — being the Self, the ego rising up, confusing himself with the body, mistaking the world to be real, differentiating the objects, covered by the ignorance of the "I"-conceit, he thinks wildly and also looks for seats. He does not understand that he himself is the Center of all and thus forms the basis for all.

If questioned, he talks of the effects of seats and footwear in terms of gravitation, magnetism, and so on. Without them, he imagines that the power of his austerities will dwindle away.

From where do they all derive their power? He looks to the effects, seeks their causes, and imagines them to be the power of seats and of footwear. A stone, thrown up, falls back to earth. Why? Owing to the gravitation, he says. Well, are all these different from his thoughts? Think and say if the stone, the earth and gravity are different from his thoughts. They are all in his mind only. He is the Power and the wielder of it. He is the Center of all and their support. He is also the Seat.

The seat is meant to make him sit firm. Where and how can he remain firm except in his own real state? This is the Seat.

D. How to conquer desire, anger, etc.?
M. Desire or lust, anger, etc., give you pain. Why? Because of the "I"-conceit. This "I"-conceit is from ignorance; ignorance from differentiation; differentiation from the notion of the reality of the world, and this again from the "I-am-the-body" idea. The last can be only after the rise of the ego. The ego not arising, the whole chain of mishaps disappears. Therefore, prevent the rise of the ego. This can be done by remaining in your own real nature; then lust, anger, etc., are conquered.
D. So, then, all these have their root in ignorance.
M. Quite so. Ignorance gives rise to error, error to conceit, etc. What is ignorance? Can it be of Pure *Brahman*, which is only the Self or Pure Knowledge? Only let the questioner know his own Self, i.e., be the Knowledge;

this question then will not arise. Because of ignorance, the person raises the question. Such ignorance is of the questioner, and not of the Self. The sun seen, no darkness persists.

Wealth is hoarded in an iron safe. The man says it is his own; the safe does not say so. It is the ownership-conceit that is responsible for the claim.

Nothing is independent of the Self, not even ignorance; for ignorance is only the power of the Self, remaining there without affecting It. However, it affects the "I"-conceit, i.e., the *jiva*. Therefore, ignorance is of the *jiva*.

How? The man says, "I do not know myself." Are there then two selves — one the subject and the other the object? He cannot admit that. Is then ignorance at an end for him? No. The rise of the ego is itself the ignorance and nothing more.

Sutra Bhashya.

The *sutras* are meant to elucidate and establish the meanings of the texts. The commentaries try to do so by bringing in the opponent's views, refuting them, and arriving at conclusions after long discussions. There are also differences of opinion within the same school of thought; again, protagonists and antagonists. Also, different schools of thought interpret the same text in different ways and arrive at different conclusions, contrary to each other.

How, then, is the purpose of the *sutras* served?

November 15, 1938

M. Coming here, some people do not ask about themselves. They ask: "Does the sage, liberated while alive (*Jivanmukta*), see the world? Is he affected by karma? What is liberation after being disembodied? Is one liberated only after being disembodied, or even while alive in the body? Should the body of the sage resolve itself in light or disappear from view in any other manner? Can he be liberated though the body is left behind as a corpse?"

Their questions are endless. Why worry oneself in so many ways? Does liberation consist in knowing these?

Therefore, I say to them, "Leave liberation alone. Is there bondage? Know this. See yourself first and foremost."

Avarana (veiling) does not hide the *jiva* in entirety; he knows that he *is*, only he does not know who he is. He sees the world; but not that it is only

Brahman. It is light in darkness (or knowledge in ignorance).

In a cinema show, the room is first darkened, then artificial light is introduced. Only in this light are the pictures projected.

For differentiation, a reflected light is thus necessary. A sleeper dreams, he is not out of sleep. Only in the darkness or ignorance of sleep can he see the unreal dream objects.

Similarly, the darkness of ignorance gives rise to the knowledge of the perceptions of the world.

This veiling is a characteristic of ignorance; it is not of the Self. It cannot affect the Self in any manner; it can veil only the *jiva*. The ego is insentient; united with the light from the Self, it is called *jiva*. But the ego and the light cannot be seen distinct from each other; they are always united together. The mixed product is the *jiva*, the root of all differentiation. All these are spoken of only to satisfy the questioners.

Avarana (veiling) gives rise to two kinds of veiling:

Within	Outside
veils *drik* (the seer)	veils the Lord's
drisya (the seen)	creation
↓	↓
"I-am-the-body" idea	Multiplicity

Jiva is not independent of *Ishvara*, nor ignorance of *maya*. Only on waking up from sleep, man perceives the body and the world. On the strength of the present knowledge, he understands that he remained in deep sleep, also. Therefore, in sleep *jiva* must be concluded to be in a pure state in which the body and the world are not perceived.

D. Is not *jiva* the reflected light, the "I"-thought?

M. *Jiva* is present during sleep and also after waking; they are related to each other as cause and effect. The sleeper *jiva* cannot be independent of *Ishvara*. On waking, he says "I am the body." If all the worlds together form *virat* (the Totality), the body is a tiny dot in it. Thus, the body is in and of *virat*. What belongs to the *jiva*, then? Only the conceit makes him claim the body as himself but not the others. He cannot be independent of *virat*.

NOVEMBER 17, 1938

A party from Rajkot came in by bus. It consisted of four chiefs and four ladies with attendants and a bodyguard. They arrived at 11:00 a.m. After lunch in their room, they had a short conversation at 12:45 p.m. and left at 1:05 p.m.

One of them said: Here is the mother of the Thakore Saheb. We have come a long way for the *darshan* of Sri Maharshi. Will he kindly give us some instructions?

Sri Bhagavan smiled and answered: Good that they have come such a long distance for the sake of *darshan*. It is enough that they have said it. What is there for me to say?

(*Lunch bell.*)

At 12:45 p.m.

D. Is a *jnani* different from a yogi? If so, what is the difference?

M. *Srimad Bhagavad Gita* says that a *jnani* is the true yogi and also a true *bhakta*. Yoga is only a *sadhana* and *jnana* is the *siddhi*.

D. Is yoga necessary?

M. It is a *sadhana*. It will not be necessary after *jnana* is attained. All the *sadhanas* are called yogas, e.g., *Karma Yoga, Bhakti Yoga, Jnana Yoga, Ashtanga Yoga*. What is yoga? Yoga means "union." Yoga is possible only when there is "*viyoga*" (separation). The person is now under the delusion of *viyoga*. This delusion must be removed. The method of removing it is called yoga.

D. Which method is the best?

M. It depends upon the temperament of the individual. Every person is born with the *samskaras* of past lives. One method will be found easy for one person and another method for another. There is no definiteness about it.

D. How is one to meditate?

M. What is meditation? It is commonly understood to be concentration on a single thought. Other thoughts are kept out at that time. Eventually, the single thought also must vanish at the right time. Thought-free consciousness is the goal.

D. How is the ego to be got rid of?

M. The ego must be held in order to get rid of it. Hold it first and the rest will be easy.

D. How is it to be held?

M. Do you mean that there is one ego to hold another ego or to eliminate the other? Are there then two egos?

D. How shall I pray to God?

M. There must be "I" who prays to God. "I" is certainly immediate and intimate, whereas God is not thought to be so. Find out that which is more intimate and then the other may be ascertained and prayed to if necessary.

NOVEMBER 19, 1938

When a child held something to be offered to Sri Bhagavan by the parents, they cajoled the child to offer it to Sri Bhagavan. The child did so gladly. Sri Bhagavan remarked: Look at this! When a child can give away a thing to *Jeja* (God), it is *tyaga* (renunciation). See what influence *Jeja* has on children, also! Every gift implies unselfishness. That is the whole content of *nishkama* karma (unselfish action). It means true renunciation. If the giving nature is developed, it becomes *tyaga*. If anything is willingly given away it is a delight to the giver and to the receiver. If the same is stolen, it is misery to both. *Dana, dharma, nishkama karma* are all *tyaga* only. When "mine" is given up, it is *chitta suddhi* (purified mind). When "I" is given up, it is *jnana*. When the nature to give away is developed, it results in *jnana*.

A little later, a young boy came all alone, unescorted by his parents. He had come from Chengam in a bus. Sri Bhagavan remarked, "The boy has left his parents to come here. This is also an instance of *tyaga*."

NOVEMBER 21 - 22, 1938

To a gentleman from Andhra Pradesh, Sri Bhagavan said: If one goes on wanting, one's wants cannot be fulfilled, whereas if one remains desireless, anything will be forthcoming. We are not in the wife, children, profession, etc., but they are in us; they appear and disappear according to one's *prarabdha*.

The mind remaining still is *samadhi*, no matter whether the world is perceived or not. Environment, time, and objects are all in me. How can they be independent of me? They may change, but I remain unchanging. The objects can be differentiated by their names and forms, whereas each one's name is only one and that is "I." Ask anyone; he says "I" and speaks of himself as "I," even if He is *Ishvara*. His name, too, is "I" only.

As long as I am identified with the body, so long a locality is distinguishable; otherwise not. Am I the body? Does the body announce itself as "I?"

Clearly, all these are in me. And upon all these having been wiped out entirely, the residual Peace is "I." This is *Samadhi*; this is "I."

Mr. V. Ganapati Sastri showed Sri Bhagavan a letter from a Spanish lady, Mercedes De Acorta, saying she would be coming here the next day. Sri Bhagavan remarked: See the trouble to so many because I am here.

NOVEMBER 23, 1938

A certain visitor began to move the punkah *(manual fan). Sri Bhagavan said*: Because it is cold, they have placed a fire by my side. Why should the *punkah* be pulled?

Then he continued: On a cold morning, when I was in Virupaksha cave, I was sitting in the open. I was feeling cold. People used to come, see me, and go back. A group of Andhra visitors had come. I did not notice what they were doing. They were behind me. Suddenly, a noise — "tak" — and water over my head! I shivered with the cold. I looked back. They had broken a coconut and poured the water on me. They thought it was worship. They took me for a stone image.

Sri Bhagavan said that this town is peculiar in that there are nine roads leading to it, not counting the railroad; *navadware pure dehe* (in the body — the city of nine gates).

An Andhra visitor asked: How is one to be quiet? It is so difficult. Should we practice *yoga* for it? Or are there any other means to it?
M. What is not difficult looks difficult. A man is prone to wander about. He is told to stay quiet at home, but finds it difficult to do so because he wants to wander about.
D. Is there any particular *upasana* that is more efficacious than others?
M. All *upasanas* are equally efficacious. But each person takes easily to one particular kind of *upasana*, which suits his *vasanas*.

NOVEMBER 24, 1938

The Spanish lady and her lady friend have come. They asked: You say the Heart is on the right. Can you explain how it is so?
Sri Bhagavan handed over the extract from the Modern Psychological Review *of Philadelphia, for her to read. He also said:* The Heart is the place wherefrom the "I"-thought arises.
D. So you mean the spiritual Heart as distinguished from the physical heart?
M. Yes. It is explained in chapter five of *Sri Ramana Gita.*

D. Is there any stage when one might feel the Heart?

M. It is within the experience of everyone. Everyone touches the right side of his chest when he says "I."

(*Both ladies kneeled before Sri Bhagavan one after another and asked for his blessings. Then they left for Pondicherry on their way to Colombo.*)

NOVEMBER 25, 1938

To a seeker from Andhra Pradesh, Sri Bhagavan said: *Sannyasa* is mentioned for one who is fit. It consists in renunciation, not of material objects, but of attachment to them. *Sannyasa* can be practiced by anyone, even at home. Only one must be fit for it.

NOVEMBER 27, 1938

Somasundara Swami, a long-standing devotee, asked: There is *akasha* in a mirror and it reflects images. How are these contained in the mirror?

M. Objects remain in space. Objects and space are together reflected in the mirror. Just as things are found in space, so they are in the reflection. The mirror is itself thin. How can these objects be contained in its compass?

D. How does the *akasha* in a pot illustrate this point?

M. There is no reflection in the *akasha* of the pot. The reflection is only in the water in it. Keeping several pots filled with water in a tank, the *akasha* is reflected equally in the water in each pot and in the water of the tank. Similarly, the whole universe is reflected in each individual.

D. The mouths of the pots must be above the surface of the water in the tank.

M. Yes, they must be so. Otherwise, how could the pots be recognized when sunk in the tank?

D. How does the reflection take place there?

M. Pure ether cannot take reflections; only the ether of water can do so. Glass cannot reflect objects; only a plate of glass with an opaque lining on its back can reflect the objects in front of it. Similarly, Pure Knowledge does not contain objects in it nor reflect objects. Only with the limiting adjunct, the mind, it reflects the world.

Neither in *samadhi* nor in deep sleep does the world remain. There cannot be illusion either in bright light or in total darkness. Only in dim light does a rope look like a snake. Similarly, Pure Consciousness remains light only; it is pure knowledge. The mind rising from it is deluded that the

442

2

objects remain apart.

D. So then the mind is the mirror.

M. Mind — mind, what is it? It is a mixture of *chit* (intelligence) and *sankalpas* (thoughts). Therefore, it forms all these — the mirror, light, darkness and the reflections.

D. But I do not see it.

M. *Chitakasha* (*chit*-ether) is Pure Knowledge only. It is the source of mind. Just at the moment of rising up, the mind is only light; only afterwards the thought "I am this" rises up; this "I"-thought forms the *jiva* and the world.

The first light is pure mind, the mind-ether or *Ishvara*. Its modes manifest as objects. Because it contains all these objects within itself it is called the mind-ether. Why ether? Like ether containing objects, it contains the thoughts; therefore, it is the mind-ether.

Just as the physical ether, though accommodating all the gross objects (the whole universe), is itself the content of the mind-ether, so also the latter is itself the content of *Chit*-ether. The last one is *Chit* Itself. There are no things contained in it. It remains as Pure Knowledge only.

D. Why call it "ether?" The physical ether is not sentient.

M. "Ether" denotes not only the insentient physical ether, but also Pure Knowledge. Knowledge does not consist in knowing objects; this is relative knowledge. But knowledge in its purity remains all alone — One, unique, transcendent Light!

D. Well — should we be imagining it in our meditation?

M. Why imagine? We can think of another only if we are independent of it, whereas here we cannot remain independent of this Pure Knowledge. Rather, only It is! How can It be imagined to be so and so or such and such?

D. How are we to proceed?

M. Only get rid of the non-self.

D. It looks all right now; but later it is all forgotten.

M. Your forgetfulness implies knowledge, for you know you forgot; otherwise, how can you speak of forgetting it? So forgetfulness also is *Chit-akasha* (Chit-ether) only.

D. How, then, is it not clear to me?

M. *Chit* is knowledge pure and simple. The mind proceeds from it; the mind is made up of thoughts. Darkness or ignorance interposing, Pure Knowledge seems different from what It really is; the same is seen as "I" and the "world" which are full of desire, attachment, hatred, etc. Therefore, the latter are said to veil the Reality.

D. How to be rid of thoughts? Is it as stated in *Atma-Vidya*, "the eye of the

443

mental eye," etc.?

M. There the mind stands for ether, Being (*sat*), and the eye for knowledge (*chit*); both *sat* and *chit* together form the universe.

D. How to realize the same?

M. As pointed out in *Atma-Vidya*, "being the eye of the mental eye, the ether of the mental ether . . ," meaning the Knowledge behind the relative knowledge, the *Chit*-ether containing the mental ether, remains as the Only One always shining bright.

D. Still, I do not understand. How shall I realize it?

M. It is also said, "Remain free from thoughts," and "It is realized only in the mind drawn within." Therefore, the mind made free from thoughts, and merged in the Heart, is *Chit Itself.*

D. Is the aforementioned mental ether *Ishvara* or *Hiranyagarbha*?

M. Can the latter remain independent of the former? The same is *Ishvara* and *Hiranyagarbha*.

D. How do they differ from each other?

M. The Immanent Being is called *Ishvara*.

D. Is not the Immanent Being *Chit-akasha* only?

M. Immanence can only be with *Maya*. It is the Knowledge of Being alone with *Maya*; from this subtle conceit *Hiranyagarbha*; from the latter the gross conceit *virat*. *Chit-atma* is Pure Being only.

DECEMBER 13, 1938

Two ladies, one Swiss and the other French, are visiting Maharshi. The younger of the ladies asked several questions, of which the most important was: Brahman is the same as jiva. If the jiva is under illusion, it amounts to saying that Brahman is under illusion. How is that possible?

M. If *Brahman* is under illusion and wants freedom from it, let Him raise the question.

DECEMBER 14, 1938

D. Seekers who are in immediate proximity of the Master can get Grace by *darshana*, *sparsana* (look, touch). But how does one get the same Grace at a distance?

M. By yoga *drishti* (yogic look).

Mr. Chopra, a Punjabi employed in Singapore, here on a visit, raised a few questions:

D. What is the efficacy of the name?

Sri Bhagavan read out an extract from *The Vision*. It was a translation of Namdev's stanzas [on the Divine Name].

D. How does the name help Realization?

M. The original name is always going on spontaneously without any effort on the part of the individual. That name is *aham*-"I." But when it becomes manifest, it manifests as *ahamkara* — the ego. The oral repetition of *nama* leads one to mental repetition, which finally resolves itself into the eternal vibration.

D. But these are all mental or physical.

M. The mind or the mouth cannot act without the Self. Tukaram, the great Maharashtra Saint, used to remain in *samadhi* during the day and sing and dance at night with large crowds of people. He always used to utter the name of Sri Rama. Once, he was answering calls of nature and also saying "Ram, Ram." An orthodox priest was shocked at the unholy mention of the sacred name and so reprimanded him and ordered him to be silent when he answered calls of nature. Tukaram said, "All right!" and remained mute. But at once there arose the name of Rama from every pore of Tukaram and the priest was horrified by the din. He then prayed to Tukaram, "Restrictions are only for the ordinary people and not for saints like you."

D. It is said that Sri Ramakrishna saw life in the image of Kali, which he worshipped. Can it be true?

M. The life was perceptible to Sri Ramakrishna and not to all. The vital force was due to himself. It was his own vital force that manifested as if it were outside and drew him in. Were the image full of life, it must have been found so by all. But everything is full of life. That is the fact. Many devotees have had experiences similar to those of Sri Ramakrishna.

D. How can there be life in stone? It is unconscious.

M. The whole universe is full of life. You say the stone is unconscious. It is your self-consciousness, which now speaks of unconsciousness. When a person wants to see if there is an article in a dark room, he takes a lamp to look for it. The light is useful for detecting the presence and the absence of the thing. Consciousness is necessary for discovering if a thing is conscious or not. If a man remains in a dark room, one need not take a lamp to find him. If called, he answers. He does not require a lamp to announce his presence. Consciousness is thus self-shining.

Now you say you were unconscious in sleep and self-conscious in the wakeful state. Which is the Reality? Reality must be continuous and eternal. Neither the unconsciousness nor the self-consciousness of the present is the Reality. But you admit your existence all through. The pure Being cannot be other than consciousness. Otherwise, you cannot say that you exist. Therefore, consciousness is the reality. When that consciousness is associated with *upadhis*, you speak of self-consciousness, unconsciousness, subconsciousness, superconsciousness, human consciousness, dog consciousness, tree consciousness, and so on. The common factor in all of them is consciousness.

Therefore, the stone is as much unconscious as you are in sleep. Is that totally devoid of consciousness?

D. But dog consciousness is different from my consciousness. I cannot read the Bible to a dog. The tree does not move, whereas I move and act.

M. Call the tree a standing man, and call the man a moving tree.

(*An American gentleman who also took part in the conversation would not allow Sri Bhagavan to explain, and so it stopped here.*)

The Punjabi gentleman referred to the popular belief of a worm being metamorphosed into a wasp (bhramarakita nyaya)*, which Sri Bhagavan had mentioned to the ladies in the course of conversation yesterday. Sri Bhagavan recalled some interesting reminiscences:*

1. I had previously heard of this *bhramarakita nyaya*. After I came to Tiruvannamalai, when I was staying in Gurumurtham, I noticed a red wasp construct a hive in which it placed five or six grubs and then flew away. My curiosity was roused, and I wanted to test the truth of the oft-quoted *nyaya*. I waited some days, maybe ten days. I then tapped the hive. It broke, and there I found that all five or six grubs had united together and taken the shape of a wasp, but it was white.

2. Later, when I was in Virupaksha Cave, I saw a red wasp construct five or six hives in each of which it placed five or six grubs and flew away. After about ten days, a black beetle, smaller than the wasp, buzzed around the hives and closed each of them with a little black mud and flew away. I was wondering at the intrusion of the beetle on the hive of the wasp. I waited a few days, and then gently opened one of the hives. Five or six black bodies came out, and each of them was a black beetle. I thought it strange.

3. Again, when I was in Pachaiamman Temple, I saw a red wasp constructing five or six hives on a pillar in the temple. It placed five or six grubs in each of them and buzzed away. I watched it for several days.

The wasp did not return. There was no black beetle, either. After about fifteen days, I opened one of the hives. All the grubs had united into a white mass of wasp-like form. It dropped down and was stunned by the fall. After a few minutes, it began to crawl. Its color was gradually changing. In a short time, there were two little specks on its sides, which grew into wings as I watched and the full-grown wasp flew away from the ground.

4. When I was in the Mango-Tree Cave, I noticed a caterpillar-like worm crawl up a wall. It stopped in one place and fixed two spots, which it later connected up with a thin filament from its body. It held the filament with its mouth and rested its tail end on the wall. It remained so for several days. I was watching it. It shriveled up in course of time and I wondered if there was life in it. So I gently tickled it with a thin stalk. There was no life within. I left it there. But a few days later, I noticed there was only a thin, dry skin left behind and the inner thing had flown away.

5. I had also seen flies carrying tiny grubs on their legs, which they deposited on waste. The grubs later flew away as flies.

D. They may be eggs laid by the flies.
M. But they move and struggle and then shape themselves as flies.
Sri Bhagavan mentioned another interesting reminiscence:
When I was a boy, I had seen the fishermen divert water from its main course and keep a pot through which the diverted water flowed. The artificial way was spread with tobacco stems. Strangely enough, the larger fishes always took the new way and fell into the pot. The fishermen, who were simply sitting quiet, used to take the fish out from the pot and throw them into their baskets. I thought at the time it was strange. Later, when I was staying here, I heard a man recite a piece from Thayumanavar, which mentioned the same trick of the fishermen.

December 15, 1938

The Spanish lady, Madame Mercedes De Acorta, wrote a letter to Mr. Hague, the American mining engineer who is staying here as a temporary resident for the past two months. She raised a few questions: If the individual self merges into the universal Self, how can one pray to God for the uplift of humanity?

(The question seems to be common among thinkers of the West.)
Sri Bhagavan said: They pray to God and finish with "Thy Will be done!" If His Will be done, why do they pray in the first place? It is true that the Divine Will prevails at all times and under all circumstances. The individuals cannot act of their own accord. Recognize the force of the Divine Will and keep quiet. Each one is looked after by God. He has created all. You are one among two billion humans. When He looks after so many, will He omit you? Even common sense dictates that one should abide by His Will.

There is no need to let Him know your needs. He knows them Himself and will look after them.

Why do you pray? Because you are helpless yourself and want the Higher Power to help you. Well, does not your Creator and Protector know your weakness? Should you parade your weakness in order to make Him know it?

D. But God helps those who help themselves.

M. Certainly. Help yourself and that is itself according to God's Will. Every action is prompted by Him only. As for prayer for the sake of others, it looks so unselfish on the surface. But analyze the feeling and you will detect selfishness there, also. You desire others' happiness so that you may be happy. Or you want credit for having interceded on others' behalf. God does not require intermediaries. Mind your own business and all will be well.

D. Does not God work His Will through some chosen person?

M. God is in all and works through all. But His presence is better recognized in purified minds. The pure ones reflect God's actions more clearly than the impure minds. Therefore, people say they are the chosen ones. But the "chosen" man does not himself say so. If he thinks he is the intermediary, then it is clear that he retains his individuality and there is no complete surrender.

D. Are not the Brahmins considered to be the priests or intermediaries between God and others?

M. Yes. But who is a Brahmin? A Brahmin is one who has realized *Brahman*. Such a one has no sense of individuality in him. He cannot think that he acts as an intermediary.

As for prayer, a realized man does not see others as different from himself. How can he pray at all, and to whom and for what? His very presence is the consummation of happiness for all. So long as you think that there are others different from you, you pray for them. But the sense of separateness is ignorance. This ignorance is again the cause of feeling helplessness.

You know that you are weak and helpless. How, then, can you help others? If you say, "By prayer to God," God knows His business and does not require your intercession for others.

Help yourself so that you may become strong. That is done by complete surrender. That means you offer yourself to Him. So you cannot retain your individuality after surrender. You then abide by His Will. Thus, Silence is the highest of all achievements.

"Silence is the ocean into which all the rivers of all religions discharge themselves" — so says Thayumanavar. He also adds that the Vedic religion is the only one that combines both philosophy and religion.

December 16, 1938

The two lady visitors returned in the morning and the younger one asked: Is the experience of the highest state the same to all? Or is there any difference?

M. The highest state is the same as is the experience.

D. But I find some difference in the interpretations put on the highest truth.

M. The interpretations are made with the mind. The minds are different, and so the interpretations are different.

D. I mean to ask if the seers express themselves differently?

M. The expressions may differ according to the nature of the seekers. They are meant to guide the seekers.

D. One seer speaks in terms of Christianity, another in those of Islam, a third of Buddhism, etc. Is that due to their upbringing?

M. Whatever may be their upbringing, their experience is the same. But the modes of expression differ according to circumstances.

A visitor asked: Sri Bhagavan said last night that God is guiding us. Then why should we make an effort to do anything?

M. Who asks you to do so? If there was truly that faith in the guidance of God, this question would not have arisen.

D. The fact is that God guides us. Then what is the use of these instructions to people?

M. They are for those who seek instructions. If you are firm in your belief in the guidance of God, stick to it and do not concern yourself with what happens around you. Furthermore, there may be happiness or misery. Be equally indifferent to both and abide in the faith of God. That will be so only when one's faith is strong that God looks after all of us.

Mr. Chopra asked: How shall I secure that firm faith?

M. Exactly. It is for such as these who want instructions. There are persons who seek freedom from misery. They are told that God guides all and so there need not be any concern about what happens. If they are of the best type, they at once believe it and firmly abide by faith in God.

But there are others who are not so easily convinced of the truth of the bare statement. They ask: "Who is God? What is His nature? Where is He? How can He be realized?" and so on. In order to satisfy them, intellectual discussion is found necessary. Statements are made, their pros and cons are argued, and the truth is thus made clear to the intellect.

When the matter is understood intellectually, the earnest seeker begins to apply it practically. He reasons at every moment, "For whom are these thoughts? Who am I?" and so forth, until he is well established in the conviction that a Higher Power guides us. That is firmness of faith. Then all his doubts are cleared and he needs no further instructions.

D. We also have faith in God.

M. If it had been firm, no questions would have arisen. The person will remain perfectly happy in his faith in the Omnipotent.

D. Is the inquiry into the Self the same as the aforementioned faith?

M. The inquiry into the Self is inclusive of faith, devotion, *jnana*, *yoga*, and all.

D. A man sometimes finds that the physical body does not permit steady meditation. Should he practice yoga for training the body for the purpose?

M. It is according to one's *samskaras* (predispositions). One man will practice *Hatha Yoga* for curing his bodily ills; another man will trust to God to cure them; a third man will use his willpower for it and a fourth man may be totally indifferent to them. But all of them will persist in meditation. The quest for the Self is the essential factor and all the rest are mere accessories.

A man may have mastered *Vedanta* philosophy and yet remain unable to control his thoughts. He may have a predisposition (*purva samskara*), which takes him to practice *Hatha Yoga*. He will believe that the mind can be controlled only by yoga, and so he will practice it.

D. What is most suitable for gaining facilities for steady *dhyana*?

M. It depends on one's *samskara*. One may find *Hatha Yoga* suitable and another man *nama japa*, and so on. The essential point is the *Atma-vichara* — inquiry into the Self.

D. Is it enough if I spend some time in the mornings and some time in the evenings for this *Atma-vichara*? Or should I do it always — say, even when I am writing or walking?

M. Now what is your real nature? Is it writing, walking, or being? The one unalterable reality is *Being*. Until you realize that state of pure being, you should pursue the inquiry. Once you are established in it, there will be no further worry.

No one will inquire into the source of thoughts unless thoughts arise. So long as you think "I am walking," "I am writing," inquire who does it.

These actions will, however, go on when one is firmly established in the Self. Does a man always say, "I am a man, I am a man, I am a man," every moment of his life? He does not say so, and yet all his actions are going on.

D. Is an intellectual understanding of the Truth necessary?

M. Yes. Otherwise, why does not the person realize God or the Self at once, i.e., as soon as he is told that God is all or the Self is all? That shows some wavering on his part. He must argue with himself and gradually convince himself of the Truth before his faith becomes firm.

December 20, 1938

A Swiss lady, Mrs. J.C. S. Hick-Riddingh, asked: Does Self-realization imply occult powers?

M. The Self is the most intimate and eternal Being, whereas the *siddhis* are foreign. The one requires effort to acquire, and the other does not.

The powers are sought by the mind, which must be kept alert, whereas the Self is realized when the mind is destroyed. The powers manifest only when there is the ego. The ego makes you aware of others, and in its absence there are no others to be seen. The Self is beyond the ego and is realized after the ego is eliminated. The elimination of the ego makes one unaware of others. How can the question of others arise and where is the use of occult powers for a Self-realized being?

Self-realization may be accompanied by occult powers or it may not. If the person had sought such powers before Realization, he may get the powers after Realization. There are others who had not sought such powers and had attempted only Self-realization. They do not manifest such powers.

These powers may also be sought and gained even after Self-realization. But then they are used for a definite purpose, i.e., the benefit of others as in the case of Chudala.

Sikhidhvaja was a pious king. His spouse was Chudala. They received instructions from a sage. The king, being busy with the administration of his kingdom, could not put the instructions into practice, whereas Chudala put them into practice and gained Self-realization. Consequently, she appeared more charming than before. The king was struck by her growing charm and asked her about it. She said that all charm was due to the Self, and he was only noting the charm of Self-realization in her. He said that she was silly. There were great *tapasvis* who could not realize the Self even after long periods of *tapas* and what about a silly woman who was all along in the family and in the worldly life? However, Chudala was not offended because she was firm in the Self and only wished that her husband should equally realize the Self and be happy. She then thought that unless she could prove her worth by manifesting some extraordinary powers, he could not be convinced and so she began to seek occult powers and gained them. But she did not betray them just then. Constant association with her made the king dispassionate. He began to dislike the worldly life, and desired to retire into the forest for performing *tapasya*. So he told his wife that he wanted to leave the world for the forest. She was delighted at the development, but pretended to be very much concerned with his unkind decision. He hesitated out of consideration for her. In the meantime, his dispassion gained in force and he decided to leave home even without her consent.

When the queen was sleeping one night, he suddenly left the palace by stealth and retired into the forest. He was seeking some solitary spot to perform his *tapas*. When the queen woke up, she did not find her husband but immediately discovered through her occult powers what had really happened. She rejoiced in her husband's determination. She called the ministers and announced that the king had gone on some important business and urged that the administration should be carried on as efficiently as ever. She herself administered the state in the king's absence.

Eighteen years passed. She then knew that the king was fit for Self-realization. So she appeared to him disguised as Kumbha. He then realized the Self and returned to rule the kingdom with the queen.

The point is that occult powers may be sought and gained for the benefit of others by Self-realized persons. But the sages are not deluded by the possession of such powers.

D. Does the sage use occult powers for making others realize the Self or is the mere fact of his Self-realization enough for it?

M. The force of his Self-realization is far more powerful than the use of all other powers.

Inasmuch as there is no ego in him, there are not others for him. What is the highest benefit that can be conferred on others? It is happiness. Happiness is born of Peace. Peace can reign only when there is no disturbance. Disturbance is due to thoughts arising in the mind. When the mind itself is absent, there will be perfect Peace. Unless a person has annihilated his mind, he cannot gain peace and be happy. Unless he himself is happy, he cannot bestow happiness on others.

When there is no mind, he cannot be aware of others. So the mere fact of his Self-realization is itself enough to make all others happy.

D. Can *samadhi* come and go?

M. What is *samadhi*? *Samadhi* is one's essential nature. How then can it come or go?

If you do not realize your essential nature, your sight remains obstructed. What is the obstruction? Find it and remove it. So one's efforts are meant only for the removal of obstructions which hide the true vision. The real nature remains the same. When once realized, it is permanent.

D. But Mr. Brunton says that he had one hour's *samadhi*. Therefore, I asked the question.

M. A practicer gains peace of mind and is happy. That peace is the result of his efforts. But the real state must be effortless. The effortless *samadhi* is the only true one and the perfect state. It is permanent. On the other hand, efforts are always spasmodic and so also their results.

When the real, effortless, permanent, happy nature is realized, it will be found to be not inconsistent with the ordinary activities of life. The *samadhi* reached after effort looks like abstraction from the external activities. A person might be so abstracted or live freely among people without detriment to his Peace and Happiness because that is the true nature or the Self.

DECEMBER 21, 1938

Sri Bhagavan shows great humor at times. He read *Upamanya Bhakta Vilas*, which contains a passage where Arunachaleswara is said to have robbed Tirujnanasambandar and his group of followers of all their possessions by his *bhutaganas* disguised as thieves.

Sri Bhagavan remarked: Shiva Himself was waylaid in *Tiruvudal Utsava* and He practiced the same trick on his devotees. Can it be so?

A saying of Lao-tzu from Tao-te Ching *was read out in the Hall:*

"By his non-action, the sage governs all."

Sri Bhagavan remarked: Non-action is unceasing activity. The sage is characterized by eternal and intense activity. His stillness is like the apparent stillness of a fast rotating gyroscope. Its very speed cannot be followed by the eye, and so it appears to be still. Yet it is rotating. So is the apparent inaction of the sage. This must be explained because people generally mistake stillness to be inertness. It is not so.

DECEMBER 24, 1938

A young man asked in broken Tamil: How long will it be before Self-realization?

M. First know what the Self means and also what Realization means, then you will know all.

D. The mind must realize in the Heart.

M. Be it so. What is mind?

D. Mind, Heart, are all *avatars* of Perumal (*Vaishnavite* term for incarnate God).

M. If so, no need to worry ourselves.

D. On this basis, how can we realize?

M. Surrender the mind to Perumal (God). His *avatar* cannot remain independent of Him. Render unto Him what is His and be happy.

D. How to do so?

M. How is the mind known to us? On account of its activities, namely, thoughts. Whenever thoughts arise, remember they are all modes of Perumal and cannot be otherwise; this is enough — the surrender of the mind. Can anything exist independent of Perumal? All is Perumal alone. He acts through all. Why worry ourselves?

DECEMBER 27, 1938

G.V. Subbaramiah, an Andhra devotee, mentioned something about "time."

M. What is *time*? It posits a state, one's recognition of it, and also the changes that affect it. The interval between two states is called *time*. A state cannot come into being unless the mind calls it into existence. The mind must be held by the Self. If the mind is not made use of, there is no concept of time. Time and space are in the mind but one's true state lies beyond the mind. The question of time does not arise at all to the one established in his true nature.

Mr. Narayana Iyer: Sri Bhagavan's words are so pleasing to hear, but their import is beyond our comprehension. That seems to be far too much for us ever to hope to realize.

Mr. GVS: Our grasp is only intellectual. If Sri Bhagavan would be pleased to direct us with a few instructions, we should benefit highly.

M. He who instructs an ardent seeker to do this or that is not a true Master. The seeker is already afflicted by his activities and wants peace and rest; in other words, he wants cessation of activities. Instead, he is told to do something in addition to, or in place of, his other activities. Can that be any help to the seeker?

Activity is creation; activity is the destruction of one's inherent happiness. If activity is advocated, the adviser is not a Master but a killer. Either the Creator (*Brahma*) or Death (*Yama*) may be said to have come in the guise of such a Master. He cannot liberate the aspirant, but only strengthens his fetters.

D. But even when we attempt to cease from activity, that very attempt is action. So activity seems to be inevitable.

M. True. Thayumanavar also alluded to it. A doctor advises his patient to take the prescribed medicine with only one condition. That condition is not to think of a monkey when taking the medicine. Can the patient ever take the medicine? Will he not think of the monkey whenever he tries not to do so?

Similarly, when people try to give up thoughts, their object is frustrated by their very attempt.

D. How then is the state to be attained?

M. What is there to attain? A thing remains to be attained if it is not already attained. But here one's very being is *That*.

Someone: Why then do we not know it?

Annamalaiswami: I should always try to think "I am That."

M. Why should one think, "I am That?" He is That only. Does a man go on thinking that he is a man?

Mr. Anantachari: The belief "I am a man" is so deeply engrained that we cannot help thinking so.

M. Why should you think, "I am a man?" If you are challenged, you may say, "I am a man." Therefore, the thought — "I am a man" — is called up when another thought, say "I am an animal," presents itself. Similarly, the thought "I am That" is necessary only so long as the other thought "I am a man" persists.

D. The thought "I am a man" is so firm that it cannot be got rid of.

M. Be your true Self. Why should you think, "I am a man?"

D. The thought "I am a man" is so natural.

M. Not so. On the other hand, "I am" is natural. Why do you qualify it with "a man?"

D. "I am a man" is so obvious whereas "I am That" is not understood by us.

M. You are neither *That* not *This*. The truth is "I am." "I Am that I Am" according to the Bible. Mere *Being* is alone natural. To limit it to "being a man" is uncalled for.

D. (*Humorously.*) If votes be taken, the majority will be on my side. (*Laughter.*)

M. I also cast my vote on your side. (*Laughter.*) I say also "I am a man"; but I am not limited to the body. It is in me. That is the difference.

Someone: The limitation (*upadhi*) of being a man cannot be got rid of.

M. How were you in deep sleep? There was no thought of being a man.

Another: So, the state of sleep must be brought about even when one is awake.

M. Yes. It is *jagrat-sushupti.*

Sri Bhagavan continued: Some people even say that while they sleep, they are enclosed somewhere in the body. They forget that such an idea did not persist in sleep but rises up only on waking. They bring their waking state to bear upon their sleep.

(*The lights went down and all retired.*)

M. The sleep, dream, and waking states are mere phenomena appearing on the Self, which is itself stationary and also a state of simple awareness. Can anyone remain away from the Self at any moment? This question can arise only if that were possible.

D. Is it not often said that one is nearer Pure Consciousness in deep slumber than in the waking state?

M. The question may as well be: Am I nearer to myself in my sleep than in my waking state?

For the Self is Pure Consciousness. No one can ever be away from the Self. The question is possible only if there is duality. But there is no duality in the state of Pure Consciousness.

Chapter Five — 1939

Dr. Emile Gatheir, S.J., Professor of Philosophy at the Sacred Heart College, Shembaganur, Kodaikanal, asked: Can you kindly give me a summary of your teachings?

M. They are found in some booklets, particularly *Who am I?*

D. I shall read them. But may I have the central point of your teachings from your own lips?

M. The central point is *the* thing.

D. It is not clear.

M. Find the Center.

D. I am from God. Is not God distinct from me?

M. Who asks this question? God does not ask it. *You* ask it. So find who you are and then you may find if God is distinct from you.

D. But God is Perfect and I am imperfect. How can I ever know Him fully?

M. God does not say so. The question is for you. After finding who you are, you may see what God is.

D. But you have found your Self. Please let us know if God is distinct from you.

M. It is a matter of experience. Each one must experience it himself.

D. Oh! I see. But God is Infinite and I am finite. I have a personality that can never merge into God. Is it not so?

M. Infinity and Perfection do not admit of parts. If a finite being comes out of infinity, the perfection of infinity is marred. Thus your statement is a contradiction in terms.

D. No. I see both God and creation.

M. How are you aware of your personality?

D. I have a soul. I know it by its activities.

M. Did you know it in deep sleep?

D. The activities are suspended in deep sleep.

M. But you exist in sleep. So you do now, too. Which of these two is your real state?

D. Sleep and waking are mere accidents. I am the substance behind the accidents.

(He looked up at the clock and said it was time for him to catch his train. He left after thanking Sri Bhagavan, so the conversation ended abruptly.)

JANUARY 8, 1939

Lady Bateman came here with her daughter to visit Sri Bhagavan. She brought a letter from Pascaline Maillert, Versailles, which read as follows:

Two years have come and gone since last I crossed the threshold of Thy Ashram and yet in spirit I have ever remained there.

Though illusion still often veils the vision of Reality revealed in the blessed Silence of Thy Presence.

Though the Silver Thread of Self-awareness be often lost midst changing light and shadows, still the inner urge to realize the Self remains and grows stronger and more insistent as Grace and search go hand in hand.

At times, yet rare, with no apparent cause, spontaneous awareness of the "I" springs up and bliss fills the heart with glowing warmth. Effortless concentration goes with this state while all desires come to rest fulfilled in utmost peace, till once more the veil is drawn and illusion seeks to blur the vision of the Real.

Yet what the soul has experienced and knows repeatedly as Truth, can neither be denied nor ever forgotten, and "That which is" gives constant strength to persevere.

I pray to Thee as to my Self for light and guidance that I know are ever there and at Thy feet lay offerings of unchanging love."

(*Signed*) Pascaline
11, Rue des Reservous
Versailles, FRANCE
November 21, 1938

JANUARY 10, 1939

A certain lady was singing a devotional song. It said among other things: "Thou art my father, Thou art my mother, Thou art my relations, My possessions and all," and so on.
Sri Bhagavan remarked with a smile: Yes, Yes, Thou art this, that, and everything except "I." Why not say "I am Thou" and finish it?

A visitor from Andhra Pradesh gave Sri Bhagavan a slip of paper containing several questions, which he wanted to have answered. Sri Bhagavan took it in his hands, went through the questions and said: All these questions arise so long as there is one who can ask questions. If the questioner is sought and found, the questions will end of their own accord.

The man said in reply: Several people raise these points, and I do not know how to meet them. Hence, I desire to know the fact (*"vishaya"* was the word he used).

M. If the *vishayi* (i.e., the basis of the facts) is understood, the *vishayas* (i.e., the facts) become clear.

Mr. Venkatakrishnaya, a lawyer-devotee, who visited Sri Bhagavan ten years before, asked him what he should do to improve himself. Sri Bhagavan told him then to perform Gayatri japa. The young man went away satisfied. When he returned after some years, he asked: If I meditate on the meaning of the *Gayatri mantra*, my mind again wanders. What is to be done?

M. Were you told to meditate on the *mantra* or its meaning? You must think of the one who repeats the *mantra*.

Again, the same man had seen another reputed Mahatma who told him to say *Om Namah* instead of *Om*, because pure *Om* is meant for *sannyasis*, whereas others can repeat *Om Namah*. When he came here, he asked Sri Bhagavan about it.

Sri Bhagavan replied casually: Should not others besides the *sannyasis* inquire into the Self and realize it?

JANUARY 17, 1939

Sri Bhagavan said to Lady Bateman: There is a fixed state; sleep, dream and waking states are mere movements in it. They are like pictures moving on the screen in a cinema show.

Everyone sees the screen as well as the pictures, but ignores the screen and takes in the pictures alone. The *jnani*, however, considers only the screen and not the pictures. The pictures certainly move on the screen, yet do not affect it. The screen itself does not move, but remains stationary.

Similarly, a person travels in a train and thinks that he moves. Realistically speaking, he sits and reposes in his seat, and it is the train which is steaming fast. He, however, superimposes the motion of the train on himself because he has identified himself with the body. He says, "I have passed one station — now another — yet another — and so on." A little consideration will show that he sits unmoved and the stations run past him. But that does not prevent him from saying that he has traveled all the way as if he exerted himself to move every foot of the way.

The *jnani* is fully aware that the true state of Being remains fixed and stationary and that all actions go on around him. His nature does not change and his state is not affected in the least. He looks on everything with unconcern and remains blissful himself.

His is the true state and also the primal and natural state of being. When once the man reaches it, he gets fixed there. Fixed once, fixed ever he will be. Therefore, that state which prevailed in the days of the Pathala Linga Cellar continues uninterrupted, with only this difference: that the body remained immobile there but is now active.

There is no difference between a *jnani* and an *ajnani* in their conduct. The difference lies only in their angles of vision. The ignorant man identifies himself with the ego and mistakes its activities for those of the Self, whereas the ego of the *jnani* has been lost and he does not limit himself to this body or that, this event or that, and so on.

There is action in seeming inaction, and also inaction in seeming action as in the following instances:

1. A child is fed while asleep. On waking the next morning, he denies having been fed. It is a case of inaction in seeming action. For although the mother saw him take his food, the child himself is not aware.

2. The cartman sleeps in the cart when it jogs along the way in the night, and yet he reaches the destination and claims to have driven the cart. This is a case of action in seeming inaction.

3. A man, appearing to listen to a story, nods his head to the speaker but yet his mind is otherwise active and he does not really follow the story.

4. Two friends sleep side by side. One of them dreams that both of them travel around the globe and have varied experiences. On waking, the dreamer tells the other that both of them have been around the earth. The other treats the story with contempt.

Lady Bateman protested that dream and sleep do not appeal to her. She said that it was for relaxation of her exhausted limbs, rather a state of autointoxication. "The sleep state is really dull, whereas the waking state is full of beautiful and interesting things."

M. What you consider to be filled with beautiful and interesting things is indeed the dull and ignorant state of sleep, according to the *Jnani*:

"*Ya nisa sarva bhootanam tasyam jagrati samyami.*"

The wise one is wide awake just where darkness rules for others.

You must certainly wake up from the sleep, which is holding you at present.

JANUARY 18, 1939

Mrs. Hick Riddingh wrote two questions on a slip of paper and asked Sri Bhagavan if her interpretations were correct.

M. The Self is beyond ignorance and knowledge. It is Absolute. These doubts do not arise to the Self, for it is Pure Consciousness and cannot admit of dark ignorance.

D. From our point of view, they arise.

M. See to whom they arise. Go to their root. See if they arise after you reach their source and hold on to it.

D. But at the present moment . . .

M. Such discussions are theoretical and there will be no end to them. One must be practical and try to solve the problems for oneself by the method indicated. Find out to whom the questions arise; they will then resolve themselves immediately.

Lady Bateman and others came to the Hall at about 3:30 p.m. In a few minutes, she asked in writing if one is nearer to Pure Consciousness in deep sleep than in the waking state.

M. The sleep, dream, and waking states are mere phenomena appearing on the Self, which is itself stationary and also a state of simple awareness. Can anyone remain away from the Self at any moment? This question can arise only if that were possible.

D. Is it not often said that one is nearer Pure Consciousness in deep slumber than in the waking state?

M. The question may as well be: Am I nearer to myself in my sleep than in my waking state?

For the Self is Pure Consciousness. No one can ever be away from the

Self. The question is possible only if there is duality. But there is no duality in the state of Pure Consciousness.

The same person sleeps, dreams, and wakes up. The waking state is considered to be full of beautiful and interesting things. The absence of such experiences makes one say that the sleep state is dull. Before we proceed further, let us make this point clear. Do you not admit that you exist in your sleep?

D. Yes, I do.

M. You are the same person that is now awake. Is it not so?

D. Yes.

M. So there is a continuity in sleep and the waking states. What is that continuity? It is only the state of Pure Being.

There is a difference between the two states. What is that difference? The incidents, namely, the body, the world, and the objects appear in the waking state but disappear in sleep.

D. But I am not aware in my sleep.

M. True, there is no awareness of the body or of the world. But you must exist in your sleep in order to say now "I was not aware in my sleep." Who says so now? It is the wakeful person. The sleeper cannot say so. That is to say, the individual who is now identifying the Self with the body says that such awareness did not exist in sleep.

Because you identify yourself with the body, you see the world around you and say that the waking state is filled with beautiful and interesting things. The sleep state appears dull because you were not there as an individual and therefore these things were not. But what is the actual fact? There is the continuity of Being in all the three states, but no continuity of the individual and the objects.

D. Yes.

M. That which is continuous is also enduring, i.e., permanent. That which is discontinuous is transitory.

D. Yes.

M. Therefore, the state of Being is permanent and the body and the world are not. They are fleeting phenomena passing on the screen of Being-Consciousness, which is eternal and stationary.

D. Relatively speaking, is not the sleep state nearer to Pure Consciousness than the waking state?

M. Yes, in this sense: When passing from sleep to waking, the "I"-thought must start; the mind comes into play, thoughts arise, and then the functions of the body come into operation. All these together make us say that we are awake. The absence of all this evolution is the characteristic of sleep and therefore it is nearer to Pure Consciousness than the waking state.

But one should not, therefore, desire to be always in sleep. In the first place it is impossible, for it will necessarily alternate with the other states. Secondly, it cannot be the state of bliss in which the *jnani* finds himself, for his state is permanent and not alternating. Moreover, the sleep state is not recognized to be one of awareness by people; but the sage is always aware. Thus, the sleep state differs from the state in which the sage is established.

The sleep state is free from thoughts and their impression to the individual. It cannot be altered by one's will because effort is impossible in that condition. Although nearer to Pure Consciousness, it is not fit for efforts to realize the Self.

The incentive to realize can arise only in the waking state and effort can also be made only when one is awake. We learn that the thoughts in the waking state form the obstacle to gaining the stillness of sleep. "Be still and know that I am God." So stillness is the aim of the seeker. Even a single effort to still at least a single thought, even for a trice, goes a long way to reach the state of quiescence. Effort is required and it is possible in the waking state only. There is effort here; there is awareness also — the thoughts are stilled, so there is the peace of sleep gained. That is the state of the *jnani*. It is neither sleep nor waking, but intermediate between the two. There is the awareness of the waking state and the stillness of sleep. It is called *jagrat-sushupti*. Call it wakeful sleep or sleeping wakefulness, or sleepless waking or wakeless sleep. It is not the same as sleep or waking separately. It is *atijagrat* (beyond wakefulness) or *astisushupti* (beyond sleep). [It is beyond *jagrat* and sleep as well as in them]. It is the state of perfect awareness and of perfect stillness combined. It lies between sleep and waking; it is also the interval between two successive thoughts. It is the source from which thoughts spring; we see that when we wake up from sleep. In other words, thoughts have their origin in the stillness of sleep. The thoughts make all the difference between the stillness of sleep and the turmoil of waking. Go to the root of the thoughts and you reach the stillness of sleep. But you reach it in the full vigor of search — that is, with perfect awareness.

That is again *jagrat-sushupti,* spoken of before. It is not dullness, but it is Bliss. It is not transitory, but eternal. From that, the thoughts proceed. What are all our experiences but thoughts? Pleasure and pain are mere thoughts. They are within us. If you are free from thoughts and yet aware, you are that Perfect Being.

Lady Bateman appreciated the discourse and thanked Sri Bhagavan. Later, she said that she would be leaving the next day. Sri Bhagavan smiled and said: You do not leave one place for another. You are always stationary. The scenes go past you. Even from the ordinary point of view, you sit in your cabin and the ship sails but you do not move. We see a picture of a man running several miles and rushing towards us, but the screen does not move. It is the picture that moves on and away.

D. I see, but I can understand it only after I realize the Self.

M. The Self is always realized. Were Realization something to be gained, there would be an equal chance of it being lost; it would thus be only transitory. Transitory bliss brings pain in its wake. It cannot be liberation, which is eternal.

Were it true that you realize it later, it means that you are not realized now. Absence of Realization of the present moment may be repeated at any moment in the future, for time is infinite. So, too, such realization is impermanent. But that is not true. It is wrong to consider Realization to be impermanent. It is the True Eternal State, which cannot change.

D. Yes, I shall understand it in course of time.

M. You are already That. Time and space cannot affect the Self. They are in you; so, also, all that you see around you is in you. There is a story to illustrate this point: A lady had a precious necklace around her neck. Once in her excitement, she forgot it and thought that the necklace was lost. She became anxious and looked for it in her home but could not find it. She asked her friends and neighbors if they knew anything about the necklace. They did not. At last, a kind friend of hers told her to feel the necklace around her neck. She found that it had been around her neck all the time and she was happy! When others asked her later if she had found the necklace that was lost, she said, "Yes, I did find it." She still felt that she had recovered a lost jewel.

Now, did she lose it at all? It was around her neck all along. But judge her feelings. She is happy as though she had indeed recovered a lost jewel. Similarly with us: we imagine we would realize that Self sometime, whereas we are never anything but the Self.

D. I feel that I am transplanted into some land other than the earth.

Sri Bhagavan, while looking into some correspondence, heard it, smiled, and said: This is the Kingdom of Heaven. The Kingdom of Heaven mentioned in the Bible and this world are not two different regions. "The Kingdom is within you," says the Bible. So it is. The realized being sees this as the Kingdom of

Heaven, whereas the others see it as "this world." The difference lies only in the angles of vision.

D. How can we deny the world and the people therein? I hear some music. It is sweet and grand. I recognize it to be Wagner's music. I cannot claim it to be mine.

M. Does Wagner or his music exist apart from you? Unless you are there to say it is Wagner's music, can you be aware of it? Without being aware of it, can it be said to exist? To make it more clear, do you recognize Wagner's music in your deep sleep? And yet you admit that you exist in sleep. So it is clear that Wagner and music are only your thoughts. They are in you and not outside of you.

D. It is beautiful.

(*Everyone is apt to be confused from time to time. Although the truth is heard and understood, at times it is forgotten, and mistakes are committed when facts confront the person. Knowledge gives way to ignorance, and confusion results. But the sage alone can give the right turn to our thoughts from time to time. That is the necessity for* Satsanga.)

A devotee came with these questions:
1. Since individual souls and *Brahman* are one, what is the cause of this creation?
2. Is the *Brahma-jnani* liable to bodily pains and rebirth? Can he extend his life span or curtail it?

M. The object of creation is to remove the confusion of your individuality. The question shows that you have identified yourself with the body and therefore see yourself and the world around. You think that you are the body. Your mind and intellect are the factors of your wrong identity. Do you exist in your sleep?

D. I do.

M. The same being is now awake and asks these questions. Is it not so?

D. Yes.

M. These questions did not arise in your sleep. Did they?

D. No.

M. Why not? Because you did not see your body, and no thoughts arose. You did not identify yourself with the body then. Therefore, these questions did not arise. They arise now because of your identification with the body. Is it not so?

D. Yes.

M. Now see which is your real nature. Is it that which is free from thoughts or that which is full of thoughts?

Being is continuous. The thoughts are discontinuous. So which is permanent?

D. Being.

M. That is it. Realize it. That is your true nature. Your nature is simple Being, free from thoughts.

Because you identify yourself with the body, you want to know about creation. The world and the objects including your body appear in the waking state, but disappear in the state of sleep. You exist all through these states. What is it then that persists through all these states? Find it out. That is your Self.

D. Supposing it is found. What then?

M. Find it out and see. There is no use asking hypothetical questions.

D. Am I then one with *Brahman*?

M. Leave *Brahman* alone. Find who you are. *Brahman* can take care of Himself.

If you cease to identify yourself with the body, no questions regarding creation, birth, death, etc, will arise. They did not arise in your sleep. Similarly, they will not arise in the true state of the Self.

The object of creation is thus clear, that you should proceed from where you find yourself and realize your true Being.

You could not raise the question in your sleep because there is no creation there. You raise the question now because your thoughts appear and there is creation. Creation is thus found to be only your thoughts.

Take care of yourself and the *Brahma-jnani* will take care of himself. If you know your true nature, you will understand the state of *Brahma-jnana*. It is futile to explain it now. Because you think that you see a *jnani* before you and you identify him with a body just as you have identified yourself with yours, you also think that he feels pains and pleasures like yourself.

D. But I must know if he is a *jnani*, for I must be inspired by him.

M. Yes, he tells you; he inspires. Do as he tells you. You want to learn and not test him.

Jnana lakshanas (signs of wisdom) are stated in the *sastras* to be an incentive to a seeker to get rid of misery and seek happiness. The methods are given. If they are followed, the result will be *jnana* having those *lakshanas*. They are not meant for testing others.

D. I think that the soul is the light within. If after death it becomes one with

Brahman, how can there be transmigration of soul?

M. Within whom? Who dies?

D. I shall then frame my question in a different way.

M. Dialectics are not wanted. Consider the answer and see.

D. How?

M. Now that you identify yourself with the body, you say that the soul is the light within. You mean there is light within the body.

Think a little and see if the body can raise any questions. It is insentient and cannot say "I." Something else says "I." What is it? Can it be the Self? The Self is pure and not aware of any other so as to be able to say "I." Who then says "I?" It is the link between the pure *chit* (the Self) and the *jada* (the body). That is the ego. Who are you now? What is it that is born? The Self is eternal and cannot be born. The body appears and disappears and your identity with it makes you speak of birth and death. See if the true significance of "I," can ever take birth. For whom is transmigration?

D. Sir, we are here to have our doubts cleared.

M. Certainly.

D. Our doubts can be cleared only when asking questions.

M. Yes. No one objects to questions being asked.

D. It is said [in the *Bhagavad Gita*] *"pariprasnena sevaya"* (by questioning again and again and by service). So we should ask questions, and the Master may kindly remove our doubts.

M. Continue your quotation, *"upadekshyanti tattvam"* (they give instructions in Truth).

D. Yes. But our doubts need to be cleared.

M. So it was with Arjuna. For he says in the end, *"nashto mohah smritirlabdha"* (lost is my ignorance; memory restored).

D. It was in the end. Before then, he asked so many questions.

M. The truth was revealed even at the start. For the very first *sloka* of Sri Krishna's *upadesa* starts, "No birth and no death; no change, etc."

D. Sri Krishna also says, "We have had many rebirths. I am aware of them; but you are not."

M. That was only because the question arose how Sri Krishna could claim to have taught the eternal Truth to Aditya. The Truth was stated at the very start, but Arjuna did not understand it. The *jnani's* state was later described and also the means of attainment. Incidentally, Sri Krishna said that the Truth was eternal and that He had originally taught the same to Aditya. Arjuna was all along identifying himself with the body and therefore thought that Sri Krishna also was the body in front of him. He therefore

468

asked, "How can that be? You (Sri Krishna) were born of Devaki some years before. Aditya was one of those who started creation. How could you have taught this Truth to Aditya?"

Sri Krishna continues to answer Arjuna's questions in that strain, "Many rebirths we have had; I know them all, but you do not," and so on.

D. We must also know the Truth.

M. You are taught the Truth. Instructions have been given. *See who you are.* That is the whole instruction.

January 19, 1939

Mrs. Hick Riddingh asked Sri Bhagavan in writing: When Bhagavan writes about the help given towards attaining Self-realization by the gracious glance of the Master or looking upon the Master, how exactly is this to be understood?

M. Who is the Master? Who is the seeker?

D. The Self.

M. If the Self be the Master and also the seeker, how can the question arise at all?

D. That is just my difficulty. I must seek the Self within myself. What, then, is the significance of the writing referred to? It seems contradictory.

M. It is not. The statement has not been correctly understood.

If the seeker knows the Master to be the Self, he sees no duality in other respects either and is therefore happy, so that no questions arise for him.

But the seeker does not bring the truth of the statement to bear in practice. It is because of his ignorance. This ignorance is, however, unreal. The Master is required to wake up the seeker from this slumber of ignorance and he therefore uses these words in order to make Reality clear to others.

The only thing that matters is that you see the Self. This can be done wherever you remain. The Self must be sought within. The search must be steadfast. If that is gained, there is no need to stay near the Master as a physical being.

The "statement" is meant for those who cannot find the Self remaining where they are.

Mr. Ward Jackson: The lady's difficulty is real and I sympathize with her. If we could see the Self within ourselves, why should we have come all the way to see him? We had been thinking of him so long and it is only right that we came here. Is it then unnecessary to do so?

M. You have done well in coming. *"Ishvaro gururatmeti"* (The Self is God and Guru). A person seeks happiness and learns that God alone can make one happy. He prays to God and worships Him. God hears his prayers, and responds by appearing in human shape as a Master in order to speak the language of the devotee and make him understand the Reality. The Master is thus God manifest as human being. He gives out His experience so that the seeker might also gain it. His experience is to abide as the Self. The Self is within. God, Master, and the Self are therefore seeming stages in the Realization of the Truth. You have doubts on reading books. You have come here to have them cleared. That is only right.

Mrs. Hick Riddingh: I understand the Self to be the Master and must be sought within. So I can do it wherever I live.
M. The understanding has been theoretical. When it is put into practice, difficulties and doubts arise. If you can feel the presence of the Master where you are, your doubts are readily overcome, for the Master's part consists in removing the doubts of the seeker.

The purpose of your visit is fulfilled if doubts do not arise hereafter, and you apply yourself steadily in the search for the Self.
D. I understand it all along.
M. Good. The objection is not to your conclusion but to your doubts.

Mr. Ward Jackson: When we read about it, we read it intellectually. But it is all too remote. When we see you in the body, we are brought nearer to Reality and it gives us courage to bring our knowledge into our everyday life.

If one realized the Self and acted upon it in the West, one would be locked up in a lunatic asylum. (*Laughter.*)
M. You will be locking yourself in. Because the world is mad, it considers you mad. Where is the lunatic asylum if not within? You will not be in it, but it will be in you. (*Laughter.*)

Uncertainties, doubts, and fears are natural to everyone until the Self is realized. They are inseparable from the ego; rather, they *are* the ego.
D. How are they to disappear?
M. They are the ego. If the ego goes, they go with it. The ego is itself unreal. What is the ego? Inquire. The body is insentient and cannot say "I." The Self is pure consciousness and nondual. It cannot say "I." No one says "I" in sleep. What is the ego then? It is something intermediate between the inert body and the Self. It has no *locus standi*. If sought for, it vanishes like a

ghost. You see, a man imagines that there is something by his side in darkness; it may be some dark object. If he looks closely, the "ghost" is not to be seen except for some dark object, which he could identify as a tree or a post, etc. If he does not look closely, the ghost strikes terror in the person. All that is required is to look closely and the ghost vanishes. The ghost was never there in the first place. So, also, with the ego. It is an intangible link between the body and Pure Consciousness. It is not real. So long as one does not look too closely, it continues to give trouble. But when one looks for it, it is found not to exist.

Again, in a Hindu marriage function, the feasts continue five or six days. A stranger was mistaken for the best man by the bride's party and they therefore treated him with special regard. Seeing him treated thusly by the bride's party, the bridegroom's party considered him to be a man of importance related to the bride's party and therefore they too showed him special respect. The stranger had altogether a happy time of it. He was also all along aware of the real situation. On one occasion, the groom's party wanted to refer to him on some point. They asked for him. He scented trouble and made himself scarce. So it is with the ego. If looked for, it disappears. If not, it continues to give trouble.

How it is to be looked for is learned from those who have already done so. That is the reason why the Master is approached.

D. If the search has to be made within, is it necessary to be in the physical proximity of the Master?

M. It is necessary to do so until all doubts are at an end.

D. If the ego is unreal and troublesome, why did we take so many pains to develop it?

M. Its growth and the trouble consequent on such growth make you look for the cause of it all. Its development is for its own destruction.

D. Is it not said that one must be like a child before advancing spiritually?

M. Yes, because the ego is not developed in the child.

D. I mean exactly the same. We could have remained like the child instead of having developed the ego.

M. The state of the child is intended to be so. No one can take lessons from a child for Realization of the Self. The Master's state is like the state of the child, yet there is a difference between the two. The ego is potential in the child, whereas it is totally destroyed in the saint.

D. Yes, I see, I understand it now.

M. The Reality is alone and eternal. To understand it is good enough. But the old ignorance should not return. Careful attention must be kept lest the present understanding of the Truth suffers later on.

A disciple served a Master a long time and realized the Self. He was in Bliss and wanted to express his gratitude to the Master. He cried tears of joy and his voice choked when he spoke. He said, "What a wonder that I did not know my very Self all these years. I suffered long and you so graciously helped me realize the Self. How shall I repay your Grace? It is not in my power to do it!" The Master replied: "Well, well. Your repayment consists in not lapsing into ignorance again but continuing in the state of your real Self."

(The Self is the Master and all else. The Realization of the Self means surrender or merging into the Master. What more can anyone do? That is the highest form of gratitude to the Master.)

JANUARY 21, 1939

A young man asked: Are thoughts mere matter?
M. What do you mean? Do you mean "matter" like the things your see around you?
D. Yes — gross.
M. Who asks this question? Who is the thinker?
D. The thinker is spirit.
M. Do you then mean that spirit generates matter?
D. I want to know.
M. How do you distinguish between matter and spirit?
D. Spirit is consciousness and the other not.
M. Can consciousness generate non-consciousness, or light generate darkness?

JANUARY 24, 1939

There were a few gentlemen in the Hall. Sri Bhagavan spoke to them some time after their arrival: What is the use of trying to remember the past or discover the future? That which matters is only the present. Take care of it and all other things will take care of themselves.
D. Is it bad to desire something?
M. One should not be elated on having his desires fulfilled or disappointed on them being frustrated. To be elated on the fulfillment of desire is deceptive, for a gain will certainly be lost ultimately. Therefore, elation must end in pain at some future date. One should not give way to feelings of plea-

sure or pain, come what may. How do events affect a person? You do not grow by acquiring something nor wither away by losing it. You remain what you always are.

D. We worldly men cannot resist desire.

M. You may desire but be prepared for any eventuality. Make effort, but do not get lost in the result. Accept with equanimity whatever happens, for pleasure and pain are mere mental modes. They have no relation to objective realities.

D. How?

M. There were two young friends in a village in South India. They were learned, and wanted to earn something with which they might afford relief to their respective families. They took leave of their parents and went to Benares on a pilgrimage. On the way, one of them died; the other was left alone. He wandered for a time, and in the course of a few months made a good name for himself and earned some money. He wanted to earn some more before returning home. In the meantime, he met a pilgrim who was going south and would pass through the native village of the young pundit. He requested the new acquaintance to tell his parents that he would return after a few months with some funds and also that his companion had died on the way. The man came to the village and found the parents. He gave them the news, but inadvertently changed the names of the two men. Consequently, the parents of the living man bemoaned his supposed loss and the parents of the dead man were happy, expecting the return of their son bringing riches, as well.

You see, therefore, that pleasure and pain have no relation to the actualities but are mere mental modes.

Another from the group asked: How is the ego to be destroyed?

M. Hold the ego first and then ask how it is to be destroyed. Who asks this question? It is the ego. Can the ego ever agree to kill itself? This question is a sure way to cherish the ego and not to kill it. If you seek the ego, you will find it does not exist. That is the only way to destroy it.

In this connection, I am often reminded of a funny incident that took place when I was living in West Chitrai Street, in Madurai. A neighbor in an adjoining house anticipated the visit of a thief. He took precautions to catch him. He posted policemen in mufti to guard the two ends of the lane, the entrance, and the back door to his own house. The thief came as expected and the men rushed him. He took in the situation at a glance and shouted, "Hold him, hold him. There he runs — there — there." Saying so, he made good his escape.

So it is with the ego. Look for it and it will not be found. That is the way to get rid of it.

January 23 - 28, 1939

M. When staying in the Skandasramam, I sometimes used to go out and sit on a rock. On one such occasion, there were two or three others with me including Rangaswami Iyengar. Suddenly, we noticed a small moth-like insect shooting up like a rocket into the air from a crevice in the rock. Within the twinkling of an eye, it had multiplied itself into millions of moths, which formed a cloud and hid the sky from view. We wondered at it and examined the place from which it shot up. We found it was only a pinhole and knew that so many insects could not possibly have issued from it in such a short time.

That is how *ahamkara* (ego) shoots up like a rocket and instantaneously spreads out as the Universe.

The Heart is therefore the center. A person can never be away from it. If he is, he is already dead. Although the *Upanishads* say that the *jiva* functions through other centers on different occasions, he does not relinquish the Heart. The centers are simply places of business (as stated in *Vedanta Chudamani*). The Self is bound to the Heart, like a cow tethered to a peg. The movements are controlled by the length of rope. All its wanderings center around the peg.

A caterpillar crawls on a blade of grass and when it has come to the end, it seeks another support. While doing so, it holds on to the blade of grass with its hind-legs, lifts its body and sways to and fro before it can hold another. Similarly with the Self: it stays in the Heart and holds other centers also according to circumstances. But its activities always center around the Heart.

There are five states for the individual. They are:
1. *Jagrat*, 2. *Svapna*, 3. *Sushupti*, 4. *Turiya*, 5. *Turyatita*. Of these, the *jagrat* is the waking state.

Deep sleep is nothing but the experience of pure Being. The three states go by different names, such as the three regions, the three forts, the three deities, etc. The Being always abides in the Heart, as stated above. If in the *jagrat* state, the Heart is not relinquished, the mental activities are stilled and *Brahman* alone is contemplated; the state is called *Turiya*. Again, when

474

the individual being merges in the Supreme, it is called thie *turyatita*. The vegetable kingdom is always in *sushupti*. The animals have both *svapna* and *sushupti*. The gods (celestials) are always in *jagrat,* man has all the three states, but the clear-sighted yogi abides only in *turiya,* and the highest yogi remains in *turyatita* alone.

The three states alternate involuntarily for the average man. The last two (*turiya* and *turyatita*) are, however, the results of practice and form clear aids to liberation. Of the other three states (*jagrat, svapna,* and *sushupti*), each one is exclusive of the other two and limited by the conditions of time and space. They are, therefore, unreal.

Our very experience of the *jagrat* and the *svapna* states proves that the Consciousness as the Self underlies all the five states, remains perfect all along, and witnesses all of them. But with regard to similar consciousness in deep sleep, every person is known to say "I was not aware of anything; I slept soundly and happily." Two facts emerge from the statement (un-awareness of anything and the happiness of sound sleep). Unless these existed and were experienced in sleep, they could not find expression by the same person in the waking state. Inference also leads to the same con-clusion. Just as the eye sees the darkness that remains enveloping all ob-jects, so also the Self sees the darkness of nescience, which remained cover-ing the phenomenal world.

This darkness was experienced when it (the Self) emerged in dots of supreme bliss, shone a trice and fleeted away in such fine subtlety as the rays of the moon which peer through the waving foliage. The experience was, however, not through any media (such as the senses of the mind), but bears out the fact that consciousness does exist in deep sleep. The unaware-ness is owing to the absence of relative knowledge, and the happiness to the absence of (seething) thoughts.

If the experience of bliss in deep sleep is a fact, how is it that no one among all the human beings recollects it? A diver who has found the de-sired thing underwater cannot make his discovery known to expectant persons on the shore until he emerges from the water. Similarly, the sleeper cannot express his experience because he cannot contact the organs of ex-pression until he is awakened by his *vasanas* in due course. Therefore, it follows that the Self is the light of *Sat, Chit, Ananda.*

Visva, Taijasa, and *Prajna* are the denominations of the experiencer in the waking, dream, and deep sleep states, respectively. The same individual underlies all of them. They do not, therefore, represent the True Self, which is pure *Sat-Chit-Ananda.* The experience in deep sleep was said to be the bliss of *Brahman*. It is only the negative aspect of such bliss, as it is the result of the absence of thoughts. Moreover, it is transitory. Such a bliss is only the *abhasa*, the counterfeit of Supreme Bliss. It is not different from the blissful feeling of sensual pleasures. In deep sleep, the *Prajna* is said to be united with the Self. So the individuality is latent in sleep.

The Self is the basis of all experience. It remains as the witness and the support of them all. The Reality is thus different from the three states — waking, dream, and deep sleep.

FEBRUARY 1, 1939

A gentleman from Hardwar: When I go on analyzing myself I go beyond the intellect, and then there is no happiness.

M. Intellect is only an instrument of the Self. It cannot help you to know what is beyond itself.

D. I understand. But there is no happiness beyond it.

M. The intellect is the instrument from where to know unknown things. But you are already known, being the Self which is itself knowledge; so you do not become the object of knowledge. The intellect makes you see things outside, and not that which is its own source.

D. The question is repeated.

M. The intellect is useful thus far, it helps you analyze yourself, and no further. It must then be merged into the ego, and the latter's source must be sought. If that is done, the ego disappears. Remain as that source and then the ego does not arise.

D. There is no happiness in that state.

M. "There is no happiness" is only a thought. The Self is bliss, pure and simple. You are the Self. So you cannot be but bliss; being so, you cannot say there is no happiness. That which says so cannot be the Self; it is the non-Self and must be got rid of in order to realize the bliss of the Self.

D. How is that to be done?

M. See from where the thoughts arise. It is the mind. See for whom the mind or intellect functions. For the ego. Merge the intellect in the ego and seek the source of the ego. The ego disappears. "Know" and "I do not know" imply a subject and an object. They are due to duality. The Self is pure and Absolute. One and alone. There are not two selves so that one may know the other. What is duality, then? It cannot be the Self, which is One and alone. It must be non-Self; duality is the characteristic of the ego. When thoughts arise, duality is present; know it to be the ego, and seek its source.

The degree of absence of thoughts is the measure of progress towards Self-realization. But Self-realization itself is not progressive; it is ever the same. The Self remains always in realization. The obstacles are thoughts. Progress is measured by the degree of removal of the obstacles to understanding that the Self is always realized. So thoughts must be checked by seeking to whom they arise. So you go to their Source, where they do not arise.

D. Doubts are always arising. Hence my question.

M. A doubt arises and is cleared; another arises and that is cleared, making way for another; and so it goes on. So there is no possibility of clearing away all doubts. See to *whom* the doubts arise. Go to their source and abide in it. Then they cease to arise. That is how doubts are to be cleared.

"*Atma samstham manah krtva na kinchidapi chintayet.*"
By merging the mind in the Self there will not arise even a single thought

D. Grace alone can help me to it.

M. Grace is not exterior. In fact, your very desire for Grace is due to the Grace already within you.

A gentleman from Andhra Pradesh read out a verse from *Viveka Chudamani,* setting forth the sense of the *Maitreyi Brahmana* of the *Brihadaranyaka Upanishad,* and asked the meaning of *Atma,* which occurred there.

M. The Self.

D. Is not *prema* (love) for something else?

M. The desire for happiness (*sukha prema*) is a proof of the ever-existing happiness of the Self. Otherwise, how can desire for it arise in you? If headache were natural to human beings, no one would try to get rid of it. But everyone who has a headache tries to get rid of it, because he has known a time when he had no headache. He desires only that which is natural to him. So, too, he desires happiness because happiness is natural to him. Being natural, it is not acquired. Man's attempts can only be to get rid of misery. If that is done, the ever-present bliss is felt. The primal bliss is obscured by the non-self, which is synonymous with non-bliss or misery. *Duhkha nasam = sukha prapti* (Loss of unhappiness amounts to gain of happiness). Happiness mixed with misery is only misery. When misery is eliminated, then the ever-present bliss is said to be gained. Pleasure which ends in pain is misery.

Man wants to eschew such pleasure. Pleasures are *priya, moda,* and *pramoda.* When a desired object is near at hand, there arises *priya;* when it is taken possession of, *moda* arises; when it is being enjoyed, *pramoda* prevails. The reason for the pleasurableness of these states is that *one thought excludes all others, and then this single thought also merges into the Self.* These states are enjoyed in the *anandamaya kosa* only. As a rule, *vijnanamaya kosa* prevails on waking. In deep sleep, all thoughts disappear and the state of obscuration is one of bliss; there, the prevailing body is the *anandamaya*. These are sheaths and not the core, which is interior to all these, and lies beyond waking, dream, and deep sleep. That is the Reality and consists of true bliss (*nijananda*).

D. Is not *Hatha Yoga* necessary for inquiry into the Self?

M. Each one finds one method suitable to himself, because of latent tendencies (*purva samskara*).

D. Can *Hatha Yoga* be accomplished at my age?

M. Why do you think of all that? Because you consider it as exterior to yourself, you desire it and try for its accomplishment. But do you not exist all along? Why do you leave yourself and go after something external?

D. It is said in *Aparoksha-anubhuti* that *Hatha Yoga* is a necessary aid for inquiry into the Self.

M. The *hatha* yogis claim to keep the body fit so that the inquiry may be effected without obstacles. They also say that life must be prolonged so that the inquiry may be carried to a successful conclusion. Furthermore, there are those who use some medicines (*kayakalpa*) with that end in view. Their favorite example is: the screen must be perfect before the painting is begun. Yes, but *which is the screen and which is the painting?* According to them, the body is the screen and the inquiry into the Self is the painting. But is not the body itself a picture on the screen, the Self?

D. But *Hatha Yoga* is so much spoken of as an aid.

M. Yes. Even great pundits well versed in *Vedanta* pursue it. Otherwise, their minds will not subside. So you may say it is useful for those who cannot otherwise still the mind.

D. *Saguna upasana* (worship of a personal God) is said to be imperfect. It is also said that *nirguna upasana* (devotion to the impersonal) is hard and risky. I am fit for the former only. What is to be done?

M. The *Saguna* merges into the *nirguna* in the long run. The *saguna* purifies the mind and takes one to the final goal. The afflicted one, the seeker of knowledge, and the seeker of gains are all dear to God. *But the jnani is the Self of God.*

D. "Not this — not this." That is the teaching to the seeker. He is told that the Self is Supreme. How is it to be found?

M. The Self is said to be the hearer, thinker, knower, etc. But that is not all. It is also described as the ear of ear, the mind of mind, etc.; and by what means to know the knower?

D. But this does not say what the Self is.

M. "Not this — not this."

D. It only negates.

(*Silence.*)

The devotee complains that the Self is not pointed out.

M. A man wants to know what he is. He sees animals and objects around him. He is told: "You are not a cow, not a horse, not a tree, not this, not that, and so on." If again the man asks saying, "You have not told me what I am," the answer will be, "It is not said you are not a man." He must find out for himself that he is a man. So you must find out for yourself what you are.

You are told, "You are not this body, nor the mind, nor the intellect, nor the ego, nor anything you can think of; find out what you truly are." Silence denotes that the questioner is himself the Self that is to be found. In a *svayamvara* (pre-marriage ceremony) the maiden goes on saying "no" to each one until she faces her choice, and then looks downwards and remains silent.

Mr. Raj Krishna found Sri Bhagavan alone on the Hill at about 5:30 p.m. and prayed: I have been desiring since my tenth year to have a glimpse of Reality. I firmly believe that I can be helped in this only by a sage like Sri Bhagavan. So I pray for thy help.

(*Sri Bhagavan looked at him for a few minutes.*)

Mr. Krishna interrupted saying: Even if I cannot realize in my life, let me at least not forget it on my deathbed; let me have a glimpse at least at the moment of death so that it may stand me in good stead in the future.

M. It is said in the *Bhagavad Gita* (chap. 8), that whatever may be the last thought at death, it determines the later birth of the person. It is necessary to experience the Reality now in life for it to be experienced at death. See if this moment is different from the last one, and try to be in that desired state.

D. I have limitations. I am unable to rise to the occasion. Grace may achieve for me what I cannot achieve by myself.

M. True, but unless there is Grace, this desire will not arise.

They were walking slowly, conversing at the same time. The Devotee said: There is a girl of eleven in Lahore. She is very remarkable. She says she can call upon Krishna twice and remain conscious, but if she calls a third time she becomes unconscious and remains in trance for ten hours continuously.

M. So long as you think that Krishna is different from you, you call upon Him. Falling into trance denotes the transitoriness of the *samadhi*. You are always in *samadhi*; that is what should be realized.

D. God-vision is glorious.

M. God-vision is only vision of the Self objectified as the God of one's own faith. Know the Self.

Sri Bhagavan has a bandage on his finger. Someone asked: What is that?
Bhagavan replied: The finger came upon a knife.
 (*The knife is inert, and relative to it the finger is a conscious agent.*)

Sri Bhagavan said to another devotee that there are five states: 1. Sleep, 2. Before waking (a state free from thoughts), 3. Sense of happiness of that freedom from thoughts (*rasasvada*), 4. The internal movement of the *vasanas* (*kashaya*), 5. Complete waking with distraction (*vikshepa*).

 The second of these should be made permanent.

FEBRUARY 4, 1939

A devotee asked Sri Bhagavan: With every thought, the subject and the object appear and disappear. Does not the "I" disappear when the subject disappears? If that is so, how can the quest of the "I" proceed?

M. The subject (knower) is only a mode of mind. Though the mode (*vritti*) passes, the reality behind it does not cease. The background of the mode is the "I" in which the mind modes arise and sink.

D. After describing the Self as *srotu* (hearer), *manta* (thinker), *vijnata* (knower), etc., it is again described as *asrota, amanta, avijnata* — non-hearer, non-thinker, non-knower. Is that correct?

M. Yes. The ordinary man is aware of himself only when modifications arise in the intellect (*vijnanamaya kosa*). These modifications are transient; they arise and set. Hence, the *vijnanamaya* (intellect) is called a *kosa* or sheath. When pure awareness is left over, it is itself the *Chit* (Self) or the Supreme. To be in one's natural state on the subsidence of thoughts is bliss; if that bliss is transient — arising and setting — then it is only the *sheath* of bliss (*anandamaya kosa*), not the pure Self. What is needed is to fix the attention on the pure "I" after the subsidence of all thoughts and not to lose hold of it. This has to be described as an extremely subtle thought, else it cannot be spoken of at all since it is no other than the Real Self. Who is to speak of it, to whom and how?

This is well explained in *Kaivalya Navaneeta* and *Viveka Chudamani*. Thus, though in sleep the awareness of the Self is not lost, the ignorance of the *jiva* is not affected by it. For this ignorance to be destroyed this subtle state of mind (*vrittijnanam*) is necessary. In the sunshine cotton does not burn, but if the cotton is placed under a lens it catches fire and is consumed by the rays of the Sun passing through the lens. So, too, though the awareness of the Self is present at all times, it is not inimical to ignorance. If by meditation the subtle state of thought is won, then ignorance is destroyed. Also, *Viveka Chudamani* states: *"ativa sukshmam paramatma tattvam na sthula drishtya"* (the exceedingly subtle Supreme Self cannot be seen by the gross eye) and *"esha svayam jyotirasesha sakshi"* (this is Self-shining and witnesses all).

This subtle mental state is not a modification of mind called *vritti*, since the mental states are of two kinds. One is the *natural state*, and the other is a transformation into forms of objects. The first is the truth, and the other is according to the doer (*kartrutantra*). When the latter perishes, *"jale kataka renuvat"* (like the clearing nut paste in water), the former will remain.

The means to this end is meditation. Though this is with the triad of distinction (*triputi*), it will finally end in pure awareness (*jnanam*). Meditation needs effort; *jnanam* is effortless. Meditation can be done, or not done, or wrongly done; *jnanam* is not so. Meditation is described as *kartru-tantra* (as doer's own), *jnanam* as *vastu-tantra* (the Supreme's own).

FEBRUARY 7, 1939

Miss Merston, an English visitor: I have read *Who am I?* While inquiring who the "I" is, I cannot hold it for any length of time. Secondly, I have no interest in the environment, yet I have hopes that I shall find some interest in life.

M. If there is no interest, it is good.

   (*The interpreter points out that the questioner hopes to find some interest in life.*)

M. That means there are those *vasanas*. A dreamer dreams a dream. He sees the dream world with pleasures, pains, etc. But he wakes up and then loses all interest in the dream world. So it is with the waking world, also. Just as the dream world, being only a part of yourself and not different from you,

481

ceases to interest you, so also the present world would cease to interest you if you awake from this waking dream (*samsara*) and realize that it is a part of your self, and not an objective reality. Because you think that you are apart from the objects around you, you desire a thing. But if you understand that the thing was only a thought-form, you would no longer desire it.

All things are like bubbles on water. You are the water and the objects are the bubbles. They cannot exist apart from the water, but they are not quite the same as the water.

D. I feel I am like froth.

M. Cease that identification with the unreal and know your real identity. Then you will be firm and no doubts can arise.

D. But I *am* the froth.

M. Because you think that way, there is worry. It is wrong imagination. Accept your true identity with the Real. Be the water and not the froth. That is done by diving in.

D. If I dive in, I shall find . . .

M. But even without diving in, *you are That.* The ideas of exterior and interior exist only so long as you do not accept your real identity.

D. But I took the idea from you that you want me to dive in.

M. Yes, quite right. It was said because you are identifying yourself with the froth and not the water. Because of this confusion, the answer was meant to draw your attention to this confusion and bring it home to you. All that is meant is that the Self is infinite, inclusive of all that you see. There is nothing beyond It or apart from It. Knowing this, you will not desire anything; not desiring, you will be content.

The Self is always realized. There is no seeking to realize what is already — always — realized. For you cannot deny your own existence. That existence is consciousness — the Self.

Unless you exist, you cannot ask questions. So you must admit your own existence. That existence is the Self. It is already realized. Therefore, the effort to realize results only in your realizing your present mistake — that you have not realized your self. There is no fresh realization. The Self becomes revealed.

D. That will take some years.

M. Why years? The idea of time is only in your mind. It is not in the Self. There is no time for the Self. Time arises as an idea after the ego arises. But you are the Self beyond time and space; you exist even in the absence of time and space.

Another devotee: Is it not that the "I" exists only in relation to a "this" (*aham-idam*)?

M. "I" and "this" appear together now. But "this" is also contained (*vyaptam*) in the "I" — they are not separate. "This" has to merge into and become one with "I." The "I" that remains is the true "I."

D. What is staying with a Guru?
M. It means studying the sacred lore.
D. But there is the special virtue of the Guru's presence.
M. Yes, it purifies the mind.
D. That is the effect or reward. I asked about how the disciple ought to behave.
M. This differs according to the type of disciple — student, householder, what his ingrained mental tendencies are, and so on.
D. If so, will it naturally come out right?
M. Yes. In former times, the Rishis sent their sons to others for education.
D. Why?
M. Because affection stood in the way.
D. That cannot be for the *jnanis*. Was it in respect of the disciples?
M. Yes.
D. If so, would not this obstacle get removed along with all the others through the Master's Grace?
M. There will be delay. Owing to the disciple's want of reverence, Grace may become effective only after a long time.

It is said that awaking from ignorance resembles awaking from a fearful dream of a beast. It is just like that. There are two taints of mind, namely veiling and restlessness (*avarana* and *vikshepa*). Of the two, the former is evil; the latter is not. So long as the veiling effect of sleep persists, there is the frightful dream. On awaking, the veiling ceases and there is no more fear. Restlessness is not a bar to happiness. To get rid of the restlessness caused by the world, one seeks the restlessness (activity) of being with the Guru, studying sacred books, and worshipping God with forms; and by these is awakening attained.

What happens in the end? Karna was ever the son of Kunti. The tenth man was such all along. Rama was Vishnu all the time. Such is *jnanam*. It is being aware of That which always is.

FEBRUARY 13, 1939

After his return from Europe, Mr. D. had a private interview with Sri Bhagavan for a few minutes. He said that his former visit had had some effect, but not as much as he wanted. He could concentrate on his work. Is not concentration indispensable for spiritual progress? Karma appealed to him because that helped towards concentration.

Sri Bhagavan: There is no karma without a *karta* (doer). On seeking for the doer, he disappears. Where is karma then?

(*Mr. D. sought practical instruction.*)

M. Seek the *karta*. That is the practice.

Mrs. D. said there were breaks in her awareness and desired to know how the awareness might be made continuous.

M. Breaks are due to thoughts. You cannot be aware of breaks unless you think so. It is only a thought. Repeat the old practice, "To whom do thoughts arise?" Keep up the practice until there are no breaks. Only practice will bring about continuity of awareness.

FEBRUARY 17, 1939

This is Shivaratri day. Sri Bhagavan was beaming with Grace in the evening. A sadhaka *raised the following question*: Inquiry into the Self seems to take one into the subtle body (*ativahika sariram* or *puriashtakam* or *jivatma*). Am I right?

M. They are different names for the same state, but these are used according to different points of view. After some time, *puriashtakam* (the eightfold subtle body) will disappear and there will be the *Eka* (One) only.

Vritti jnana alone can destroy *ajnana* (ignorance). Absolute *jnana* is not inimical to *ajnana*.

There are two kinds of *vrittis* (modes of mind): 1. *vishaya vritti* (objective), and 2. *atma vritti* (subjective). The first must give way to the second. That is the aim of *abhyasa* (practice), which takes one first to the *puriashtaka* (subtle body of eight phases), and then to the One Self.

In the course of conversation, a devotee said in passing: Sivaprakasam Pillai, who is such a good man, such an ardent devotee and a longstanding disciple, has written a poem saying that Sri Bhagavan's instructions could not be carried out by him effectively in practice. What can be the lot of others then?

M. Sri Acharya [Shankaracharya] also says similar things when he com-

poses songs in praise of any deity. How else can they praise God?
(*Saying this, Sri Bhagavan smiled.*)

The sadhaka *repeated his question in a different way:* The inquiry into the Self
seems to lead to the *ativahika,* the *puriashtaka,* or the *jivatma.* Is it right?
M. Yes. It is called *sarira* (body or abode, city or individual, *puri* or *jiva,*
according to the outlook). They are the same.

Vritti-jnanam is usually associated with objective phenomena. When
these cease, there remains the *atma-vritti* or the subjective *vritti* that is the
same as *jnanam.* Without it, *ajnanam* will not cease. The *puriashtaka* also will
not be found associated with anything outside, and the Self will shine forth
uniform and harmonious.

FEBRUARY 18, 1939

Mr. Satyanarayana Rao, a teacher in Vellore Mahant School, is a well-known
devotee of Sri Maharshi. He is suffering from cancer of the throat and the
doctors have no hope for him. He was given a room in the Ashram, and the
Sarvadhikari (manager) is very kind to him. He has been here about two
months and is very weak.

At about 9:00 a.m., Sri Bhagavan was reading the *tapals* (newspapers).
Mr. Rao's brother appeared in the Hall with an anxious look to ask Sri Bhaga-
van about the patient, who was gasping. The *Sarvadhikari* also came to the
Hall on behalf of the sufferer. Sri Bhagavan continued to read the *tapals.* A
few minutes later, another devotee also came there for the same purpose.
Sri Bhagavan asked: Did you call the doctor?
D. Yes, but he is too busy at the hospital.
M. What can I do?
(*After a short time.*) They will be pleased if I go there.

Soon Bhagavan left the Hall and went to the patient's side, massaged
him gently and placed his hand on the patient's heart and the other on his
head. Rao, whose tongue was protruding, mouth open, and eyes fixed,
showed signs of relief and in about twenty minutes gently murmured, "Oh
Help of the helpless, how I have troubled Thee! What return can I make for
this kindness?" The people felt relieved.

Sri Bhagavan returned to the Hall. Someone offered soap and water to
Sri Bhagavan to wash his hands. *But he declined them and rubbed his hands
over his body.* However, the patient passed away a few days later.

A well-known devotee remarked: Sri Bhagavan appears so unconcerned under all circumstances. But He is all along so loving and gracious.

FEBRUARY 23, 1939

A visitor from Dindigul said: I suffer in both mind and body. From the day of my birth, I never had happiness. My mother, too, suffered from the time she conceived me, I hear. Why do I suffer in this manner? I have not sinned in this life. Is all this due to the sins of past lives?

M. If there should be unrelieved suffering all the time, who would seek happiness? That is, if suffering were to be the natural state, how could the desire to be happy arise at all? However, the desire does arise. So to be happy is natural; all else is unnatural. Suffering is not desired, only because it comes and goes.

(The questioner repeated his complaint.)

M. You say the mind and body suffer. But do they ask the question? *Who is the questioner?* Is it not the one that is beyond both mind and body?

You say the body suffers in *this* life; the cause of this is the previous life, its cause is the one before it, and so on. So, like the case of the seed and the sprout, there is no end to the causal series. It has to be said that all the lives have their first cause in ignorance. That same ignorance is present even now, framing this question. That ignorance must be removed by *jnanam*.

"Why and to whom did this suffering come?" If you question thusly, you will find that the "I" is separate from the mind and body, that the Self is the only eternal being, and that It is eternal bliss. That is *jnanam*.

D. But why should there be suffering now?

M. If there were no suffering, how could the desire to be happy arise? If that desire did not arise, how could the quest of the Self be successful?

D. Then is all suffering good?

M. Quite so. What is happiness? Is it a healthy and handsome body, timely meals, and the like? Even an emperor has troubles without end though he may be healthy. So all suffering is due to the false notion "I am the body." Getting rid of it is *jnanam*.

A gentleman from Andhra Pradesh, who retired from Government Service, asked: I have been doing omkara upasana (meditation on *Om*) for a long time. In the left ear, I am always hearing a sound. It is like the piping of a *nadaswaram* (pipe instrument). Even now I hear it. Some luminous visions are also seen. I do not know what I should do.

M. There must be one to hear sounds or see visions. That one is the "I." If you seek it, asking "Who am I?", the subject and objects would coalesce. After that there is no quest. Till then thought's will arise, things will appear and disappear; you ask yourself what has happened, and what will happen. If the subject is known then the objects will merge in the subject. Being without that knowledge, one applies the mind to objects, because these objects appear and disappear, and one does not know that one's true nature is that which remains over as the Self. On the vanishing of objects, fear arises. That is, the mind being bound to objects, there is suffering when the objects are absent. But they are transient and the Self is eternal. If the eternal Self is known, subject and object merge into one and the One without a second will shine.

D. Is there the merger of the *Omkara?*

M. *Om* is the eternal truth. That which remains after the disappearance of objects is *Om*. It does not merge into anything. It is the State of which it is said: "Where one sees none other, hears none other, knows none other, that is Perfection" (*Yatra nanyat pasyati, nanyat srunoti, nanyat vijanati sa bhuma*). All the *upasanas* are ways to winning it. One should not get stuck in the *upasanas*, but must query "Who am I?" and find the Self.

D. I have no pleasure in the house. There remains nothing for me to do in the family. I have finished doing what I had to do. Now there are grandsons and granddaughters. May I remain in the house, or should I leave it and go away?

M. You should stay just where you are now. But where are you now? Are you in the house, or is the house in you? Is there any house apart from you? If you get fixed in your *own* place, you will see all things have merged into you, and there will be no cause for questions such as these.

D. Yes. Then it seems as if I may remain at home.

M. You must remain in your real state.

A gentleman from Hospet has returned from pilgrimage to Kailas, Amarnath, etc. He described how fine those places are and how difficult the journey was. He finally asked for something to remind him of Maharshi, meaning some instruction.

M. You have been to Kailas, etc. Have you been to Muktinath?

D. No. It was too difficult a journey for me. I have, however, been to Nepal. Have you been to those places?

M. No, no. I mentioned Muktinath casually.

To go to Kailas and return is just a new birth. For there the body-idea drops off.

Mrs. Kelly Hack asked if the waking and the dream states might be imagined to be excursions from the natural state of the Self.

M. There must be a place for excursions. The place must also lie outside oneself. That is not possible in the true nature of the Self.

D. But I meant that it might be imagined to be so.

M. One might as well imagine the true nature of the Self.

D. The illustration of the screen is very beautiful.

M. The cinema screen is not sentient and so requires a seer, whereas the screen of the Self includes the seer and the seen — rather, it is full of light.

The pictures of the cinema show cannot be seen without the help of darkness, for you cannot have a show in broad daylight. Similarly, the mind thinks thoughts and sees objects owing to an underlying ignorance (*avidya*). The Self is pure knowledge, pure light where there is no duality. Duality implies ignorance. The Knowledge of the Self is beyond relative knowledge and ignorance; the Light of the Self is beyond the ordinary light and darkness. The Self is all alone.

There was a question about progress.

Sri Bhagavan said that progress is for the mind and not for the Self. The Self is ever perfect.

MARCH 2, 1939

For the past few days, a rule is in force by which visitors are not allowed to enter the Hall between noon and 2:30 p.m. A few Muslim visitors came to the Ashram during the interval today. The attendant promptly told them that they should not disturb Sri Bhagavan's rest at this hour. Sri Bhagavan quietly got down from the sofa and came out of the Hall; he sat on the stone pavement adjoining the wall and asked the visitors to sit close to him. He went on reading a newspaper and also laid himself on the stone. He was finally requested to go in.

While speaking to Mr. K.L. Sarma of Pudukotah, Sri Bhagavan said: Leaving out what is intimate and immediate, why should one seek the rest? The scriptures say "That Thou art." In this statement, "Thou" is directly experienced, but leaving it out they go on seeking "That"!

D. In order to find the oneness of "That" and of "Thou."

M. "Thou" is the Inner Self, immanent in all; in order to find the same, he leaves himself out and sees the world objectively. What is the world? What is immanent in it? It is "That." These ideas arise only on forgetting one's own Self. I never bothered myself with all that. Only after a time, it occurred to me that men had investigated such matters.

MARCH 3, 1939

At about 4 p.m. Sri Bhagavan, who was writing something intently, turned his eyes slowly towards the window to the north; he closed the fountain-pen with the cap and put it in its case, he closed the notebook and put it aside; he removed the spectacles, folded them in the case and left them aside. He leaned back a little, looked up overhead, turned his face this way and that; and looked here and there. He passed his hand over his face and looked contemplative. Then he turned to someone in the Hall and said softly:

"The pair of sparrows just came here and complained to me that their nest had been removed. I looked up and found their nest missing." Then He called for the attendant, Madhava Swami, and asked: "Madhava, did anyone remove the sparrow's nest?"

The attendant, who walked in leisurely, answered with an air of unconcern: "I removed the nests as quickly as they had been built. The last one I removed this very afternoon."

M. That's it. That is why the sparrows complained. The poor little ones! How they take the pieces of straw and shreds in their tiny beaks and struggle to build their nests!

Attendant: But why should they build here, over our heads?

M. Well, well. Let us see who succeeds in the end.

(*After a short time, Sri Bhagavan went out.*)

Explaining the opening stanza of Sad-Vidya, *Sri Bhagavan observed*: The world is always apparent to everyone. All must know "I and this world exist." On inquiry, "do these always exist?" And, "if indeed real, they must remain even unrelated to time, space, and differentiation; are they so?" It is evident that only in the waking and dream states are these perceived, but not in deep sleep. Therefore, "I" and the world appear sometimes and disappear, also. They are created, have their being and later vanish. From where do they arise? In what way do they remain? Where do they go on vanishing from view? Can such phenomena be recognized to be real?

Furthermore, I and the world, objects of creation, sustenance and destruction, are perceived in the waking and dream states only, but not in

489

deep sleep. How does deep sleep differ from the other two states? In sleep, there are no thoughts, whereas in the other two states there are. There the thoughts must be the origin of the "I" and the world.

Now, what about thoughts? They cannot be natural; otherwise, they would not appear at one moment and disappear at another. From where do they arise? Their source, ever-present and not subject to variations, must be admitted to be. It must be the eternal state as said in the *upadesa mantra,* "That from which all beings come forth, that in which they remain, and that into which they resolve."

This stanza is not in praise or adoration, but only an expression of Reality.

Mr. K.L. Sarma asked: *Svasvarupanusandhanam bhaktirityabhidhiyate.* Again, *Svatmatattvanusadhanam bhaktirityapare joguh.* What is the difference between the two?

Whatever differences among people one sees, they are only different forms of the Self.

When one sees all people as the form of God, then devotion spontaneously arises in the mind.

M. The former is *vichara* (inquiry) — Who am I? (*Koham?*) It represents *jnana.*

The latter is *dhyana* (meditation) — Whence am I? (*Kutoham?*) This admits a *jivatma,* which seeks the *Paramatma.*

An elderly, learned person from Andhra Pradesh, asked: Are the two methods *Karma Marga* and *Jnana Marga* separate and independent of each other? Or is the *Karma Marga* only a preliminary, which after successful practice should be followed by *Jnana Marga* for the consummation of the aim? Karma advocates non-attachment to action and yet an active life, whereas *jnana* means renunciation. What is the true meaning of renunciation? Subjugation of lust, passion, greed, etc., is common to all and forms the essential preliminary step for any course. Does not freedom from passions indicate renunciation? Or is renunciation different, meaning cessation of the active life? These questions are troubling me and I beg for light to be thrown on those doubts.

Bhagavan smiled and said: You have said all. Your question contains the answer also. Freedom from passions is the essential requisite. When that is accomplished, all else is accomplished.

D. Sri Shankara emphasizes the *Jnana Marga* and renunciation as preliminary to it. But there are clearly two methods (*dwividha*) mentioned in the *Gita*. They are karma and *jnana* (*Lokesmin dwividha nishtha . . .*).

M. Sri Acharya has commented on the *Gita* and on that passage, also.

D. The *Gita* seems to emphasize karma. For Arjuna is persuaded to fight; Sri Krishna himself set the example by an active life of great exploits.

M. The *Gita* starts by stating that you are not the body, that you are not therefore the *karta* (doer).

D. What is the significance?

M. That one should act without thinking that oneself is the actor. The actions go on despite his egolessness. The person has come into manifestation for a certain purpose. That purpose will be accomplished whether he considers himself the actor or not.

D. What is *Karma Yoga*? Is it non-attachment to karma or its fruit?

M. *Karma Yoga* is that yoga in which the person does not arrogate to himself the function of being the actor. The actions go on automatically.

D. Is it the non-attachment to the results of actions?

M. The question arises only if there is the actor. It is being said all along that you should not consider yourself the actor.

D. So *Karma Yoga* is *kartrtva buddhi rahita karma* — action without the sense of doership.

M. Yes. Quite so.

D. The *Gita* teaches active life from beginning to end.

M. Yes, the actorless action.

D. Is it then necessary to leave the home and lead a life of renunciation?

M. Is the home in you? Or are you in the home?

D. It is in my mind.

M. Then what becomes of you when you leave the physical environment?

D. Now I see. Renunciation is only action without the sense of being the *karta*. Is there not action for a *jivanmukta*?

M. Who raises the question? Is he a *jivanmukta* or another?

D. Not a *jivanmukta*.

M. Let the question be raised after *jivanmukti* is gained, if found necessary. *Mukti* is admitted to be freedom from mental activities, also. Can a *mukta* think of action?

D. Even if he gives up action, the action will not leave him. Is it not so?

M. With what is he identified in order that this question might apply?

D. Yes, I see all right. My doubts are now cleared.

A District Official, a Muslim: What is the necessity for reincarnation?

M. Let us first see if there is incarnation before we speak of reincarnation.
D. How?
M. Are you now incarnated that you speak of reincarnation?
D. Yes. Certainly. An amoeba developed into higher organisms until the human being has been evolved. This is now the perfection in development. Why should there be further reincarnation?
M. Who is to set limits to this theory of evolution?
D. Physically it is perfect. But for the soul, further development may be required which will happen after the death of the man.
M. Who is the man? Is he the body or the soul?
D. Both put together.
M. Do you not exist in the absence of the body?
D. What do you mean? It is impossible.
M. What was your state in deep sleep?
D. Sleep is temporary death. I was unconscious and therefore I cannot say what the state was.
M. But you existed in sleep. Did you not?
D. In sleep, the soul leaves the body and goes out somewhere. Then it returns to the body before waking. It is therefore temporary death.
M. A man who is dead never returns to say that he died, whereas the man who had slept says that he slept.
D. Because this is temporary death.
M. If death is temporary and life is temporary, what is it that is real?
D. What is meant by the question?
M. If life and death are temporary, there must be something which is not temporary. Reality is that which is not temporary.
D. There is nothing real. Everything is temporary. Everything is *maya* (illusory).
M. On what does *maya* appear?
D. Now I see you; it is all *maya*.
M. If everything is *maya*, how does any question arise?
D. Why should there be reincarnation?
M. For whom?
D. For the perfect human being.
M. If you are perfect, why do you fear to be reborn? It indicates imperfection.
D. Not that I fear. But you say that I must be reborn.
M. Who says it? You are asking the question.
D. What I mean is this. You are a Perfect Being; I am a sinner. You tell me

that I being a sinner must be reborn in order to perfect myself?

M. No, I do not say so. On the other hand I say that you have no birth and therefore no death.

D. Do you mean to say I was not born?

M. Yes, you are now thinking that you are the body and therefore confuse yourself with its birth and death. But you are not the body and you therefore have no birth and death.

D. Do you not uphold the theory of rebirth?

M. No. On contrary, I want to remove your confusion that you will be reborn. It is you who think that you will be reborn.

See for whom this question arises. Unless the questioner is found, the questions can never be set at rest.

D. This is no answer to my question.

M. On the other hand, this is the answer to elucidate the point and all other doubts, as well.

D. This will not satisfy all others.

M. Leave others alone. If you take care of yourself, others can take care of themselves.

(*Silence followed. He left in a few minutes, apparently dissatisfied with the discourse.*)

Sri Bhagavan said after a few minutes: This will work in him. The discourse will have its effect.

He does not admit any Reality. Well, who is it that has determined everything to be unreal? In that case, the determination also becomes unreal.

The theory of evolution is enlarged upon by the person in this state. Where is it if not in his mind?

To say that the soul must be perfected after death, the soul must first be admitted to exist. Therefore, the body is not the person. It is the soul.

To explain evolution, Sri Bhagavan continued: One sees an edifice in his dream. It rises up all of a sudden. Then he begins to think how it should have been already built brick by brick by so many laborers during such a long time. Yet he does not see any builders working. So also with the theory of evolution. Because he finds himself a man, he thinks he has developed to that stage from the primal state of the amoeba.

Another devotee: It is an illustration of the saying that he sees the universe full of cause and effect (*Visvam pasyati karyakaranataya*).

M. Yes. Man always traces an effect to a cause; there must be a cause for the cause; the argument becomes interminable. Relating the effect to a cause makes the man think. He is finally driven to consider who he is himself. When he knows the Self, there is Perfect Peace. It is for that consummation that man is evolved.

Later in the evening, another devotee said to Sri Bhagavan that the Muslim official continued to speak of the same topic to the Municipal Commissioner. Sri Bhagavan said: He says that body and soul together form the man. But I ask: what is the state of the man in deep sleep? The body is not aware, whereas the man is there all along.

D. But he says that sleep is temporary death.

M. Yes, so he says. But he qualifies the word death by the word "temporary," so that the man returns to the body. How does he find the body to re-enter it? Moreover, he is sure to return. That means he must exist to return to the body or to claim the body for himself.

The scriptures, however, say that the *prana* protects the body in sleep. For when the body lies on the floor, a wolf or a tiger may feed on it. The animal sniffs and feels that there is life within and therefore does not feed on it as on a corpse. That again shows that there is someone in the body to protect it in deep sleep.

General remarks by Sri Bhagavan:
All knowledge is meant only to lead the person to realization of the Self. The scriptures or religions are well known for that purpose. What do they all mean? Leave alone what they say of the past or of the future, for it is only speculative. But the present existence is within the experience of all. Realize the pure Being. There is an end to all discourse and disputes.

But the intellect of man does not easily take to this course. It is only rarely that a man becomes introverted. The intellect delights in investigating the past and the future but does not look to the present.

D. Because it must lose itself if it sinks within in search of the Self. But the other investigation gives it not only a lease of life but also food for growth.

M. Yes. Quite so. Why is intellect developed? It has a purpose. The purpose is that it should show the way to realize the Self. It must be put to that use.

MARCH 12, 1939
A man of about thirty, of good appearance, came to the Hall with a few companions.

The man abruptly began: To say "I-I" cannot help anyone to reach the goal. How can "I" be pointed out?

M. It must be found within. It is not an object to be shown by one to another.

D. When the instruction to find the "I" is given, the instruction must be made complete by showing what it is.

M. The instruction here amounts to direction only. It depends on the seeker to use the direction.

D. The seeker is ignorant and seeks instruction.

M. He is therefore guided to find the Truth.

D. But it is not enough. The "I" must be pointed out specifically.

(The man assumed an aggressive attitude and did not listen. Sri Bhagavan tried to explain, but he would not allow Sri Bhagavan to do so.)

Finally Sri Bhagavan said: This is not the attitude of the seeker. When someone teaches humility to the seeker, he will reach the way and not until then.

(The chanting of the Vedas *began.)*

The previous conversation was casually referred to by a devotee present.

Sri Bhagavan again said: The seeker must listen and try to understand. If on the other hand he wants to disprove me, let him do so by all means. I do not argue.

The man again began: My attitude was not properly understood. I want to know the "I." It must be pointed out to me.

(But he displayed considerable malice. The others did not like it and so tried to bring him round. He became worse.)

Sri Bhagavan finally said: Go back the way you came. Do it externally or internally, as it suits you.

(The man grew excited and others also were equally excited. He was finally led out of the Hall and sent away. Later, it was learned that the man was an adherent of yoga and that he used to abuse all other methods. He used to vilify jnana *and the* jnanis.*)*

At night, after supper, Sri Bhagavan spoke of Govinda Yogi, a Malayali Brahmin pundit of some repute, who used to extol yoga and vilify other methods. He always cited the *Gita*, the *Upanishads*, etc., to support his statements. Others, e.g., Sri Narayana Guru, used to refute him on the same grounds.

Later, Sri Bhagavan spoke appreciating the amiability of Amritanatha.

He is a great *tapasvi,* who had made considerable *japa.* He had fed the poor on many occasions in many places. He could easily gain the goodwill of others, including great men like Sir P. Ramanathan and Pundit Malaviya.

MARCH 13, 1939

Sri Bhagavan referred to the following passage from Gandhiji, in the current issue of the Harijan:

"How mysterious are the ways of God! This journey to Rajkot is a won-der even to me. Why am I going, whither am I going? What for? I have thought nothing about these things. And if God guides me, what should I think? Why should I think? Even thought may be an obstacle in the way of His guidance.

The fact is, it takes no effort to stop thinking. The thoughts do *not* come. Indeed, there is no vacuum, but I mean to say that there is no thought about the mission."

Sri Bhagavan remarked how true the words were and emphasized each statement in the extract. Then He cited Thayumanavar in support of the state free from thoughts:

"Although I had often heard that all the *Srutis* declare the state of stillness to be one of Bliss, all Bliss — yet I continued to be igno-rant. Again, I did not follow the advice of my Lord — the Silent Master — because of my folly. I wandered in the forest of illu-sion; alas! it was my fate.

"Bliss will reveal itself if one is still. Why, then, this illusory yoga practice? Can it (i.e., Bliss) be revealed by directing the in-tellect in a particular way? Do not say so, you who are given to the practice and are therefore an innocent babe.

"The eternal Being is that state where you have disappeared. Are you not in it, too? You, who cannot speak of it, do not be perplexed. Although you do not manifest, yet you are not lost. For you are eternal and also still. Do not be in pain. Here is Bliss — come on!"

MARCH 15, 1939

D. Is not what Gandhiji describes, the state in which thoughts themselves become foreign?

M. Yes, it is only after the rise of the "I"-thought that all other thoughts

496

arise. The world is seen after you have felt "I Am." The "I"-thought and all other thoughts had vanished for him.

D. Then the body-sense must be absent in that state.

M. The body-sense also is a thought, whereas he describes the state in which "thoughts do not come."

D. He also says, "It takes no effort to stop thinking."

M. Of course no effort is necessary to stop thoughts, whereas it is necessary for bringing about thoughts.

D. We are trying to stop thoughts. Gandhiji also says that thought is an obstacle to God's guidance. So it is the natural state. Though natural, yet how difficult to realize. They say that *sadhanas* are necessary and also that they are obstacles. We get confused.

M. *Sadhanas* are needed so long as one has not realized it. They are for putting an end to obstacles. Finally there comes a stage when a person feels helpless notwithstanding the *sadhanas*. He is unable to pursue the much-cherished *sadhana*, also. It is then that God's Power is realized. The Self reveals itself.

D. If the state is natural, why does it not overcome the unnatural phases and assert itself over the rest?

M. Is there anything besides that? Does anyone see anything besides the Self? One is always aware of the Self. So It is always Itself.

D. It is said, because It shines forth, It is directly perceived. I understand from it that It becomes *pratyaksha* (directly perceived), because It is *pradeepta* (shining). Since it is not realized by us, I take it to be not shining. It is only *pradeepta*, and hence admits of obstacles and goes under them. If the *Atma* becomes *prakarshena deepta* (very shining), it will shine over the rest. So it seems necessary to make it shine more.

M. How can it be so? The *Atma* cannot be dull at one moment and blazing at another. It is unchanging and uniform.

D. But Chudala says to Sikhidhvaja that she simply helped to trim the wick.

M. That refers to *nididhyasana*.

- By *sravana*, Knowledge dawns. That is the flame.
- By *manana*, the Knowledge is not allowed to vanish. Just as the flame is protected by a windscreen, so the other thoughts are not allowed to overwhelm the right knowledge.
- By *nididhyasana*, the flame is kept up to burn bright by trimming the wick. Whenever other thoughts arise, the mind is turned inward to the light of true knowledge.
- When this becomes natural, it is *samadhi*.

- The inquiry "Who am I?" is the *sravana.*
- The ascertainment of the true import of "I" is the *manana.*
- The practical application on each occasion is *nididhyasana.* Being as "I" is *samadhi.*

D. Although we have heard it so often and so constantly, yet we are unable to put the teaching into practice successfully. It must be due to weakness of mind. Is it possible that one's age is a bar?
M. The mind is commonly said to be strong if it can think furiously. But here the mind is strong if it is free from thoughts. The yogis say that realization can be had only before the age of thirty, but not the *jnanis.* For *jnana* does not cease to exist with age.

It is true that in the *Yoga Vasishta,* Vasishta says to Rama in the *Vairagya Prakarana,* "You have this dispassion in your youth. It is admirable." But he did not say that *jnana* cannot be had in old age; there is nothing to prevent it then.

The *sadhaka* must remain as the Self. If he cannot do so, he must ascertain the true meaning of the "I" and constantly revert to it whenever other thoughts arise. That is the practice.

Some say that one must know "*tat*" because the idea of the world constantly arises to deflect the mind. If the Reality behind it is first ascertained, it will be found to be *Brahman.* The "*twam*" is understood later. It is the *jiva.* Finally, there will be *jivabrahmaikya* (union of the two).

But why all this? Can the world exist apart from the Self? The "I" is always *Brahman.* Its identity need not be established by logic and practice. It is enough that one realizes the Self. It is always *Brahman.*

According to the other school, *nididhyasana* will be the thought *Aham Brahmasmi* (I am *Brahman*). That is diversion of thought to *Brahman.* No diversion should be allowed. Know the Self and there is an end of it.

No long process is necessary to know the Self. Is it to be pointed out by another? Does not everyone know that he exists? Even in utter darkness when he cannot see his hand, he answers a call and says "I am here."
D. But that "I" is the ego or the "I"-thought and it is not the Absolute Self that answers the call, or is otherwise aware of oneself.
M. Even the ego can become aware of itself in the absence of light, sight, etc. Much more so should be the Pure Light of the Self.

I am saying that the Self is self-evident. One need not discuss the *tattvas* to find the Self. Some say there are twenty-four *tattvas,* others more and so on. Should we know the *tattvas* before we admit the existence of the Self?

The *sastras* elaborate upon them to point out that the Self is untouched by them. But the seeker can straightaway admit the Self and try to be That, without having recourse to the study of the *tattvas*.

D. Gandhiji adhered to *satya* (Truth) so long, and won realization of the Self.

M. What is *satya* except the Self? *Satya* is that which is made up of *sat* (Existence). Again, *sat* is nothing but the Self. So Gandhiji's *satya* is only the Self.

Each one knows the Self yet remains ignorant. The person is enabled to realize only after hearing the *mahavakya*. Hence the *Upanishadic* text is the eternal Truth to which everyone who has realized owes his experience. After hearing the Self to be *Brahman*, the person finds the true import of the Self and reverts to it whenever he is diverted from it. Here is the whole process of realization.

MARCH 17, 1939

Sri Bhagavan said that Tatva Rayar was the first to express *Advaita* philosophy in Tamil.

He had said that the Earth was his bed, his hands were his plates for taking food, the loincloth was his clothing, and thus there was no want for him.

In *Maharaja Turavu* (Renunciation of the King), he says: He was seated on the bare ground; the earth was his seat, the mind was the *chamara* (fan); the sky was the canopy, and renunciation was his spouse.

Then Sri Bhagavan continued: I had no cloth spread on the floor in earlier days. I used to sit on the floor and lie on the ground. That is freedom. The sofa is bondage. It is a jail for me. I am not allowed to sit where and how I please. Is it not bondage? One must be free to do as one pleases, and should not be served by others.

"No want" is the greatest bliss. It can be realized only by experience. Even an emperor is no match for a man without want. The emperor has got vassals under him. But the other man is not aware of anyone beside the Self. Which is better?

MARCH 18, 1939

Mr. Thompson, a very quiet young gentleman who has been staying in India for some years and studying Hindu Philosophy as an earnest student, asked: Srimad Bhagavad Gita says, "I am the prop for Brahman"; in another place: "I am in the heart of each one." Thus the different aspects of the Ultimate Principle are revealed. I take it there are three aspects, namely 1. the transcendental, 2. the immanent, and 3. the cosmic. Is Realization to be in anyone of these or in all of them? Coming to the transcendental from the cosmic, the *Vedanta* discards names and forms as being *maya*. But I cannot readily appreciate it because a tree means the trunk, branches, leaves, etc. I cannot dismiss the leaves as *maya*. Again, the *Vedanta* also says that the whole is *Brahman* as illustrated by gold and ornaments of gold. How are we to understand the Truth?

M. The *Gita* says: *"Brahmano hi pratishtaham"* ("I" is rooted in *Brahman* alone). If that *aham* is known, the whole is known.

D. It is the immanent aspect only.

M. You now think that you are an individual, there is the universe and that God is beyond the cosmos. So there is the idea of separateness. This idea must go. For God is not separate from you or the cosmos. The *Gita* also says:

> "The Self am I, O Lord of Sleep,
> In every creature's heart enshrined.
> The rise and noon of every form,
> I am its final doom as well."
> — *Bhagavad Gita* 10.20

Thus, God is not only in the heart of all, He is the prop of all, He is the source of all, their abiding place and their end. All proceed from Him, have their stay in Him, and finally resolve into Him. Therefore, He is not separate.

D. How are we to understand this passage in the *Gita*: "This whole cosmos forms a particle of Me."?

M. It does not mean that a small particle of God separates from Him and forms the Universe. His *Shakti* is acting; as a result of one phase of such activity, the cosmos has become manifest. Similarly, the statement in *Purusha Sukta*, "All the beings form His one foot" (*Padosya viswa bhutani*), does not mean that *Brahman* is in four parts.

D. I understand. *Brahman* is certainly not divisible.

M. So the fact is that *Brahman* is all and remains indivisible. He is ever realized. Man does not, however, know it. He must know it. Knowledge means the overcoming of obstacles, which obstruct revelation of the Eternal Truth that the Self is the same as *Brahman*. The obstacles form altogether your idea of separateness as an individual. Therefore, the present attempt will result in the truth being revealed that the Self is not separate from *Brahman*.

A middle-aged gentleman asked Sri Bhagavan how he should make his japa.
M. The *japa* contains the word *namah*. It means that state in which the mind does not manifest apart from the Self. When the state is accomplished, there will be an end of the *japa*. For the doer disappears and so also the action. The Eternal Being alone is left. *Japa* should be made until that state is reached. There is no escape from the Self. The doer will be automatically drawn into it. When once it is done, the man cannot do anything but remain merged in the Self.

D. Will *bhakti* lead to *mukti?*
M. *Bhakti* is not different from *mukti*. *Bhakti* is being as the Self (*Svarupa*). One is always that. He realizes it by the means he adopts. What is *bhakti?* To think of God. That means: only one thought prevails to the exclusion of all others. That thought is of God, which is the Self, or it is the Self surrendered unto God. When He has taken you up, nothing will assail you. The absence of thoughts is *bhakti*. It is also *mukti*.

The *jnana* method is said to be *vichara* (inquiry). That is nothing but "supreme devotion" (*parabhakti*). The difference is in words only.

You think that *bhakti* is meditation on the Supreme Being. So long as there is *vibhakti* (the sense of separateness), *bhakti* (reunion) is sought. The process will lead to the ultimate goal as stated in *Srimad Bhagavad Gita*:

> "*Chaturvidha bhajante mam, janah sukrtino 'rjuna,*
> *arto jignasuh artharthi, jnani cha Bharatarshabha.*"
> The virtuous ones who worship me are of four kinds, the man
> in distress, the seeker for knowledge, the seeker for wealth,
> and the man of wisdom [*jnani*].

> "*Tesham jnani nityayukta, ekabhaktir visishyate,*
> *priyo hi jnanino 'tyartham, aham sa cha mama priyah.*"
> Of these the *jnani*, who is ever attuned, whose devotion is
> centered in One, is the most excellent; because to the *jnani* I
> am exceedingly dear and he is dear to me.
> — *Bhagavad Gita* 7.16-17

Any kind of meditation is good. But if the sense of separateness is lost, and the object of meditation or the subject who meditates is alone left behind without anything else to know, it is *jnana*. *Jnana* is said to be *ekabhakti* (single-minded devotion). The *jnani* is the finality because he has become the Self and there is nothing more to do. He is also perfect and so fearless, *dwitiyat vai bhayam bhavati* (only the existence of a second gives rise to fear). This is *mukti*. It is also *bhakti*.

MARCH 23, 1939

Major A.W. Chadwick is copying the English translation of the Tamil Kaivalya Navaneeta. *He came across several technical terms and felt some difficulty in understanding them, he asked Sri Bhagavan about them. Sri Bhagavan said*: Those portions deal with theories of creation. They are not material because the *Srutis* (scriptures) did not intend to set forth such theories. They mention the theories casually so that the inquirer may please himself if he is so inclined. The truth is that the world appears as a passing shadow in a flood of light. Light is necessary to see that shadow. The shadow does not deserve any special notice, analysis or discussion, for the book deals primarily with the Self and that is its purpose. Discussions of creation may be omitted for the present.

Later, Sri Bhagavan continued: *Vedanta* states that the cosmos springs into view simultaneously with the seer. There is no detailed process of creation. This is said to be *yugapat srshti* (instantaneous creation). It is quite similar to creations in a dream where the experiencer springs up simultaneously with the objects of experience. When this is stated, some people are not satisfied because they are so rooted in objective knowledge. They seek to find out how there can be sudden creation. They argue that an effect must always be preceded by a cause. In short, they desire an explanation for the existence of the world, which they see around them. Then the *Srutis* try to satisfy their curiosity by such theories of creation. This method of dealing with the subject is called *krama srshti* (gradual creation). But the true seeker can be content with *yugapat srshti* — instantaneous creation.

MARCH 24, 1939

A certain person had composed verses in praise of Sri Bhagavan in which the word Avartapuri *occurs. Sri Bhagavan said that it means "Tiruchulli" (the birthplace of Sri Bhagavan).*

The place goes by different names, such *Avarta chuli*, which means "an eddy". There had been several deluges. God Shiva saved this place from

502

three of them. On one occasion, when the whole land surface was flooded, Shiva planted His spear there. All the waters were drawn into that hole. Then an eddy formed, hence the name. Again in another deluge, He held the place aloft on the top of the spear. Hence, *Sulapuri*.

Mother Earth was once carried away by Hiranyaksha into the waters. When recovered by Vishnu, she felt that she had *papasparsa* (touch of sin) by that Rakshasa. As an expiation of that impure touch, she worshipped Shiva in that place. Hence, *Bhuminatheshwara Kshetra*.

Gautama is prominent in Arunachala, as well as in Tiruchulli. Shiva showed Himself to the saint in the dancing posture and also re-enacted the wedding of Gauri Shankar.

Kaundinya was another *rishi* for whose sake the sacred river began to flow there. It goes by the name of the *rishi*, i.e., Kaundinya river (which in Tamil is was corrupted into Kundaru). It is otherwise called Papahari, i.e., the destroyer of sins. There lies a story behind it: A King's daughter was hysterical (i.e., possessed). She was taken on a pilgrimage to various sacred places and *tirthas* (sacred waters). On one occasion, the party heard the name of Papahari as a *tirtha* in a *sankalpa* before bathing. They inquired where the *tirtha* was and went to Tiruchulli. The girl bathed in that water and was made free from the spirit.

The Pandya king also became free from *brahmahatya* (sin of killing a Brahmin) in this place. It happens to be the center of the Pandya Kingdom, which comprised the Madurai, Ramnad, and Tirunelveli districts.

The village had a sacred tank in front of the temple, which was the spot of the eddy created by the spear of Shiva. Even now, the waters in the tank rise at the rate of about a foot every day for ten consecutive days preceding the full moon in the Tamil month Masi (*Maghasuddha Pournami*) and then gradually fall during the succeeding ten days. This phenomenon can be observed every year. It is noted with wonder by the young people of the village. Pilgrims gather to bathe in those waters on that occasion. That water is sulphurous, as indicated by silver jewels of the bathers tarnishing after bathing in it. Sri Bhagavan said he had noted it when he was a boy.

The village has the river on one side and a huge lake on the other side. The embankment of the lake is full of clay and runs about three miles in all. The lake strangely enough is twenty feet above the level of the village. Even when it is overfull, the waters escape in other directions, leaving the village unaffected.

APRIL 1, 1939

Some teachers who attended the Teacher's Guild meeting in town came on a visit to the Hall. One of them asked Sri Bhagavan: I seem to be wandering in a forest because I do not find the way.

M. This idea of being in a forest must go. It is those very ideas, which are at the root of the trouble.

D. But I do not find the way.

M. Where is the forest and where is the way unless they are within you? You are as you are and yet you speak of a forest and ways.

D. But I am obliged to move in society.

M. The society also is an idea similar to that of the forest.

D. I leave my home and go and mix in society.

M. Who does it?

D. The body moves and does all.

M. Quite so. Now that you identify yourself with the body, you feel the trouble. The trouble is in your mind. You think you are the body or that you are the mind. But there are occasions when you are free from both. For example, in deep slumber you create a body and a world in your dream. That represents your mental activities. In your waking state, you think that you are the body and then the idea of forest and the rest arise.

Now, consider the situation. You are an unchanging and continuous being who remains throughout all these states that are constantly changing and therefore transient. But you are always there. It follows that these fleeting objects are mere phenomena, which appear on your being like pictures that move across a screen. The screen does not move when the picture moves. Similarly, you do not move from where you are, even when the body leaves home and mixes in society.

Your body, the society, the forest, and the ways are all in you; you are not in them. You are the body also, but not this body exclusively. If you remain as your pure Self, the body and its movements need not affect you.

D. This can be realized only by the Grace of the Master. I was reading *Sri Bhagavatam*; it says that Bliss can be had only by the dust of the Master's feet. I pray for Grace.

M. What is Bliss but your own being? You are not apart from Being which is the same as Bliss. You are now thinking that you are the mind or the body which are both changing and transient. But you are unchanging and eternal. That is what you should know.

D. It is darkness and I am ignorant.

M. This ignorance must go. Again, who says "I am ignorant?" He must be

504

the witness of ignorance. That is what you are. Socrates said, "I know that I do not know." Can it be ignorance? It is wisdom.

D. Why, then, do I feel unhappy when I am in Vellore and feel peace in your presence?

M. Can the feeling in this place be Bliss? When you leave here, you say you are unhappy. Therefore this peace is not permanent; nay, it is mixed with unhappiness, which is felt in another place. Therefore, you cannot find Bliss in places and in periods of time. It must be permanent in order that it may be useful. Such permanent being is yourself. Be the Self and that is Bliss. You are always That.

You say you left Vellore, traveled by train, arrived in Tiruvannamalai, entered the Hall and found happiness. When you go back, you are not happy in Vellore. Now, do you really move from place to place? Even considering you to be the body, the body sits in a cart at the gate of the home, the cart moves on to the railway station. Then it gets into a railway carriage that speeds on from Vellore to Tiruvannamalai. There it gets into another cart, which brings the body here. Yet when asked, you say you traveled all the way from Vellore. Your body remains where it was, and all the places went past it. Such ideas are due to the deep-rooted false identity.

Another asked: Should we understand the world as transient (*anitya*)?

M. Why so? Because you are now considering it to be permanent (*nitya*), the Scriptures tell you that it is not so in order to wean you off wrong ideas. This should be done by knowing yourself to be eternal (*nitya*) and not by branding the world as transitory (*anitya*).

D. We are told to practice indifference (*udasina*), which is possible only if the world is unreal.

M. Yes, "*Oudasinyam abhipsitam*". Indifference is advised. But what is it? It is absence of love and hatred. When you realize the Self on which these phenomena pass, will you love or hate them? That is the meaning of indifference.

D. That will lead to want of interest in our work. Should we do our duty or not?

M. Yes, certainly. Even if you try not to, you will be compelled to do so. Let the body complete the task for which it came into being.

Sri Krishna also says in the *Gita*, whether Arjuna liked it or not he would be forced to fight. When there is work to be done by you, you cannot keep away; nor can you continue to do a thing when you are not required to do it, that is to say, when the work allotted to you has been done. In short, the work will go on and you must take your share in it — the share allotted to you.

D. How is it to be done?

M. Like an actor playing his part in a drama, free from love or hatred.

ओम तत सत

Om Tat Sat

GLOSSARY

Abhasa: Reflection; appearance.

Abhijna: Direct perception.

Abhimana: Attachment; conceit.

Abhisheka: Pouring water, etc. over a sacred image.

Abhyasa: Practice.

Abhyasi: One who practices.

Achala: Unmoving; a hill or a mountain.

Achamana: Sipping of water associated with a religious ceremony.

Achit: Not sentient.

Adhara: Support.

Adhistana: Substratum.

Adhridha: Weak; not firm.

Adhyaropa: Superimposition of bliss.

Adhyasika: Superimposed.

Advaita: "Not two"; nonduality; affirms the nondifference between the individual soul and *Brahman.*

Adyatmika shakti: Power of the Self.

Agami (agami karma): Actions expected to bear fruit in future births.

Aham: I; embodied self; soul.

Aham Brahmasmi: I am Brahman. One of the four *Mahavakyas.*

Ahamkara (ahankara): "I"-sense; the ego-self.

Ahamvritti: The "I"-sense; the objective "I."

Ahimsa: Nonviolence.

Ajatavada: The theory of *advaita* that denies creation; nonorigination; nonexistence.

Ajna: Direction; injunction.

Ajnana: Ignorance; nescience.

Ajnani: One who is ignorant; who has not realized the Self.

Akahsa: Ether; space.

Akara: Form or shape.

Akashavani: Voice coming from the sky.

Akhanda: Undivided.

Akhandakara vritti: Unbroken experience.

Akritopasaka: One who has not practiced meditation (*upasana*).

Amrita: Immortal; Nectar of Immortality.

Amrita nadi: The name of a yogic nerve.

Anadi: Without beginning.

Anahata: Name of yogic *chakra.*

Ananda: Bliss.

Anandamaya kosa: The sheath of bliss.

Anandatman: Self in the state of bliss.

Ananta: Infinite; endless.

Anatman: Non-Self.

Anava: Limitation.

Anichcha: Involuntary.

Anitya: Transitory.

Annamalai: The Tamil name for Arunachala.

Annamaya kosa: Sheath of gross matter.

Antah (antar): Inner; internal.

Antah karanam: The inner organ; the mind.

Antah pranayama: Internal breath-regulation.

Antardhana: Disappearance from sight.

Antarmukhi manas: Inward-turned mind.

Anu: Atom.

Ap: Water.

Apana: The life force that goes down.

Apara: The lower.

Apara vibhuti: Inferior *vibhuti*.

Aparoksha: Direct; immediate.

Apavada: Removal; refutation, as in repudiation of a wrong belief.

Aruna: Red.

Arupa: Formless.

Asamshakti: Nonattachment; one of the seven stages of enlightenment.

Asana: Sitting posture; seat.

Asat: Not real; nonbeing; nonexistence.

Asesha sakshi: Witness of all.

Asrama (ashrama): Stage of life; a place where hermits and sages live.

Asthira: Unsteady.

Asuddha: Impure.

Asukavi: One who can spontaneously create verse.

Asura: Demon.

Ati jagrat: Beyond waking.

Ati sunya: Beyond the void.

Atiasrama: Beyond the four traditional stages of life.

Atita: Beyond.

Ativahika sarira: The subtle body which remains after the physical body perishes, and which carries the individual to other worlds.

Atma (Atman): Self; the basis of all; the substrate of the individual, and identical with *Brahman* (the Absolute).

Atma jnani: One who has realized the Self.

Atma nadi: The name of a yogic nerve.

Atma nishta: Abiding as the Self.

Atma-vichara: Inquiry into the Self.

Atmanusandhana: Continuous contemplation on the Self.

Atyanta vairagyam: Total dispassion.

Avarana: Covering.

Avastha traya: The three states of consciousness, namely waking, dream, and sleep.

Avatar: Incarnation of God.

Avidya: Ignorance; nescience.

Avritta chakshus: Introverted look.

Ayatana: Repository.

Bahir mukhi manas: Outward turning mind.

Bahir pranayamam: External breath regulation.

Bahudaka: A spiritual mendicant (*sannyasin*) who wanders about.

Bahya: External.

Bala: Child.

Bandha: Bondage.

Bandha hetu: Cause of bondage.

Beeja: Seed.

Bhajana: Singing God's praises, especially in chorus.

Bhakta: Devotee; lover of God.

Bhakti: Love; devotion to God.

Bhakti Marga: The spiritual path of realizing the Absolute through love and devotion.

Bhakti Yoga: See *Bhakta Marga.*

Bhashya: Commentary.

Bhashyakara: Commentator.

Bhavana: Idea.

Bheda: Difference; differentiation.

Bhoga: Enjoyment.

Bhoga hetu: Cause of enjoyment.

Bhoga vastu: Object of enjoyment.

Bhogyam: That which is enjoyed.

Bhokta: Enjoyer.

Bhuma: All-comprehensive; the Absolute.

Bindu: A dot, or spot; symbol for the universe in its unmanifest form.

Brahma: A name for God in his role as creator of the universe.

Brahmachari: A celibate; a student.

Brahmacharya: Celibacy; continence in thought, word, and deed.

Brahmahatya: The sin of killing a Brahmin.

Brahmaivaham: *Brahman* am I.

Brahmajnana: Knowledge (Realization) of *Brahman,* the Supreme Reality.

Brahmajnani: One who has realized the Self.

Brahmakaravritti: Concept in the form of *Brahman.*

Brahman: The ultimate Reality; the eternal imperishable Absolute, ungraspable by thought and inexpressible by speech.

Brahmanishta: One who is established in *Brahman.*

Brahmavid: One who has realized *Brahman.*

Brahma-vid-vara: One who is a superior among the knowers of *Brahman.*

Brahma-vid-varishta: The very best among the knowers of *Brahman.*

Brahma-vid-varya: The best among the knowers of *Brahman.*

Brahmin: A member of the priestly class.

Buddha: One who is aware; awakened.

Buddhi: Intellect.

Chaitanya: Consciousness.

Chakra(s): Wheel; center; the seven yogic centers located in the subtle body.

Chakshus: Eye.

Chamara: A flywhisk made of the bushy tail of *Bosgrunniens* and used as a badge of royalty.

Chanchala: Changing; fickle creation.

Chidvyoman (chitta vyoman): Expanse of consciousness.

Chinmaya: Full of consciousness.

Chinta: Thought or idea.

Chintamani: A mystical wish-fulfilling gem; an epithet for God.

Chit: Consciousness.

Chitta: Memory; mind.

Chitta suddhi: Purity of mind.

Chitta vilasa: Play of mind.

Chittaikograta: One-pointedness of mind.

Chitta-nirodha: Control of mind.

Crore: Ten million.

Daharakasha: Ether of the heart.

Dakshinamurti: The young sage who guided disciples older than himself through a profound, silent influence (*mouna*) on the heart.

Dana: Gift; charity.

Darshan: To have sight of; vision; especially of saints and sages.

Dasi: Courtesan.

Deha: Body.

Dehatma buddhi: I-am-the-body consciousness.

Dehavasana: Attachment to the body.

Devas: Celestial beings.

Dharana: Concentration; single-mindedness.

Dharma: Righteousness; that which holds together; the basis of social and moral order.

Dharma sastri: One who is well versed in the scriptures relating to *dharma*.

Dhriti: Steadfastness.

Dhyana: Meditation; absorption; unbroken contemplation.

Diksha: Spiritual initiation.

Divya chakshus: Divine eye.

Drashta: Seer.

Dridha: Firm.

Drik: The subject; he who sees.

Drishti: Look; seeing.

Drishti srishti: Simultaneous creation.

Drisya: The object; that which is seen.

Drisya vilaya: The disappearance of the objective world.

Drisyanuviddha: Associated with something seen.

Dukha: Suffering; misery.

Dvaita: Duality; dualism.

Dvandva: Pair of opposites.

Dvividha (dwividha): Two-fold.

Eka: One.

Ekagrata: One-pointed concentration or attention.

Ganja: Hashish.

Gayatri: A well-known Vedic mantra originating from the *Rigveda*.

Gopuram: Temple tower.

Granthi: Knot (knot of ignorance).

Grihastha: Householder.

Grihini: Housewife.

Gunas: The three fundamental qualities or tendencies that underlie all manifestation — *Sattva, Rajas,* and *Tamas* (Purity, Activity, and Inertia).

Gunatita: One who has transcended the *gunas*.

Guru: A spiritual master; preceptor; one who removes the darkness of ignorance.

Halahala: The poison (in Hindu mythology) which arose when the milky ocean (covering the earth) was churned.

Hamsa: A *sannyasi* who has advanced to a spiritually elevated stage.

Hasta: Hand.

Hatha Yoga: A system of yoga involving bodily postures and breath control.

Hetu: Cause; reason.

Hiranyagarbha: Universal consciousness; totality of minds.

Homa: *Vedic* ritual of sacrificial offering to a fire.

Hridaya: Heart; the spiritual center in the body.

Hridaya granthi: Knot of the heart.

Hrit: Heart.

Hrit pundarika: The heart lotus.

Ichcha: Desire.

Idam: This; also refers to the substratum or basis upon which an illusory perception is projected.

Indriyas: Senses.

Ishta devata: The form of God that one prefers to worship or contemplate.

Ishvara: God; the Supreme Being in manifestation as the entire world.

Ishvara anugraha: God's grace.

Ishvara aradhana: Worship of God.

Ishvara drishti: Seeing everything as God.

Ishvara prasada: God's grace.

Jada: Insentient.

Jagat: The world.

Jagrat: Waking state.

Jagrat sushupti: Wakeful sleep.

Jai: Victory.

Jala: Water.

Janma: Birth.

Japa: Repetition of a sacred word or syllable or name of God.

Japa karta: One who does *japa*.

Jirna: Decay; breakdown.

Jiva: The individual soul; the ego.

Jivanmukta: One who is liberated even while alive.

Jivanmukti: Liberation while one is alive.

Jivatman: The individual self.

Jnana: Knowledge of the Self; wisdom.

Jnana bhumikas: Stages of knowledge, of which there are seven.

Jnana chakshus: Eye of wisdom.

Jnana drishti: Eye of wisdom.

Jnana lakshana: Sign of wisdom.

Jnana Marga: The spiritual path of realizing the Absolute through Knowledge.

Jnana Yoga: See *Jnana Marga*.

Jnanagni: Fire of wisdom.

Jnanendriya: Sense organ.

Jnani: A Sage; one who has realized the Self.

Jyoti: Light; effulgence.

Kaivalya: The state of liberation.

Kala: A term used to denote time; the phenomenal cause of things passing away.

Kalpana: Idea; imagination; presumptive knowledge.

Kama: Sensual desire; pleasure.

Kantha: Throat.

Kanthabharana: Ornament worn

around the neck.

Kanya: Virgin.

Karana: Cause.

Karana sarira: Casual body.

Karma: Action; work; deeds; also the accumulated effect of deeds.

Karma Marga: The spiritual path of realizing the Absolute through selfless action.

Karma samya: Good and bad actions in equal proportions.

Karma traya: The three kinds of karma, namely *sanchita, agami,* and *prarabdha.*

Karma Yoga: See *Karma Marga.*

Karmendriya: Organ of action.

Karpura arati: The waving of lighted camphor during worship.

Karta: Doer; he who does an act.

Kartrtva: Doership.

Kartrtva buddhi: The sense of doership.

Kashaya: Latent impurity.

Kashayam (kashaya): Ochre colored garment, usually worn by a *sadhu* or *sannyasi.*

Kasiyatra: Pilgrimage to Kasi; an ancient marriage rite among Brahmins.

Kasturi: Musk.

Kayakalpa: A medicinal preparation for prolonging life.

Kayasiddhi: Making the body proof against injury.

Kevala kumbhaka: Stoppage of breathing, whether in the midst of inhaling or exhaling.

Kevala samadhi: The state of consciousness in which activities of

body and mind are only merged.

Khanda: Division.

Khyati: Theory.

Kousalam: Skill.

Krama mukti: Liberation by degrees.

Krama srishti: Gradual creation.

Krida: Play; pastime.

Kritopasaka: One who has done *upasana* or meditation.

Krodha: Anger.

Kshetra: Temple; field; the body.

Kshipta: Active.

Kumbha: A pot used for keeping water.

Kumbhaka: Retention of breath.

Kumkuma: Vermilion powder applied to the forehead.

Kundalini: Yogic principle called the serpent power; the sleeping spiritual force in every human being that lies coiled at the base of the spine.

Kutichaka: A *sannyasin* who lives permanently in a hut.

Kuvasana: Bad tendency.

Laghu: Light; easy; simple.

Lakh: One-hundred thousand.

Lakshana: Sign; definition.

Lakshya: Aim; goal; target.

Lakshyartha: Implied meaning.

Laya: Dissolution; disappearance.

Lila: Divine play in the manifest world.

Linga: Symbol; usually ascribed to Shiva (the formless Reality).

Linga sarira: Subtle body.

Loka: World; that which is seen.

Loukika: Worldly.

Madhya: Center; mixed; middling.

Madhyama: Middle; middling.

Maharshi: Great *rishi* (seer or sage).

Mahasunya: Great void.

Mahatma: Enlightened person.

Mahavakyas: The four main statements proclaiming the truth of *Brahman*, one taken from each *Veda*.

Malaparipaka: Complete removal of impurity.

Malina: Impure.

Manana: Reflecting over what has been heard (such as an exposition of the Truth).

Mani: Jewel.

Manikavachakar: A South Indian Poet-Saint, who wrote prolifically on the nature and bliss of Realization in ancient Tamil verse. These outpourings form the popular work known as *Tiruvachakam*.

Manolaya: Subsidence of the mind.

Manomaya kosha: Sheath of the mind.

Manonasa: Extinction of the mind.

Manta: Thinker.

Mantra: A scared word or phrase of spiritual significance; sound forms of the *Vedas* used for worship and prayer; seed letters or words used for meditation on the Absolute.

Mantra japa: Repetition of a mantra.

Marga: Path; way.

Maru marichika: Mirage seen in a desert.

Mati: Thinking power.

Maya: The principle of appearance; illusion; the power inherent in *Brahman* by which it manifests the world (not ultimately real).

Maya vada: The doctrine of *maya*.

Medha: Intellect.

Moda: Joy, which is higher than *priya*.

Moksha: Liberation; spiritual freedom; the ultimate goal of human life.

Moodha: Dull.

Moola: Root; source.

Mouna: Silence; the inexpressible.

Mriga trishna: Water as seen in a mirage.

Mukta: One who is liberated.

Mukti: Liberation (see *moksha*).

Muladhara: One of the yogic centers of the body.

Mulavidya: Primal ignorance.

Mumukshu: One who aspires for liberation.

Mumukshutva: The desire for liberation.

Muni: Sage.

Muppall: Three voids.

Na medhaya: Not by the intellect.

Nabhi: Navel.

Nada: Subtle sound accompanied by an effulgence, a term used in *Tantra*.

Nadaswaram: The musical pipe of the South Indian piper.

Nadi: Yogic nerve.

Naham: I am not; not I.

Naishtika brahmacharya: Lifelong celibacy.

Nama: Name; usually refers to the name of God.

Nama japa: Repetition of the name of God.

Nama sankirtan: Singing the names of God.

Nama smarana: Remembering and repeating the name of God.

Namaskar: Prostration before God or Guru.

Nana: Plurality; diversity.

Naraka: Hell.

Nasa: Destruction.

Nava: New.

Nididhyasana: Uninterrupted contemplation; the last of the three stages of vedantic realization.

Nijananda: True bliss.

Nirakara upasana: Meditation on the formless aspect of the Absolute.

Nirguna: Without attributes; devoid of qualities.

Nirguna upasana: Meditation on the attributeless *Brahman*.

Nirodha: Control.

Nirvana: Liberation; perfection.

Nirvikalpa samadhi: The highest state of contemplation in which the soul loses all sense of being different from the universal Self, yet a temporary state from which there is a return to ego-consciousness.

Nishkama karma: Action done without a motive; desireless action.

Nitya: Permanent; eternal; unchanging.

Nitya siddha: Ever present.

Nivritti: Turning away from activity.

Nivritti Marga: Negation or renunciation; turning away from activity toward Self-recollection.

Niyama: Observance; discipline; law.

Oupacharika: In a worldly sense.

Padarthabhavini: Absolute nonperception of objects; one's state in deep sleep.

Panchakshari: A mantra of five syllables sacred to Shiva.

Panchikarana: Theory that every physical object contains all the five elements in various proportions.

Para: Higher; Supreme; in Tantra it refers to unmanifest sound.

Para nadi: The name of a yogic nerve.

Para vibhuti: Superior *vibhuti*.

Param: Transcendental; highest.

Paramahamsa: A renunciate who has attained Self-realization.

Paramarthika: The Absolute.

Paramarthika satyam: Absolute truth.

Paramatma: The Supreme Self.

Paranchi khani: Outgoing.

Pareccha: By another's will.

Parinama vada: The theory of *Brahman* changing itself into the world.

Paroksha: Indirect or nonperceptional knowledge.

Pasyanti: A level of sound that ultimately manifests toward speech.

Phala: Fruit; the result of an act.

Phala chaitanyam: Results of spiritual realization.

Phala data: Dispenser of the results of our acts.

Phala sruti: Description of the results of an act.

Pisachas: Demons.

Poorna: Full; complete.

Pradakshina: Going round a sacred place or holy person.

Pradeepta: Shining brightly.

Prajna: The individual in deep sleep.

Prajnana: Wisdom; knowledge.

Prajnana ghana: Firm in wisdom or knowledge.

Prakriti: Primal nature; the phenomenon of *Maya*.

Pralaya: Dissolution (of the world).

Pramana: Means of valid knowledge.

Pramata: Knower; cognizer.

Pramoda: Joy, which is higher than *moda*.

Prana: Vital air; the breath of life.

Pranayama: Regulation or control of the breath; one of the eight limbs of *Raja Yoga*.

Pranamaya kosa: The sheath of vital air (*prana*).

Pranashakti: The power of the vital forces.

Pranava: A name for the sacred syllable OM.

Pranayama: Regulation of breath (*prana*), one of the eight-limbs of *Raja Yoga*.

Prapatti: Surrender.

Prapti: Attainment.

Prarabdha: That part of one's karma to be worked out in this lifetime.

Prasad: Grace; also food etc., which is first offered to God then distributed among devotees.

Prasthana traya: The three primary works of *Vedanta:* the *Upanishads*, the *Bhagavad Gita*, and the *Brahma Sutra*.

Pratibhasika satya: Reality appearing as illusory to an individual.

Pratikam: Symbol.

Pratikriya: Remedy.

Pratyabhijna: Recognition.

Pratyahara: Withdrawal of the senses from objects; one of the steps in *Raja Yoga;*.

Pratyaksha: Direct; immediate perception.

Pravritti Marga: Path of active involvement in the world.

Prayaschitta: A rite for expiating sin.

Prayatna: Effort.

Prema: Love.

Prithvi: The earth.

Priya: Joy; dear.

Puja: Ceremonial worship with flowers, water, etc.

Punya: Merit; meritorious deeds.

Puraka: Inhalation of breath; as practiced in *pranayama*.

Purana: Ancient narratives; legendary histories of Hindu religious gods and heroes, embodying religious symbolism.

Puri: Place; city.

Puriashtaka: Subtle body (city) consisting of eight entries.

Purna: Full; complete.

Purusha: Individual soul; from the

nondualistic (*advaitic*) perspective, there is only one *purusha*.

Purushakara: Personal effort.

Purva paksha: Arguments advanced by the opponent.

Purva samskara: Latent tendency.

Raja Yoga: The principal system of Yoga as taught by Patanjali.

Rajas: One of the three primal qualities (*gunas*); the principle of activity and passion.

Rajju-sarpa: Rope-snake; a rope that appears as a snake in a dim light.

Rasa: Bliss; spiritual delight; the essence of things.

Rasasvada: Taste of bliss in the absence of thoughts.

Ravi Marga: Path of the sun.

Rechaka: Out-breath, exhalation; as practiced in *pranayama*.

Rishi: A seer; a sage.

Sabdanuviddha: Associated with sound.

Sadguru: The true guru — who is one with the Divine consciousness.

Sadhaka: A spiritual aspirant; one who follows a method of spiritual discipline (*sadhana*).

Sadhana: Self-effort; spiritual discipline; practice as a means toward Liberation.

Sadhana-chatushtaya: The four qualifications expected in an aspirant.

Sadhu: Ascetic; holy man; renunciate.

Sadhu seva: Service rendered to saints.

Sadyomukti: Immediate liberation.

Saguna: With attributes; contains qualities.

Saguna upasana: Meditation on *Brahman* with attributes.

Sahaja: Natural; one's natural state.

Sahaja samadhi: Samadhi that comes naturally and is present always.

Sahasrara: The highest yogic center located in the brain.

Sajatiya: Of the same kind.

Sakshatkaram: Direct realization.

Sakshi: Witness consciousness; the observer.

Sama: Equal; common.

Samadhi: Absorption; deep spiritual contemplation. A state beyond expression and above all thought; beyond the states of waking, dreaming, and deep sleep.

Samanya: Common; ordinary; class. The common characteristic by virtue of possessing which an individual becomes a member of a class.

Samashti: Whole; cosmic; collective.

Samatva: Equality; equanimity under all circumstances.

Samjnana: Awareness; perception.

Samrajya: Empire.

Samsara: Empirical existence; the cycle of birth and death.

Samskara: Impression; innate tendency; predisposition.

Samvit: Consciousness; knowledge.

Samyamana: One-pointedness of mind.

Sanchita (sanchita karma): Accumulated karma to be worked out in a future birth.

Sandeha: Doubt.

Sanga: Association.

Sankalpa: Intention; will; self-willed thought leading to action.

Sannidhi: Presence; proximity.

Sannyasa: Renunciation of all worldly attachments and ties.

Sannyasi (sannyasin): An ascetic; one who has taken to the path of renunciation (*sannyasa*).

Sarira: The body.

Sarira traya: The three bodies, namely the physical, subtle, and causal.

Sariri: Dweller in the body.

Sarva: All; everything.

Sarvajna: Omniscient.

Sarvajnatvam: Omniscience.

Sastra: Scripture; teaching.

Sat: Existence; Being; Reality.

Sat-Chit-Ananda (satchitananda): Being-Consciousness-Bliss.

Satsanga: Association with the wise.

Sattva: Purity; one of the three primal qualities (*gunas*); the principle of harmony and goodness.

Sattvapatti: Realization; one of the seven stages of enlightenment.

Sattvic: Pure; relating to *sattva*, one of the three constituents of *prakriti*.

Satya: The true; the real.

Satyam: Truth; reality.

Savikalpa samadhi: A state of deep concentration in which there is still a distinction between the knower, knowledge, and the known.

Shadadhara: The six yogic centers.

Shaiva: One devoted to Shiva; relating to Shiva.

Shakti: Primal energy; power; the dynamic aspect of the Absolute.

Shaktipata: Descent of divine power on a person.

Shankara (Shankaracharya, Adi Shankara): One of India's greatest sages and philosophers, and the primary representative of *Advaita Vedanta*. He was instrumental in reestablishing the nondualistic teachings of the *Upanishads*, *Brahma Sutra*, and the *Bhagavad Gita*, after the rise of Buddhism. Shankara is also a name for Shiva.

Shanti: Peace.

Shiva: Auspicious; A name for God in his role as destroyer of ignorance.

Shivoham: I am Shiva.

Siddha: A perfected being; one who if fully accomplished; may also mean one who has acquired supernatural abilities and can use them for the welfare of others.

Siddhi: Psychic or supernatural abilities; can also mean realization, attainment.

Sishya: Disciple.

Sloka: A stanza (verse) in Sanskrit poetry.

Smriti: Memory; scriptures based on traditional scriptural texts.

Soham: I am He (*Brahman*).

Sparsa: Touch.

Sphurana: Manifestation; vibration.

Sraddha: Faith; belief; an inner attitude reflecting earnestness of purpose.

Sravana: Hearing of the truth from a qualified teacher, such as the Guru.

Srishti drishti: Gradual creation.

Srota: Hearer.

Srotra: The ear.

Sruti: Revealed scriptures; directly perceived by the sage or seer, such as in the Vedas.

Sthitaprajna: One who is firmly established in spiritual knowledge.

Sthiti: Being.

Sthula: Gross; body.

Sthula sarira: Physical body.

Stotram: A hymn of praise.

Subhechcha: Desire for enlightenment.

Suddha: Pure.

Sukha: Happiness.

Sukha asana: Easy and comfortable posture of sitting.

Sukshma: Subtle state beyond waking, dreaming, and sleeping.

Sukshma sarira: The subtle body.

Sunya: The void; nonbeing.

Sushumna: The name of a yogic nerve.

Sushupti: Dreamless sleep.

Sutra: Aphorism; concise statements that usually require a commentary for understanding.

Suvasana: Good tendency.

Svagata: Within itself.

Svapna: Dream state during sleep.

Svarga: Heaven.

Svarupa: Natural form.

Svechcha: Of one's own will.

Swaraj: Independence.

Swatantra: Independence.

Taijasa: The individual being in the dream state.

Tamas: Darkness; one of the three primal qualities (*gunas*); the principle of inertia and dullness.

Tamil: A South Indian language and the earliest branch of the four Dravidian languages. It is not related to the Indo-Aryan languages of which Sanskrit is based.

Tanha: Thirst (for living).

Tanmatras: Subtle essence of the five elements.

Tanmaya: Full of the Self.

Tantra: A spiritual practice that involves symbolic ritual, *mantras*, *mudras*, and *mandalas* (symbolic diagrams); the philosophical approach centered around divine energy and creative Power.

Tantric: Relating to or having the qualities of *tantra*.

Tanumanasa: Tenuous mind; one of the seven stages of enlightenment.

Tapas (tapasya): Austerity; concentrated discipline; intense spiritual practice undertaken for the purpose of spiritual attainment.

Tapobhrashta: One who has fallen away from austerity.

Tapta-aya-pindavat: Like a red-hot

iron ball.

Tattva: Truth; the essence of a thing; the essential "is-ness" or true being.

Tejas: Effulgence; glow.

Tejo rupa: Of the form of light.

Tejomaya: Full of light.

Tirtha: A sacred river or tank.

Tirujnanasambandar: A revered child-saint from South India.

Triputi: Triad; triple form; the knower, the known, the act of knowledge.

Turavu: Renunciation.

Turiya: The fourth state of consciousness; the supreme reality; that which underlies the passing states of waking, dreaming, and sleeping.

Turyaga: Beyond words; one the seven stages of enlightenment.

Tyaga: Giving up; letting go; renunciation.

Udasinam: Indifference.

Upadesa: Spiritual instruction; initiation; usually given by a Guru.

Upadhi: Limiting adjunct or attribute; everything that is superimposed on *Brahman*, the Reality.

Upasaka: One who meditates; an aspirant.

Upasana: Meditation; worship.

Upasana sthana: Seat of meditation.

Vachyartha: Literal meaning.

Vada: Theory; debate.

Vaikhari: One of the stages in the formation of sound; audible

(manifest) sound.

Vaikuntha: The abode of Vishnu.

Vairagya: Dispassion; nonattachment.

Vaishnavite: A worshipper of Vishnu.

Varnasrama dharma: Dharma of the various castes and stages of life.

Vasana: Latent tendencies or impressions that cling to the individual.

Vasana kshaya: Cessation of *vasanas*.

Vasishta: A famous sage and author of the *Rigveda*. His instructions to Sri Rama form the basis of the Sanskrit work, *Yoga Vasishta*.

Vastutah: In reality.

Vayu: Air; life-breath.

Vedanta: The "end" or consummation of the *Vedas*; based on the teachings in the *Upanishads* on the nature of *Brahman*.

Vibhakti: Separation.

Vibhuti: Sacred ash; manifestations of divine power.

Vichara: Inquiry into the nature of the Self.

Vichara Marga: The spiritual path of Self-Inquiry.

Vicharana: Investigation; one of the seven stages of enlightenment.

Videha mukta: One who is liberated after death.

Videha mukti: Liberation after death.

Vidya: Knowledge; wisdom; learning.

Vijatiya: Of a different kind.

Vijnana: Spiritual knowledge; realization.

Vijnanamaya kosa: Sheath of the intellect.

Vijnanatma: The ignorant self.

Vijnata: Knower.

Vikshepa: Dispersion; false projection.

Vikshipta: Distracted; unsteady.

Viparita: Contrary; contrary to what is.

Virat: Totality of gross beings; the cosmic form of the Self.

Visesha: Particular; distinguishable.

Vishaya: Object.

Vishnu: All-pervading; a name for God in his role as preserver of the universe.

Vishva: The individual being in the waking state.

Vishvarupa (darshan): God seen as comprising the form of the universe.

Visishta: Qualified; determinate.

Visishtadvaitin: One who believes in a modified form of nonduality, based on the teachings of the South Indian saint, Ramanuja.

Visranti: Repose.

Vivarta vada: Theory of apparent change; *Brahman* appears as the world, soul, and God, like a rope appears as a snake, without itself undergoing any change.

Vivechana: Discrimination.

Viyoga: Separation.

Vritti: Modification of the mind; it is what makes knowledge possible.

Vyaptam: Pervaded.

Vyashti: Part.

Vyavahara (vyavaharika): Empirical; from the relative viewpoint.

Vyavahara satya: Phenomenal existence.

Yaga: See *Yajna.*

Yajna: Sacrificial ceremony.

Yoga: Union; a spiritual process or discipline leading to oneness with the Divine.

Yogabhrashta: One who has slipped from the discipline of yoga.

Yogarudha: One who has attained yoga.

Yogiraja: King of yogis.

Yugapat srishti: Simultaneous creation.

REFERENCED WORKS

Akshara Manamalai (Aksharamanamalai): "The Marital Garland of Letters." One hundred and eight joyful verses spontaneously composed by Maharshi, and often sung by devotees as they did *pradakshina* around the Arunachala Hill.

Arunachala Ashtaka: "Eight Stanzas on Sri Arunachala." One of the hymns to Arunachala composed by Ramana Maharshi, and later published as part of the *Five Hymns to Arunachala.*

Arunachala Mahatmya: A portion of the *Skanda Purana* that expresses the glory of Sri Arunachala and its uniqueness as a center for Spiritual Knowledge.

Arunachala Pancharatna: "Five Stanzas to Arunachala." One of several hymns that reflect the ecstasy of Divine Union, written by Ramana Maharshi. The *Arunachala Pancharatna* forms part of the collection of additional hymns, titled *Five Hymns to Arunachala.*

Atma Bodha: "Knowledge of the Self." Originally written in Sanskrit verse, by Shankaracharya. Maharshi translated this work into Tamil in 1949.

Atma-Vidya: "Self-Knowledge." A song of six stanzas written by Maharshi, at the request of a devotee. It expresses the ease and immediacy of Self-knowledge, and begins with the lines "Self-knowledge is an easy thing, the easiest thing there is."

Bhagavad Gita: A philosophical work of 700 verses, which is often considered to contain the essence of Hinduism. This profound dialogue between Sri Krishna and Arjuna comprises the sixth book of the great Indian epic, the *Mahabharata.*

Dakshinamurti Stotra: Shankaracharya's "Hymn to Dakshinamurti." Ramana Maharshi rendered this original Sanskrit hymn into Tamil verse.

Five Hymns to Arunachala: A collection of hymns to Arunachala, most of which were written by Ramana when he was about thirty-five years old. These poems express profoundly and symbolically, the love and union between the individual soul and God.

Kaivalya Navaneeta: "The Cream of Emancipation." A classic work originally written in Tamil, in which the principles of *Advaita* and the way to Liberation are clearly presented.

Mahabharata: The great epic of Hinduism. Containing 106,000 verses in eighteen books, it is a narrative of the battle between two powerful, related families and portrays the triumph of truth over evil. Book Six contains the *Bhagavad Gita,* one of the most important Indian philosophical texts.

Maha Yoga: A book written by K. Lakshmana Sarma that expresses the core teachings of *Vedanta,* and the traditional approach to Self-realization, in the light of the teachings of Ramana Maharshi.

Nan Yar: (Tamil) See *Who Am I?*

Ramayana: A large and important work of verse, which contains the life and exploits of Sri Rama, who is considered to be a divine incarnation. It was originally written in Sanskrit by the Sage Valmiki.

Reality in Forty Verses: See *Sad-Vidya.*

Ribhu Gita: This work forms the sixth part of the Sanskrit work known as *Shiva Rahasya.* It contains the teachings of Shiva to his devotee Ribhu. This *Gita,* named after Ribhu, contains a clear and direct exposition of the Truth in the clearest tradition of *Advaita.*

Sat-Darshanam: The Sanskrit rendering of *Reality in Forty Verses*, by Vasishta Ganapathi Muni.

Sad-Vidya: "Forty (verses) on That which Is." Known more popularly as *Reality in Forty Verses*, this original Tamil work was written by Ramana Maharshi and later translated into Sanskrit (*Sat-Darshanam*) and English (*Sad-Vidya* or *Truth Revealed*).

Self-Enquiry: The first work that Maharshi ever wrote, around 1901-1902. This work represents a collection of answers to questions asked by an earnest seeker.

Self-Realisation: The first English biography written on the life and teachings of Sri Ramana Maharshi. It was by B.V. Narasimha Swami and published in 1931.

Song of the Poppadum: A poem written by Maharshi, that gives instruction for spiritual development under the symbolism of making *poppadum* (a thin, round, crispy cake).

Spiritual Instruction: A booklet that contains answers to questions by Sri Natanananda, one of Maharshi's devotees.

Sri Ramana Gita: A collection of Ramana Maharshi's answers given to different questioners on various occasions. The entire work was compiled and commented on by the eminent scholar and yogi, Vasishta Ganapathi Muni.

Supplement to the Forty Verses: Forty additional verses, which supplement the original *Forty Verses on Reality* (*Sad-Vidya*).

Tiruvachakam: A popular Tamil work by the respected Poet-Saint, Manikavachakar. These poems express the joy and ecstasy borne of union with the Divine.

Ulladu Narpadu: (Tamil) See *Sad-Vidya*.

Upadesa Saram: "The Essence of Instruction." Legend has it that these thirty verses were given to the Rishis of Daruka Forest by Shiva. Bhagavan wrote out these verses at the request of a devotee and later translated them into Sanskrit. The instructions to the Rishis reveal the way to Liberation through renunciation of action.

Upadesa Undiyar: (Tamil) See U*padesa Saram.*

Upanishads: The last portions of the *Vedas,* which deal with spiritual and philosophical subjects. There are ten principal *Upanishads,* and these form the principal basis of *Vedanta.*

Vedas: The oldest (revealed) texts of Indian philosophical literature. The four books, which make up the *Vedas,* represent every aspect of religious life, from ritual and its practice to the achievement of philosophical and spiritual knowledge.

Vichara Mani Mala: "Jewel Garland of Enquiry." Compiled by Ramana Maharshi, this is a compilation that captures the essential teachings in the work, *Vichara Sagara* (Ocean of Enquiry).

Vichara Sagara: Originally written in Hindi, this small work represents a dialogue between Guru and disciple on the means to Liberation through Self-knowledge.

Vicharasangraham: See *Self-Enquiry.*

Vivekachudamani: "The Crown Jewel of Discrimination." Written by Sri Shankaracharya, it reveals the way to Liberation through the discrimination of the Real from the unreal.

Who Am I?: Written around 1902, *Who Am I?* is the title given to twenty-eight questions and answers concerning the practice of Self-Inquiry. The answers found in *Who Am I?* form the basis of Ramana Maharshi's teaching on Self-Inquiry.

Yoga Sutra: A collection of aphorisms by the sage Patanjalai that represent the oldest textbook on the system of Yoga.

Yoga Vasishta: A work of about 32,000 Sanskrit couplets, traditionally attributed to Valmiki, author of the Ramayana. It represents a dialogue between Sri Rama and Sage Vasishta and imparts the purest teachings of
advaita, the principle of *ajatavada* (nonorigination).

INDEX